Pee Wee Reese

Pee Wee Reese
The Life of a Brooklyn Dodger

GLEN SPARKS

McFarland & Company, Inc., Publishers
Jefferson, North Carolina

LIBRARY OF CONGRESS CATALOGUING-IN-PUBLICATION DATA

Names: Sparks, Glen, 1964– author.
Title: Pee Wee Reese : the life of a Brooklyn Dodger / Glen Sparks.
Description: Jefferson, North Carolina : McFarland & Company, Inc., Publishers, 2022. | Includes bibliographical references and index.
Identifiers: LCCN 2022001725 | ISBN 9781476677903 (paperback : acid free paper) ∞
ISBN 9781476644387 (ebook) ∞
Subjects: LCSH: Reese, Pee Wee, 1918-1999. | Brooklyn Dodgers (Baseball team)—History. | Baseball players—United States—Biography. | BISAC: SPORTS & RECREATION / Baseball / History | BIOGRAPHY & AUTOBIOGRAPHY / Sports
Classification: LCC GV865.R4 S73 2022 | DDC 796.357092 [B]—dc23/eng/20220126
LC record available at https://lccn.loc.gov/2022001725

BRITISH LIBRARY CATALOGUING DATA ARE AVAILABLE

ISBN (print) 978-1-4766-7790-3
ISBN (ebook) 978-1-4766-4438-7

© 2022 Glen Sparks. All rights reserved

No part of this book may be reproduced or transmitted in any form or by any means, electronic or mechanical, including photocopying or recording, or by any information storage and retrieval system, without permission in writing from the publisher.

Front cover: Brooklyn Dodgers shortstop Pee Wee Reese
(National Baseball Hall of Fame Library, Cooperstown, New York)

Printed in the United States of America

McFarland & Company, Inc., Publishers
Box 611, Jefferson, North Carolina 28640
www.mcfarlandpub.com

To my mom, Barbara Sparks (1937–2017)

Acknowledgments

Thank you to McFarland for giving me the opportunity to write this biography of Hall of Fame shortstop Pee Wee Reese. Thank you especially to Gary Mitchem, who provided counsel and much patience along the way.

Many thanks to the friends and baseball fans who read parts of my manuscript and offered valuable feedback. Thank you to Joe Elstner, Jay Knehans, Cory Ritterbusch, Steve Taylor, and Doug Wilson for being so generous with your time.

Thank you to the many hard-working people at the St. Louis Public Library and the St. Louis County Library. I am always amazed at how much our libraries offer in the way of books, magazines, movies, and other items. I encourage everyone out there to get a library card and to take advantage of these valuable community resources.

One great service I need to mention is the interlibrary loan (ILL) program. Through ILL, patrons at one library can check out material owned by another library from across the country or around the world. I used ILL many times in the course of completing this book. Thank you to Kathi Buckner at the St. Louis County Library for her hard work in finding what I requested. I can truly say that she batted 1.000.

So many reporters covered Reese and the Dodgers during that great era of the 1940s and 1950s. Brooklyn's beloved Bums remain alive today in part due to the hard work of Dave Anderson, Harold C. Burr, Tommy Holmes, Roger Kahn, Jim McCulley, Tom Meany, Joe Trimble, Hy Turkin, Dick Young, and others. Thank you all for meeting the deadline.

Carl Erskine spent 10 seasons as a pitcher for the Dodgers. He won 122 games and threw two no-hitters. The right-hander from Anderson, Indiana, also gained a deserved reputation for being one of the game's great gentlemen. I thank him for his time and patience as he graciously answered my questions one afternoon about his life in baseball.

More than anyone, I want to thank my wife, Pam. Her love and support is one of the great blessings of my life. She encouraged me every step of the way on this project, from the time I sent off my proposal until I completed the final page. This is her book as much as it is my book.

Table of Contents

Acknowledgments — vi
Preface — 1

1. "Man, Pee Wee ought to be your middle name" — 5
2. "Brooklyn's in the major leagues, isn't it?" — 14
3. "Skip, where do you buy your clothes?" — 26
4. "I'm trying to teach him to holler" — 39
5. "Another guy I'll have to beat out for a job" — 52
6. "As boyish as ever" — 66
7. "I looked at it, and I just flatly refused" — 80
8. "Reese? Now, you're talking about a ballplayer" — 95
9. "Just don't make me out to be a hero" — 108
10. "That's why we called him 'Captain'" — 116
11. "(Pee Wee Reese) will be the 1951 skipper" — 129
12. "I don't believe it" — 141
13. "Not guilty" — 156
14. "One hundred and eighty pounds of dynamite" — 169
15. "He's not swinging a bat" — 182
16. "I said to myself, 'This can't be true'" — 194
17. "You're getting good in your old age" — 208
18. "So, Pee Wee did it for Walter" — 222
19. "Let's see, folks. Where were we?" — 234
20. "He was the heart and soul of the boys of summer" — 246

Chapter Notes — 257
Bibliography — 287
Index — 291

Preface

Pee Wee Reese never wrote an autobiography. Baseball fans can only shake their heads in disappointment. What a book it would have been! Pee Wee could have spun countless tales about himself and his Brooklyn Dodgers teammates—outstanding players like Jackie Robinson, Duke Snider, Roy Campanella, Gil Hodges, Carl Erskine, and Carl Furillo. Alas, Reese, who granted many interviews through the years and spoke to dozens of reporters, declined to write a full-length memoir. Perhaps he was simply too modest a man to sit down and put his life story to paper.

I hope this book offers a satisfactory substitute and is one that readers will enjoy. Reese's story is one worth telling. Pee Wee was not only a fantastic baseball player during one of the game's great eras. He also was a leader of men and the Bums' long-time captain. Branch Rickey chose him for that role following the 1948 season and said, "You're not only the logical choice. You're the only choice."[1]

Harold Henry "Pee Wee" Reese entered the Brooklyn baseball scene in the spring of 1940. He hailed from Kentucky and spoke with a soft drawl. The writers joked that he looked like a high school kid, not like the future Dodgers shortstop and Leo Durocher's replacement.

Of course, Pee Wee did indeed succeed Leo the Lip. The one-time marble shooter went on to play 16 seasons, missing three years due to his service in World War II, and made 10 All-Star teams. He collected 2,170 hits, belted 126 home runs, and stole 232 bases. The Dodgers teams during his tenure won seven pennants and a championship—finally—in 1955.

In his book *The Cooperstown Casebook*, published in 2017, author Jay Jaffe rated Reese as the 17th-best shortstop of all time. Jaffe put him one spot behind Joe Cronin and two behind Lou Boudreau but ahead of Hall of Famers Joe Sewell (ranked 19th), Luis Aparicio (22nd), Dave Bancroft (25th), Hughie Jennings (29th), Travis Jackson (31st), and Phil Rizzuto (35th). Jaffe wrote that "for a perennial All-Star who keyed seven pennant winners and played a pivotal role in the fall of the color line, Reese is quite underrated." Reese, according to Jaffe, boasted "a league-average bat—no small matter for a shortstop," with "elite" baserunning skills and "an excellent glove."[2]

In recent years, advanced statistics have gained a foothold even within the baseball establishment, and Wins Above Replacement, or WAR, has become the metric of choice for many inside and out of the research community. Intended to sum up a player's overall contribution to his team, WAR determines how many wins he is worth relative to a replacement-level player at the same position. In 2018, for instance, Mookie Betts led all of baseball with a 10.7 WAR, indicating that Betts was worth nearly 11 more wins to his team than a replacement-level right fielder would have been.[3]

Babe Ruth, not surprisingly, leads all MLB players with a career WAR of 182.5, followed by Walter Johnson (164.5), Cy Young (163.8), Barry Bonds (162.8) and Willie Mays (156.2) in the top five. Honus Wagner is first among shortstops with a value of 130.8, followed by Alex Rodriguez (117.5), Cal Ripken (95.9), George Davis (84.7), and Arky Vaughan (78.0). Reese has a career WAR of 68.2 and ranks 16th among shortstops. However, no shortstop who ranked higher than Reese missed three years due to military service. He had a WAR of 6.1 in 1942, his last year with Brooklyn before going into the Navy, and a 6.0 WAR in 1946, his first year back from service. "It's not unthinkable that he lost 15–18 WAR to World War II," Jaffe wrote, "which would have pushed him well into the top 10 here." Jaffe called the Veterans Committee election of Reese to the Hall of Fame "one of its best moves."[4]

Of course, as Brooklyn Dodgers historian Bill Borst once wrote, echoing the comments of many, "The box score never truly reflected the many intangible contributions Pee Wee Reese made to the Dodgers and to the history of baseball."[5] Yes, Pee Wee Reese lined big base hits, stole hundreds of bases, and made countless acrobatic plays from his spot in the infield. All Brooklyn Dodgers fans know that. They know Reese belongs in the Hall of Fame on the numbers alone. They also know that "his value to the club far exceeded his baseball statistics."[6]

Pee Wee Reese grew up in Louisville when segregation and Jim Crow ruled the land. He rarely spoke to a Black resident and never shook of the hand of a Black man until he shook the hand of Jackie Robinson. Mark Reese, looking back on those different times, once said that his dad did some "soul searching" and "listened to his heart" when Robinson joined the Dodgers. Pee Wee demonstrated his empathy right away. In the fresh spring of 1947, some players bandied about a petition meant to keep Robinson out of baseball. Pee Wee Reese refused to sign it. He just wanted to "play ball,"[7] he said. Talk of a petition quickly ended. Later, Reese put his arm on the shoulder of Robinson in a show of support when fans and opposing players let loose a torrent of boos and hatred. The details remain murky. Did it happen in 1947 or 1948? In Cincinnati or Boston? Some say it never happened. Robinson said it did.

The Dodgers of Reese's vintage played exciting baseball and thrilled their passionate fans, who yelled encouragement—and, yes, sometimes booed—while seated (occasionally) or standing (often) inside a merry bandbox of a ballpark located at 55 Sullivan Place. More than one writer described Reese as "the glue" that held the Dodgers together. "He was the man who cooled tempers and soothed bruised egos,"[8] according to one writer. Hall of Fame slugger Duke Snider called Reese "the finest person I've ever met."[9]

Only one man played in every inning of every World Series game that pitted Brooklyn against the New York Yankees. That man was Pee Wee Reese. He took the field in 44 classic October games. He also watched as Bobby Thomson hit that most famous of pennant-winning home runs in 1951.

Pee Wee Reese was, as they like to say about the truly dedicated, a baseball lifer. Following his career, he did some coaching and then enjoyed a successful stint as a broadcaster, much of that time spent alongside the whimsical Dizzy Dean. He also worked for his hometown's most famous company, Hillerich & Bradsby, maker of the Louisville Slugger.

The biography that follows should be of interest both to the casual fan and to anyone who ever cheered for the Brooklyn Dodgers. This is the first book that covers the entire life of one of baseball's most popular players. Before writing it, I looked at newspaper articles and magazine pieces, as well as many books on Dodgers history. I also spent time talking to Carl Erskine, a Dodger for 12 years and a gentleman for life. These sources helped me gain a better understanding of the player known by some as The Little Colonel.

Pee Wee Reese still liked to watch baseball in his final years, mostly from the comfort of his easy chair at home, placed just a few feet from the television set. He noted the better equipment and the bigger gloves of the modern era and how fielders liked to dive for balls. He couldn't recall the great Joe DiMaggio ever diving for a baseball. The playing surfaces looked faster, too, slicker. Baseballs skipped and bounced around on concrete-hard artificial turf. Good pitching still thrilled him. He admired Greg Maddux, a control artist and winner of 355 games. "He can throw the ball on a dime anywhere,"[10] Reese marveled.

Of course, he wore his world championship ring from 1955. He had not played for the Dodgers in decades, but he still liked to talk about those long-ago pennant races. Teams battled it out on warm summer days when players wore heavy wool uniforms, pitchers hurled hot fastballs and knee-buckling curveballs, and stories about baseball ruled the sports page. "It was a beautiful time," Pee Wee Reese said. "A beautiful time to play ball."[11]

1

"Man, Pee Wee ought to be your middle name"

Carl Reese grew corn and tobacco on a small farm outside Ekron, Kentucky.[1] Located in the central part of the Bluegrass State, Ekron lies about 45 miles southwest of Louisville, in Meade County. Brandenburg, the county seat, is just a few miles away, along the Ohio River.

Pioneers, most of them with ancestral roots in England and Scotland, settled this area in the late-1700s, attracted not only by the mighty Ohio, but also by the great number of wild buffalo, deer, and elk. Frontiersman Daniel Boone, along with his younger brother, Squire, bought land there after blazing a trail through the Cumberland Gap in southern Appalachia. Tom Lincoln, a local stonemason and the father of future U.S. president Abraham Lincoln, helped build one of the early grinding mills. John James Audubon, the ornithologist and prolific painter of American birds, visited in the early 1800s.[2]

The county, founded on December 17, 1823, is named for Kentucky native and U.S. Army Captain James M. Meade.[3] Meade died in the Michigan territory at the Battle of Raisin River, "one of the bloodiest battles of the War of 1812."[4] The captain "was conspicuously in the forefront, occupied a very exposed position, and was mortally wounded while gallantly leading his company in a charge."[5]

Today, Meade county spans 325 square miles and, according to the 2010 census, has 28,602 residents.[6] "Our telecommunications are the latest as is the machinery that that tills our soil, milks our cows, and provides our transportation."[7] Life was much different, and a great deal more difficult, in the first half of the 19th century. The men and women who put down roots in the rugged hills faced many dangers. "The winters were hard. Cords of wood were stored up and the fires were banked at night, so they could be quickly relit in the morning. … Children who went barefoot all summer now had shoes that were mended by their fathers and handed down as long as there was any usefulness left in them." Newcomers traveled on roads "muddy and often impassable." The injured rarely saw doctors. Instead, "bad lacerations were cauterized to stem the flow of blood by searing the wound with a red hot poker." Many died from infection and disease. "But through it all, Meade County people, nay, all Kentuckians were hearty souls."[8]

Reese family history runs deep in this part of the Bluegrass State. Carl Marion Reese, born on March 18, 1886, in Meade County, grew up the son of Blent Marion[9] and Elizabeth "Lizzie" Reese, also Meade County natives.[10] Carl Reese married Emma Allen, the daughter of Gus and Bettie Allen, in December 1906. Emma was born on August 10, 1888, in Meade County, the birthplace of her parents.[11]

Harold Henry Reese, known later as "Pee Wee" and a big league shortstop, entered the world in high summer, on July 23, with the exact year in question. Carl had drawn the shades in a bedroom next to the kitchen as a way to keep out the midday sun. Hours later, Emma cradled her new-born child. Tired, she sat on a large iron bed. "He isn't very big, is he, Carl?" Mr. Reese just smiled. "Big enough for a baby, I guess."[12]

The doctor who delivered the child rode a horse-drawn carriage back into town. He stopped long enough for a storekeeper to ask, "What was it, Doc?" The doctor looked over at the man. "A boy." The horse and carriage trotted away. A few hours later, Carl took another look at his son and decided, "You do look kinda small for your age."[13]

Some accounts list Harold Reese's birth year as 1918. Others list it as 1919. According to the Kentucky birth index, he was born in 1918.[14] The 1930 U.S. census records indicate his birth year as "abt. 1919."[15] The Dodgers gave him a humdinger of a birthday party in 1955. Reporters listed his age as 36, giving him a birth year of 1919. *Baseball Digest* published a first-person article on Reese in its May 1954 issue. The ballplayer told readers, "I was born on July 23, 1919."[16] Most stories about Reese during his playing career report him as being born in 1919, or they use the corresponding age.

Etched onto the headstone of Reese's plot at Resthaven Cemetery in Louisville is the year 1918. Further, most articles about Reese in his post-playing days list his birth year as 1918, or, again, use the corresponding age.

Carl Reese gave up his dream of farming the Kentucky land when Harold was seven years old.[17] Hoping to find better economic opportunities in the big city, he took his wife and children to Louisville. As Pee Wee recalled, "Farming was difficult. We were very poor, trying to make a living on not too good of a farm."[18]

Louisville grew as a portage site along the Ohio River. Boats passing through the area unloaded their cargo before navigating the nearby rapids-strewn Falls of the Ohio. This proved a boon for local businesses. "By 1820, Louisville was a thriving and prosperous little town."[19] Nearly 700 buildings lined local streets. "Of these, sixty-five were licensed stores and the remainder small shops and homes."[20] Caleb Atwater, an antiques dealer from Ohio, wrote of a Main Street that "presents a proud display of wealth and grandeur. ... Stores are filled with commodities and manufactures of every clime and every art, dazzling the eye."[21]

During the Civil War, Kentucky was a state divided. The Unionists "favored neutrality because they disapproved of both southern succession and northern coercion of southern states. Confederate sympathizers backed neutrality because they feared if Kentucky chose a side, she would choose the union." The state had a large slave population. By 1830, slaves "constituted 24 percent of all Kentuckians." In 1860, about 38,000 residents owned slaves, a figure exceeded only by Virginia and Georgia. Most owned four or fewer slaves.[22] In May 1861, just one month after the official start of the Civil War, Kentucky governor Beriah Magoffin issued a proclamation of neutrality and told residents to stay at home and avoid the fighting. "We are a border state. We have the brunt of the battle," he said. In a letter to one of the state's newspapers, Magoffin wrote that Kentucky would "take her position calmly, fearlessly, wisely, with her whole heart beating for the Union and her whole soul overflowing with patriotism and loyalty to that Union under the compact of the Constitution." Armies, though, from both sides entered the state and recruited volunteers. All told, about 100,000 Kentuckians put on the blue uniform of the North, and between 25,000–40,000 suited up in the grey garb of the South.[23]

Louisville surpassed the 100,000 mark in population during the 1870s. "It was considered, along with Chicago, St. Louis, and Cincinnati, one of the country's great interior cities. Paddle-wheelers, flatboats, and barges, carrying cotton, cast-iron pipe and passengers tied up along the city's cobblestone wharf."[24] By 1920, the city had grown to 234,891 residents.[25] The Reese family settled in the Old Louisville section of town. Census records from 1930 indicate that they lived in a house at 1252 Sixth Street. Pee Wee had three older sisters—Pauline, Willie, and Elizabeth, and an older brother, Carl Jr. The youngest child in the family was Mary, who was born in 1925.

For a while, Carl Reese worked at the Ford Motor Company in Louisville. Later, he found a job as a detective with the Louisville & Nashville Railroad, chasing vagrants off the property. "My dad had no education," Pee Wee said. "There was not a lot of education in my family."[26] Pee Wee later described his dad as a "dark-haired, intense man" who liked to drink. Emma Reese also held down a "full-time job," as Pee Wee recalled. Which was? "Keeping my father sober."[27]

Carl played semi-pro baseball when just about every city and town across the country fielded at least a few teams. "I'm no small potatoes," he said at one point. "I make more than five dollars a game."[28] Pee Wee later confirmed, "He was a pretty good second baseman."[29]

Baseball in Kentucky dates to July 19, 1865. On that day, the Louisville Greys beat the Nashville Cumberlands in the first game west of the Alleghenies that was played under "standard rules."[30] Louisville knocked off Nashville, 22–5. Several reporters covered the game "because of the business rivalry between the towns."[31] About 200 fans enjoyed the action, "but many didn't have a clue about what they were watching."[32]

The Greys joined the National League as a charter member in 1876 and finished in fifth place with a 30–36 record. They improved to second place the following year, with a 35–25 mark, but not without scandal. The ballclub lost nine straight games in August and blew the pennant. Rumors grew that crooked players, rather than bad luck, led to this sudden downturn. Bill Craver, Jim Devlin, George Hall, and Al Nichols were thrown off the team and banned from professional baseball for life. The Greys franchise subsequently folded. The Louisville Eclipse, later called the Colonels, played in the American Association from 1882–1891 and the National League from 1892–1899.[33]

One of Louisville's most notable contributions to baseball began as a woodworking shop in 1859. J. F. Hillerich, famous for his long-flowing beard, knew little about the game. Native to Germany, he settled in Louisville in 1842.[34] His company, J. F. Hillerich Job Turning, "was known for custom-carving wood everything from bedposts to chairs, railing, and butter churns." The shop, filled with lathes, "served America's expanding need and desire for furnishings during the country's robust growth period in the latter half of the 19th century."[35]

John A. "Bud" Hillerich began working at his father's company as a 14-year-old in 1880. "He had completed grade school, which was all the education most boys were given in those days."[36] Bud "was a bit of a black sheep in the family, in part because he loved baseball." Many in the 1880s disparaged baseball as a game for ruffians and ne'er do wells.

J. F. Hillerich got into the bat-making business in the 1880s. The origin story is still something of a mystery. A popular version is that Bud Hillerich left the shop one afternoon to cheer on his beloved Eclipse. On that day, Pete Browning supposedly broke his bat.[37] Nicknamed the "Gladiator" and the "Louisville Slugger," Browning ranked as one of the great hitters from his era. He led the American Association with a .378 batting average as a rookie in 1882. He struggled as a fielder, though, and he drank too much. (He called beer "German tea.") Browning also was nearly deaf. "He spoke to everyone in a booming, quirky voice because he could not hear himself speak."[38] In addition, Browning "was remembered for being one of the first players who cared about his bats, taking many of them home to his basement late in his career, apparently believing there were no hits left in them." He named many of his bats. He swung pieces of lumber that he dubbed Mary, Joe, Kate, and even Lazarus.[39]

Bud Hillerich invited the local star to his dad's shop. Supposedly, Browning left with a new bat and lined three hits the next day. He topped the Association with a .362 mark in 1885, "and word spread throughout baseball about the Hillerich-made bats."[40]

Another story is that St. Louis Browns third baseman Arlie Latham, the so-called "Freshest Man on Earth," swung the first Hillerich-brand bat in 1883 or 1884. Fans knew Latham more for his base stealing than his great hitting (724 career steals, a .269 average). Supposedly, he—like Browning—broke his bat one afternoon while on a road trip to Louisville. Unable to find a replacement for sale, he turned to J. F. Hillerich.[41]

Yet another version is that J. F. Hillerich made a bat for Bud, who showed it off to friends, including local pitching star Gus Weyhing. "As Weyhing's teammates tried the bat, they found it superior" to others "and requested Hillerich deliver more."[42] Bud Hillerich registered Louisville Slugger as a trademark in 1894. J. F., though, still preferred making bed posts to baseball bats. "J. Frederich thought the sport of baseball was beneath the dignity of the family business, and the making of bats was a distraction."[43] (Frank Bradsby joined Hillerich's firm in 1911 as a sales and marketing expert. Five years later, the company changed its name to Hillerich & Bradsby.)

Often, Carl Reese worked the night shift for the L&N. That left him free in the afternoon to play catch and hit grounders to his young son. One can easily imagine a pint-sized Harold shifting his feet in the loose dirt at a local park, staring at his dad, maybe pounding his right fist into a worn baseball glove and wiping a stream of perspiration from his face on a hot summer day. "Get down," Carl instructed. "You got to dig that ball out of the ground! Stay with it. Play the ball. Don't let it play you!"[44] Father and son did this for hours.

One day, Carl Reese brought home an old pair of spiked baseball shoes. Harold laced up the shoes and hurried to the park. "I could hear them scrape the concrete when I walked on the sidewalk," he recalled decades later. "They sounded so good. I felt as if I were in the big leagues."[45]

Harold held down a part-time job at the rail yard, hawking newspapers and selling box lunches. Later, he said, "We all worked. My sisters, they worked. You could work at any age, and they worked for the telephone company. ... We all lived together and threw the money into the pot."[46] On at least one occasion, Carl walked with his son to a particular tree that stood on the rail yard grounds. "He said that's where a rope had been thrown over [a] limb [and] there's been quite a few blacks hanged there."[47]

The writer Roger Kahn described Reese in his childhood days as "fair-haired, a pale, thin boy," but one "gifted with extraordinary hand-eye coordination."[48] He played a tough game of marbles. The neighborhood boys and girls watched in awe as he unpacked his bag and got ready for yet another match. Nobody could beat him. Harold especially liked a small marble, one known as a peewee. "Man, peewee ought to be your middle name," one boy said, "the way you use that shooter."[49] A peewee, Reese explained in 1956, "is a small marble that's not worth much of anything. It's much smaller than the crystals and agates and much less valuable."[50] One year, when he was about 12, Harold—now, Pee Wee—entered a marbles tournament sponsored by the *Louisville Courier-Journal*. Many articles and books have claimed that Reese won the tournament. In truth, he was runner-up. At least one writer later asked him if he was robbed of a championship. "I was not robbed," Reese affirmed. "The other kid was better."[51]

America's youth loved to shoot marbles. "The decade that spanned the late 1920s and 1930s is referred to by collectors as the Golden Age of Marbles,"[52] and with good reason. Clyde R. Miller, director of education services at Columbia University in New York City, said in 1932 that "marbles teach skill, self-control and fair play. These are the prime attributes of success in any field of endeavor. A lad who has never played marbles graduates from boyhood with a serious handicap. ... The marbles champion has poise and complete control of himself. The training he receives is invaluable in later years when self-control becomes one of the most important weapons with which to face the issues of life."[53]

Pee Wee began classes at duPont Manual High School as a nearly 100-pound freshman. Opened in 1892 as a vocational school for boys only, duPont is renowned for its Gothic architecture and five-story tower "framed by three double doors set between gothic pilasters with huge stone arched transoms."[54] The school began admitting female students in 1950.

Reese's first mention in *The Sporting News* probably came in the July 27, 1934, issue. Known by many as the baseball bible, the weekly publication ran a team photo of a "Louisville amateur team." Carl Reese, Jr., is shown in uniform, as is everyone else in the photo. Except for the kid in the front. Harold Reese, 15 years old at the time, is wearing street clothes. He was serving as the team's batboy.

He played second base for an American Legion squad and for the New Covenant Presbyterian Church team, coached by Keith Sparks.[55] Finally, in his junior year,

Pee Wee worked up the courage—almost—to try out for the duPont Manual varsity. He walked onto the field and heard the crack of the bat and the thump of baseballs colliding with gloves. He saw the other players, all of them big and strong. They were staring at him, he was sure. Staring and chuckling at the little guy, still not much more than 100 pounds. Pee Wee stepped closer to the duPont coach, Ralph Kimmel, on this first day of practice. He wanted to introduce himself. Maybe he wanted to ask a question. And then he couldn't. He ran off the field and fled for home.

His baseball career continued with New Covenant. The kid kept playing and practicing. He finally made the duPont team as a senior. Kimmel put him at second base. The youngster lasted a handful of games, until a spike wound injured his hand. He headed back to the church league.

Over the summer, after graduation, Reese took a job splicing cables for the Southern Bell Telephone Company. Every day, he shimmied up and down telephone poles, gaining muscle in his legs and shoulders. The job "really built me up,"[56] Reese said. He added about 30 pounds and four inches in just a few months. Sparks took one look at Reese in the spring of 1937 and shifted him from second base to shortstop, a position that requires a more powerful throwing arm.

New Covenant, in large part due to Reese's sparkling play, won the city amateur championship. Sparks decided that Cap Neal, owner-manager of the Louisville Colonels minor league team, should know a few things about Reese. "I've got a boy for you to look at," Sparks said. What position does he play, Neal asked. Sparks told him, "A whale of a shortstop." The Colonels didn't need a shortstop, Neal said. They had plenty. Sparks kept up the sales pitch. "I don't care who they are," he said. "They couldn't carry my boy's glove."[57] Sparks invited Neal to drop by and watch Reese play ball the following day at one of the local parks. "Take a look for yourself," Sparks said. "Then you can buy me a box of cigars for tipping you off." Neal just shrugged. "Maybe I will, Sparks. Maybe I will."[58]

Neal picked a good game to watch. In the third inning, Reese "made a great stop on a smash up the middle" and "flipped to second to start a double play." Two innings later, he singled to left field and stole second, reaching the base "well ahead of the catcher's throw." In the sixth, Reese ran with his back to home plate and made an over-the-shoulder catch "on the dead run" in short left field. He completed the day by ringing a double against the left-field wall. "Neal's eyes were glinting now." He told Sparks to "bring that Reese kid into my office next week. And tell him to bring his father with him. We'll need his signature on the contract."[59]

First, though, Reese left for New York to watch the Yankees and Giants play in the World Series. The trip was New Covenant's prize for winning a championship. While in the Big Apple, Reese asked for and secured an autograph from the great Giants slugger, Mel Ott. The Yankees beat the Giants in five games. New York center field Joe DiMaggio batted .346 (9-for-26), and first baseman Lou Gehrig hit two home runs with seven RBIs. Roger Kahn, in his book *Into My Own*, wrote that this was "a week full of firsts" for Reese. "He had never before seen a subway, or a concrete and steel ballpark or playing fields so vast."[60]

Yankee Stadium at its deepest point in the outfield was 466 feet from home plate. "I noticed the power hitting," Reese recalled. "That series, Gehrig. DiMaggio, and [Tony]

Lazzeri all hit home runs. I remember thinking these fellers looked pretty strong." Many years later, Kahn asked Reese whether he imagined himself playing at that park one day. "Absolutely not," he answered. "If you had told me in 1937, I'd be playing in a World Series four years later, I would have thought you'd had too much to drink."[61]

Back home, contract negotiations began in Neal's office. Reese hoped to sign fast and start playing for the Colonels right away. Sparks, though, wanted to bargain. At least one other minor league team had shown interest in Reese. Neal offered $65 a month for the church league star. Reese leaned forward to sign. It sounded like good money. Sparks, though, just scoffed at the figure. "I thought you were interested in signing this boy," he said. "I guess I was wrong." How about $100 a month, he countered. Neal argued that Reese still needed some seasoning but agreed to the price. "I better say okay before you ask for a piece of the Colonels, too," he said. As a matter of fact, Sparks asked for just that. He wanted Reese to get five percent of the purchase price just in case Louisville decided to sell the new player's contract. "It's only fair that a kid share in the profit made on a deal involving him," Sparks argued. Neal grumbled but, once again, agreed to the demand.

Reese promptly quit his job with the telephone company. His supervisor told him to think it over before leaving. The phone company offered a steady salary, benefits and, upon retirement, a pension. "I'm young, sir," Reese said. "I can afford to take a chance."[62]

Neal advised his young player not to dream big. "You're kinda small," he told Pee Wee. Furthermore, "the pitching in our league is a helluva lot better than the amateur stuff you've been seeing. But do your best. Maybe we can work you into the lineup in two or three years." Two or three years! Reese offered his new skipper a frank scouting report on both himself and the infield competition. "I've watched your team, Mr. Neal," he said. "Right now, I can play better infield than anyone you've got."[63]

He finally got his chance after one of the team's veterans suffered a serious injury. Determined to prove he belonged, and maybe pressing a bit, Reese got off to a slow start, especially in the field. If he wasn't kicking a grounder, he was throwing wildly to first. Neal offered some encouragement. "Don't let it get to you, kid," he said. "Tomorrow's another day." And, unfortunately, another chance to make an error. Reese booted baseball after baseball. "I was fortunate it wasn't a good club," he recalled. "It was independently owned, so consequently we didn't have a lot of good players, so I got to stay with the team and play."[64] Gradually, his fielding improved.

Scouts from several teams watched Reese play throughout the season. Billy Evans, farm director for the Boston Red Sox and a former umpire, "had practically set up camp at the Louisville club that season."[65] Following one game, Evans walked into Neal's office and announced that he wanted to make a deal for Reese. "I think I can beat anybody's offer," he said. Neal looked up at Evans. Just how badly did the Red Sox want Reese? Neal had an idea, however outlandish. He suggested that the Red Sox purchase, not just Reese, but the entire Colonels ballclub.

"It's not as crazy as it sounds," Neal insisted. He confessed, "I haven't been feeling too well lately. I've got to slow down. I'd like to sell my club, take it easy, go fishing someplace." Neal called Reese "an important asset to the Colonels. Naturally, whoever buys the team would want Reese to go with it. So, I don't know that I'd like to deal him off to anybody, unless the rest of the club went with the deal. Buy the Louisville club and you get Reese."[66]

Evans listened and probably scratched his head as he thought about Neal's proposal. Buy an entire team just to secure the rights to one player? He wasn't sure how Red Sox owner Tom Yawkey might react to that proposal. Yawkey, though, known for being a free spender, gave his approval. He bought the Colonels for $195,000.

The Sporting News reported that "the deal was guarded with such secrecy that some officials of the Louisville club actually did not know that [the Red Sox] were interested in the Colonels." The new ownership group also included former big league shortstop Donie Bush and Indianapolis banker Frank E. McKinney. William E. Smith, the outgoing president of the Colonels, said, "A new era of baseball is dawning for Louisville; the new owners have ample resources and capable management. We did the best we could, but we were handicapped financially."[67]

Reese played 138 games for the Colonels in 1938 and batted .277 with 23 stolen bases. Catchers threw him out just one time. Even so, McKinney suggested to Bush that he try "softening Reese up a little before we sit down with him and talk money" for the 1939 campaign. Good idea, Bush said. He and Reese met for a few minutes and, instead of softening up the shortstop, Bush gave him a big raise. Bush waved him off an incredulous McKinney. "Well, when I was a kid, I'd have been tickled silly if somebody paid me that much," Bush said. "Besides, he called me 'mister.' I like that in a youngster."[68]

Pee Wee's dad lived long enough to see his son turn into a top-notch minor leaguer. He did not, however, get to see the glory years that followed. Carl Marion Reese died on December 3, 1938, at the age of 52, after his left kidney ruptured.[69]

The following spring, Red Sox officials asked their manager and star shortstop, Joe Cronin, to drive from the team's spring training camp in Sarasota, Florida, to the Colonels' camp in nearby Arcadia, and watch Reese play ball. Cronin was 32 years old and already a 13-year veteran. The

Reese joined the Louisville Colonels in 1938 after playing for New Covenant Presbyterian Church. Louisville manager Donie Bush called him the best-fielding shortstop he had ever seen (National Baseball Hall of Fame Library, Cooperstown, New York).

San Francisco, California, native broke in with the Pittsburgh Pirates as a 19-year-old in 1926. Pittsburgh sold him to the Kansas City Blues of the American Association in April of 1928. He struggled and hit just .245 in 74 games. Cronin worried about another possible demotion. Instead, the Washington Senators purchased his contract in July. The right-handed batter soon established himself as one of the game's top sluggers. He drove home more than 100 runs in five straight seasons (1930–1934) and topped the American League with 45 doubles in 1933, his first year as both player and manager.

The Senators sold Cronin to the Red Sox following the 1934 campaign. Yawkey sent shortstop Lyn Lary and $250,000 to Washington. Cronin signed a five-year deal to serve as Boston's player-manager at $30,000 per season. He continued to make life tough for opposing pitchers. In 1938, Cronin batted .325 and topped the AL in doubles for a second time, this time with a career-high 51.

Only Cronin stood in the way of Reese getting a starting job with the Red Sox. But the veteran wasn't budging. He had no plans to put away his potent bat and middling glove. "So, that's the guy who's going to take my place," Cronin said. "He's too small."[70] Maybe. Cronin also liked his job security. He continued to give Pee Wee Reese a bad rap. "The kid won't do," he said. "I'm still good for a couple of years. Better years, I'm sure, than Reese can give you."[71] With that, Cronin suggested the Red Sox rid themselves of their new acquisition.

Bush already had told *The Sporting News* that Reese was "the best fielding shortstop he's seen in his thirty-one years in the game,"[72] and Bush knew a few things about that position. He played shortstop for 16 years in the big leagues, for the Detroit Tigers and the Senators. The Indianapolis, Indiana, native hit .250 over his career and stole 406 bases. He led the American League in walks five times and in runs scored twice. The 5-foot-6-inch, 140-pound switch-hitter also was known as a top-flight bunter and top defender. Following his retirement, Bush returned to Indianapolis and managed the local affiliate of the American Association, the Indians. Later, he managed in the big leagues for the Pirates, Chicago White Sox, and Cincinnati Reds before taking over dugout duties in Louisville.

In late July, the Red Sox sold Reese to the Brooklyn Dodgers for $35,000 and four players to be named later.[73] (The headline in *The Sporting News* called this transaction a $75,000 deal. The Dodgers paid $35,000 in cash. A value of $10,000 was given to each of the four players headed to Louisville.)[74] MacPhail declared it the largest deal in American Association history.[75] Tommy Fitzgerald, a columnist for the *Louisville Courier-Journal*, reported Reese's birth year as 1919 and said that he moved to Louisville "when he still was in short pants."[76] Reese was batting .278 and leading the Association with 25 steals. St. Paul Saints manager Babe Ganzel said, "He goes to his left and gets in front of balls that other shortstops can get to with only one hand." While Reese was error-prone, Ganzel said, "He makes the hard chances look easy and is charged with miscues on balls that others wouldn't catch up with."[77] The article listed Reese as 5-feet-10-inches and 158 pounds. Terms called for him to stay with Louisville for the rest of the season. Fitzgerald praised Reese as "probably the most popular player to ever wear a Louisville uniform."[78]

Pee Wee Reese heard about the deal and just about threw a fit. "Brooklyn?!" he exclaimed. "No! I don't want to go to Brooklyn!"[79]

2

"Brooklyn's in the major leagues, isn't it?"

Pee Wee Reese joined a franchise that many fans and some sportswriters jokingly called the "daffy Dodgers." Certainly, a majority of Brooklyn ballclubs over the previous few decades deserved that cheeky moniker. After winning the National League pennant in 1920, Brooklyn finished in the first division just five out of the next 19 years.

Headline writers enjoyed the struggle. "Dodgers Still Daffy Outfit,"[1] claimed one newspaper. "Daffy Dodgers Take Twin Bill Off Cardinals,"[2] reported another. Sometimes, it didn't even matter if Brooklyn knocked off an arch-rival—by a 15-7 margin, no less. "Daffy Dodgers Wallop Giants,"[3] the *Muncie Star Press* informed readers on September 4, 1937. St. Louis-based columnist Sid Keener insisted that no one—not even the most diehard Brooklyn fan—should take offense at this deflating nickname. The Daffy Dodgers deserved it. "They were appropriately named by the boys in the press box because they were always doing the wrong thing at the wrong time—those Brooklyns," Keener wrote.[4]

Floyd Caves "Babe" Herman, more than anyone, inspired the headline-making daffy material. One reporter tabbed him "the daffiest of the Daffy Dodgers of the late 1920s and early 1930s."[5] Born June 26, 1903, in Buffalo, New York, Herman grew up in southern California. The lanky, left-handed swinger (6-foot-4-inches, 190 pounds) batted .324 over 13 campaigns (1926–1937, 1945), including a .381 mark in 1929 and a career-high .393 in 1930. During that latter season, he also set career highs with 35 home runs, 130 RBIs, 241 hits, 48 doubles, and 143 runs scored.

Babe Herman posed a danger to opposing teams any time he held a bat in his hands. He presented a hazard to himself and teammates whenever he ran the bases or put on a glove. Herman retired with a fielding percentage of .961 and led the National League in errors committed by a right fielder in 1928, 1929, and 1931 with 16, 16, and 13, respectively. In 1927, he also topped the circuit in first-base miscues, with 21. Official scorers marked Herman with 96 errors over his career. Brooklyn teammate Fresco Thompson, later a front-office executive for the Dodgers and other teams, said, "He [Herman] wore a glove for one reason; because it was a league custom."[6]

Some Babe Herman stories remain the stuff of baseball lore. Probably the most famous one took place August 15, 1926, at Ebbets Field, against the Boston Braves. Herman stepped into the batter's box with two outs and the bases loaded in the seventh inning. Chick Fewster stood near first base, Dazzy Vance crept a few feet off second, and Hank DeBerry looked in from the third base bag. The game was tied, 1–1. Herman ripped a pitch that crashed into the right field wall. He sprinted to first and headed for second. DeBerry scored easily. Vance rounded third base as Fewster stepped across second. Herman charged ahead, right behind Fewster. Realizing what was about to happen, Brooklyn third base coach Mickey O'Neil yelled, "Back! Back!"[7]

"He meant Herman, but it was Vance who paid attention," according to the *Brooklyn Daily Eagle*. It got awfully crowded 90 feet from home plate. "The Dazzler rumbled back to third and fell on the bag just as the Babe, with a beautiful slide, arrived from the opposite direction. Fewster? He fell and was momentarily pinned to third base, between Vance and the Babe. Disgusted, he tore himself loose and trudged toward his position as second baseman."[8] Eddie Taylor, Boston's quick-thinking infielder, tagged all three Brooklyn base runners. There already was one out, but why take any chances? Taylor even tagged O'Neil. Umpire John "Beans" Reardon ruled it this way: Vance was entitled to the base. Fewster and Herman were out. The inning was over.

That famous episode led to a popular joke. "The Dodgers have three men on base." "Oh yeah? Which base?" Years later, Babe's son, Bob Herman, recalled a silver lining to the incident, at least for the sake of Herman family history. Brooklyn won the game, 4–1, thanks largely to Babe's bat. "The thing that most people forget about that story is that the run which scored was the winning one in that game," the younger Herman said in 1971. "My dad drove in the game-winning run."[9]

Herman sometimes ignored the goings-on. During one game against the Pittsburgh Pirates, a batter's line drive smashed into the left field corner at Forbes Field. Brooklyn manager Wilbert Robinson lost sight of the ball as runners sprinted along the base paths. He looked over at Herman, who had the day off. "What just happened out there?" the skipper asked. "I don't know, Robbie," Herman answered. "I was reading the paper."[10]

Some reporters made it a practice to write about the latest Herman escapade, much to the star player's chagrin. "You make me look like a clown," Herman told Joe Gordon of the *New York American*. Some of the stuff was funny, sure. But "give me a break, will you," Herman pleaded. He thought fans might think of him as a clown rather than a solid big leaguer. Gordon listened, agreed that Herman had a point, and promised to stop writing so many unflattering stories. Then Herman pulled a cigar from his pocket, and Gordon held out a match. "Don't bother," Herman said. "It's lit." Well, that did it. "It's all off," Gordon said about the agreement reached less than a minute earlier. "Nobody who carries around lighted cigars in his pocket can tell me he isn't a clown."[11]

"Daffy" jokes notwithstanding, baseball in Brooklyn had enjoyed a long—and mostly successful—tradition, one beginning in the first half of the 19th century. Civic leaders built parks and baseball grounds in Williamsburg, Bedford, and other neighborhoods. Newspaper writers encouraged city residents to get some exercise and enjoy the afternoon sunshine, at least on the weekend. The famous poet Walt Whitman wrote on June 23, 1846, about young people playing "base," a game of ball. "We wish such sights were more common among us," he continued. "In the practice of athletic and manly sports, the young men of nearly all our American cities are very deficient—perhaps more so than those of any other country that could be mentioned. ... Let us enjoy life a little."[12]

Between 1835 and 1855, this former Dutch settlement—originally called "Breuckelen" from the Dutch word for "Marshland"—grew from 24,592 to 205,250 people. Immigrants poured into the area, mostly from Ireland and Germany. Many workers built ships or stocked goods such as tobacco, wool, sugar, and grain in the warehouses that lined the shore. By the mid–1850s, Brooklyn had grown into the third-largest city in the United States, a busy place just across the East River from Manhattan.

Baseball flourished on the 71-square-mile tract of land. By the time Union and Confederate forces had fired the opening shots of the U.S. Civil War in April 1861, Brooklyn could boast of fielding more than 70 teams, compared with about 25 in Manhattan.[13] The earliest ones included the Excelsiors, the Atlantics, the Eckfords, and the Putnams. Each squad set up shop in a different Brooklyn neighborhood. The Excelsiors, for instance, represented South Brooklyn, and the Atlantics claimed the Bedford area. Some clubs fielded multiple teams, each one suited for a different age and skill level. "It seemed that nearly every male inhabitant of the city with the leisure time and athletic proclivities was playing baseball."[14]

Some squads swung bats and fielded balls on frozen ponds at Prospect Park and other places. These games attracted crowds of curious fans. The Atlantics beat the Charter Oaks, 37–27, in one high-scoring matchup held on February 4, 1861. The *Daily Eagle* frowned on the entire, icy affair. Baseball, it stated, should be played on grassy fields on warm summer days, not on frozen ponds during the dead of winter. "We hope we shall see no more ball games on ice," one writer sniffed. "The ballplayers have their season, and a long one; playing on skates is mere tom foolery; it interferes with the rights of the ticket holders and creates dissatisfaction.... If any of the ball clubs wants to make fools of themselves, let them go to Coney Island and play a game of stilts."[15] That tough stand did nothing to melt the ice among local fans. Teams kept playing baseball during the deep freeze, slippery as it may have been.

The story of the Dodgers goes back to 1883. That year, New York businessman Charles Byrne, along with his brother-in-law, Joseph Doyle, and Rhode Island casino operator Ferdinand Abell, bought a franchise in the Inter-State Association of Professional Baseball Clubs, a minor league. Known as the Brooklyn Grays, the team played its first game on May 1 and lost, 9–6, to the Quickstop club in Wilmington, New Jersey. The Grays opened at their home yard, Washington Park, on May 12 and beat a squad from Trenton, New Jersey, 13–6, thanks in part to 12 Trenton errors.[16] Brooklyn went on to win the league title and promptly joined the American Association, then a major league. By 1889, fans had thought up a new name for their team—"the Bridegrooms"—after six players got married over the off-season. That franchise joined the National League in 1890.

Two years later, team owners hired a 23-year-old New York City native and former architecture student named Charles Hercules Ebbets. The young man handled a number of chores for the ballclub. He began by hawking tickets and game-day programs and worked his way into the front office. He took over as team president in

1898, following the death of Charles Byrne, and even managed the club for a short time. Ebbets sat in the dugout and directed a group of tobacco-chewing tough guys while wearing a top hat.

As early as 1895, some fans began calling Brooklyn's baseball team the "Trolley Dodgers." Three years earlier, the first of many fast-moving trolley trains began to crowd borough streets. These trains replaced the much slower, horse-drawn trolleys. Soon, and before many citizens could take cover, "trolley car tracks were decorating every street in Brooklyn and crisscrossing every intersection in Brooklyn."[17] The darned things could be dangerous. On June 23, 1892, the *Evening World* reported, "Run into by a trolley car. This time in Brooklyn. The record of events keeps furnishing arguments against the perilous railway system, as applied on city streets." Three days later, "The Trolley's fatal score. Score three more dead for the trolley." By September 20, 1893, an *Evening World* writer exclaimed, "We were dodging the dorned [sic] trolleys at every corner, and couldn't get clear of them. We will never go near Brooklyn again." Some people, probably those from outside the borough, tabbed Brooklyn residents as "Trolley Dodgers," or, in time, just "Dodgers."

Ebbets dreamed of building a new ballfield, one to replace rickety Washington Park, and found the ideal spot in a borough neighborhood with the odd name of Pigtown. Hogs, goats, and other farm animals scampered through the dusty streets. Rickety housing stood—sometimes just barely—in this section of Brooklyn. A stinking pit made the area even less attractive. Residents tossed their garbage into the hole, which became a popular place for swine and other animals to feed. "But," Frank Graham wrote, "in his mind's eye, he [Ebbets] could see it cleared and leveled, and soaring about it, the structure of a modern baseball plant."[18] Unfortunately, about 40 different people held deeds to this property. Ebbets began buying parcels one at a time, keeping his intentions as secret as possible. It took about three years to complete all the deals.

Reporters and city officials attended the groundbreaking ceremony on March 4, 1912. A writer asked Ebbets what he planned to call the team's new home. Probably Washington Park, he said, the same name as the last one. Leo Wooster of the *Brooklyn Times* had a better idea. "Why don't you call it Ebbets Field?" Wooster suggested. "It was your idea and nobody else's, and you've put yourself in hock to build it. It's going to be your monument, whether you like to think about it that way or not."[19] Ebbets agreed.

The ballpark hosted its first big league game on April 5, 1913, in an exhibition against the Yankees. Genevieve Ebbets, Charles' daughter, threw out the first pitch. "An overflow crowd of 30,000 fanatical Brooklyn fans screamed in delight"[20] when Casey Stengel put his team ahead with an inside-the-park home run hit over the head of center fielder Harry Wolter. Brooklyn went on to win, 3–2. Four days later, "before a chilled crowd of 10,000 diehard fans,"[21] Brooklyn lost, 1–0, to Philadelphia in the team's regular-season opener. Tom Seaton tossed a six-hit shutout for the Phillies. In the *Eagle*, a writer known simply as "Rice" reasoned, "One game does not make a season, and an opening day is 153 games from the closing day, the President of the Don't Worry Club reminds us, in a champagne-tinted note, but doggone it, we wanted to win that first game!"[22]

Brooklyn hired Wilbert Robinson as manager in 1914. Born on June 29, 1863, in Boston, Robinson worked for a while in the family butcher shop before pursuing a baseball career. The good-natured catcher put together a fine career, batting .273 over 17 seasons (1886–1902), driving home 722 runs, and stealing nearly 200 bases. In 1909, he took a coaching job with John McGraw's formidable New York Giants. "His main duties were keeping the club loose, jockeying the opposition, and helping the pitching staff."[23] Robinson's friendship with McGraw ended just hours after the final out of the 1913 World Series against Connie Mack's Philadelphia Athletics. McGraw, now drunk, lambasted Robinson for some coaching decisions made that day. Robinson, in turn, tore into McGraw's dugout skills. "This is my party," McGraw bellowed. "Get the hell out of here."[24] The rift lasted for nearly two decades.

Players called Robinson "Uncle Robbie" and enjoyed his good humor. He is most famous for trying to catch a grapefruit dropped from the sky one spring training in Daytona Beach, Florida. Casey Stengel, a young Brooklyn outfielder and part-time dental student from Kansas City, Missouri, supposedly encouraged Robinson on this escapade.[25] The manager swore that he would grab the falling citrus with his mitt. How hard could it be?

Local aviator Ruth Law flew the plane on the big day, March 13, 1915. Decades later, she made no mention of Stengel in her account of the stunt. Law explained she had received a message to drop a baseball from about 500 feet to a waiting Dodger on the ground. With the plane ready for takeoff, though, Law realized that she had forgotten the ball. "A young man working in [her] outfit" handed Law a grapefruit, and "I thought what difference would it make if I dropped the pretty yellow fruit." She buzzed over the field, and Uncle Robbie looked to the sky. Suddenly, something—surely just a speck at first—dropped from above. Robinson looked up. He had it, he had it. Then, he didn't. The grapefruit hit him in the chest and splattered all over his uniform. The force knocked him to the ground. "Oh, God," he cried. "I'm bleeding. Somebody go get a doctor—quick!"[26]

Brooklyn earned its first pennant in 1916 and met the Boston Red Sox in the World Series. Boston took the opener, 6–5, and, behind a young, husky left-hander named Babe Ruth, won the second game, 2–1, in 14 innings. The 21-year-old Ruth, who led the American League with a 1.75 ERA and nine shutouts, went the distance. Brooklyn won its first World Series game ever on October 10 at Ebbets Field. Veteran "Colby Jack" Coombs, a 31-game winner for the Philadelphia Athletics in 1910 and famous for his drop curveball, beat Carl Mays, 4–3. A two-run triple in the fifth inning by shortstop Ivy Olson secured the victory. Boston took the next two games, 6–2 and 4–1, and the best-of-five championship.

Four years later, Brooklyn met the Cleveland Indians in a best-of-nine Series. This one featured the first triple play in fall classic history (turned by Cleveland second baseman Bill Wambsganss), the first Series grand slam (Cleveland's Elmer Smith), and the first World Series home run hit by a pitcher (Elmer Bagby, again, of Cleveland), all in Game Five. Brooklyn won two of the first three games, then lost four straight. The Indians outscored the Robins, 21–8.

Robinson never made it to another World Series. His later clubs usually struggled to get out of the second division. The Robins still boasted some talent. Outfielder

Zack Wheat, for instance, made a habit out of hitting .300 and twice batted as high as .375. Pitcher Dazzy Vance, who battled arm problems for years before going to Brooklyn in 1922, led the National League in strikeouts seven times. The 6-foot-2-inch right-hander threw a ferocious fastball and tumbling curveball. Following one game, Bill Corum of the *New York Times* wrote that "Vance had all the vaunted speed and a dizzy curve, which looped the loop, twisted and twirled and cut capers like a toy balloon in a Kansas cyclone."[27] Vance won 28 games in 1924 and posted a 2.16 ERA. The Robins stayed in the pennant chase before finishing in second place with a 92–62 mark, Robinson's best post–1920 club.

The following year, on April 25 in New York City, Charles Ebbets died at the age of 65, soon after doctors had ordered him to his suite at the Waldorf-Astoria Hotel for some much-needed rest and relaxation. Robinson called his late boss "a remarkable baseball man." National League President John A. Heydler said Ebbets' death "will have a marked effect on organized baseball. He was a great visionary who made his dreams come true."[28]

Brooklyn's 1925 squad finished in sixth place once again. Robinson, now team president in addition to manager, had grown tired of the buffoonery and comic misplays that plagued his team. So he instituted a Bonehead Club. He decided to charge players $10 for every miscue, a decent sum in those days. On the first day of this new order, Robinson messed up the team's batting lineup. Eddie Murphy of the *New York Sun* probably laughed as he typed these words: "The manager of the Dodgers formed a Bonehead Club before yesterday's game and promptly elected himself a charter member."[29]

Robinson's reign as Dodger skipper ended after the 1931 campaign. The team's five directors voted not to renew his contract. Supposedly, he got the news while he was inspecting the dairy cows on his Georgia farm.[30] Tommy Holmes of the *Daily Eagle* wrote, "Eighteen years is a long time in baseball reckoning to stick at the head of one ballclub, and the last one-third of Wilbert Robinson's reign was studded with trials and tribulations. The longer it lasted, the tougher it became for the 68-year-old pilot. … He made Brooklyn baseball, but the change had to come, next year if not this year."[31]

Uncle Robbie won 1,375 games and lost 1,341. When he retired, only McGraw and Fred Clarke had won more games as National League skippers, with 2,652 and 1,602 victories, respectively. John Kieran of the *New York Times* wrote about Robinson: "His conversation was a continuous flow of homely philosophy, baseball lore, and good humor. He knew baseball as the spotted setter knows the secrets of quail hunting, by instinct and experience."[32]

The Dodgers shuffled through a trio of managers over the next several seasons. Only Max Carey, a former outfielder who held a .285 career batting average and stole 738 bases, led the team to a winning record. The Terre Haute, Indiana, native, did that in his first year. His 1932 Brooklyn squad finished 81–73, in third place. The following season, the team fell to 65–88 and sixth place. Brooklyn fired Carey and hired Stengel, who turned to managing after his 14-year playing career ended in 1925. Stengel led the Toledo Mud Hens, the New York Giants' top affiliate in the American Association, for six seasons before getting the Brooklyn job. Stengel hoped to put a layer of polish onto the young Dodgers. "What else are you going to do when you get a second-division ballclub?" he asked. "You've got a couple of good players on it, you work on them. Who else are you gonna work on?"[33] Stengel lasted three seasons with Brooklyn, never finishing higher than fifth.

Next up was retired pitcher Burleigh Grimes. A native of Emerald, Wisconsin, Grimes began practicing his trademark spitball at the age of 13. Five years later, he began his professional career as a member of the Eau Claire Commissioners of the Class D Minnesota-Wisconsin League. Grimes made his big-league debut, as a member of the Pirates, late in the 1916 campaign. By then, he was chewing slippery elm and rubbing the goop onto the baseball. "However, he said the juice from the wood irritated his skin, so he refrained [from shaving] on the mornings of the days he was scheduled to pitch." Players began calling the pitcher Ol' Stubblebeard. Brooklyn traded for him in January 1918. Grimes spent 19 seasons in the big leagues, including nine with Brooklyn during the daffy years, and won 270 games. In his first few days as Brooklyn skipper, Grimes told writers, "I don't want you fellows to be writing about this club as the Daffiness Boys. This time it's going to be different. There will be strict training rules and a curfew at eleven o'clock, and nobody is going to get away with the things my old pals got away with on Robbie."[34] Brooklyn finished, 62–91, in sixth place. Again.

The Dodgers needed a new boss. They needed someone brash, talented, intelligent, and hard-driving. They needed a man bold enough to have attempted the kidnapping of a world leader, and they found just such a man in Leland Stanford "Larry" MacPhail of Cass City, Michigan. Born February 3, 1890, MacPhail grew up the son of a successful bank owner and did turns as an attorney and department store manager before getting into the baseball business. During World War I, he entered the Army as a private and rose to captain of an artillery division.

Among his outlandish activities, MacPhail and a group of fellow officers tried to arrest Germany's Kaiser Wilhelm II, transport him to the Paris Peace Conference, and have him tried for war crimes. MacPhail and Army Col. Luke Lea hatched the plot, attempted on New Year's Day 1919. The two, along with six other soldiers, traveled in touring cars from Paris to a palace in Holland. The plan failed, and MacPhail barely escaped arrest. "Their fantastic venture came within a few seconds of success," according to one report. "Lea and MacPhail managed to get inside the palace in which the Kaiser was housed and were just about to pounce on their quarry when lookouts outside sounded the signal that the guards were approaching with bayonets ready."[35] The conspirators high-tailed it off the palace grounds. MacPhail swiped a palace ashtray for his troubles.

MacPhail cut quite a presence. He combed slick-backed red hair; looked into the mirror at a face filled with freckles; and opted for loud, often checkered suits, bold ties, and two-toned dress shoes. He talked non-stop and spoke in a voice that echoed as loudly as his wardrobe. He was Larry MacPhail, damn it, a man filled with ideas and opinions, and he was more than willing to share them—like it or not. Why not use yellow baseballs instead of white ones, MacPhail thundered. Hitters can see yellow ones better. Oh, and MacPhail cussed a blue streak, as big and blue as a summer sky.

In 1930, MacPhail took over as president of the Columbus (Ohio) Red Birds, which soon became part of the St. Louis Cardinals' vast farm system. The always energetic executive led the effort to build a new stadium and introduced a popular Ladies Day season-ticket program. In 1934, he took over as vice-president and general manager of the Cincinnati Reds. MacPhail hired cigarette girls and brought in workers to repaint the ballpark. He also convinced owner Powel Crosley, Jr., to broadcast Reds games on the radio. MacPhail hired a smooth-talking broadcaster out of Florida named Walter "Red" Barber to do play-by-play work for $25 a week, less than what he was making as the voice of University of Florida football. When Barber took his seat in the Crosley Field booth, he not only broadcast his first major league baseball game, he also watched his first major league baseball game. "That was the most joyous day of my life, next to my wedding day,"[36] he said.

On May 24, 1935, MacPhail introduced night baseball to the majors. President Franklin D. Roosevelt pushed a button from the White House at 8:30 p.m., signaling MacPhail to flip the light switch at Crosley Field. One reporter asked MacPhail how much it cost to light up the stadium for a ballgame. "I hate to tell you," MacPhail answered. "Possibly $250, but that is cheap if the public likes it." That night, 20,422 fans attended the game. Ever wary of the team's financial bottom line, MacPhail told Crosley, "Night baseball will give you a mid-week Sunday."[37] That is, the Reds could count on at least approaching Sunday attendance figures, the most popular game attendance day of the week.

It took just a couple of years for MacPhail to wear out his welcome in Cincinnati. Crosley could not tolerate his executive's colorful lifestyle. Many years later, MacPhail's son, Lee, offered more specifics on his dad's firing. "It was just because of his personal activities, which Crosley couldn't put up with. The personal activities included alcohol and women. My father lived a full life."[38]

Following one season working as a banker in Michigan, MacPhail took over as general manager of the Dodgers. He vowed to toss those daffy Dodgers days into the scrap heap. Sports writers, though, were not ready to let go of the nickname. "Larry MacPhail's first edition of the Daffy Dodgers is beginning to look like a peppy and dangerous ballclub," reported the *Cincinnati Enquirer*. "They have an air about them now."[39] MacPhail felt confident enough to declare that his new club could beat his old team. "On the field, I have a pretty fair club, pretty fair," he declared. "At least good enough to beat out the Reds. I'll bet you 3 to 1 on that."[40]

In March, MacPhail acquired Dolph Camilli, a power-hitting first baseman with the Phillies, in a $75,000 cash deal. The lefty batter had slugged at least 25 home runs in the three previous seasons. On July 11, Brooklyn picked up veteran pitcher Whitlow Wyatt. Up to that point in his career, Wyatt was 26–43 for three teams, with a 5.22 ERA, but MacPhail had been scouting him and liked what he saw.

MacPhail, with the help of $200,000 from the Brooklyn Trust Company, gave Ebbets Field a much-needed facelift. He had the infield rebuilt and re-sodded. He ordered every seat and railing repainted and had 1,500 reserve seats added behind home plate. Plus he requested that new flags for each National League team be installed and new concession stands built on the first and third bases sides. That wasn't all. "On the belief that the Ebbets Field ushers lacked glamour, Larry dressed them up in flashy green-and-gold uniforms,"[41] according to author G. Richard McKelvcy.

The Roaring Redhead, as some called him, even hired the great Babe Ruth as a Brooklyn coach midway through the 1938 season. Fans whooped it up for the retired Sultan of Swat, baseball's all-time home-run king. The Babe, still able to take a mighty cut, walloped homers in batting practice and exhibition games. A rumor began circulating. Maybe the Babe could swat some homers in a real game. Grimes, though, shot down any talk of a Ruthian comeback. "He can't see," said the 44-year-old, retired since 1934. "If he can hit, I can still pitch." Years later, Grimes said, "Sometimes, he couldn't see pitches. ... I knew he had trouble when I threw batting practice. So, we used to have Merv Shea, a catcher, throw to him. Shea just sort of flipped his arm when he threw, and it was easy to follow the ball. But you put him in a game? He might have been killed."[42] Brooklyn got some fun out of Ruth, plus 24 home runs and 100 RBIs out of Camilli, but finished in seventh place with a 69–80 record. MacPhail fired Grimes and asked Leo Durocher to do double duty as shortstop and manager. What a match, Larry and Leo.

Leo Ernest Durocher of West Springfield, Massachusetts, born July 27, 1905, grew up the son of French-Canadian parents from Quebec and often spoke French at home. He hustled pool as a kid and began playing semi-pro baseball as a teen. The New York Yankees signed him in 1925. Durocher wore snazzy suits and had a big mouth. Even as a rookie, in 1928, teammates were calling him "Leo the Lip." Babe Ruth couldn't stand him. He called Durocher the "All-American Out" for his woeful batting skills. Once, Ruth accused Durocher of swiping his watch.

The Yankees, much to Ruth's relief, put Durocher on waivers in February of 1930. Cincinnati picked him up, eventually grew tired of his boorish personality, as well as his fondness for gambling and speakeasies, and shipped him to the Cardinals halfway through the 1933 campaign. The Redbirds needed a new shortstop. Charles Gelbert, who held that position for St. Louis, accidentally shot himself in the ankle during an off-season hunting accident in Pennsylvania. Branch Rickey, the bushy-browed, cigar-smoking, Bible-quoting Redbirds executive, made the deal.

Rickey liked Durocher's competitive fire and defensive talents. He could put up with the mediocre hitting. The ever-quotable Rickey once said, about Durocher's fiery side, "He's still that kid from West Springfield with a pool cue butt in his hand."[43] Durocher served as captain of the Cardinals' fabled Gas House Gang, a group of hard-living, fun-loving ballplayers who won the World Series in 1934. "We fought as much among ourselves as with the opposition,"[44] Durocher wrote in his memoir, *Nice Guys Finish Last*.

In time, Leo Durocher wore out his welcome in St, Louis. MacPhail traded for him following the 1937 season, after Durocher hit a career-low .203 in 135 games. The scrappy veteran batted .219 in 1938, but that hardly mattered. In October, MacPhail appointed him—to the surprise of many—as player-manager for the upcoming season. The announcement was made, Hy Turkin wrote in the *Daily News*, "at a lovefest luncheon given by Larry MacPhail at a midtown hotel." Turkin added, "The pact will call for the usual one-year term of 'produce or get out,' it was reported."[45] MacPhail announced Durocher's promotion on the same day that Durocher caught a train for West Springfield to bury his dad. Holmes asked MacPhail why Durocher was the right man for the job. "Morale," MacPhail answered. "Our club did not have it. I don't intend to blame Burleigh Grimes for that, but our team did not have a hustling get-together spirit as a team. A few of the Brooklyn players felt that way and others hustled as individuals. But there was too little of this 'C'mon gang, let's up and at 'em fight."[46]

At least early on, the 1939 squad looked like most of the other Brooklyn teams from that era. The Dodgers got off to a disappointing 11–17 start. On July 27, following

Larry MacPhail (left) made the trade that brought Pee Wee Reese from the Red Sox to the Dodgers. Leo Durocher managed Reese for parts of five seasons (National Baseball Hall of Fame Library, Cooperstown, New York).

a 3–1 loss to the Chicago Cubs, Brooklyn dropped to 13½ games out of the top spot. That same day, Dixie Walker made his first start for the Dodgers. MacPhail had purchased the outfielder's contract from the Detroit Tigers. Over 61 games so far that season, the Villa Rica, Georgia, native was batting .280 with two home runs and 38 RBIs. He pinch-hit and struck out in his Brooklyn debut on July 25. A bum right knee bothered him all season.

"I was hobbling around when I reported in Chicago that July day in 1939," Walker recalled. "I hobbled all year. The fans didn't know what to expect. They had been told I was all wired together."[47] Brooklyn fans, though, quickly made Walker one of their favorites. "There was something about the guy—big, blond, smiling, affable—that caught the fancy of the mob at Ebbets Field almost as soon as he went to the plate for the first time," Frank Graham wrote. In time, fans began calling Walker "The People's Choice," or, in fluent Brooklynese, "The People's Cherce."

Brooklyn enjoyed a 37–24 stretch over August and September and finished in third place with an 84–69 won-loss record, a great improvement over the previous season. Camilli led the Brooklyn attack. He slammed 26 home runs, drove in 104 runs, and batted .290. Infielder Harry "Cookie" Lavagetto, a California product like Camilli and acquired from Pittsburgh in December 1936, batted .300 with 87 RBIs. Luke Hanlon, from Michigan, won 20 games, while Georgia native Hugh Casey, plucked off the Memphis Chicks roster after the 1938 season, added 15 victories. MacPhail earned *Sporting News* Executive of the Year honors.

Writers complimented Durocher and his Dodgers for their surge from seventh place to third. "This gent Durocher has done just about as nice and tidy a job as was performed by nobody anywhere in the recent baseball wars," said Bill Ritt. Durocher himself batted .277, one of the highest averages of his career. Ritt expected Brooklyn to climb a few more notches in 1940. "Yes, that Durocher fellow's done right smartly in his first year a manager and we wouldn't be surprised if he'll have something to say about the disposition of that National League pennant next year."[48]

Brooklyn scout and former infielder Harry "Ted" McGrew had begun following Pee Wee Reese over the summer, or since rumors spread that Boston might be interested in dealing him. One afternoon, MacPhail—decked out in white flannel pants, navy blue sport coat, and a yachting cap—summoned a group of sportswriters to his cabin cruiser, parked on the calm waters of Long Island Sound.[49] He wanted to talk about the young shortstop from Louisville.

McGrew had told MacPhail all about Reese. McGrew praised his speed on the bases, his range on defense, and his strong throwing arm. Supposedly, though, he could not hit an outside curveball. Now he could. "A couple of days later, I get a telegram from Ted," MacPhail continued. It read: "Just saw Reese hit two outside curves against the right field wall for triples. And he still runs the bases like [Ty] Cobb."[50]

MacPhail set out for himself and pronounced his scouting venture a great success. "I've just returned from Louisville, gentleman, and I will tell you this Reese is the greatest prospect I've ever seen," MacPhail exclaimed. "Furthermore, I think this kid could mean the pennant for Brooklyn. Not this year—but mark my words, in a couple of years, Reese will make us a winner."[51]

At least three other teams had wanted to acquire Pee Wee Reese, MacPhail said.

The Cubs offered $30,000 and two players, well below the Dodgers' bid. "And when I put the proposition to them, they accepted readily." Reese had played just two seasons of professional baseball. MacPhail acknowledged that the deal was "a risk" and "and a big gamble," but "I think we've got a great buy."[52]

New York Daily News reporter Jack Mahon introduced Reese to local readers. His article in the August 13, 1939, edition included a picture of Reese, wearing a Colonels uniform, with a caption headline: "Future Great?" Mahon continued, "To hear the old hands talk, this kid is a combination of Honus Wagner, Leo Durocher, Dave Bancroft and all the good short fielders of recent years." The Dodgers expected Reese to compete for a starting job in spring training. McGrew said, "The boy learns so fast he will probably be able to stick with the Dodgers in his first trial."[53]

Late in August, during a hot train ride from Washington, D.C., to St. Louis, Joe Cronin asked Charley Wagner and Wilfred LeFebvre to help pick an American Association All-Star team. The two young pitchers had spent much of the season in Louisville. Both chose New York Yankees farmhands Johnny Sturm and Jerry Priddy as the top first baseman and second baseman, respectively. They both picked Reese as the most talented shortstop.

Maybe Cronin felt a little cranky. Maybe he already had heard too much about Pee Wee Reese. He interrupted the two players. "That's because he was your teammate. How can you pick Reese over [Phil] Rizzuto, also of Kansas City, who is hitting .360, and [Jimmy] Pofahl, Minneapolis, who is hitting over .300?" Wagner didn't change his mind. "In a tight spot, I'd rather pitch to either of the other two than Reese," Wagner insisted. "Pee Wee is small, but he's a tough customer up there at the plate, especially since he's learned to hit a curveball into right field."[54]

Reese batted .279 in his 147 games with Louisville in 1939. He added four home runs and 18 triples, and he swiped 35 bases in 36 attempts. MacPhail, in another note of praise for his new acquisition, called Reese "the most instinctive base runner I've ever seen."[55] Did all this mean Leo Durocher was through as a player? McGrew wouldn't say. "But this kid is a real wonder," he insisted. "When this kid is at shortstop, you won't need a second baseman or a third baseman. He'll cover that much ground."[56] At last, Reese decided that going to Brooklyn might not be such a bad deal after all. He said, "I don't care who I play with, so long as I get to the big leagues."[57] He added, "Brooklyn's in the major leagues, isn't it?"[58]

3

"Skip, where do you buy your clothes?"

Pee Wee Reese arrived late to the Dodgers' spring training camp in Clearwater, Florida. Team officials had mailed him three letters over the winter. Each correspondence indicated a different reporting date. When Reese reported to Clearwater Athletic Field, a security guard stopped him. He said he was there to play ball for Brooklyn. The guard looked him over, shook his head, and called a team executive: "Say, look, there's a kid here who claims he's one of the team. ...just a skinny kid.... Yeah, I told him to beat it. ... His name is Reese.... Harold Reese.... No! Him? I never would have believed it. ... You can go in, kid."[1]

The winter flu bug had taken a bite out of him. He dropped a few pounds, and that wool uniform sagged on his already small frame. He looked like a bat boy with a head cold. One writer asked Reese whether he packed a razor. The young shortstop, who was by now his full adult height of 5 feet, 10 inches tall, said he shaved about once a week. "My chin gets a little fuzzy, that's all,"[2] he said, not bothered at all by the question.

Eddie Murphy glanced at Reese, turned to Ted McGrew, and scratched his head. Shouldn't a future star be healthy and tan? Why was Pee Wee so pale? McGrew, one of Reese's biggest supporters, scoffed at the question. "Well, heck, the kid's only been in Florida a couple of days,"[3] he said. Murphy didn't miss a beat. "Where'd he spend the winter? In jail?"[4]

Maybe Reese felt a bit anxious. If so, it was understandable. Just a few years earlier, he was starring for a church league team in his hometown. Now he was fighting for a spot on the Brooklyn roster. Was he even big enough to play ball at this level? That job as a telephone line splicer had packed some meat onto his bones. Still, no one described him as muscle-bound. "I weighed all of 155 pounds soaking wet. Looking like I was sixteen, I guess," Reese said in *Bums*. "When I got there, I didn't know any of the fellas on the team, and I was scared to death."[5]

He answered a few questions just by taking the field. He dashed to his left and to his right, stepped deep into the hole, and threw to a waiting first baseman. Following 30 minutes of this, the writers peeked at Leo Durocher. They wanted to get the skipper's opinion. Can the kid play? Was he ready to take on a starting job? Reese made a quick believer out of Durocher. "Ab-so-lute-ly. He's the greatest prospect I've seen in 15 years. Hell, maybe he's the best I've ever seen."[6] Durocher praised Reese's range and strong arm. "Yes, sir," he said. "I've seen some pretty good ones come up, but this kid has got 'em all beat. He'll be a sensation."[7] Durocher told reporters, "You can tell the way a kid moves after the ball, the way he gloves it and the way he gets it over to the first baseman. You can tell like that whether he's a shortstop or a bum. This kid is a shortstop."[8]

Really, no one worried about Reese's talents as a defender. The debate centered around his bat. Could he get around on a fastball and drive it into the outfield? Or slap a decent curveball past alert infielders? Durocher decided that Reese boasted not just a major league glove but a big league bat as well. "Your Uncle Leo may get a long spell of bench-sitting. … He [Reese] has a nice, smooth swing. Nothing jerky about it."[9] The youngster smacked line drives and lifted his batting average above the .400 mark. Reese could do it all. "He broke up game after game with a timely hit, ran the bases like a deer, and stole opposing catchers frantic,"[10] said one biographer.

Harry Ferguson, sports editor for the United Press, wrote that Pee Wee Reese "is a kid who seems on the way to great things." He wasn't familiar with National League pitchers, he said, "But I don't know why I shouldn't be able to hit in this league. I don't think I've got any particular weaknesses at bat." Reese, according to Ferguson, "hit curveballs pretty good and fastballs, too, although everybody is going to miss a fastball every now and then."[11]

Teammates appreciated Reese's friendly manner. Lavagetto, Camilli, and infielder Peter Coscarart invited him to movie nights and out to dinner. Reese laughed at their jokes and listened to their stories about life inside the club houses and dugouts of major league baseball. "Wherever they went, they took me with them," Reese said. "Why did they do it? Beats the hell out of me. I was just a scared kid from Kentucky, and those guys had been up in the majors for a while. I guess it was because I was just a helluva nice kid—if you'll accept that."[12]

Reese joined a "rough, tough brawling group of ballplayers," Charles Dexter wrote in 1952 in *Baseball Digest*. Reese, though, looked "like a high school junior, wore corduroy slacks and a cream-colored sports jacket, his honey-colored hair slicked back." Furthermore, according to Dexter, and maybe with some exaggeration, Reese "ate ice cream by the pint." Another writer cited by Dexter tabbed "Harold" as the "the All-American boy."[13]

Only a couple of minor injuries kept him from enjoying a nearly perfect spring. First, he split open a hand against the Detroit Tigers on March 10. That mishap cost him two weeks. On March 30, the wound re-opened, forcing him to sit out a few more games. Between ailments, Reese continued to impress Durocher and other observers. Tommy Fitzgerald of the *Louisville Courier-Journal* left for Florida to enjoy some warm weather and watch the hometown player he called the "No. 1 publicized rookie of the year" and "Louisville's contribution to major league shortstopping." After Reese displayed great range on one play and "almost flagged a ground hit over second," Durocher yelled out, "S-a-a-y, did ya see dat? The kid almost got it. Yes, sir."[14] Earlier in the game, when an umpire called Reese out at second base, Durocher barked, "The kid was safe by a mile!" He said to Reese, "Geez, Peewee, ya was sitting on the bag when he touched ya." Reese agreed. "Yeah, I think I was safe."[15]

Maybe the Dodgers didn't need a new shortstop, at least not yet, said Whitney

Martin of the Associated Press. Durocher certainly could play the position for a while longer. Soon, though, Martin continued, "Manager Leo Durocher is going to discover that Shortstop Leo Durocher has reached a point where his spirit is willing, but his legs are weak." Anyway, the skipper had run "plumb out of words" in figuring out ways to compliment Reese. "He's a gangly kid," Durocher admitted. "Looks like a junior in high school, but he doesn't play at shortstop. He just floats out there."[16]

Tommy Holmes pointed out that while Pee Wee Reese wore uniform number 35 in spring training, he'd be switching to number 1 when the season began. Teams don't assign that numeral to just any rookie. The gesture, Holmes wrote, indicated "what Manager Durocher thinks of him."[17] Even Hillerich & Bradsby took a bullish stance on Reese's future and featured him in an advertisement placed inside *The Sporting News*. The copy read that "Harold 'Pee Wee' Reese [decked out in a Brooklyn uniform and carrying a piece of company lumber] with the Louisville Colonels in 1939, now at the Brooklyn training camp, stands a good chance of carving a permanent place for himself with the Dodgers. Reese is one of the younger users of Louisville Sluggers."[18]

Yankees manager Joe McCarthy pronounced Reese a future star the first time he saw him. His club met the Dodgers in an exhibition game April 8 in Owensboro, Kentucky. Reese scored two runs, drove in two, and hit a home run to help the Dodgers win, 10–6. McCarthy said, "You don't have to worry about Reese. The boy's got it." George Kirksey speculated that Pee Wee Reese "may take shortstop away from Manager Leo Durocher for at least one-third of the schedule."[19] Durocher himself said, "I'll start the season at short and then slip Pee Wee in now and then."[20]

Brooklyn's top nemesis figured to be the Cincinnati Reds, who won the pennant in 1939 with a 97–57 mark before getting swept by the Yankees in the World Series. The Reds featured pitchers Bucky Walters, a 27-game winner with a 2.29 ERA, and 25-game winner Paul Derringer. First baseman Frank McCormick led the offense. He batted .332 with 18 home runs, 41 doubles, and 128 RBIs. Veteran catcher Ernie Lombardi added 20 homers and 85 RBIs.

The St. Louis Cardinals also boasted a strong team. They finished in second place the previous season with a 92–61 mark, 4½ games behind Cincinnati. First baseman Johnny "Big Cat" Mize topped the NL with 28 homers and a .349 batting average. Leftfielder Joe "Ducky" Medwick hit .332, cracked 14 homers and drove in 117 runs. Right fielder Enos "Country" Slaughter, from rural Roxboro, North Carolina, batted .320 and topped the circuit with 52 doubles.

Durocher admitted to some worries about his club. Many players still fit into the team's old daffy tradition. "We had an outfielder [Joe Vosmik] who wore a pink corset because he had a bad back," he recalled, "and a relief pitcher [Vito Tamulis] who whizzed through our training camp base in Clearwater on a motor bike, giving vent to wild cowboy yells." Durocher also mentioned outfielder Roy Cullenbine, acquired by Brooklyn from the Tigers in January. Cullenbine hit .240 in limited action for Detroit in 1939. He blamed his subpar campaign on a diet that leaned heavily toward salads. So why was Cullenbine munching on salads all season? "My wife was having a baby," he said. Durocher was confused. "You know how they eat at a time like that," Cullenbine went on. "Salads, salads, salads. That's all we had at home. Leo, funny thing I noticed about salads. You eat one, and you're still hungry."[21]

Dolph Camilli groused about his contract just about every day. He wanted a $1,000 raise, to $15,000, plus travel expenses to Florida from northern California for his wife and children. MacPhail relented after a good deal of arguing. He grumbled to Durocher, "Tell Camilli he is going to get that extra thousand bucks he is crying about, but don't let him know it is coming from me. This is one argument I want to win."[22]

Leo the Lip, usually eager to share his opinion, refused to offer a strong prediction for the upcoming season. "But I will say this," he began. "It was hustle, not luck, that gave the Dodgers third place last year and we'll be the same hustling club this year."[23]

Pee Wee Reese's big league career began during a time of great tension around the globe. War news dominated the airwaves and front-page headlines throughout the season. Germany invaded Denmark and Norway on April 9, just months after smashing into Poland. The Wehrmacht soon forced its way through the Netherlands, Belgium, and Luxembourg. A few months later, on June 13, German soldiers marched into Paris with scarcely a shot fired in that great city's defense. Across the English Channel, the Battle of Britain continued for months. Spitfire pilots defended their homeland against Luftwaffe planes that bombed cities, towns, and industries. ("Again, the Germans have been sending their bombers over singly or in pairs," CBS Radio broadcaster Edward R. Morrow reported on September 13. "The antiaircraft barrage has been fierce but sometimes there have been periods of twenty minutes when London has been silent."[24]) In another ominous note, Germany, Italy, and Japan signed the Tripartite Pact on September 27, creating an unholy alliance, or "Axis." In southwestern Poland, the first Jewish prisoners arrived at a concentration camp called Auschwitz.

At home, the Great Depression, which began shortly after the stock market crash in 1929, still raged. The unemployment rate in 1940 averaged 14.6 percent, down from 24.9 in 1933 but still a crippling figure.[25] Following baseball offered a respite from some of the bleak news of the day.

Brooklyn opened its regular season on Tuesday, April 16, at Braves Field against the Boston Bees. (Following a woeful 1935 campaign, Braves owner Bob Quinn staged a contest to rename his ballclub. Fans chose the Bees and nicknamed the team's home field "The Beehive." The Bees buzzed around the hive from 1936–1940 and then went back to being the Braves.) Whit Wyatt tossed a five-hitter, and Camilli drove in three runs. The Dodgers won, 5–0. Durocher played shortstop, batted eighth, and knocked a double in four at-bats. Reese watched the action from a seat on the bench. In the second game, three days later at Ebbets Field, Brooklyn whipped the Giants, 12–0. Hugh Casey scattered nine hits, and Lavagetto drove in four runs. Durocher notched two hits, both singles. Once again, Reese stayed seated in the dugout.

Finally, on April 23, Pee Wee Reese played his first game, Brooklyn's third. He started at shortstop and, batting eighth against the Bees, went 1-for-3 with a walk and two runs. He drew the base on balls in his first plate appearance, with one out in the second inning, off starter Nick Strincevich, a 25-year-old from Gary, Indiana, who also was making his big league debut. Catcher Herman Franks had just smashed a three-run home run to tie the score, 3–3.

Reese advanced to second base after Brooklyn starter James "Tex" Carleton grounded out. He scored when Charlie Gilbert homered to give Brooklyn a 5–3 lead. Reese grounded out in the third inning against reliever Dick Errickson. In the sixth, he singled off Errickson for his first hit and, two batters later, trotted home once again following Gilbert's second home run. Carleton, an eight-year veteran from Comanche, Texas, near Fort Worth, scattered 10 hits and gave up three runs in the team's third straight complete game. Reese handled five chances but also committed an error. "Peewee Reese in his first major league start fielded brilliantly in spite of one low throw,"[26] Tommy Holmes wrote.

He made another error in his next game, also against Boston. That one led to an unearned run. Cullenbine, though, free now to eat some red meat and not just salads, muscled up and hit a three-run homer that powered the Dodgers to an 8–6 win. Durocher kept writing Reese's name into the starting lineup, and Brooklyn kept winning. The Dodgers boasted a perfect 8–0 mark when they went into Crosley Field on April 30 and played the Reds. Reese's batting average had plunged to .176, and he had committed three errors. He also made a miscue in this one, as did Coscarart and Lavagetto.

It hardly mattered. Carleton hurled a masterpiece. The 33-year-old held Cincinnati hitless. He struck out four and walked two. Coscarart belted a three-run homer in the fifth inning to account for all the scoring. Cincinnati right-fielder Ival Goodman flew out to end the game. Carleton jumped off the mound and "clicked his heals"[27] as soon as Goodman's ball landed in Walker's glove. The last Brooklyn pitcher to throw a no-hitter had been Dazzy Vance, against the Philadelphia Phillies on September 13, 1925.[28]

Brooklyn's winning streak ended the following day. The Reds knocked Hugh Casey around for eight runs in just four innings and won, 9–2. Reese played error-free ball. He also went hitless in two at-bats, and his batting average fell to just .130. MacPhail insisted that Durocher bench Reese. Durocher urged his boss to be patient, not one of MacPhail's strong suits. The Dodgers boss was as patient as a dog with a bone. "I'm paying out $5,000 for you to play shortstop," MacPhail cried. Durocher retorted, "Reese is going to be our shortstop." MacPhail just shook his head. "He'll get his chance some other time. Right now, I'm not paying you to collect splinters on the bench while he kicks away ballgames." Furthermore, he thundered, "If you're not out at shortstop tomorrow, you're fired!"[29] MacPhail fired Leo Durocher a lot through the years. And quickly hired him back.

MacPhail, despite his dramatic pronouncement, had not given up on Reese. Far from it. In fact, he swore that the Dodgers could get the talented but temperamental Joe Medwick straight up for Reese. That was quite a statement. Medwick, a six-time All-Star and three-time RBI champ, won the NL's Most Valuable Player Award in 1937. Not surprisingly, MacPhail's comment, according to writer Eddie Brietz, "made everyone's hair stand straight up today."[30]

Over the next couple of weeks, Reese started a handful of games and appeared a few times as a late-inning replacement. Durocher started the other games. That routine lasted until Durocher—off to a hot start with a .371 batting average—hurt his arm May 15 against the Reds. The skipper had no choice but to make Pee Wee Reese his full-time shortstop once again. The Dodgers sported an impressive 15–5 won-lost record, but they had fallen out of first place, half a game behind the Reds. Walker led the team with a .395 average.

The rest did Reese some good. When he returned to the starting lineup, his batting average rose and, more importantly, his fielding steadied. He made just 11 errors the rest of the season, albeit an injury-shortened campaign. He also delighted the Brooklyn faithful before each game. Durocher liked to end infield practices by hitting a grounder up the middle. Reese would sprint from near third base, snatch the ball, and fire to first. "He was a joy to watch,"[31] longtime fan Bill Reddy said.

The rookie gained the reputation as one of baseball's top clutch hitters. Late in the season, E. C. "Doc" Osborn wrote a column on the "slim, straw-haired stripling"[32] and reviewed every home run from Reese's rookie campaign. In Osborn's opinion, "the Dodgers are never licked until Pee Wee Reese is out in the 9th."[33] Reese, "that mass of muscles,"[34] belted his first long ball on May 26. He picked a dramatic moment against the Philadelphia Phillies at Shibe Park, under gray skies.

The teams were tied, 1–1, after nine innings. Ernie Koy popped out to start the Brooklyn 10th. Reese followed by hitting Kirby Higbe's first pitch into the left-field upper deck. "There was no fluke about it," the *Eagle* reported. "The pale-faced kid's first major league home run was a rifle shot and into the teeth of a wind to boot."[35] Reese gushed to the *Brooklyn Citizen* about his big hit. He called the homer "the biggest thrill of my life" and told Lee Scott that "Higbe threw up a fast ball and I was ready. I put everything I had behind it and the ball traveled into left field. At first, I didn't know if it was a home run, but when I got to first [pitcher]) Freddie Fitzsimmons gave out such a howl and then told me to go on home. Boy, it sure was a big moment in my life."[36] Vito Tamulis, in relief of starter Luke Hamlin, preserved the victory.

For much of the early going, Reese batted in the seventh or eighth slot. He led off for the first time on May 20 at home against the Cubs—following three straight Brooklyn losses—and went 1-for-4 with a double. The Dodgers lost again, 6–4. After batting in the seventh spot over the next three games, Reese once again stood atop the order on May 27. On a day when the Dodgers beat the Phillies, 6–0, Reese notched three singles and scored three runs.

Near disaster—by way of an errant fastball—struck Reese on June 1 at Chicago's Wrigley Field. In the top of the 12th inning, with the score tied, 3–3, he stepped to the plate against Cubs right-hander Jake Mooty. It was a warm day. Summer had all but officially arrived. Fans, many of them wearing white shirts, anticipated the next pitch. Mooty looked to his catcher, Al Todd, for the sign. He unleashed a fastball that rode high and inside. Reese may have lost the heater amid all those white shirts. "Look out!"[37] Mooty yelled from the mound.

The ball smacked Reese behind the left ear. He spun around and fell in the batter's box. "Mooty released the ball, and I never saw it," Reese said decades after the beaning. "I never thought anyone could hit me in the head, but he did."[38] Durocher sprinted onto the field. "Get out of the way!" he yelled. "Give the kid some air! Get the doctor!"[39] Dr. John F. Davis rushed to the scene from his seat in the stands. Reese left on a stretcher with what Davis feared was a severe concussion.

An ambulance rushed him to the hospital. Durocher worried that a promising career may have just ended. He liked the kid's talent—"Covers the left side of the field like an octopus,"[40] he once said. Most of all, he liked his heart. Some players return after getting hit in the head, "but there are some that are always plate shy after they've been hurt like that," Durocher said. "They're finished as hitters. And before long, they're finished in baseball."[41] Davis said the woozy rookie apparently did not suffer a fracture, but the following day, he said more tests were needed. "When Reese moves around, he becomes dizzy and nauseated," the doctor said. "We couldn't take all the X-rays we wanted to today."[42]

While Reese recuperated, MacPhail traded for none other than Ducky Medwick. Brooklyn sent Ernie Koy, pitcher Carl Doyle, minor league infielder-outfielder Bert Haas, and minor league pitcher Sam Nahem, plus $150,000, to St. Louis on June 12, 1940, in exchange for Medwick and pitcher Curt Davis.[43] Medwick hailed from Carteret, New Jersey, about 25 miles from Brooklyn, and would take over for journeyman Joe Vosmik in left field. The Dodgers sat in a first-place tie with Cincinnati when the deal was made and had won 11 of 12 games. Maybe Medwick could seal a pennant for Brooklyn. Many fans and sportswriters hoped so. Ed Hughes declared, "Flatbush was as happy as a goat in a tin can factory, as a clam at high tide and a bug in a rug last night."[44]

Maybe so. Some St. Louis players still may have cheered as Medwick left their team and town. Author Derrick Goold described Medwick as "ornery" and wrote that he "earned a reputation for being as hard on his teammates as he was on opposing pitchers." Once, Ducky—a nickname he hated and which was given to him because of his unusual gait (he preferred "Muscles.")—punched Ed Heusser after the Cardinals pitcher accused Medwick of loafing. "Durndest man I've ever seen," the legendary and colorful Redbirds hurler Dizzy Dean once said of Medwick. "Before you even get to do enough talking…. Joe whoops you and the fight's over."[45]

Medwick even started a brawl in the seventh game of the 1934 World Series against the Detroit Tigers. The Cardinals led, 7–0, in the sixth inning. It was all over except for the victory party. Medwick ripped a two-out triple, and as he slid safely into third base, he apparently kicked at Marv Owen, the Detroit third baseman. Owen took offense at Medwick's aggressive move, and the two players engaged in a brief scuffle. When Medwick trotted out to left field in the bottom half of the inning, irate fans at Navin Field pelted him with empty soda bottles, oranges, apples, other food, and assorted garbage. Commissioner Kenesaw Mountain Landis ordered Medwick back to the dugout (Landis nearly forfeited the game to the Cardinals, who went on to win, 11–0.)

Medwick quickly put himself into the middle of some commotion in Brooklyn. The Cardinals arrived in town on June 17, less than one week after the big trade. St. Louis won the opener in the three-game set, 3–1. The next morning, Durocher and Medwick ran into Bob Bowman, the Cardinals' scheduled starting pitcher that day, in the lobby of the Hotel New Yorker. One wisecrack led to another, and Medwick stuck the needle a bit too far into Bowman. The pitcher, tired of being razzed by his former teammate and the opposing manager, said, "I'll take care of both you guys. Wait and see!"[46] Did that constitute a threat of some kind?

3. "Skip, where do you buy your clothes?" 33

Ducky Medwick (right) and Reese talk over a game situation. The Dodgers acquired Medwick from the Cardinals early in the 1940 campaign (National Baseball Hall of Fame Library, Cooperstown, New York).

A few hours later, the first three Dodgers reached base against Bowman. Dixie Walker led off with a single, and Cookie Lavagetto doubled him home. Joe Vosmik followed with a base hit, bringing up Medwick. Bowman unfurled a pitch that crashed into Medwick's head. Fans screamed and booed, and Durocher sprinted toward Bowman. Larry MacPhail rushed from his seat in the stands and headed straight for the Cardinals' dugout, ready to fight. Players stormed onto the field. New York's finest followed soon after and broke up the brawl. Once calm was restored, MacPhail called National League president Ford Frick and demanded that Bowman be banned from baseball for life. He raged that Bowman's pitch to Medwick was a "deliberate"[47] assault and even more than that. "It's the worst thing I've seen in all my baseball experience," MacPhail insisted. "This guy comes to the ballpark with a premeditated notion of committing murder and I can call six witnesses to prove it."[48] (MacPhail also was unhappy that his team blew a 4–0 first-inning lead and lost, 7–5, in 11 innings.)

The borough's district attorney, William O'Dwyer, agreed that the incident merited some attention but not a "wild-eyed" investigation.[49] O'Dwyer, born in Ireland and the future mayor of New York City, did not flinch at tough prosecution. A few years earlier, he helped topple Murder Incorporated, a name given by the media to organized crime groups and gangsters such as Louis Lepke, Martin "Buggsy" Goldstein, and Vito "Socko" Gurino. O'Dwyer appointed Assistant District Attorney Barton Turkus to lead the beanball inquiry. Turkus took some testimony, but the hubbub ended there. No one was fined or suspended, and no criminal charges were filed. Cardinals manager Billy Southworth denied that Bowman hit Medwick on purpose. "That incident of the morning was just kidding," he said. "Jack Russell and Mort Cooper, two of our other players who heard it all, told me that Bowman wasn't serious and merely joking."[50] Bowman said the beaning left him "scared stiff."[51] He told reporters, "I thought I killed Joe. I got up to him first after he fell, and, boy, he sure looked like he was gone."[52]

Decades later, Durocher said Medwick never fully recovered from that knock to his head. He returned "shaky and gun-shy,"[53] according to Durocher. "Many think that the beaning ruined one of the greatest free-swingers the game has ever known, and that Medwick was never the same after it."[54] The Dodgers also worried about Reese. They feared he might be timid about facing tough pitchers with terrific fastballs and sharp-breaking curves. Hitters did not wear helmets in those days, at least one time with fatal consequences. Yankees pitcher Carl Mays struck Cleveland Indians batter Ray Chapman in the head on August 16, 1920, at the Polo Grounds. Rushed to the hospital, Chapman died 12 hours later.

Pee Wee Reese answered any questions about his courage right away. In his first appearance post-beaning, on June 21 against the Pittsburgh Pirates, he belted a single, double, and a triple. "The little gamester showed he wasn't plate shy,"[55] Harry Forbes wrote in the *Daily News*. The Dodgers won, 10–8, and advanced to 34–17, still just one game better than the Giants and Reds. Reese, batting .237 on the morning of June 21, raised his mark 40 points by month's end.

Reese rarely asked Durocher for advice that season. He did at least one time. He walked up to his manager, who figured "finally, the kid was coming over to the old master about playing shortstop."[56] Durocher smiled and looked at his protégé. "OK, kid, shoot. What do you want to know?" The old master waited for an answer. Reese asked, "Skip, where do you buy your clothes?"[57]

Pee Wee Reese smacked his second home run on July 3 against the Giants. New York led, 3–1, going into the final frame. The Dodgers scored six times in the ninth "to humiliate"[58] their opponent, 7–3. Reese recorded the biggest hit, a grand slam off Hy Vandenberg, a 6-foot-4-inch, 220-pound right-hander. According to

The Sporting News, Reese "rammed" a Vandenberg fastball "against the foul pole of the upper left tier [of the Polo Grounds] to clear the sacks and sink the Giants."[59] After Reese crossed home plate, his teammates "all but carried" him into the dugout. Hy Turkin—"Ye humble scribe"—wrote that he "hadn't seen a player hugged and back-slapped and handshaken so much since Cubs catcher Gabby Hartnett"[60] hit his pennant-winning home run in the ninth inning on September 28, 1938, at Wrigley Field.

A reporter asked Giants player-manager Bill Terry about Reese. Now, Terry knew how to razz the Dodgers. He hit .340 over 14 seasons, all with the Giants, and a league-leading .401 in 1930, but he may be most famous for his wisecrack about Brooklyn's chances at winning the 1934 pennant. Terry, in mock surprise, asked, "Is Brooklyn still in the league?" Even so, Terry gave Pee Wee Reese his due. "I don't know whether or not Reese can hit enough to stick with Brooklyn," Terry said. "But I do know he knocked one of my pitchers right out of the major leagues."[61] Following the game, New York demoted Vandenberg to the team's Triple A farm club in nearby Jersey City, New Jersey.

The Dodgers stood 41–21, in first place by one game. They slipped out of the top spot on July 7 and began losing ground to the surging Reds. By July 27, following a 6–13 stretch, they had fallen behind by nine games. Their pennant-winning dreams were slipping away. In its August 1 edition, *The Sporting News* decided that "it seems only a train wreck or an overdose of over-confidence can keep them [the Reds] out of the 1940 World Series."[62] But was MacPhail, the "ivory manipulator extraordinary," ready to wave a white flag? Not a chance. He released outfielder Charley Gilbert and sent pitchers Newt Kimball and Lou Fette to the team's Triple A affiliate in Montreal. He also promoted a young infielder named Harold Patrick "Pete" Reiser, "the slugging sensation of the Brooklyn training camp in 1939."[63]

The St. Louis native, born on May 17, 1919, first made his name as a sandlot superstar. He earned $50 a game playing semi-pro soccer while still a 14-year-old student at Holy Ghost Parochial School on the city's north side. Reiser even turned himself into a top-notch bowler and ice skater. As a teenager he wanted to be "the greatest football player Notre Dame ever had," he told Donald Honig.[64] The hometown Cardinals signed Reiser out of Beaumont High School in 1937. He had turned some eyes while attending a Cardinals tryout camp when he was just 15.

Reiser, though, never put on a Redbirds uniform. Commissioner Landis ordered the Cardinals to release him and other farmhands, saying that St. Louis was tying up too many young ballplayers. The Dodgers signed Reiser for about $200, but with a gentleman's agreement of sorts to bury him in the low minors and trade him back to St. Louis. It never happened. Reiser was too good. MacPhail liked him too much, and Durocher absolutely fell in love with "Pistol Pete." (Reiser enjoyed watching western movies as a boy and patrolled the neighborhood while carrying a pair of toy six-shooters at his side.) Reiser had played a three-game series against St. Louis in spring training and reached base 11 times, seven times via a hit. He belted four home runs. The performance mesmerized Durocher. "I kept staring at him, wondering if it was all a dream," Durocher recalled. "Holy cats, I'm thinking. 'What have I stumbled onto here? This is a diamond, Leo. All you have to do is polish him.'"[65]

Pistol Pete Reiser began his Brooklyn career by going hitless in his first nine at-bats. He watched from a seat in the dugout on August 3 as Pee Wee Reese bashed his third homer, a solo shot in the ninth inning off Chicago left-hander Ken Raffensberger. This long ball came with one out and some controversy. According to the *Daily News*, "A fan reached over the railing for the catch," and the Cubs argued that Reese's hit should have counted only as a ground-rule double, "but Umpire [George] Barr wouldn't budge."[66] The dramatics only sliced Chicago's 2–0 lead in half. Walker, the next batter, flied out. Vosmik tripled, but Medwick grounded out to end the game.

The next day, Reiser put himself into the hit column in the second game of a doubleheader versus Chicago. He singled with one out in the second inning with Claude Passeau on the mound. Reese hit a ball much harder and farther against Passeau in the ninth inning. His bases-empty blast tied the score, 6–6. Brooklyn won, 7–6, on Camilli's homer in the 11th. Harry Forbes reported that "the mob" at Ebbets Field "was just as crazy" over Reese's homer "as it was when Dolf hit the jackpot at 7:30 last evening."[67] The Dodgers had lost the first half of the twin-dip, 11–3. "It was almost a disaster day for the Dodgers, who still entertain pennant hopes," said Forbes. In fact, after the Cubs took a 6–1 lead in the second game, "many of the 29,298 customers started to leave for the happier surroundings."[68]

Reese notched his fifth and final homer on August 8 against the Giants at the Polo Grounds. With two out in the seventh inning of a 3–1 game, Reiser ripped a pinch-hit single to bring up Reese, who knocked a Bill Lohrman pitch over the left-field fence. The Dodgers went on to win, 6–3, in 12 innings. Once again, Camilli hit the game-winner, this time a three-run blast.

Besides contributing his big hit, Reese pulled off some nifty plays in the field. Brooklyn's enthusiastic third-base coach, Chuck Dressen, let loose a string of praise for the rookie shortstop. He predicted a pennant for the Dodgers "and when we win, you can bet that shortstop Pee Wee Reese, the greatest rookie of the year, will rate plenty of the credit." Dressen said that Reese "has everything a brilliant shortstop needs. He's all over the field and a peril at the plate to any pitcher."[69]

Unfortunately, Reese's season ended in the middle of the diamond, amid a whirl of dust, on August 15 at Ebbets Field. He hurt his left ankle while sliding into second base in the seventh inning against Philadelphia. The next day, Forbes reported that Reese had suffered a broken bone in the 4–2 loss. "When Pee Wee limped off the field, it was hoped the injury was nothing more than a severe sprain and he would be out only a week." Forbes called Reese a "popular little dynamo shortstop."[70]

The Dodgers' pennant chances now seemed as shaky as Pee Wee Reese's impaired ankle. One pessimistic reporter put it this way: "The horrible spectacle of third or even fourth place stares them in the face. That's how much the kid meant to them."[71] During Reese's stay at New York Hospital, "the telephone rang constantly. Most of the calls were from girls, not excluding the hospital's phone operator, for Pee Wee was just about the most eligible bachelor in the metropolis. The girls sighed and wisecracked."[72]

A few days later, Reese, "the boy wonder who is more shy and reticent than Joe Palooka," flew home to Louisville. About 200 people, including his mom, two sisters, and brother Carl, greeted Pee Wee at Bowman Field. H. L. Nations wrote, "Peewee is the little man who proved that you don't have to be able to grow heavy whiskers to do a big job playing shortstop for the Brooklyn Dodgers." Reese hobbled along on a pair of crutches. "I don't know exactly what it is that's broken," he said. "The doctor told me in a lot of big words that I can't remember and couldn't explain if I did." Nations called Reese a "hotshot shortstop" and a "dynamo."[73]

The Dodgers' record stood at 63–44 following the games of August 15, good for second place in the National League, five games behind the Reds and seven games in front of the third-place Giants. Without Reese, Brooklyn dropped eight of its next 12. A combination of Durocher, Reiser, Eddie Miller, and Johnny Hudson shared shortstop duties.

The MacPhail-Durocher soap opera continued to play out in that final month of the season. The Brooklyn executive had not decided whether to bring Durocher back in 1941. Despite the development of Reese, MacPhail still envisioned Durocher as a player-manager, not simply as the skipper. "Evidently, he wants to be a bench manager, and that changes things," MacPhail said. "I don't know yet what we'll do about it."[74]

Brooklyn finished 88–65, in second place and 12 games behind the Reds, who won a second straight pennant and beat the Tigers in a seven-game World Series. The Dodgers attracted 975,978 fans and topped the National League in attendance for the second straight year. Reese hit .272 in his rookie campaign, with a .366 on-base percentage. Besides knocking five home runs, he collected 28 RBI and 85 hits. Reese stole a team-high 15 bases and scored 58 runs.

Camilli led the Brooklyn offense with 23 home runs and 96 RBI. He finished 12th in the MVP race. Walker topped the team with a .308 average. Durocher, meanwhile, hit .231 in 160 at-bats over 62 games. He also smacked the last of his 24 career home runs, on June 16 in the second game of a doubleheader against the Reds, a solo job in the eighth inning off Jim Turner. Medwick batted .300 in his 106 games as a Dodger, with 14 home runs and 66 RBI, while Reiser hit .293 in 225 at-bats.

The 38-year-old Fitzsimmons, known by many as "Fat Freddie," compiled a 16–2 record in just 134⅓ innings. *The Sporting News* selected him as its Veteran of the Year. Fitzsimmons, acquired by the Dodgers in June of 1937, threw a knuckle curveball that baffled hitters. Brooklyn fans loved the former Giant, and Fat Freddie loved them back. More than 33,000 fans attended a special night for him on August 16, one game after Reese's season-ending injury. Fans pooled enough money to buy the right-hander a new car. Teammates bought him a shotgun, and the writers gave him a set of pipes. The choked-up pitcher told the crowd, "I'll keep doing all I can for the team; I'll never let you down."[75]

Things were looking up for the Dodgers. It was time to put those Daffy days behind them. MacPhail looked forward to a long string of winning seasons. He wrote a letter on team stationery to fans, addressed December 16, 1940. "Over one million dollars has been expended during the past three years to improve the playing personnel [citing the contracts of Reese, Medwick, Camilli, and Wyatt, among others]." In addition, "more than $250,000 has gone into the improvement of Ebbets Field, which, although built in 1912, is now a modern, comfortable ballpark with all the facilities of a present-day stadium. Our lighting system is regarded as the best in baseball."[76] In the next-to-last paragraph (before wishing fans "a very Merry Christmas and a prosperous New Year"), MacPhail wrote that "our main object is to bring a pennant and a World's Championship to Brooklyn and all the efforts of our entire organization are directed toward that goal."[77]

4

"I'm trying to teach him to holler"

Brooklyn's popular young shortstop waited for his foot to mend. Doctors told him to take it easy. He couldn't even go bowling, one of his favorite pastimes. In mid–December, feeling a bit more spry, he booked a train to New York City—nattily attired in a "felt hat, camel's hair coat, knit tie, and saddle-colored high-top shoes"[1]—for an X-ray and brief examination. Dr. Frank Glenn pronounced him okay and said, "The only way Reese can break his heel-bone again is to slide into a base and catch his spike in the bag in exactly the same manner. And that's almost impossible."[2] Therapists gave Reese applied massages and infra-red treatments. By late January, he could start swinging his golf clubs. Newspapers carried a picture of him out on the links with Cincinnati Reds catcher Dick West and, reportedly, he felt "no ill effects"[3] after playing 18 holes.

While Reese recuperated, MacPhail pored over opposing rosters and made telephone calls to rival executives. The Brooklyn executive targeted Phillies pitcher Kirbe Higbe and Cardinals catcher Mickey Owen. First, he called St. Louis general manager Branch Rickey and asked about Owen, a 23-year-old prospect from rural Missouri. Touted as a catcher who could both hit and play defense, he also boasted a touch of brashness. (While still in the minor leagues, he held up his mitt to teammates and declared, "That's the glove that's going to catch the next World Series for the St. Louis Cardinals."[4]) Owen's bat, though, never matched his mitt or his self-confidence. Over his first four big league seasons (1937–1940), he hit a pedestrian .257 with just seven home runs in 1,282 at-bats. Maybe Rickey was growing impatient. It was a worth a shot. "How about a deal for that young punk, Owen?"[5] MacPhail asked.

Rickey hemmed and hawed. He liked Owen despite the ballplayer's struggles. MacPhail wanted to get his target on the cheap, and the talks stalled. A short time later, MacPhail ran into Phillies owner Gerry Nugent and asked what he wanted for Higbe. "A hundred thousand dollars,"[6] Nugent decided, plus Tamulis, pitcher Bill Crouch, and catcher Mickey Livingston. Deal. In Higbe, MacPhail had purchased a hard-throwing, hard-drinking 26-year-old from Columbia, South Carolina, who compiled a 14–19 record in 1940 and posted a 3.72 ERA. MacPhail liked his new prize's live, but often wild, right arm. Higbe topped the National League in strikeouts with 137. He also led the circuit with 121 walks.

Just one thing, MacPhail said to Nugent. Keep this trade a secret. If Rickey finds out that the rival Dodgers have acquired Higbe, he'll never let go of Owen. Nugent agreed, and MacPhail went back to the Cardinals. Rickey, undoubtedly waving around a cigar and raising one or both of his famous bushy eyebrows, said he could only part with Owen at a high price. It would cost the Dodgers $60,000, plus catcher Gus Mancuso and minor league pitcher John Pintar. Deal.

The Brooklyn president already had acquired a future Hall of Famer in Ducky Medwick, albeit one with some mileage. On January 31, he signed outfielder Paul Waner, aka "Big Poison," the older brother of Lloyd Waner, or "Little Poison." A 15-year veteran, Big Poison sported a .340 lifetime batting average with 2,868 career hits for the Pittsburgh Pirates. Injuries, including a ligament pull in the right knee, limited his playing time in 1940. The three-time batting champion appeared in just 89 games but still hit a solid .290. Pittsburgh released him on December 5. Durocher envisioned the left-handed batter as both a pinch-hitter and frequent starter. "You can't tell me that a guy who hit around .330 in 1939 [.328 to be exact] is all through at the plate,"[7] the skipper said.

Besides doing all that wheeling and dealing, MacPhail worked on a safety measure that is a mandatory part of today's game. He told reporters that during spring training, several of his players would go to bat while wearing a protective helmet, one lightweight but strong enough to withstand big league fastballs. "And I want to make a prediction," he continued, "that within a year, every player in the major leagues will be wearing it."[8]

Walter Dandy and George Bennett, doctors at Johns Hopkins Hospital in Baltimore, designed the helmets. They patterned them after ones worn by jockeys. MacPhail wrote a letter to Dandy on February 7 and asked that the headgear be ready for spring training "regardless of the expense involved in getting out the samples."[9] The doctors cut a zippered pocket into the sides of a regulation baseball cap (most players wore a size 7–7½ cap, so MacPhail ordered cap bands a half-inch larger)[10] and inserted a hard-plastic plate, about an inch thick but weighing just more than one ounce. The helmets were meant to protect "the vulnerable area from the temple to about an inch behind the ear."[11]

Columnist Victor O. Jones wrote that a plethora of beanballs over the past few seasons—such as those aimed at Reese and Medwick—should make tough-minded baseball players more sympathetic to safer headgear. Jones reminded readers that fans "loudly hooted" at Roger Bresnahan when the Giants catcher began wearing a chest protector in the early 1900s. Additional so-called "tools of ignorance" were added through the decades. "Should a catcher appear behind the plate today without chest protector, mask and shin guards," Jones wrote, "a psychologist would be called by the manager."[12] He added that a helmet might have saved Chapman's life. "The purpose of baseball has never been to show [that] a batter could 'take it' on the head, that his skull was harder than the ball."[13] Reese and Medwick tried on the hard hats and liked them. "Both Pee Wee and Joe pronounced the helmets 100 percent okay,"[14] MacPhail said.

A whirlwind pre-season tour awaited. MacPhail booked a 50-game schedule, both in the United States and abroad, starting in Miami and going from there to Cuba, to Houston and Fort Worth, Texas, before concluding in Clearwater. Jack

Miley of the *New York Post* wrote that the journey would "make the Lewis and Clark expedition seem like a short walk."[15]

The Cuban leg began with a touch of drama. Veteran catcher Ernest "Babe" Phelps was a no-show at the Miami airport. He hated to fly and made that clear in 1940. MacPhail, always open to new ideas, had booked the Dodgers on a few commercial flights. Phelps took one jaunt on an airborne contraption and decided that his flying days were done. The other Dodgers could cruise above the clouds. He would take the train. The burly veteran (6-foot-2-inches, 225 pounds) also hated boats, making it nearly impossible for him to get from Miami to Havana. He stayed at home in Maryland and insisted that he had caught a cold. Durocher undoubtedly rolled his eyes.

Years later, the skipper wrote that Phelps suffered from hypochondria. Supposedly, the catcher once stayed up all night, counting his heartbeats. "Babe's theory was that the body could continue to function if your heart missed one beat, or even two or three, but that if it missed four beats in a row, you were dead,"[16] wrote Durocher. MacPhail summoned a doctor to examine Phelps. The verdict? He was "in great shape."[17] MacPhail fumed. "I forbid him to come here," the general manager declared during a press conference in Havana. "He's no sicker than I am."[18] MacPhail ordered Phelps to the team's minor league camp in Macon, Georgia.

Reese, on the other hand, couldn't wait to get going. He agreed in February to a contract worth about $9,000. The *Eagle* recounted Reese's injuries from the previous season and decided that while he was a "standout player," he also "fell victim to several disastrous incidents." Even so, "Durocher is hoping that Reese can step in as the regular shortstop."[19] Associated Press correspondent Gayle Talbot noted that Durocher was beginning to "show a sprig of white at each temple"[20] and predicted that Reese would get most of the playing time. Durocher seemed to agree. After all, he figured, "Why should I get out there when I've got a great player like Reese to take my place?"[21]

The early signs looked good. Reese went through some drills in Havana and declared himself ready for the upcoming season. That ankle was not bothering him at all, he said. "Boy, I feel swell," he insisted. "Say, you can just forget about that injury."[22] Reese reminded Ted McGrew of the great Cobb. "If nothing happens to Pee Wee Reese, he is going to be the greatest all-around player I ever saw,"[23] McGrew boasted to reporters in February 1941, nearly echoing MacPhail's comments from a few years earlier. McGrew insisted that Reese was as "fast as Cobb ever was, and he has a better arm, and give him a ball up around his shoulders and he'll knock it out of sight. Furthermore, he's one of the nicest kids [who] ever came into baseball."[24]

Talk about putting pressure on a young ballplayer. Cobb, an outfielder (more irascible than nice), played 24 seasons in the big leagues and batted .366 with 4,189 hits. The Georgia Peach won 12 batting titles, topped off by a .420 campaign in 1911. Baseball enshrined the left-handed hitter, along with a handful of other greats, at the first Hall of Fame induction ceremony, held on June 12, 1939, in Cooperstown, New York. Cobb gained 98.2 percent of the vote, more than any other player on the ballot, including home-run king Ruth (95.1 percent).

Reese's .272 rookie batting average hardly hinted at any future offensive greatness. (Of course, Cobb only hit .240 over 41 games in his first season, with the Tigers in 1905.) Gayle Talbot, who wrote the newspaper article that featured McGrew's optimistic prediction, described Reese as a "fragile-looking little shortstop,"[25] but one who "played sparkling ball for the Dodgers last season."[26] Fortunately, the Dodgers did not need Reese to be Cobb. They needed him to provide steady play and, they hoped, stay healthy.

Durocher wanted to hear more from Reese in 1941. The skipper hoped to put a bit of Leo the Lip into the reserved Pee Wee. The kid was too quiet, something Durocher never was. Holmes agreed that Reese should learn how to take charge. "He will be better when he makes more noise, becomes a leader, directs the infield operations on complicated plays."[27] Whitney Martin wrote that Reese "still has a pip-squeak voice."[28] Martin quoted Durocher on the situation. "I'm trying to teach him how to holler. I broke in hollering, and the other players used to ask me what I was hollering about. I said, 'Never mind. I'll keep on hollering,' and I did."[29]

Brooklyn's top competition once again figured to be the World Series champion Reds, plus the Cardinals and Giants. Tom Meany offered a rundown on the Dodgers in the March 20 edition of *The Sporting News*. He called the Brooklyn infield "about the defensive tops in the league." He wrote that Reese's foot had healed, but "the shortstop didn't take kindly to the Cuban food and was eight pounds underweight in Havana. He can't afford to shed any poundage and as a result didn't look too well, but the important thing is that his foot is OK." Meany liked the new pitching combo of Kirbe Higbe and Whitlow Wyatt. "The pair rates among the league's top-flight pitchers," Meany wrote. As for the new man behind the plate, "Catching undoubtedly has been improved with the addition of Mickey Owen." The writer concluded, "Personally, I'll be disappointed if the Dodgers don't win the pennant."[30]

Away from the baseball field, the U.S. Congress passed something called the Lend-Lease Act, which gave President Franklin D. Roosevelt the authority to send arms, airplanes, ships, and other materials to countries at war with Germany. During a speech at the Mansion House in London, British prime minister Winston Churchill said, "The Lend-Lease Bill must be regarded without question as the most unsordid act in the whole of recorded history."[31] Firms such as Curtiss-Wright, Douglas Aircraft, Kaiser Shipyards, American Locomotive, and Ford Motor Company built airplanes, tanks, trucks, and ships. Many hailed this "Arsenal of Democracy."[32]

In the summer of 1940, FDR stopped the shipment of oil, gasoline, and metals to Japan and transferred the Pacific Fleet from San Diego, California, to Hawaii, then a U.S. territory. The fleet included nine battleships, all stationed at Pearl Harbor on the island of Oahu. Hawaiians from ancient times called this area "Wai Momi" or "Waters of Pearl." Oysters, ripe with pearls, rested below the quiet, blue-green water. Fisherman and divers often visited Wai Momi. The U.S. Congress officially created a naval base at Pearl Harbor in 1908. According to legend, a "benevolent shark goddess" watched over and protected the bay.[33]

During spring training, Leo Durocher settled on a starting outfield of, left to right, Medwick, Dixie Walker, and Pete Reiser. Paul Waner, though, had put himself through a rigorous off-season training program and showed that he could still rip his fair share of line drives. He earned more and more playing time and, it seemed, a starting outfield job, with Reiser now the probable center fielder and Medwick staying in left. Where, the writers asked, did that leave Walker, the popular "People's Cherce"? Durocher gave a straight answer. "On the bench,"[34] he said. That comment threw the Brooklyn fans into a tizzy. The faithful sent off a Western Union telegram to the Dodgers' front office, threatening to stay away from Ebbets Field if Durocher stopped penciling Walker's name into the starting lineup. And what did MacPhail think about that? "Keep Waner in there," he barked at Durocher. "If you play Walker, I'll fire you."[35]

As it worked out, Brooklyn opened at home against the Giants on April 15 with Medwick in left, Walker in center, and Waner in right. Reese took his spot at shortstop and batted leadoff, with Wyatt on the mound. Reese went hitless in four at-bats, drew a walk, and scored a run. The Giants won, 6–4. Brooklyn lost three straight to the Giants and then swept a three-game series from the Braves (back from being the Bees). The Bums won the first game, 11–6, on April 18 and took a doubleheader April 19, winning both games 8–0. In the first half of that double dip, Reese hit a home run, a double, and two singles. He also scored three runs. "Pee Wee Reese was a ball of fire all morning," Hy Turkin proclaimed.[36]

Brooklyn and St. Louis battled it out all season. Even after the Dodgers improved to 22–6 on May 14, they still led the talented Redbirds by just two games. MacPhail shuddered at each Brooklyn defeat. "Every time we lost a game," according to Durocher, "the reasons were monotonously the same. I yanked a pitcher too late. I yanked a pitcher too soon. Or I was on the bench when I should have been playing short instead of Reese."[37]

By the third game, Reiser had taken over the center field spot in place of Walker. Soon, though, Walker found his way back into the starting lineup. Waner had left that smooth swing in Florida, fell into a deep slump, and lost his job. The Dodgers released Big Poison and his .171 batting average on May 11. Pistol Pete Reiser started hot and stayed that way all season. He batted .355 in April and .382 in May. Reiser expected nothing else. During spring training, he said "I can hit any pitcher who ever threw a baseball."[38]

Reiser also made fast friends with Brooklyn's shortstop. Writers began calling the two young players "The Gold Dust Twins." They had much in common. Both grew up in river towns, started in organizations other than the Dodgers, and were christened with the first name of "Harold." They also boasted nicknames that harkened back to childhood—"Pee Wee" and "Pistol Pete." The pair shopped together, exchanged clothes, and "helped each other through batting and fielding slumps."[39] Late in the season, *Sporting News* editor and publisher J. G. Taylor Spink wrote a column about the Dodgers duo and their close friendship. "We're together as much off the field as on it," Reese told Spink. "And it gives me a laugh when I read in the papers that I'm the lively guy and Pete's the deadpan. Why, that guy keeps me in stitches all the time. …the gags he pulls. … You got to know him, that's all."[40] Camilli liked Reese and Reiser so much that he told teammates not to put them through any of the hazing rituals most young ballplayers endured, like it or not. "Leave these kids alone," Camilli said. "They're going to help us win the pennant."[41]

Through 21 games, Reese had lifted his batting average to .284 with a .437

on-base percentage. He also had committed 11 errors. Durocher could see how much each slip-up was wreaking havoc on his shortstop. Reese sometimes sat slouched over in the clubhouse after the game, palms in his face, probably replaying every bad throw or bobble dozens of times. Durocher acknowledged, "He was having a tough year, making the mistakes all youngsters make. The only difference was that they attracted special notice because every play meant so much in a pennant race."[42]

Meanwhile, the Dodgers' second baseman, Pete Coscarart, had fallen into a deep slump. His batting average dropped to just .227 on May 4, low enough to spark trade talk. Durocher had told MacPhail during spring training that Brooklyn needed just one more player to help win a championship. Oh, yeah, MacPhail answered, who might that be? Billy Herman, a standout second baseman with the Chicago Cubs (and a friend of Durocher's), was the chosen ballplayer.[43]

In early May, Durocher answered a telephone call at four o'clock on the morning. It was, not surprisingly, MacPhail, who asked if he was awake. Durocher couldn't resist a bit of sarcasm ("No, I'm bowling."[44]) before MacPhail handed the phone to his new acquisition—Billy Herman. "Hello, buddy," Herman said, sounding a bit tired. "I'll see you at the ballpark if this boss of yours will let me get back to sleep."[45] MacPhail had sent Charlie Gilbert, Johnny Hudson, and $65,000 cash to Chicago for Durocher's friend.

Hours later, Durocher's mood had brightened. Herman might indeed be the answer to one of Brooklyn's problems—Reese's up-and-down play. Durocher told the *Eagle*, "He'll steady the kid at shortstop. He'll take charge of the infield. And he gives us sustained power on attack."[46]

Herman, 32 years old, began the 1941 season slowly, slumping to .194 through his first 11 games. Even so, the seven-time All-Star, a "classic No. 2 hitter,"[47] had batted .292 the previous season and boasted a .310 career mark. He figured to start scorching line drives any game now. Why would Chicago deal such a valuable commodity? Turns out, the veteran had lost out on a promotion. He was unhappy after the Cubs fired skipper Gabby Hartnett following the 1940 campaign and hired Jimmy Wilson. Herman had wanted the job.

The new Dodger hailed from New Albany, Indiana, in the southern part of the state, just a few miles from Louisville, and, like Reese, had played youth baseball in a local church league. If anyone could help Reese relax, it was Herman. Well, that was the idea. Reese, though, kept on kicking baseballs. Gene Schoor wrote, "His [Herman's] presence didn't seem to help Reese at all. … The youngster was playing terrible ball, worse than he had early the season before."[48] Newspapers printed the graphic details of Reese's sophomore slump. On May 4, he bobbled a ball, leading to four unearned runs in a 6–4 loss to Pittsburgh.

By May 20, Reese's batting average had dropped to .244, and he was battling a 2-for-17 slump. The Dodgers were playing the Cubs at Wrigley Field. Chicago put two runners on base with two out and rookie infielder Lou Stringer at bat. Kirbe Higbe began his wind-up, and Reese ran toward second base, ready to grab the throw for a presumed pickoff attempt. Rather than a pickoff, though, Higbe hurled a pitch. Stringer, in turn, knocked a base hit through the spot Reese had just vacated, scoring a run. "I don't know what Reese was thinking about when he ran for second," a perplexed Durocher said after the game. "Ever since Higbe's been in the league, I've never seen him try to pick a runner off second. He never throws to that bag when he's pitching. I think it's time to give Reese a rest."[49] The Dodgers also had lost four straight games. "Lippy realizes something must be done," the *Brooklyn Citizen* reported, "so he has benched Pee Wee Reese, the sensational shortstop, for the time being."[50] The *Daily News* called Reese "slump-ridden."[51]

Durocher's tenure lasted not even an entire game. Reese took over for Durocher in the bottom of the sixth inning against St. Louis on May 21 after Jimmy Wasdell batted for his skipper and popped out. Reese flied out in the ninth as the Cardinals secured a 9–3 victory. Reese started the following day and went 1-for-5. He also committed another error, his 15th of the campaign, in a 7–6 loss to St. Louis. The shortstop fumbled[52] a grounder hit to him by Jimmy Brown in the first inning. The Redbirds' leadoff batter scored on Mize's sacrifice fly. Brooklyn slipped to 22-12, while St. Louis improved to 22-9.

Reese played errorless ball for the next couple of weeks, until he made two miscues on June 7 against the Reds with Luke Hamlin on the mound. The first only served to prolong the fifth inning. He bobbled a grounder hit by Ernie Koy (the former Dodger, acquired from the Cardinals less than a month earlier) with one out and Bucky Walters on first. The scoring threat ended after both Lonny Frey and Jimmy Ripple grounded out.

That second error led to a big mess. With two out in the eighth inning and Brooklyn ahead, 3–2, Frank McCormick hit a roller that Reese mishandled. What followed was, according to an Associated Press report, "a painful chain of events." The Reds scored six runs, all unearned, before the inning mercifully ended, but with the Reds ahead by the final score of 8–3. Lou Smith ended his account of the game on a stinging note. He wrote, "It wouldn't be fair to sign off without saying: 'Thanks for the donation, Mr. Pee Wee Reese!'"[53]

Dodgers fans, loyal but passionate, let Reese have it. Tommy Holmes wrote. "For the first time in his young career, Peewee Reese, the boy shortstop, listened to the baying of the Flatbush wolfpack in full cry. His ears must have burned as he came to bat in the last of the ninth."[54] (Reese grounded out to end the game. He went 0-for-5 at the plate and nearly got beaned in the seventh inning. It was an all-around lousy day.) Hy Turkin referred to the young shortstop as "pee yew."[55] The defeat, coupled with the Cardinals' 11–3 win over the Giants at the Polo Grounds, moved St. Louis into first place.

Pee Wee Reese had now committed 17 errors. He was on a horrific pace. His teammates, he was sure, had lost all faith in him. "I know the only one the players weren't sure of was me," Reese told writer Frank Graham. "They were afraid that I might blow the pennant. If they had been able to conceal their feelings, it would have been easier for me, but they couldn't. ... I know they never intended to hurt me, but I could tell, just the way they looked at me, how they felt."[56] He admitted, "There were days I dreaded to go to the ballpark."[57]

Reese, who recorded just 22 RBI through the first four months, drove home 13 runs in August and 11 more in September. Unfortunately, his fielding woes continued. He made two big mistakes in the second game of a doubleheader against the

Cardinals on August 26. Brooklyn won the opener, 8–3, and he notched a couple of hits and drove in a run. In the seventh inning of the nightcap, with the game still scoreless and Fitzsimmons on the mound, Creepy Crespi led off by hitting a ball that "squirted through [Reese's] legs" for one error. The next batter, Marty Marion, hit a grounder to Reese, who "threw wild"[58] for the second miscue. Three unearned runs scored before the frame finally ended. St. Louis went on to win, 3–1. A headline above that day's box score lamented "Poor Pee Wee!" Afterward, "Reese cried in the clubhouse," according to the *Brooklyn Citizen*. "The kid felt badly about it."[59] Jack Smith of the *Daily News* wrote about "the jittery hand of Pee Wee Reese."[60]

Several teammates, even Freddie Fitzsimmons, patted a discouraged Reese on the back and offered their kind words. Dick McCann of the *Daily News* told readers that "the saddest man in all the world last night was Pee Wee Reese,"[61] who now had 38 errors. A few hours after the final out, Reese sat alone in a nearly empty clubhouse. Leo Durocher thought about what to do. Finally, he barked at the kid. "Come on, Reese! Do you think that's the last error you're ever going to make for the Dodgers?" Reese "glared" at his skipper, but "as it sank in, he got dressed, and seemed to feel somewhat better."[62]

Reporters asked Durocher if the skipper planned to sit down his error-plagued shortstop. He brushed aside any talk of another benching. "Why rest him?" Durocher challenged the press. "Sure, he made a couple of errors—but I wouldn't have him on my club if he didn't make errors. I wouldn't have a player who didn't try. The kid's always trying. I think he's a great shortstop."[63]

St. Louis and Brooklyn met for the final time in a three-game series that began September 11 at Sportsman's Park with the Dodgers up by just one game in the standings. The Dodgers won the opener in 11 innings, 5–4. The Cardinals took the next game, 4–3. Wyatt, enjoying the best year of his career, pitched another gem in the series finale. He threw a three-hit shutout and beat Mort Cooper, 1–0. Cooper held Brooklyn hitless until Dixie Walker doubled with one out in the eighth. Billy Herman followed with a run-scoring two-base hit of his own. J. Roy Stockton of the *St. Louis Post-Dispatch* called the contest "one of the best hurling duels baseball could present."[64]

From St. Louis, the Dodgers traveled by train east to Cincinnati. Reese knocked home three runs in a 7–5 win against the Reds on September 14 at Crosley Field. He hit a two-run single in the sixth inning and added an RBI double in the eighth, both off losing pitcher Bucky Walters. "All season long, the Louisville Kid has been twice the ballplayer away from Flatbush than he has been in the ball club's back yard,"[65] according to the *Eagle*. About 500 Pee Wee Reese fans made the trip to Cincinnati on what many called the Peewee Reese Special. "And what a show Reese put on from them,"[66] the *Eagle* gushed.

Reese dazzled the crowd with his defensive play. He "roamed all over the left side of the infield." In the ninth inning, with Brooklyn holding on to a slim lead, Bill Werber hit a grounder far to the shortstop's left. Reese got in front of the ball, "which took a bad hop," and snagged it over his left shoulder. "He had to transfer the ball to his bare hand for the long peg to first." Reese threw low to first base, but "Camilli scooped it up just in time for the putout."[67] Brooklyn led St. Louis by 1½ games with two weeks to go. Tommy Holmes warned Brooklyn boosters not to celebrate quite yet. "Although the Dodgers won what might be their last super-crucial series of the most hectic of all National League races," he wrote, "the St. Louis villains still pursue them."[68]

Dodgers fans, more confident than Holmes, looked forward to a pennant and took to the road. Many descended on Shibe Park for a five-game series against the Phillies that included consecutive doubleheaders. "Thirty-nine busloads unloaded outside the park," reported Rud Rennie in the *New York Herald Tribune*. "They came in costume, with a band, bells, horns, bottles, banners, placards and boundless enthusiasm. ... The people from Brooklyn took charge. They moved right onto the field for the Dodger batting practice."[69]

The Dodgers took four out of the five games and improved to 97–53 through September 22. The Cardinals were 94–53, still just 1½ games away. Finally, on Thursday, September 25, Dodgers players and fans could celebrate. Reiser knocked a two-run homer and Wyatt threw his league-leading seventh shutout as the Dodgers won, 6–0, in Boston. St. Louis, meanwhile, lost 3–1 in Pittsburgh and dropped 2½ games out of first place with two games to play. The Bums won a pennant race in which no team ever held more than a four-game lead. Brooklyn and St. Louis stood atop the standings eight times apiece. The Dodgers finished 100–54, the Cardinals 97–56. (The defending champion Reds struggled early and did not get above the .500 mark for good until June 24. They ended up 88–66, in third place, 12 games behind.)

The victory party began quickly and in earnest. "Peewee Reese, at the dinner," Durocher wrote, "received a chocolate ice-cream shampoo."[70] Reese recalled, "There was enough victory champagne to float the Queen Mary. Everybody was pouring ketchup on everybody. Shirts were ripped off backs and somebody went around with a carving knife, cutting off neckties below the knot. Strangely enough, nobody's throat was cut."[71] Reese said that winning a pennant was "the biggest thrill of my life"[72] and probably a great relief after he batted just .229 with two home runs and committed a league-high 47 errors. On the plus side, Reese led circuit shortstops with 346 putouts.

Brooklyn boasted a fine balance of pitching and hitting. No National League team scored as many runs as the Dodgers (800), hit as many home runs (101), or slugged at a higher percentage (.405). Reiser led the circuit with a .343 batting average and a .558 slugging percentage. He topped all NL hitters with 39 doubles, 17 triples, 299 total bases, and 117 runs scored. He also missed some time after getting beaned, not once, but twice. The Phillies' Ike Pearson "zonked" him early in the season, as he recalled, and Paul Erickson "hit me in Chicago." "That was some kind of year, '41," Reiser said in *Baseball When the Grass Was Real*. "Everything happened."[73] Camilli mashed 34 home runs and drove in 120 runs.

Dodgers pitchers posted the lowest team ERA (3.14) in the league and struck out 603 batters, the second-highest figure. Wyatt and Higbe, as hoped, gave Brooklyn a tough one-two starting combination. Both pitchers won 22 games, and Wyatt fashioned a sparkling 2.34 ERA. Higbe completed 19 games but still ended the year with more walks (132) than strikeouts (121). Hugh Casey posted solid numbers as both a starter (27 games) and reliever (18 games). The hard-living right-hander won 14 games and saved seven. The Dodgers led the NL in attendance for the third straight year. More than 1.2 million fans flocked to the ballpark at 55 Sullivan Place.

Brooklyn's baseball heroes boarded a train headed back to New York City. Thousands of boisterous fans gathered at Grand Central Station. Some players asked the conductor to stop at the 125th Street station so they could get out and avoid the pandemonium. Durocher wanted none of that. The faithful had waited decades to applaud a pennant-winning team. Durocher longed for a celebration as grand as the fabled station itself. Skip the 125th Street stop, Durocher ordered, and head straight to Grand Central. The conductor obliged, passing not just the station, but also MacPhail. The GM had taken a cab to 125th Street in hopes of climbing aboard and joining the party. Imagine how steamed he was as the train ran past him. MacPhail left the station, hailed another taxi, and headed for the New Yorker Hotel. There, he awaited an explanation and loathed the one he got from Durocher. "You're fired," MacPhail roared.[74]

Durocher, ecstatic just a few minutes earlier, turned glum. He refused to pose for pictures or face the newsreel cameras. The next day, MacPhail ordered Durocher into his office. The sharp-tongued executive looked quite dapper. He wore a blue suit with a carnation pinned to the lapel. Fired? Of course, Leo Durocher, the first pennant-winning Brooklyn manager in 21 years, wasn't fired. "Pull up a chair here, and we'll figure out how to beat those Yankees,"[75] MacPhail said.

The Bronx Bombers won their 11th American League pennant in 1941 with a 101–53 record, 17 games better than the second-place Red Sox. The Yanks boasted three outfielders who clubbed at least 30 home runs—Charlie Keller (33), Tommy Henrich (31) and Joe DiMaggio (30). Second baseman Joe Gordon added 24. DiMaggio enjoyed a magical season. He is most famous for his 56-game hitting streak, one that began May 15 at Yankee Stadium and ended July 17 at Municipal Stadium in Cleveland. DiMaggio, the son of Italian immigrants, won the AL MVP Award. He batted .357, well behind the league leader in that category. Red Sox left fielder Ted Williams put together a magical campaign of his own. The "Splendid Splinter" from San Diego hit .406 in just his third season.

Most baseball experts favored the Yankees to claim their fifth championship in the past six years. "The Yankees were established as 5-to-3 odds-on favorites for the first game and 1-to-2 favorites for the series," Judson Bailey of the Associated Press reported. "In other words, you would have to put up eight dollars to win five on the Yanks in the first game and 10 dollars to win five on the series."[76] But, Harry Grayson noted, "the beautiful Bums can't be written off."[77]

The *Eagle* quoted several borough citizens about their beloved team, from District Attorney O'Dwyer to telephone operator Jane Morrison to the honorary president of the Pride and Judea Home and Jewish Sanitarium for Chronic Diseases, Max Blumberg. They all pledged their allegiance to the hometown Bums. "It will be Brooklyn all the way," Blumberg predicted. "Every patient in our hospital is confident of victory."[78] Durocher worried that two of his top young players might be nervous as they prepared for their first World Series. "Reese is just a kid," he said. "Two years and boom—he's in a World Series. You got to expect him to be nervous. And Reiser may be a little jittery."[79]

Pee Wee Reese, though, could barely contain his glee or marvel too much at his good fortune. Just a few years earlier, he was working as a line splicer for the hometown telephone company. "I'm four years off a utility pole," he recalled in later life. Suddenly, "I'm in Yankee Stadium, and I look around and say, 'What the hell am I doing here?'"[80]

Curt Davis faced Red Ruffing in the opener on October 1. The Yankees took an early lead and won, 3–2, in front of 68,540 fans. Ruffing walked Dixie Walker to lead off the game and retired 14 straight batters before Reese lined Brooklyn's first hit, a single in the top of the fifth that sparked a two-out rally. Owen followed Pee Wee by lining a triple into left-center field and driving home the Dodgers' first run. Later, Reese added two more singles. His base hit in the seventh inning advanced Lavagetto to second, and he scored Brooklyn's second run on a single by third baseman Lew Riggs. "Pee Wee Reese was the big hitter of the day,"[81] Jack Smith wrote in the *Daily News*.

Unfortunately, Reese committed a base-running gaffe in the seventh inning that may have cost Brooklyn dearly. Lavagetto reached base on an error to lead off the frame. Reese followed with a base hit. Lew Riggs, batting for Owen, hit a first-pitch single to center that brought home Lavagetto and sent Reese to second. Durocher asked Jimmy Wasdell to bat for Hugh Casey. The 27-year-old utility man missed a bunt sign and popped to Rolfe in foul territory. Reese took off for third base "without orders and was thrown out easily."[82] Walker grounded out to end the inning. Al Del Greco, in his column for the *Hackensack Record*, wrote that Reese "was caught by three city blocks. ... A double play on a pop foul."[83] Coach Charley Dressen said he never ordered Reese to advance. "But don't blame Pee Wee," Dressen said. "He took a chance. It looked like a good one." Reese told reporters, "I thought I could make it." Durocher said, "We just played lousy ball, that's all."[84]

The Dodgers squeaked out a 3–2 victory the next day in the Bronx. Whitlow Wyatt faced Spurgeon Ferdinand "Spud" Chandler, a former star halfback at the University of Georgia. Once again, the Yankees broke out on top with an early 2–0 lead. The Dodgers tied the game in the fifth inning on Reese's RBI groundout and Owen's run-scoring single. Camilli provided the go-ahead base hit the next inning. Maybe this win could propel the Dodgers to a championship. Tommy Holmes thought so. The players, he wrote, were "full of pepper and they think that the Yankees are worried. Perhaps, they're right."[85]

The Series shifted to Flatbush.[86] Were the Yankees ready for such an exuberant home crowd? Brooklyn fans poured their heart and soul into every pitch and every play. "The Yankees are slated to spend three games in the midst of more noise than they have ever heard before, and the Dodgers at home are tougher than they are on the road," famed columnist Grantland Rice wrote. "One reason is the terrific support they get from the most emotional crop of fans that baseball has ever known."[87]

Freddie Fitzsimmons, who battled arm injuries much of the season and pitched just 82⅔ innings (though with a 6–1 mark and a sublime 2.07 ERA), started for the Dodgers against Marius Russo, a Brooklyn native and graduate of Richmond Hill High School in nearby Queens. Both pitchers threw shutout baseball for six innings. New York managed four hits, the Dodgers only one. The Yankees caught a break—almost literally—with two outs in their half of the seventh. Russo ripped a line drive that smacked into Fitzsimmons' left leg. The ball ricocheted and landed in Reese's waiting glove. Fitzsimmons left the game limping. Hugh Casey quickly warmed up for the eighth inning. The reliever retired Sturm, but after that, in the words of Frank Graham, "the enemy smote him heavily."[88] Red Rolfe and Tommy Henrich lined base hits, and DiMaggio followed with a run-scoring single. Keller's base hit scored Henrich to make the score 2–0.

Reese knocked in Brooklyn's only run. He "shot a sizzling single into the right-field corner,"[89] off Russo, with two out in the eighth inning. Walker, after opening the frame with a double, came around to score. Brooklyn needed a win to even the Series. Game Four, though, featured a play that has survived in baseball lore, in the same infamous, embarrassing manner as Merkle's Boner during the 1908 pennant race and Fred Snodgrass's dropped fly ball in the 1912 World Series.

October 5 broke hot and steamy in New York City. The afternoon temperature soared into the 90s. Kirbe Higbe faced off against Atley Donald, a right-hander from Mississippi nicknamed "Swampy." Brooklyn led, 4–3, going into the final frame. Casey, who entered the game with two outs in the fifth inning, hoped to close out the Yankees. The 27-year-old got New York's first two batters, Johnny Sturm and Red Rolfe, to ground out. Henrich, the next hitter, worked the count full. Casey then unloaded a "a hard sinker breaking low on the outside corner of the plate,"[90] according to Durocher. Henrich swung and "missed the ball by a foot."[91] It should have been strike three. Umpire Larry Goetz even bellowed out the call. Owen, though, one of the game's top defensive catchers, missed the pitch and let it trickle through his legs. He ran back to retrieve the most famous passed ball in baseball history but not before Henrich reached first base.

The Dodgers still had a chance. Judson Bailey of the Associated Press wrote, "This was a small thing on the surface, but everyone sensed deep down that this was a storm signal and the fans settled back into their seats for the big blow. They were stunned, but still hopeful."[92] Hope, though, faded fast. Charlie Keller hit a two-run double to right field that gave New York a 5–4 lead. Two batters later, after Bill Dickey walked, Joe Gordon added another two-run double.

Reliever Johnny Murphy, a New York City native and graduate of Fordham University, made quick work of the Dodgers in the bottom of the ninth. Brooklyn, instead of tying the Series at two games apiece, now trailed three games to one. Yankees first baseman Johnny Sturm said, "Don't tell me you ever saw a world series game like that. There'll never be another game like that played."[93] Bailey called the contest "more surprising than any fiction and more heartbreaking than any melodrama."[94] Tommy Holmes lamented that "it was the saddest crowd I ever saw, the one that silently filed out of Ebbets Field yesterday afternoon."[95]

Owen committed just two passed balls in 128 regular-season games. Still, he accepted his fate as the Series fall guy. "I would rather be the goat than anybody else on this ballclub," he told reporters. "How I happened to miss that third strike, I will never know, I am quick with my hands, but this one got away from me."[96] Even Henrich offered a note of sympathy. Sorta. "That was a tough break for poor Mickey to get," he said. "I bet he feels like a nickel's worth of dog meat."[97]

MacPhail broke down after the final out. Alfred Vanderbilt, Jr., a horse racing enthusiast and the president of Belmont Park in New York, watched as the emotional executive wept. He stepped toward MacPhail and mentioned his own recent disappointment on the sporting field. Cheer up, Vanderbilt said. "Only last week," he relayed, "I had a horse five lengths in front down the home stretch and he jumped the fence."[98]

An entire devoted fan base shared MacPhail's anger, astonishment, and tears. The heart-crushed group included 11-year-old Joel Oppenheimer, who was walking down a street in his Yonkers, New York, neighborhood, listening to the radio broadcast that rang out from house to house. Owen's passed ball hurt him deeply. What a nightmare for a young fan. "I thought, 'Why God, why?'" Oppenheimer said decades after the ball slipped through Owen's legs. "Why had God done it to us and given it to them. Why?"[99]

A debate began. Just what kind of pitch did Casey throw to Henrich? Casey insisted that he unfurled a curveball. Owen agreed. "It was a good pitch, maybe the best curveball Casey threw all afternoon. It squirted out of my glove somehow."[100] Tommy Holmes called the pitch "a sharp, sweeping curve." He wrote that Henrich "missed the big one by a foot" and that "catcher Mickey Owen was fooled, too."[101] Reese, though, said the pitch left Casey's hand with some moisture on it. "It was a little wet slider," he said, "and the ball kind of broke real sharply to the right and kinda got by his glove."[102] Durocher sided with Casey and Owen on this one. Casey, Durocher insisted, did not boast a spitball in his repertoire. "Why should he?" Durocher asked. "Casey had a natural sinker—that's why he was a relief pitcher. A good spitball acts exactly the same way. It breaks down and away. Common sense tells you that a man wouldn't bother to develop a pitch that acts the same as a pitch he's already throwing."[103]

Game Five, played the next day on another hot afternoon at Ebbets Field, barely mustered a hint of suspense. Ernest "Tiny" Bonham (actually 6-foot-2, 215 pounds with a "torso like a blacksmith,"[104] according to *The Sporting News*), making his first appearance in the Series, started against Game Two winner Whitlow Wyatt. New York took a 2–0 lead in the second inning en route to a 3–1 victory. Brooklyn punched across its lone run on a Reiser sacrifice fly in the third inning. The Dodgers managed just one hit over the final six innings off Bonham's nasty forkball, a Walker single in the eighth.

The Yankees celebrated their ninth world championship. The Dodgers were still looking for their first. Reese made three errors and batted just .200 in his Series introduction. He also contributed some big hits and drove in two runs. Gene Schoor decided, perhaps a bit optimistically, that Reese had "emerged as a full-fledged Dodger star, a World Series star."[105] Maybe more accurately, he added, "it was an empty, hollow triumph."[106] For Reese and all of Brooklyn, it was the first of many disappointing October endings against the powerful ballclub from the Bronx.

5

"Another guy I'll have to beat out for a job"

The attack began at 7:48 a.m. Hawaiian Standard Time on December 7, 1941. More than 350 Japanese aircraft descended on the U.S. Navy base at Pearl Harbor, about 11 miles north of downtown Honolulu. Fighters and bombers, launched in two waves from six aircraft carriers, damaged much of the Pacific fleet and killed more than 2,400 people, including 1,177 sailors aboard the battleship USS *Arizona*.[1] Congress, at the behest of President Roosevelt, declared war on Japan the following day.

Brooklyn, like much of the country, fell into a state of anger and outrage. Recruiters at the borough's Federal Building stayed busy signing up future sailors, soldiers, and Marines. The headline in an *Eagle* editorial declared, "American People Are United by the Treachery of Japan." According to the newspaper, "If war had to come—and we have fervently hoped it would not—we can hardly conceive of a way which would so speedily arouse the patriotism of all loyal Americans."[2] John Harrocks, 22, a graduate of local Erasmus Hall High School, joined the Army just hours after learning about the news in the Pacific. Before that day, he had "given no thought to it until the draft collected me, if those [Japanese] hadn't gone haywire."[3]

A few days later, the fight expanded into Europe. "U.S. DECLARES WAR ON AXIS," screamed the *Eagle* in a front-page headline on December 11. "The greatest war in the world's history became a full reality for an America which has been on a basis of undeclared shooting with Germany and Italy,"[4] reported the United Press. Draft-eligible young men filled rosters in the major leagues and the minors. Baseball, some thought, might go on hiatus until the shooting stopped. During World War I, teams played a shortened schedule in 1918 due to fuel restrictions that made travel difficult. The Red Sox, with a 75–51 record, took the AL pennant, while the Cubs, 84–45, earned the NL flag. Boston, behind ace pitcher Babe Ruth (2–0, 1.06 ERA in two starts), won the World Series.

This time around, FDR, with his Green Light letter, gave the go-ahead for teams to play ball. The president wrote, in part, "I honestly feel that it would be best for the country to keep baseball going. There will be fewer people unemployed, and everybody will work longer hours and harder than ever before. And that means they ought to have a chance for recreation and for taking their minds off their work even more than before."[5]

Many newspapers across the country printed copies of Roosevelt's dictate. J. G.

Taylor Spink agreed with the message and wrote that "well in advance of the 1942 pennant season, baseball could designate Franklin Delano Roosevelt, President of the United States, as its Player of the Year."[6] Baseball executives expected this war to last awhile. It might take years to defeat the powerful Japanese and German armies. "We are in for a long war, and there is no use in trying to make ourselves believe anything else,"[7] said Philadelphia Athletics owner and manager Connie Mack.

The Dodgers announced plans to aid in the Allied effort. National League pennant winners in 1941, "today they're first again in the much more important fight to preserve national unity and aid national defense." Larry MacPhail promised to donate the receipts from one home date to a service relief society or group of societies as well as the Dodgers' share from one road game. MacPhail also told all employees to accept 10 percent of their salary in defense bonds or stamps, or, he insisted, "We will not open the gates this season." Finally, the club expected to invite 150,000 servicemen to Ebbets Field over the coming months. "With this as a model," the INS reported, "it is believed the other major league clubs will soon fall in line with a similar plan."[8]

Pee Wee Reese signed his 1942 contract on February 12. The "colorful and cocky little Dodger" agreed to a deal worth $9,000. "I'm going to have my greatest year," he predicted. He didn't mention anything about taking 10 percent of his salary in the form of defense bonds. Even so, he told a reporter, "I certainly will be glad to do it."[9]

MacPhail made a big move over the off-season. Back in December, he traded for the talented Pirates infielder Joseph "Arky" Vaughan, a native of Clifty, Arkansas, who earned his nickname after the family moved to California. The Vaughans lived for a while in Mendocino County, not far from San Francisco, and settled in Orange County, south of Los Angeles. Arky's dad, Robert, found work in the local oilfields. Arky played ball at Fullerton Union High School, where a California transplant from an earlier generation—the great Walter Johnson, native to Kansas—once starred. Vaughan broke into the big leagues in 1932 and boasted a .324 lifetime batting average, He hit a career-high .385 in 1935 and batted .316 with six home runs in 1941. According to Lee Scott in the *Brooklyn Citizen*, the Dodgers "landed the player they had been trying to get for some time." MacPhail sent Luke Hamlin, Babe Phelps, Jimmy Wasdell, and Peter Coscarart to the Pirates. Scott called Wasdell, a .298 batter in 94 games, "the most valuable member of this foursome."[10]

Vaughan, Scott noted, was 30 years old and married, and thus unlikely to be called into military service. He might play third base for Brooklyn, or he could see action at shortstop "if Pee Wee Reese, now classed 1-A, is inducted into the Army." Scott reiterated to readers in early January that Reese was 1-A, meaning that he was fit for military duty. Less than two weeks later, Scott reported that Reese "is now 3-A for the draft" meaning that military service might cause financial hardship to his family. The reporter added, "he is single and may be called for duty when re-examined."[11]

In February, Leo Durocher told reporters that Reese was 3-A but "classification doesn't mean much. He might go even with his dependents. You know the government is going to look after dependents. Any of us might go now."[12] The April 16 edition of *The Sporting News* further reported Reese's draft status as 3-A, but acknowledged, like Durocher, that "The Service may decide to grab him, as well. However, let us say that Pee Wee and Pete [Reiser] will linger through the season."[13]

The Dodgers lost Cookie Lavagetto to the Navy before the season even began. He reported for duty to the Alameda Naval Air Station near his hometown of Oakland, California, as an aviation machinist's mate. Lee Scott wrote that while "Lavagetto was far from sensational last year, he was considered by his boss [Durocher] to be one of the outstanding third baseman in the league." Durocher insisted that the war effort trumped any talk of pennant races. "Baseball men," he said, "stand at the beck and call of the government, are ready to do whatever they can to assist, and if it tells us to throw down our bats and go marching to war, we'll do it with a smile."[14]

Players headed to Daytona Beach, Florida, for spring training. Reese invited his fiancé, Dorothy "Dottie" Walton, for a warm-weather getaway. Pee Wee had met Dottie on a summer morning in 1939. She lived next door to one of his sisters in Louisville. When Pee Wee first saw her, Dottie was "sitting cross legged on a bench chair, the sun glinting on her dark hair." She was, according to *The Pee Wee Reese Story*, "one of the most beautiful girls he had ever seen."[15] Reese could barely say a word. Finally, he managed to blurt out his name. He said, "That … is the moment I decided: 'That's the girl for me.'"[16]

Reiser also had a girlfriend, Patricia Hurst, who was visiting from her home in St. Louis. The young players, along with their dates, went out to dinner one night with Dixie and Estelle Walker. Pee Wee announced that he and Dottie planned to get married in the fall, after the season. Estelle had a different idea. "Why don't you get married now?"[17] she suggested. A few days later, on March 29, the couple found a justice of the peace and became Mr. and Mrs. Harold Henry Reese.[18] Reiser served as best man, and Hurst acted as bridesmaid. Pete and Patricia got married a few hours later in nearby Titusville, Florida.

Pee Wee and Pistol Pete stopped by MacPhail's office and broke the news. MacPhail, his face most likely turning an unpleasant shade of red, leaped from his desk. He began pointing at the window, like "There. There, can you see it? Can you see it?" The Gold Dust twins stood in place, maybe at attention. They didn't get it. They couldn't see anything except for an angry boss. Why was he pointing? Did a bird just fly by? No. No. No. "Did you see that?" MacPhail said. "It was the National League pennant—it just flew out the window."[19] What a romantic. MacPhail even fined Reese and Reiser $200, much to the chagrin of fan Jack Schwebel, who wrote a letter to the *New York Times*. "Now, who does MacPhail think he is? Ballplayers are human, too, and getting married is just as important to them as to anyone else. In fact, it is a lot more important than winning a few games."[20] In his biography of Reiser, Sidney Jacobson put forth this theory: "Somehow, he [MacPhail] believed that marriage—like those participated in by most of the players he had traded for and coveted—sucked the athletic skills out of ballplayers."[21]

Several sportswriters asked why Durocher stuck with Reese at shortstop during a tight pennant race the previous season. Simple, Durocher said. He wanted to boost the young player's confidence. Shaky infielders do not turn into steady ones by sitting on the dugout bench. "What would it have done to the kid?" Durocher asked. "It would have killed his spirits, that's all." Durocher called Pee Wee Reese a "great

Pee Wee and Dorothy "Dottie" Walton were married March 29, 1942, during spring training in Florida, much to the chagrin of Dodgers GM Larry MacPhail (National Baseball Hall of Fame Library, Cooperstown, New York).

player." The 37-year-old also said, "I'm going to get in shape, so I'll be ready to step in if I'm needed this year."[22] He vowed that Reese would improve over his shaky sophomore campaign, or, he told at least one writer, "I'll buy you a $10 hat."[23]

A journeyman outfielder offered Reese some fielding tips. In December, MacPhail had purchased the contract of Johnny Rizzo. Brooklyn was the fourth stop in five seasons for the 29-year-old from Houston, Texas. Rizzo enjoyed his best season as a rookie in 1938 when he hit .301 for the Pirates with 23 home runs and 111 RBI. He played on three teams in 1940 (the Pirates, Reds, and Phillies) and batted a meager .217 for Philadelphia in 1941. Rizzo watched Reese field ground balls one sultry afternoon in Florida and noticed something. "You got a name around the league as a hot shortstop," Rizzo said. "But you got a scatter arm. Hitters like to hit the ball your way. You might throw the ball into the grandstand." Well, that probably did little to cheer up the young shortstop. All the same, Reese asked whether Rizzo had any advice. "Your trouble, Pee Wee, is that you're trying to get the ball away too fast. You're throwing it even before you've got it. You're off balance." Rizzo suggested that Reese learn how to throw sidearm or three-quarters as a way to save some time. Reese did it Rizzo's way for the rest of the day and liked it. "Maybe, you got something there, Johnny,"[24] Reese decided.

The Sporting News predicted Cincinnati to finish first in the National League, followed by the Cardinals and Dodgers. Spink said Cincinnati boasted the "best pitching in the old circuit" but might have trouble scoring runs. "The Cards," Spink continued, "are sure to miss [Johnny] Mize," who was sold to the Giants, and might be expecting too much out of Stan Musial, the outstanding prospect with an unusual corkscrew batting stance from the left side. Musial hit a whopping .426 (20-for-47) as a 20-year-old rookie in 1941. The article called Reese "quite vulnerable in regards [to] the draft."[25] Brooklyn, Spink decided, had too many older players, and "very likely saw their best year in 1941, and will skid in 1942."[26]

Brooklyn began the season April 14 with a 7–5 win against the Giants at the Polo Grounds. Curt Davis beat veteran Carl Hubbell, who lasted just 3⅔ innings and allowed six runs. Reese batted leadoff and enjoyed the best Opening Day of his career. He went 2-for-5, scored twice and had two RBI. He doubled to start the game, and the season, and hit a two-run homer in the fourth inning. Brooklyn led, 7–0, after five innings. New York staged a near-comeback in front of 32,653 fans by scoring five times in the seventh. "On opening day, Reese was 'the difference,'"[27] Tommy Holmes wrote. Dolph Camilli said, "We picked up right where we left off [last] season. We win, but we scare everybody half to death, including ourselves."[28]

On April 22, "Pee Wee Reese rose to glory"[29] against the Braves. Magnificent pitching had ruled much of the day. Whitlow Wyatt threw nine scoreless innings before giving way to Hugh Casey. Boston knuckleballer Jim Tobin, meanwhile, kept the Dodgers baffled. In the 12th inning of a scoreless game, and with Tobin still on the mound, both Camilli and Walker reached base. Pee Wee Reese stepped to the plate. The shortstop lined a pitch "sharply"[30] to left field, scoring both runners. The Dodgers added two more runs and won, 4–0. Brooklyn led the NL pennant race by four games at the end of April with a 14–3 record.

Newlywed Dottie Reese followed the team. She knew little about the game, she confessed, but planned to visit Ebbets Field and other ballparks "practically every day." She already had developed a strong opinion on baseball fashions. She disliked them. Pee Wee "is really a handsome man," she said, "but you'd barely know that by looking at him in a baseball uniform. Why, even Tyrone Power would look like a second-story man in those clothes."[31]

Reese, who hit .250 in April, matched that mark in May. He only batted .204 in June and drove home four runs. After stealing six bases in May, he swiped just one in June. He did, however, help win a game in thrilling fashion against the Reds on June 26 at Ebbets Field. The score was tied, 4–4, in the 10th inning. Cincinnati reliever Clyde Shoun gave up a one-out triple to Babe Herman and intentionally walked Mickey Owen and Babe Dahlgren to load the bases, bringing up Reese. On a two-ball, one-strike count, he laid down a squeeze bunt that "completely fooled" Shoun. Herman dashed home with the winning run. Turkin wrote that "a crescendo of shrieks, such as only a ladies' day crowd of 16,616 could emit, greeted an unorthodox play, as only the Dodgers would commit."[32] Brooklyn improved to 46–17 and took a 9½ game lead over the second-place Cardinals.

Pee Wee Reese made his first All-Star team in 1942. Lee Scott applauded the selection. "Pee Wee Reese improves with every game," he wrote in the *Brooklyn*

Citizen. "Right now, we can honestly say that the Brooklyn shortstop is the best in the league. He is playing right smart ball and the pitchers are grateful."[33] The Brooklyn contingent for the July 8 game also included Herman, Medwick, Owen, Reiser, Vaughan, and Wyatt, more than any other NL team. A driving rainstorm delayed the opening pitch at the Polo Grounds for about an hour. The AL scored three times in the first inning on a Lou Boudreau solo home run and Rudy York two-run homer, and won, 3–1, before not even 34,000 fans. Reese smacked a line drive with two runners aboard in the seventh inning that Boudreau snagged with a "spectacular, stabbing catch."[34]

Following the break, Brooklyn traveled to Cincinnati for a four-game series and won two of the first three. The finale went into extra innings. Reese led off the top of the 15th with a walk. Lew Riggs put down a sacrifice bunt that advanced him to second base. Augie Galan popped out, bringing Medwick to the plate. Shoun hurled a pitch that bounced off catcher Ray Lamanno's glove and squirted to the backstop. Reese took off in a sprint, rounded third, and scored the go-ahead run. Hugh Casey retired Cincinnati in order in the bottom of the 15th. Dick McCann wrote that "Pee Wee's feet twinkled and fled him across the plate."[35]

The next day in Pittsburgh, Reese pulled off what Brooklyn pitcher Larry French called "one of the greatest plays I have ever seen on a ballfield." The Dodgers were leading, 2–1, with two outs in the bottom of the ninth inning. Maurice Van Robays hit a grounder that Reese scooped up deep in the hole and made a "bullet-like peg" to nail Robays at first base, ending the game with the tying run at third. French, in the final season of a 14-year career, gave Reese a big hug. Davis called Reese "the best in the league. ... Reese is better than any man I have ever seen at making plays behind second. And the way he gets under short flies to the outfield is positively marvelous."[36]

On July 24, Hy Turkin wrote that Reese had "nailed shut the coffin on Leo Durocher's shortstopping career." Turkin also called Reese the team's "iron man." Thus far, the shortstop had played in every inning of every game. "The tow-headed kid, deemed 'erratic,' 'brittle' and 'reckless' by armchair generalizers, did more than answer the roll call every inning—he meshed the Dodger infield gears into a machine that has committed [the] fewest errors in the majors."[37] Reese joked to reporters about his sudden durability. "Credit my wife, Dorothy," he said. "She sees to it that I get lots of rest and serves swell steaks and chicken."[38]

Over July, Reese hit—yes—.250, the third full month in which he finished with that mark. Finally, in August, he heated up a bit, batting .283 with a .357 on on-base percentage. On August 4, he smacked a bases-loaded, inside-the-park homer in the 10th inning of a twilight game against the Giants. Dodgers fans at the Polo Grounds smiled, screamed, and applauded as the shortstop ran a 360-foot sprint with three teammates ahead of him. It was maybe the most exciting play of the season. And it didn't count. It was the grand slam that got away, a big hit stolen by the rules of the day and an ever-ticking clock. Pee Wee was "cheated,"[39] Scott claimed.

The score was tied, 1–1, after nine innings. Reese already had driven home Brooklyn's lone run with a single in the fifth inning that scored Owen. Umpires gave the go-ahead for the 10th inning to start, although the Army's wartime curfew was fast approaching. Brooklyn loaded the bases with nobody out. Reese stepped to the plate against starter Bill McGee. "Pee Wee looked at a couple of pitches—then wham!" The shortstop "blasted the ball and the bases emptier than a horse player's pocketbook after the eighth race."[40] Reese sprinted around the bases as the ball traveled to the far reaches of center field. He "easily beat the relay home,"[41] according to the *Brooklyn Citizen*. Then the Dodgers got some bad news. The umpires conferred, and the big hit was "washed out" before could even catch his breath in the dugout. It was the third time that the Dodgers played a game that was shortened due to blackout restrictions. Innings could not begin after 9:10 p.m.[42]

Brooklyn led the NL by nine games in mid–August. Leo Durocher complimented his ballclub's spirit. "Everybody's happy," Durocher said to MacPhail, who just grumbled. That was just the problem. "Everybody's *too* happy," MacPhail sneered. "Nobody's worried. Nobody's hustling. You've got a fat complacent ballclub there, Leo. And I don't think you're going to win the pennant with them." Durocher waved off his boss's pessimism. The Dodgers led the Cardinals by five games with just one month to go. "You should be twenty games in front," MacPhail roared. "And you would be if those guys would hustle. Durocher, we're going to lose this pennant."[43]

Soon enough, MacPhail began to look like a prophet. St. Louis chipped away at the frontrunner by winning five straight games to close out August and five out of six to start September. The Dodgers met the Redbirds for a final two-game series starting September 11 at Ebbets Field. Brooklyn led the pennant chase by two games. Mort Cooper outdueled Wyatt in the opener and won his 20th game of the season, 3–0. Brooklyn managed just three singles, including one in the third inning by Reese. Jack Smith complained in his *Daily News* column about the stumbling Dodgers offense. The team had averaged less than four runs over its past 19 games. "Base hits, brothers—and nothing else will bring that pennant to Brooklyn." If the Dodgers did fly another pennant, Smith wrote, "it will be raised to the rhythm of base hits rattling off the right-field wall."[44] Sid Keener of the *St. Louis Star and Times* wrote, "Our Cardinals are staging another dramatic finish to a National League pennant race."[45]

St. Louis boasted a talented group of mostly young ballplayers. Stan Musial picked up where he left off as a rookie and was mashing line drives at ballparks around the league. He, along with outfielder Enos Slaughter (25 years old on Opening Day), shortstop Marty Marion (25), third baseman Whitey Kurowski (24), catcher Walker Cooper (27), and outfielder Terry Moore (the old man at 29), comprised the heart of a formidable team. Twenty-nine-year-old Mort Cooper, Walker's older brother, anchored a strong starting staff that also included 23-year-old Johnny Beazley and 26-year-old Max Lanier. Years later, Marion explained the 1942 Redbirds this way: "We were not a home-run-hitting team, and we didn't steal a lot of bases. We weren't a running team, although we were fast. We stole very few bases. We didn't even try to steal. We were a first-to-third team. We got a walk and a single, and if we got another hit, we took the extra base. We were aggressive on the base paths. And we had speed in the field for defense."[46]

The Cardinals finally caught up with the Dodgers on September 12. Lanier outdueled Max Macon, a starter and reliever and occasional first baseman and left fielder. Judson Bailey of the Associated Press wrote that St. Louis "stormed to another victory over the bewildered Dodgers." In truth, the final score was 2–1, hardly a storm. Both teams got their scoring out of the way quickly, in the second inning. Kurowski hit a two-run homer in the top of the frame. Reese "fired a screeching double"[47] that scored Owen in the bottom half. The 27,511 fans in attendance included 1,573 servicemen.[48] J. Roy Stockton reported on the Cardinals' "amazing drive to the top." The Redbirds appeared "hopelessly out of the competition just a few weeks ago."[49]

That loss ended the Dodgers' 144-day run with "uncontested control"[50] of first place. The Cardinals had won 29 of their past 34 games. United Press lauded "one of the most brilliant stretch drives in baseball history."[51] Cincinnati swept a doubleheader against Brooklyn the following day, 6–3 and 4–1. After losing to the Pirates, 3–2, on September 17, the Dodgers fell three games behind the Redbirds. In the words of Tommy Holmes, "Our weary Dodgers are a beaten ball club unless a miracle intervenes."[52] Alas, the Bums faced only a cold reality. They ended the year with an eight-game winning streak but still finished two games out of first place with an impressive 104–50 record. MacPhail, who predicted the downfall, nevertheless reportedly told his team, "Last year, you fellows won a pennant. This year, you have won more games than any team in the history of the Brooklyn ball club. I don't know which was the greater achievement. It took a miracle team to catch you."[53]

The Dodgers drew 1,037,765 fans, tops in the league. Hilda Chester "a plump, pink-faced woman with a mop of stringy grey hair,"[54] counted herself among the most faithful. She was certainly among the loudest. Born September 1, 1897, she began following the Dodgers as a little girl. In her teen years, she waited outside the *Brooklyn Chronicle* to get the latest score. By the 1930s, Hilda Chester was a fixture at Ebbets Field. She liked to clang her "10-cent bell" and preferred a seat in the bleacher section to one up close. "They are the real fans," she said. "Y'can bang the bell all y'darn please. The 55-centers don't fuss so much about a little noise."[55] She yelled in leather-lunged Brooklynese to the Dodgers players. "Pee Wee! Pee Wee!" she'd scream. "Have you had your milk today?" And so, Reese recalled, "I'd have to look up and smile and say, 'Yes, Hilda, I've had my milk today.'"[56]

Reese hit .255 overall, a 26-point improvement over 1941. Displaying a keen eye at the plate, he walked 87 times and boasted a .350 on-base percentage. He hit only three home runs, but he collected 53 RBI and crossed home plate 87 times. Maybe most importantly, he cut his error total from 47 to 35. He also led all NL shortstops in putouts for the second straight year with 337 and topped the circuit with 482 assists.

Camilli led the Brooklyn offense with 26 home runs and 109 RBI. Reiser batted .310 and stole a league-leading 20 bases. On the mound, Wyatt won 19 games and posted a 2.73 ERA. The Georgia native had found a home, as well as a better curveball, in the big city. Reiser remarked of Wyatt, "If I could sculpt a statue of what a pitcher should look like, for form and grace and style, it would look like Whitlow Wyatt. I said it before, for those few years there in the early '40s, he was the best right-handed pitcher I ever saw. He could do just anything he wanted."[57]

War raged throughout the season. In April, Gen. Jimmy Doolittle led a squadron of B-25s on a short raid into Japan. The mission did little real damage but boosted morale for U.S. citizens still angry over Pearl Harbor. In early June, the United States scored a major victory at the Battle of Midway in the Pacific. U.S. forces sank four

Japanese fleet carriers and one heavy cruiser in what military historian John Keegan called "the most stunning and decisive blow in the history of naval warfare."[58] The United States lost the carrier *Yorktown* and the destroyer *Hamman*.

In October, MacPhail exchanged his business suit for an Army uniform. He told reporters that the Pentagon needed him more than the Dodgers did.[59] The Brooklyn Trust Company turned to Branch Rickey as MacPhail's replacement. Regarded as a cheapskate by some and a great judge of talent by almost everyone, Rickey created the modern farm system and built a powerhouse in St. Louis. His Cardinals teams won six pennants and four World Series.

Born on December 20, 1881, in Portsmouth, Ohio, Wesley Branch Rickey grew up the son of a Methodist minister and retained his father's pious nature. Throughout his life, he refused to play or attend ball games held on Sunday. After graduating from Ohio Wesleyan University, Rickey spent parts of four seasons in the majors and is most famous—or infamous—for the game he played—or misplayed—on June 28, 1907, while with the Yankees. A catcher, he gave up 13 stolen bases against the Senators. The record still stands today, surely never to be broken. The *Washington Post* said, "Rickey threw so poorly to bases that all a man had to do to put through a steal was to start."[60] Rickey appeared in just 120 games as a major leaguer and retired with a modest .239 batting average.

Discouraged, Rickey enrolled in law school at the University of Michigan and then took a job with the St. Louis Browns, first in the front office and then also on the field. He managed the team in 1913 and 1914 and for 12 games in 1915 but struggled amid accusations that he was "too intellectual in dealing with his players."[61] Rickey left the Browns early in the 1917 season but stayed in St. Louis as president of the Cardinals. He spent part of 1918 overseas, serving as a major in the Army's Chemical Corps during World War I. His unit included Ty Cobb and the great pitcher Christy Mathewson and "supported a number of attacks on the Germans."[62] Upon returning stateside, Rickey also took on managerial duties with the Cardinals. His teams compiled a 458–485 won-lost mark (.486 percentage) over parts of seven seasons. In 1925, Rickey shed his role as field manager but remained as the Cardinals' GM. He performed better at the office than he did in the dugout. Managing "tended to make Rickey tense and anxious."[63] On the other hand, "It was as an executive that he blossomed; his imagination stirred, and his dreams proved fruitful."[64]

Rickey's 1926 Redbirds ballclub won a pennant, the first in team history, and then knocked off the Yankees in seven games to capture the World Series. The Redbirds featured first baseman Jim Bottomley, who drove home 120 runs; third baseman, Les Bell, who hit .325; and Rogers Hornsby, maybe the greatest second baseman in baseball history, who batted .317, a disappointing figure after he averaged .397 over the previous six campaigns and posted a 20th-century-best .424 mark in 1924. Following the final out in the Series, "St. Louis abandoned itself to tumultuous celebration,"[65] reported the *Post-Dispatch*. No, not just the city. "The celebration spread itself throughout the city, beyond the city into the suburbs, beyond the suburbs into the state, beyond the state into the Southwest and Southeast. Telephones and telegraph brought word that hundreds of loyal Cardinal towns were celebrating."[66]

One week later, more than 350 prominent St. Louisans toasted Rickey for his championship work. Former team president James C. Jones said that Rickey "worked tirelessly in building up the team." Rickey himself "spoke in highest terms of the present-day Cardinals." Afterward, guests gave the Redbirds executive a "handsome" gold watch.[67]

Rickey, prone to pontificating and self-congratulation, insisted that he gave more to players and teams than simply his baseball genius. "I offered mill hands, plowboys, high school kids a better way of life," he said at least once, probably many times. "They rose on sandlots to big city diamonds. In a month, they earned more than they could have earned in a year. And no man who signed a contract with me has ever suffered—educationally or morally. If he chose to remain in school, I helped him. When he quit the Cardinals chain, he had learned the lessons of clean living and moral stamina."[68]

In one of his wisest moves, Rickey bought a handful of minor-league teams—in Houston, Fort Smith, Arkansas, and other places—and put each one under the Cardinals' umbrella. That way, St. Louis could sign and develop hundreds of players at one time and prepare the best of them for the major leagues. Critics called this innovation "the farm system." Others called it "chain store baseball" and "Rickey's plantation." A defensive Rickey said, "Starting the Cardinal creation was no sudden stroke of genius. It was a case of necessity being the mother of invention. We lived a precarious existence. Other clubs would outbid us; they had the money and the superior scouting system. We had to take the leavings, or nothing at all."[69]

Rickey loved St. Louis. Unfortunately, he and Cardinals owner Sam Breadon clashed as often as fox and hound. At one point, Rickey yelled, "Sam, I will dig ditches at a dollar a day rather than work for you one minute beyond the expiration of my contract."[70] Rickey resigned from the Cardinals on October 19, 1942, and took a job with the Dodgers less than two weeks later. Harold Parrott offered an introduction to *Eagle* readers. "Rickey–well, he's a card," Parrott wrote. "He may not make Brooklyn fans forget MacPhail—but I guarantee he'll make 'em remember Rickey." Sure, Rickey never let his lips touch booze, Parrott acknowledged. He did not, however, look for polite teetotalers to play on his baseball team. Rickey, after all, had assembled the Gas House Gang, "the roughest, toughest, most swash-bucklin,' tobacco-chawin' team in modern baseball history,"[71] a group that included, in addition to Durocher, such characters and talented ballplayers as Dizzy Dean, Ducky Medwick, and Pepper Martin.

Marion described Rickey as a "kind of phantom. Not many ballplayers talked to Mr. Rickey in his presence. The only time he got involved with you was during contract time, and he would send you letters. ... I was kind of glad when Mr. Rickey left. The players always talked about him behind his back. He was a demon. He was the law. We respected him, don't forget that, but we didn't like him. He was keeping us from getting the money."[72]

A Branch Rickey workday began at about 8 a.m. and lasted for 12 hours or more. He sometimes toiled until midnight or later and rousted associates out of bed in the wee hours of the morning. Rickey received and responded to a voluminous amount of mail. He read great works of literature, box scores, scouting reports, and more. He studied the Bible and quoted from it freely. Once, a reporter asked him, "Mr. Rickey, what will abide?" Rickey held up a Bible. "This," he said, "will abide."[73] In time, Rickey earned the unusual nickname of "The Mahatma," given to him by sportswriter Tom Meany, who "read a portrait of Indian political leader Mohandas 'Mahatma' Gandhi that described Gandhi as a combination of 'your father and Tammany Hall.'"[74]

Rickey wanted to build a farm system in Brooklyn, one just as deep and talented as the one he built in St. Louis "while every club was cutting back drastically," mostly because of the war. In his biography of Rickey, Murray Polner wrote, "His idea was to find and sign as many young and gifted athletes as possible so that when the war ended, their pool of talent would be the largest in the sport."[75]

He also turned his attention to the Dodgers' clubhouse, a space "overrun with gamblers, bookies, ticket scalpers, and racing handicappers,"[76] wrote Durocher biographer Paul Dickson. Durocher's groupies "scurried from dugout to locker room like happy, squealing vermin in the rat runs of an aging barn."[77] Years later, Reese admitted, "It seemed like we always had someone hanging around that was a gambler or a bookie. All the Dodgers, it seemed, knew a bookie named Memphis Engleberg,"[78] who was, according to Durocher, "probably the best horse handicapper I had ever come across."[79] The Brooklyn manager also ran with Connie Immerman, one-time owner of the fabled Cotton Club in New York City and operator of a gambling house in Cuba. "I had known him through the years," Durocher admitted, "seen him occasionally, and I had always liked him."[80]

Many Dodgers indulged in high-stakes poker games, with Durocher often dealing the cards. This was not, wrote Bob Dunbar in the *Boston Herald*, common practice among teams. "A lot of big-league managers will not permit poker playing, even for a dime limit,"[81] he asserted. Not every Dodger took a seat at the table. Durocher named several players, including Reese, who "never turned a card all season."[82] Commissioner Landis told Rickey to "clean house."[83]

In January, Draft Board No. 135 in Brooklyn ordered Reese to appear for a physical. The shortstop asked to take the exam in Louisville, a request that the board granted. According to the *Daily News*, "Draft boards recently have been calling men with 'collateral dependents,' such as these."[84] Reese called it "highly improbable"[85] that he would be playing for the Dodgers in 1943.

Reese, "the blond, baby-faced favorite of Ebbets Field fans," enlisted in the Navy on January 31, 1943, and reported for boot camp at the Gene Tunney School in Norfolk, Virginia. "The Little Colonel became a gob yesterday," Dick McCann wrote, "raising the right hand that has scooped up so many hot grounders and whipped so many clothesline pegs to first base."[86] He was sworn in as an apprentice seaman and hoped for a quick promotion to chief petty officer. "Harold (Pee Wee) Reese will play on Uncle Sam's team for the duration,"[87] said an AP story. McCann wrote that "His absence from the Dodger lineup will be sorely felt."[88]

The Dodgers mostly struggled the next three years. As expected, Arky Vaughan took over at shortstop in 1943 and put together a strong season. He hit .305 with 39 doubles, 20 stolen bases, and 112 runs scored. Billy Herman batted .330 and collected 100 RBI despite hitting just two home runs. The team began on a strong note, going 5–1 in April and 20–12 in May. By the end of June, Brooklyn boasted a 42–26 record and led the pennant chase by 1½ games. No Brooklyn club had ever won back-to-back pennants. Neither did this one. The Bums endured a 10–19 stretch in July and sank out of contention. By the start of August, they trailed the first-place Cardinals by 10½ games, and they finished with an 81–72 mark, in third place.

Durocher signed a new deal with the Dodgers on November 19. Rickey expected him to be on his best behavior. The Brooklyn president forbade gamblers or gambling in the clubhouse. "I don't care what Leo does so long as he puts the welfare of the team first," Rickey said. "What I won't tolerate is professional gambling."[89] Durocher prohibited players from even bringing the *Daily Racing Form* into the clubhouse.

The new-model, squeaky-clean 1944 Dodgers stumbled almost from the start. They lost, 26–8, in the first game of a doubleheader against the Giants on April 30 (Tommy Warren gave up 15 runs, 11 earned, in five innings of supposed relief work, while Giants first baseman Phil Weintraub drove in 11 runs; the Dodgers trailed, 16–7, after four innings) and slipped below .500 for good on May 16 after losing, 7–6, to the Cubs. By season's end, Durocher's squad sported a 63–91 mark and looked up from seventh place. Only the most long-suffering Brooklyn fan could recall a more wretched five and a half months, when the Dodgers of 1912 finished 46 games behind the pennant-winning Giants. Dixie Walker topped Brooklyn with 13 home runs and led the National League with a .357 batting average. Some said that Walker won the batting title in a watered-down war year. He offered a great reply: "I beat out a pretty fair hitter named Musial,"[90] who hit .347.

Durocher employed a team of shortstops. Vaughan had retired—at least for the time being—to his cattle ranch in northern California. The story behind that departure is another Durocher classic. The previous July, Durocher suspended pitcher Bobo Newsom for insubordination after Newsom supposedly hurled an unannounced spitball that crossed up catcher Bobby Bragan. After the game, a 2–1 Brooklyn victory in 10 innings, Durocher accused Newsom of making Bragan look bad on purpose. Newsom denied the charge. Durocher suspended him anyway. Vaughan took Newsom's side, cleaned out his locker, and threw his uniform at Durocher. "Take this uniform and shove it,"[91] Vaughan barked at his manager. Only the soothing words of Rickey kept Vaughan from leaving right away. At season's end, though, the respected player said he preferred ranching to ballplaying. Bragan, Eddie Stanky, Tommy Brown, Bill Hart, and a few others saw action at shortstop for the Dodgers in 1944.

Brooklyn rebounded from that mess and finished 87–67 the next season, in third place, 11 games out of first. Outfielder Luis Olmo, the second major leaguer to hail from Puerto Rico, batted .313 with 110 RBI.[92] Dixie Walker hit .300 and drove home 124 runs. Eddie Basinski, a 22-year-old infielder from Buffalo, handled most of the shortstop chores. He hit .262 in 108 games but without a stolen base or a home run.

Some teammates called Basinski "The Fiddler." He trained as a classical violinist in his youth and earned a chair with the Buffalo Symphony Orchestra while a freshman at the University at Buffalo. Basinski got off to a fast start with the Dodgers and boasted a .305 batting average going into July. Whenever he made a good play in the field, broadcaster Red Barber liked to exclaim, "The violin is playing sweetly today!"[93] After Basinski threw out one runner by several feet, Durocher labeled his player "Bazooka."[94] Alas, the Fiddler/Bazooka hit a sour note in the summer months. He plunged into a severe slump, saw less and less action, and batted just .197 in the second half of the season.

Durocher said that only the war kept his club from hoisting a pennant flag. He told reporters, "You would be coming to Brooklyn for the National League half of the World Series if we were stronger on the left side of the field. Two men would have made us pennant winners. They are Pee Wee Reese and Arky Vaughan."[95] The Dodgers could count on Reese and others to return in 1946. Vaughan might be content to raise cattle.

While in the Navy, Reese, according to one writer, had "an easy war."[96] He did not serve in combat aboard a battleship, destroyer, or submarine. Mostly, he did what he did best, albeit on military bases and Pacific islands rather than major league ballparks. He played baseball. In 1943, Reese turned double plays and lined base hits for a team based at the Norfolk, Virginia, Naval Air Station.

The Sporting News gave extensive coverage to the Armed Forces games. On June 16, Reese's Air Station squad knocked off the Norfolk Naval Training Station, 5–1. Reese collected four hits and scored two runs. One week later, he hit a game-winning double in the ninth inning and helped the Air Station win, 4–3.[97] Besides playing shortstop, Reese saw occasional action at third base while with Uncle Sam. At least one time, he tried out his fastball and breaking stuff. Norfolk Air Station led Camp Pickett by the comfortable margin of 22–0, in front of a few thousand soldiers. "Pee Wee, by popular demand," according to a report, "pitched the last inning."[98]

Reese, along with Hugh Casey, left for Hawaii in February 1944 and reported to Lt. Commander Edwin Haislet. Before shipping out, he traveled home to Louisville and met a new member of the family. Dottie Reese gave birth to Barbara Lee Reese on January 20, 1944. Many newspapers across the country carried a picture of the proud new mom and dad along with their first-born child. Barbara Lee was about five weeks old when the picture was taken. The caption noted that Pee Wee Reese "used to play shortstop for the Brooklyn Dodgers before he entered the armed forces."

In Hawaii, Reese once again spent much of his time playing baseball. He and Casey sometimes competed against one another in Honolulu. Once, Casey, as ornery as always, buzzed a fastball near Reese's head, forcing the shortstop to hit the dirt. Reese drilled the next pitch right through the box, getting the best of that battle. The next time up, Casey threw Reese another high-and-tight heater. Afterward, Reese walked up to the veteran pitcher and said, "You ought to be ashamed of yourself. Don't you remember me—Pee Wee, your old teammate." Casey just laughed. He told Reese that the ball kept "slipping." You'd throw at your own mother, Reese told Casey. "Well," Casey decided, "only if she was crowding the plate."[99]

In May 1944, Reese and a large group of big league stars (Johnny Mize, Vern Olsen, Johnny Lucadello, and others) met for two games in front of 25,000 "rabid"[100] fans at Honolulu Stadium. Reese managed three hits in the opener and "in the other fracas," he enjoyed another "terrific game." Months later, the *Honolulu Advertiser* reported that Reese earned the Williams Equipment Company Award as "outstanding athlete of the week" after he hit a game-winning home run to help his Aiea Hospital squad beat the Aiea Receiving Barracks team, 4–3. According to the *Advertiser*, "Reese has been one of the sparkplugs of the team and his consistently fine fielding at shortstop has borne out his reputation as one of the finest infielders to hold down a Brooklyn post in the National League."[101]

More than 500 major leaguers and thousands of minor leaguers served in World War II.[102] Most, like Reese, never strayed into enemy fire. Some, though, saw heavy action. Sgt. Warren Spahn, a young pitcher in the Boston Braves system and a future Hall of Famer, dodged German bullets at the frozen Battle of the Bulge and the Bridge at Remagen. Lt. Hank Greenberg, the great Tigers slugger, flew airplanes in the China-India-Burma Theatre, and Bob Feller, star pitcher for the Indians, served aboard the USS *Alabama* in the Marshall Islands, Saipan, and New Guinea. Feller led an anti-aircraft gun crew and survived the great storm that swept through the South Pacific in late 1944, known by many as Halsey's Typhoon, named for U.S. admiral William "Bull" Halsey. Three destroyers capsized and nearly 800 sailors died. Twenty-nine more warships suffered damages.[103] "The hurricane lasted for several days, with winds of 180 miles an hour and gusts up to 200,"[104] Feller wrote in *Now Pitching, Bob Feller*.

Yankees prospect Hank Bauer earned 11 campaign ribbons, including two Bronze Stars and two Purple Hearts, for his heroics at Guadalcanal and Okinawa. He suffered through 23 outbreaks of malaria. Two major league players were killed during the war. Capt. Elmer Gedeon, a former track and football star at the University of Michigan who played five games with the Senators in 1939, died when German artillery shot down the B-26 he was piloting over France in April 1944. Marine Corps Lt. Harry O'Neill, who caught one game for the Athletics on July 23, 1939, was killed by a sniper in March 1945 at the Battle of Iwo Jima. Both men were 27 years old when they died.

The fighting in Europe ended May 8, 1945, just a few weeks after German chancellor Adolf Hitler committed suicide while ensconced and raving inside his underground bunker in Berlin. "IT'S OVER," the *Daily News* headline shouted. Joyful crowds gathered at Times Square in New York City, Piccadilly Circus in London, and other cities. President Harry Truman, in office since the death of FDR on April 12, 1945, reminded radio listeners that the German surrender in Europe was "a victory half won."[105] Fierce fighting continued in the Pacific. On August 15, 1945, Japanese officials signed a surrender document aboard the USS *Missouri* in Tokyo Bay. The *Eagle* headline read: "JAPS ORDERED TO CEASE FIRE." Once again, celebrations broke out around the world. More than 60 million people, including at least 45 million civilians, lost their lives during World War II.[106]

In late 1945, Reese boarded a ship in Guam bound for the United States. A sailor walked up to him with a newspaper and pointed out an article. The Dodgers had just signed an infielder. His name was Jackie Robinson. What's more, he was a Black player. He was supposed to play in the upcoming season for Brooklyn's Montreal affiliate in the International League. What's more, he was a shortstop, Reese's position. Maybe Reese learned this news as he stood on deck and looked out at the vast Pacific Ocean, the only scenery for hundreds of miles. "How do you like that?" he said. "Another guy I'll have to beat out for a job."[107]

6

"As boyish as ever"

The ship continued its long cruise across the ocean. Pee Wee Reese spent at least some time thinking about Jackie Robinson and what lay ahead. Reese was 26 years old, a three-year Dodgers veteran, and hoping to re-establish himself as an All-Star shortstop. The competition for a starting job, maybe not in 1946 but certainly in 1947, figured to be fierce if Brooklyn planned to keep Robinson at shortstop. Then there was that other part. The part about Robinson being Black. Lose his job to a Black man? Play on the same team with a Black man? How might that go over with friends and family back in Louisville? He kept thinking about it as that ship cut through the waves and sailed closer to home. Finally, Reese decided, as he explained to a reporter in later years, "If he's man enough to take my job, I'm not going to like it, but, dammit, black or white, he deserves it."[1]

Pee Wee Reese mustered out of the Navy in San Francisco and headed for Kentucky. The start of spring training was just a few months away. He told reporters that he planned to do "some light"[2] workouts before joining his teammates March 1 in Daytona Beach.

The neighbors, who also read newspapers, asked Reese, "What about Robinson?" … "You going to play ball with a Negro?" … "You going to room with him?" … "You going to eat and sleep in the same hotel with a Negro?"[3] Reese lay awake at night. He was thinking about Jackie Robinson, of course. He had never met the man. Really, he knew almost nothing about him. He knew Branch Rickey, though. Reese decided, much as he had during that long voyage home, "if he signed Robinson, then he must be good enough to play for the Dodgers. And, again, if I know Rickey, Robinson must be a pretty good guy."[4]

Reese, late for camp in his rookie campaign, made it to spring training earlier than forecast in 1946. He arrived on Sunday, February 18, "as boyish as ever," according to Jack Smith of the *Daily News*, "and with the same infectious smile."[5] Reese expected to fit right in even after being away for three seasons. "Of course, I'll have to work hard to regain top shape," he said. "It will take time to know the league again, but after a while, and not too long a while either, I think I'll be able to play like I used to."[6] Yankees catcher Bill Dickey, about to begin the final year of a Hall of Fame career, predicted a big season ahead for the Brooklyn shortstop. "Reese was the best ballplayer I saw in the Pacific," Dickey said following a spring exhibition game when Reese notched two doubles and a single in a 10–6 win against New York. "And it looks like he's going to be just about the best shortstop around the major leagues, too."[7]

He had gained some weight while overseas and tipped the scales at 172 pounds, "about 15 pounds more than when I went in."[8] According to Hugh Casey, "[Reese] was one of the biggest chow hounds in the Navy."[9]

Rickey split the team into two squads, one composed of veterans—tabbed the "Brooklyn" group—and the other made up of younger players, or the "Dodgers." Each squad would play a different schedule and then meet up for the annual three-game spring series against the Yankees, set for April 12–14. Rickey put Reese on the Dodgers squad. "Pee Wee is still a youngster," he said, "and we'll probably group him with the younger players."[10]

Many Brooklyn stars from the old days—the ones acquired by MacPhail for the 1941 pennant winner—were now gone. Rickey dealt Dolph Camilli to the Giants in July of 1943. The hard-hitting first baseman, however, refused to go, and the reason was simple. He hated the Giants. "This was no put-on stuff," he said. "Their fans hated us, and I hated them."[11] Instead, Camilli went home to California. He played in 1944 for the Oakland Oaks of the Pacific Coast League and hooked on with the Red Sox in 1945. He batted .212 in 63 games and took his release. Joe Medwick also got traded to the Giants in the summer of 1943. Unlike Camilli, he joined Brooklyn's rival and made the All-Star team in 1944.

Freddie Fitzsimmons left the Dodgers in 1943 to manage the Phillies. The oft-overlooked pitcher won 217 games in a 19-year playing career but flopped in his chores as a skipper. He compiled a 104–180 record and got fired midway through the 1945 campaign. Whitlow Wyatt also left Brooklyn for Philadelphia, in the spring of 1945. The 37-year-old lost all seven of his decisions and retired with a career mark of 106–95 in 16 campaigns. Wyatt boasted an 80–45 record in six summers with the Dodgers and a 26–50 record in 10 seasons with four other clubs.

Finally, Mickey Owen, the goat of the 1941 World Series, left Brooklyn—and the country—in that spring of 1946. Jorge Pasquel, a millionaire from Mexico and a sports mogul, offered him $15,000 to jump from the Dodgers to the Veracruz Blues. Pasquel, the proud owner of six Lincoln automobiles and a haberdashery at his home, made the rounds that spring. Subtle, he was not. "Pasquel carried a suitcase full of cash, the contents of which he would offer players for agreeing to play in his league."[12]

Whether Pasquel ever opened his suitcase to Reese is unknown. Certainly, Reese was putting together an impressive spring. His batting average surged above the .400 mark at one point. "Reese has looked extremely good," said one report. "He is hitting," and "maturity has made him more certain and has given him poise that he lacked in the old days when he was a kid beset by the major league jitters."[13] Durocher proclaimed that Reese would overtake Mr. Shortstop himself, the Cardinals' Marty Marion.

Marion, who, like Reese, made his big league debut in 1940, put together some solid seasons during the war years. (A childhood leg injury kept him from being drafted. He suffered a compound fracture as a 10-year-old and spent several months in traction. He couldn't walk for more than a year.) "Slats," as some called Marion, led the National League in doubles with 38 in 1942 and won the MVP Award in 1944. A so-so hitter, Marion earned the most praise for his outstanding defense.

The South Carolinian stood 6-foot-2, tall for a shortstop in those days, and relied on his long arms and legs to snare elusive baseballs. Red Smith wrote that Marion "could go and get balls nobody else could reach."[14] Even so, Durocher blanched at all that Mr. Shortstop stuff. "All this talk about Marion being Mr. Shortstop is a lot of idle babbling," he said in typical, straightforward Leo-the-Lip fashion. "He is not Mr. Shortstop is my book. Sure, he makes plays, but there are other shortstops who make plays and who will outhit Marion. ... I'm not saying he is not a good shortstop—I'm just saying he has no patent at that position. There are others who can play it even with him. I'll take Pee Wee Reese."[15]

The Sporting News predicted the Dodgers to finish in third place, behind the Giants and the favored Cardinals. Harold C. Burr, in a capsule preview, listed Pee Wee Reese as, among Dodgers, the "only man sure of an infield post" and wrote that Brooklyn was in the "rebuilding stage and anything can happen to it."[16] Ready or not, the Brooklyn players and coaching staff boarded a train bound for Boston.

Jack Roosevelt Robinson, the grandson of slaves, was born January 19, 1919, in Cairo, Georgia. His middle name honored Theodore Roosevelt, the 26th president of the United States, who had died less than two weeks earlier.

Cairo is the Grady County seat, located about 30 miles north of Tallahassee, Florida. Blessed with streams and sandy loam soils, the area is ideal for growing peas, turnip greens, striped watermelon, and other crops. Jerry Robinson, Jackie's dad, worked the land for $12 a month. Later, he negotiated a deal with the plantation owner and was made a half-cropper, meaning that he shared in the profits from his labor rather than earning a flat sum. That promotion eased some of the financial burdens as Jerry and Mallie Robinson raised their five children. Jerry, though, left for Texas in the summer of 1919 and supposedly took a neighbor's wife with him. Mallie's brother, Burton McGriff, encouraged the family to leave Georgia, a state that offered little hope for Black residents. "If you poor Georgia folks want to get a little closer to heaven, come out to California," he said.[17]

The following summer, Mallie took Jackie and his four siblings out west. Upon arriving, Mallie delighted at the lights of Los Angeles that twinkled at night. She called it "the most beautiful sight of my whole life."[18] The Robinsons settled in a mostly white neighborhood in Pasadena. Many residents bullied the new family and made regular calls to police for even the slightest indiscretion, real or imagined.

Robinson and some young friends from school—Black, Mexican, and Asian—formed something called the Pepper Street Gang. "All of us came from poor families and had extra time on our hands," Robinson said. More mischievous than anything, the boys hurled dirt clods at passing cars and swiped golf balls from nearby courses. In due time, a local auto mechanic named Carl Anderson and a pastor, the Reverend Karl Downs, turned Robinson away from the gang and toward more useful activities. Anderson told Robinson that "it didn't take guts to follow the crowd, that courage and intelligence lay in being willing to be different." Downs encouraged Robinson to teach Sunday School. Robinson remembered that the pastor "didn't preach and he didn't talk down like so many adults or view you from some holy distance. He was in there with you."[19]

Mostly, Robinson turned to his supreme talent as an athlete. "Sports had been a big thing with me ever since I was a little boy," Robinson wrote in *I Never Had It Made*. "In grammar school, some of my classmates would share their lunches with me if I played on their team."[20] A letter-winner in football, basketball, baseball, and track at John Muir Technical High School, he earned a scholarship to Pasadena Junior College and later to UCLA, where he started in the Bruins backfield with future NFL player Kenny Washington and averaged more than 11 yards per carry his junior season. As a basketball player, Robinson topped the Pacific Coast Conference in scoring both his junior and senior years.

In his preview for an upcoming basketball game between UCLA and USC, Rob Ray of the *Los Angeles Times* opined that "the problem is how to stop Jackie Robinson, UCLA's great all-around athlete." Ray added, in the racial tone of the times, that Robinson's "black magic on the basketball courthouse has made him the leading scorer in the Southern Division scoring race."[21] Robinson also won the NCAA long-jump championship and advanced to the semifinals of the national Negro tennis tournament. He played just one year of baseball for the Bruins. A shortstop, he lined four hits and stole four bases in his debut but soon found himself in an epic slump. He finished the year with a lowly .097 batting average.[22]

"I guess I didn't put as much effort into baseball as I did into the other sports," Robinson acknowledged. "Like most Negro athletes, I just assumed baseball was a sport without a professional future. I played it solely for the fun of it. Football, on the other hand, held out some kind of a future. Professional teams in the Pacific Coast Leagues did not discriminate against Negro players. The same was true of basketball."[23]

While at UCLA, Robinson met a young nursing student named Rachel Isum. Born in Los Angeles on July 19, 1922, Rachel graduated from Susan Miller Dorsey High School. Smitten from the start, Robinson asked her for a date. "I was immediately attracted to Rachel's looks and charm, but as in many love stories, I didn't have the slightest idea I was meeting a young lady who would become the most important person in my life,"[24] he said. The couple got married February 10, 1946.

Robinson dropped out of college before graduating, "convinced that no amount of education would help a black man get a job." Soon after, he left for Hawaii and played football with the Honolulu Bears, an integrated, semi-pro squad. When the season ended, he boarded a ship bound for California. Two days into the journey, the ship's captain ordered all passengers on deck and told them about the attack at Pearl Harbor. "Being drafted was an immediate possibility," Robinson said, "and like all men in those days I was willing to do my part." The Army sent Robinson an "Order to Report for Induction" on March 23, 1942. He did his basic training, and, later, completed Officers' Candidate School, at Fort Riley, Kansas.

Robinson wanted to try out for the base football team. Unfortunately, he never played a down. Fort Riley had scheduled its opening game against the University of Missouri, which "made it quite clear to the Army that they would not play a team with a black player on it." Robinson also asked about suiting up for the Fort Riley baseball squad. An officer told him not to bother. He had to play for the "colored team." Pete Reiser, also at Fort Riley, recalled what happened next. "That was a joke," Pistol Pete said. "There was no colored team. [Robinson] stood there for a while watching us work out. Then he turned and walked away." That was the first time Reiser saw his future Brooklyn teammate. "I can still remember him slowly walking away."[25]

Later, Robinson reported to Fort Hood, Texas, as leader of the 761st Tank Battalion. How he got that job remains a mystery. "I had no knowledge, background, or experience in whatever it was a tank battalion did," Robinson admitted. The most famous—or infamous—incident in the military career of Jackie Robinson took place on a bus at Ford Hood, located in central Texas and named for Confederate general John Bell Hood. Robinson took a seat near the front of the bus one evening. The driver yelled for him to get up and move to the back. Robinson ignored the order. That led to a heated exchange and eventually to a court martial, with a dishonorable discharge on the line. "I was naïve about the elaborate lengths to which racists in the Armed Forces would go to put a vocal black man in his place,"[26] Robinson recalled. Several Black officers wrote letters of support, and some Black newspapers—including the influential *Pittsburgh Courier*—advocated for him. The panel decided in Robinson's favor and awarded him an honorable discharge in November of 1944.

About that time, Robinson ran into a friend and former player with the Kansas City Monarchs, one of the top teams in the Negro Leagues. The friend told him "there was good money in black baseball," and Robinson needed a job. He wrote to the Monarchs, who, following a tryout, offered him a contract for $400 a month, "a financial bonanza for me."[27] He also said, "I never dreamed of becoming a professional baseball player. All the time I was playing, I was looking for something else."[28] He assured Rachel that he held no grand plan to make baseball a long career. He told her, "All I want to do is make some money. They're going to pay me a hundred dollars a week. I've got to help my mother out and I don't know anywhere I can make that much money right away."[29]

The Monarchs' roster included luminaries from the Negro Leagues such as Hilton Smith, Ted "Double-Duty" Radcliffe, and Satchel Paige. About the tall, slender Paige, who was 40-something years old (his exact age varies with the source, along with the legend), Robinson said, "I remember thinking to myself what a wizard he must have been in his prime—he could still do anything he wanted to with a baseball."[30]

Life on the road was rough, especially for Robinson, who refrained from drinking, smoking, and chasing women. He called the hotel rooms "dingy and dirty, and the restrooms were in such poor condition that players were unable to use them."[31] Players spent long hours traveling on bumpy roads in rickety buses. Teams looked hard for decent meals and accommodations. "Some of the crummy eating joints would not serve us at all," Robinson remembered. "You could never sit down to a relaxed hot meal. … You were really living when you were able to get a plate of cold cuts."[32] All in all, he concluded, "It turned out to be a pretty miserable way to make a buck."[33]

Despite all that, Monarchs center fielder Sammie Haynes said Robinson tried hard to fit in with the team. He'd say, "'Look, I'm here to learn. I know I don't play the brand of baseball you guys play. But help me."[34] Robinson started at shortstop for the Monarchs, although Haynes said, "He didn't have that strong of an arm."[35] Robinson expected little more than a paycheck for all of his work. "The black press, some liberal sportswriters, and even a few politicians were banging away at those Jim Crow barriers in baseball," Robinson wrote. "I never expected the walls to come crumbling down in my lifetime."[36]

Branch Rickey, though, hoped to take a wrecking ball to those walls. He wanted to sign a Black player and put him in a Dodgers uniform. No Black man had played major league baseball in the 20th century.[37] Rickey's pursuit "was a product of his religious beliefs [Methodism], his desire to win and draw fans, and his ability to see baseball in the context of American society."[38] Rickey said, "The very first thing I did when I came into Brooklyn in late 1942 was to investigate the approval of ownership for a Negro player."[39] He outlined his proposal to George V. McLaughlin in January of 1943. McLaughlin controlled 50 percent of the Ebbets family stock in the ballclub. Rickey needed McLaughlin's approval to go forward. Maybe, Rickey suggested, the Dodgers could expand their scouting staff and find some additional talent, and, he added, "That might include a Negro player or two."[40] McLaughlin mulled over the idea and nodded. He also stuck on a condition. "If you're doing this to improve the ballclub, go ahead," he said. "But if you're doing it for the emancipation of the Negro, then forget it."[41]

Rickey told his scouts to look for Black players in the United States, Cuba, Puerto Rico, and elsewhere. To help the plan along, he announced the creation of the Brooklyn Brown Dodgers, a ballclub to play in a new Negro League. That was a ruse. Now, though, Rickey could more easily dispatch scouts to find his ideal player. He sent Clyde Sukeworth—or "Sukey"—a former catcher and proud New Englander—to Comiskey Park in Chicago and told him to watch Jackie Robinson, the Monarchs' shortstop.

Sukeworth sat behind the Kansas City dugout. He walked up to Robinson before the game. The Brown Dodgers needed some players, Sukeforth said. He suggested that Robinson go to Brooklyn and talk to Mr. Rickey about this new opportunity. "I shrugged and said I'd make the trip," Robinson said. "I figured I had nothing to lose."[42]

Robinson met Rickey at the Dodgers' team headquarters on Montague Street. Robinson's first impression was that Rickey was "an impressive-looking man" with "a classic face, an air of command, a deep, booming voice, and a way of cutting through red tape and getting down to basics."[43] Rickey inquired, "You got a girl?" Next, Rickey wanted to know what Sukeworth had told the young ballplayer. The Brown Dodgers were looking for players, Robinson said. "That's what he was supposed to tell you," Rickey answered. "The truth is you are not a candidate for the Brooklyn Brown Dodgers. I've sent for you because I'm interested in you as a candidate for the Brooklyn National League Club. I think you can play in the major leagues. How do you feel about that?"[44]

Reese, batting leadoff against Johnny Sain, popped up to Braves second baseman Connie Ryan in his first at-bat post–World War II. He struck out in the third inning and reached on a bunt single in the fifth. Two innings later, he popped out again. In Boston's half of the seventh, Reese "booted"[45] a "sharp grounder"[46] by Boston catcher Phil Masi. The next batter—Skippy Roberge—hit an RBI double. Second-year outfielder Gene Hermanski added to the fielding woes. He "muffed"[47] a flyball hit right at him, allowing two unearned runs to score. Boston went on to win, 5–3. Carl Furillo, a hard-hitting prospect with a rocket arm, made his big league debut in center field and collected two base hits. Dick Young still decided, "Branch Rickey's ballyhooed Brooklyn youth movement cost the Dodgers their opening game at chilly Braves Field."[48]

Maybe. If so, the youth grew up fast. Following that defeat, they reeled off eight straight wins. On April 18, in Brooklyn's home opener, Reese notched a single and an RBI triple as the Dodgers beat the Giants, 8–1. He enjoyed four more two-hit games that month and belted his first home run, off Hal Schumacher, in a 7–3 loss to New York on April 28. Over in St. Louis, the Cardinals also began the season by winning eight games out of nine. Even in the opening few weeks, this was shaping up just like 1941.

Through Sunday, May 12, Reese's batting average stood at a lofty .411 (30-for-73), with an on-base percentage of .511, thanks to 14 walks. Many newspapers took note of Brooklyn's "dashing shortstop"[49] who was leading the league in hitting, 23 points better than runner-up Musial. Reese's double-play partner, Billy Herman, was batting .368 with a .446 on-base percentage. Lee Scott wrote that "Billy Herman and Pee Wee Reese are setting a torrid pace in the hitting department.... Reese is the pleasant surprise of the team."[50] Durocher sounded cautiously optimistic about his ballclub. "I don't say we can win the flag," the skipper said. "I haven't seen the Cards yet. But these boys of mine feel they can win it and I'm not going to tell them different."[51]

The Dodgers could hit. They could pitch. They could also throw some punches. On May 22, they met the Cubs for a two-game series at Ebbets Field. Joe Hatten and Johnny Schmitz hooked up in a great duel. Brooklyn scored a run in the first inning on Herman's RBI single. The Cubs matched that in the second. Both pitchers then put up a succession of zeroes. Dixie Walker smacked a game-winning double in the 13th inning, the only other score of the game, off Schmitz, still in the game during this rubber-armed era.

All the pugilism took place in the 10th inning. Schmitz led off that frame with a ground-ball single. Lennie Merullo followed with a bunt that forced Schmitz at second base. The pitcher slid hard with Reese covering the bag. According to Tommy Holmes, Schmitz stopped "with his spikes on our dashing shortstop's foot."[52] The next batter, Don Johnson, hit into an inning-ending double play. This time, Eddie Stanky covered the bag. Merullo came charging down the baseline and smacked right into "The Brat." "Well sir," Holmes began, "as Stanky landed on his back, he threw his leg in the air and applied a neat body scissors upon Merullo, dragging the Cub down with him."[53] Benches cleared, and a melee ensued. Players scraped and wrestled one another to the ground and even swung a few punches. Order at last restored, Stanky and Merullo headed to the showers, per the umpires' orders. Close to 20,000 fans (19,733 to be exact) enjoyed this nail-bitter of a game and "real knockdown brawl."[54]

Two days later, Hy Turkin offered a follow-up to what he called "one of the hottest slugfests in recent baseball seasons." Twenty-five city police officers had raced onto the field to break up the scrum and "prevent a complete riot." Officers threatened several players with arrest. Cubs manager Charlie Grimm issued his own stern warning to New York's men in blue. "Don't you dare lay a hand on my boys!" he yelled. Turkin reported that "Walker lost a tooth in the mix-up, thanks, apparently to the fist of Merullo." Even so, Walker proclaimed, "I'm all right."

While Merullo and Walker fought it out, Pee Wee Reese and Cubs captain Phil Cavarretta got into a scrap that was squelched quickly. National League President Ford Frick fined Merullo $150 and suspended him for eight games. He also took $150 out of Walker's next paycheck and gave him five games off, the same punishment as Cubs coach Red Smith, who prevented police from breaking up the free-for-all. Reese and Cavarretta drew $100 fines apiece but no suspensions.[55]

Bad blood continued between the two teams when they met on June 8 at Wrigley Field. The Cubs won, 2–0, behind former Dodger Bob Chipman, and "war almost broke out again," according to Harold Burr. With Reese covering the second-base bag, Cubs runners refused to slide "any too gently." Harry "Peanuts" Lowery, at least in Reese's mind, hit the bag particularly hard in the eighth inning. "The Dodger shortstop resented what he thought was dirty works at the crossroads and told Peanuts so," Burr wrote. "Umpires had to separate the blistering belligerents. It was the first time a Dodger had spoken to a Cub in the series. The 36,229 paying patrons got their money's worth booing Reese."[56]

No matter. The Dodgers kept winning. Brooklyn looked to pull away from St. Louis for good after knocking off Philadelphia, 3–2, on July 2 at Shibe Park and jumping ahead by 7½ games. The Dodgers had won seven straight and improved to 45–23. Art Herring, a one-time Dodger 2–4 with an ugly 6.20 ERA in 1934) now back with his old team, earned the win in relief and upped his record to 5–1. Brooklyn relievers now had 19 wins against just seven defeats. Lee Scott praised the "high-flyin' Brooklyns" for their "knack of winning ball games in late innings" and Durocher's "uncanny knack of getting relief pitchers into the game at the right time."[57] The streak led right into a quick tailspin. The Dodgers struggled through a 4–10 stretch and lost six in a row at one point.

Reese, batting .312 with a .416 on-base percentage, earned his second All-Star Game selection. The American League enjoyed a lopsided 12–0 victory on July 9 at Fenway Park. Ted Williams, playing in front of his home crowd, hit two home runs, including one off Rip Sewell's famous blooper—or "eephus"—pitches. Reese missed the one-sided affair after suffering a chipped vertebrae in his neck two days earlier. While Reese was pivoting to turn a double play in the second game of a doubleheader, a Braves runner slid and bowled him over at second base. "The hard bellywhop shook the neck severely," Dick Young wrote, although Reese stayed in the game and felt okay until the next morning. A doctor, upon examination, fitted the shortstop's neck with a plaster cast, "which would make you think the worst." Young wrote to his readers about a "frightening sight."[58]

On October 23, 1945, Rickey announced the signing of Jackie Robinson to a contract with the Montreal Royals, the franchise's International League affiliate. Observers reacted in different ways. Dan Parker of the *New York Mirror* wrote, "Why a good, responsible Negro athlete shouldn't fit in just as well into organized baseball as he does into college football, basketball, boxing and cricket (to drag an ally into the argument), is something I have never been able to figure out in view of the record of amicable inter-racial relations in these sports."⁵⁹ *The Sporting News* took a more pessimistic view and predicted, "The waters of competition in the International League will flood far over his head."⁶⁰

Rickey signed Robinson only after the two men spoke for quite some time. The Brooklyn executive wanted to know whether Robinson could withstand the great pressure and abuse he was sure to take. Rickey was thinking about the fans, the belligerent players and, yes, Robinson's own teammates. The new player could not retaliate, at least for a few years. "What I am saying to you, Jackie, is that you will have to be more than just a good ballplayer,"⁶¹ Rickey said. The executive stood up and made this his test. He hurled racial epithets. He sprang into Robinson's face, into his very breath. Rickey stormed. He yelled. He challenged. He demanded to know. Could Robinson turn the other cheek? Robinson said quietly, but with determination, "Mr. Rickey, I've got two checks. Is that it?"⁶² Yes, that was it. Only then did Rickey offer a contract, for $600 a month with the Montreal Royals and a $3,500 bonus.

He gave Robinson few encouraging words as he sent him to the Montreal training camp in Daytona Beach, Florida, a pretty town by the ocean but a segregated Southern town, nonetheless. Rickey, famous for his grand speaking, gave his new player a shot of reality. "There's virtually nobody on our side," Rickey said. "No writers, no umpires, very few newspapers."⁶³

Robert Clay Hopper, Mississippi born and bred, managed the Royals. A former minor league star (he played from 1926--1941 and hit four home runs on July 17, 1927, for the Danville Veterans of the Three-I League), Hopper wanted nothing to do with his new infielder. Once, Rickey and Hopper nearly came to blows after both saw Robinson make a sensational diving stop in the infield and throw out a batter. Rickey watched the play unfold and marveled that Robinson looked "superhuman." Hopper, looking on, glanced at Rickey and asked, "Do you really think a n------'s a human being?'"⁶⁴

Florida pulled out the unwelcome mat for Robinson. One police officer in DeLand, about 40 miles northeast of Orlando, waited until Robinson slid across home plate in the first inning of an exhibition game and told the Dodgers to get out of town. "No n------ don't play with no white boys," the officer said. "Get off the field now, or you're going to jail."⁶⁵ Hopper refused to argue. He just asked the umpire for a quick explanation.

Playing games several hundred miles north of the Mason-Dixon Line—even in Syracuse, New York, of all places—did not guarantee a warm reception. There, baseball historian Robert Smith wrote, "the fans reacted in a manner so raucous, obscene, and disgusting that it might have shamed a conclave of the KKK."⁶⁶

Rickey had signed another Black player, a right-handed pitcher named Johnny Wright. Born November 29, 1918, in New Orleans, Louisiana, Wright began playing professional baseball in 1936 for the New Orleans Zulu Social Aid and Pleasure Club. The Newark Eagles signed him in March 1937, and he began a successful career in the Negro Leagues. Wright threw hard and featured an outstanding curveball. Rickey signed him on January 29, 1946, three months after cutting the deal with Robinson. The constant rain of vicious taunts from fans at International League ballparks and from opposing players humiliated the young hurler. "He couldn't withstand the pressure of taking insult after insult without being able to retaliate," according to Robinson. "It affected his pitching that he had to keep his temper under control all the time." Wright soon left the team. Robinson vowed to succeed. "I was conscious every minute of every day," he said, "and during many sleepless nights that I had to make good out there on the field."[67]

Jackie and Rachel Robinson rented an apartment in the French-speaking East End of Montreal. They found the cosmopolitan city to their liking. "We were stared at in the street, but the stares were friendly,"[68] Jackie recalled. On the ballfield, Robinson excelled. In his first game, on April 26, he collected four hits, including a three-run homer, and led the Royals to a 14–1 victory. He also stole a base and forced the opposing pitching to commit a balk. The next day, Wendell Smith wrote in the *Pittsburgh Courier* that Robinson "entered the fray with a big question mark dangling over his bronze, curly head." By game's end, "all doubt was removed as Robinson stole the show from established stars."[69] According to Joe Bostic of the *Amsterdam News*, Jackie Robinson "did everything but help the ushers seat the crowd."[70]

It was the first of many big games for the former Monarch, who went on to lead the International League with a .349 batting average. He also walked 92 times, which gave him a .468 on-base percentage. Robinson scored 113 runs in 124 games, stole 40 bases, and struck out just 27 times. Wendell Smith wrote that "[Robinson] has done everything that you could ask a ballplayer to do, plus a lot of other things that weren't expected him. … [He] is head and shoulders above the rest of the second basemen in the league. His brilliant performances have provided sportswriters with plenty of good copy this year."[71] Robinson, who possessed a so-so arm, mostly played second base for Montreal.

The Royals compiled an admirable 100–54 record and won the pennant by 19½ games. They beat the American Association champ Syracuse Chiefs in the Little World Series. Afterward, excited fans rushed to congratulate Robinson after such a fantastic season. They pursued him for three blocks. "Sam Malton in the *Pittsburgh Courier* wrote a story saying it was the first time a mob had chased a Negro to love him instead of kill him," Rachel Robinson said. "And it literally happened. He was running because he had to catch a plane, and fans were chasing him down the street."[72]

Reese's injury only cost him five games. He returned to the lineup July 15 against St. Louis and singled in the third inning off Harry Brecheen. The Cardinals knocked around Dodgers pitching and won, 10–4. They edged them, 5–4, the next day and swept the four-game series. (St. Louis took the opener, 5–3, and the second game, 2–1.)

Brooklyn stumbled in the next two contests as well, both against Cincinnati. The Reds scored four times in the eighth inning of the series opener and won, 5–2. Carl Lundquist of the *Brooklyn Citizen* called the Dodgers "demoralized."[73] Cincinnati took the next game, 4–2, and knocked the Bums out of first place, a lofty spot they had occupied since May 24. St. Louis took over as the league's top team. Harold Burr sounded a warning. "Today, even the lowly second division Reds recognize the pallid creatures for what they are—just a tired old ball club that has been living on borrowed time too long."[74] Only 4,913 fans watched the action, "but the Dodgers would have preferred that no one had seen their shame. ... The team is down mentally wandering around in a daze on and off the field." Leo Durocher insisted that he wasn't worried. Reese said nearly the same. "Of course, we have to hit the ball and cut down on those errors," he told reporters, "but we'll do that all right, and just watch us when we get back to Brooklyn."[75]

The Cardinals stayed alone in first place for exactly one day. On July 19, with St. Louis traveling by train from Philadelphia to Boston, Reese contributed three hits and three RBI as Brooklyn won, 8–4, against Cincinnati. Dick Young insisted that Reese's "particular bitterness" over a called strike in the seventh inning motivated the shortstop to snack a triple that brought home two runs. The Reds led, 4–3, going into the frame. The Dodgers were playing "somewhat spiritless ball under the broiling sun."[76] Eddie Stanky began the inning by singling off third baseman Grady Hatton's glove. Carl Furillo popped out, and Reiser hit a grounder that forced Stanky. Reds reliever Clyde Shoun had nearly wiggled out of the inning. Dixie Walker saved the rally by singling to left field and advancing Reiser to third. Howie Schultz's base hit brought home one run and sent Shoun to the showers.

New pitcher Harry Gumbert started off Reese with two called strikes, the second one being the object of Reese's scorn. After that, according to Young, "Reese, fuming over ump [Lou] Jorda's call, stepped out of the batter's box, slammed a fistful of dirt angrily to the ground, and was so mad that he slammed the ball over center fielder Dain Clay's head."[77] The Dodgers took a 6–4 lead. They added another run in the eighth inning on Dick Whitman's sacrifice fly and a final one in the ninth on Reese's squeeze bunt.

Next, the Reds pulled into Brooklyn. The Dodgers won the opener, 3–2, and lost the second game by that same score. The rubber game headed into extra innings with the score tied, 4–4. In the bottom of the 14th, Brooklyn loaded the bases, bringing Reese to the plate nearly 3½ hours after the game's opening pitch. He took the first pitch from reliever Joe Beggs for a called strike. Schultz, the lead runner, crept off third base. Durocher signaled for Reese to "lay that fat pitch down," and "that's how Durocher caught them flat-footed." The shortstop tapped a ball to one side of Beggs, who fired home, "but had no chance on a play for Schulz, who crossed standing" on a "nifty squeeze bunt."[78] Fans ran onto the field to celebrate. Reese high-tailed it to the dugout.

Brooklyn enjoyed a small lead, or at least a share of the top spot, for much of July and August. St. Louis, though, cruised through August with a mark of 22–9 and led the race by 2½ games going into September. Stan Musial batted .403 in August with 11 doubles and five triples.

On September 11, the Dodgers played their longest game of the year and still couldn't score. Neither could the Reds. Both pitching staffs put up goose eggs for 19 innings, a major league record since broken. Hal Gregg threw 10 shutout innings for Brooklyn, while Johnny Vander Meer hurled an amazing 15 scoreless frames for Cincinnati. Reese recorded two of Brooklyn's eight hits, a single in the sixth and another single in the 11th. The Dodgers "truthfully feel that they were fortunate to escape with a tie," Young wrote. "They never came close to scoring."[79] Two Reds, meanwhile, were thrown out at home plate.

Reese played a big role in one of those plays. In the fifth inning, Eddie Luken ripped a line drive that punched the right-center fence and bounded away from Walker and Furillo. Reiser sprinted toward Luken's hit from his spot in left field and "whipped the ball to Reese." Luken sped around the bases, kicked up dirt, and hoped to stretch a triple into an inside-the-park home run. "Pee Wee whirled and fired a one-bounce bullet to Edwards for the photo-finish out." No Brooklyn player visited third base the entire game. In fact, only four made it as far as second. Reese did make a loud out. In the 19th inning, he drove a "smash to deep left center which brought the fans to their feet with a gasp."[80] Max West ran down the drive in front of the wall.[81]

Lou Smith wrote about Pee Wee Reese in his September 15 column in the *Cincinnati Enquirer*. He said former slugger and current Giants manager Mel Ott already thought of Reese as one of the greatest shortstops in baseball history. Ott called Reese "Durocher's standout performer" and "this column agrees heartedly." Smith noted Reese's improvements as a hitter. "However," he wrote, "it is his sensational fielding that has made him a standout. Pee Wee has been a great shortstop since the first day he came to Brooklyn from Louisville in 1940, of course, but today he is a super star." If Marty Marion claimed any edge over Reese on defense, Smith concluded, "it is only the advantage of a 6-foot-2 acrobat over a 5–10 wizard."[82]

Reese shows off his acrobatic flair. He topped National League shortstops in putouts four times and in assists once. He also led the circuit in double played turned by a shortstop in 1942 and 1948 (National Baseball Hall of Fame Library, Cooperstown, New York).

Brooklyn and St. Louis ended the year with identical 96–58 marks, tied for first place. The Dodgers headed to Sportsman's Park for the start of a best-of-three play-off series. Durocher had won the coin toss. It was his call. Start the series in St. Louis or begin it in Brooklyn? He wanted to play the final two games at home. So the Dodgers boarded a train for a 22-hour, nearly 1,000-mile trip to the only destination in major league baseball located west of the Mississippi River. "The longest trip we had in those days," Branca said. "That trip was a killer."[83]

Howie Pollet, a left-hander from New Orleans, took the mound for St. Louis in the opener. Durocher gave the ball to the 20-year-old Branca. Hometown product Joe Garagiola drove home two runs and led the Cardinals to a 4–2 victory. Pee Wee Reese smacked two singles and scored a run.

The Dodgers dressed in slow-motion quiet following the game. Columnist Jimmy Cannon wrote that "it was as though putting on their clothes was something they had not done before, and they found the task complicated and mysterious." Durocher ordered photographers and writers out of the locker room. He ran from the shower and yelled, "No comment. No comment at all. No comment. That's the whole story. No comment!" Durocher's repeated refusals to speak barely a word—except, of course, for "no comment"—gave at least one reporter a bright idea. "Leo not talking should be the lead story on every paper in [the] country," the scribe cracked. Pollet pitched in and out of trouble all day. The Cards scored their runs thanks to some "fluky hits," coach Chuck Dressen said. Reese told the writers, "A break is all we needed and he's out of there 15 times. I've seen Pollet when he had a lot more stuff."[84] Reese singled twice in four at-bats.

Sid Keener wrote that the Cardinals enjoyed "a joyous train ride" to Brooklyn. The Dodgers, meanwhile, were "hanging on the ropes, in the fashion of any of Joe Louis' heavyweight fistic challengers."[85] Joe Trimble wrote nothing to make his *Daily News* readers feel better. "It doesn't look good folks, because the Brooks didn't look good today."[86]

St. Louis walloped Brooklyn, 8–4, in front of 31,437 fans, to wrap up the pennant. Whitey Kurowski, Marty Marion, and Enos Slaughter drove home two runs apiece. Durocher congratulated Cardinals skipper Eddie Dyer. In typical Durocher fashion, though, he gave the other team only so much credit and yelled in the locker room that his Brooklyn players "did a better job than the Cards."[87] Tommy Holmes told readers, "The Dodgers went down fighting. They were beaten by a better ballclub."[88] Reese grounded out, struck out, and walked twice.

The Dodgers drew 1,796,824 fans in their first season after the war, tops in the National League. They nearly won a pennant despite boasting a starting staff that rarely threw complete games (52, seventh in the league) and a lineup that rarely hit home runs (55, also seventh). Walker led the team with a .319 batting average. Reiser batted .277 and led the league with 34 stolen bases. He stole home seven times and topped Brooklyn with 11 long balls. He also crashed into the left field wall at Ebbets Field on August 1, one of several such mishaps that plagued him throughout the years. Reiser spent much of his career black-and-blue. Not that he made any big deal out of it. "Hell, any ballplayer worth his salt has run into a wall," he once said. "More than once. I'm the guy who got hurt doing it. That's all."[89] Second-year first baseman Ed Stevens smacked 10 homers, the only other Dodger to reach double figures. Kirby Higbe won 17 games and lost nine. Both Joe Hatten and Vic Lombardi threw a team-high 13 complete games.

Reese batted .284 with five home runs and 60 RBI. He scored 79 runs, boasted a .384 on-base percentage, and stole 12 bases. He finished sixth in the MVP race, won by Musial for the second time. Milt Gross of the *New York Post* wrote that "Reese entered the Navy in 1943 as a brilliant, but scatter-armed shortstop. He came out ten or fifteen pounds heavier and as the best shortstop in the National League. ... He was the Dodgers' most consistent performer of the season."[90]

7

"I looked at it, and I just flatly refused"

Pee Wee Reese said "no." He refused to sign a petition meant to keep Jackie Robinson from joining the Brooklyn Dodgers. The shortstop, only a couple of years out of the Navy and with a young family to support, said he "just wanted to play ball."[1]

In 1947, Rickey sent his club to Havana, Cuba, for spring training, and, later to Panama, instead of Florida. He hoped to avoid all the racial animosity that plagued the Jim Crow South. Cuban police officers did not break up baseball games after Black men slid across home plate. Rickey, though, resisted any temptation to promote Robinson from the Montreal roster. "If Robinson merits being with the Dodgers, I'd prefer to have the players want him, rather than force him on the players," he said. "I want Robinson to have the fairest chance in the world without the slightest bit of prejudice."[2] The plan began as smoothly as a well-turned double play. Warm days gave way to sultry nights, palm trees swayed in the gentle breeze, and Robinson's batting average soared past the .600 mark. He stole base after base against hapless catchers.

Some players still refused to welcome this most talented of athletes. The exact group of players in the anti–Robinson camp varies with the telling. Most accounts point to Dixie Walker as the ringleader, with catcher Bobby Bragan, Eddie Stanky, Hugh Casey and Ed Head also part of the cabal. Each of them grew up in the South. Many sources say Carl Furillo, a Pennsylvania native, also opposed Robinson. The outfielder always denied the claim. "He and I, as far as I was concerned, were always friendly," Furillo said. "I always spoke to him no matter where I saw him, and I talked to him on the side and everything."[3]

The conspirators searched out more players to support their ill-advised cause. Maybe they could talk a polite young shortstop into joining them. How much arm-twisting might this take? Not much, Walker figured. After all, Reese grew up in Kentucky, not a Confederate state during the Civil War, but one close enough to Dixie. Reese, though, shook his head and declined. He liked and respected Walker; the two were friends. What he disliked was that petition.

> Dixie came to the room, and he asked Pete [Reiser] and me to sign that I wouldn't play with a black man. I looked at it, and I just flatly refused. I just said, "Hey, look, man, I just got out of the service after three years. I don't care if this man is black, blue, or whatever the hell color he

is. I have to play baseball." I wasn't trying to be the Great White Father. I just wanted to play ball. And Pete refused to sign it, too.[4]

Reese said later, "It was a terrible moment. I knew what these fellers were doing was wrong, just plain wrong, but they were my buddies."[5]

Reiser offered a personal reason for not signing the petition. During his Army tour, he spent some time at Camp Lee, Virginia. While there, his daughter, Sally, got sick. The baseball player turned temporary soldier brought the girl to an African American physician. The man gave Sally a shot of penicillin, which quickly improved her condition. Reiser told all this to Walker, who looked bewildered. Reiser asked, "What would you have done?" Walker actually thought about it for a minute. He finally answered, "I would have turned around and walked out of that neighborhood."[6] Reiser called Walker a fool.

The plot quickly unraveled. One night at the hotel bar, Kirby Higbe, maybe after a few drinks, began to talk. He told Harold Parrott, now the Dodgers' traveling secretary, about the petition. Higbe stumbled through his words. "The old man [Rickey] has been fair to Ol' Hig. Ol' Hig ain't going to join any petition to keep anybody off this club."[7] Parrott hurried to Durocher. The skipper, replete in a yellow bathrobe, hustled a group of players into a late-night meeting that turned noisy. Durocher's voice grew louder and his language more profane as the room filled. "I don't care if the guy is yellow or black, or if he has stripes like a *bleeping* zebra," Durocher thundered. "I'm the manager of this team, and I say he plays. What's more, I say he can make us all rich. And if any of you can't use the money, I'll see that you're traded."[8] Durocher told the offending players just what they could do with their petition.

Branch Rickey, upon learning about the offending piece of paper, met with Walker at the Hotel Nacional. The Dodgers executive tore into his veteran outfielder. "He really reamed me out," Walker said. "I was so mad at him accusing me of being a ringleader that a few days later I wrote him a letter requesting to be traded."[9] The letter, addressed "Dear Mr. Rickey," read: "Recently, the thought has occurred to me that a change of ball clubs would benefit both the Brooklyn Dodgers and myself. Therefore, I would like to be traded as soon as a deal could be arranged. For reasons I don't care to go into, I feel my decision is best for all concerned."[10]

In Dixie Walker's version of events, Rickey "tried his dead-level best to get me to say that I wanted to be traded because of Jackie Robinson. I would not say it then, and I have never said it."[11] Walker acknowledged that, being "a southern boy," he "didn't think much of the idea of Robinson joining the club. I'd be a liar if I said I did." He blamed his feelings on "the climate of the times."[12] Later, he told Tommy Holmes, "Frankly, I cannot recall a petition of any sort that was signed. The charge is completely false."[13] (Jules Tygiel, adamant about Walker's role, wrote in *Baseball's Great Experiment* that Walker "initiated a protest petition."[14] Tygiel wrote, without explanation, that "Reese's refusal, perhaps more than any other, doomed the petition."[15])

Bobby Bragan also denied that a petition ever existed. "I don't know who started that rumor," he said. "I was Dixie's roommate [and] I never did see it. I'm sure I would have seen it."[16] Gene Hermanski, a young outfielder in the spring of 1947, said no one asked him to sign a petition, maybe due to his New Jersey roots. "We had Negroes in our classes,"[17] he said. No one asked 21-year-old pitcher Ralph Branca, either. "I guess they figured I was a northerner,"[18] he said.

In *The Era*, Roger Kahn relayed a further note about the petition. Walker was working as a Dodgers coach in 1976 and invited Kahn for a glass of wine after the game. While sipping "a marvelous Margaux," Walker, according to Kahn, admitted, "I organized that petition in 1947, not because I had anything against Robinson personally or against Negroes generally." Walker explained that he owned a hardware store in Birmingham and "people told me I'd lose my business if I played ball with a black man. That's why I started the petition. It was the dumbest thing I did in my life. If you ever get a chance, sometime, please write that I am deeply sorry."[19]

The baseball season in Brooklyn promised to be an eventful one, filled with drama, excitement, and—fans, players, and the manager hoped—lots of wins. Leo Durocher missed it all. Baseball Commissioner Happy Chandler suspended Durocher for one season on April 9. Chandler handed down his decision less than a week before Opening Day. The reason for the suspension? Or, as Durocher kept asking, "For what?"[20] Chandler said he gave Durocher the year off following an "accumulation of unpleasant incidents detrimental to baseball."[21]

Durocher still liked to gamble. That was hardly a secret. He counted the actor—and gambler—George Raft as a friend. Raft grew up in the gritty Hell's Kitchen neighborhood of New York City and had appeared in movies such as *Scarface* (1932), *Bolero* (1934), and *Johnny Angel* (1945). A few years earlier, New York City District Attorney Frank S. Hogan investigated a complaint made by an aircraft company executive that Raft ran an illegal—but highly profitable—dice game out of Durocher's Manhattan apartment. Supposedly, Raft cheated the man out of $18,500. According to Durocher biographer Gerald Eskenazi, Durocher swore ignorance about the entire affair "and soon he no longer was the focus of the criminal investigation. But baseball didn't forget."[22]

Chandler vowed to keep an eye on Durocher. The two men met in November 1946 on a California golf course. Chandler ordered Durocher to break off all ties with Raft, along with Engleberg, Immerman and any other unsavory characters. Durocher promised to find a higher class of friends. Chandler inquired, did Durocher know the notorious West Coast mobster Bugsy Siegel? Yes, Durocher admitted, he had a "nodding acquaintance" with Siegel. "Don't nod at him anymore,"[23] Chandler ordered.

Durocher had complicated matters even further by falling in love. With a married woman, no less. The object of his affection, Laraine Day, hailed from a wealthy Mormon family in Utah that later moved to Long Beach, near Hollywood. Day embarked on an acting career and appeared in, among other films, the Alfred Hitchcock suspense classic *Foreign Correspondent* and *Dr. Kildare Goes Home*. Day's husband was Ray Hendricks, a former bandleader who ran the Santa Monica municipal airport. Supposedly, Hendricks and Durocher argued in Day's bedroom one night about who should have the actress's hand. Chandler told Durocher not to pull that kind of stunt in Kentucky. Why not? Durocher asked. "They'll kill you,"[24] Chandler said.

California state judge George A. Dockweiler granted Day an "interlocutory degree" on January 20, 1947. She could not marry again for one year. Day and Durocher found a way around the order. Day drove to Juarez, Mexico, got a "quickie divorce," crossed back over the border and, in El Paso, married Leo. Judge Dockweiler, none too happy, threatened to void Day's divorce and throw her in jail for bigamy if she and Durocher lived under the same roof.[25]

Three thousand miles away, the Reverend Vincent J. Powell, director of the Catholic Youth Organization (CYO) in Brooklyn, threatened to pull 50,000 CYO boys from the team's Knothole Club. Powell accused Durocher of "undermining the moral training of Brooklyn's Roman Catholic youth."[26] In a letter to the Dodgers brass, Powell wrote, "The present manager of the Brooklyn Baseball team is not the kind of leader we want for our youth to idealize and imitate."[27]

At one point, Chandler asked Rickey in a telephone conversation, "Can you handle Leo Durocher?" The commissioner decided to make the question a rhetorical one. "Well, I don't believe you can. … I've given you your chance, Branch. Now, I'll handle him."[28] Maybe Durocher could appeal. Or could he? "To whom?"[29] Rickey answered when Durocher made that very inquiry. Baseball's commissioner ruled with near-absolute authority.

Durocher walked into the Brooklyn clubhouse, wished the players good luck, and told them goodbye. It must have been tough. "It was my team," he said. "Rickey had built it for me, sure, but I had suffered with it through the diaper stage. I had thrilled to see it grow and improve, and now that it was striding about on its own legs, I had to leave it."[30]

One day after Chandler suspended Durocher, Rickey made an important announcement of his own. It happened in the sixth inning of an exhibition game between the Dodgers and Royals and right after Jackie Robinson hit into a double play. The short, low-key press release read: "Brooklyn announces the purchase of the contract of Jack Roosevelt Robinson from Montreal. He will report immediately. Signed Branch Rickey."[31]

The Dodgers began the regular season April 15 at Ebbets Field. The day broke chilly and cloudy, typical for Brooklyn in the early spring. Robinson left for the ballpark from his room at the McAlpin Hotel in Manhattan and took the subway. He said to his wife that morning, "Just in case you have trouble picking me out, I'll be wearing number 42."[32]

When Robinson walked into the Brooklyn locker room, only 22-year-old pitcher Rex Barney and Ralph Branca shook the new player's hand. "The rest of the Dodgers ignored him."[33] Bobby Bragan, though, in his memoir *You Can't Hit with the Bat on Your Shoulder*, recalled, "To Pee Wee's everlasting credit, he was Jackie's friend from day one." Reese "talked to him just as friendly as he did to the rest of his teammates."[34] One day earlier, Stanky spoke to Robinson about just where he stood on the matter of baseball integration. "You're on this ballclub," Stanky acknowledged. "But before I play with you, I want you to know how I feel about it. I want you to know I don't like it. I want you to know I don't like you."[35]

Rickey asked Clyde Sukeworth to manage the Dodgers in place of Durocher, at least temporarily. As expected, Sukeforth penciled in Robinson at first base, a position he had only begun playing—reluctantly—during spring training. "I think he's a great enough all-around athlete to play any position, in time,"[36] Sukeworth said. As for any advice he may have offered, the interim skipper said, "I didn't tell Jack anything special [before] the game. Jack had enough to think about."[37] Hopper, now one of Robinson's most enthusiastic fans, told the *Daily News*, "I know he'll hit .300 in the majors. He'll bunt third basemen crazy, and he'll hit enough line drives to all fields to keep the opposition guessing. He has no real weakness at bat and is one of the most amazing judges of the strike zone I ever saw."[38]

Stanky took his spot beside Robinson at second base. Reese, still recovering from a minor ankle injury that he suffered April 6 in Cuba, trotted out to shortstop, while Spider Jorgenson jogged out to third base. Before the game, photographers snapped pictures of the infield quartet in front of the Brooklyn dugout. Stanky put his hand on Robinson's shoulder. Reese stood second from the left, between Jorgensen and Stanky.

Hermanski, Reiser, and Walker began the day in the Brooklyn outfield, from left to right. Bruce Edwards crouched behind the plate, and Joe Hatten, a 14-game winner as a 29-year-old rookie in 1946, walked out to the pitcher's mound. Johnny Sain, the "Man of a Thousand Curves," drew the pitching assignment for Boston. Sain, a right-hander from Havana, Arkansas, won 20 games in 1946 and posted a handsome 2.21 ERA.

Robinson, placed second in the Brooklyn order, grounded out in his first at-bat and went hitless on the day. "Jackie is very definitely brunette,"[39] Red Barber said on the radio broadcast. Reiser drove in two runs and scored three times as the Dodgers came from behind to win, 5–3. Reese, batting eighth, doubled in the fifth inning and reached on an intentional walk in the sixth. Sain gave up five runs (three earned) in six innings but certainly impressed Robinson. "What pitching," Robinson said in the *Daily News*. "If they're all like this, I'm going to have a tough time making this league." Pee Wee Reese offered some comforting words. "You were looking at one of the best,"[40] he said.

Only 26,623 fans showed up at Ebbets Field, far short of capacity. "The crowd was disappointing," the *Eagle* reported. "But Flatbush misses its pepperpot manager and the team didn't look right out there on the field without Durocher to drive 'em to victory."[41] Some fans probably stayed away due to a local smallpox scare. New York City health officials had declared the outbreak in early March and inoculated more than six million adults and children against the dreaded, contagious disease. "Nobody knew if his neighbor in the seat had been vaccinated or not,"[42] the newspaper decided.

Jonathan Eig, in *Opening Day*, wondered whether another factor kept the stadium count below capacity. According to one estimate, about 60 percent of the crowd was Black.[43] On most days, Black fans "made up five percent of the crowd, but probably not 10."[44] Eig suspects, "White Brooklynites were not accustomed to being surrounded by black Brooklynites, and they were not eager to discover how it felt."[45] Bill Reddy confessed, "It was strange to go to Ebbets Field and root for a guy of another color. We had never seen this before."[46] Another fan, Tom "Duke" Bunderick, said, "When Jackie Robinson came up, there were a lot of adults who dropped their allegiance to the Dodgers. There was a lot of bigotry, among the working class more than anything: the Irish, the Italians, the Swedes." Bunderick insisted, though, "The young kids didn't care, 'cause we felt, 'here's another great ballplayer.'"[47]

The Dodgers still needed a full-time manager. Rickey found one in 62-year-old Burt Shotton of Lorain County, Ohio, not far from Cleveland. Shotten and Rickey went way back. They met in 1913 when Rickey was the Browns' skipper and Shotton was a speedy outfielder for St. Louis, with a solid bat and a good eye at the plate. Nicknamed "Barney" after the great race-car driver Barney Oldfield, Shotton coached for several teams following his playing days and managed the Phillies from 1928–1933 and the Reds in 1934. Now, he was happy and semi-retired in Florida—or so he thought—doing some scouting for Rickey, but mostly relaxing in the sunshine.

Rickey sent him a telegram. Not surprisingly, it revealed little, more like something out of a spy novel than an invitation to manage the Dodgers. "Be in Brooklyn in the morning," the note read. "Call nobody, see no one."[48] John Drebinger of the *New York Times* wrote that Shotton "appeared on the scene like something whisked out of a magician's closet by Prof. Branch Rickey."[49] Bespectacled and grandfatherly, Shotton told reporters that he planned to manage the Dodgers while wearing street clothes, much like Charles Ebbets once did in Brooklyn and Connie Mack still did while leading the Athletics.

Brooklyn won 10 of its first 13 games. Furillo boasted a .450 batting average in the early going, Walker, .400. Reese started off in a 2-for-19 funk and hit .152 in April with just the one Opening-Day extra-base hit. He drew 10 walks and sported a .349 on-base percentage.

The Phillies visited Ebbets Field for the first time on April 22. Come game time, Philadelphia manager Ben Chapman let loose a string of loud, racial hatred. Chapman hailed from Alabama and played 15 seasons in the big leagues. He batted .302 lifetime and gained a well-deserved reputation as one of the game's nastiest bench jockeys. Following one noxious rant directed at Robinson, Eddie Stanky of all people yelled from the Brooklyn dugout, "Why don't you guys go to work on somebody who can fight back?"[50] Afterward, Chapman said he treated Robinson the same way he treated the Jewish Hank Greenberg, the German-American Clint Hartung, and the Irish-American Connie Ryan. Poorly.

Rumors swirled that the Cardinals planned to go on strike against Robinson and the Dodgers. Stanley Woodward of the *New York Herald Tribune* broke the story. The Redbirds, he wrote, had decided to sit out the May 6 game at Ebbets Field. "Subsequently, the St. Louis players conceived the idea of a general strike within the National League on a certain date," Woodward wrote in a follow-up article in *The Sporting News* on May 21. National League president Ford Frick and Cardinals owner Sam Breadon worked to avert the stoppage. Frick issued a stern warning to players. "If you do this, you will be suspended from the league. You will find that the friends you have in the press box will not support you, that you will be outcasts. I do not care if half the league strikes. Those who do it will encounter quick retribution." Frick said the suspensions might wreck the National League "for five years." Even so, "This is the United States of America, and one citizen has as much right to play as another."[51] Woodward labeled his article "thoroughly substantiated."[52]

Bob Broeg of the *St. Louis Post-Dispatch* called the entire controversy balderdash.

"There was no threat to strike against Robinson," Broeg said. "There was talk on all clubs, but the Cardinals had no plans to strike. I know because I was with them."[53] Stan Musial agreed with Broeg. "We never had a meeting or talked about anything of that nature," he said. "We never considered it, talked about it, or had any ideas about it."[54] Marty Marion said, "I never heard such a stupid thing in my life. Nobody is their right mind would do a thing like that. ... Sure, we didn't like Jackie Robinson. We didn't like anybody. That had nothing to do with Jackie Robinson being black."[55] Players knew all about Robinson and how he made of habit of hitting line drives and stealing bases for the Royals. Marion said, "Everybody knew he was coming to the big leagues."[56] Dick Sisler, a young outfielder and the son of Hall of Famer George Sisler, offered a slightly different take from the others. He called the strike talk more than just idle chit-chat. "Very definitely there was something going on at the time whereby they said they weren't going to play."[57] In the end, neither the Cardinals nor any other team struck to protest Robinson.

That game that went forward on May 6 turned into a big one for Reese. Brooklyn took an early 2–0 lead, only to watch St. Louis roar back with three runs in the third inning and three more in the fourth. The Dodgers scored once in the fifth inning and three times in the sixth to tie the score. Reese, batting with one out in the seventh inning against reliever Johnny Grodzicki, "rammed his game-winning circuit smash into the left-field seats, and the paper poured onto the field like some hero's reception along Broadway,"[58] Among the witnesses in the stands were Durocher and Day, who, Dick Young speculated, "may have inspired the boys to that old Brooklyn fight-from-behind spirit." The Dodgers improved to 11–3 on the young season. The "groping, stunned"[59] Cardinals, the defending World Series champions, fell to 3–12.

Reese, who hit just .225 in May, got hot in June. He batted .326 over the month with a .453 on-base percentage and .589 slugging percentage. He also slammed six homers and drove in 22 runs, numbers more indicative of a middle-of-the-order hitter than an eighth-hole batter. On June 4, he ripped a grand slam in the second inning off Elmer Singleton in a 9–4 win over the Pirates. "Pee Wee, who's batting the most deceptive .248 in baseball, unleashed his fifth homer to take the circuit swat lead among his teammates,"[60] Young wrote. Reese added an RBI single in the eighth. The next day, he lined a run-scoring hit that put Brooklyn ahead, 1–0, against the Bucs, en route to a 3–0 victory.

On June 19, Shotton moved Reese to the third spot in the batting order "because the Cubs happened to be pitching a left-hander [Johnny Schmitz]—and all Pee Wee did was win today's 5–1 ball game"[61] with his three hits and two RBI. Reese doubled in the first inning and tripled in the sixth. His three-base hit—"Reese rammed the serve down the right-field alley"[62]—drove home Robinson, who had walked. Reese scored when Furillo lifted a sacrifice fly to left-center field. One inning later, Reese singled "sharply"[63] to score Hodges.

Altogether, Reese collected two hits in eight games during June and three hits in two others. He ended the month by going 3-for-5 with a homer and four RBI in a 7–4 road win against the Phillies. Reese now had nine home runs on the season. His previous high was five, accomplished in 1940 and 1946. "He's eating something different these nights,"[64] Dick Young decided. Reese could not explain his sudden fondness for the outfield fences. "I don't know what it is," he told a reporter. "I'm swinging the way I always have. The ball just seems to be going into the stands."[65]

On July 3, Indians owner Bill Veeck purchased the contract of Larry Doby, the first African American player in the American League. Born December 13, 1923, in Camden, South Carolina, Doby graduated from high school in Paterson, New Jersey, where he earned 11 varsity letters. He accepted a basketball scholarship to Long Island University and later served in the Pacific during World War II. After hearing that Jackie Robinson had signed with Brooklyn, Doby changed his career plans. "My main thing was to become a teacher and coach," he said. "But when I heard about Jackie, I decided to concentrate on baseball. I forgot about going back to college."[66]

Doby, who hit a home run in his final at-bat with the Newark Eagles, struck out in his first big league at-bat, on July 5, and made his first hit the following day. Initially, many of Doby's teammates gave him the cold-shoulder treatment. Player-manager Lou Boudreau told him to "shrug it off."[67] (Doby played just 29 games in that opening campaign and hit .156 in 32 at-bats. He gained a starting job the following year and played 13 seasons in the big leagues. He belted 253 long balls over his career, leading the league twice, and was elected to the Hall of Fame in 1998.)

"Neglected by the fans in the recent balloting,"[68] Reese earned a spot on the National League All-Star team after the Reds' Eddie Miller begged out due to a sore throwing arm. Reese joined a Brooklyn party that also included Ralph Branca, Bruce Edwards, Eddie Stanky, and Dixie Walker. The AL won, 2–1, on RBI singles by DiMaggio and Stan Spence. Reese struck out in the seventh inning, against Walt Masterson, and walked in the ninth against Joe Page.

Going into the break, Brooklyn led the pennant race by one game. Harold Burr wrote that Shotton "has had to overcome a wobbly staff and an injury-riddled outfield." Branca, in his first full season, had won 12 games by the traditional midway point and had posted a 2.73 ERA. Harry Taylor, also pitching in his first full season, was 7–2 with a 2.65 ERA. Hal Gregg, though, had an astronomical ERA of 7.64, and Rex Barney's was 5.64.

On June 4, Pistol Pete Reiser did it again. He crashed into an unforgiving outfield wall, again at Ebbets Field. The Dodgers led, 7–2, in the bottom half of the seventh inning. Cully Rikard hit a long fly ball against Branca. Reiser went back to make the catch. He was thinking, he told Donald Honig many years later, "Hell, this is an easy out." He kept going back on the ball. "I'm going full speed," he said. "And, oh, My God."[69] Reiser hit the outfield wall head-first and collapsed onto the grass as Rikard circled the bases. Reiser left the field on a stretcher. A priest gave him last rites in the clubhouse. Reiser admitted later, "I almost died. When I woke up, I couldn't move. For 10 days, I was paralyzed."[70] A few weeks later, and miraculously back with the Dodgers, the outfielder was talking one night with Reese on a hotel porch in Chicago. Reese asked his roomie whether he felt okay. Yes, Reiser said he felt fine. "What's that big knot on your head?" Reese asked. Reiser called the doctor and was soon on his way by airliner to Johns Hopkins University Hospital in Baltimore to have a blood clot removed. The doctor told him, "You're lucky. If it had moved just a little more, you'd have been gone."[71] Reiser returned to the lineup July 12.

Carl Furillo, meanwhile, had emerged as an up-and-coming star. He went into the break with a .312 batting average and .382 on-base percentage. Furillo was 25 years old and the son of Italian immigrants Michael and Filomena Furillo. He quit school after the eighth grade and earned money as a youth by picking apples and working in a local mill. The Great Depression hit the family hard. "Sometimes, we didn't even have a loaf of bread on the table for Christmas dinner,"[72] he said. Furillo played baseball in a local recreation league and "immediately earned a regular outfield berth."[73] He signed in 1940 with the Pocomoke City (Maryland) Chicks, an unaffiliated team in the Class D Eastern Shore League, and batted .319 in 71 games. He also played eight games for the Reading Brooks, another unaffiliated team, this one in the Class B Interstate League. The Dodgers purchased the Brooks following the 1940 season. Furillo hit .313 for Reading in 1941 and .281 for the Montreal Royals in 1942. He spent the next three years in the Army and earned three battle stars for his service in the Pacific Theater.

Furillo got into 117 games as a Dodgers rookie in 1946 and batted .284 with a .346 on-base percentage. He earned the nickname "Skoonj," from the Italian word *scungilli* (snail), one of his favorite dishes. He also earned a reputation for blunt speech. "He spoke with honesty rather than discretion."[74] Furillo even mailed back his 1947 contract to the Dodgers after the team offered just a modest raise from his rookie campaign. "I'm sure I helped keep the Dodgers in the thick of the scrap with the St. Louis Cardinals and what do I get, a minor league contract," he said to Doc Silva of the *Reading Times*. "Now is the time to get the extra money."[75]

Stanky and Reese were providing consistent, sometimes spectacular, play up the middle. "The pitchers owe a debt to Stanky and Reese, the little chaps who guard the midway for the Flock," Harold Burr wrote time and again. "They have been rescuing the faltering moundsmen by coming up with double plays to kill dangerous rallies, and the expert speed with which they execute 'em has been a joy to watch."[76]

Following the All-Star break, the Dodgers began a five-game series at home against the Cubs. Brooklyn won the first four games and improved to 46–31. The Dodgers also took the finale, 6–5, on July 12, coming from behind and scoring twice in the bottom of the ninth. The game is most notable for an embarrassing moment, at least for Pee Wee Reese. In the third inning, he walked with one out. Furillo followed by flying out to center field. That brought up Dixie Walker, who swung and missed for strike two and let the bat fly out of his hands, near Reese's feet. Being a polite sort. Reese walked over a few feet and picked up the bat to give it back to Walker. No one on the umpiring crew had stopped play, though. Cubs catcher Clyde McCullough threw down to first baseman Eddie Waitkus, who tagged Reese for the final out of the inning.[77] Leo Durocher sent Reese a telegram that read, "Next time, don't be such a nice guy."[78]

Brooklyn closed out July with a 13-game winning streak that began with a doubleheader sweep of the Reds at Ebbets Field, 7–4 and 4–3, on July 21. Reese notched two hits in the opener, including a go-ahead base hit in the seventh inning. On July 30, "in the sweltering heat of St. Louis,"[79] Reese, "a great clutch player,"[80] singled in the 10th inning to drive home Gene Hermanski and put Brooklyn ahead for good, 11–10, after the Bums managed to blow a 10–0 lead. St. Louis scored four runs in the sixth inning and six in the ninth. Joe Reichler of the Associated Press wrote that the game boasted "all the thrills and pathos of a World Series encounter."[81]

The next day, Reese tripled with one out in the ninth inning to drive home Bruce Edwards and give the Dodgers a 2–1 victory. Reese collected two other hits on the day and improved his batting average to .288. Cornelius Ryan wrote, "Always mentioned when star shortstops are discussed but always overlooked when talk gets around to 'the very best,' Pee Wee Reese of Brooklyn could point to the record and demand justice today."[82] The Dodgers improved to 63–36 and moved 10 games ahead of the second-place Giants (49–42) and Cardinals (51–44). "With only 55 games to play and the feared champs floundering in serious trouble, the Brooks appear headed for another subway World Series with the New York Yankees,"[83] said one newspaper. The Yankees led the Red Sox by 12 games at that point.

Jackie Robinson endured many death threats in his rookie campaign. He read aloud one hate-filled rant while the team traveled by bus to Macon, Georgia, for an exhibition game. The disturbed writer threated to shoot Robinson if the Dodgers took the field that day. Hours later, during pre-game warmups, Robinson inched closer and closer to Pee Wee Reese. Finally, Reese joked, "Hey, get away from me, you human target. With my luck, that guy'll take a shot, and hit me by mistake." Off-the-wall comments like that eased Robinson's raw nerves. "When Pee Wee started kidding me, everything kind of loosened up. I didn't feel so alone anymore. I felt that at last I finally was a member of the ballclub."[84] In interviews through the years, Reese often brushed aside any praise for helping out a lonely teammate. "I get a lot of credit and I appreciate it," he said. "But, after a while, I thought of him as I would Duke Snider or Gil Hodges or anyone else."[85]

Jules Tygiel, in *Baseball's Great Experiment*, wrote, "During the course of the 1947 season and subsequent campaigns, Robinson developed his closest friendship with Pee Wee Reese. The alliance emerged out of mutual respect and Reese's unaffected acceptance of Robinson as a teammate."[86] In *Opening Day*, Jonathan Eig called Reese, at least in 1947, "an ally" of Robinson's, "but not a strong one, and certainly not an outspoken one."[87] Reese's interactions with Black people through the years had been limited. "In the park that I grew up in, there were no blacks allowed," Reese recalled years later. "Blacks got in the back of the bus. They had a special fountain to drink from. I don't guess that I ever shook the hand of a black person" until he shook hands with Robinson. Like some other white players, Reese thought that Black athletes could not cope with pressure situations. "You hear that all your life, you believe it,"[88] Reese said.

Going into the season, Robinson did not know what to expect from his Kentucky-born teammate. "When I first joined the club, I was aware that there might be a real reluctance on Reese's part to accept me as a teammate," Robinson wrote in *I Never Had It Made*. He knew about the young veteran's roots in a border state and that "mischief makers" had bandied about a petition that they asked Reese to sign. Reese, though, Robinson wrote, "from the time I joined Brooklyn, had demonstrated a totally fair attitude." The first-year infielder praised "the courage and decency of a teammate who could easily have been my enemy rather than my friend."[89]

Reese watched as opposing pitchers hurled fastballs high and inside at Robinson.

Other players hurled racial slurs. "You'd hear a lot of insults from the opposing benches during games, guys calling him things like 'n-----' and 'watermelon eater,' trying to rile him," Reese said. "You began to put yourself in his shoes. You'd think of yourself trying to break into the black leagues, maybe, and what it would be like—and I know that I couldn't have done it. In a word, he was winning respect."[90]

Reese's role in helping Robinson gain acceptance on the team cannot be overstated. One player put it this way (anonymously): "Most of us weren't in favor of Robinson playing against us, and we rode him pretty hard—and rough. But everybody in this league's got a lot of respect for Reese. And when we'd see him out there, talking and laughing with Robinson like they were the best of buddies, we began to figure, well, maybe Robinson isn't too bad a guy after all."[91] In *Rickey and Robinson,* Roger Kahn described Pee Wee Reese as "a practicing Christian" in a "quiet, nonevangelical way." He quoted Reese as saying, "As a Christian, how could I deny another human being the right to inherit a small portion of the earth? That was what was in my heart. Jackie Robinson had that right."[92]

Unfortunately, controversy followed Brooklyn throughout that summer of 1947. One of the most talked-about incidents happened on August 20 against the Cardinals. In the seventh inning of a scoreless game at Ebbets Field, Enos Slaughter hit a dribbler down the first-base line. As he ran past the bag, Slaughter remembered, "My spikes clipped [Robinson's] ankle."[93] The Dodgers infielder needed just minor medical attention. The big question was, did Slaughter spike Robinson on purpose? Stanky thought so. "I always had the highest respect for Slaughter," he said. Now, "I've lost all my respect for him." Slaughter, for his part, said, "I've never deliberately spiked anyone in my life. Anyone who does doesn't belong in baseball. It was an accident, pure and simple. I hope it is not serious."[94]

Bob Broeg said, "[Slaughter] cut him, but it was so minor that I hardly even remember it."[95] The Redbirds won, 3–2, in 12 innings on a Whitey Kurowski home run but still trailed the Dodgers by five games. Years later, Slaughter said he gained a bad-guy reputation over a bang-bang play in which he meant no harm. "The two teams had been fighting like cats and dogs for the entire decade, but now that Jackie had been promoted to Brooklyn, the writers said the two teams fought because the Cardinals were prejudiced. … People started calling me a dirty player."[96]

Reese also suffered a spike wound that summer. He, like Robinson, earned no sympathy from the opposing team. In fact, Reds infielder Augie Galan, a former Dodger, called Reese and the rest of the Dodgers a bunch of "cry babies." Cincinnati had pulled into Brooklyn for a three-game set beginning August 21. The Dodgers took the opener, 8–1. Reese walked twice and scored a run. In the fifth inning, Reiser collided with Reds starter Ewell Blackwell at home plate while trying to score from second base on a wild pitch. Instead of sliding, Reiser charged at the pitcher and bowled him over. Blackwell hurt his leg, but, "we didn't say anything,"[97] Galan told reporters.

Reese contributed an RBI double in the second game as part of a two-run eighth inning. Brooklyn won, 6–5, in 12 innings. The next day, the Reds' Tommy Tatum slid into Stanky, spiking him and sending him to the bench. In the ninth inning, with Brooklyn ahead, 8–5, Bert Haas "collided" with Reese, who also had to leave the game. Reiser saw the play and insisted that Haas's hard slide "was deliberate and malicious."[98] Galan acknowledged, "We waited out turn, and we gave two or three of their boys a going over, they shouted to blue heaven. If they can't take it, they shouldn't try to dish it out."[99]

Stanky "didn't cry" after getting spiked, Galan said. "But Reese, who is usually a pretty good, game guy, snorted around, pulled out the crying towel, and started to holler. And the Brooklyn bench! Oh, my, I thought we would have to send over a bottle of smelling salts to Burt Shotton for his pets." Galan said, "Haas could have wrecked Reese the clumsy way Pee Wee came to the bag to tag it"[100] In an article for *The Sporting News*, Reese insisted, "He went out of his way to get me! I was on the other side of the bag. I hope he's satisfied."[101]

The injury cost Reese 10 games. He hit a home run in his first game back, September 4 against the Giants at the Polo Grounds. Brooklyn led 1–0 when Reese deposited an Andy Hansen pitch over the left-field fence. The solo shot gave starter Vic Lombardi an insurance run. The 5-foot-7 left-hander allowed five hits and improved to 11–9. He also lowered his ERA to 3.21.

Reese enacted a bit of revenge against the Reds in a doubleheader on September 14 at Crosley Field. He drove home four runs in the opener as the Dodgers cruised to a 13–2 victory. In the second game, he belted his 12th home run of the season. Brooklyn came from behind and won, 6–3, to go ahead of St. Louis by 7½ games. The *Cincinnati Inquirer* offered a frank assessment of the home team after it lost twice and was outscored, 19–5, on the day. "The Brooks did everything better than the Reds, who appeared to be tight and jittery."[102]

When the Dodgers returned from a long trip on September 19, and with the pennant nearly at hand, thousands of full-throated fans greeted their baseball heroes at Penn Station. It was a raucous scene. Members of the Dodgers faithful slapped players on the back, shouted words of encouragement, and even hoisted a few, including Reese, onto their shoulders. The shortstop took a short ride and then looked for his wife, who stood somewhere in the crowd. Dottie Reese had an idea. She walked over to the station announcer and gave him a message. A voice boomed out, "Mr. Reese, meet your party in the station master's office." When Mr. and Mrs. Reese finally caught up with one another and embraced, photographers snapped away. One newsman asked them to do it again. "You bet," Reese agreed. A different photographer asked for another shot. The couple obliged. Finally, some cameramen shouted, "Now, let's have it for the newsreels."[103] Finally, someone asked Reese, "What are you, the new Clark Gable?" The happy ballplayer offered only a slight correction. "No," he said. "The new Barrymore."[104] Over to one side, the Brooklyn Symphony—a band of musicians, some talented, others off-key, all of them Dodgers fans—cranked up a tune.[105]

The Dodgers ended the year with a mark of 94–60, five games better than the runner-up Cardinals. Despite that disappointing Opening Day crowd, Brooklyn played in front of 1,807,526 fans at Ebbets Field and led the NL in home attendance. Over in the American League, the Yankees took their 15th pennant and ended up 97–57, a dozen games ahead of the second-place Tigers.

Game One was set for September 30 at Yankee Stadium. "We aren't worried about the Dodgers," New York's first-year skipper, Bucky Harris, said before the first pitch. "But then they don't seem to be worried about us."[106] Reese was one of five Dodgers still on the roster from the 1941 pennant-winning team, along with Reiser, Walker, Lavagetto, and Casey. The returning Yankees contingent included Spud Chandler, Joe DiMaggio, Tommy Henrich and Phil Rizzuto. Three of the four baseball writers from the *Daily News*—Jim McCulley, Hy Turkin, and Joe Trimble—predicted another championship in the Bronx. "It's an old Yankee habit," Trimble wrote. "They'll win in four straight!"[107] Only Dick Young favored the Dodgers.

Ralph Branca and Spec Shea drew the Game One pitching assignments. Dixie Walker gave the Dodgers an early lead on an RBI single in the first inning. Branca cruised through four innings without allowing a hit. He ran into big trouble in the fifth, though. The Yankees posted five runs en route to a 5–3 victory. Reese singled in the seventh inning, stole second, and scored after reliever Joe Page unleashed a wild pitch. The ball skipped to the screen and Yogi Berra "fell on his face against the stands as he retrieved the ball." Reese "easily beat the catcher's wide throw, which was made from a prone position. Yogi looked like a battered rag doll as he lay on the cold ground,"[108] reported the *Daily News*.

New York knocked off Brooklyn the following day, 10–3. The Yankees led, 6–2, after six innings and scored four more times in the seventh. Reese enjoyed another solid game. He singled twice, walked, and scored a run. In the field, he waited all game for a ball to travel his way. It never happened. "With all their slamming the ball about, the Bombers did not hit a single chance to Pee Wee Reese."[109] The Brooklyn shortstop matched a mark set by the Phillies' Dave Bancroft in Game Four of the 1915 Series and the Athletics' Joe Boley in Game One of the 1929 fall classic.[110]

The series shifted to Ebbets Field for Game Three. The 40-year-old former Dodger (and veteran of many other teams) Bobo Newsom started for New York against Joe Hatten. Both pitchers got clobbered. Brooklyn scored six runs in the second inning and led, 9–4, going into the fifth inning. Reese hit an RBI single as part of that big second frame. The Yankees chipped away but ultimately fell short, losing 9–8.

Brooklyn edged the Yankees, 3–2, in Game Four, which, Gene Schoor wrote, "combined heartbreak and heroics, real drama that had baseball fans talking about nothing else for weeks afterward."[111] Harry Taylor started for the Dodgers against the hard-throwing Bill Bevens and could not retire a single batter. He gave up two hits, one walk, and an unearned run before being pulled for Gregg. The Yankees took a 2–0 lead in the fourth inning on a Johnny Lindell RBI double.

Brooklyn pushed across one run in the fifth without the benefit of a hit. Bevens walked Jorgensen and Gregg to open the inning. Stanky advanced both runners on a sacrifice bunt. Reese followed by grounding into a fielder's choice that scored Jorgensen. Reese stole second and made it to third after Berra airmailed his throw into center field. Robinson struck out to end the inning. Bevens was still ahead and still throwing a no-hitter—albeit a wild one. He already had walked six.

Going into the bottom of the ninth, Brooklyn still had not recorded a safety and still trailed, 2–1. Edwards led off that final frame by flying out. Bevens then gave up his ninth walk of the day, this one to Furillo. Jorgensen, though, popped up to George McQuinn at first base. Bevens was one out away from a victory and the first

World Series no-hitter. Shotton sent Reiser up to bat for Casey and told 25-year-old Al Gionfriddo to pinch-run for Furillo.

Gionfriddo stole second, and Bevens intentionally walked Reiser to bring up Lavagetto who swung and missed on the first pitch and then ripped a line drive against the right field wall for a double, Brooklyn's first hit. The liner bounded off the sign advertising Gem Single-Edged Razor Blades.[112] Henrich fielded the ball, hesitated for just an instant, and threw into the infield, too late, as Eddie Miksis, pinch-running for Reiser, scored easily. The 5-foot-6 Gionfriddo, known by some as Little Al, followed Miksis and slid into home plate with the winning run. Moments later, Lavagetto burst into the locker room and enjoyed the greeting of a lifetime from his teammates. "After five mad minutes of kissing, cussing, and slapping, it was a disheveled Italian-American guy who was dumped in front of his locker, tears in his eyes and a mile-wide grin on his usually impassive face,"[113] Hy Turkin wrote. Branch Rickey "chuckled" at the misfortune of Bevens, nearly a hero for all time. "Just one pitch away, and he's the winning pitcher of a World Series game. That's wonderful."[114] The *Eagle* described it as "the craziest, most wonderful baseball game in history."[115]

The World Series excitement and suspense continued the next afternoon at Ebbets Field. The Dodgers and Yanks played their third straight one-run game. This time, New York came out ahead, 2–1, with solo tallies in the fourth and fifth innings. Brooklyn mustered its lone run in the sixth. Gionfriddo walked, and, with one out, Reese did the same. Robinson followed with an RBI hit to center field.

Back at Yankee Stadium, the fabled House that Ruth Built, Reese enjoyed his best game of the Series. He singled and scored as part of a two-run first inning and doubled and scored in a two-run third. Vic Lombardi, a 12-game winner in the regular season with a 2.99 ERA, gave it all back. The Yankees scored four times in their half of the third and jumped ahead, 5–4, on Berra's RBI single in the fourth. Brooklyn waited until the sixth inning to stun the 74,065 fans at Yankee Stadium. Reese singled home two runs as part of a four-run outburst that put the Dodgers ahead, 8–5. The Yankees scored once in the ninth. "The Dodgers are still the darlings of the baseball gods," Harold Burr wrote. "But they have been making their own breaks and have fought the American League champions to a standstill. They don't look like the same ballclub that blew the first two games at the Stadium."[116]

Hal Gregg and Spec Shea faced off in Game Seven. Brooklyn took a 2–0 lead in the second inning on a Bruce Edwards RBI single and Spider Jorgensen's run-scoring double. Gregg, though, squandered the favor. New York scored once in the second inning and twice in the fourth. The Yankees added solo runs in the sixth and seventh, one off Hank Behrman and another off Hugh Casey. The Dodgers managed just two base hits over the final seven innings and lost, 5–2. "Brooklyn is a borough of three million pallbearers today," Joe Trimble began his story in the *Daily News*. The Dodgers, he wrote, "went down almost without a struggle."[117]

Reese walked once but went hitless in the finale. He batted .304 (7-for-23) with a .448 on-base percentage in his second World Series. He also drove home four runs and scored five times. The Dodgers, though, hit just .230 as a team. Furillo led Brooklyn with a .353 mark (6-for-17), while Robinson batted .259 (7-for-27). Walker knocked the team's lone home run. Cheer up, Holmes wrote to Dodger fans in his *Eagle* column. "Everyone knew or should have known that the 1947 Dodgers are still in the formative stages, should get better in time, and need additions here and there. ... There will come a day."[118]

Pee Wee batted .284 and had 73 RBIs over the regular season. He tied for the team lead in home runs with 12. Robinson batted .297 in 151 tension-filled games, with a .383 on-base percentage and 125 runs scored. He led the league with 29 stolen bases and, like Reese, hit 12 home runs.[119] The infielder finished fifth in the MVP voting and won the first-ever Rookie of the Year award. Robinson thanked Reese for helping him get through such a stressful campaign. "Pee Wee did so many things to help me," Jackie said. "So many things for which I'll be eternally grateful to him."[120]

Rickey hoped to add more talent and boost his club's prospects in 1948. Brooklyn had advanced to the World Series twice in the past seven seasons and fallen short both times. "We haven't got a pitcher who can go the distance," Rickey said. "I've got the best second baseman in the game in Robinson, but I've got to play him on first. The Dodgers are going to have a good club eventually, but it's still in the making."[121] He clarified to the press, "There are some Brooklyn players who will not be traded. Two of these are Pee Wee Reese and Jackie Robinson."[122]

8

"Reese? Now, you're talking about a ballplayer"

Pee Wee Reese smacked a two-run single in the seventh inning on July 3, 1948, to help the Dodgers beat the Giants, 7–5, at Ebbets Field. The following day, he added three more hits and scored four times as Brooklyn knocked off New York, 13–12.

An improbable pennant drive began with those two victories. The Dodgers had stumbled through the first part of the season and even spent some time in the National League cellar. In July, a cold team turned hot. Loyal fans rooted for their club to make back-to-back World Series appearances for the first time in franchise history. Some worried that it might be too late. The Bums sported a 27–33 record through June, stuck in sixth place, eight games behind Boston.

Trying to figure it all out from the dugout was Leo Durocher, back with Brooklyn. Branch Rickey and Happy Chandler met shortly after the 1947 season concluded. Was Durocher's suspension finally over, Rickey wanted to know. Did the banishment conclude after the final out of the World Series? Or did it last until April 9, 1948, the one-year anniversary of Chandler's decree? The commissioner hadn't officially said. Rickey and Chandler talked, and Chandler grumbled a bit. He already had nixed Rickey's plan to give Durocher a full World Series share even after Brooklyn paid its exiled skipper his entire regular-season salary.

Couldn't Rickey just re-sign Shotton—or someone else, anyone but Leo the Lip—to manage the Dodgers? That's what Chandler hoped. Rickey, though, wanted Durocher. The Mahatma and Happy, both strong-willed men, went back and forth. They were a formidable duo, both blessed with the gift of great rhetorical skills, both eager to show off that gift. Finally, Chandler just about threw his hands into the air in surrender. What was the use in arguing? "Do what you damn please,"[1] he said.

Rickey said he kept Durocher "because it was the right thing to do, and I still consider him a good manager. Durocher was a good manager on the day he was suspended and as far as I know, nothing has happened to alter his ability on the ballfield."[2] Rickey and Durocher made for an odd couple. Durocher spoke profanely, preferred flashy clothes, and enjoyed a stiff drink. Rickey quoted Bible verses, dressed in rumpled suits, and abstained from alcohol. The two found common ground in the game of baseball and a mutual passion for winning. That was enough.

A surprised Tommy Holmes wrote in his column, "Well, sir, you could have knocked me over with a Cadillac convertible when I picked up the paper and read that Leo Durocher had been re-appointed Brooklyn manager."³ Shotton returned to Florida. Ricked asked him to oversee all 26 managers in Brooklyn's vast farm system. "As usual, there is no need for a contract between Rick and myself," Shotton said. "We've never discussed money. But I'll have enough to live on."⁴

Brooklyn's rebuilding plan continued. In December, Rickey sent 37-year-old Dixie Walker to the Pirates, along with pitchers Vic Lombardi and Hal Gregg. Upon leaving, Walker called Dodgers fans "the most sincere group of people a man could hope to play before."⁵ The Pirates sent infielders Billy Cox and Gene Mauch, plus veteran hurler Elwin "Preacher" Roe, to the Dodgers.

The 22-year-old Mauch bunted well, hit to the opposite field, and liked to break up double plays with aggressive slides. "He was always described as 'brash,' a baseball term that seems to mean pushier than your humble ability would normally allow for,"⁶ Maury Allen wrote. Cox, 28, flashed a fancy glove, one of the best in the game. He broke in with Pittsburgh in 1941 but missed four seasons due to World War II. Cox hit 15 home runs in 1947. Primarily a shortstop, he figured to move over a few feet—to third base—if he expected to see much action in Brooklyn. "Cox is a shortstop for whom the Dodgers have little need with Pee Wee Reese around,"⁷ said the *Eagle*.

Roe, a slender left-hander (6-foot-2-inches, about 165 pounds), hurled an intimidating fastball early in his career and led the National League with 148 strikeouts in 1945. After fracturing his skull in February 1946, Roe lost the zip on that heater. Headaches and dizzy spells left him weak and unable to throw hard for more than a few pitches every game. Over the next two seasons, he struggled with a 7–23 record and a 5.21 ERA. Maybe the 32-year-old Arkansas native, the son of a country doctor, could resurrect his career by developing a new pitch—or harnessing an old one.

On March 1, Reese signed a $20,000 deal, making him the highest-paid Brooklyn player.⁸ Stanky agreed to a $17,000 contract, up from $14,000 in 1947. The Brat, though, like Reese, had asked for $20,000. Durocher didn't exactly help his friend's cause. "Sure, [Stanky's] a great team man, a great hustler, a fine influence on the rest of the players, but now let's talk about his ability." Durocher said. "He's no [Joe] Gordon or [Bobby] Doerr, and I'm sure if Eddie calmly took stock of the situation, he'd realize that. I don't think Mr. Rickey has been a bit unfair to him."⁹

As for Reese, well, Pee Wee Reese was a whole other story. Durocher said, "Reese? Now, you're talking about a ballplayer. One of the best in the game."¹⁰ Hy Turkin gave this round of wheeling and dealing to Rickey. "The double-play combination of Pee Wee Reese and Eddie Stanky," Turkin wrote, "has pulled some breathtaking maneuvers in their time, but never one to approach the hypnotic job pulled on them yesterday by prexy Branch Rickey."¹¹

Maybe. Even so, Reese said he liked negotiating with Rickey more than he did with Larry MacPhail in those early years. After Reese's dad died in 1938, "I had no one to consult when I came to Brooklyn." MacPhail refused to help out in a "fatherly" way. As Reese recalled, "MacPhail said, 'I am sitting on this side of the desk, and you are sitting on that side of the desk. I have a job to do, and you have a job to do. I cannot help you at all.' The net result was no good, and you can bet I gave up the fatherly approach then and there." Reese said he "never made any money" off MacPhail. As for Rickey, a man known as El Cheapo by many sportswriters, "He was very good to me. There were times when I think he could have given me less, but he went up."[12]

Eddie Stanky's time in Brooklyn ended shortly after the ink on that contract turned dry. On March 6, the Dodgers traded him to the Braves in exchange for utility infielder/outfielder Carvell "Bama" Rowell, first baseman Ray Sanders, and $40,000. An angry Stanky ripped Durocher in the press. He told Jack Cuddy, a United Press writer, "I played 146 games last year when he wasn't even here. So how does he know what I was worth? In short, he knifed me in the back, he really put the skids under me."[13] Maybe Durocher wanted to go back to a life of leisure in California. "My return to the Dodgers," he later wrote, "had turned sour from the beginning."[14]

The ballclub began its spring training regimen in Ciudad Trujillo, Dominican Republic. (General Rafael Trujillo, nicknamed "El Jefe" or "The Chief," ruled the country during this era, often with an iron fist. In 1936, Dominican officials voted to rename the capital and historic city of Santo Domingo, founded in 1498, after their leader. Following the assassination of Trujillo in 1961, Cuidad Trujillo went back to being Santo Domingo.) Reese walked up to popular columnist Jimmy Powers in the hotel lobby. "Jimmy, this is the best baseball camp I have ever seen," he said. "The weather is great, and so is the park. That is a combination that can't be beat anywhere."[15]

Several teammates joked that Reese was a "rich man" after signing his new contract. He just laughed. "If I am a rich man, I just feel sorry for the rest of the players," he said. Powers wrote that the shortstop boasted a nice suntan and looked "hard and lean. This club unquestionably will be the best sun-tanned club in either circuit."[16] With the gregarious Stanky gone, Rickey said the Dodgers needed some "glue." Bill Roeder asked what that meant. Rickey explained. "To hold the team together, to make it an aggressive unit," Rickey said. "I will encourage men like Reese to take over, speak up more, go in and talk to the pitchers."[17] Rickey even gave Reese a copy of Dwight Eisenhower's *Crusade in Europe* "so Harold may develop into a leader of men."[18]

Jackie Robinson showed up to camp flabby and out of shape. He reported about 20 pounds overweight due in large part to a sweet tooth that he indulged on the winter banquet circuit. Durocher was furious. After all, the skipper had supported Robinson and ordered Dixie Walker to toss that petition into the trash can. Now, Durocher felt betrayed. As punishment, he told coaches to hit ground ball after ground ball to Robinson under the tropical sun. The temperature hit 90 degrees and soared even higher. Durocher didn't care. "Move, Robinson, move," Durocher yelled. "There's plenty of fat back in the states. Leave some of your fat in Santo Domingo."[19] The workouts lasted for hours. "That's enough for the fat boy today, fellas," he'd finally say. "He's done. Stick a fork in him."[20]

Durocher boiled as he watched Robinson sweat off those extra pounds. Seeing Roy Campanella hit line drives and ably maneuver himself behind home plate made life easier. "Leo liked my style," Campanella wrote in *It's Good to Be Alive*. "He told me he'd open the season with me behind the plate. That's what he told Mr. Rickey, too."[21]

Born November 19, 1921, in Philadelphia, Campanella grew up the son of a

Sicilian American father, John, and an African American mother, Ida. Burly, muscular, and surprisingly athletic, young Roy quit school at age 16 and signed with the Washington (D.C.) Elite Giants, one of the top Negro Leagues teams. When the U.S. entered World War II, he found work at an armor-plate factory in north Philly. By spring, the local draft board had given him permission to resume his baseball career. He joined the Monterrey Sultans of the Mexican League and then returned to the Elite Giants, who had moved a few miles north, to Baltimore, in 1938. Rickey met with the catcher to gauge his interest in playing for Brooklyn. Campanella, thinking that Rickey wanted him to suit up for the Brown Dodgers, declined.

Soon after, Campanella ran into Robinson, who asked whether Rickey had signed the catcher. No, Campy said, he hadn't. "I told him I didn't want to play for his Brown Dodgers."[22] Robinson sprang the news. "I signed," he said. But, he added, "I didn't sign with the Brown Dodgers. I'm going to play for Montreal." Campanella looked a bit puzzled. "I'm going to be the first negro in organized baseball," Robinson said. "It's the end of Jim Crow in baseball." Campanella could hardly believe it. "I sat dumbfounded," he remembered. "My cigar went out, but I didn't realize it and kept puffing away. For the longest while, I didn't say a word. I just sat and stared at Jackie."[23]

Rarely dissuaded, Rickey sent a telegram to Campanella. "Please report [to] Brooklyn office by March 10. Very Important. Branch Rickey."[24] That was a week away; Campanella couldn't wait. He caught a plane to New York City that day. The Dodgers assigned him, along with African American pitching prospect Don Newcombe, to the Nashua (New Hampshire) Dodgers of the New England League. Campanella took a pay cut, from $600 a month with Baltimore to $185 a month for Nashua. He could handle the drop in income. Now he could dream about playing in the major leagues. Campanella batted .290 for Nashua with 96 RBI and won league MVP honors.

He spent the 1947 season in Montreal and kept his batting average above the .300 mark for much of the campaign before tailing off in the final weeks and finishing at .273. Once again, he took home an MVP trophy. Next stop, Brooklyn? Campanella wasn't sure. He looked around in the spring of 1948 and felt discouraged. His competition behind home plate included veterans Bobby Bragan and Bruce Edwards and a top prospect named Gil Hodges. "The team was crawling with catchers,"[25] Campanella remembered.

Following two weeks in the Dominican Republic, the Dodgers moved to their new spring-training facility on an old military base in Florida, next to the Atlantic Ocean. Bud Holman, who opened the Vero Beach Cadillac Company in 1925, led the development of this marshy scape. He and other prominent residents built the Vero Beach Airport, which by 1935 had grown into a fueling stop for Eastern Airlines.[26] During World War II, many Navy and Marine pilots trained at U.S. Naval Air Station, Vero Beach.

After the war, Holman thought the old base might make a great place for a baseball facility, even though, according to his son, Bump Holman, "My dad didn't know first base from second base."[27] Bud contacted Rickey, who dispatched his 31-year-old executive, Emil "Buzzie" Bavasi, to check out Vero Beach, plus sites in Fort Pierce and Stuart. "To make a long story short, I never made it to Fort Pierce or Stuart," Bavasi said. "Bud Holman met me at the train, and he wouldn't let me go any farther south. The facilities were already there. All we had to do was put in the ball fields."[28]

In just a couple of months, the Dodgers built a baseball factory of sorts, complete with manicured fields, offices, dressing rooms, batting cages, pitching mounds, sliding pits, and more. The place needed a name. One New York sportswriter suggested "Dodgertown,"[29] which quickly won Rickey's favor. Among the road signs put in place were Flatbush Avenue, Rickey Boulevard, and Durocher Trail. Citrus trees surrounded the complex, and cattle grazed in nearby fields. The McKee Jungle Gardens attracted tourists, as did the beaches. "The future of the Brooklyn baseball team is here,"[30] Rickey declared.

The Dodgers' spring schedule included a couple of road games against the Fort Worth Cats, the organization's Texas League affiliate. Fans flocked to the ballpark. About 7.500 watched the first match-up, and an overflow crowd of 15,597 bought tickets for the second. Many saw something for the first time. "Sportswriters traveling with the Dodgers wondered what brought out the tremendous throngs for the exhibitions, and local observers agreed it probably was the unprecedented appearance of Negro players on a major league club in games in Texas," said one report. Fortunately, the writer continued, "There wasn't a single untoward incident in either game insofar as the presence of Robinson and Campanella in the Dodger lineup was concerned."[31]

In fact, the only squabble involved Pee Wee Reese and a rookie first baseman named Dee Fondy, who at one point found himself in a rundown between second base and third. After he nearly knocked over Reese, the shortstop offered a few choice words. Moments later, Fondy threw a punch. Durocher, Fort Worth manager Les Burge, "and several others raced between the belligerents and broke it up."[32]

On April 17, just a few days before Opening Day, CBS radio aired a special on the life of Brooklyn's' popular shortstop. The program, titled "Play Ball," ran from 8–9 p.m. on the East Coast and was "radio's first full-scale study of the national pastime."[33] Red Barber served as narrator and asked Reese several questions about life in the big leagues. "Reese started the drama rolling," *The Sporting News* noted, "by explaining that ballplayers are no different from anyone else; they have nerves, families, income taxes, and worries." Honus Wagner, the great former shortstop, spoke for a few minutes about how the game was going soft. Not like back in his day. "You had to be tough in my day to play ball," the Flying Dutchman told listeners. Modern players look like "a bunch of college boys. Why, some of them even wear ties."[34]

Babe Ruth, retired since 1935, made an appearance. The fabled Sultan of Swat encouraged the kids to "get into the game." Ralph Kimmel, Keith Sparks, and others offered their thoughts and perspectives on Pee Wee Reese. They told stories about his days on the Louisville sandlots, about how he only reluctantly tried out for the high school team, and other familiar tales. Emma Reese sat down for a short interview and offered a memorable, blunt scouting report on her son. "Pee Wee is good," she said, "but I'll tell you this: he'll never be the ballplayer his daddy was."[35]

Exactly how many listeners tuned into the program is unknown. Gene Schoor wrote, "One thing about Pee Wee—though he's probably the most embarrassed guy on earth right now on account of last night's broadcast, he doesn't have to set out to justify all the nice things said about him. ... And if we know Pee Wee, he'll go on being what he is, a great baseball player and a great guy, without giving a thought about being either."[36]

Brooklyn began the regular season on April 20 with a 7–6 win against the Giants at the Polo Grounds. Leo Durocher gave the Opening Day ball to Rex Barney, who went 5–2 for Brooklyn in 1947 with a 4.75 ERA. Over his three seasons in the big leagues—with two years spent in World War II service—Barney had thrown 176⅔ innings and walked 151 batters. Barney once described his repertoire this way: "I had a good curveball, hardly any change-up, and a fastball that never went straight in its life. Gene Mauch says my fastball traveled the most explosive last six feet he ever saw, as if an afterburner kicked in just before it reached the plate."[37] Rickey called Barney "conveniently wild."[38] During spring training, Barney said, "I guess I impressed Leo."[39]

Reese, batting fifth, knocked an eighth-inning double and scored on third baseman Cox's two-run homer. Robinson started at second base, his "preferred position"[40] and one now open with the trade of Stanky. He led off and managed a double and two RBI in his five at-bats. Hodges started at catcher, while Campanella took over late in the game and got hit by a Ken Trickle pitch in his first big league at-bat. Barney gave up three runs over six innings.

The following day, Durocher mixed and matched about as much as a manager can mix and match. He sent 24 players onto the field, a major league record. Only Barney, Casey, and oddly enough, Campanella, remained on the bench. Durocher called on five pitchers, "who lavishly gave up 13 bases on balls,"[41] five pinch-hitters, and four second basemen. All the hubbub still produced a loss. New York built a 6–1 lead through six innings and won, 9–5. Reese singled in four at-bats. "It was a game you had to see to believe," Harold Burr wrote in the *Eagle*. "No agate type in a box score could possibly give its rich and full flavor."[42] Durocher just shrugged. What was the big deal? "Twenty-four, eh?" he said. "Hell, I'd use 100 if it was legal and it would help me win a ballgame."[43]

Through the first seven games, Reese boasted a .385 batting average. He scored three runs in a 6–3 win against the Giants on April 22 and had three hits, including two doubles, in a 6–3 loss to the Phillies on April 25. In the eighth inning of the eighth game, on April 27 against Boston, he suffered a charley horse injury and missed five starts, although he did pinch-hit in two games before returning to the starting line-up May 7. Dick Young argued that Reese needed more healing. "Leo has been gambling with Pee Wee Reese's condition, and gambling with Reese is as reprehensible as cutting the cards with your home as the prize,"[44] Young wrote.

Just a couple of days later, though, Reese enjoyed one of the best games of his career. He drove in a career-high six runs on May 9, in the first game of a doubleheader against the Pirates at Forbes Field. Brooklyn led, 3–1, after seven innings and then exploded for 11 runs in the final two frames to win, 14–2. Reese cracked a grand slam off Mel Queen with one out in the eighth inning and added a two-run double in the ninth. Earlier, he made an eye-popping play in the field when power-hitting Ralph Kiner walked to open the fourth. Kiner broke to second on a hit-and-run play with Dixie Walker, playing in his first game against his former teammates, at bat.

Walker lined a shot up the middle. Reese "found himself right in line with Dixie's drive, made a spectacular leapfrog grab between his legs, and stepped on second to start the DP,"[45] reported the *Daily News*.

Even after going 1-for-5 in a 9–3 win on May 13 at Cincinnati, Reese's batting average stood at a robust .351 with a .456 on-base percentage. Several other Dodgers also got off to hot starts, including Furillo (.396), Robinson (.338), and Edwards (.340). The team, though, owned just an 11–10 record, in part due to weak pitching. Managers in those days expected starting pitchers to go the distance. Too many Brooklyn hurlers needed early relief.

The Dodgers promptly lost eight straight games and slipped into a last-place tie with the Reds on May 23. Dick Young let his readers know that the Bums had collapsed like a cheap roof. "That loud crash heard in the vicinity of Ebbets Field at 5:12 P.M. yesterday was not Leo Durocher committing suicide. It was the Brooks hitting the bottom of the NL."[46]

Brooklyn wallowed in the lower reaches of the National League over the next several weeks. Reese provided one of the few bright spots in a game against the Cubs on May 27. He led off the fifth inning with a walk, advanced to second on a Jorgensen sacrifice bunt, and raced to third as Robinson grounded out. That brought Arky Vaughan up to bat against Russ Meyer. The Cubs starter went into his long wind-up, and Reese "lit out for the plate and stole it cleanly."[47] Brooklyn won, 4–2. About that steal of home, the *Eagle* reported, "The Little Colonel is following in the cold spike marks of his roomie, Pete Reiser, who specialized in purloining the hardest base of all to reach." In a hopeful note, the article concluded, "Brooklyn is displaying symptoms, slight as yet, of being on the march—if they don't stub their spikes. It's a better ball club than it has shown."[48]

May also coincided with the publication of Leo Durocher's controversial memoir, *The Dodgers and Me*. Ghostwritten by Harold Parrott and published by Ziff-Davis of Chicago, the book sold plenty of copies and made the skipper few friends. Much of the book seems mild by contemporary standards and is devoid of foul language and graphic material. Even so, Durocher did get in his shots throughout the more than 250 pages. He insisted that former Brooklyn skipper Wilbert Robinson "must have been the blunderingest of all baseball men"[49] and that Larry MacPhail "could not identify the players, even when they were in uniform, and was constantly asking who this was, who that was."[50] He called former pitcher Bobo Newsom "one of the biggest windbags the game has ever known."[51]

Many writers gave an enthusiastic thumbs-down to *The Dodgers and Me*. Columnist Red Smith called the book "dishonest. ... because on the pretext of telling the actual, inside story of his years in Brooklyn, and his one year out of it, Durocher makes this tale a medium for the expression of private animosities, and his version is at times one-sided."[52] Bill Roeder wrote, "Few feelings are spared, and the list of persons who consider themselves abused is growing every day."[53] Durocher, not surprisingly, defended his tell-all bio as being something close to the gospel truth. He ignored the book critics. All that controversy helped sell more copies, he reasoned. Anyway, he claimed, "It wouldn't be much of a book if I didn't unload a few blasts."[54]

So, Leo Durocher had a book. Now he needed a winning streak. Brooklyn, just

11–15 in May, also sputtered through June, going 11–13. It hardly pleased Durocher or the fans when Rickey sent Campanella to St. Paul in the American Association on May 15. Rickey, though, planned for Campanella to integrate the AA, with teams located mostly in Midwest cities. "But," the catcher said, "Leo did get Mr. Rickey to promise that if he needed me for the pennant race around midseason, I would be recalled."[55] Campanella had only played in three games, going 0-for-4.

Talk about a frustrating season. On June 20 at Ebbets Field, Reese hit a home run in the third inning against the Cubs. Or so he thought. Reese ripped a pitch that landed in the left field stands near the foul pole. Umpire Scotty Robb called the ball fair. The Cubs protested, and fellow ump Bill Stewart sided with the road team, taking away two bases from Reese. Stewart ruled that the ball hit a top rail in left field, "four feet fair, and took [a] freak backward carom into protruding seats in foul territory." Any ball that hit below the green mark, like Reese's did, was a double according to the ground rules. "If it hits on or above that strip," Stewart said, "it's a homer."[56]

Boos poured down from the 21,919 fans on hand. One fan took it a bit too far with his profane ranting and raving. Stewart ordered the man removed from the ballpark. "I've never heard such language [in] all the years I've been in baseball," Stewart said. "Ladies sitting nearby thanked me for what I'd done."[57] The Dodgers lost, 6–3, and dropped to 23–29. The end appeared near for Durocher, who seemed distracted at times. Maybe it was his marriage, Rickey speculated, which was still in the newlywed stage. He put it in a way that few others could. "The management of a baseball club," he said, "is a jealous mistress. In earthly terms, he can have no other god."[58]

On July 2, Brooklyn blew a 4–3 lead when the Giants scored three times in the ninth inning, sending 33,104 fans at Ebbets Field home in a melancholy mood. Once again, the Dodgers fell to last place, percentage points behind the Cubs (.439 to .435). On a bright note, Campanella, just promoted from St. Paul, went 3-for-4. Reese also collected three hits.

The following day, Brooklyn began a lengthy run of spectacular baseball. The Giants led the Dodgers, 5–2, in the bottom half of the seventh, when Gil Hodges (who took over at first base on June 29) and Campanella reached base against Larry Jansen. Giants manager Mel Ott signaled for Sheldon Jones to provide some relief. Jones, though, walked Vaughan to load the bases and gave up a single to Reese that brought home two runners. Four batters later, with the score tied, Reese sprinted home with the game-winning run on a wild pitch. Brooklyn added another run when Robinson scored on a bases-loaded walk to Furillo.

The next game got even wilder. Once again, New York grabbed a lead. Once again, Brooklyn staged a seventh-inning rally, down 8–3. Reese already had doubled and scored in the third inning. In the seventh, he singled with two out and scored as part of a three-run frame. The Dodgers took a 9–8 lead in the following frame. Reese added another base hit and the tying run scored. New York refused go away quietly and leaped ahead, 12–9, going into the bottom of the ninth.

Hodges led off with a base hit. Campanella followed by belting a two-run home run, his second of the day. Brooklyn then loaded the bases, Reese getting aboard via a walk. "Firecrackers popped throughout the stands," as he trotted to first, while "the crowd let loose a mounting frenzy"⁵⁹ on this national holiday. Reiser stepped to the plate as a pinch-hitter against Sheldon Jones, the Giants' seventh pitcher that day.

Before the game, the oft-injured Reiser was frustrated and—he insisted—ready to hang up his spikes. His ankle hurt, and he limped around the field during batting practice. "I think I'll quit,"⁶⁰ he said. Against Jones, Reiser promptly banged a base hit to right field, bringing home two runners, including Reese, who, along with Robinson, began "jumping in the air and smothering Reiser with their joyous slaps and embraces. … You would never have believed that this was just another winning ball game for a second-division outfit that doesn't seem to be going anywhere in particular. If the Brooks do happen to catch fire and step out from here, they can always look back to this game and say: 'That's where we re-captured the old spark.'"⁶¹

Durocher missed most of the action. He got tossed early and turned on the clubhouse radio. While the crowd roared in the late innings, Harold Parrott paid him a visit. Rickey had ordered Parrott to ask for Durocher's resignation. Durocher, always a bit of a firecracker himself, refused. "You can tell him I am not going to resign, and nobody is going to fire me by messenger."⁶² Durocher turned his attention back to the radio broadcast.

The Dodgers won eight out of the next 10 games and broke for the All-Star Game with a 35–37 mark. Only Reese and Branca represented Brooklyn on the National League squad. The AL prevailed, 5–2, in front of 34,009 fans at Sportsman's Park. Branca started for the senior circuit and gave up two runs over his three innings. Reese went hitless in two at-bats.

Following the break, Mel Ott resigned as Giants manager. The one-time slugger had taken the job in December 1941, replacing Bill Terry. His club was struggling with a 36–37 mark and in fourth place. Owner Horace Stoneham asked Ott ten days earlier what the team needed to get back into the pennant race. He got a blunt answer. "Maybe it's a new manager,"⁶³ Ott said. Now, "one of the best-liked members of the baseball fraternity"⁶⁴ planned to take a short vacation and return to the Giants in a front-office capacity.

Stoneham, searching for a fresh dugout boss, got in touch with Rickey and asked whether Shotton might be available. Rickey thought about it and decided that he needed his former manager and current scout. "How about Durocher?"⁶⁵ Stoneham countered. Rickey perked up. "You'd be interested in Leo?" Sure, Rickey told Stoneham, you can talk to Durocher. The Lip met Stoneham, along with former Giants pitching great Carl Hubbell, at the Durocher apartment on 46 East 61st Street in Manhattan and, following a short talk, agreed to terms. (As a matter of trivia, Durocher took over as Giants skipper exactly 46 years after the Giants hired John McGraw as skipper. McGraw led New York to 10 National League pennants and three World Series championships, in 1905, 1921, and 1922.)⁶⁶

Once again, Rickey asked Burt Shotton to put on a suit and tie and lead the Brooklyn Dodgers. Shotton, probably to no one's surprise, agreed to his boss's request. "I'm glad to be back," he said, although he had hardly left. "It seems like coming home. Why sure I think we're going to win the pennant. … The fans of Brooklyn think the same way."⁶⁷ Reporters scurried around the locker room to solicit opinions from Brooklyn's players. Robinson, predictably, welcomed the change. He and

Durocher two never gelled, in part due to Durocher's mandatory weight-loss regimen back in the Caribbean. "I sure like to play for that man," Robinson said of Shotton. "I can hardly wait."[68] Reese put it simply and directly. "I'm a Durocher man, myself." He added, "Leo was on the spot. He had to win or quit, and he never would have quit. But I'll play my head off for Shotton. He's one great guy."[69] A writer asked Reese how he thought the Giants might fare under Durocher. He said to "throw out this year." He looked for New York to be "tough" in future campaigns. "They've got to get better," Reese said. "Leo's a great manager."[70]

The Dodgers won seven of their first eight games under Shotton, including a 13–4 blowout against the Cardinals on July 18 at Sportsman's Park. Reese went 3-for-4, with two RBI and two runs scored. He cracked a run-scoring single in the first inning to give the Dodgers a 4–0 advantage and an RBI double in the second to put Brooklyn ahead, 10–0. Reese hit .347 over the month with a .421 on-base percentage. He slugged 10 doubles, drove in 20 runs, and crossed home plate 32 times.

A polite, teetotaling right-hander from Anderson, Indiana, joined the Dodgers in late July. Carl Erskine sported a 15–7 record and 2.59 ERA for Fort Worth. The 21-year-old threw overhand benders, a pitch taught to him by his dad, Matt, who once put on a clinic in the family living room. He stood next to the family sofa, a baseball in one hand, an instructional book in the other. "Suddenly, he made a full arm motion and accidentally released the ball," Carl recalled. Seconds later, Matt Erskine's pitch smashed into the china cupboard. He broke out in a big grin. "Son," he said, "that's the biggest break I ever got on a curveball."[71] Brooklyn also called up a strong-armed outfielder from Youngstown, Ohio. George "Shotgun" Shuba boasted a robust .389 batting average for the Mobile (Alabama) Bears of the Class AA Southern Association.

The August heat and humidity did nothing to stop Brooklyn. The Dodgers won 20 games and only lost 11 over that sultry month. Reese hit just .222 but knocked three homers, including a "towering drive over the left field wall"[72] in the fourth inning on August 25 at Crosley Field. Brooklyn knocked off the Reds, 6–1, behind Joe Hatten, who improved to 10–7. Following two more wins against Cincinnati, the Dodgers headed to St. Louis for a doubleheader on August 29. They entered the action in third place with a 64–52 mark, 2½ games behind the Braves and one game in back of the Redbirds.

Pee Wee Reese drove home three runs in the first game and helped Brooklyn to a lopsided 12–7 win. Jackie Robinson, "spurred by constant boos" from the 33,826 fans at Sportsman's Park, hit for the cycle. The Dodgers won the second game, 6–4, and moved past St. Louis into second place, a half-game behind Boston. "It was invigorating to watch the manner in which the Brooks stepped up the plate, swinging from the heals, as though the Cards were just another bunch of guys named Joe and Schmoe,"[73] Dick Young wrote.

The teams hooked up for another doubleheader the following day. In the opener, Brooklyn scored four runs in the ninth inning and came back from a 5–2 deficit. The "rampaging"[74] Dodgers took the nightcap, 6–1, and vaulted over the Braves and into first place with a 68–52 mark. "Brooklyn's Dodgers have accomplished what many experts said would be impossible,"[75] wrote Joe Reichler of the Associated Press.

Brooklyn had now won seven straight games. Harold Burr told *Eagle* readers, "Your first-place Dodgers today have that old championship look."[76]

Unfortunately, the celebration ended quickly. Brooklyn lost its final two games in August and six of its first eight games in September. After the Leo-led Giants beat the Bums three times in a four-game series, the Dodgers fell to 71–62, 6½ games behind league-leading Boston. A team that climbed into first place just 11 days earlier had now dropped to fifth, just three spots from the bottom. Jim McCulley asked, "Are the Dodgers dead?"[77] For all intents and purposes, they probably were.

The ballclub that powered through the National League with a 41–17 mark from July 3 through August 30 faded fast and won just 16 of 34 games to close the season. Reese hit .204 over that disappointing stretch. Brooklyn ended up 84–70, in third place. Nearly 1.4 million fans flocked to Ebbets Field and watched this roller-coaster of a pennant chase.

Reese enjoyed a solid all-around campaign. He batted .274 with a .363 on-base percentage and hit nine home runs. He collected 75 RBI and scored 97 times. Pee Wee also hit 31 doubles and stole 25 bases. He led the NL in shortstop putouts with 335 and finished third in assists with 453. The writers voted him sixth in the MVP Award race, well behind Stan Musial, who enjoyed the best season of his extraordinary career. The St. Louis superstar topped the league in batting average (.376), on-base percentage (.450), slugging percentage (.702), hits (230), doubles (46), triples (18), RBI (131), and total bases (429).

Among National League clubs, only the Giants scored more runs than the Dodgers, 780 to 744. Still, Brooklyn lacked the requisite long-ball pop to intimidate most opponents, tying Philadelphia for sixth in the league with 91 home runs. Hermanski topped the Dodgers with 15 round-trippers. Robinson led the team in RBI (85), doubles (38), and runs scored (108). Billy Cox struggled in his first season in Brooklyn. He played just in 88 games and hit .249 with three homers and 15 RBI. Looking back, Rex Barney wrote that Cox boasted "the most unbelievable arm you've ever seen." He also "had suffered some sort of shell shock in the army. He had terrible problems and seemed close to a nervous breakdown all the time. He could not play a day game after a night game, nor a doubleheader."[78]

Barney led the Brooklyn pitching staff with 15 wins, 12 complete games, and four shutouts to go with a 3.10 ERA. He struggled early on, with a 4.21 ERA through June. At one point, following a tough outing, Durocher vowed never to allow Barney on a pitcher's mound again. Reese told Barney not to worry. "Hang in there. He changes his mind a lot. He's a big hunch man."[79] Barney, though, did his best pitching after Leo left. He posted a 2.28 ERA in August and 2.57 in September. Barney pitched the best game of his career on September 9 at the Polo Grounds. After loading the bases on two walks and an error with one out in the first inning, he retired the next 26 straight batters. "I knew it!" Barney yelled minutes after finishing off his no-hitter. "I just knew I was going to pitch one of those things this year."[80] Durocher walked up to his former pitcher. He said, "I'm proud of you, kid."[81]

Preacher Roe, meanwhile, completed quite a comeback season. He finished 12–8 with a 2.63 ERA and won five of his final six decisions. He was now a finesse pitcher. He could no longer throw the hot fastball of his youth. Instead, he hit the corners and changed speeds, baffling batters. Campanella said, "They can cut the middle out [of the strike zone] and throw it away. Ol' Preach ain't gonna use it."[82] Roe also toyed with an illegal pitch. He threw the occasional spitball but not as often as some batters thought. A deliberate worker, he liked to tug at his jersey or his cap, just to "play with hitters' minds."[83] He once said, "You don't have to throw it [a spitter]. Just make 'em think you're going to throw it."[84] Shotton said that Roe discovered how to pitch instead of just firing hard stuff. "He knew where to throw the ball and had a change of speed, though not his old speed," Shotton said. "Didn't seem like the same pitcher."[85] Roe got the job done, wet or dry.

Pete Reiser, a shell of his former, all-world self, despite that big Fourth of July base hit, played in just 64 games. He hit one home run in 149 at-bats and batted a disappointing .236. Following the season, Reiser told Arch Murray of the *New York Post* that he wanted to cut all ties with Brooklyn. It was time to move on. "You can say that if they don't trade me, I'll quit," he said. "And I mean that from the bottom of my heart. I'll never wear a Dodger uniform again."[86]

UPI's Oscar Fraley offered a blunt opinion of Reiser's future: It was bleak. The 29-year-old had crashed into too many walls and suffered too many concussions. His list of injuries included shoulder separations, ankle fractures, a twisted back, and more. "They are saying around the National League today—again—that Pistol Pete Reiser is through," Fraley wrote. Reiser, he continued, "is in the doldrums." Reiser himself admitted, "I can't throw. I can't swing a bat, and I can't run."[87] Maybe he could find a fountain of youth somewhere outside of Flatbush. In December, Branch Rickey broke up the Gold Dust Twins. He shipped Reiser to the Braves in exchange for outfielder Mike McCormick and a player to be named later. Tommy Holmes wrote that "Rickey, in his heart, feels that Reiser is through."[88]

One columnist asserted that Reese told Reiser to stop sulking over his injury problems. Reese took offense at that remark. "Anybody that says Pete Reiser and I ever had an argument is a liar," Reese told reporters after the trade. "Pete's the best friend I've got in baseball. And he always will be. But Pete asked to be traded—in print. You can't do that and not expect to get action." As for Reiser's future, Reese said, "I hope he hits .500 at Boston. But not against the Dodgers, of course."[89]

Might Reese also be on the move? To a hated rival, no less? "It's being bruited about by men in baseball that Pee Wee Reese is headed for the Giants in a big deal," Harold Burr reported, presumably to replace six-year veteran Buddy Kerr. Supposedly, Rickey already had talked to the Pirates. He offered $125,000 and any shortstop in the Brooklyn system except Reese. In turn, Rickey asked for Stan Rojek, the one-time Dodger, who hit .290 in his first season with Pittsburgh. "This would indicate that Reese is headed to the Polo Grounds," Burr asserted. Reese supposedly entered the Brooklyn doghouse after he declared himself a "Durocher man" following Durocher's firing. Was a reunion in the works? "There's no doubt," Burr continued, "that Durocher would like to have his boy back with him at short on the Giants."[90]

The deal didn't happen, and Rickey scoffed at the rumor. "Pee Wee is a fixture at short," he told the press. "I can't conceive how the story started that he was going to the Giants. He's one of our untouchables."[91]

Reese could be a lifesaver while on the baseball diamond, with his sure glove, strong bat, and swift feet. He also could be a lifesaver off the field. *The Sporting News* posted an interesting note in its November 24 edition. The 10-year-old son of Brooklyn Trust Company employee Jack Bunn had undergone a tonsillectomy. While recovering at home, the boy began bleeding and was rushed back to the hospital for transfusions. Doctors grabbed a bottle of donated blood labeled "Pee Wee Reese," and "the boy's life was saved." Reese had donated blood earlier that year. "Young Bunn is strong and well once more," *The Sporting News* concluded, "and eager to see his hero perform in the Dodger infield again."[92]

9

"Just don't make me out to be a hero"

The two men—teammates, one white and the other Black—met near second base and faced a loud, nasty crowd at Crosley Field in Cincinnati. Fans spewed racial epithets at the Black man and directed profane questions at the white man. The pair stood side by side on that spring day in 1947. The crowd grew louder and more insulting. Finally, in a gesture of friendship, the white man—shortstop Pee Wee Reese—put his arm on the shoulder of the Black man—first baseman Jackie Robinson. Within seconds, the ballpark fell quiet.

Famed writer Roger Kahn called this—the Embrace—"baseball's finest moment."[1] Stuart Miller, in the *New York Times,* labeled it "a wonderful folk tale."[2] Rachel Robinson told columnist Ira Berkow in 2005, "I remember Jackie talking about Pee Wee's gesture the day it happened. It came as such a relief to him, that a teammate and the captain of the team would go out of his way in such a public way to express friendship."[3]

Writers, historians, filmmakers, and others continue to debate this moment in time. Filmmaker Ken Burns, a one-time believer, now says, "It didn't happen,"[4] at least not in 1947. Burns released his nine-part *Baseball* series in 1994, which, among other subjects, takes a close look at the racial history of the game and includes an interview with Red Barber. "The first time the Dodgers showed up at Cincinnati [in 1947], there was a very hostile crowd," Barber said. "A lot of booing," During a lull, "Pee Wee just walked over to where Robinson was standing on the infield and put his arm on his shoulder and just talked to him for a minute. And then, he went back, which said to the crowd, 'This is my friend.'"[5]

In 2016, Burns released another documentary, this one titled *Jackie Robinson.* By then, the filmmaker had decided that the story of a Robinson/Reese embrace was simply an episode of hopeful fiction. "It's too convenient," he asserted. Burns pointed out that nobody in the Black press, "which would have done 15 related articles,"[6] wrote a single piece.

Even so, most books by and about Robinson include an account of Pee Wee Reese's on-field embrace. The exact site varies with the source, as does the year. Robinson biographer Arnold Rampersad wrote that Reese's act of friendship took place "in full view of the public."[7]

As fans screamed from the safety of their seats, Reese "dared to put his white hand on Robinson's black shoulder in a gesture of solidarity." Rampersad acknowledged that the exact date and location this happened is "uncertain." It took place "either in Boston [as Robinson recalled] or in Cincinnati [as others remembered it]." Rampersad offered this quote from Robinson: "Pee Wee kind of sensed the sort of helpless, dead feeling in me and came over and stood beside me for a while. He didn't say a word, but he looked over at the chaps who were yelling at me and just stared. He was standing by me, I could tell you that."[8] The author added, "Reese over the years became Jackie's closest friend on the Dodgers."[9]

A life-size statue that depicts Reese with an arm on Robinson's shoulder stands outside a minor league ballpark in Coney Island, Brooklyn, not far from the former site of Ebbets Field. An engraved inscription on the statue base reads:

> This monument honors Jackie Robinson and Pee Wee Reese: teammates, friends, and men of courage and conviction. Robinson broke the color barrier in Major League Baseball. Reese supported him, and together they made history. In May 1947, on Cincinnati's Crosley Field, Robinson endured racial taunts, jeers, and death threats that would have broken the spirit of a lesser man. Reese, captain of the Brooklyn Dodgers, walked over to his teammate Robinson and stood by his side, silencing the taunts of the crowd. The simple gesture challenged the prejudice and created a powerful and enduring friendship.[10]

Brooklyn played one two-game series against Cincinnati in May 1947, on Tuesday the 13th and Wednesday the 14th, about a month after Robinson's debut. The

Jackie Robinson and Pee Wee Reese played together on the Brooklyn Dodgers for 10 seasons. They celebrated six pennants and a World Series championship in 1955 (National Baseball Hall of Fame Library, Cooperstown, New York).

Dodgers arrived in town with a record of 12–8, although they had lost five of their previous seven games. Robinson's batting average stood at .263, Reese's just .175 with only two RBI.

The Reds, struggling with a 9–14 won-loss mark, had lost six of eight. Lou Smith reported in the *Cincinnati Enquirer* that "a capacity crowd of 30,000" was expected for that night's game despite rain in the forecast and the home team's recent woes. Smith waited until the last two paragraphs to mention Robinson, writing only that the rookie might not continue much longer as a starting first baseman. "But for the fact that he is the first acknowledged Negro in major league history and so much attention has been focused on him," Smith asserted, "he would have been benched a week or two ago."[11]

Harry Taylor started on the mound for Brooklyn. Johnny Vander Meer got the call for Cincinnati. The Dodgers made three errors and lost, 7–5. Robinson went 1-for-4, scored a run, and drove in one. He extended his hitting streak to 10 games. Reese hit a double and single in three at-bats. He also walked, scored, and collected two RBI. Rex Barney pitched two innings in relief. In his memoir, the hard thrower recounted a raw, ugly scene at Crosley.

While warming up, Barney heard some Reds players unload a nasty string of insults at both Reese and Robinson. "I could hear the Cincinnati players screaming at Jackie, 'You n----- sonofabitch, you shoeshine boy,' and all the rest, and then then they started to get on Pee Wee," Barney wrote. "They were yelling at him, 'How can you play with this n----- bastard?'"[12] That's when, Barney recalled,

> Pee Wee went over to him [Robinson] and put his arm around him as if to say, "This is my boy. This is the guy. We're gonna win with him." Well, it drove the Cincinnati players through the ceiling, and you could have heard a gasp from the crowd as he did it. That's one reason Pee Wee was such an instrumental person contributing to Jackie's success. Pee Wee more than anyone else because Pee Wee was from the South.[13]

Lester Rodney, a staff writer for the *Daily Worker*, the Communist party newspaper, also said he witnessed the embrace that day at Crosley Field. But, to his life-long regret, he did not report on it. In Rodney's latter-day account, the insults began pouring out before Vander Meer even threw his opening pitch. "A bunch of men before the game were shouting," he said. "Pee Wee dropped his glove at shortstop and walked over. I was there that day. That kind of drama, how do you measure it?"[14]

Jonathan Eig, in *Opening Day*, recounted a far different scene at Crosley Field, one more festive than angry. The 27,164 fans on hand included a large contingent of African Americans. Eddie Erautt, a rookie pitcher with the Reds, put it bluntly: "The place was packed—all with blacks." Most rooted for the visiting team. According to Erautt, "All Robinson had to do was foul a ball off and they cheered. You'd have thought he hit a home run."[15] Donald Spencer, who taught at a local all-Black junior high school, said the game "was like a picnic, like a holiday."[16]

Cincinnati's African American population had been growing for many years, from approximately 56,000 in 1940 to 78,000 in 1950.[17] In 1947, about 75 percent of Black residents lived in the city's west end, a place Eig described as a "sprawling slum filled with falling-down houses, aging factories, and empty lots. About 80 percent of black families lived in homes that the city deemed beneath acceptable standards."[18]

Also in the west end, at the corner of Findlay Street and Western Avenue, stood Crosley Field, opened on April 11, 1912.

The *Enquirer*, in its May 14 edition, did not report any incidents of booing or untoward actions directed at Robinson. In fact, the newspaper informed readers, "Jackie Robinson was applauded every time he stepped to the plate" and earned compliments for his defensive work at first base. "He already has mastered all the fine points of playing the bag. Jackie is not an overpowering hitter, but he hits the ball hard."[19] The New York newspapers also did not point out any reckless fan behavior. Harold Burr, in the *Eagle*, focused his story on the sloppy play of Brooklyn fielders and the eight walks issued by Dodgers pitchers. "Your Dodgers—and you can have 'em—found another way to lose a ball game at Crosley Field last night."[20] Dick Young wrote, "Despite heavy showers throughout the afternoon, a near-capacity crowd of 27,000—many of them drawn by Jackie Robinson's first appearance—attended."[21]

Cincinnati won the next day, 2–0. Ewell Blackwell tossed a six-hit shutout and beat Joe Hatten. The Reds scored once in the first inning and added another run in the fourth. This time, only 6,688 fans watched the action. Robinson hit two singles. Reese added a base hit and a walk but committed his fourth error of the season. Again, Wendell Smith did not write about any booing or unruly behavior. Concerning the infielder, he reported, "Jackie Robinson was the only Flatbusher to get more than one safety off Blackie's blazing fastball and exploding curve. He beat out an infield single in the sixth and drilled another to center in the eighth. He has now hit safely in the last eight games."[22]

Maybe Pee Wee Reese's embrace of Robinson took place a little later in the 1947 season. The 2013 Robinson biopic *42* includes a scene set at Crosley Field that shows Reese talking to Robinson and, later, putting an arm around him. According to the movie, the episode happened on June 21, 1947. At that point, the Dodgers were 30–25 and in third place but just 1½ games out of first. They were coming off a 5–3 win against the Cubs two days earlier at Wrigley Field.

As the players make their way onto the infield, as depicted in the movie, a chorus of booing begins. The crowd is mostly white and hardly jovial. Reese walks over to Robinson, and the booing gets louder.

ROBINSON: What's up?
REESE: They can say what they want; we're here to play baseball.
ROBINSON: Just a bunch of crackpots still fighting the Civil War.
REESE: Hell, we'd have won that son of a gun if the cornstalks had held out. We just ran out of ammunition.
ROBINSON: Better luck next time, Pee Wee.

Then, to the shock of the crowd, Pee Wee Reese puts his arm around Robinson. The packed ballpark goes quiet.

REESE: Ain't gonna be a next time. All we got is right now. This right here. Know what I mean? ... Thank you, Jackie.
ROBINSON: What're you thanking me for?
REESE: I've got family here from Louisville up from somewhere. I need them to see who I am.

The Dodgers won that game, 6–5, in front of 11,807 fans. Robinson doubled and scored in three at-bats. Reese went hitless, walked, and scored a run. Newspaper accounts made no mention of an embrace between Reese and Robinson or of heckling fans. A notes column in the *Enquirer* pointed out, "Jackie Robinson was proving to be quite a gate attraction. The typewriter athletes traveling with the Dodgers estimated that the husky Negro first-sacker lures an average of 5,000 extra fans a day through the turnstiles. Incidentally, he is playing much better than he did when the Dodgers appeared here last month."[23]

Dick Young wrote that "Robinson smashed a blue darter down the left line, which the umpire called fair after a moment's hesitation."[24] (The newspaper also ran a short AP article that day under the headline "Chapman Praises Jackie Robinson." Just a month after the Phillies manager unleashed his tirade, Chapman said, "Robinson is a major leaguer in every way. He can run, he can hit, he is fast, he is quick to the ball—and his fine base-running keeps the other team in an uproar."[25])

Ken Burns believes that the "myth" of Reese's embrace has persisted because "the fish gets bigger the farther you get away from the lake."[26] Certainly, the skeptics can make a good case. The absence of any newspaper coverage or any photograph of an embrace may be their most compelling point. Also, Eig pointed out a flaw in Barney's version of events. The Dodgers pitcher wrote that he witnessed the ugly events at Crosley Field while he stood on the mound in the first inning. Barney, though, did not appear in that game until the seventh frame.[27] And while Barber told a moving story, he did not witness it. Broadcasters from that era only called games at their home ballpark.

Some writers and historians cite geography as another reason for their disbelief. Robinson played first base in his rookie campaign. Would Reese really have walked across the field from his position on the left side of the infield to show support for a teammate? Baseball historian John Thorn doubts it. "We don't know that this happened," he said about the embrace. "We don't know when it happened. It is likely that if it happened, it didn't happen in 1947, because Reese would have had to traipse across the diamond to first base to throw his arm around Jackie."[28]

Those more inclined to believe that Reese did indeed show on-field support for Robinson can offer their own strong cases. Joe Posnanski acknowledged that no newspaper from 1947 or 1948 printed an article or photograph that showed Reese embracing Robinson while in the middle of a baseball diamond. "But like everything else," he added, "it might not be so simple." Posnanski pointed out that "now, we find every element of Robinson's struggle to be fascinating and historic. There have been dozens and dozens of books written about it, countless articles, millions and millions of words. We now view it as the single most important sports story of the last 100 years." Even so, he continued, "The 1947 coverage of Jackie Robinson's struggle was, to say the least, not so probing. We may celebrate Robinson's first game every year but at the time, it garnered almost no attention in newspapers around the country."[29] That is certainly true.

Dick Young wrote the April 15 game story in the *Daily News*. Except for a brief mention early on, he waited until near the end of his story to write about Robinson's debut. "Jackie Robinson, the majors' most-discussed rookie, fielded flawlessly at first base but went hitless in three official trips to the plate," Young informed readers.[30] Arthur Daley wrote in the *New York Times*, "The muscular negro minds his own business and shrewdly makes no effort to push himself. He speaks quietly and intelligently when spoken to and already has made a strong impression."[31]

Brad Snyder, in a column titled "Jackie Robinson Myth-Busting Gone Wrong," praised Burns' documentary about the Dodgers infielder but took exception to the filmmaker's conclusion that the embrace never happened. Snyder conceded that "there is some mythology around the event"[32] and that the inscription on the Coney Island statute "like most other accounts of the event, repeats the mythical part of the episode as fact." He suggested, "It would be better to just update the inscription below the statue than to tear it down entirely."[33]

Snyder wrote, as others have, that an embrace most likely took place in 1948 at Braves Field in Boston. Snyder cited as his source Robinson himself. Baseball's first African American player of the 20th century wrote several times about an embrace, or at least a show of on-field support from Reese.

In the summer of 1949, Robinson wrote in the *Eagle* about a day "I'll never forget." Reese "faced a few loudmouth guys on the other team." The opposing players started "joshing him very viciously because he was playing on the team with me and was on the field nearby. Mind you, they were not yelling at me; I suppose they did not have the nerve to do that, but they were calling him some very vile names and every one bounced off of Peewee and hit me kind of like a machine-gun bullet. Pee Wee kind of sensed the sort of helpless, dead feeling in me and came over and stood beside me for a while." Reese didn't say anything. Instead, he stood on the field and stared at the dugout troublemakers. "He was standing by me, I could tell you that." The yelling stopped. "It was wonderful the way this little guy did it. I will never forget it."[34]

This account—like many—does not give an exact date that the bench jockeys yelled at Reese and Robinson. Snyder writes that "it makes sense that the incident occurred in April 1948,"[35] one month after Boston traded for Eddie Stanky. The Dodgers and Braves met for a two-game series at Braves Field, starting on Monday April 26. Bill Voiselle shut out Brooklyn in the first game, 5–0, with only 8,006 fans in attendance. Robinson entered the game as a defensive replacement in the eighth inning and did not bat. Reese singled in the second inning. The next day, in the second game, Boston edged Brooklyn, 3–2, in front of 6,902. Robinson started at second base and went hitless in four at-bats. He got credit for an RBI on a groundout in the seventh. Reese hit a single and drew two walks.

Talking to *Focus* magazine in 1952, Jackie Robinson said, "We were in Boston in '48, and the Braves were 'giving it' to Reese for playing shortstop alongside me. Peewee came over from shortstop, put his arm around my shoulders, as if he had something to say. Actually, he just wanted to show where he stood. The jeers subsided …."[36]

In 1955, Robinson told *Look* magazine,

> Pee Wee was great to me in 1948 when Eddie Stanky went to the Boston Braves and I moved to second base. He took a lot of bitter abuse around the circuit because of it. Pee Wee comes from Louisville and the bench jockeys kept asking him how it felt to be playing alongside a negro. The first day we played in Boston that spring the Braves tried to give me a real bad time. But Pee Wee shut them up, He walked over to me and put his arm around me and talked with me in a friendly manner, smiling and laughing. There was no more trouble after that from the Braves. He did the same thing later in other parks.[37]

Finally, Robinson spoke in 1962 to Cardinals broadcaster Jack Buck. Robinson called Reese "a real man" who walked to his side during a game against Boston when there was "considerable jockeying" pouring out from the Braves bench. Reese "put his hand on my shoulder and said something in my ear. Immediately, all the noise stopped. ... His action indicated that the only thing that he was asking was that Jackie Robinson continue to play baseball in the best manner that he could." Robinson told Buck that this happened "the first time in Boston that we played together as a double-play combination."[38]

Robinson wrote several books through the years. *Jackie Robinson: My Own Story*, co-written by Wendell Smith and published in 1948, is a slim volume—less than 200 pages—and covers, among other subjects, his childhood in Pasadena, his days at UCLA and in the Negro Leagues, and his season with the Montreal Royals. *My Own Story* mentions several episodes from the 1947 season, including the unfortunate one with Chapman and the Phillies players. "As the jockeying continued on this level, I almost lost my head," Robinson wrote. "I started to drop my bat and go over and take a sock at them. But then I remembered Branch Rickey's warning me of what I'd have to take without losing my temper. So, I pretended I didn't hear them. I gritted my teeth and vented some of my anger on a solid single." The book, though, relates nothing about Reese putting an arm on Robinson's shoulder at Crosley Field or any other ballpark. In fact, *My Own Story* only mentions Reese a few times in passing.

Carl T. Rowan wrote a book with Robinson in 1960 titled *Wait Till Next Year*. Rowan related that "the incident Robinson remembers best as illuminating Reese's innate decency occurred in Boston ... shortly after Jackie was shifted to second base." Several of the Braves' top bench jockeys "decided that rather than giving Robinson the works, they would goad Reese." They yelled stuff like, "Hey out there, Kentucky boy. When yo' grandpappy finds out how you up heah socializing and fraternizing with cullud folks, he's gonna cut you off from yo' mint juleps." Reese turned away from the catcalls for a time. Then, Rowan wrote, he stepped toward Robinson and "put his arm around his shoulder. They talked for a minute in buddy-buddy fashion— oddly enough, neither Robinson nor Reese remembers a single word they said—and the Braves' players fell silent. Reese had said, simply but with force: Robinson and I are teammates, and we came here to play baseball. ... That ended the race heckling."[39]

Wait Till Next Year devotes an entire chapter to Reese, titled "The Colonel from 'Old Kaintuck.'" Robinson, Rowan wrote, enjoyed such a strong rookie campaign in part due to Reese, "whose decency and courage in seemingly insignificant situations had buoyed him up and kept him believing that America is populated mainly by decent people who justify the Negro's continued optimism." Rowan acknowledged that Reese was not "a crusader, a lecturer about the heritage of freedom or the rights of a minority, or the necessity for baseball to operate on a democratic basic."[40]

Robinson released his last book, *I Never Had It Made*, in 1972. The first half focuses on his baseball career, the other half on his work in politics and the civil rights movement. He mentions an incident at Braves Field but does not provide a year when Reese "put his hand on my shoulder and began talking to me. His words weren't important. I don't even remember what he said. It was the gesture of comradeship and support that counted. As he stood talking with me with a friendly arm around my shoulder, he was saying loud and clear, 'Yell. Heckle. Do anything you want. We came here to play baseball.'"⁴¹

Even Eig, so skeptical about an embrace happening in 1947, acknowledges that one may have taken place in 1948 after Robinson moved over to second base and the two players "enjoyed frequent chats on the infield between innings and during time-out in action. Perhaps Reese, as warm and kind a man as there was in baseball, sometimes put an arm around Robinson's shoulder." Reese may have done this, Eig wrote, "intentionally to show support when catcalls were raining down, or simply to remind fans that black and white men were now playing side by side."⁴²

Maybe someone will craft a new statue of Reese and Robinson, one of them playing a round of golf. In late June of 1947, on an off-day from the regular season schedule, and with an exhibition game scheduled that evening in Danville, Illinois, near the Illinois-Indiana state line, some Dodgers and newspaper writers enjoyed an afternoon on the links. Robinson and Wendell Smith went out together. The pair soon caught up with Rex Barney, Harold Parrott, Roscoe McGowen, and Reese. The shortstop saw Robinson and Smith heading their way and invited them to turn a foursome into a somewhat unheard of "sixsome." Later, Smith wrote that Reese and Barney "joked and kidded with Jackie and he did the same with them. They were three baseball players and without actually saying it to each other, they admitted that each had something in common."⁴³ Bill Roeder included a note about the episode in his Robinson bio and wrote that Reese "invited" Robinson and Smith "to join the party" and "they finished the round as a jolly sixsome." Reese, Roeder wrote, was "one of the most popular men in the trade. The Brooklyn players adored him, and he had friends all around the league. Everyone liked to kid him, but everyone respected him as a player and as a good joe."⁴⁴

Gene Schoor's bio of Reese also relates the golfing story, with Reese saying to Robinson and Smith, "Hey Jackie, don't be so darned exclusive. Come on over and play join us."⁴⁵ (In this version, Reese is on the links only with catcher Bruce Edwards, thus turning the twosome into a more traditional foursome.) Rampersad called the episode "a remarkable sign of progress."⁴⁶

Reese spoke many times about his friendship with Robinson but always shied away from making a fuss over any help he offered at Crosley Field or anywhere else, in 1947 or any other year. He did what he did out of a simple sense of decency. Jules Tygiel, in *Baseball's Great Experiment*, relayed a story in which Reese once said to Robinson, "You know, I didn't go out of my way to be nice to you," to which Robinson responded, "Pee Wee, maybe that's what I appreciated most."⁴⁷

Dave Kindred wrote about the two players in 1997, on the 50th anniversary of Robinson's debut. Reese sounded reluctant to participate. "You know the Jackie stories better than I do by now," he said. Kindred pleaded with the former player. "But, Pee Wee, I need your voice,"⁴⁸ he said. Reese agreed to talk. But, he said, "Just don't make me out to be a hero. It took no courage to do what I did. Jackie had the courage. If it had been me, a white man, trying to be the only one in the black leagues, I couldn't have done it. What he had to endure, the criticism, the catcalls—I wouldn't have had the courage."⁴⁹ Reese once told Roger Kahn, "I was just trying to make the world a little bit better. That's what you're supposed to do with your life, isn't it?"⁵⁰

10

"That's why we called him 'Captain'"

A young Duke Snider stood in the batter's box and fell behind in the count, no balls and two strikes. Mired in a slump and determined not to strike out, the fair-haired kid from southern California took a meek swing at the next pitch. He hit a weak grounder to shortstop for an easy out. Pee Wee Reese waited as Snider walked back to the dugout. "What were you doing up there?" he asked. "Giving up?"[1]

Snider kind of grunted. "What are you talking about?" Reese insisted, "That wasn't your swing." Snider, a left-handed hitter, explained that he wanted to punch the ball to the opposite field rather than pull it to right. Reese shook off the alibi. "Look," he began. "I'm the guy who's supposed to punch the ball and move it around. That's because I'm the lead-off hitter. I'm supposed to get on base any way I can. But you're not supposed to do that. You're supposed to drive me in."[2]

Through the years, Reese gave his teammate many lessons in the finer points of playing smart baseball. Snider, for example, hated to charge ground balls that came skipping to him in the outfield. "C'mon, Duke," Reese encouraged. "Be aggressive out there."[3] In *The Duke of Flatbush*, Snider wrote, "[Pee Wee] helped me tremendously with the mental approach to the game. So much of baseball is the mental alertness and anticipation to make the right play. And you had to maintain that level of mental sharpness over a season of 154 games. That's not easy even if you have the physical tools, and that's why Pee Wee was so important to the Dodgers as a team and to so many of us individually. That's why we called him 'Captain,'"[4]

Branch Rickey named Reese the Dodgers' captain in January 1949. Brooklyn had been without an official team leader since Dolph Camilli left after the 1943 season. According to *The Pee Wee Reese Story*, Rickey met with Reese in Louisville and began the conversation, as he often did, in a roundabout manner. "Pee Wee," Rickey began, "sometime during the next baseball season, you will be thirty years old. Not a young man by baseball standards. Already you are being talked of as 'the last of the old Dodgers.'"[5]

Talent filled the Brooklyn roster, but so did youth. Players like Snider, Gil Hodges, and Carl Erskine stood on the brink of stardom. Rickey wanted a leader who could guide this team to a championship. "I'd like to think of you as the first of the new Dodgers,"[6] he said to Reese. That's when Rickey sprang his news. "You're not only the logical choice," to serve as team captain. "You're the only choice; the players all respect you."[7]

There was just one problem. Reese didn't want the job, and he blamed Eddie Stanky. The former Brooklyn second baseman and unofficial infield captain yelled at and razzed both friend and enemy. Stanky could be a bundle of nerves. Reese liked getting along with everyone, from the writers to the fans to teammates and front-office personnel. He thought of the captain's role as a contentious one and, undoubtedly, a big headache. "Some of the players resented [Stanky's] attempt at authority," Reese said. "I wouldn't want any of the guys to feel that way about me or feel that I was showboating or anything like that."[8]

Rickey, eloquent to a fault, kept making his case. "You'd be acting with my expressed authority on the field," he said. "An official captain."[9] Finally, Reese agreed to the boss's request. He also agreed to a new contract, one for $24,000, plus $500 to fill the role of captain, making him the highest-paid Dodger of all time.[10] The players supported Rickey's decision. "Don't print this because it would only embarrass Pee Wee," one veteran said to a reporter. "But there's not one of us who has any gripe about his being captain. Everybody on this club knows Pee Wee's a real team man. Nobody puts more heart into the game than he does."[11]

Captain Reese arrived early to spring training, mostly to relax and play golf before the real work began. Some writers asked him what the captain's role might entail. He smiled and shrugged. Maybe he twirled a seven iron as he spoke. "How do I know?" he said. "I guess I'm supposed to be the take-charge guy."[12]

Branch Rickey named Reese as captain of the Dodgers in 1949. The shortstop served in that role for the rest of his career (National Baseball Hall of Fame Library, Cooperstown, New York).

More than 150 players dressed out in Dodger blue and white at Vero Beach, the first full season they trained in that sun-blessed city. Rickey urged reporters and fans to be patient while the club took shape. Whittling down the roster would not be easy. "All of these boys in a Dodger uniform have a chance to make the team," Rickey said.[13] The Brooklyn starting lineup, though, appeared set at several positions. Gil Hodges had nailed down the first-base job, with Jackie Robinson the likely second baseman. Robinson spent much of the off-season working out in New York and watching his diet. He reported at about 200 pounds, 20 pounds less than the previous spring.

Billy Cox figured to start at third base, alongside Reese, on the left side of the infield. Shotton predicted a strong comeback season for his 29-year-old infielder. "Cox is a changed man from last year," Shotton said. "He can hit, field, and run. All he needed was a little spark."[14] Cox confessed, "I was all mixed up last year. I just couldn't seem to do anything right. It wasn't that island malaria that I picked up in the south Pacific—that's left me for good."[15] Rather, Cox said, he felt tired physically and mentally. Now he felt much better. He gained seven pounds over the winter and cracked jokes with teammates in Florida.

Roy Campanella and Bruce "Bull" Edwards battled for work behind the plate. Shotton expected Edwards, just two years removed from an All-Star appearance, to win the starting job. "I'd be willing to bet right now," he said in March, "that Edwards catches one hundred games."[16] Snider hoped to gain a starting job in the outfield, alongside Gene Hermanski and Carl Furillo. "If Snider clicks, we're in," Shotton told reporters. "That boy has the makings of a great player. He has lots of power, can run like a deer, throws with a rifle arm and can go and get them. All he needs is confidence and a little more experience."[17]

Edwin Donald Snider was, like Pete Reiser before him, an outstanding natural athlete. Born September 19, 1926, in Los Angeles, the only child of Ward and Florence Snider, he threw a no-hitter and struck out 15 batters in his first game at Compton High School and once hurled a 63-yard touchdown pass for the football team. He counted future NFL commissioner Pete Rozelle as one of his closest boyhood friends.

Snider earned a spot on youth all-star teams at every level. "From the time I started playing softball in the fourth grade at George Washington Elementary School, I rarely experienced any frustration or failure,"[18] he recalled. Snider's dad began calling him "Duke." The Dodgers signed him for $250 a month plus a $750 bonus following a tryout in nearby Long Beach, and ordered him to Bear Mountain, New York, in the Hudson Highlands, one of those makeshift spring training sites made necessary due to wartime travel restrictions. A snowstorm greeted Snider as he stepped off the train. Making things worse—and himself that much colder—he forgot to bring a coat. Soon enough, he left New York for the Newport News (Virginia) Dodgers of the Class B Piedmont League, where he hit .294 with 34 doubles and a league-leading nine homers. Hitting soft, re-covered baseballs—another wartime oddity, this one due to the rationing of leather goods—wasn't easy. "You couldn't get the ball out of the park if you fired it with a cannon,"[19] he said.

Following the season, and just one day after getting home to California in mid–September, Snider opened a telegram. The Navy requested his services. He spent much of 1945 on a ship in the Pacific Ocean. His dad also was serving on a Navy ship, one much closer to harm's way. "Poor mom,"[20] Snider wrote. Unscathed, he mustered out of the military on June 26, 1946, and reported to the Fort Worth Cats of the Class AA Texas League. He started slowly but soon began ringing hard hits in ballparks all over the Lone Star State. He spent the next two seasons with the St. Paul Saints and the Montreal Royals, getting late-season call-ups to Brooklyn both years. He hoped to stick with the Dodgers from the start in 1949.

Each day in Florida, coaches ordered veterans to the sawdust sliding pits and led them through a series of drills. "It's just another example of how highly specialized this unique camp is,"[21] the *Daily News* reported. Red Smith called Dodgertown "a vast industrial plant which Branch Rickey built to turn out Dodgers on a stamping machine, so many per hour with every item cut to the same size and pattern."[22] Ballplayers from throughout the system put on their assigned uniform and number, while coaches studied mimeographed sheets of paper that secretaries typed up throughout the night "because this is a factory that operates around the clock."[23]

Some players hit off tees. Others ran 60-yard sprints on a six-lane cinder track. Several pitching machines hurled fastballs. Smith labeled those contraptions "bazookas." Some threw knuckleballs and assorted off-speed selections. Whistles blew, and players moved to the next station. "Generalisimo" Rickey sat in a chair near one of the batting cages and fired questions at prospects. Lots of questions. "What's your first name, son?" ... "What does your father do?" ... "You married?" ... "Any brothers?" ... "Where were you in your first year [in the Brooklyn organization]?"[24] On and on.

At one point, Burt Shotton ordered all 40 players on the Brooklyn roster into the locker room. He asked each of them what they hoped to accomplish in Florida. Snider, for instance, wanted to gain a better idea of the strike zone. Hermanski needed to improve his defense, while Hodges planned to work on hitting off-speed pitches. Finally, Pee Wee Reese stood up to speak. First, he promised to improve his all-around game. "But I know the one thing you want me to do the most of all, Barney," Reese said. "I won't mention it, and if you don't, I'll just concentrate on overcoming it."[25] What could it possibly be? The veterans knew. Reese had gotten into a bad habit of taking too many first pitches, often for strikes, making an at-bat that much tougher.

As the Dodgers broke camp, Reese began complaining of abdominal pains, which increased whenever he made a quick stop or start. "I don't know how I got it, originally," he said. "There's no particular play I can put my finger on. It just came down on me—sort of a pulldown here, low on my right side."[26] Doctors, concerned that Reese was suffering from a hernia, ordered him to the bench. Dick Young wrote that Reese might not be ready for Opening Day. On April 14, the shortstop talked his way into an exhibition match-up against the Senators. "I've got to find out some time, so why wait any longer?" he said. "The darned thing was supposed to keep me out only three days, and I've gone almost two weeks without playing now. If I can't play, then it must be something more than just a simple muscle pull. If that's the case, I want to know about it right now."[27] He couldn't get the ball out of the infield in any of his at-bats but pronounced himself ready to go.

Reese jogged out to his customary spot at shortstop for the opener on April 19 at home against the Giants, with Hodges heading to first, Robinson to second and Cox to third. Cal Abrams, a graduate of James Madison High School in Brooklyn, enjoyed a strong spring and earned the left field job over Hermanski. Snider started in center, with Furillo in right. Campanella, who endured racial taunts in small towns throughout Dixie as the ballclub headed north, won Shotton's favor and crouched behind home plate. Left-hander Joe Hatten, fresh off a 13–10 campaign, drew the mound assignment. The Dodgers won, 10–3, in front of 34,530 fans. Campanella belted a three-run home run. Furillo and Robinson added solo round-trippers. Reese hit leadoff and went 1-for-3 with two walks and a run scored. He batted .388 over 12 April games. On April 28, in a 15–2 blowout win at the Polo Grounds, he collected four hits, drove in three runs, and took over the team RBI lead with 13.

In closing out the season's opening month, Reese hit two home runs against the Phillies. He ripped a solo long ball in the first inning off Hank Borowy, deep into the left-center field seats, and another in the ninth inning, this one into the left field corner, again off Borowy. Philadelphia still pasted Brooklyn, 12–4. Pitching continued to be a worry for Shotton's club and, as the *Daily News* noted, "even a grand competitor like Pee Wee Reese," unfortunately, "can't pitch a lick."[28]

Few teams in baseball, though, could match the powerful Brooklyn offense. On May 18, the Dodgers notched 20 hits and beat the Cubs, 14–5, at Wrigley Field. Every player in the Brooklyn lineup, including pitcher Hatten, recorded at least two hits. Reese smacked a single and a triple and drove in two runs. Three nights later at Sportsman's Park, Brooklyn trounced St. Louis, 15–6. Robinson collected six RBI. Reese notched four hits, including a three-run homer off Ray Yochim, and scored five times. "Pee Wee's homer was the big blow,"[29] Young wrote.

From St. Louis, the Dodgers left to play a doubleheader against the Reds. As usual, plenty of Pee Wee Reese fans were expected at Crosley Field. "A few hundred Louisville baseball fans will stampede by special train and private car into Cincinnati this afternoon to see the darling of the Dodgers," Dean Eagle wrote in the *Louisville Courier-Journal*. Eagle called Reese "the David among Goliaths."[30] In the opener, Reese hit a seventh-inning double but was overshadowed by a 6-foot-4-inch right-hander making his first start. Don Newcombe allowed just five hits and shut out the Reds, 5–0.

Born on June 14, 1926, in Madison, New Jersey, Newcombe weighed 200 pounds as a 15-year-old. Roland Newcombe thought his son should pursue a boxing career. Young Don, though, frowned at the idea of getting hit in the face for a living. He preferred baseball. As a junior, he dropped out of high school to play for the Newark Eagles. Brooklyn signed him in late 1945. "He was by no means the best pitcher in Negro baseball," Wendell Smith wrote, "but Rickey signed him because he's young, big, and has all the natural ability necessary to get him into the big leagues."[31] Newcombe played for Nashua in 1946 and 1947 and Montreal in 1948.

The 22-year-old made his Dodgers debut on May 20, in the opening game of a doubleheader against the Cardinals in St. Louis. He struck out the first batter he faced—Chuck Diering—but gave up three runs on four hits before exiting. "He fired a fierce fastball," Dick Young wrote. Even so, Newcombe "certainly did not look like the guy who is going to straighten out the Dodger pitching problem."[32] Two nights later, after Newcombe dispatched the Reds, Harold Burr decided, "The Dodgers have found the man whose strong right arm may lead 'em out of their pitching wilderness."[33] Brooklyn lost the second game of the twin bill and dropped to 17–15, in third place.

Not until the weather turned warm did the Dodgers get hot. They posted an 18–9 record in June. Reese batted .383 over the month. He notched at least two hits in 12 of 13 games from June 3–16. The Dodgers won 10 of those contests and swept a three-game series at home against the Reds by a combined score of 41–15. Reese reached base eight times. Cincinnati's general manager, Warren Giles, took notice of Reese's fine play and made this pronouncement: "If I had my choice of any single player in our league, I'd jump at the chance to get Reese. Day in and day out, that boy does everything for you and does it better than well." Giles even said that he preferred Reese over Stan Musial. That was quite a compliment. The Cardinals outfielder already had won three MVP Awards and three batting titles. "[Reese] can run, throw, hit and field," Giles continued. "And he does it so consistently that people come to expect it. They say: 'Reese? Oh yeah, sure, he's a good little ballplayer.' Good? He's the best."[34]

Harry Grayson, sports editor for the Newspaper Enterprise Association, also praised Reese, both as a player and as a team leader. Reese had taken over the captain's role with gusto. The shortstop, Grayson wrote, "talks pitchers out of the jitters" and "tells who to take what in the infield." Grayson called Reese "a vastly under-rated and under-publicized ballplayer for a half-dozen years. … The one-time marble champion is a real stand-up-and-cheer ballplayer."[35]

On June 25 at Forbes Field, Reese contributed two hits and scored twice as the Dodgers beat the Pirates, 17–10. The Bums posted nine runs in the third inning. The following day, Brooklyn scored 10 times in the seventh inning and knocked out Pittsburgh, 15–3. Reese hit three singles and a double. UPI's Carl Lundquist wrote that the Dodgers "put on another terrifying display of power." He added, "Agonizing is the news a pitcher gets these days when his manager says, 'Tomorrow you start against the Brooklyn Dodgers.'"[36]

Brooklyn ended June by losing, 4–2, to the Phillies at Shibe Park. Reese hit a two-run homer in the third inning. His average stood at a robust .320, and Dick Young wrote, "You just can't sit silently by and let the long-subdued appreciation Pee Wee Reese's greatness go unpublicized."[37] One of the few Dodgers outplaying Reese was Robinson, who hit .374 in June with 11 steals after batting .431 with six homers and 34 RBI in May.

Robinson was a "fearless" ballplayer, Reese recalled. On defense, "He had only a fair arm but made up for it at second base by never backing down when a runner came barreling in."[38] It should be noted that Robinson's agreement with Rickey to turn the other check, even in the most vile of circumstances, had run its course by 1949. He could now talk back and fight back. He liked to razz the competition. "He could be a tough bench jockey,"[39] Reese said. Robinson insisted that pitchers hurled fastballs at his head because they were racists. Reese corrected him, slightly. "You know, Jack, some of these guys are throwing at you because you're black. But others are doing it because they just don't like you."[40] Robinson admitted, "You've got a point."[41]

Teams broke for the annual All-Star Game with Brooklyn in the top spot by just a half-game over St. Louis. Ebbets Field hosted the midsummer contest for the only time, on July 12. This was the first All-Star Game to feature African American players. Local fans cheered on many of their heroes. Campanella, Newcombe, and Robinson earned roster spots for Brooklyn, in addition to Branca, Hodges, Roe, and Reese. ("Captain Pee Wee Reese is having one of his greatest years at short, which is just about all that could be said in praise of the greatest shortstop in the game,"[42] wrote Harold Burr.) Larry Doby played four innings as an AL All-Star.

For most Brooklyn players, it was a day to forget. The AL's best pitchers held Reese hitless in five at-bats, and the Dodgers ended up a collective 2-for-15. Newcombe allowed two runs in 2⅔ innings. On the plus side, Robinson scored three times, and Roe pitched a scoreless ninth. Musial went 3-for-4 and smacked a two-run homer. NL fielders made a whopping five errors in an 11–7 AL victory. Neither team managed a hit over the final two frames. "The pitching got better toward the end, because it couldn't have very well gotten worse,"[43] Burr reported.

Following the break, Brooklyn won five of six games. Reese's batting average stayed above the .300 mark throughout July. Bill Corum asked in the July 13 edition of *The Sporting News*, "What can't the 'Little Colonel' do?" Corum called Reese "practically a player-manager. … He's that smart." On the base paths, he was tougher to catch "than a mosquito in a pitch-black bedroom."[44]

The Cardinals, in second place by 2½ games, arrived in Brooklyn on July 22 for a four-game series. St. Louis won the opener, 3–1, and took the second game, 5–4. The Redbirds pummeled the Dodgers, 14–1, in the third game and vaulted into first place. Musial hit for the cycle and drove in four runs. Harold Burr speculated, "The 34,042 fans sat in the stands, wondering if the honeymoon is over for their favorite ballclub."[45] (Umpires called the final game with the score tied, 4–4, after nine innings so that both teams could make late-afternoon train connections.)

Except for a few days in mid–August, the Cards enjoyed a lengthy run in the top spot, although they never pulled ahead by more than 2½ games. Musial, as he often did, powered the St. Louis offense. He batted .383 in August with nine homers and 25 RBI. Burr called Musial "Missouri Murder Inc. in human form" and labeled the entire Redbirds team "the maddened marauders from across the Mississippi."[46] But what did that make the Dodgers? Both Brooklyn and St. Louis played .645 baseball in August (20 wins, 11 losses).

The Dodgers opened the final month of the season by winning 15 of 20 games. Reese played a key role in several of the victories. He drove in three runs in an 11–8 win at home against Cincinnati on September 1. A few days later, he reached base five times and had two RBI as Brooklyn trounced Boston, 13–2, in the second game of a doubleheader. In the opener, he scored twice and drove in a run as Brooklyn won, 3–2.

On September 11, Reese crumpled to the ground in the seventh inning of a home game against New York. Teammates worried that he had taken another pitch to the noggin and might be out for a while. Actually, Larry Jansen's fastball had glanced off Pee Wee's elbow. The shortstop missed one game and promptly rapped two hits and scored twice against the Reds. "Sparked by their captain and shortstop,"[47] Brooklyn edged Cincinnati, 4–2. Later, Reese said "the elbow didn't bother me so much. I had a far worse worry."[48]

The very word "polio" terrified people, especially the parents of young children. The disease, known by some as infantile paralysis, dates back to ancient times. The first large-scale epidemic in the United States struck in 1916. By the time it ended, doctors had counted 27,000 cases. More than 6,000 victims died, about one-third of them in New York City.[49] In 1949, approximately 40,000 polio cases were reported in the United States, or one for every 3,775 people.[50] The small town of San Angelo,

Texas, suffered the most. There, the city reported 420 polio cases, or one for every 124 people. David M. Oshinsky, in *Polio: An American Story*, wrote that "per capita, San Angelo had the worst polio epidemic in world history."[51]

Researchers determined that the virus was primarily transmitted through fecal matter, often in swimming pools. Some had blamed flies, mosquitoes and even car exhausts, cats, and Italian immigrants. Doctors and scientists warned against "polio hysteria."[52] Symptoms included sore throat, fatigue, headache, stomachache, and other maladies often associated with the flu.[53] Most children recovered and developed an immunity. For some, though, polio affected the brain and spinal cord, and, in approximately one out of every 200 cases, led to paralysis.[54] The 1949 epidemic left "its most tragic sign: children with wheelchairs, crutches, leg braces, and deformed limbs."[55] Paralyzed patients were often forced to lie inside a so-called iron lung—"an airtight metal tank that encloses all of the body except the head and forces lungs to inhale and exhale through regulated changes in air pressure"[56]—in order to breathe. The virologist and medical researcher Dr. Jonas Salk developed the first reliable polio vaccine in 1955.

Pee Wee Reese's five-year-old daughter, Barbara Lee, showed signs of polio in the late summer of 1949. "Fortunately, Dr. Morris Steiner got the disease under control," Reese said in a 1954 article for *Look* magazine, later adapted for *Baseball Digest*. "Today, thank the Lord, Barbara Lee is a fine, healthy young lady."[57]

Brooklyn's pennant chances took a direct hit on September 16 in a game against the Pirates when Roy Campanella suffered a mild concussion from getting hit in the head with a pitch. The catcher had refused to wear a protective helmet, unlike Reese and many other Brooklyn players. Campanella often kidded Reese about going to bat with "military"-style headwear. "You'll wear it too after you get a ball stuck in your ear," Reese said. Campanella always laughed and insisted that he could duck away from any pitcher's errant fastball. Only after getting beaned did he look around the dugout for a hard hat that fit. "They ain't never gonna get me to take this off," he said. "How do I look?" Reese glanced at his teammate. "Like a doll," he said. "A real doll."[58]

The Dodgers boasted a 91–54 won-lost mark when they pulled into St. Louis' Union Station for a final three-game series against the Cardinals. The first-place Redbirds, 92–52, stood 1½ games in front. No other team was close. The Phillies sat mired in third place, 16 games out of the top spot.

Don Newcombe matched up against Max Lanier in the opening game of a doubleheader on September 21. Both pitchers held opposing hitters scoreless over the first eight innings. Lanier put up another scoreless frame in the top of the ninth. Enos Slaughter began the bottom half by doubling to left field. Newcombe gave Ron Northey a free pass and allowed a single to Bill Howerton that loaded the bases. Joe Garagiola grounded a hit through the infield that scored the winning—and only—run. Roe blanked St. Louis in the second game, 5–0. He tossed a two-hitter and improved his record to 14–5. Brooklyn scored all of its runs in a big fourth inning against Harry Brecheen. Luis Olmo led the way with a two-run triple.

The Dodgers put on a powerful display in the finale and won, 19–6, in front of 30,765 stunned fans. Carl Furillo made five hits, including three doubles, and drove in seven runs. Gil Hodges added five RBIs. Brooklyn narrowed the Cardinals' lead to a half game with six to play. Harold Burr wrote that "the Dodgers are really back in the pennant race with both spikes." Brooklyn, he continued, was "breathing hotly on the clammy necks of the frightened Red Birds, half a length away."[59] The Dodgers split their next series at home against the Phillies. They won the opener, 8–1, but lost the nightcap 5–3. The Cardinals, meanwhile, swept the Cubs to open another 1½-game advantage. Was the pennant chase finally over? Many in the Gateway City thought so. "Practically everybody in St. Louis, from the big banker to the little hat check girl, thinks the Cardinals won the National League pennant yesterday,"[60] Joe Reichler wrote.

St. Louis closed out the schedule with two games in Pittsburgh and three in Chicago. Brooklyn, also on the road, had a doubleheader left against Boston and a two-game set versus Philadelphia. The Dodgers won both games against the Braves, 9–2 and 8–0. Furillo and Snider slammed three-run homers in the opener. Newcombe tossed a four-hitter in the finale. Four Brooklyn hitters, including Reese, collected two hits apiece. St. Louis, meanwhile, lost both games against the Pirates, 6–4 and 7–2. The Dodgers took over first place and went ahead by a full game after the Cubs beat the Cards, 6–5, on September 30, an off-day for Brooklyn.

Both Brooklyn and St. Louis lost on Saturday, October 1. The Cardinals could force a playoff with a win on the final game of the season, coupled with a Dodgers loss. St. Louis did its part by winning, 13–5. The Dodgers, though, outslugged the Phillies, 9–7, and earned the NL pennant with a 97–57 mark. The game was knotted, 7–7, after nine innings. Reese, 0-for-4 up to that point, led off the 10th with a single, advanced to second on an Eddie Miksis sacrifice, and scored on a Snider single. Luis Olmo added an RBI base hit. Jack Banta held Philly scoreless in the bottom half of the frame. A pleased Burt Shotton told reporters, "My boys always win the game they have to win."[61] An emotional Reese sat on a chair in front of his locker and told reporters, "I feel like crying, and I don't think anyone would blame me."[62]

Reese hit just .225 in September and finished with a .279 batting average. Thanks in part to his 116 walks, he boasted a .396 on-base percentage and crossed home plate a league-high 132 times. He also hit a career-high 16 homers, drove in 73 runs, and stole 26 bases. Catchers nabbed him just four times. In the field, he led the National League in shortstop putouts (316) for the second straight year. His double-play partner, Robinson, also hit 16 homers and led the NL with a .342 batting average and 37 stolen bases. Number 42 drove home 124 runs and scored 122 runs. Hodges and Snider topped the team with 23 home runs apiece.

Billy Cox played in 100 games and batted just .233 but provided excellent defense. In his seven seasons with the Dodgers, Cox played in more than 140 games just one time. Injuries and other ailments often kept him on the bench. At least once, he begged out of the second game of a doubleheader. He was "bushed," he said. No other Dodger said a word. At last, Reese spoke. "What are you saving something for?" he asked. "An exhibition game in Altoona?" Cox played the game.[63]

Don Newcombe led the pitching staff. He won 17 games, completed 19 starts, and threw five shutouts. Preacher Roe won 15 games and finished with a 2.79 ERA. Brooklyn attracted 1,633,747 fans, tops in the league.

The Yankees took home the AL flag with a mark of 97–57, one game better than the second-place Red Sox. Casey Stengel earned a pennant in his first season as New York skipper. In his three years as a Dodgers manager and six with the Boston Braves (1938–1943), Stengel's teams had never finished higher than fifth place. He spent 1948 as manager of the Oakland Oaks and won a pennant. Editors at *The Sporting News* tabbed him as Minor League Manager of the Year. He was 58 years old, happy in California, and, in truth, mulling over retirement. Then, the Yankees offered him maybe the best job in baseball, certainly the most prestigious. How could he turn it down? "I at once commenced not thinking about retirement,"[64] Stengel said.

Page One of the October 5 *Eagle* proclaimed in large type "Newcombe Faces Reynolds," the scheduled starting pitchers for Game One on a chilly afternoon at Yankee Stadium. One day earlier, an estimated 375,000 fans watched as "Dodger players in white and royal blue uniforms sat in open cars, two to a car, with trucks, a horse and wagon and a slaphappy kid winding up the rear" on a parade route from Grand Army Plaza to Borough Hall, "which was packed shoulder to shoulder with yelling, screaming delirious men, women and children." Confetti poured down from office buildings and onto the street. "When the cavalcade finally came to a halt, the watchers broke through though barriers and snake-danced through the plaza until it was one huge waving, dancing panorama."[65]

Joe Gabionwitz, a 26-year-old textile worker and Dodgers fan from Newark, stood all night in the rain just to buy a bleacher seat for one dollar. He told *Eagle* reporter Violet Brown, "I like to be the first at these things. I'm going to head up the line over at Ebbets Field, too."[66] Gabionwitz and more than 66,000 others watched two hard-throwing right-handers engage in a high-pressure duel. The game remained scoreless after eight innings. Reynolds had given up just two hits; Newcombe had scattered five. Brooklyn went down quickly in the top of the ninth. Tommy Henrich hit a solo homer in the bottom half. A dejected Newcombe said afterward, "It's the biggest disappointment of my life." Stengel said that Henrich hit a Newcombe heater. "It was a fastball," Stengel said. Nope, Campanella told reporters. "It was Don's best curveball."[67]

The Game Two starting pitchers, Preacher Roe, "so skinny you can almost see through him,"[68] and Vic Raschi, the "Springfield Rifle," nearly matched Newcombe and Reynolds. The teams played another 1–0 ballgame at Yankee Stadium in front of more than 70,000 fans. This time, Brooklyn came out on top. Brooklyn scored the game's lone run in the second inning. Jackie Robinson led off with a double and advanced to third on Gene Hermanski's popup in foul territory. He sprinted home when Gil Hodges lined a single to left.

Roe, sailing along for much of the way, ran into some trouble in the eighth inning. Johnny Mize, acquired a few weeks earlier in a $40,000 cash deal from the Giants, led off with a single. Phil Rizzuto reached on an error with one out, and Henrich stepped to the plate. Reese called time-out and walked to the mound. "Preach, let's you and me have a little talk," he said. Okay, Roe said. "What should we talk about?" "Heck, Preach," Reese said, "anything at all. Hunting, fishing. How's the weather in Arkansas? Just let's keep Henrich waiting up there and wondering how you're going to pitch to him."[69] Henrich proceeded to fly out, and Hank Bauer hit into a force play. Joe DiMaggio singled to lead off the New York ninth before Roe retired the next three batters. Afterward, he sat on his locker-room stool and relayed the story about Reese's mound visit. "How about that guy?" Roe said. "Ain't he a daisy?"[70]

The World Series moved to cozy Ebbets Field for Game Three. Nearly 33,000 fans jammed into one of baseball's coziest ballparks on October 7 to watch Tommy Byrne, the so-called "Wild Man" (he led the AL in walks in 1949 with a whopping 179 in 196 innings), take on Ralph Branca. The Yankees took a 1–0 lead in the third inning on a Rizzuto sacrifice fly. Reese led off the fourth with a "circuit smash into the left-center steerage deck"[71] for his first World Series home run and the first hit off Byrne.

Branca gave up just the one run, plus two hits and two walks, through eight innings. He unraveled in the final frame and loaded the bases with two outs. Stengel called on Mize to pinch-hit for Cliff Mapes. Baseball's "Big Cat," from Demorest, Georgia, pounded an inside, letter-high fastball—"just the way we're supposed to pitch him," according to Branca—into right field for a two-run single. Jerry Coleman added an RBI base hit. Olmo and Campanella hit solo homers for Brooklyn in the bottom of the ninth. New York held on to win, 4–3. The *Daily News* reported that afterward, despite a near-comeback, "the entire Dodger dressing room reeked of mourning, but Branca was sadder than anyone else." He stood by his locker and kept saying "just one more out. One more damn pitch."[72] In his column for the International News Service, Reese confirmed that Branca followed the scouting report on Mize, a four-time NL home run champ. The starter "pitched the best ball game he has pitched all season," Reese said. Branca "got the ball exactly where he wanted to get it. Mize hit it. That's baseball. Such things happen."[73]

Burt Shotton sent Don Newcombe to the mound for Game Four on two days' rest against Eddie Lopat, a 15-game winner "with a bag of soft tricks,"[74] unlike his hard-tossing teammates. Both pitchers struggled. Newcombe, pitching his fourth game in 10 days, "couldn't take the grueling grind any longer"[75] and allowed three runs in the fourth inning. Joe Hatten entered the game in relief but offered little. He gave up three runs on a base-loaded triple by Bobby Brown. The Dodgers mustered a four-run sixth inning to make the game close. "They got two big innings and we just got one,"[76] Shotton explained to reporters. Reese doubled in the first inning and singled and scored in the sixth.

Brooklyn's manager hoped that Preacher Roe could start Game Five on two days' rest. Roe, though, hurt a finger on his non-throwing hand in the second game. Now he couldn't fit his glove over the swollen digit. Branch Rickey showed his hurler no sympathy and asked whether fear or a tired arm had simply gotten the best of him. "Ah, can't pitch with this finger, Mr. Rickey, in Brooklyn or anywhere else," Roe said. Rickey called Roe a "coward."[77]

With that, the Dodgers turned to Rex Barney, who struggled much of the season. He posted a 9–8 record with a 4.41 ERA and walked 89 batters in 140⅔ innings. Against the Yankees, he gave up five runs in 2⅔ innings. His cringe-worthy pitching line included six walks. "When you think of walks, you think of Rex Barney,"[78] chirped the *Daily News*, piling on to the pitcher's misery. Banta and Erskine offered little in the way of relief. The Yankees led, 10–2, after six innings. Reese produced an RBI single in the third frame. Brooklyn cut the lead to 10–6 following a four-run seventh. By that point, much of the once-filled Ebbets Field had emptied. "Clusters of fans began to wend their way toward the exit gates" in the sixth,[79] according to the *Eagle*.

Once again, reporters gathered around Pee Wee Reese, who batted .316 over the five games, and asked him to explain another October disappointment. "It's tough to lose, but they beat us," he said. "The score tells the story."[80] Shotton gave all the praise to his dugout counterpart, a man who "capped a brilliant season."[81] The Brooklyn skipper then took a divine turn. "The good Lord himself couldn't have gotten more out of those Yankees than Casey Stengel," Shotton said. "In my book, he's a truly great manager."[82] Stengel insisted that he did nothing over the past season to change the way he ran a ballclub. But, he added, "Nowadays, I seem to get a little more assistance from my help."[83] Rickey, for his part, said, "We didn't go into the Series at our peak. I'm concerned now with building a pitching staff to beat the Yankees."[84]

Two weeks later, Louisville honored one of its favorite citizens. City leaders chose October 24 as the start of Pee Wee Reese Week and issued a proclamation that read, in part, "Whereas Pee Wee Reese is regarded as one of the outstanding players in the field of organized baseball today … and, is an example to and inspiration for the youth of America … the City of Louisville is proud to proclaim Pee Wee Reese as a native son."[85]

On October 27, about 400 people crowded into the fashionable Brown Hotel in downtown Louisville to salute Reese. Tom Fitzgerald wrote that several local bigwigs wanted to present Reese with membership in a local club, "where he could indulge his hobby of playing golf." The shortstop demurred. "I already belong to one private club," he said. "If I belonged to two, my friends might think I'm trying to put on the dog." Reese's tastes were simple. He enjoyed golf, playing bridge, and going to movies. The Reese family lived during the off-season in an "unpretentious apartment" in Louisville. Emma Reese told Fitzgerald that success hadn't changed her son "one bit. You can't say that about everybody. Pee Wee certainly appreciates what his friends are doing for him, but he'd prefer to just go along unnoticed."[86]

Speakers at the dinner, which benefited the local polio fund, included Branch Rickey, Ted McGrew, Dodgers executive Fresco Thompson, and others. Reese's old sandlot coach, Ralph Kimmel, recalled a time that his slender, undersized player "couldn't hit a ball into the left-field stands, only 180 feet away, unless a strong wind was behind him." Reds executive Gabe Paul looked over at Reese, who wore a suit and tie to the formal event. "You don't know what a pleasure it is to see Reese in civilian clothes," Paul said. "Unfortunately, we're forced to see him in a baseball uniform all season."[87]

Finally, Rickey hinted that Reese not only fit the requirements of an ideal team captain The shortstop also fit the requirements to someday take over as manager. "He's more than a fine player and more than a fine citizen," Rickey said. "He's a person qualified to do a fine job in anything his judgment will lead him to seek or accept." Rickey paused for a few seconds. "If you have a certain thing on your mind," he continued, "you can make the most of this statement."[88] Reese, with characteristic modesty, spoke for just a few minutes. "I'm not deserving of this," he insisted. "I've just been lucky and have gotten a lot of breaks to get where I am. If I've succeeded, I owe plenty to a lot of people. I thank you."[89]

Soon after, a couple of Dodgers picked up some postseason hardware. On November 3, the Baseball Writers' Association of America chose Don Newcombe as National League Rookie of the Year. He earned 105 of a possible 116 votes, easily beating out Phillies third baseman Willie Jones, who picked up four votes. A few weeks later, on November 18, the BBWAA selected Jackie Robinson as the NL's Most Valuable Player. He captured 264 votes, 38 more than runner-up Stan Musial. Pee Wee Reese was fifth with 118 votes. Carl Furillo (sixth place, 68 votes) and Newcombe (ninth place, 55 votes) also finished in the top 10.

Robinson doubted he would play much longer. All that stress over the past few years had taken a toll. "Not that I have anything to worry about, but I'm jumpy and nervous all the time,"[90] he told reporters. About the MVP award, he said, "I'd have picked Pee Wee Reese as the most valuable player on our club."[91] Reese took to his role of captain much like a ship's captain takes to life on the high seas. "He took charge out there," Robinson said. "When Pee Wee told us where to play or gave some of us the devil, somehow it was easy to take. He just has a way about him of saying the right thing."[92]

11

"(Pee Wee Reese) will be the 1951 skipper"

Pee Wee Reese underwent hernia surgery on January 3 in Louisville. Dr. George Leachman performed the "highly successful"[1] 40-minute procedure and expected his patient to be ready for Opening Day on April 18. Reese had played with pain throughout the previous season. According to the *Daily News*, "the condition grew considerably worse throughout the campaign," probably one reason why he batted just .245 over his final 77 games. "It [the pain] was very bad during the World Series, so he went to see the doctor at home,"[2] Dottie Reese told reporters.

While Pee Wee recuperated, he could read the latest Cold War news. A jury in New York City convicted alleged spy Alger Hiss of perjury on January 21. Four days later, federal judge Henry Goddard sentenced Hiss, a former U.S. State Department official, to five years in prison. On January 31, President Harry Truman ordered scientists at the Atomic Energy Commission to develop a hydrogen bomb, just months after the Soviet Union detonated an atomic weapon. Truman made the decision according to what he called his "responsibility as commander-in-chief of the armed forces to see to it that our country is able to defend itself against any possible aggressor."[3] Physicists expected the world's first H-bomb to be ready for testing in one year and said it would be "two to 10 times as powerful as today's best plutonium bomb, itself the equivalent of nearly 200,000 tons of TNT."[4]

A piece of sports news also demanded the attention of Reese and everyone else in the Brooklyn baseball community. Supposedly, the Dodgers wanted to unload Jackie Robinson, possibly to the Braves. Gayle Talbot conceded that the idea seemed "preposterous." Even so, he added, Robinson's supposed demand for a $50,000 contract might be the impetus for a deal. "The Robinson-to-Boston report," Talbot wrote, "possibly owes its refusal to die to the well-known fact that Rickey never has paid that kind of money to ball players—that he will sell them rather than submit to the financial pain."[5] Rickey laughed at the scuttlebutt and insisted that he had no plans to part with his reigning MVP. The infielder agreed to a contract in late January, not for anything close to $50,000, but for $35,000. "Robinson will be the highest paid Dodger in my Brooklyn experience,"[6] Rickey said.

On February 3, Brooklyn inked the other half of its All-Star double-play combination. Reese signed a contract for $30,000, a salary that trailed only Robinson among Dodgers.[7] The shortstop pronounced himself a "new man" following surgery, although, he told *The Sporting News*, "I don't expect to jump in the first week at top speed."[8] Rickey joked that Reese need not worry. The Dodgers, after all, had a few other shortstops in camp. "I hope they're not too good,"[9] Reese replied.

Rumors about Reese taking over the managerial reins in Brooklyn served as a subplot to the season. Dick Young scoffed over reports that Clay Hopper or Walt Alston, two of the organization's minor league skippers, might get the Dodgers job whenever Shotton stepped down. Montreal Royals president Hector Racine had spread those rumors, which Young called "a nice-tasting mouthful of mush designed to make everybody feel good. Everybody except Reese, that is."[10] Reese, according to Young, hoped to lead the Dodgers someday. He refused to lobby for the job, though, because "that wouldn't be in good taste, and Reese is certainly ever the perfect gentleman." Shotton might wait a few years before hanging a "Gone Fishin'" sign on the front door of his Florida home, but, Young continued, "When that time comes, Rickey knows the fans would burn down Ebbets Field if anybody but Reese were named as manager, and the Brook players would help them."[11]

Rickey sounded confident about his latest Brooklyn ballclub. In January, he said "the 1950 series will be played right here"[12] at Ebbets Field. He added, "It is always anybody's pennant in January. It will not be a two-club race. I expect troubles from St. Louis, Boston, New York, Pittsburgh, and Philadelphia."[13] Phillies skipper Eddie Sawyer already had made a prediction of his own, back in October, on that final game of the season, following his squad's 9–7 loss to the Dodgers at Shibe Park. "We are going to win it all in 1950. Come back next year ready to win,"[14] Sawyer said, according to young outfielder Richie Ashburn.

Some writers labeled Philadelphia's club "the Whiz Kids." Harry Grayson, sports editor for the Newspaper Enterprise Association (NEA), may have coined the term. He liked what he saw from the youthful team. "He was probably the only national writer to pick us to win the pennant,"[15] Hall of Fame pitcher Robin Roberts wrote. Not every Philadelphia player felt so confident. "Although we knew we were talented, I am not sure many of us really thought we could beat the Dodgers or the Cardinals for the pennant over the long haul,"[16] according to Roberts.

Philadelphia had last hoisted a flag in 1915, a fact not altogether surprising. "The Phillies had been plagued for decades by what have been described as 'five and dime' ownerships,"[17] said Roberts. William H. Baker, a former New York City police commissioner, owned the team from 1913–1930. In December 1917, Baker sent Grover Cleveland "Pete" Alexander, one of baseball's top pitchers, plus starting catcher Bill Killefer, to the Cubs for pitcher Mike Prendergast, catcher William "Pickles" Dillhoefer, and $75,000. Alexander already had led the NL in wins five times and ERA three times. The *Philadelphia Inquirer* reported that "The Phillies lose their two most valuable players, who constitute the greatest battery in either major league today."[18] According to the *Inquirer*, "Mr. Baker, in parting with his only famous players, stated that he expected to be very severely criticized, but he was sure that time would show that the move was a wise one, even if Philadelphia was wrecked for the time being."[19]

Despite an ongoing battle with the bottle, Alexander retired in 1930 with 373 victories and a 2.56 ERA. Prendergast, meanwhile, pitched five seasons in the majors, compiled a 41–53 record, and won just 13 games in two seasons as a Phillie. Dillhoefer managed one hit in 11 at-bats in his lone year with Philadelphia (1918) and retired with a .223 batting average over 247 big-league games. Later, Baker admitted that he traded Alexander and Killefer because "I needed the money."[20] Killefer played four seasons in Chicago and 13 years altogether. He batted .238 lifetime and drove home 240 runs.

Robert Ruliph Morgan Carpenter, a business executive and graduate of the Massachusetts Institute of Technology, known by many as "Ruly," bought the Phillies in 1943 and began pouring money into player development. Scouts signed Roberts, Ashburn, Granville "Granny" Hamner, Del Ennis, Curt Simmons, and others. Midway through the 1948 season, Carpenter promoted Eddie Sawyer to Phillies manager. The Rhode Island native and one-time minor league outfielder had been leading the organization's International League affiliate in Toronto and had mentored many of the team's future stars. "We did things pretty fast," said Sawyer, who held a master's degree in biology from Cornell University in New York. "Our scouts signed a lot of good young players. Of course, we rushed them to the major leagues pretty quickly, but we made sure they had a good foundation."[21] The Phillies, 43–48 when Sawyer came on board, took a nosedive and went 23–40 the rest of the way. They rebounded the following season, going 81–73 and finishing above .500 for the first time since 1932.

Brooklyn and Philadelphia met on Opening Day at Shibe Park. The home team knocked around Newcombe, who retired just three batters and gave up four runs. Roberts went the distance and won, 9–1, before 29,074 fans. Reese finished the afternoon 0-for-4. The following day, in front of a much smaller crowd of 8,450, Brooklyn overcame an early 3–1 deficit and roared back to win, 7–5. Reese recorded a single and a double and scored the game's opening run after stealing second base and sprinting home on a Robinson hit. The Dodgers rolled out of the gate with a 7–2 record in April. Reese batted .316 over the month.

Fans tuning in on WMGM Radio and WOR-TV were hearing a new voice in the broadcast booth. Vincent Edward Scully, just 22 years old and less than one year out of Fordham University, began calling Dodgers games in 1950. The team hired him to replace Ernie Harwell, who left for the Giants. Scully grew up in the Washington Heights area of upper Manhattan and followed Brooklyn's rival as a young boy. He listened to Giants games on an oversized radio in the family living room and imagined himself as a great sportscaster.

Red Barber liked how Scully sounded on a college football radio broadcast that pitted Boston University against the University of Maryland, a game played on a frigid afternoon at Fenway Park. "I always had the dream of taking an untutored kid who showed some promise and of putting him on the air for what he was, a neophyte learning the trade," Barber wrote in *Rhubarb in the Catbird Seat*. "Scully was the perfect choice. He was a green pea, but he was a very appealing green pea. It was obvious that he had something on the ball."[22] Scully, a redhead like Barber, joined a booth that also included Connie Desmond, who, besides working Dodgers games, called New York Giants football and New York Knicks basketball.

Another man—burly, bespectacled, and decked out in a plus-size Dodgers uniform, with microphone in hand—also made his way onto the local baseball scene in

1950. A musician, actor, comedian, master of ceremonies, and former vaudevillian, Francis Joseph "Happy" Felton from Bellevue, Pennsylvania, outside of Pittsburgh, also had hosted some comedy and quiz shows. (He even took a turn as a violin soloist in the Pittsburgh Symphony Orchestra at the tender age of seven.)

In 1949, while on a tuna-fishing trek, Felton pitched his idea to then-Dodgers VP Walter O'Malley for a pre-game show aimed at young baseball fans. O'Malley, in turn, took Felton to see Branch Rickey. "Mr. Felton," Rickey said, "Your idea has merit."[23] The first episode of *Happy Felton's Knothole Gang* aired April 21 on WOR-TV. The 42-year-old Felton weighed 260 pounds, maybe more. He employed a big smile and hearty laugh to win over the kids. The show was an almost instant hit. The basic format went like this: Felton would introduce a young man from the area—usually a seventh- or eighth-grader—who wanted to work on his ball-playing skills. The kid would warm up for a few minutes, and Felton would ask a Brooklyn player to join the show and offer some batting or fielding tips. Columnist Red Smith gave the program a favorable review. "It is, in this book, a solid show because it brings kids into the ballpark; it sells baseball," he wrote.

Most copies of *Happy Felton's Knothole Gang* have been lost through the years. At least one exists, from 1956. In this episode, a young ballplayer from Jersey City named Ronald Ferraris peppers Reese with several questions, including one on how to bunt for both a sacrifice and base hit. Reese, with bat in hand, demonstrates both techniques. He was passing on some tips from Yankees shortstop Phil Rizzuto, "the best bunter I ever saw in baseball." When trying to bunt for a hit, Reese said, "All he does is, and I've talked to him quite about it and I do it, I wait as long as I possibly can. When the pitcher lets the ball go, I drop this [right] foot back. The bat goes down in the same motion." If sacrificing, "I don't give myself up. I just wait 'til the last minute, just like I'm going to hit the ball. The main thing is to get the big part of the bat in front of you. … When you get ready to bunt the ball, just act like you're going to catch it with the bat."[24]

Carl Erskine recalled that players were rewarded with a $50 check for appearing on *Happy Felton's Knothole Gang*. "And we used to joke with Pee Wee about all the money he made on that show. The kids would pick Pee Wee all the time. He was so popular. Part of it was that name. Pee Wee. It was just kind of magical to the kids."[25]

On May 4, Reese added something new to his baseball resume. An umpire gave him the heave-ho. It happened in the 1,000th game of his career, at Wrigley Field, with the Dodgers holding a comfortable 4–0 lead. Reese had two hits, a single in the first inning and a double in the third. It hardly seemed like a day to get sore. But in the fifth, he took a three-and-two pitch for strike three. He whirled around and exchanged unpleasantries with home-plate umpire Babe Pinelli, a former third baseman for the White Sox, Tigers, and Reds. No cursing or anything. He did, however, flip his bat high into the air in a fit of anger. That was enough for Pinelli to toss Reese, who turned around and said, "Well, I hope you're satisfied. This is my thousandth game, and I've never been tossed out before."[26]

Pinelli explained that tossing a bat meant an automatic ejection. Dick Young wrote in his own inimitable style, "Just when everybody was expecting Pee Wee Reese to sprout wings, and fly away, he turned out to be human after all."[27] As Reese headed to the showers, Clyde Sukeworth, now serving as a Brooklyn coach, ran out to argue with Pinelli. Reese waved him off. "Let it be, Sukey," he advised. "It's the first time. Maybe it makes me a man."[28] The Dodgers won, 10–2, in front of only 7,459 fans.

Fresh off that milestone, Pee Wee Reese reached another one just a few days later. On May 8, "the scrappy Brooklyn captain"[29] collected the 1,000th hit of his career, a single in the third inning off Pirates starter Cliff Chambers at Forbes Field. The base knock to center field scored Duke Snider, who led off that frame with a base hit. Brooklyn won, 7–5, and improved to 11–6.

The Dodgers swept a doubleheader May 20 against Pittsburgh. Gil Hodges' two-run double in the eighth inning of the opening tilt gave the Dodgers a 3–2, come-from-behind win. In the second half of that twin bill, Reese injured himself while trying to steal second base. Harold Burr wrote that Reese "caught his spikes in the bag and suffered his sprain in the right ankle."[30] Eddie Miksis and Billy Cox shared shortstop duties over the next couple of weeks as Reese recuperated. The duo scored just five runs in 13 games. Reese made it home safely 132 times in 1949, Joe King reminded readers, and drew 116 walks. "There is none other on the squad who can hold the No. 1 spot where run production should start,"[31] he wrote. Pee Wee Reese returned to action June 4 against Chicago.

Later that month, the Dodgers once again picked on the Pirates. They collected 19 hits and beat up Pittsburgh, 15–3, on June 23. An eight-run seventh inning broke open the game. Carl Furillo capped off the frame with a three-run homer. Reese contributed a double, single, RBI, and run scored. The following day, the hard hitting continued. Brooklyn led, 19–12, as the clock struck 11:59 p.m. According to the Saturday baseball rule, umpires were forced to halt the game. (When the teams picked up on August 1, the Dodgers scored two more times and won, 21–12. They collected 25 hits, with Robinson, Campanella, and Furillo getting four apiece. Reese added two singles, drove in one run, and scored three times.)

Just a few weeks earlier, President Truman ordered U.S. air and sea forces into South Korea following an invasion from the North. According to a wire-service report, U.S. fighter jets shot down four North Korea planes near Seoul on June 26, "where a South Korean counter-offensive hurled the Communist invaders back from the gates of the capital."[32] On June 30, Truman ordered a naval blockade of the Korean peninsula and authorized General of the Army Douglas MacArthur to send ground troops into the fray. Marine troops entered the battle a few days later.[33]

An average of 15,300 fans attended Dodgers games in 1950, a fair drop-off from 1949 although still runner-up to Philadelphia. Not too long ago, most fans took the trolley or walked to Ebbets Field from their house or apartment in the borough. Now, more and more arrived in cars from nearby suburbs. Many lived in a place called Levittown, a planned housing development built on old potato farms in Nassau County, Long Island, not far from the Brooklyn ballpark and fully imagined by William J. Levitt, president of Levitt & Sons. A Navy Seabee during World War II, Levitt knew how to build things fast. His team could assemble a house in one day. "The houses were simple, unpretentious, and most importantly to its inhabitants, affordable to both white and blue-collar workers,"[34] Crystal Galyean wrote. Levitt, a Brooklyn native, called his product "the best house in the U.S."[35] In the fervor of the day, Levitt further declared, "No man who owns his own home and lot can be a Communist. He has too much to do."[36]

Dodgers fans of all political persuasions grimaced as their team dropped to third place following a 6–4 loss to the Phillies on July 1. Just a few days later, Brooklyn fell to fourth, although just a handful of games out of the top spot. The Dodgers played 15–14 baseball in July, not nearly as good as the Phillies, who won 22 games and lost 13.

Following a stretch of four straight losses in early August, including three by one run, Branch Rickey began to fume. He "blasted his players mercilessly" at the Brooklyn-Against-the-World sandlot dinner, held August 9 at the Hotel St. George. "The Dodgers of a year ago were the result of this organization when the players sweated and toiled," the Mahatma preached. "The Dodgers of 1950 are what is left of a team with complete satiety and where complacency sets in. … I won't apologize if the Dodgers don't win. You can make excuses, but excuses or apologies never do any good."[37] Several Brooklyn players attended this event. All of them left before Rickey stepped to the podium. Their early departure rankled the team executive. "Next year," Rickey said, "when I post a note on the bulletin board inviting the team to attend this dinner, I will add a footnote about staying until the end."[38]

Less than two weeks later, the Bums swept a doubleheader against the Giants and moved into second place. They withstood a three-run rally in the eighth inning and won the first game, 8–6. Reese, batting leadoff, went 2-for-3 with a walk and scored twice. He crossed home plate two more times in the nightcap as Brooklyn won, 5–1. Jim McCulley wrote about "the sad tears at the Polo Grounds," which "reflected what could be a Dodger resurgence toward the top of the NL."[39]

Gil Hodges enjoyed the game of his life on August 31 in a 19–3 shellacking of the Braves in Boston. Warren Spahn lasted just two innings and gave up five runs on seven hits. Hodges belted four home runs and drove in nine runs. He went 5-for-6 and scored five times. Reese contributed two hits and three RBI in a 19-hit Brooklyn attack. Hodges hit his long balls in the second, third, sixth, and eighth innings. "Fast ball, curveball, fast ball, curve,"[40] Hodges said afterward, explaining the pitches that he ripped for each round-tripper. No right-handed batter in the 20th century had hit four home runs in one game.[41] "Did I think I was going to hit the fourth one?" the slugging first baseman asked a reporter. "I didn't think I'd even hit three."[42]

He was the Dodgers' big, strong Marine. Born April 4, 1924, in Princeton, Indiana, Gilbert Raymond Hodges grew up the son of a coal miner, Charles, and a homemaker, Irene. He played four sports at Petersburg High School and enrolled at St. Joseph's College in Rensselaer, Indiana, on an athletic scholarship, opting for that over a minor league contract in the Tigers organization. One year later, the Dodgers signed him to a deal. He made his big league debut in the final game of the 1943 season. Just a few weeks later, Hodges joined the Marine Corps and left for Hawaii. He landed at Tinian and later earned a bronze star for his actions at Okinawa. Reports about Hodges' heroics circulated back in the United States. "We kept hearing about this big guy from Indiana who killed [Japanese] with his bare hands,"[43] Don Hoak recalled.

The soft-spoken, hard-hitting first baseman married a Brooklyn girl, Joan

Lombardi, on December 26, 1948, and made his year-round home in the borough. Fans respected Hodges so much they didn't boo him, not even when he fell into the most epic of slumps on baseball's biggest stage in October of 1952. "Not getting booed at Ebbets Field was an amazing thing," Clem Labine said. "Those fans knew their baseball, and Gil was the only player I can remember whom the fans never, I mean, never booed."[44]

At least a few boo birds sang at Ebbets Field in the late summer. The Dodgers lost, 9–7, to the Cubs on September 18 and dropped to nine games behind the first-place Phillies. Preacher Roe looked terrible in this one. He gave up seven runs in 6⅔ innings and walked eight. His record fell to 18–11. The Dodgers were muddling their way toward the end of the season. Then they swept a four-game series from the last-place Pirates and boarded a train bound for Philadelphia. Maybe it wasn't all over yet.

Don Newcombe and Robin Roberts hooked up September 23 at Shibe Park. Roberts was putting together the first big year in a Hall of Fame career that would produce 286 victories and six 20-win seasons. Ralph Kiner said that Roberts, from Springfield, Illinois, threw the best fastball he ever saw. Red Schoendienst said Roberts' heater "seemed to skid across the strike zone as though it were on a sheet of ice."[45]

The Dodgers, though, touched up Roberts for three runs in the third inning and won, 3–2. Reese singled in the third and in the eighth. The next day's game belonged to Erv Palica, who hit a grand slam in the sixth inning off Bubba Church and tossed a "brilliant"[46] two-hit shutout, all part of an 11–0 Dodgers victory. Brooklyn now trailed the Phillies by five games but with just 11 to go. On the plus side, the Brooks had completed their road schedule. They would play the rest of their games at Ebbets Field.

The homestand began September 25 with a three-game set against the Giants. Brooklyn won the opener, 3–2, thanks in large part to a two-run homer by Reese and a complete-game effort by Roe. Brooklyn lost the second game, 4–3, but won the following day, 8–4. Philadelphia, meanwhile, won a three-game series against the Braves in Boston and maintained a five-game lead. The Phillies had six games left to play. The Dodgers were down to eight, including six against the Braves.

Brooklyn and Boston split the first four games in the set, both doubleheaders. The teams met for a final twin bill on September 29, and Brooklyn got the sweep it needed. The Dodgers roared back from a 5–2 deficit in the first game and won, 7–5. Brooklyn took the second game, 7–6. Roy Campanella blasted his 30th homer and ripped an RBI double.

Baseball's schedule makers ended the year on a dandy note. The Dodgers, with an 88–64 record, closed out the season with two games against the Phillies. Brooklyn could set up a playoff by winning both. The hard-throwing Palica matched up in the first game against Bob Miller, a 6-foot-3-inch right-hander equipped with "a deceiving fastball, sweeping curve, and baffling sinker."[47] Brooklyn broke out on top, 4–0, in the fifth inning. Cal Abrams singled home Billy Cox for the first run. Reese followed with a triple that ended Miller's day. Eddie Sawyer brought in Jim Konstanty to provide some relief.

The Phillies had counted on Konstanty all season. The 33-year-old from Arcade, New York, had toiled for several seasons in the minor leagues and taught gym classes in the winter. He found his pitch in the palm ball, a type of change-up, and enjoyed a solid year in 1949, winning nine games and saving seven with a 3.25 ERA. He pitched even better in 1950. Going into that final game, he sported a 2.36 ERA to go with 16 wins and what would be 19 saves using today's criteria.

"I have never seen him get hit real hard," Sawyer said. "He is murder to good hitters."[48] The game on September 30 marked his 74th appearance. Konstanty, that year's MVP Award winner in the National League, had logged nearly 150 innings. "I had to pitch Konstanty an awful lot, and they were getting used to him and he was wearing down a little," Sawyer said. "But he always wanted that ball. He literally wanted to pitch every day."[49] Duke Snider stepped to the plate and, after fouling off one pitch, hammered a Konstanty offering "over the chicken wire in right field and into Bedford Ave."[50]

The Phillies answered by scoring three runs in the top of the sixth inning. With two runners on base, Dick Sisler (acquired from St. Louis in early 1948) looped a single to center field. Snider "unwisely refused to play it safe" and "came tearing in for a shoestring catch." Unfortunately, Harold Burr continued, "all he accomplished was to stand on his head, spikes wildly waving, while the ball rolled through the fence." Erv Palica took the throw from the outfield, but in continuing this mess of a play, fired wildly to third base, toward the stands. In all the excitement, "a feminine fan reached over the rail and picked up the ball." The umpires ruled fan interference and awarded Sisler home plate.[51]

Roy Campanella iced the game with a three-run homer in the eighth inning off Konstanty. Burr told fans the next day, "The fabulous Dodgers continued to chase the Whiz Kids up an alley at Ebbets Field…. It's becoming the most gruesome fairy tale a bunch of kids ever listened to and the Whiz Kids from Philadelphia didn't sleep to soundly last night, stuffing the corners of hotel pillows in their mouths to keep from screaming and hiding under their bedclothes."[52]

More than 35,000 fans filled Ebbets Field on the final game of the year. One unidentified man looked around the packed ballpark. The Dodgers had drawn several crowds of fewer than 10,000 during this exciting stretch, including just 2,051 on September 18 and 1,011 on September 20. "Look at you Brooklyn fans today," he said. "Where were you the last ten days? What wuz ya—resurrected or something?"[53] Dodgers business manager Jack Collins looked forward to the season's final day. "It's just the greatest fight in the history of baseball," he declared. "I'm confident we'll win and, more important, the team is confident."[54]

Appropriately, the big game pitted two aces, Roberts and Newcombe. Neither pitcher gave up a run through the first five innings. Newcombe allowed three singles. Roberts walked Cal Abrams in the first inning and allowed a line-drive double to Reese in the fourth. Both teams pushed across a run in the sixth inning. Philadelphia scored on a Willie Jones RBI single in the top half. In the bottom half, Reese hit the most unusual of home runs.

Reese knocked a lazy fly ball that stopped short of clearing the right-field fence. The ball stuck in the screen and dropped to a narrow ledge below, a home run according to that year's ground rules. Roger Kahn explained some of the nuances of Ebbets Field in *The Era*: "The right field wall in Brooklyn angled back for about eight feet, then rose vertically to a point fifteen feet high, where it was topped off by a stiff screen that went forty feet into the air. Right field in Brooklyn wasn't deep—297 feet down the line and 344 in right-center—but it was high."[55]

Stan Baumgartner of the *Philadelphia Inquirer* wrote that it looked, at least for an instant, like Reese's drive might clear the fence. "Instead," the ball "dropped dead on the wire and remained on the ledge."[56] Reese raced around the bases. Frank Dascoli, the second-base umpire, told him to slow down. "The ball is stuck," he said. Reese kept going at full speed. "I knew the ground rules," he said later. "If that ball started rolling down the right field wall, it was in play."[57] The ball, though, stayed steady. Richie Ashburn said, "Pee Wee ran around the bases, laughing at his good fortune."[58] Carl Lundquist, covering the game for the United Press, called the hit "a crazy homer."[59]

Neither team mustered a run over the next three innings. Brooklyn came the closest. Cal Abrams walked to lead off the ninth. Reese lined a single, and Snider hit a Roberts pitch into center field. Ashburn scooped up the ball as Abrams rounded third. Brooklyn third-base coach Milt Stock waved him home. Ashburn, not known for possessing a strong throwing arm, threw a dart to catcher Stan Lopata and nailed Abrams at the plate. Later, Burt Shotton defended his coach's decision. "Stock played it right," the manager insisted. "That's the sort of set-up when you send in the big run." The Dodgers, though, would have had the bases loaded with nobody out if Stock had held Abrams. "We still had runners on second and third with one out and our big hitters coming up,"[60] Shotton pointed out. In fact, Roberts gave Jackie Robinson a free pass to load the bases and set up a possible double play. Carl Furillo and Gil Hodges flied out to end the threat. Stock saw it this way: "Reese was coming around fast, and if I had held up Abrams, there might have been a jam at third base." For his part, Abrams, with hindsight in his favor, said, "I think they should have held me at third."[61]

Roberts and Eddie Waitkus singled to open the Phillies' half of the 10th. Dick Sisler batted after Ashburn grounded out. Newcombe, still in the game, tried to keep the ball inside but left one pitch over the plate. Sisler hit a long fly ball the opposite way, to left field. "I was past first base when I saw that it was a home run," Sisler said. "Boy, that was the greatest feeling in the world. That was the greatest thrill I ever had in baseball."[62]

The Dodgers failed to launch a rally of any sort in the bottom half of the inning. Tommy Brown ended the game—and the Brooklyn season—by popping out to Waitkus at first base. Ten-year-old Dodgers fan and Brooklyn resident Hank Lieberman watched from a box seat near the home team's dugout. Years later, he spoke about his "vivid memory" of watching another boy retrieve Reese's home run from that spot on the ledge. After the game, the boy leaned into the dugout and tried to give the ball to Reese. The kid was yelling, "but," Lieberman rightly recalled, "the Dodgers had lost. . ."my recollection is Reese didn't even look up."[63] Minutes later, Brooklyn players sat "slumped down in front of their dressing staffs after the game, staring at the floor."[64] Shotton told the press, "They had to be a good team to beat us. This will be the best team the Dodgers come up with for the next 50 years."[65]

Young Dodgers fans seemed to flock to Reese. Here, the Brooklyn shortstop offers a few tips on how to play better baseball (National Baseball Hall of Fame Library, Cooperstown, New York).

Once again, Brooklyn's offense dominated the National League leaderboard. The Dodgers topped the circuit with 847 runs scored, 62 more than the next most powerful offense, the Braves. They led the NL in home runs (194), batting average (.272), on-base percentage (.349), and slugging percentage (.444). Three Dodgers hit more than 30 homers, led by Hodges with 32. Campanella and Snider belted 31. Robinson topped the regulars with a .328 batting average, followed by Snider at .321 and Furillo at .305. On the mound, both Newcombe and Roe won 19 games. Newcombe threw 20 complete games and tossed four shutouts.

Reese batted .260 with a .369 on-base percentage. He hit 11 home runs, had 52 RBI, scored 97 runs, and stole 17 bases. He did fall to fifth place among NL shortstops in putouts (282) after leading the circuit the past two seasons. Joe King more than hinted that Reese had lost a step in the field. "Robinson is a peerless double-play man, an artist at the feat," King wrote. "But he is no longer protected in some measure on his right his year, with Pee Wee Reese no longer a genius a short. The captain is still a classic performer in the short field but does not execute the miracle plays of old."[66]

A fabulous era in Brooklyn baseball history ended on October 26. Branch Rickey resigned after directing a letter to the team's board of directors. He wrote in part, "The past eight years of my association with you have been full of interest and challenge."[67] Rickey sold his share in the team for just over $1 million.[68] On his final day as a Dodgers employee, Rickey spoke to the assembled press at the Hotel Bossert in downtown Brooklyn. Tommy Holmes described him as "almost radiant." Rickey called Walter O'Malley, the team's new president, "a man of youth, courage, enterprise and desire." O'Malley, in turn, said, "I have developed the warmest possible feelings of affection for Mr. Rickey as a person."[69]

In the story of the Brooklyn Dodgers, Walter Francis O'Malley remains, at least for some, the villain of the piece. Born on October 9, 1903, in the Bronx, he grew up the son of Edwin and Alma O'Malley. Edwin worked in the dry-goods business and fostered political connections in the local Democratic party. Walter attended prep school at the pricey Culver Academy in Indiana and graduated in 1926 from the University of Pennsylvania, where fellow students elected him class president in his junior and senior years. He earned a law degree from Fordham University and joined the Dodgers in the winter of 1943–1944 as team attorney. O'Malley, a "thorough behind the scenes operator,"[70] often opposed Rickey, usually over matters of finance. Rickey, for instance, wanted to present a new Studebaker car to every player and coach following the 1946 season. O'Malley squawked so much that Rickey cancelled the order.[71] Near the end of Rickey's time in Brooklyn, he could see the future. "I'm doomed,"[72] he said. Just a couple of days before his resignation, he said, "I'd prefer to stay. I'll be 69 years old in December. My tentacles have struck deep down in Flatbush. I've enjoyed myself. Everybody has been kind to me."[73]

O'Malley requires a little more description. Jowls hung from his face, "so heavy," according to one writer, "they swallowed his chin."[74] He kept his dark hair oiled and combed straight back. His fashion sense directed him toward dark, double-breasted suits and frameless glasses. Of stout frame, he preferred talking and making deals to strenuous exercise. The tightly built Durocher took notice of O'Malley's girth and labeled him "whale belly."[75] O'Malley loved cigars and smoked cigarettes from a holder. "His first act upon rising was to light a cigarette," Michael Shapiro wrote. Next, O'Malley, "a devout Catholic," promptly "dropped to his knees and said his morning prayers."[76] He and his wife, Kay, lived in Amityville on Long Island, near the beach, and liked to garden. They built a hothouse on the property and grew orchids. The couple had two children, a daughter, Terry, and a son, Peter. A family man, O'Malley "always tried to be home for dinner."[77]

A few weeks after the Yankees swept Philadelphia in the World Series, some reporters speculated that Pee Wee Reese's managerial career might begin the following spring, assuming the team did not retain Burt Shotton. O'Malley said nothing to squash these rumors. "I will have to be shown the hard way that there is a job that can't be filled by a man in our organization,"[78] O'Malley said.

Back in May, Jimmy Powers, in his popular newspaper column "The Powerhouse," wrote that most fans would be "shocked at the lack of prospective skippers" among the 400 or so big leaguers. He mentioned Reese as one of the few strong candidates. "Pee Wee is destined to take over the Flock when Shotton retires, which may be sooner than anyone thinks.... Pee Wee is well liked by the players. That is half the battle in succeeding as a big-league mentor or a straw boss on a ditch-digging gang."[79]

AP writer Fred Hayden reported on some recent changes in the Brooklyn front office, such as the appointments of Buzzie Bavasi and Fresco Thompson to vice-presidential roles. According to Hayden, "the hottest tip seems to be that Dodgers' Captain and veteran shortstop Harold (Pee Wee) Reese will be the 1951 skipper."[80] But did Reese even want the job? He appeared to be waffling, just like when Rickey asked him about accepting the captain's role one year earlier. "I'm not sure I'd take it if it was offered to me,"[81] he confessed.

The *Daily News* ran a graphic on November 4, titled "Flatbush Futurity Field," that handicapped a group of potential Brooklyn skippers. Press room oddsmakers made Clyde Sukeworth and "classy maiden"[82] Reese the co-favorites at 5–2. Other names on the list included Dixie Walker at 4–1, Burt Shotton at 8–1, and Clay Hopper and Bobby Bragan at 10–1. Walter Alston trailed the pack at 30–1 ("No chance," according to the newspaper).[83]

12

"I don't believe it"

Bobby Thomson stepped into the batter's box on a warm, gray afternoon at the Polo Grounds. The temperature hovered in the upper 70s. Many New Yorkers expected some rain. That morning, local newspapers devoted much of their front-page space to stories about the big game, the one going on right now in upper Manhattan, near a place called Coogan's Bluff, next to the Harlem River. "This is an unprecedented and almost unbelievable situation, but it has happened,"[1] Tommy Holmes wrote in the *Eagle*. It was Wednesday, October 3, 1951.

Thomson peered toward the mound at Ralph Branca, just summoned into this autumn thriller. Two runners stood on base. One batter was out. Thomson and the Giants trailed the Dodgers, 4–2. Fans at the half-filled ballpark waited for the next pitch, in the bottom of the ninth inning of the 157th game of the season, the National League pennant at stake.

Pee Wee Reese watched the action unfold from his spot at shortstop. Most likely, he looked over at Clint Hartung, pinch-running for Don Mueller, at third base, and Whitey Lockman, standing off second base. He probably glanced at Jackie Robinson, to his left, and Billy Cox, just to his right. Branca waited for catcher Rube Walker, acquired just a few months earlier and playing in place of the injured Roy Campanella, to give the sign.

How did it even get to this point? The Giants waited until June 9 to climb above the .500 mark for good. The Dodgers went to bed on the evening of August 11 with a 13-game lead.[2] Now, these two teams were playing for a chance to meet the Yankees in the World Series. The Yanks had fought off a tough Indians squad and won the AL flag by five games. Duke Snider put it this way in *The Duke of Flatbush*: "An injury here, a short slump there, and all of a sudden the machine that had been breezing toward a championship is beginning to cough and sputter. If another team gets hot at that same time, the whole world can turn upside down." In 1951, Snider lamented, "that's what happened."[3]

In *The Home Run Heard 'Round the World*, Ray Robinson called Reese "the last link to the storied Brooklyn teams of pre–World War II, with those colorful personalities who produced more anecdotes than victories." Reese never played with Babe Herman or Dazzy Vance, Robinson conceded, "but they were all somehow connected with Reese—and you couldn't really say that about any of the other Dodger stars of the fifties." Reese was now, Robinson asserted, "the glue of the Dodgers, the man who made the plays every day like clockwork."[4]

He was not, however, the team's new manager. In late November, O'Malley replaced Burt Shotton with Chuck Dressen, the former Brooklyn third-base coach. Shotton was tied too closely to the old regime. He and Branch Rickey were friends. The two even went on a hunting trip to Virginia over the off-season. "This action indicated that the skipper had remained in Rickey's corner,"[5] Rob Edelman argued in his SABR biography of Shotton.

The 57-year-old Dressen, from Decatur, Illinois, stood 5-foot-5 and weighed less than 150 pounds. As a young man, he thought about becoming a horse jockey. He later turned to baseball (and, yes, football), and played eight seasons in the major leagues, mostly as a third baseman for the Reds. He batted .272 lifetime and hit 11 home runs before embarking on a managerial career. Dressen led Cincy for parts of four seasons and compiled a 214–282 mark. The club fired him with about a month left in the 1937 campaign.

Dressen spent the 1938 season as skipper of the Nashville Vols, the Dodgers' affiliate in the Southern Association. Larry MacPhail added him to the Brooklyn staff the following season and brought him to the Yankees in 1946. Two years later, following MacPhail's retirement, Yankees general manager George Weiss let go of the high-spirited coach, labeling him as not "Yankee material."[6] Dressen took over as the Oakland Oaks manager, a job that opened up after Weiss summoned Casey Stengel to the Bronx. Under Dressen, Oakland took second place in 1949 and won the PCL pennant in 1950.

Walter O'Malley told reporters, "When Chuck left us for a similar job with the Yankees, I did my best to stop him. When I realized I could do nothing about keeping him in Brooklyn, I told him I'd get him back when I was in position to."[7] Always confident that he could get his team out of a jam, Dressen liked to tell players, "Just stay close. I'll think of something."[8]

Dressen said the Dodgers boasted "good strength up the middle, with the exception of pitching. We are strong in catching, first, second, and shortstop and in centerfield." The new skipper, without elaborating, told the press, "I'll be running the training camp my way, which I understand is completely different from the Branch Rickey system." He added, "I don't know how the team was handled last year under Burt Shotton, and I don't know anything about a curfew—yet. But you bet we'll have a hustling club. We have a lot of good talent and I believe if the pitchers come through, we will be in the thick of the pennant race."[9]

Pee Wee Reese signed a contract for $30,000 in January[10] and reported to camp in February at just north of 175 pounds. He felt completely healed from the hernia surgery that bothered him throughout the previous season. "I had no problem whatever during the winter with my legs," he said. He played some golf, "but not too often, and not as often as I used to. I never had any bother all winter. I don't think I'll have any trouble doing what I am supposed to do."[11] Maybe he really could go on forever. At one point, he mashed three homers in a five-game span down in Florida. His defense, shaky at times the previous season, looked improved. He was ranging all over the infield and "gobbling up grounders." Reese, "taken more for granted than the air you breathe," had, Dick Young wrote, "never looked better."[12]

Brooklyn began the regular season April 17 at home against Philadelphia.

Dressen penciled in Hodges at first base, Robinson at second, Reese at short, and the rookie Everett "Rocky" Bridges at third base in place of Billy Cox. Don Thompson, Duke Snider, and Carl Furillo started in the outfield, from left to right. The Dodgers had acquired Thompson from the Braves organization after the 1949 season. In 1950, the Swepsonville, North Carolina, native led Montreal with 24 home runs, 87 RBI, and a .311 batting average. Roy Campanella took his usual spot behind home plate, and Carl Erskine walked to the mound for the first of his four career Opening Day assignments. Philadelphia scored three runs in the first two innings and won, 5–2, behind Robin Roberts. Reese, batting seventh, singled and walked. The game attracted 19,217 fans. Tommy Holmes called it a "cold and raw" day, one typical of major-league openers. "It is always a gray day with winds that seem to generate in the general vicinity of the Arctic Circle," he wrote. "The sun, when it appears at all, flashes only briefly and then runs away and hides as though chased by the special police."[13]

The Dodgers withstood those early brisk winds and won eight of 13 games in April. (Billy Cox regained his starting job the second week of the season. Bridges spent much of the campaign as a solid utility man.) Reese picked up where he left off in spring and enjoyed five two-hit games over the season's opening month. He boasted a .359 batting average going into May, with a .510 on-base percentage. Despite that hot start, some writers had taken to calling the 31-year-old an "old man" on the baseball diamond, much to the shortstop's chagrin. "Old man!" Reese barked. "Shucks, I'm almost a year younger than Phil Rizzuto of the Yankees, and I don't hear anybody calling him an old man."[14]

The Giants, meanwhile, began the season on a woeful note. They lost 12 of their first 14 games. It certainly was not the start they had envisioned. Back in spring training, Leo Durocher turned his ambitious thoughts toward taking a pennant. He told reporters in St. Petersburg, Florida, "I got my team now. We're going to win it."[15] He kept his cool as the losses mounted. Following one game, he told reporters, "We have too many pros, standouts such as Whitey Lockman, Bobby Thomson, Alvin Dark, Eddie Stanky (traded, along with Dark, by the Braves to the Giants on December 14, 1949), and others, not to get untracked soon."[16]

Brooklyn knocked off New York in five of the teams' first six meetings. That included a three-game sweep from April 20–22 at the Polo Grounds. Campanella smashed a three-run homer in the opener, and Robinson drove home three runs in the second game. New York grabbed a 3–1 lead in the finale before Brooklyn charged back with solo runs in the eighth, ninth, and tenth innings off Sal Maglie, an ornery 6-foot-2-inch right-hander with a heavy beard and a penchant for hurling high, inside fastballs. (Maglie, in time, earned a nickname "The Barber." Some batters swore that his close, brisk pitches nearly gave their chins a shave.) Reese singled in the tying run. Furillo hit the game-winning homer. Later in the month, the Dodgers won two of three games against the Giants at Ebbets Field. Reese collected six hits in nine at-bats, going 2-for-3 each day.

Reese ripped his first home run on May 6 against the Cardinals. It was the fourth grand slam of his career. He clubbed it in the seventh inning off Cloyd Boyer, far over the center field fence at Ebbets Field to put Brooklyn ahead, 7–5. Dodgers relievers squandered the lead and surrendered six runs in the top of the eighth as St. Louis won, 11–7. Dick Young described it as "a screwy sort of game."[17] Just how screwy? Well, Brooklyn not only blew a big lead, but Stan Musial, the usual Dodgers-killer, made two outs in that big eighth inning while his teammates handled the heavy hitting. He popped out to lead off the frame and also struck out. Of course, Stan the Man doubled and tripled in two of his three other at-bats.

The Dodgers' long run with at least a share of first place began May 13. They beat the first-place Braves, 12–6, that day in Boston. Furillo drove home four runs, and Snider brought in three. Reese hit a trio of singles, scored three times, and drove home a run. One week later, the Dodgers swept a doubleheader from the Reds at Crosley Field. They won the opener, 10–3. Reese went 2-for-4 with two RBI. Brooklyn took the night-cap, 14–4. Reese notched two more hits and drove in four run.

The violent harassment of Jackie Robinson continued. Several death threats in writing were leveled at him during the Reds series. Robinson said he was "a little bit concerned" but doubted that a potential shooter would warn him in advance. Even so, police kept a close eye on the crowd and the tall buildings overlooking Crosley Field. Robinson acknowledged, "When I came to the plate for the first time today, it was a little bit uncomfortable." Later, he made a few jokes about the hateful correspondence. "I told the boys not to get to close to me on the field, and Pee Wee said he was going to take a step or two backward before throwing to me on a double play."[18] Reese offered his own darkly comical suggestion. "I think we should all wear 42. Then they will have a shooting gallery."[19] The Dodgers left Ohio with a mark of 18–13.

On May 25, a highly touted prospect joined the Giants at Shibe Park in Philadelphia. Willie Howard Mays, Jr., from Westfield, Alabama, outside Birmingham, could do it all. The one-time star for the local Black Barons club hit for average, hit for power, stole bases, threw darts from his spot in center field, and made spectacular catches. He was batting a ridiculous .477 (71-for-149) for the Minneapolis Millers of the American Association. Mays, though, started his big-league career by making 12 straight outs. He followed that by hitting a home run off Warren Spahn before plunging into another slump. His batting average slipped to a worse-than-woeful .038. During that spell, Durocher spotted his protégé weeping in the locker room. Mays begged Durocher to send him back to the minors. "I knew I couldn't hit big-league pitching," he said. Durocher reassured Mays, "You are my center fielder." He also told Mays to quit crying.[20]

The Dodgers made a blockbuster trade with the Cubs on June 15. Eight players changed uniforms. Brooklyn acquired outfielder Andy Pafko, pitcher Johnny Schmitz, infielder Wayne Terwilliger, and Rube Walker in exchange for Gene Hermanski, Eddie Miksis, Bruce Edwards and Joe Hatten. "From the Dodger viewpoint, Pafko is the key man in the deal," Dick Young wrote. "Pafko is fleet of foot, a sure-handed ballhawk, and the possessor of a powerful arm." He also could hit pitches a long way. The 30-year-old slugger already had ripped 12 home runs in 49 games after smashing 36 in 1950. Pafko would take over for Hermanski in left field. (Thompson lost his starting job early in the season and was batting .190 when the trade was made. Hermanski had a .250 average with just one home run.) Young wrote, "The Brooks now possess by far the finest outfield in baseball."[21] Reese recalled, "When we got

Pafko, I can remember some of the opposing players saying, 'My God, you guys are way out in front and you pick up a guy like Andy Pafko. Now, you're going to win it by 30 games."[22]

Chuck Dressen proclaimed the current Dodgers to be Brooklyn's all-time best. "When we won the pennant in 1941, everyone said that was the greatest club Brooklyn ever had," he said. But, he insisted, "This is a better club than the '41 team." He offered a position-by-position breakdown of the two teams. He preferred the newer model at six of nine spots, choosing the 1941 squad only at third base (Lavagetto over Cox), in center field (Reiser over Snider, although, Dressen said, Snider "is getting better all the time.") and in the pitching department. ("We have been winning with seven pitchers. In 1941, all 10 pitchers were major leaguers.") Reese was the lone holdover. Dressen acknowledged that the Pee Wee Reese of 1941 was younger and faster, but "he wasn't the smart competitor then that he is today. Nor was he anything near the .300 batter he is this season."[23]

Reese enjoyed one of the best months of his career in July. He batted .356 (42-for-118) with six home runs and 26 RBI. His hit total also included five doubles and three triples. He scored 23 runs and stole six bases. Reese began his offensive binge right away. On the first day of the month, Brooklyn knocked off Philadelphia, 2–0, at Ebbets Field. With two outs and two runners on base, Reese tripled into right field, bringing home the only runs of the game. The next day, he smacked three hits and scored three times in a 6–1 win against the Braves. On July 16, he hit a three-run homer in an 11–2 shellacking of Cincinnati.

The Sporting News, in its August 8 edition, hailed the 1951 Dodgers as "the finest baseball club since the pre-war Yankees and Cardinals" and "probably the most valuable team in history." The baseball weekly estimated the combined value of the Brooklyn players to be approximately $3 million. One source said that Reese, Robinson, and Campanella might bring $200,000 each if put up for sale. Furillo and Roe could fetch $150,000. "The age of players does affect the price," the source said. "A Reese, a Robinson, a Roe, does not have long expectancy of star rating, but the experience and poise such as man has through the stress and strain of flag races makes him most desirable to a contender." Hodges might net the Dodgers as much as $300,000. "He doesn't hurt easily, he is always in A-1 condition," said *TSN*. "He is even-tempered and consistent, and altogether he is a guy you know will help you, on a pennant level for years."[24]

The Dodgers were running away from the competition. They completed a three-game sweep of the Giants on August 9 and jumped in front by 12½ games. Reese drove home three runs in the series and scored twice. During a celebration afterward, several players broke out in song. "Roll out the barrel. … We got the Giants on the run."[25] New York players listened through the locker room walls. Some swore that Robinson said to Reese, "Hey, Pee Wee … have a beer. When we win, Dressen buys the beer."[26] The manager, ever so sure of himself, told reporters, "The Giants is dead."[27]

Robinson also reportedly yelled, "Eat your heart out, Leo!" He started slamming a bat, "as if beating a drum at what he thought was the Giants' funeral." Eddie Stanky hollered at Robinson, telling him exactly what to do with that stick of lumber. Leo Durocher stood in the locker room while all this happened. He didn't yell or cuss. He said to his players, "I don't have to make any speeches. If that doesn't wake you up, nothing will."[28]

Apparently, the impromptu concert did indeed awaken the Giants, although they sank another half-game in the standings the following day. On August 12, New York swept a doubleheader from the Phillies and won another 14 straight games. After taking two from the Cubs on August 27, the Giants stood just five games out of the top spot. "We began to look over our shoulders, which you should never do," Furillo admitted. "And things began happening."[29] Ardent Brooklyn fan Donald Honig blamed everything that he suffered through over the next few months on that off-key locker room sing-along. "The Giants heard what the Dodgers were saying," he said, "and they simmered with hatred for what they felt was a very unprofessional attitude. Personal invective was coming through the wall, and the Giants' fury rose, and this added to their superhuman effort."[30]

So famous is the rivalry between these two New York clubs that baseball historians can pinpoint—or insist they can—when it all began, down to the minute. Lee Allen, in *Giants and the Dodgers*, put the time at 3:07 p.m. on October 18, 1889, at the old Polo Grounds, Fifth Avenue and 110th Street. It was the first game of the World Series, one pitting the National League champion Giants against the American Association champ Dodgers (known by many that year as the Bridegrooms). Brooklyn won the opener, 12–10, but lost the lengthy, best-of-11 series, six games to three. Allen wrote, "it is appropriate, considering the fury that would attend the subsequent history of the rivalry, that the competition began blatantly with an absurd dispute." Tom Lynch, one of two umpires scheduled to work Game One, demanded $800 for the entire Series, or twice the original agreement. Both teams balked at Lynch's demand, and the game continued sans the renowned arbiter.[31]

That first game being a high-scoring affair, the action continued as the sunlight dimmed. In the eighth inning, while holding a two-run advantage, Brooklyn's players "stalled. The umpires did not call the game, but merely walked aimlessly around, and finally the spectators became tired and wandered down to the field, settling the question for themselves by making further play impossible."[32] The following day, Lynch, the so-called "King of the Umpires," took his proper spot on the field but, Allen wrote, "he could not render decisions that pleased either side."[33] And while Brooklyn won three of the first four games, all but one ended before nine innings had been played as fans swarmed onto the field. Following one contest, New York manager John Day yelled to Brooklyn skipper Charles Byrne, "We will never play your team again. Your players stall and complain."[34] Day accused the Brooklyn nine of being "dirty" and of winning by "trickery."[35]

Both teams celebrated "victory banquets" before the match-up even ended. Brooklyn held its soiree at the Academy of Music following the fifth game (and after New York won, 11–3). According to Allen, "Someone had sprayed perfume over the linen at the head table, and the players sniffed nervously and frowned at each as they sat down." Byrne introduced his players—his "brave boys,"—and labeled Brooklyn "the greatest baseball city in the world." The Giants, though, won the final five games in the series and the championship. "Perhaps in Brooklyn," Allen wrote, "in the winter that followed, the cry, 'Wait til next year!' was first heard."[36]

12. "I don't believe it"

T.S. Eliot is famous for writing, in his epic poem "The Waste Land," that "April is the cruelest month." In baseball, though, September has April beat by a mile, especially during a tight pennant race. Vin Scully once called it "the month of sweating palms, pounding hearts, and acid stomachs. I've seen players sit in the dugout, their heads in their hands for many minutes, crushed in spirit, after making a bad play or a crucial out in a critical game."[37]

The Dodgers and Giants began a two-game set on September 1 at the Polo Grounds, with Brooklyn holding a seven-game advantage. Maybe the Giants could make one final push. "Don't count us out," Durocher said. "Baseballs can bounce as funny as footballs."[38] Gene Ward wrote that before the game, "you could feel the tension in the air a block from the ballpark, and it wasn't that electrical storm bouncing around the atmosphere, either." For the Giants, Ward wrote, "now was the time. Do or die!" Reese, like the other Brooklyn batters, took a few pre-game swings in the batting cage. He asked reporters about a recent boxing match. "Nothing about baseball," Ward wrote. "The real 'old pro' has another 30 minutes before he starts worrying about the Giants, and meanwhile, he's loose and easy."[39]

The contest turned lopsided fast. New York rocked Ralph Branca for five runs over four innings and won, 8–1. Don Mueller, with 10 homers going into the game, knocked three pitches out of the ballpark and collected five RBI. Reese went 3-for-4 but was left stranded after each base hit. He gained the most attention for his line drive out in the fifth. Cal Abrams reached on an error to lead off the frame. Carl Furillo followed by singling down the left field line. Reese, the next batter, smashed a liner right to Al Dark, who tossed the ball to second baseman Stanky and doubled off Abrams. The Brat tagged Furillo to complete the triple play. Ward wrote that the action happened "as fast you throw a one-two punch,"[40] or, more appropriately, a one-two-three punch.

Several "beanball incidents"[41] kept hitters from getting too comfortable in the box. Umpires at one point ordered both teams to knock off the noggin-thumping pitches. Brooklyn scored its lone run after Maglie hit Robinson with the bases loaded in the third inning. Later, Dodgers pitchers nailed Lockman in two at-bats.

The Giants won the second game by another lopsided margin, 11–2. New York pummeled Don Newcombe, whose record dropped to 17–8. Newcombe allowed seven runs (just three earned) and 10 hits over six innings. Reese went 0-for-3 with a walk. Don Mueller, a "southpaw slap hitter suddenly turned killer," according to Jim McCulley, enjoyed another terrific game. He hit a two-run homer in the eighth inning that made the score 9–1 and "sent the Brooklyn fans home in tears."[42] Mueller, a fourth-year player from St. Louis, posted a second-straight five-RBI game.

New York, Duke Snider wrote, "started coming on like gangbusters"[43] and won 17 of its first 22 games in September. Brooklyn played 11–10 baseball, not nearly as good. The rivals split a two-game set in Brooklyn on September 8–9. The Dodgers won the opener, 9–0. Newcombe tossed a two-hitter. Pafko, Hodges, and Cox each had two RBI. The Giants, behind Maglie, won the second game, 2–1. Reese bunted for a single in the sixth inning after going hitless the previous day.

On September 26, Reese told reporters, "We're still in front. That's all I know. We're trying to stay there."[44] Two days later, the Dodgers blew a 3–0 lead and lost,

4–3, to the Phillies at Shibe Park. Carl Erskine gave up all four runs. He "half-sobbed" afterward and swore "I'd have given my year's pay to have won that one."[45] The Dodgers slipped into a first-place tie with the Giants, who were off that day.

Both teams entered the final weekend of the season with marks of 94–58. Brooklyn won both its remaining games, against Philadelphia. Newcombe tossed a seven-hit, 5–0 shutout on September 29. Pafko hit a two-run homer, and Reese notched two singles. The next day, the Dodgers won, 9–8, when Jackie Robinson slugged a home run in the 14th inning off Robin Roberts, who was pitching his seventh inning of relief after going eight innings as a starter one day earlier. Brooklyn managed 17 hits, including two singles and triple by Reese, who also scored a run. The Giants, meanwhile, beat the Braves, 3–0, behind Sal Maglie, and then won, 3–2, with Larry Jansen on the mound. A three-game playoff awaited.

Jim Hearn faced off against Ralph Branca in the opener at Ebbets Field with 30,070 fans screaming and cheering. Andy Pafko gave the Dodgers an early lead on a solo home run in the second inning, his 18th in 84 games for Brooklyn. Bobby Thomson, with the count full, cracked a two-run homer in the third inning. It was the 31st long ball of the season for the 27-year-old. "I thought I had Thomson struck out when I broke his wrists on a 3–2 pitch," Branca said afterward. "Then he hit a high fastball into the stands."[46]

Thomson was a hometown product by way of Scotland. Born October 25, 1923, in Glasgow, he arrived in the United States with his family in the summer of 1926 and grew up on Staten Island, the smallest of New York City's five boroughs. James Ray Thomson struggled to support his wife and six children as a cabinet maker. Bobby, tall and with a thick set of dark, curly hair and dark brown eyes, excelled in sports as a youngster. Scouts from the Dodgers and Giants watched him play ball at Curtis High School and on a local industrial league team. Both teams talked contract with the 6-foot-2 teenager. The Dodgers offered him more money, $125 a month versus $100 from the Giants, but "I was a Giants fan, and I wanted to play for them."[47]

He hit 29 home runs and batted .283 in 1947, his first full season in New York, and, following a sophomore slump (16 homers, a .248 batting average in 1948), smacked 27 home runs in 1949 and 25 in 1950. Thomson still lived in his boyhood home. Dave Anderson, in *Pennant Races*, described how Thomson took the Staten Island Ferry across the New York bay and past the Statue of Liberty. He then drove the West Side Highway to the Polo Grounds parking lot. "It takes me an hour and half to get here," Thomson said. "But Staten Island's worth it."[48]

Monte Irvin added a solo homer in the eighth inning, again off Branca, as the Giants won, 3–1. Branca had now given up 18 home runs on the season, 10 against New York. "Giants bats must be highly magnetized when they go swishing against the offerings of Ralph Branca,"[49] the *Eagle* offered. Reese singled in the first inning and walked in the ninth with one out. He also grounded out and struck out. Roy Campanella hobbled around throughout the contest. His right leg hurt so much he could barely run. "Unless he's much better tomorrow, he won't catch,"[50] Dressen said.

Brooklyn, with Rube Walker behind the plate, won a laugher the next day, 10–0, at the Polo Grounds. Clem Labine tossed a six-hit shutout, and Jackie Robinson paced a 13-hit attack with a home run and three RBI. Hodges, Pafko, and Walker also homered for the Dodgers. Reese singled twice, walked, and scored a run in the eighth inning on a wild pitch. Reese, who booted a grounder hit off Stanky's bat in the third inning, "made one of the greatest plays of his career," on the next batter, Al Dark. The New York shortstop lashed a grounder that looked like a "sure base hit," according to Tommy Holmes. Reese, though, "dashed to his right for an unbelievable stop" and "executed an off-balance throw to Robinson for a force play at second."[51]

The game lasted three hours, 25 minutes. Joseph Wilkinson wrote that the lopsided loss made Giants fans feel "dazed, doubtful and disillusioned." Brooklyn fans, on the other hand, were walking the streets with "calm, satisfied smiles, looking as though they had just accepted a pleasant inevitability."[52] One Brooklyn fan insisted that in Game Three, Newcombe would turn the Giants and their fans "every way but loose."[53]

On October 3, a *Daily News* headline on the top of Page 3 proclaimed in large, bold type: THIS IS IT! MAGLIE AGAINST NEWCOMBE. The article began, "Today it's sudden death. The Dodgers have now carried the greatest of all pennant races as far as it can go."[54] Branca stood next to Reese and Robinson during batting practice. A reporter asked the three men whether they felt any nervous butterflies. Only Reese answered. "No matter how long you've been playing," he said, "you still get butterflies." Robinson smiled and Branca nodded.[55] Campanella wanted to play. Dressen shook his head. "You can't run, Roy," the manager said. Walker started again.

Brooklyn broke on top in the first inning. Reese and Snider reached base on one-out walks. Robinson, the next batter, jumped on Maglie's first pitch and lined an RBI single into left field. The game settled into a pitchers' duel over the next several innings with Brooklyn holding on to a 1–0 lead. New York finally put across a run in the seventh inning. Monte Irvin led off with a double and advanced to third on a fielder's choice. That brought up Thomson, who drove a pitch into center field, deep enough for Irvin to score. "As he had done so often in recent weeks, Bobby came through again," Ray Robinson wrote.[56] Thomson batted .440 with nine homers and 24 RBI in September and October.

Willie Mays grounded into a double play to end the inning. The score now tied, Newcombe walked back to the bench and said he was through for the day. Robinson, who "liked to light fires under people, especially Newcombe,"[57] challenged the pitcher to keep going. At least Newcombe could catch his breath. The Dodgers scored three times in the eighth inning. Reese singled with one out and, after advancing to third base on a base hit by Snider, sprinted home when Maglie unfurled an ill-timed wild pitch. Andy Pafko and Billy Cox added RBI base hits to put the Dodgers ahead, 4–1. Eddie Stanky tried to rev up his teammates. "The big guy's losing it," meaning Newcombe. "We'll get him. He's losing it."[58] Newcombe, though, maybe encouraged after Jackie Robinson's pep talk and a three-run lead, retired New York in order. The game headed into the ninth.

Larry Jansen, in relief of Maglie, made quick work of the Dodgers. An All-Star and 23-game winner, the 6-foot-2-inch right-hander from Verboort, Oregon, was making his fifth appearance that season out of the bullpen. He got Newcombe and Furillo to ground out and Reese to fly out. At the end of that quick frame, Leo Durocher told his club, "You guys have come this far. Let's give 'em a finish."[59] Al

Dark led off by knocking a single past Hodges and down the right field line. Dressen wanted to keep any drama to a minimum. He phoned Clyde Sukeforth, now the Brooklyn bullpen coach. Who was ready?

Erskine and Branca had been throwing since the fifth inning. Labine also got up and threw for a while. Dressen kept phoning Sukeforth. Who was ready? Don Mueller came to bat and creamed a base hit into right field. Dark sprinted to third. Monte Irvin stepped to the plate. The 32-year-old from New Jersey (he earned 16 varsity letters at East Orange High School) and one-time star for the Newark Eagles drove in a league-high 121 runs in 1951. He couldn't get the job done this time, though, and popped out to Hodges. One away. The lefty-swinging Whitey Lockman came up to bat. The blond-haired, 24 year old from rural North Carolina, already playing in his sixth big league season, crashed a stand-up double into the left-field corner that scored Dark and put Mueller on third. The score was now 4–2. Dressen looked again to the bullpen. Who was ready?

Sukeforth caught all three pitchers in the bullpen that day. "I kept telling Dressen that Branca looked ready to me." Labine, Sukeforth reminded his boss, had pitched a day earlier. "I didn't want him in that spot, with no rest," Sukeforth said. "And I didn't think Erskine was ready, either. Carl had a doubtful arm all his life, and he hadn't shown me his best curve or fastball that day."[60]

Dressen called time-out and walked to the pitcher's mound. The infielders gathered around Newcombe and the skipper. Then, surprisingly, the ever-so-confident Dressen took a humble turn. "What do you want to do? It's your money as well as mine," he said. Reese "couldn't believe" that the manager was soliciting opinions from his players. Finally, Reese offered one. "Newk's given us all he's got for the last week. Why don't you get somebody fresh in here?"[61] Who was ready?

The skipper waved for Branca. He seemed like the safer pick. Erskine had just bounced a curveball and, according to Sukeforth, "Branca's throwing hard." Dave Anderson, though, wrote in *Pennant Races* that "when his curveball bounced in the dirt, Erskine was elated." It meant that the pitch was "dipping through the strike zone."[62] Dressen, though, feared the pitch might get away from Walker. Campanella usually grabbed it. Looking back, Erskine said, "Was I ready? Yes, absolutely. That was my job."[63]

While Branca warmed up, Durocher called for Thomson. The batter ran over to his manager. "If you ever hit one," Durocher said, according to *Pennant Races*, "Hit one now." Meaning, hit a home run. Durocher, though, in *Nice Guys Finish Last*, wrote that "a home run never occurred to me." Instead, he continued, "this is the last inning, we've got to get that tying run in, that's all I'm thinking about." Durocher told Thomson, "I think he'll throw you a fast one. High and tight like they always try to pitch you. Be ready for it, Bobby! Go to ripping at it! Get a base hit here!"[64] Anderson contradicted Durocher's scouting report, at least to some extent. Thomson had hit a fastball for his Monday homer. "This time," Anderson wrote, "Branca hoped to get him to hit a curveball."[65] First, though, the pitcher figured to hurl a hard one, just as Durocher expected. According to Anderson, "Branca needed to get ahead in the count with some good mustard."[66]

Willie Mays kneeled in the on-deck circle. The 20-year-old played 121 games in his rookie campaign and batted .274 with 20 home runs and 22 doubles. He hit just .233 in September and knocked a lone homer, on September 15 against the Cubs and Paul Minner. (Thomson also homered that day against Minner, a 28-year-old junk-ball artist.) "So, do you pitch to Bobby Thomson or do you pitch to Willie Mays?" Reese asked years later. Anderson wrote that "Willie Mays was worrying." Mays put it simply, "I was sure they were going to pass Bobby,"[67] But, Anderson pointed out, "Mays didn't know that the intentional walk had seldom been one of Dressen's tactics. Especially when it meant putting the winning run on base, in this case the pennant-winning run."[68]

Thomson was nearly the goat of this game. In the second inning, he came to bat after Whitey Lockman singled with one out and drove a Newcombe pitch down the left field line. It looked like a sure double. Thomson put his head down and rushed past first base. Lockman, though, watched as Andy Pafko, known for his strong arm, fielded the ball in the corner. While Thomson headed toward second, Lockman opted to stay put. Billy Cox took the throw from Pafko, fired to Robinson at second, and nailed Thomson. "It was my mistake all the way," Thomson said. He really wanted that double. "I was so determined to get to second base that I didn't even watch [Lockman]."[69]

He also struggled in the field. Pafko's RBI hit in the eighth ricocheted off his glove. The official scorer, maybe in a generous mood, gave Pafko a base hit rather than charging Thomson with an error. "It was one of those play where you either do or you don't," Thomson said. "The ball hit my glove as I tried to grab it between hops, and I just didn't come up with it."[70] Cox's base-scoring hit, meanwhile, shot past Thomson, who tried to block the ball. He never had a chance. "It was a blur," he said.[71]

Thomson tried to forget all that. "Let's face it," Thomson wrote in his memoir. "If you think about the possibility of being a goat, it's going to take away from your performance. The only motivating factor for me was the chance to get up to bat."[72] Thomson got ready in the batter's box. Branca toed the rubber. Fans crept to the edge of their seats. Some watched from a nearby hill—Coogan's Bluff—that overlooked the ballpark.

Branca threw a first-pitch fastball down the middle. Thomson watched as it popped into Walker's mitt for strike one. "I should have swung," Thomson said later.[73] Branca threw his next pitch a little high and inside. Thomson ripped it. "Hit solidly, the ball rose on a low line toward the lower leftfield stands,"[74] Dave Anderson wrote. According to Thomson, "I was quick with my hands. After I hit it, I watched it go,"[75] Cox began yelling, "Get down! Get down!"[76] Thomson said, "I knew it was a home run as soon as I hit it." But then he didn't. "The ball started to sink and for a split second, I thought it was gonna hit the wall. Then it disappeared."[77] Duke Snider also thought the ball might stay in the park. Pafko ran to the wall "to make the catch if humanly possible," Snider wrote. "I dashed over to play it off the wall and hold the runners to two bases."[78] (The next day, many newspapers carried a picture of Pafko standing at the wall, as he "looked up hopelessly"[79] in front of the 315-foot sign and watched the ball rush into the stands.)

Durocher said "very few home runs" ever landed in the lower deck of the Polo Grounds "because of the overhang from the upper deck. Only a line shot—a rising line drive—ever went in there."[80] Jackie Robinson stood near second base with hands on hips and watched to make sure Thomson touched each base and, finally, home plate. Like his teammates, Robinson could hardly believe what he just witnessed. "We are three runs ahead going into the ninth inning," he said. "We see ourselves in the World Series."[81]

Reese watched the ball sail, sail, and finally leave the ballpark. "It was the toughest thing I ever went through in baseball," he said. Russ Hodges, the voice of Giants broadcasts since 1949, screamed into his microphone: "There's a long drive … it's gonna be…. I believe … the Giants win the pennant! The Giants win the pennant! The Giants win the pennant!"[82] Thomson, in a column for the United Press, swore, "I didn't run around the bases—I rode around 'em on a cloud."[83]

The Dodgers, their season complete, walked across the field and into the visiting clubhouse. Gayle Talbot described the ending "as heart-stabbing" and wrote that "few madder scenes have ever been seen on the baseball diamond." Following Thomson's "great blow," Talbot continued, "the stricken Dodgers, who less than two months ago were being hailed as one of the National League's greatest clubs, shuffled across the grass toward their dressing room with the misery of the world on their shoulders."[84]

Robinson tossed his glove into the back of his locker. Dressen tore off his uniform shirt, the buttons spilling to the floor. Reese saw the tears in Branca's eyes. "I had a few tears in my eyes, too,"[85] Reese said. Branca lay in agony on the locker room floor. Snider remembered the pitcher crying, "Why me? Why me?"[86] In one of the more understated comments on this most melodramatic of afternoons, Dressen told reporters, "Well, that's what makes baseball the game that it is. You never know what's going to happen."[87] Erskine recalled, "You just had the wall separating the two locker rooms for the two teams. You could start to hear the players yelling and celebrating. Our locker room was like a tomb. I can still vividly recall Ralph sprawled out on the steps, so upset."[88]

Red Smith began his memorable column in the *New York Herald Tribune*: "Now, it is done. Now, the story ends. And there is no way to tell it. The art of fiction is dead. Reality has strangled invention. Only the utterly impossible, the inexpressibly fantastic, can ever be plausible again."[89] Scores of Giants fans, predictably, ran onto the field to celebrate. "They stood at least a thousand deep, before the clubhouse in center field, and chanted for a personal appearance from every Giant, but mainly and repeatedly for Thomson, and all obliged,"[90] Joe King wrote in *The Sporting News*.

Dressen walked to the New York locker room and congratulated the victorious Durocher. "Leo threw his arms around me and hugged me," Dressen said. "Guess he loves everybody today."[91] The Dodgers skipper said Thomson hit "a good pitch, that is, a strike. I thought it was just about the same pitch as the one he hit in Brooklyn."[92] The day's hero disputed Dressen's account, or at least his judgment of the strike zone. "It was a bad high pitch," Thomson said. "If I was a good hitter, I would have laid off it altogether."[93] Well, nuts to that, Dressen said. "Thomson's crazy! It was belt high, the same kind of pitch Bobby beat us with in the first game at Ebbets Field."[94]

Leo Durocher never saw the legendary hit. "I blanked out," he wrote in *Nice Guys Finish Last*. Instead, "the last picture I have in my mind, I'm seeing the fans reaching and jumping in the left-field bleachers, frozen and unmoving, like a still photo."[95] He also recalled Reese leaning over at his shortstop position, hands on his knees, looking over his head at the traveling baseball, "his mouth open in surprise." Durocher, though, doubted his own memory. "Logic told me that Pee Wee had to have gone out to take a possible relay"[96] in case Thomson's ball fell short of the seats.

Later that fall, Reese confirmed his former manager's recollection. The two spoke at a luncheon in Louisville. Reese said he froze after Thomson connected on Branca's pitch. He had "gone into shock." Then he walked off the field and into the clubhouse. Reese spoke softly to Durocher as he relived the heartache. "I just sat in front of my locker and said to myself.... I said to myself, 'It's not so. They just called time for a minute. We're going to go back and play. They ... can't ... do ... this ... to ... us. They can't beat us with one swing of the bat like that after we were up by thirteen and a half.'" He sat in front of his locker ... for how long? "It's not over," he kept saying. "I don't believe it. It's not so. We're going out in a few minutes to finish the game. They just called time for a minute. They called time...." At that moment, as Reese spoke, Durocher said he felt sorry for Pee Wee, Campy, Gil, "and all the rest of my old boys."[97]

Branca insisted that "it wasn't a bad pitch" that he threw to Thomson. "I didn't think he hit it too well. It was sinking when it went into the stands."[98] Thomson may have gotten some help as he stood in the batter's box. In later years, rumors circulated that the Giants stole signs throughout the summer and early fall of 1951. Joshua Prager wrote about New York's race to the pennant—and Brooklyn's downfall—in a 2001 article for the *Wall Street Journal*, later expanded into a full-length book, *The Echoing Green*.

According to Prager, Durocher called a team meeting on July 19. Famous for uttering the remark "nice guys finish last," Durocher also wrote, "Win any way you can as long as you can get away with it."[99] Henry Schenz, a middling infielder and first-rate bench jockey, had given the manager an idea. The Giants acquired Schenz on June 30. During his days with the Cubs, Schenz liked to hang out in a spot behind the Wrigley Field scoreboard, prop up his sophisticated 35-millimeter Wollensak telescope, and steal opponents' signs. Schenz confessed all this to Durocher, who grew intrigued and overjoyed.

The powerful telescope could "pick a crystal out of the water,"[100] Durocher told his players. Durocher explained how a telescope placed inside the Giants' clubhouse (located behind center field) could spot, say, a catcher flashing signs—fastball, curveball, brushback—to the opposing pitcher. A smart team could figure out the signs and how to relay them back to the batter. Bingo! Instant offense. Durocher wasn't kidding. "We've got to start stealing signs," he said.[101] Who wants signs, he asked? Who wants to know what's coming? Several players wanted signs. Others did not. Irvin said, "No thanks, coach."[102]

Durocher also enlisted the help of a lifelong Dodgers fan named Abraham Chadwick, one-time shortstop for Brooklyn Boys High School and a former cab driver. Chadwick took a job repairing New York City streetlights in 1943 and earned some extra money by working the lights at the Polo Grounds. Could Chadwick rig up some sort of contraption to relay signs from the clubhouse to a batter nearly 500 feet away,

Durocher asked? Chadwick, happy for the attention, figured out a way. He installed a bell-and-buzzer system in the clubhouse and ran it to some wall-box phones in the bullpen and dugout. "Now, with the press of a button beside the fourth window in the clubhouse, two phones buzzed—one in the bullpen, one in the dugout."[103]

The plan went something like this: Schenz, joined later by Giants coach and former catcher Herman Franks, sat in the clubhouse and directed the telescope at the opposing catcher. Chadwick sat beside them. When the catcher put down his sign, Chadwick pressed a buzzer as instructed. "One buzz meant a fastball was coming," the *Times* reported. "Two meant a curveball."[104] According to James Elfers, "Schenz had no problem discerning even the smallest of catchers' gestures"[105] with his telescope.

Durocher stationed backup catcher Sal Yvars in the bullpen. Durocher and Yvars loathed one another. During spring training in 1949, the two got into an argument. Players broke up the squabble but not before Yvars committed assault. He nailed Durocher in the head with a shin guard. Yvars provided one important asset for a ballclub. Durocher "made it clear that the only reason he was in the majors was his skills at stealing signs."[106]

In this case, though, Yvars' job was not to decipher signs. He just had to listen for the buzzer and signal the batter, who could look over or not. "Watch me in the bullpen," Yvars instructed. "I'll have a baseball in my hand. If I hold on to the baseball, it's a fastball. If I toss the ball in the air, it's a breaking ball."[107] In the words of Giants pitcher Al Gettel, "Every hitter knew what was coming," at least the ones who wanted signs. "Made a big difference."[108]

Bobby Thomson played 15 years in the majors and retired with 264 home runs, 189 of them for the Giants. He told *USA Today*, about that most famous of clouts, "We did steal signs, and I did take some, and I don't feel good about it." As for that epic clout off Branca on October 3, "I didn't get the sign on that pitch," he insisted. "Ralph says I did, and if that erases the burden of what he's carried around all these years, I'm glad for that." Branca told the *New York Times*, "I don't want to diminish a legendary moment in baseball. And even if Bobby knew what was coming, he had to hit it. … Knowing the pitch doesn't always help."[109]

William F. McNeil, author of *The Dodgers Encyclopedia*, called October 3, 1951, "the darkest day in Brooklyn Dodgers history."[110] A few years after Thomson deposited his epic long ball into the seats, Reese said, "That was the only game of my career that I refused to discuss in the clubhouse afterward. It was like a nightmare, and I wanted to forget it as soon as possible."[111] He did talk for a moment to Monte Irvin. Reese said, "I was planning to be at Yankee Stadium tomorrow. I can't believe you guys have done this to us." Irvin offered a simple suggestion. He said, "Pee Wee, don't go to the stadium tomorrow. You'll be the only Dodger there."[112]

The discouraged shortstop got dressed and left the ballpark. He hit 10 home runs on the season and collected a career-high 84 RBI. He batted .286 and rebounded on defense after his sub-par 1950 campaign. He finished second among NL shortstops in putouts (292) and third in assists (422). Gil Hodges led the team with 40 home runs, while Roy Campanella collected a team-high 108 RBI and batted .325. Jackie Robinson hit .338 and drove in 88 runs. Preacher Roe led the pitching staff with a marvelous 22–3 record. Newcombe won 20 games. The Dodgers played before more fans than any other team in the league, drawing 1,282,628.

Outside the Polo Grounds, Reese spotted Dottie, along with a few friends from Louisville. "Then," he said, "we all went out to Gallagher's Restaurant [228 W. 52nd Street] for a roast beef dinner."[113] Later, Reese described Thomson's fabled "Shot Heard 'Round the World" as "probably my saddest moment in baseball."[114]

13

"Not guilty"

Bobby Thomson and the Giants lost the 1951 World Series. The Yankees knocked off Brooklyn's arch-rival in six games. Thomson batted .238 against New York pitching. He managed four singles and a double. Casey Stengel's ballclub celebrated the franchise's 14th title and third straight. "Yankees Again ('49), Again ('50) and Again ('51),"[1] proclaimed one newspaper. Again, again, and again. Rooting for the Yankees, some liked to say, was like rooting for U.S. Steel, then a symbol of American industrial might.

The Dodgers—the pride of the borough—suffered through what was surely an agonizing off-season. Chuck Dressen spoke to reporters during spring training. "I hear the Giants are laughing at us," he said on March 30. "Let 'em laugh. Let 'em holler at us. Let 'em holler at Ralph Branca. I hope they do. I've got some clippings waiting for the Giants." They were all at Dressen's house, inside a trunk. He kept them in storage over winter. "Then," he vowed, "they'll go up on the clubhouse wall."[2] Robinson said, "I think every player on the team will be putting out a little more this year because he feels that we let the fans down in bad finishes the two previous years."[3]

"Wait 'til next year," Brooklyn fans were heard to cry following yet another round of October disappointment. As in, "We'll win the World Series yet. Wait 'til next year." But how many "next years" did some players have left? Pee Wee Reese would turn 33 years old on July 23, nearly a grizzled veteran by some baseball standards. A few writers speculated that he might be slowing down. Jackie Robinson, who turned 33 on January 31, faced the same charge. "Not guilty," Reese said. The Brooklyn shortstop pointed out that he played in all 154 games the previous season and "I didn't get tired. Unless I'm hurt, I expect to play as many this year." Robinson added, "Numbers don't mean anything. It's how you feel that counts. I've taken pretty good care of myself."[4]

By February 14, Reese and all the other Dodgers had signed contracts for the upcoming season. Reese, "who had a whale of a year a year in '51,"[5] agreed to a $32,500 deal, making him the second-highest paid member of the team, next to Robinson.

Before the season began, Brooklyn said goodbye to one of its top pitchers. Uncle Sam wanted Don Newcombe for the next two years. On February 26, the big right-hander reported to the Newark induction center for his Army swearing-in. Additional pressure now fell on the 34-year-old veteran, Preacher Roe. Even he speculated that repeating his 22-win campaign might be asking too much. "I figure that if I can win 18, it'll be a good year," he said. "I can still take my regular turn, every fourth day or so, but I just can't do much of that two-day-rest stuff anymore, I guess."[6]

Maybe the Dodgers could get some quality innings from a local kid with a nasty curveball and an eccentric manner. Born December 13, 1929, in Long Island City, Billy Loes grew up in Astoria, Queens, about a 30-minute drive from Ebbets Field. The son of Greek immigrants, he tossed four no-hitters during his senior year at William Cullen Bryant High School. Brooklyn outbid several interested teams and signed him to a contract that included a $21,000 bonus. Loes, assigned to Nashua, won 11 games in his first year in professional ball and posted a 2.43 ERA.

He looked like a future star. And a self-confident one at that. This is the guy who as a prep star compared himself favorably to Giants star pitcher Larry Jansen. "I forgot more [about pitching] than he ever knew,"[7] Loes declared. The Dodgers added Loes to the major league roster in 1950. Mostly he sat on the bench, getting into just 10 games and pitching only 12⅔ innings. He gave up 11 earned runs, 16 hits, five walks, and five home runs. His ERA? A whopping 7.82. Loes did an Army stint in 1951. Now he wanted to pitch for the Brooklyn Dodgers, not in the minor leagues. "I've learned all any minor league manager can teach me," he said to Dressen. "I'd be wasting my time down there."[8] Maybe he forgot about that nearly 8.00 ERA from just a few years earlier.

According to a poll of managers and club owners, the Dodgers boasted "the most solid team" in the National League. Bob Carpenter, president of the Phillies, said, "I can see only [one] player in the league, Stan Musial, who could make the Dodger team, outside [of] the pitching staff." Brooklyn-born Braves manager Tommy Holmes (not to be confused with the *Brooklyn Eagle* sportswriter of the same name) said, "Most clubs are glad to have four true major leaguers for the eight positions. But the Dodgers have eight-for-eight."[9]

Roger Kahn, a 24-year-old sportswriter for the *New York Herald Tribune*, began his two-season tour on the Dodgers beat. A graduate of nearby Erasmus Hall High School, he made his rounds during spring training. "I walked into the clubhouse, trying to choke back awe, and introduced myself to Reese." Pleasant, Reese welcomed Kahn. "But you don't want to hang around me," the shortstop said. "Why not, Mr. Reese?" Kahn asked. Reese said, "I'm not good copy."[10] Thus began a long friendship.

They spoke frequently as the train whistled north from Florida to the various barnstorming stops en route to New York. They shared drinks, and Reese asked as many questions as Kahn did. How did such a young man get a job covering a major-league baseball team for a large-circulation daily newspaper in New York City? Was it always Kahn's dream to be a sportswriter? "No, Pee Wee," Kahn admitted. "My first dream was to have your job." As a boy, Kahn longed to be a big league shortstop. Ah, that would be the life, or so he imagined. Reese set the young writer straight. Playing baseball isn't easy, he said. Even catching an infield pop fly is no simple chore. "Look at me carefully the next time I'm under a pop fly," Reese instructed. "The play isn't routine at all. Every cord in my neck is sticking out. That routine pop-up is ten stories high." Kahn asked Reese whether playing baseball was still fun. Pee Wee offered a straightforward answer. "Not really," he said. "It's work. I don't enjoy playing under pressure, or the night games. I like meeting new people like you. But I don't like baseball too much during working hours."[11]

The two men, born eight years apart in different parts of the country—one a great shortstop, the other a great writer—also talked about poetry and literature. Reese asked Kahn whether he knew Robert Frost and admired him. Kahn recited some lines from one of Frost's poems. "That's very beautiful," Reese said. "It must be something to be able to write that beautifully." Who, Reese asked, is the best current sportswriter? "Right now, I'd say Red Smith," Kahn answered. They kept talking on that day and throughout the season, on trains bound for Brooklyn, St. Louis, and similar destinations, past small towns and open farmland. "That was the beginning," Kahn wrote. "With his innate grace and unpretentious nobility toward Jackie Robinson, Reese enlarged my understanding of what it was to be a major league ballplayer and what it was to be a man."[12]

The Dodgers added more color to their jersey front in 1952, a red uniform number placed underneath the blue "Dodgers" script. Walter O'Malley had wanted to debut the new feature for the 1951 World Series. Thomson's home run postponed that plan. *The Sporting News* called the innovation "a particular benefit to television fans, who often obtain only a front view of a player before he passes out of camera range."[13] (Another version of the story is that a Brooklyn front-office executive suggested adding the red numeral to make it easier for home fans to recognize players. Red numbers first appeared on the team's road uniform in 1959.)[14]

Brooklyn opened with a 3–2 win in Boston on April 15. Only 4,694 fans watched as Preacher Roe beat Warren Spahn. Both pitchers threw complete games. Pee Wee Reese hit a double and a single in five at-bats. The next day, he notched two more hits and drove in two runs as the Dodgers beat up the Braves, 14–8. Brooklyn carved out an 8–2 record in April. Reese, however, slipped into a terrific slump after those first two games and batted just .179 over the month.

Home fans witnessed his frustration during the first game of a doubleheader against Boston on April 22. Reese already had struck out twice that day and was battling a 2-for-22 slide. The Dodgers led, 1–0, in the eighth inning thanks to a Campanella homer and had filled the bases, looking to add more runs. Reese stood in the on-deck circle, swinging a couple of bats, determined to break out of his doldrums. Dressen, though, sent in George Shuba to pinch-hit. Reese growled over the move. The normally mild-mannered shortstop stalked back to the dugout and slammed down his bat before taking a seat on the bench.

Fans at Ebbets Field booed, not because of Reese's temper tantrum, but for Dressen's decision to lift one of Brooklyn's favorite players. The booing grew louder when Shuba struck out on three pitches. Easing the pain, Brooklyn held on to win, 2–1 and took the nightcap, 3–1. The next day, Dick Young came to Reese's defense. "True, the shortstop hadn't been hitting—he failed in four previous attempts last evening," Young conceded. "But, Reese, hitting or not, is great in the clutch. ... The booing Dressen took in the opener was brought on the manager by his insatiable desire to win—regardless of personalities. There are no sacred cows, in Chuck's opinion, when it comes to a ballgame."[15]

Reporters looking for juicy quotes from a struggling ballplayer walked away disappointed. A contrite Reese took his manager's side. "I guess Dressen was right," he said. "I've been going lousy. Maybe I shouldn't have gotten angry." But, he continued, "Any player who doesn't want to get up to bat in a tight spot isn't worth a darn" Reese paused. "You know, I sympathize with Dressen. I feel sorry for him the way the fans booed him."[16] Dressen conceded that Reese was a top-notch clutch hitter, but a slump is a slump, and 2-for-22 is most definitely a slump. "Of course, the fans got on me," the manager said. "They like Pee Wee. But you can't let the fans run your ball game."[17]

On May 11, Reese still boasted just a .215 batting average. On this day, though, he let his feet do the important work at home against the Phillies. With one out in the 10th inning and the score tied, 3–3, he reached on an error. After Billy Cox lined out, Reese stole second with Jackie Robinson at bat. Philadelphia starter Howie Fox intentionally walked Robinson to set up a force play with Campanella up next. The Brooklyn catcher lined a base hit into center field. Reese rounded third and headed for home, safe at the plate with the winning run. The *Philadelphia Inquirer* called it "a daring bit of running."[18]

While Reese struggled in the early going, Robinson began the season on fire. He hit .448 in April and stayed above the .400 mark until May 10. "Several newspaper stories" over the winter had included quotes from Branch Rickey saying both Reese and Robinson "should have been traded by now," reported *The Sporting News*. Walter O'Malley disagreed with the former Dodgers boss. He pointed out that both members of the Brooklyn double-play combo put up excellent numbers in 1951. "We do not agree with the feeling that Reese and Robinson have their best years behind them." Besides, O'Malley said, "I would never think of trading players of the stature of Reese and Robinson without first consulting them. Because of their long service with the club, I think they are entitled to that consideration."[19]

Both players did their part in a record-breaking inning on May 21 at Ebbets Field, when the Dodgers posted 15 runs in the opening frame. Twenty-one Brooklyn hitters stepped to the plate against four all-but-helpless Reds pitchers. The onslaught began with one out on a walk to Reese. Snider followed by smashing a home run off Reds starter Ewell Blackwell. The torrent of offense continued. Reese went to bat three times. He singled in his second trip, scoring Chris Van Cuyk, and walked again in his third at-bat, bringing home Rube Walker. Robinson doubled in his first at-bat and got plunked with the bases loaded in his second. Snider ended the inning—at last—by striking out. Back-up infielder Bobby Morgan added a two-run homer in the third inning and another in the fifth. The Dodgers won by the lopsided margin of 19–1. "It was murder, plain murder!" Lou Smith, the *Cincinnati Enquirer* sports editor, called it. "That's all one could call what happened to the hapless Reds tonight in plain view of 11,850 screaming and hilarious witnesses at Ebbets Field."[20] Some fans "began drifting toward the exits even before it became an official game," according to the *Eagle*.[21]

The Bums, "in one of the wildest rounds ever beheld at Flatbush,"[22] recorded 10 hits in that first inning, seven walks, and two hit batsmen (in addition to Robinson, Cox got plunked.) They set modern-day major league records for most runs scored in one inning (15), most plate appearances in one inning (21), most consecutive batters to reach base (19), most RBI in one inning (15), and most runs scored after two outs (12). Reese set a record for reaching base three times in one inning. He, Cox, and Snider equaled a record by coming to bat three times in one frame.[23] In a preview of the next day's game, Sid Frigand wrote, "The blooded, battered Cincinnati Reds will be in Ebbets Field this afternoon, it was reliably reported, to take their turn at bat."[24] (The Dodgers won again, this time, 8–7. The Reds blew a 7–3 lead in the eighth inning. Brooklyn scored four times. Reese began the rally with a base hit.)

On June 1, the Dodgers beat the Cubs, 3–2, and the Giants lost to the Cardinals, 8–7, lifting Brooklyn into first place. Hodges hit a two-run homer in the second inning, while Reese drew a bases-loaded walk later in the frame. Joe Black threw 1⅓ innings of scoreless relief and struck out three Chicago hitters. The 6-foot-2-inch right-hander from Plainfield, New Jersey, had thrown 14 innings, covering seven games, and had an ERA of 0.00.[25] "Pretty soon, they'll be calling Joe Black 'Joe Blank,'"[26] Dick Young wrote. Black was 28 years old. The Dodgers had purchased his contract from the Baltimore Elite Giants in 1951 and assigned him to Montreal and, later, St. Paul. He compiled a middling 11–12 mark for the Royals and Saints but posted a solid 3.28 ERA. During spring training in 1952, Black "had to sweat out the last cuts."[27] Dressen liked what he saw from Black and pegged him for bullpen duty. Broadcaster and former pitcher Dizzy Dean offered some kind words about the Dodgers' rookie. "He's got a nice follow through, and he's loose," Dean said. "He has the makings of a nice pitcher."[28]

Billy Loes also got off to a hot start. He notched a win in relief on June 18 against the Cubs and lowered his ERA to 2.31. The following day, 25-year-old Carl Erskine took the mound against the Cubs and was nearly perfect. He allowed only a walk in the third inning to Willie Ramsdell. Other than that, nearly all the sneaky fastballs and overhand curveballs that the Cubs hit into play found their way into the glove of a Brooklyn defender. Erskine struck out just one batter—Dee Fondy, Reese's one-time sparring partner—with one out in the eighth inning.

Erskine induced 16 ground balls in a 5–0 win. Reese notched two hits and scored twice. "My control did it," Erskine said afterward. "I threw a lot of curves and some fastballs. I had them hitting the pitch I wanted them to."[29] As for that lone walk, Erskine explained that he looked to the sky above Ebbets Field and saw some fearsome clouds. "The rain was coming on fast," he said. "We had a 4–0 lead at the time, and we wanted to get in 4½ innings to make it an official ballgame. ... I threw him [Ramsdell] four fastballs. But I pitched so fast I couldn't get them over the plate."[30] Walter O'Malley gave Erskine a $500 check after the game and ordered a case of champagne to the clubhouse, although the day's star did not drink.

The Dodgers averaged 14,048 fans in 1952, tops in the league. The enthusiastic faithful reached far beyond the borough of Brooklyn. Alistair "Butch" Forbes hailed from Scotland, an ocean away from the City of Churches. Forbes began following the Dodgers during World War II on the Army's European Radio Network. He wrote to O'Malley that he planned to visit Brooklyn and "look over the dames ... and the Dodgers."[31] Forbes worked at a grain mill in his native country. He advertised himself to any unattached woman. "I am 23 years old, six foot one and one-half inches, weigh 185 pounds, don't smoke, don't drink or dance. But I do breathe sometimes." Forbes looked forward to seeing the sites around New York City. "First of all," he wrote, "I want to get the low down proper on this baseball business."[32]

The *Eagle*'s Robert M. Grannis wrote a column about Forbes, who once yelled to an umpire, "Hey, Cricket-head, why don't you get a pair of glasses?" Forbes hoped someday to make the United States his home. He wanted to live in Brooklyn, of course, near Ebbets Field. Grannis decided, "To Butch, I say you'd be a darn good Brooklynite. You're a 'holler guy' and when you yell, the sound suggests you are one of us in the name of freedom, good fellowship and good clean fun."[33]

Pee Wee Reese broke out of his slump in early June. He collected two hits in five of the first nine games that month and "unleashed two booming triples"[34] on June 6 against the Reds, to go with three RBI. "Pee Wee Reese was the big man for the Dodgers"[35] in the 6–4 Brooklyn victory. Reese raised his average to .279 after going 4-for-6 in a 14–4 blowout at home against the Pirates on June 21. Over the month, he hit .333 with a .412 on-base percentage and eight stolen bases. He slammed one home run and had 13 RBI.

In July, Reese put up even better numbers. He batted .346 and nearly matched his on-base percentage from June, with a .409 mark. He raised his season's average above .300 on July 12 after going 5-for-5 in a 12–2 win against the Cubs. One report that day complimented the Dodgers for "spraying 22 hits to every conceivable corner of Wrigley Field."[36] On July 19, against the Pirates at Forbes Field, Reese hit a grand slam in a 9–1 victory.

During hot streaks and slumps, Reese served as a leader on the field, a coach planted on the left side of the diamond. He offered a pat on the back or a kick in the butt. Words of wisdom? If Reese had them, he shared. He refused to help in only one small way. He would not raise any fingers into the air to indicate the number of outs, as was the custom. "This is the major leagues," he'd say. "You're supposed to be able to keep track of the outs yourself. Besides, they're on the scoreboard."[37]

Reese liked to give a gentle needle to teammates and the newspaper beat writers. Roscoe McGowen covered the Dodgers for the *New York Times*. He also liked to play cards. By all accounts, he did better with writing and reporting than he did at poker. McGowan usually blamed bad luck for his losses. Following one more lousy hand, McGowan again cursed his misfortune within ear shot of Brooklyn's veteran shortstop. Reese, in a pleasant manner, offered his own take. "Roscoe," he began, "did it ever occur to you that you might be a horseshit poker player?"[38]

In late April, the Brooklyn shortstop, "one of the diamond game's most popular players," had begun hosting a Saturday afternoon radio program called, appropriately enough, "The Pee Wee Reese Show." A critic called it "probably one of the fastest-moving, most informative baseball shows on the air, a natural for fans of the national pastime and for boys learning the rudiments of the game."[39] Reese liked nothing more than to talk baseball, on the air or in the locker room. Carl Erskine wrote that despite Reese's fast footwork on the diamond, he "was one of the slowest players to get dressed and leave the clubhouse." Following games, Reese sat in his chair, smoked a pipe, read the newspapers, and talked to his teammates. Some players got dressed and left for home as fast as they could, usually to the admonishment of their captain. "When you hurry in and out of the clubhouse," he'd say, "you hurry in and out of baseball."[40]

Brooklyn traveled to Crosley Field for a doubleheader on August 19 and celebrated Pee Wee Reese Night at the ballpark closest to Reese's off-season home. The special event attracted 25,543 fans, one of the biggest crowds of the year, including about 1,000 admirers from Louisville. Reese responded by getting three hits in the first game and stealing a base in both contests. Brooklyn won the first game, behind Preacher Roe, 3–0, and lost the second, 5–3. "Reese showed that 33 years have exacted little of the fleetness from his nimble legs," Tommy Fitzgerald wrote in the *Courier-Journal*. "Experience has even added to his skill and danger as a runner."[41]

NL President Warren Giles told the *Courier-Journal* that umpires often "commend" Reese "for his sportsmanship." During his time as general manager of the Reds, Giles said, "I always thought greatly of Reese as a player." Now, "in my new job as league president, my relationship toward him as a player is different, but my regard for him has grown. What the game needs is more Reeses. I often wonder whether the Dodgers fully appreciate what he really means to them."[42]

The Dodgers built a 10½-game lead after sweeping a doubleheader on August 25 in St. Louis, 3–1 and 9–5, and coasted the rest of the way, going just 13–15 in the final month. Brooklyn clinched the pennant on September 23 after beating the Phillies, 5–4, at Ebbets Field. Brooklyn fans had witnessed clinching games in years past, but the excitement never dimmed. Dick Young reported on the raucous scene at the ballpark. Some fans ran onto the field "and hugged Johnny Rutherford, who had hurled a snappy seven-hitter for the wrap-up win … Some clawed affectionately at Duke Snider, whose fifth-frame double had cracked across the tying and winning runs. … Some pawed at Pee Wee Reese, who has played on four of Brooklyn's six pennant-winning clubs."[43] Someone raised an unofficial pennant—a white flag with blue lettering that read "Brooklyn Dodgers, National League Champions." In red lettering, the pennant read: "1952." Gladys Gooding played "Follow the Dodgers" on the stadium organ.[44] Brooklyn finished 96–57, in front by 4½ games. Umpires called the final game on account of darkness after 12 innings against the Braves, the score tied, 5–5.

Reese fell into a late-season slump and finished with a .272 batting average, a 14-point drop from 1951. He walked 86 times, though, and boasted a .369 on-base percentage. The shortstop also scored 94 runs and led the league with 30 stolen bases. Catchers threw him out just five times. Branch Rickey once described Pee Wee Reese as a base stealer in this way: "He doesn't tip and tear, spike and upset, bluff and bully as did Cobb in his heyday." Instead, "Reese does it smartly. He steals a base before the opposition is aware it is being stolen." Rickey added, "He doesn't make the pitcher watch him. He makes the pitcher unwatch him if I may coin a word."[45] Reese also hit six home runs, his lowest total since 1946, and had 58 RBI. In the field, he finished third among NL shortstops in putouts (282).

The Dodgers led the National League in runs scored (775), home runs (153), total bases (2,102), and on-base percentage (.348). Brooklyn finished tied with New York for the top spot in slugging percentage (.399). Gil Hodges hit 32 home runs with 102 RBI. Roy Campanella drove in 97 runs, while Duke Snider knocked in 92. Jackie Robinson batted .308 (.440 on-base percentage) and stole 24 bases. The Dodgers scored in double figures 16 times and gave up 10 or more runs just four times.

Brooklyn pitchers posted the lowest ERA in the league (3.53) and struck out the most batters (773). Brooklyn beat up the league's bottom dwellers, going a combined 54–11 against the Braves, Reds, and Pirates. *The Sporting News* decided that "the Dodgers established some sort of record" with that impressive achievement.[46]

Major league hitters belted 55 grand slams in 1952. The Red Sox and the Dodgers hit eight apiece. Furillo, Hodges, and Campanella all hit two.[47] Oh, and this team could play defense. Brooklyn finished with the highest fielding percentage in the league (.982) and the fewest errors (106). The Bums could do it all. But could they win a World Series, finally?

This year's Series pitted the Dodgers against … yes, once again, the New York Yankees, celebrating their 50th season in the Bronx. (The American League began play in 1901 with eight teams, one of them the Baltimore Orioles, who finished in fifth place with a 68–65 record. Baltimore slipped to last place the following season, going 50–88. AL president Ban Johnson requested that the Orioles move to New York in 1903, giving the circuit an important presence in the nation's biggest city. Dubbed the "Highlanders," the team played for a decade at Hilltop Park, located at one of the loftiest points in Manhattan. The "Yankees" name became official in 1913.)

Bronx's Bombers won the 1952 pennant by two games over the Cleveland Indians, although this crew relied as much on pitching as power. New York's staff posted the best ERA in the American League (3.62), while the offense finished second in runs scored (727). Allie Reynolds enjoyed probably the best season of his career, going 20–8 with a league-leading 2.08 ERA at the age of 35. Vic Raschi (16–6, 2.78 ERA), Eddie Lopat (10–5, 2.53), and former Braves star Johnny Sain (11–6, 3.46) rounded out a solid staff. Yogi Berra led the club with 30 home runs and 98 RBIs.

A marvelous young outfielder named Mickey Mantle slugged 23 homers and hit .311 in his first full season as a Yankee. The 20-year-old grew up in little Commerce, Oklahoma, in the far northeast corner of the state. As a boy, Mantle listened to Cardinals games on the family radio. "My two idols were Stan Musial and Pee Wee Reese,"[48] he told reporters. The son of Elvin "Mutt" Mantle, who worked in the area's lead and zinc mines, Mickey smashed tape-measure homers and sprinted from home plate to first base in 3.1 seconds.[49] Casey Stengel stared and marveled. "He has more speed than any slugger I've seen and more slug than any speedster—and nobody has ever had more of both of them together," Stengel once said. "This kid ain't logical."[50] The Yankees began a new chapter while closing another. Joe DiMaggio retired after the 1951 campaign.

Billy Loes, as if on cue, made another head-scratching comment on World Series eve. He predicted the Yankees to win it all in six games. Imagine how that went over in the Brooklyn clubhouse. Not surprisingly, the pitcher issued a clarification. "I never told that guy the Yanks would win it in six," he insisted. "I said they would win it in seven." Okay, then. Chuck Dressen, predictably, sided with his own club. "I think we've got a helluva chance to take them,"[51] he said.

J. Henry Weber at the *Daily News* forecast "continued balmy weather"[52] through at least the first five games of the Series, with high temperatures between 70 and 80 degrees. Although fans could listen to the action at home on the radio or watch it on television, ticket demand for the Series was "overwhelming. Speculators were getting

$100 for a strip of three Dodger boxes, face value of $32. The scalpers were doing business at $30 for a single box seat and $20 each for six-buck reserved seats."[53]

Ford Frick, who took over from Happy Chandler as baseball's commissioner in 1951, laid out a few rules for each team and for reporters. "The scribes" could not go into either clubhouse until five minutes after the final out of each game, except for the finale. "Newsmen bent on gathering pre-game morsels will be permitted in the dressing room at the discretion of the managers," Joe Trimble reported. Also, Frick expected players, coaches, and managers to speak like gentlemen. "Frick," wrote Trimble, "warned both managers against profanity, by themselves or the players, and banned arguments over balls and strikes calls."[54]

During a workout at Ebbets Field, two days before the Series opener, Reese spoke at length on the field with his Yankee counterpart, Phil Rizzuto. The competing shortstops also posed for a picture. Rizzuto, born on September 25, 1917, in Brooklyn, grew up in Queens and graduated from Richmond Hill High School. The Yankees signed the 5-foot-6 "Scooter" in 1937 and promoted him to the big club in 1941. Like Reese, Rizzuto missed three seasons during World War II. Rizzuto earned MVP honors in 1950 when he batted .328 and collected 200 hits, including 38 doubles, seven triples, and seven homers. He hit .254 with 17 stolen bases in 1952. "A couple of pretty fair shortstops over there, Case," a reporter said to Stengel. The skipper picked up on the hint and began talking. "You say he [Reese] stole 30 bases last year?" he asked.

All-Star shortstops Pee Wee Reese (left) and Phil Rizzuto competed against each other six times in the World Series. Rizzuto's Yankees came out on top every year except 1955 (National Baseball Hall of Fame Library, Cooperstown, New York).

"Led the league, huh? That's not surprising. He knows how. Watches the pitcher. Gets the break, which is the difference between Pee Wee and the guys who can outrun him. But that isn't all he does. Just like my little guy over there, he does all the things a good shortstop should do. Makes that double play when you need it. Good bunter and a pretty good hitter in the clutch."[55]

The Series began on Wednesday, October 1, at Ebbets Field. The headline at the top of the *Eagle* screamed "D (DOOM) DAY FOR YANKS." Lower on the front page, an article in this afternoon daily reported on loyal fans who were "jammed to the rafters today." Among the boosters was Carrie Koschnick of 217 Madison Street in Brooklyn, "who sported a large black derby and a large white coverall apron with the names of the Dodger players. Carrie started cheering early and often for the team she has followed for 42 years."[56]

Still lower on Page 1, the *Eagle* ran an article titled "O'Malley Stresses Need for Arena." The Brooklyn sports executive wrote the piece as part of a 10-part feature on the borough's future. "My business is baseball," O'Malley declared in his opener. "Brooklyn," he wrote, "has an international reputation as a baseball town." Now, "to capitalize on the fact," he wanted to replace Ebbets Filed with "the first all-purpose, all-weather sports and convention arena." He envisioned a parking lot large enough to fit 5,000 cars and a stadium capable of holding 55,000 fans for baseball and 90,000 for boxing. He expected every seat to face the pitcher's mound, and he suggested a "600-foot roof"—yes, a dome—to eliminate costly rainouts. Besides baseball and boxing, the complex could play host to football, ice skating, roller skating, and other events. And that wasn't all. Underneath the stands—"wasted space in most ballparks"—O'Malley foresaw shops, supermarkets, and fire-proof storage areas.

The price tag for all this? About $6 million. If built, the Dodgers could boast of playing in "the most up-to-date home in the major leagues and provide Brooklyn with the largest covered convention hall in the world." O'Malley did not offer a specific site for his project but wrote that it should be "strategically located" near public transportation. The plan was beyond the "pipe-dream stage." The architect Norman Bel Geddes already had sketched a design.[57]

Chuck Dressen gave the Game One ball to Joe Black, who started just two games all season, September 21, and September 27, his last two appearances. Stengel went with Reynolds. Brooklyn took a quick lead on a Robinson solo homer in the first. With two out in the sixth and the game tied, 1–1, Reese singled to right field. Snider followed by slamming a home run deep over the right-center field fence. Two innings later, with Brooklyn clinging to a 3–2 advantage, Reese hit a solo homer off relief pitcher Ray Scarborough. It was his second home run in World Series play. He was the first Dodger to accomplish that feat. The clout, though, did nothing to impress Yankees fan Jack Allen, who was sitting in the stands that day. "That wouldn't have gone into the stands anywhere else in the majors," Allen declared. "This is a joke ballpark."[58]

The Dodgers held on to win, 4–2. Black threw a complete game. He gave up six hits, struck out six, and walked two. "Nervous? Was I nervous?" Black responded to reporters. "I'm always nervous out there. My stomach was full of butterflies."[59]

In the sixth inning, Mantle crashed hard into Reese's left knee "and knocked him sprawling"[60] while trying to break up a double play. Hy Turkin, sitting in the bleachers, reported that, following the collision, Dodgers fan Richard Largione yelled out, "The next time he slides in, Pee Wee, spike his head off!"[61] Mantle worried, "Oh, my God, I've killed my idol."[62] Reese did sprints in the dugout runway between innings to keep his muscles from tightening and remained in the game. He told reporters afterward, "I believe I'll be able to play [in Game Two]. It feels good right now."[63]

Carl Erskine opposed Vic Raschi, with Reese in the starting lineup, though probably nursing a black-and-blue left knee. Brooklyn broke out on top in the third inning. Reese singled with one out and, after advancing to second, scored on a Campanella base hit. That was it for the Brooklyn offense. The Dodgers couldn't push across another run—or even a hit. The Yankees, meanwhile, collected 10 hits and scored seven times, highlighted by a five-run sixth inning. With one out and two runs already across home plate, New York's volatile infielder, Billy Martin, hit a three-run homer off reliever Billy Loes, who refused to offer much credit. The pitch headed almost straight down the middle with hardly a break on it. "You could have hit it out of the park,"[64] Loes told a reporter. Martin also hit a run-scoring single off Erskine in the fifth inning.

Eddie Lopat and Preacher Roe faced off in Game Three at Yankee Stadium. The home club took an early lead, 1-0, on Lopat's RBI single in the second inning. Brooklyn managed solo runs in the third, fifth and eighth innings, the second tally coming on Reese's hit to left field. Roe kept the New York hitters guessing for much of the way. With one out in the eighth, Yogi Berra guessed right and slammed a pitch for a solo home run.

In Brooklyn's half of the ninth, Reese and Robinson knocked back-to-back RBI singles against Yankees reliever Tom Gorman. With Campanella at the plate, Reese took off for third base while Robinson sprinted to second. Moments after the duo pulled off their double steal, and after Campanella popped out, Gorman unleashed a pitch to Andy Pafko that eluded Berra, allowing both base runners to score. The Yankees put across a solo run in the ninth, on Johnny Mize's round-tripper, to make the final score 5-3. About the passed ball, Stengel just said, "I can't be sure, but I think there must have been some mix-up," Berra confessed, "It was my fault."[65] Holmes reported that Berra "seemed too bewildered to start in pursuit. Reese scored easily. And here was Robinson galloping around third and over the plate standing up."[66] Pee Wee Reese, in a joyful clubhouse, told reporters, "We're not playing safety-first baseball." Reese said he took off for third base on his steal "knowing that Jackie would follow when he saw me go."[67]

Joe Black and Allie Reynolds hooked up again in Game Four. Black pitched better than he did in the opener. So did Reynolds. Both gave up four hits. Black allowed one run over seven innings. Reynolds tossed a shutout. Johnny Mize, now 39 years old, cracked a solo home run to open the fourth inning. "The big fella still is a real good hitter,"[68] Stengel said. Mickey Mantle tripled in the eighth off Johnny Rutherford, who relieved Black, to make the score, 2-0. Reese recorded half of Brooklyn's hits, a single in the first inning and another in the third. A devastated Black said afterward, "I threw that long ball" to Mize. "I'm always failing." Reese, who overheard, said, "What's the guy supposed to do? Pitch a shutout every time he's in there? Always failing? My gosh."[69]

In Game Five, Brooklyn broke out on top on Pafko's RBI single in the second inning off Ewell Blackwell. The Dodgers added three runs in the fifth on Reese's sacrifice fly and Snider's two-run homer. Carl Erskine's curveball, meanwhile, kept the Yankees baffled. He gave up just a bunt hit to Mantle over the first four frames. "I had first-class stuff,"[70] he said. Then he lost it. The Yankees posted five runs in the fifth inning. At one point, Charlie Dressen marched out to the mound and spoke to his starter. "See if you can get this game over before it gets dark," the skipper said. Brooklyn knotted the score in the seventh inning on Snider's RBI single off Johnny Sain.

Erskine went back to throwing his Grade-A curveball. He retired the Yankees in order in the sixth, seventh, eighth, ninth, and, yes, the 10th inning. Brooklyn finally broke through in the 11th. Sain, in his sixth inning of work, gave up one-out base hits to Cox and Reese. Snider drove home the game-winning hit with a double that bounced off the bullpen railing in right field. Erskine set down the Yanks one-two-three in the bottom half of the frame. He retired 19 straight batters to complete a game that Roger Kahn called the "most enjoyable I've seen."[71] The contest featured outstanding glove work by Furillo, Cox, Pafko, and Snider. "I've never [seen] so many great plays in a Series," Reese said. "Not all season, have there been as many great catches." Through the first five games, Reese had a .429 batting average. "I'm no gloveman," he proclaimed. "I'm a slugger."[72]

Just one more win and Brooklyn could celebrate a championship. Billy Loes and Vic Raschi matched zeroes over the first five innings of Game Six. In the bottom of the sixth, Duke Snider hit a solo home run. New York responded by scoring twice in the seventh inning and once in the eighth. Snider crushed another solo homer in Brooklyn's half of the eighth, his fourth of the Series, to conclude the scoring with the Yanks ahead, 3–2. Snider joined legends Babe Ruth and Lou Gehrig as the only players to smash four round-trippers in a single World Series. "No foolin?" Snider asked. No foolin'. Reese went hitless in four at-bats, and the Dodgers failed to mount any big threats except for Duke's dramatics. No one else even made it to third base. The offense needed to get going. "That's what we need and that's what we've got to have tomorrow," Dressen said. "Some hitting."[73]

Once again, fans looked forward to—nervously anticipated?—a World Series seventh game. Allie Reynolds and Joe Black matched up for a third time. The Dodgers scored single runs in the fourth and fifth innings, the first on Gil Hodges' sacrifice fly, the second on Reese's RBI single. The Yankees matched them in both frames. New York added solo runs in the sixth and seventh innings and won, 4–2. Brooklyn had the bases loaded with one out in the seventh. Snider, though, hit a weak pop-up to Gil McDougald at third base, while Robinson popped up a ball near the pitcher's mound that Martin raced in and caught just above his shoelaces to end the threat. Relief pitcher Bob Kuzava easily retired the Dodgers in the final two frames. Pee Wee Reese made the last out of the Series on a fly ball to Gene Woodling in left field.

With that, Clarence Greenbaum wrote in the *Eagle*, "All Brooklyn was ready to become a vast snake pit of celebration of the World's Championship that never came. The Yankees snafued the deal."[74] At least one newspaper offered no sympathy for the disappointed Dodgers, only praise for the mighty Yankees. According to a headline in the *Coos Bay Times* of little Marshfield, Oregon, "Yankees Are Still the Champions; Brooklyn Dodgers are Still 'Bums.'"[75]

Johnny Mize led the Yankees with a .400 batting average, three home runs and six RBI. Mantle collected a Series-high 10 hits, batted .345, and hit two home runs. A disconsolate Robinson blamed the loss on the blond-haired wunderkind from Commerce. "They didn't miss Joe DiMaggio," Robinson insisted. "It was that Mantle, that Mickey Mantle killed us."[76]

It hurt that the high-powered Brooklyn offense all but disappeared in the World Series. The Dodgers batted just .215 over the seven games and scored 18 times. They hit six home runs; Snider belted four of them. Reese batted .345, the third straight Series in which he hit above .300 and his best-ever Series mark. Campanella (.219), Pafko (.190), Furillo (.174), and Robinson (.174) all struggled. No one suffered as much as Gil Hodges. The big first baseman ended up 0-for-21, with that lone sacrifice fly as his Series highlight.

Brooklyn lost one game by one run and two by two runs. Reese sat in the clubhouse, dejected. The veteran brushed aside any talk of moral victories. "I don't go for that stuff,"[77] he said. Just once, he wanted to celebrate following the last out of that final October game. He wanted to jump up and down and laugh and pour champagne over Jackie and Duke and the rest of his teammates. Would he ever get that chance? This one hurt. "If we couldn't beat them after having them down three games to two, we just don't deserve to win," he said. "We have no one to blame but ourselves. We had the chances, and we failed to cash in on them."[78]

Reese reminded writers that in that disappointing final game, Brooklyn also filled the bases with nobody out in the fourth inning and only scored one run. "Yep," Reese continued, "we lost it ourselves. Don't get me wrong, the Yankees have a great team. They outplayed us. They took advantage of their opportunities. We didn't."[79] A little while later, after all the other players had put on their street clothes, Reese still sat in front of his locker, still wearing his baseball uniform. "I thought for sure we had them," he said to a reporter. "We had all the better of it. We had them, and we let them get away."[80]

Some Dodgers fans gathered near Ebbets Field after the final out. They yelled encouragement to their baseball heroes, who walked out of the ballpark and into their cars. Another long off-season awaited. "Wait'll next year," the faithful shouted.[81] Maybe. As Roger Kahn wrote, "Every year is next year for the Yankees."[82]

14

"One hundred and eighty pounds of dynamite"

Brooklyn's Bums of 1953 turned the pennant race into a high-scoring march to the World Series. They conquered teams during the cool days of spring, through the muggy months of summer, and into the early glow of fall. Duke Snider, Roy Campanella, and other heavy hitters made opposing pitchers cringe at ballparks from St. Louis to Cincinnati to 55 Sullivan Place. The Dodgers won a franchise-record 105 games and clinched the pennant earlier than any team in National League history.

Few lineups in baseball ever boasted the brawny power of this one. Gil Hodges collected 122 RBI and still finished third on the club. Snider cracked 42 home runs; Campanella, the MVP Award winner, hit 41. The Dodgers slugged .474, a figure topped up to that point in league annals only by the 1930 Chicago Cubs. Brooklyn's eight regulars hit a collective .308. The entire team batted .285, 20 points better than the NL average. Reese scored 108 runs, one of six Dodgers to reach the century mark. Carl Erskine, who certainly benefited from such a prolific offense, said "the 1953 Brooklyn team was the greatest team I played on."[1] William F. McNeil, author of *The Dodgers Encyclopedia*, called the 1953 squad "one of the most devastating wrecking crews in major league history."[2]

This dynamic ballclub led all National League teams in scoring for the fifth straight year and reached double figures 26 times.[3] The Dodgers averaged 6.2 runs per game. Only one pitcher—a rookie right-hander—shut them out. Roger Kahn said, "The Dodgers of 1953—the eight men on the field—can be put forth as the most gifted baseball team that has yet played in the tide of times."[4]

Walter O'Malley began the new year in grand style. On January 12, he invited reporters to the Lexington Hotel in midtown Manhattan and announced the signings of Robinson, Reese, and Campanella for, respectively, $38,000, $35,000, and $25,000. Dana Mozley added up the total ($98,000) and called this event "the most expensive luncheon in baseball history." Reese, who spent much of the winter indulging his passion for golf, "looked as if he could begin playing right now."[5]

A few weeks later, Pee Wee Reese picked up the 1952 Player of the Year trophy, also known as the Sid Mercer Memorial Award, given by the Baseball Writers of New York. Nearly 1,400 people gathered inside the grand ballroom of the swanky Waldorf Astoria on Park Avenue. Reese did not put up the gaudiest numbers in all of baseball the previous season. He did not bat .336, like Musial did, or hit 37 home runs, like the

Pirates' Ralph Kiner and the Cubs' Hank Sauer did. Undoubtedly, Reese took home a shiny plaque for reasons other than just his statistics. "His character and his qualities of leadership, plus his defensive and offensive skills, make him worthy of any award that any group might choose to bestow upon him," Roscoe McGowen wrote. Reese spoke to the crowd but just briefly. "Gentleman," he began, "if I possessed the oratorical fire of Demosthenes or the linguistic elasticity of Branch Rickey, I could wow you with superlatives. But, frankly, fellers, I ain't got it. Thank you very much."[6]

Arthur Daley wrote about Reese in his *New York Times* column. "Deep has been the affection for him since he first reported at training camp in 1940, a slim blond youngster who tried to hide a scared look behind an engaging grin." Even after 10 seasons in the big leagues (not including his service time during World War II), "There is still a boyish look about him, and the mischievous twinkle still flickers in his eyes." The columnist complimented Reese for his adept work as a team captain. "He has been a superb choice, a perfect liaison man between the players and the front office since he has been able to hold fast to the respect and trust of both."[7]

The Dodgers made a few moves in the off-season. In a surprising one, in January, they traded Andy Pafko to the Braves for second baseman Roy Hartsfield and an undisclosed amount of cash.[8] Pafko, nearing his 32nd birthday, said he felt "keenly disappointed but not disheartened" about leaving Brooklyn. He added, "I more or less expected something like this when the Dodgers delayed in sending me my 1953 contract."[9]

"Handy Andy," though, never played a game in Boston. On March 19, the National League approved owner Lou Perini's relocation plan to Milwaukee. Perini made his money in the construction business and had purchased a majority share of the Braves in 1943. His ballclub won a pennant in 1948 and attracted a franchise-best 1,455,439 fans. Soon, though, the slide began. The Braves tumbled to fourth in 1949 and attendance dropped by almost 35 percent. Support dwindled even more in 1950 and continued to fall. The Braves played in front of only 281,278 fans in 1952. At one point, Perini visited Milwaukee, a beer-and-factory town with a strong economy and a great desire for big league baseball. He said to his Braves staff, "I'm going to tell you fellows something, and I don't even want you to tell your wives. We're going to have to move the team to Milwaukee."[10]

Of note, Pafko grew up in rural northwest Wisconsin and gave the Braves an immediate home-state product. Andrew Paul Mele, in *Tearin' Up the Pea Patch*, wrote that Perini made his move "with the full support and aid of Walter O'Malley" and that "O'Malley was sure to take notice of the 43,000 seats at the new Milwaukee County Stadium and the 10,000 parking spots."[11] Ebbets Field, to O'Malley's chagrin, only had spaces for about 700 cars.

Brooklyn also acquired a Phillies pitcher with the curious nickname of "The Mad Monk." Russ Meyer, a temperamental but talented fireballer, landed in Brooklyn as part of a four-team deal. He went 13–14 in 1952 but sported a decent 3.14 ERA. The Dodgers needed Meyer to bolster a so-so starting pitching staff. He and Jackie Robinson, though, had engaged in some nasty battles through the years. Once, Robinson began jockeying back and forth at third base during a game at Ebbets Field, threatening to steal home. An unnerved Meyer yelled, "Go ahead, you n-----, try to steal." The

Mad Monk also hurled beanballs at the Dodger a few times, and the two nearly came to blows. When Meyer walked into the locker room for the first time as a Brooklyn hurler, Robinson held out a hand. "We've been fighting one another," he said. "Now, let's fight them together." Meyer smiled. "OK, pal."[12]

Another problem down in Florida proved more complicated. Dressen told reporters that he planned to convert Billy Cox into a utility infielder, move Robinson to third base, and install up-and-coming prospect Jim "Junior" Gilliam as the team's new second baseman. Dressen liked Gilliam's speed and knack for getting on base. Not surprisingly, the decision angered Cox, one of the game's top defenders. Kahn wrote that "while Charlie Dressen fiddles with his infield, Billy Cox burns."[13]

Some pitchers probably grumbled that such a sensational glove man might not be there to make a key play behind them. Also, Gilliam had come up through the Negro Leagues. That meant the Dodgers would have three Black players—also Robinson and Campanella—in the starting line-up on most days. Would that be a source of trouble? Robinson hoped not. He told Milt Gross of the *New York Post*, "I know Cox is upset. Someone has moved him out of his position, and he has a right to be upset. I don't think it makes a difference to him whether that someone is white or Negro." Kahn, though, wrote that "Remarks by some Dodgers in the clubhouse and at the hotel indicate that the problem of Negros in baseball is still to be finally resolved."[14]

Indeed, Stanley Woodward wrote a story about how "racial tension could tear apart the Dodgers."[15] Reese promised to "do my best" to calm any troublemakers. That vow was good enough for Robinson, who said, "There's not a man on this team that doesn't have a world of respect for you." According to Gene Schoor, Robinson said, "The few malcontents were straightened out, without any hardness or resulting friction."[16] Later, Don Newcombe recalled, "Pee Wee was one of the guys on the Dodgers who we—I mean the black guys—could look to for leadership. Jackie would tell us who the nice guys were and who wasn't. And Pee Wee was surely one of the nice guys—one you could trust."[17]

Brooklyn hoped to get a comeback year from Carl Furillo. Vision problems had forced him to step out of the batter's box throughout the 1952 season and rub his eyes. He underwent cataract surgery on January 3 in New York City. "Skoonj" sounded eager to take his swings in Florida. "I'm seeing the ball real good now," the outfielder said in late February. "I used to see it leave the pitcher's hand—then I'd lose it—then I wouldn't see it again, sometimes, until it was right on top of me. Now, I follow it all the way. It's clear, not blurry."[18]

The Dodgers opened on April 14 at home with an 8–5 victory against Pittsburgh. Duke Snider and Roy Campanella both drove in three runs. Reese singled and scored in the fourth inning. Joe Black earned the win in relief of Carl Erskine. The following day, Reese hit a two-run single in the eighth inning off Johnny Lindell, an outfielder turned knuckleball pitcher, to break up a 2–2 tie. He "cracked the knuckler for a solid single through the box,"[19] Lester J. Biederman wrote in the *Pittsburgh Press*. The Dodgers won nine games and lost four in April. Robinson batted .375; Snider hit .345 with four home runs. Three times, Brooklyn beat teams by a score of 12–4, including on April 19, a dreary day in Pittsburgh. The Dodgers made "a shambles of the muddy field."[20] Reese hit a two-run single, walked four times, and scored three runs.

Reese, as he had the past few seasons, batted second in the Brooklyn order. Jim Gilliam occupied the top spot. Reese said he preferred the two-hole over the lead-off position. Especially early in his career, he let too many good pitches go by. He explained later, "if you're batting lead-off, it means that you follow the pitcher on all trips to the after the first one." If the pitcher makes the second out and the leadoff hitter makes an out on the first pitch, "the pitcher has to get back to the mound without really having had a chance to draw his breath."[21]

On May 1, Reese belted a dramatic two-run homer against the Cubs and 43-year-old right-hander Emil "Dutch" Leonard, a six-time All-Star who pitched for Brooklyn from 1933–1936. Chicago led, 5–2, going into the bottom of the eighth inning at Ebbets Field. A two-run single by Rube Walker made it a one-run game. After Gilliam flied out, Reese "hammered"[22] his game-winning round-tripper on a 3–2 pitch. The Dodgers improved to 10–5.

Now, if Gil Hodges could just get going. That dreadful World Series slump had carried over into the regular season. By the start of May, his batting average had dropped to .227, and he still had not homered. Finally, on May 6, against St. Louis, he deposited a Joe Presko pitch into the seats. It was the 140th home run of his career, breaking the all-time team mark set by Dolph Camilli.[23] The 18,178 fans at Ebbets Field gave Hodges a loud ovation as he rounded the bases. "It was wonderful," Hodges said. "Imagine them cheering me when they should be razzing me. I'll never forget that."[24]

Jim Gilliam, meanwhile, handled big league pitching almost from the start. After going 3-for-3 in a 9–4 loss against the Braves on May 4, the 24-year-old raised his batting average to .344 and his on-base percentage to .506. "He's rapidly showing himself to becoming the best lead-off man Brooklyn has had in years," Harold Burr wrote in the *Eagle*.[25]

Born October 17, 1928, in Nashville, Tennessee, Gilliam began playing for the local Crawford ballclub in 1944. Two years later, he earned a starting job with the Baltimore Elite Giants but struggled to hit curveballs thrown by right-handed pitchers. "Hey, Junior, get over on the other side of the plate," Giants manager George "Tubby" Scales told Gilliam. "Junior." The nickname stuck. So, too, did Gilliam's dedication to batting from both sides of the plate. He played in the Negro Leagues All-Star game from 1948–1950. Harry Postove, a scout for the Cubs, wrote a report on the switch-hitter and called him "the best young prospect in the Negro American League."[26] Brooklyn signed Gilliam before the 1951 season and assigned him to Montreal. The following year, he won the International League MVP Award after hitting .301 (.411 on-base percentage), driving in 112 runs, and stealing 18 bases.

Reese liked what he saw from his new double-play partner. He had played alongside Eddie Stanky and Jackie Robinson, and set a high standard for Brooklyn second basemen. "I think I know a good second baseman when I see one," Reese told Milt Richman in late April. "He [Gilliam] moves quick and gives you the ball well on double plays. He covers half an acre around second base, and he's a shrewdie, too."[27]

Brooklyn's powerful offense grabbed many of the headlines in 1953. On May 17, in the second game of a doubleheader, the Bums pounded out 20 hits and beat the Reds, 10–0, at Crosley Field. Reese recorded two singles and two doubles. He also scored three runs. On this day, though, Carl Erskine earned much of the press attention. "The young gentleman from Indiana"[28] tossed a one-hitter. He gave up just a bunt single to Gus Bell in the sixth inning. Some insist that bunting to break up a no-hitter, especially later in the game, goes against one of baseball's unwritten rules, not that it bothered Erskine. "I don't blame him a bit," the pitcher said. "It was good baseball."[29]

On May 22, New York knocked off Brooklyn, 5–1. It was the Dodgers' final loss of the month. They reeled off 10 straight wins and entered June with a mark of 27–14. Their most lopsided win during that streak came May 24 against the Phillies. The Dodgers led 3–2 going into the eighth inning. By the end of the frame, they were ahead, 15–2. Reese contributed to the pounding with a bases-loaded triple. No one even made an out until Erskine, the 14th man to bat, struck out looking against Kent Peterson, the fifth Phillies pitcher that frame. "This was one of those everything-happens-where-Brooklyn-happens-to-be games," Dick Young wrote. No team had ever scored a dozen runs in one inning before making an out. Young called the 44-minute offensive explosion a "concentrated traipsing."[30] The Dodgers added one more run in the ninth for good measure.

In June, many newspapers nationwide ran an article that included thoughts and opinions from several National League shortstops on "who was the tops at his trade." Reese, for his part, selected Al Dark from the Giants. "He's a good hitter, he's fast, and he gives himself up a lot to advance runners. [The Braves' Johnny] Logan has as good a pair of hands as I've seen on a shortstop, but he's not quite as good a hitter as Alvin." Dark, in turn, touted Reese for his all-around play. "From the time he put on his uniform until the time he took it off, Pee Wee Reese is the best shortstop I've ever seen. That takes in everything—covering ground, throwing, making double plays, power-hitting, bunting, making the hit-and-run play, walking, running bases, and stealing. There's nothing he can't do." Solly Hemus of the Cardinals said, "For day in and day out play, Reese is the most dependable guy in the league."[31]

Pee Wee Reese even did nice turns for sports writers. During one game at Ebbets Field, Roger Kahn's wife, Joan, got clocked by a foul ball while sitting in the stands. As she was being treated in the first-aid room, O'Malley sent a note to the press box, informing Kahn that the Dodgers could not be held responsible for Joan's injuries. "If you sue me, you will lose," O'Malley warned. Following the game, Reese asked Kahn about his wife. How was she getting home? "I'll drive her," the scribe said, "but I have to write my story first." Reese told Kahn to take his time with the story. "I'll drive Joan home."[32]

In *Into My Own*, Kahn shared a story about one of his many road adventures with Reese. This one took place at the Victoria Club, a piano bar in East St. Louis, Illinois, just across the Mississippi River from downtown St. Louis. Late one night—or, maybe early one morning, near closing time nonetheless—the two men, filled with drink, pondered a cab ride home. Kahn, looking around at the evening's delight, ordered a final libation. Reese thought Kahn had indulged quite enough and told him so. Nearby, a lady named Gwen sat at the piano, ready to play one more song. Kahn mulled over last call. "Most of the writers I knew who took that extra drink and another and another, died young," he wrote later. Gwen knew lots of songs. She offered to play any of them in her book. Kahn need only place a five-dollar bill into her ample cleavage. Reese saw the lights of an awaiting cab and took his sportswriter pal by the arm. The shortstop, older and wiser than his drinking buddy, put an end to the party. "Gwen was damn good-looking," Kahn said from the safety of a taxi headed just a few miles west. Reese, as usual, knew what to say. "Day game tomorrow."[33]

The Bums took over first place on June 28. They beat the Braves, 11–1, to complete a three-game sweep. Brooklyn hitters pounced on Warren Spahn for four runs over 2⅓ innings and kept going. They notched two runs in each of the final three frames. Robinson drove home three runs, and Hodges hit a "400-foot poke into the Brooklyn bullpen."[34] Reese contributed to a 16-hit attack with three singles and an RBI.

Brooklyn won three of its next four games and took a drubbing on July 5. The Giants smacked five home runs and beat up their rival, 20–6, at the Polo Grounds. Hank Thompson, a former Negro Leagues star and a machine gunner at the Battle of the Bulge, hit two homers and drove in seven runs. Sal Maglie took his lumps but still threw a complete game. One reporter tried to console Charlie Dressen. A lopsided game is much easier on the nerves than a 1–0 defeat, the writer declared. The Brooklyn skipper just scoffed. "Lose 1–0 to Maglie?" Dressen said. "No sir." Sure, Maglie won this day, Dressen said, but "he needed a flock of runs to do it. Heck, anybody can win with the kind of hitting he got behind him today." Dressen looked at the reporter. "Even you."[35]

True to form, the Dodgers met Pittsburgh the next day and won, 14–2, at Forbes Field. Billy Cox, enjoying a solid season as a semi-regular, hit a three-run homer and led a 15-hit Brooklyn attack. Furillo and Hodges also hit home runs. Dodgers batters had now slugged at least one homer in 19 straight games, equaling an NL mark set by the Giants in 1947. The streak began June 18 when Gilliam ripped a pitch into the seats in the fifth inning of a 12–4 loss to St. Louis. Reese kept the long-ball barrage going on June 27. He hit a solo home run off Jim Wilson in the top of the 10th inning to beat Milwaukee, 4–3. Dick Young wrote that Billy Loes was "kissing Reese on the cheek" for slamming that game-winner and "many of the 34,360 fans [at County Stadium in Milwaukee] must be starting to kiss off the brazen Braves, who have now lost six straight."[36]

The streak reached 21 as the Dodgers swept a doubleheader on July 7 against the Pirates. Hodges, Snider, and Robinson homered in the first game. Cox belted two in the nightcap. Even the light-hitting Preacher Roe hit a home run, the first of his career. He entered the day with a .110 lifetime batting average. In the third inning, he sent a Bob Hall pitch into the left-field bleachers. "Hall let up on a fastball, and I really cut loose," Roe said to reporters. "I warned you guys before the game I was going for the fences."[37] Brooklyn swept the twin bill, 5–4 and 9–5. Reese collected four hits on the day and scored three runs.

On July 11, the Giants did something that no other team did against the Dodgers all season. They held the Bums scoreless. Al Worthington, making just his second career start, tossed a four-hit, 6–0 shutout. Worthington, who blanked the Phillies in his debut five days earlier, allowed only one batter to get past first base. Reese walked with one out in the fourth inning and advanced to second on a single by Snider.

Campanella followed by hitting into a double play. The Bums' streak of 24 games with at least one home run ended one short of the major league record set by the 1941 Yankees. Brooklyn batters hit 39 homers during that long-ball run. Hodges led the way with eight. Furillo hit five, and Reese and Campanella both knocked out four. Snider and Cox each hit three. Gilliam slugged two, and Robinson, George Shuba and Rube Walker, along with Roe, hit one apiece.

Reese earned a spot on his ninth All-Star team. Campanella, Hodges, Robinson, Furillo, and Snider joined him on July 14 at Crosley Field. Reese was still looking for his first hit in the midsummer classic. Thus far, he was 0-for-13 with two walks. His first two at-bats in this one were just more of the same. He grounded out both times. At last, in the fifth inning, against Allie Reynolds, he singled with two outs and drove home Enos Slaughter. In the seventh inning, with the Indians' Mike Garcia on the mound, Reese doubled with two outs and once again brought home Slaughter. The National League won, 5–1, giving the senior circuit four straight victories. Afterward, Reese, according to one newspaper article, was "the grinningest man in the room."[38]

Following the All-Star Game, Brooklyn won eight out of 10, all part of a 23–8 mark in July, a .742 pace. The Dodgers outscored the opposition, 204–124. St. Louis pitchers looked all but helpless during a four-game set. Brooklyn swept the series and outscored the Redbirds, 44–12. In the first inning of the second game, the Dodgers posted seven runs. In the fourth inning of the finale, they scored nine. Reese reached base eight times in the series. Going into August, the Dodgers boasted a 65–34 record and led the second-place Braves by eight games.

On July 27, after three years and one month of carnage, the Korean War ended with a ceasefire. The *Eagle* proclaimed in large type: "FIGHTING ENDS." Ernest Horbrect wrote, "The bitter, costly, and stalemated war in Korea ended in a truce at 10:01 yesterday, and 12 hours later [at 9 p.m. Brooklyn time], the shooting died out." The war cost 33,629 U.S. lives, with 103,284 wounded and 5,178 captured or missing. Horbrect wrote, "So ended a 'police action' which developed into one of the longest and most expensive wars in United States history."[39]

The Sporting News provided an in-depth profile of the Brooklyn offense in its August 26 issue. Bill Roeder wrote that the Dodgers of 1953 compared favorably with the Yankees of the 1920s and 1930s, the Cubs and A's of 1929 and 1930, and the New York Giants squads in the years just after World War II. "This classy combination of sluggers and sprinters will go down in baseball history as one of the greatest attacking forces of any era," according to Roeder. "It is an authentic murderers' row."[40]

The Dodgers also had a chance to break the single-season record for most total bases, set by the 1936 Yankees (2,703), or at least surpass the National League mark of 2,684, set by the 1930 Cubs. "It should add up to the most devastating one-year display of power," since the 1936 Yankees club that boasted five players with 100 or more RBI, led by Lou Gehrig with 152 and Joe DiMaggio with 125. Some critics argued that Brooklyn hitters were benefiting from a lively baseball, and Roeder conceded, "There has been dispute about that all season." However, "[the Dodgers] have a handicap which none of the old slugging teams faced—for years, the balance of Brooklyn power has been righthanded, so that most of the time the Dodgers operate against right-handed pitchers." Indeed, of the Brooklyn regulars during this era, only Duke Snider batted left-handed.[41]

Reese ripped two home runs on August 28 against the Reds. He hit the first with two out in the second inning. That round-tripper, off Cincinnati starter Herm Wehmeier with Jim Gilliam on base, put the Dodgers ahead, 5–1. The Reds charged forward and scored five times in the third inning. Reese hit his second long ball, again with Gilliam aboard, in the eighth off reliever and former Dodger Clyde King, to break a 7–7 tie. "Even Pee Wee Reese is muscling in on the strong-arm act as the Dodgers come down the pennant stretch aiming their artillery at 100 victories and 200 home runs," said the *Eagle*. Reese called the first homer "the hardest ball [I] ever hit." Reese joked with Snider in the clubhouse and showed off his muscles. "One hundred and eighty pounds of dynamite," he said. "Say Snider, how many [home runs have you got, 33? Sorry, I've only got 11. It looks like the season is going to run out on old Pee Wee."[42] The Dodgers had hit 12 home runs over their past four games.

On the same night that Reese hit two home runs, Carl Furillo also hit one, his 20th of the season, joining Campanella, Snider and Hodges with at least that many. Brooklyn tied the National League mark for having four players with at least 20 home runs in one season.[43] The Dodgers had now hit 174 homers. The all-time single-season homer mark of 221, set by the 1947 Giants, might be out of reach, but the Dodgers could still eclipse the team record of 194, set in 1950. Also, no team had ever won 100 games in a single season and slugged 200 homers. The 1953 Dodgers had a chance. "And beat Babe Ruth and them?" Charlie Dressen asked. Dave Anderson answered, "Yep, even the Yankees' Murderers' Row never did it."[44]

Brooklyn saved its largest offensive explosion for an August 30 game against St. Louis. The teams met on a sweltering day at Ebbets Field. The thermometer soared into the 90s. While 16,781 fans watched and fanned themselves to stay cool, the Dodgers stayed hot and enjoyed a 20–4 lopsided win. They scored 12 times in the seventh inning, the second time that year they put up a dozen runs in one frame. "Up to that moment, it was a fairly respectable game," Dick Young wrote. Reese contributed an RBI single. The dozen runs tied a record for runs by a National League team in the seventh inning. The Cubs scored 12 times in the seventh frame on May 28, 1925. The Red Sox held the major league record. They posted 14 runs in the seventh inning on July 4, 1948.[45]

Roy Campanella drove in five runs and now had 122 RBI, tying him with Gabby Harnett and Walker Cooper for the most by an NL catcher in one season.[46] Gil Hodges, utility infielder Bobby Morgan, and starting pitcher Carl Erskine all had three RBI. Bob Broeg wrote that "At Ebbets Field, Redbird hurlers appeared to suffer from an exaggerated case of claustrophobia caused probably (1) by the closeness of the outfield fences and (2) an apparently unconquerable desire to get the blanketly-blank off the mound as soon as possible."[47] The Dodgers improved to 89–40 and led the second-place Braves by 10 games.

Reese posted his second four-hit game of the 1953 campaign on September 11, albeit in a 9–8 loss to Milwaukee. The following day, Brooklyn clinched the pennant with a 5–2 victory against the Braves. Erskine won his 19th game and scattered seven hits over nine innings. No team had ever wrapped up a flag this early. The 1931

Cardinals held the previous mark for a 154-game schedule, September 16.[48] O'Malley made his way through the locker room to congratulate his victorious charges. Happy Felton and Connie Desmond set up TV cameras. Reese and Cookie Lavagetto hoisted Charlie Dressen onto their shoulders for a moment. The table spread included some local beer and Wisconsin cheese. Players waited "about an hour and half" to begin the traditional champagne celebration, or until they boarded a train bound for Chicago, Tommy Holmes reported.[49]

The Dodgers concluded their regular season with an 8–2 win against the Phillies at Connie Mack Stadium. On the year, the Dodgers scored 955 runs, almost 200 runs more than the Cardinals and the Giants, both of whom scored 768. Brooklyn hitters pounded out 208 home runs, 32 more than the runner-up Giants, and set a new team mark. Duke Snider had whacked the team's 200th long ball on September 15 versus the Cardinals. Two days later, against St. Louis once again, Brooklyn won its 100th game. The Dodgers beat Murderers' Row and every other team in history. They fell just a bit short of the NL record for total bases, finishing with 2,545.

The Bums could also run. They topped the circuit in stolen bases with 90, or 41 more than the next-speediest team, the Cubs. In the field, the Dodgers finished with the highest fielding percentage of any NL team (.980) and the fewest errors (118). And to top it all off, Dodgers pitchers posted the third-lowest ERA (4.10) and struck out the most batters (817).

Pee Wee Reese enjoyed another solid season. Besides scoring 108 runs, he batted .271 and sported a .374 on-base percentage. He also hit 13 homers, had 61 RBI, and stole a team-high 22 bases. Brooklyn first-base coach Jake Pitler said, "[Pee Wee] is still absolutely the smoothest guy taking a lead off first that I ever saw. … His secret is no tipoff. He's just moving. That's all. It's the timing, I guess, with Reese knowing his pitchers, and making his move to take the fullest advantage."[50] Jim Gilliam led the National League with 17 triples, batted .278, and scored 125 runs. Carl Furillo rebounded from his lackluster 1952 season and topped NL hitters with a .344 batting average. Carl Erskine led the pitching staff with a 20–6 mark and a 3.54 ERA. The 26-year-old also set career highs with 187 strikeouts and 16 complete games. The Dodgers finished second in league attendance, with 1,163,419 fans passing through the Ebbets Field turnstiles.

Reese called this squad "a real pro team." He rated it above the 1941 Dodgers. Dolph Camilli, Dixie Walker, and Billy Herman provided the pop on that ballclub. "There were great hitters on that '41 club," Reese said. "But I think this present club has as good hitting and a little more power." As for pitching, Reese said Erskine compared well with Whitlow Wyatt, and while Hugh Casey provided strong work out of the bullpen in 1941, the corps of Clem Labine, Bob Milliken, and Ben Wade handled that job for the 1953 team. In addition, Reese said, "Our defense has been so darn good this year that I would have to sum up by saying this club is better all around, with more balance than any I have played with in Brooklyn."[51]

Once again, the Dodgers got ready to play the Yankees in the World Series. The Bronx Bombers easily won the American League pennant, finishing 8½ games ahead of the Indians, who got a career year out of Al Rosen. The 29-year-old third baseman just missed out on the Triple Crown. He led the circuit in home runs (45) and

RBI (145) and finished .001 points behind Washington Senators first baseman Mickey Vernon with a .336 batting average. Yogi Berra led the Yanks with 27 home runs and 108 RBI. Whitey Ford, a 24-year-old lefty with a wicked curveball, won 18 games. Veteran Eddie Lopat won 16 with a 2.42 ERA.

Businesses throughout Brooklyn offered their support to the borough's ballclub. Citizens Bank took out an advertisement that offered a "Good Luck to Our Dodgers." Fountain Pen Clinic wished a "Good Luck to Dem Bums." Ebinger's, a local bakery, placed the figure of a ballplayer atop a cake with the line, "Hail to the Brooklyn Dodgers."[52]

Dick Gifford, a newspaper mailer, counted himself among the Dodgers faithful. He reported for jury duty at the local courthouse at 120 Schermerhorn Street, ready to make his case to City Court Justice George Eilperin. Gifford held a jury notice in one hand and a copy of the *Brooklyn Eagle* in the other. He planned his vacation around going to the World Series and already had bought tickets. Gifford pleaded to the judge, who had just lectured prospective jurors on the importance of performing their civic duty, "I knew it wasn't even a good excuse," Gifford said. "But I reminded the judge I wasn't trying to skip out. I just wanted a delay. I assured him the series wouldn't go seven games and would he put it over to October 5." Judge Eilperin nodded and intoned, "I hope you're right. Be here next Monday."[53]

Now, could the Dodgers finally break through and celebrate a championship? The team had lost six World Series in franchise history, three since 1947. The manager and players promised a different ending this time. Charlie Dressen said, "We've been hot against good pitchers all year. There's no reason why we can't be hot for another week." Jackie Robinson said, "I've never felt so confident about a World Series in all my life." Carl Furillo even announced how long it would take before the celebration began. "In six games. That's the lucky number, six." Pee Wee Reese said, "How do I feel about the Series? I feel like we're going to win it."[54]

The Series began at Yankee Stadium and, at least for the Dodgers, on a sour note. Carl Erskine gave up four runs in the first inning. New York led, 5–1, before Brooklyn scored three times in the sixth inning. The Dodgers added another run in the seventh but still lost, 9–5. Making it all worse, an Allie Reynolds fastball ran into Campanella's right hand, although the catcher stayed in the game and refused an X-ray. Reese, 0-for-3 with two walks, said the Dodgers "just had the hell beat out of us" but added, "We're not downhearted. But, of course, the Yanks aren't either. This isn't going to be easy."[55]

The task got even tougher the following day. Mickey Mantle belted a two-run homer in the eighth inning off Preacher Roe to break a 2–2 tie. Mantle hit "a heck of pitch," Roe said, a "changeup screwball" that dipped below Mantle's knees. One inning earlier, Billy Martin whacked a solo home run into the left field stands. He hit a high curveball, and Roe could only shake his head. "Nobody ought to pitch anybody a high curve" he lamented. "It was the greatest mistake since they invented buttermilk."[56] Brooklyn wasted Reese's out-out triple off Lopat in the first inning. Duke Snider popped out, and Robinson flied out to end the threat. It looked bad for the Dodgers. No team had ever won a World Series after losing the first two games.

Dressen asked Erskine to rebound in Game Three at a packed Ebbets Field. A headline in the *Eagle* encouraged the Bums to get going: "Egad, Men! Wake up!" Erskine told Snider, "I gotta pitch like there's no tomorrow."[57] Up to the challenge, he baffled Yankees hitters in the early going and struck out six through the first three innings. The Dodgers led, 2–1, going into the eighth inning, when New York tied the score on Gene Woodling's RBI single.

Roy Campanella, playing with a "painfully puffed right hand,"[58] following his Game One injury, batted with one out in Brooklyn's half of the eighth and hit a solo home run deep into the left field bleachers. The Dodgers held on to win, 3–2. Erskine allowed six hits and struck out a World Series-record 14 batters. "Erskine had better stuff than any pitcher we saw all year in the American League,"[59] Mantle said. Erskine felt exhausted. He told reporters, "I didn't know how many strikeouts I had. I just knew we had our backs to the wall, and I had to keep pumping 'em in."[60]

Brooklyn's vaunted offense show up at last in Game Four. Like the earlier games, this one was played on "beautiful day, the fourth great weather day in a row in New York."[61] The Dodgers scored three first-inning runs off Whitey Ford and won, 7–3. Snider led a 12-hit attack with a home run and four RBI. Gilliam added three hits and two RBI. "The Dodgers," Oscar Fraley wrote, "were operating with the same murderous intent that marked their efforts all season."[62] The World Series was now tied at two games apiece. A confident Dressen shouted in the Brooklyn locker room that "we have a terrific chance now."[63]

All that enthusiasm quickly turned to disappointment. By the third inning of Game Five, the Yankees led, 6–1, en route to an 11–7 victory. Johnny Podres allowed five runs (just one earned) in 2⅔ innings of work. The following day, New York celebrated another championship. Erskine, making his third start, could not repeat the magic from Game Three. He allowed two runs in the first inning and one more in the second. He gave up six hits and three walks in his four innings of work. "Erskine was in more trouble than a prisoner of the Soviet secret police,"[64] Tommy Holmes wrote.

The Dodgers still made the game interesting. They pushed across one run in the sixth inning and tied the score in the ninth after Carl Furillo slugged a two-run homer off Allie Reynolds. Dressen sent out Labine for his third inning of work in the bottom half of the ninth.

The Brooklyn pitcher gave up a lead-off walk to Hank Bauer and, after getting Berra to line out, allowed a single to Mantle. New York had runners on first and third. Billy Martin stepped to the plate. The 25-year-old had put together a strong regular season. He hit 15 home runs with 75 RBI. Thus far in the Fall Classic, he was 11-for-23 (.478) with two homers and seven RBI. Martin took Labine's first pitch for a strike. "The next one, he belted squarely just to the left of second base into center field," said the AP. "Snider came tearing in to take it on the hop but didn't even bother to try a throw to the plate."[65] Bauer, "one of the fastest base runners in the game," easily scored the Series-winning run. He "couldn't have been tagged with a rocket gun."[66]

Walter O'Malley, magnanimous in the moment, walked into the Yankees clubhouse, put one of his burly arms around the skinny Martin, and shouted "Billy, you're the hero of the series!" Martin called his game-winning hit "the biggest kick in my life."[67]

Overall, the Dodgers hit .300, better than the Yankees' .279 mark. New York still outscored Brooklyn, 32–26. Pee Wee Reese batted just .208 (5-for-24), with the lone triple and no RBI. Reese, in a Tommy Holmes column headlined "Yanks On Their Game—Our Guys Weren't," said, "We lost because the Yanks played their usual game in the Series and our nine didn't. We're better than we showed."[68] Roy Campanella, as upbeat as ever, told reporters, "It was a wonderful season," while still conceding "It ended in a heap of nothing."[69] Reese, disconsolate, searched for the right words to explain why the Dodgers kept falling short in October. "I've been trying to find out for 12 years now," he said. "Wait til next year? Who knows? Maybe I won't even be here next year. Anything can happen in this racket, you know."[70]

Sometimes even the manager resigns after winning back-to-back pennants. Dressen left Brooklyn "in a huff" on Wednesday, October 14. O'Malley rejected the skipper's request for a three-year contract but did offer a one-year deal "at a substantial increase." Dressen and his wife, Ruth, wrote a letter to O'Malley, stating the skipper's desire for greater job security. The letter included one paragraph that was, according to Dressen, "pretty strong. But I'm not going to second guess my wife." Harsh words did nothing to move O'Malley. While he ran the Dodgers, managers should only expect one-year contracts. Even so, O'Malley liked Dressen and invited him back to Brooklyn. "Charlie can sign a contract with me right this minute if he agrees to a one-year term," O'Malley said. "Unless he agrees to sign for one year, however, the Dodgers will have a new manager next year."[71]

At the very least, Dressen wanted a two-year agreement. "All my friends tell me I'm crazy to sign a one-year contract," Dressen said. "I win two pennants, something no other manager ever did in Brooklyn, and they want to give me one year. I'm not going to do it." O'Malley acknowledged that, yes, some teams had signed managers to long-term deals. The Dodgers held no plans to follow suit. "I am a firm disbeliever in long-term contracts," he said. O'Malley owned stock in the club when it was still paying Casey Stengel, Burleigh Grimes, and Leo Durocher after each was terminated. "The Brooklyn club has paid more managers more money for not managing than any team in major league history." O'Malley vowed, "It will never happen again."[72]

Just a few days later, Dressen left Brooklyn for California. He signed on to manage the Oakland Oaks, his old ballclub and also Stengel's. A gleeful Dressen bragged about his new salary, larger than he earned with the Dodgers. "Honest," he said, "I'm pleased as heck."[73] O'Malley offered a curt bon voyage message. "I'm sure Mrs. Dressen will be very happy in Oakland."[74]

Attention now turned to Dressen's successor. Fans made telephone calls and mailed hundreds of letters to the team's headquarters on Montague Street, most of them in favor of giving Reese the job. Even Dressen put in a plug for his now-former shortstop. "I think Pee Wee is the logical man for the job," he said. "Of course, I don't know what they'll do, but Reese ought to make them a good manager. If he gets the job, I wish him all the luck in the world, and I'll be rooting hard for him."[75]

In *Off the Record*, Buzzie Bavasi confirmed that the "search for a new manager began in Louisville." Of course, that meant the search began with Reese. "Walter O'Malley wanted someone the public could relate to, as well as a man the players would respect," Bavasi said. "Reese seemed to be the perfect choice. He was Walter O'Malley's choice, too."[76] O'Malley counted himself as one of the shortstop's biggest

14. "One hundred and eighty pounds of dynamite"

fans. "When people ask me to name my favorite player," he said, "I always answer 'Pee Wee Reese.'"[77]

Bavasi flew to Louisville and talked to the captain. Over lunch, Bavasi asked Reese about his interest in managing the Dodgers. Reese thought about it and turned down any offer. "Well, number one, I still think I can play some more," he said. "Number two, we just won the pennant for two straight years. How can you improve on that? I don't think I'm ready to manage now."[78] Later, Bavasi admitted, "I did not try to talk [Reese] out of his decision to refuse the offer."[79]

Jackie Robinson, after hearing of Reese's decision, decided that "maybe it's for the best. Pee Wee has all the baseball sense in the world, but I'm afraid he's too close to the players. ... Whenever any of us had a problem, Pee Wee was the first guy we'd go to. It couldn't work that way if he's managing. He'd get complete cooperation—everybody loves the guy." But, Robinson added, "I'm afraid we'd try too hard to win for him and tighten up."[80]

In early November, Reese spoke to a reporter about turning down the managerial job. "Maybe I made a mistake," he said. "I will know that in a couple of years." He added, "I think I have done the right thing. Anyway, that's the way it is, and I'll never be sorry, no matter now things might turn out."[81] Now, fans and reporters turned to another question: Who would lead the Dodgers in 1954?

15

"He's not swinging a bat"

"Gentleman, our new manager, Walter Alston."[1] Walter O'Malley introduced Charlie Dressen's replacement at a press conference held November 24 at team headquarters. Reporters scribbled notes, photographers snapped pictures, and newsreel cameramen jockeyed for position. O'Malley told the assembled media that he expected to hoist a championship trophy in October. "No sense kidding about it," he said. "We're dedicated to winning a World Series. We think Walter is the man who can do it."[2] Furthermore, "Do you realize that we have lost more World Series than any club in major league history? I'm getting a little tired of it."[3] Even so, he insisted, addressing his skipper, "Walter, no one is breathing down your neck."[4]

It was Wednesday afternoon. O'Malley hired Alston on Tuesday.[5] A 42-year-old grandfather and one-time minor league power hitter, Alston had been with the Brooklyn organization for a decade, most recently as skipper of the Montreal Royals. The locals knew almost nothing about him. On November 25, a *Daily News* headline read: "Alston (Who's He?) To Manage Dodgers."

Tommy Holmes described the 6-foot-2-inch Walter Emmons Alston as a "tall, bald, nice-guy type."[6] Born December 1, 1911, in Venice, Ohio, near Cincinnati, the Dodgers' new skipper grew up on a farm in nearby Morning Star and, later, in Darrtown. For a while, he rode a pony bareback to grade school. During his teen years, he earned the nickname "Smokey," one he kept for the rest of his life. A pitcher in those early days, "I used to have a real fast fireball,"[7] he explained. It had plenty of smoke on it.

Following high school, Alston enrolled at Miami University in Oxford, Ohio. He drove a laundry truck and hustled pool games to help pay tuition. He also starred in a nearby county baseball league. The Cardinals signed Alston as an infielder in 1935 and assigned him to the Greenwood (South Carolina) Chiefs of the Class C East Dixie League. He recorded his lone major league at-bat on September 27, 1936, at Sportsman's Park, against the Cubs and Lou Warneke, a right-hander known as "The Arkansas Hummingbird". He fouled off a few pitches and then struck out. After that, "I went in to play first [base] and didn't do too well."[8]

Alston successfully handled one chance and muffed the other. The Cardinals lost, 6–3. "He's not particularly responsible for what happened," the *Post-Dispatch* reported. "But he was the goat."[9] Alston never appeared in another big league game. Johnny Mize held claim over the first-base job in St. Louis. Alston retired with a career fielding percentage of .500 and a .000 batting average. He hit 176 home runs as a minor leaguer. Brooklyn hired him in 1944 as player-manager of the Class B Trenton (New Jersey) Packers in the Interstate League. He won his first title two years later while leading the Nashua Dodgers and moved on to the Class A Pueblo (Colorado) Dodgers, then to Saint Paul, and, finally, to Montreal.

Only after Pee Wee Reese turned down the job did Alston emerge as a leading candidate. Buzzie Bavasi gave Alston a strong endorsement. "O'Malley hired Alston entirely on my recommendation," Bavasi wrote in *Off the Record*. "Maybe I was going out on a limb, but I never thought so. I believed in what Alston could do. No matter which club we gave him, he had always done an excellent job."[10] Brooklyn's general manager called Alston in Ohio and told him to catch the next plane to New York City. O'Malley thought that Alston, once in the big city, should register at the McAlpin Hotel under an assumed name. What would be a good one? "Alston," Bavasi said. "That's an assumed name here. Nobody knows who Alston is."[11]

Throughout the press conference, O'Malley puffed on a cigar and answered questions about his team's new skipper. Reporters asked about the length of Alston's contract. O'Malley held up a lone finger. One year. He anticipated no problems from Pee Wee Reese, the popular choice to manage Brooklyn's baseball team. "Reese is no threat," O'Malley said, addressing Alston as well as the press. "Pee Wee is a fine little gentleman and will give you his best, as he has done with every manager before you. He can round out his career as a player and then start in our organization [as a manager] in a lower classification. If he prefers, he can leave us and start at the top as a manager for some other big-league club."[12]

Reporters called Reese at his Louisville home. The shortstop said he only knew Walter Alston through comments from players such as Roy Campanella, who offered good reports. Reese wished the manager "all the luck in the world,"[13] and added, maybe with a bit of false modesty, "I only hope that I'm his shortstop."[14] Negotiations on a new contract for the shortstop took about "two seconds,"[15] Bavasi said. Reese signed a deal worth $33,000, according to the *Daily News*, a $1,000 raise from 1953.[16]

The March 2 edition of the *Eagle* included a picture of Reese and Alston shaking hands, plus an article on Reese's thoughts about the upcoming season. He expected the pennant race to be a close one, not a Brooklyn runaway this time. "You can't expect all our players to hit as well this year as we did last [year]," he told Dave Anderson. "That'd be impossible. But we've got Don Newcombe back [from his tour in the Army] and maybe he'll take up that slack. If anybody can do it, he can."[17]

The often "roly-poly"[18] Roy Campanella arrived in Florida at a slim 189 pounds. Campanella shrugged off reports that the Dodgers might be complacent after winning back-to-back pennants. This was a team, after all, that had lost four World Series in seven years. How could it possibly be complacent? "This is a hungry camp," the Brooklyn catcher insisted. Alston said that eight of his players had arrived in Florida one or two weeks early. "We all want another World Series cut and another crack at those Yankees,"[19] Jackie Robinson explained. Reese reported at 172 pounds, three pounds lighter than he weighed at the end of the 1953 campaign. "Did some hunting, bicycle riding, and played a little golf,"[20] he said. He expected to play "154 games," or all of them.[21] He wanted to bat .300, something he had never done but "I've been expecting to for the last 14 years."[22]

Some players, predictably, tested the rookie manager. Early on, Alston talked hitting with Duke Snider. Did the Brooklyn slugger always stand that way in the batter's box? Undoubtedly, Snider knew all about Alston's dubious legacy as a big league ballplayer and shrugged off his skipper. "Where did you make your mistakes?"[23] Snider asked. Nevertheless, Reese told a reporter, "It's my impression that all the boys like Walter and that they have respect for him, which he deserves, so far as I'm concerned. He's not going to have any trouble with me—that's for sure. And I don't think he's going to have any trouble, period."[24]

Of course, no one expected Reese to cause problems. Back in January, *The Sporting News* asked writers to pick each team's fastest runner, wittiest player, best dressed, etc. The writers selected Reese as the least temperamental Dodger. He also took top marks for being most relaxed on the field, most cooperative with writers, best student of the game, most helpful to rookies, most popular off the field, and having done the most for his team. (Among the other winners: Billy Loes, worst dressed and best pinball player; Jackie Robinson, most nervous on the field and most ambitious; Roy Campanella, happiest and biggest eater; and Carl Erskine, best looking and happiest marriage.)[25]

Roscoe McGowen called Reese "absolutely honest and frank." He affirmed that "anybody who knows Reese would know that Alston will get all the cooperation from Pee Wee that any manager possibly could hope for—the same cooperation the Little Colonel previously had given to Leo Durocher, Burt Shotton and Chuck Dressen."[26] In an article for *Baseball Digest*, the veteran shortstop acknowledged that Alston was in a "rough spot. The only way he can improve on Dressen is to win a World Series."[27]

Pitching, not slugging, might carry Brooklyn to a pennant, Reese said. He cited, in addition to the return of Don Newcombe, a bullpen that included Clem Labine, Johnny Podres, and Jim Hughes. Bob Milliken and Ben Wade had also provided solid relief for the Dodgers in 1953. "I've never seen a team with the depth that we have in the bullpen," Reese said. "If our starter gets knocked out, in comes another guy who throws even harder. The guy who just left was throwing aspirin tablets; the guy who's coming in throws peas—with streamers. That's where we're going to win this thing."[28]

Certainly, Brooklyn hoped for a comeback season from Joe Black. The pitcher suffered through a dreadful sophomore slump. He compiled an admirable 6–3 record but with a 5.33 ERA over his 72⅔ innings. Black blamed some of his problems on Dressen. The former skipper had wanted him to add a trick pitch to an arsenal of fastballs and curveballs. Maybe a knuckleball of all things. With that, columnist Bill Lee wrote, "Black stopped throwing free, loose and fast. His control was beyond redemption." Now, Lee reported, "Black is throwing fast again."[29]

Later, Walter Alston wrote that he never worried about duplicating the pennant-winning 1953 campaign. Instead, he "wanted each man to have the best year he can. ... We were solid at every position. I had three dependable leaders in Reese, Hodges, and Campanella."[30] Of note, Alston failed to mention Jackie Robinson. The two men clashed almost from the start. Robinson sometimes went through morning exercises in a half-hearted way, talking with reporters rather than building up a good sweat. During a clubhouse meeting, "Our conversation got a little rough," Alston admitted. "I called him on it and told him and everyone else that they could talk to me any time, any place and about anything. Now, some of the players felt that was a physical challenge by me of Jackie. Possibly it could have been interpreted that way."[31]

Anyway, the 35-year-old Robinson talked as though this might be his last season, "no matter how good a year I have," due to the continued wear and tear on his legs. "It's just too tough to keep on going," he said. He hoped to find work in radio or television, something he had dabbled in part-time over the past few years. "Now, we've built the show to the point where it could pay off in real money," Robinson said. "But even if that job doesn't pan out, I hope to get another, so I can get out of the game while I'm still at my peak."[32]

The Dodgers cruised through their spring training schedule. On March 19, they won their 10th straight game, knocking off the Yankees, 2–1, in front of 9,032 fans in Miami. Reese's run-scoring single in the 10th inning broke a 1–1 tie. Two days later, Campanella slid into second base and jammed his left wrist. A subsequent X-Ray revealed some bad news. "My hand is broken," the catcher told Buzzie Bavasi. Campanella decided against surgery and hoped to play through the pain, at least while he could.[33]

The Giants spoiled Walter Alston's Brooklyn debut. Dodgers nemesis Sal Maglie beat Carl Erskine, 4–3, with 32,397 fans on hand on April 13 at the Polo Grounds. Campanella, sore hand and all, started behind the plate and slugged two solo home runs. Willie Mays undid a 3–3 tie when he led off the sixth inning by walloping an Erskine pitch deep into the stands. Reese went hitless in two at-bats but walked three times. He struck out once, in the fifth inning, on a bender courtesy of "Sal the Barber". "Nobody throws a curve like Maglie," Reese said. "It stays in the same plane. Most curves drop. Not his. It stays level and just shoots off at an angle."[34]

This being a Giants-Dodgers series, inside fastballs and tough words soon ruled the day. In the second game, baseball's fiercest rivalry heated up once again. Supposedly, Leo Durocher told his relief pitcher, Mario Picone, to hurl a beanball at Reese, the skipper's one-time protégé. Durocher, according to the *Eagle*'s Dave Anderson, had begun fuming that Reese "was playing too rough when he tagged Mays after the Giants' glamour boy jockeyed around"[35] during a rundown play in the seventh inning. Reese led off for Brooklyn in the eighth inning. Durocher yelled to Picone, or at least Dodgers players said he did, "Stick it in [Reese's] ear."[36] Picone, a Brooklyn native, obeyed and sent a "high, inside fastball"[37] that the shortstop ducked away from at the last instant.

Reese didn't make a big deal out of Picone's brushback pitch or his own tag on Mays. He wasn't trying to injure the Giants' young superstar-in-the-making. "[Mays] was going away from me," Reese told reporters, "and then he came back, so I ran into him hard. And I wound up straddling him. That's all."[38]

The two were involved in another play that game. Reese walked to lead off the sixth inning and made it to third base on Snider's double. With one away, Gil Hodges hit a soft fly ball to Mays in shallow left-center. Reese tagged up and faked going home. He was explaining all this afterward, and Snider chimed in, "You faked me, too."[39] In a moment that harkened back to Brooklyn's Daffy days, while Reese feigned his dash for home plate, Snider tagged up and sprinted toward third. After recognizing the bluff, Sniswe scrambled back to second, but too late. Mays threw him out.

Even so, Reese insisted, New York's "Say-Hey Kid" made just a so-so throw, not a "Mays throw," to get Snider for the double play. "What's the matter with Mays' arm?" Reese asked reporters. "Mays is supposed to have a good arm and he wasn't too deep." The Dodgers still won the game, 6–4. Don Newcombe, making his first start since October 3, 1951, threw a complete game and drove in two runs. Besides drawing a walk, Reese singled and tripled. All of that made the Daffy-like episode a little easier to digest. "It's funny now," Reese said. "But it wouldn't have been so funny if we lost because of that play." Alston, doing double duty as both manager and third-base coach, blamed himself for the gaffe. "I forgot to hold up Snider," he confessed. "You can't say he wasn't hustling."[40]

Reese put his long-ball swing on display in the early part of the season. He homered four times in April and three times in May. He drilled his first pitch into the seats on April 19 against Bob Miller and the Phillies. That two-run shot cut the Philadelphia lead to 5–4. Brooklyn went on to win, 9–7. He hit a solo homer the next day off Murry Dickson. This time, the Phillies came out ahead, 6–3.

The Dodgers tormented Cincinnati starter Harry Perkowski on April 29. Batters knocked five of the veteran left-hander's pitches into the seats at Crosley Field. Reese deposited a homer with two out in the sixth inning. Jim Gilliam hit two pitches out of the park that day. Duke Snider and Dick Williams, a young utility player and future manager of two World Series champions, also homered. Si Burick of the *Dayton Daily News* called the Cincinnati pitching "shabby." No one could argue with that barb. Reds hurlers had allowed 31 home runs over the previous 15 games.

Brooklyn dropped to 9–7 after losing, 7–6, to the Reds on May 1. Worse, the pain in Roy Campanella's hand had not dulled, and extra padding in his catcher's mitt did nothing to help. Neither did sticking his hand into a bucket of ice water after every game to ease the swelling. Surgery was the only option. "Okay," Campanella finally said to Buzzie Bavasi, "Let's get it over with."[41] One week later, Johnny Podres hurled a three-hit, 3–0, shutout. Reese made three hits and drove in two runs. He ripped his second homer of the season off Dickson, a two-run shot, in the fifth. The game lasted just six innings due to a major rainstorm that soaked the field. The *Philadelphia Inquirer* reported, "Rain and Pee Wee Reese were too much for Murry Dickson."[42]

Pee Wee Reese celebrated a couple of milestones over the next few weeks. On May 29, he stole second base in the seventh inning against the Giants at the Polo Grounds. It was just his third theft of the year but the 200th of his career.[43] Reese was the top base stealer among active players and the first National Leaguer to reach the 200 mark since Kiki Cuyler, who retired after the 1938 season with 328 career thefts for the Cubs, Pirates, Reds, and, in his final campaign, the Dodgers. Cuyler, an outfielder, led the NL in steals four times and swiped a career-high 43 bases for Chicago in 1929.

A few innings before getting his stolen base, Reese walked with the bases loaded to put the Dodgers ahead, 1–0. His two-run homer in the ninth inning off Sal Maglie gave Brooklyn a 4–2 win behind Erskine. "The Barber threw a curve that was aimed for the outside corner," Jim McCulley wrote. "Reese also took aim—for the rightfield stands. He stuck his bat out and popped the ball up against the façade. It was not a vicious rap, but it was enough to win."[44]

On June 16, Reese ripped the 100th home run of his career. Ray Crone, a rookie right-hander, served up the pitch that sailed out of Ebbets Field in the seventh inning with Gilliam on base. Reese also roped a double and lined a run-scoring single to help the Dodgers beat the Braves, 8–4. The shortstop "practically mopped up Ebbets Field." Afterward, Reese joked that he only had 105 RBI to go along with a century's worth of homers. (Actually, he had driven home nearly 700 runs at that point in his career.) He looked over at Gil Hodges, his muscular teammate, and said, "Shame on you, Hodges. If I was as big and strong as you, I'd probably hit 100 a year. Shame on you for only hitting 30 or 40." Reese, "in mock seriousness," predicted that he would hit 100 more home runs before retiring. Just how long might that take, a reporter asked. "About 10 years," Reese said, when he would be 45 years old.[45]

The Dodgers and Giants bumped against one another in the standings throughout June. Brooklyn took a turn in first place early in the month before New York moved into the top spot. The rivals met for a three-game series at the Polo Grounds starting June 29. New York grabbed an early lead in the opener with solo runs in the second and third innings. Roy Campanella, who returned to action May 30, hit a two-run homer in the ninth and sent the game into extra innings.

Reese singled with one out in the 12th. The next batter, rookie outfielder Walt Moryn, muscled a base hit to center field. Reese rounded second, headed for third and slid into the bag. He made it there safely but not without injury. His left thigh muscle barked from pain. "It looks bad," he told reporters. To make matters worse, two innings earlier, Duke Snider took a Marv Grissom fastball directly on the right elbow. "I can't bend my arm,"[46] he said. The final insult? The Giants won the game, 4–3, on a Dusty Rhodes' RBI single in the 13th.

Initially, Reese thought he hurt the same muscle that he pulled a few days earlier. The next morning, he decided, "This one is higher up and deeper. Of course, you can never tell how long it'll take for these things to heal. Some are fast, some are slow."[47]

As it turned out, Reese missed just nine games and promptly began making trouble again for opposing pitchers. (Snider sat out two games following his elbow plunking.) Over the next three weeks, he hit .402, with a .474 on-base percentage, and raised his batting average to .311. He cleared the bases with a double in the ninth inning on July 9 versus the Phillies and helped the Dodgers to a 7–5 win. The following day, again against Philadelphia, he drilled a double and two singles in a 10–5 victory. Snider called Reese "the best ball player on the Dodgers, and I've said it for five years. In the clutch, he's the man. When Brooklyn loses him, they're really going to lose something."[48]

Reese made the NL All-Star team for the 10th and final time. Other members of the Brooklyn party included Erskine, Campanella, Hodges, Robinson, and Snider. Walter Alston, by virtue of managing the reigning pennant winner, led the NL squad, which lost a slugfest at Cleveland Municipal Stadium, 11–9, on July 13 before nearly 70,000 fans. Al Rosen, at his home ballpark, collected three hits, including two homers, and drove in five runs. Alvin Dark played the entire game at shortstop for the National League. Reese sat on the bench. The *Eagle* only reported that Reese missed the game but offered no explanation.[49] He had played in both ends of a doubleheader against Philadelphia on July 11, the final two games before the All-Star Game, and went a combined 2-for-7 with two walks and a run scored. Brooklyn split the twin bill, taking the opener, 8–7, and losing the nightcap, 3–1. He lined three base hits in the Dodgers' first game after the break, a 2–1 win in Milwaukee. Most likely, Alston simply took advantage of the three-day pause for the midsummer classic and rested his shortstop, whose leg probably needed more healing.

Following that victory against the Braves, Brooklyn lost the next three games in the series. Newspaper reporters filed into the locker room and asked what was wrong with the team. Jackie Robinson said Alston should give a fiery speech. Reese disagreed. He preferred hot bats to loud speeches. "It's up to us," he said. "We all certainly know that." Gil Hodges said that Little Leaguers need pep talks, not grown-up baseball players. "Who's Alston going to spank, anyway?" Hodges asked. Duke Snider argued that a tough speech might be just what this team needed. He doubted that Alston could give it. "The only two managers I've played for who could do it," according to Snider, "were Leo Durocher and Dressen."[50]

Pee Wee Reese left Milwaukee with a .304 batting average. On July 23 in St. Louis, he turned 35 years old. Eddie Stanky, now in his third year as the Cardinals' manager, watched that evening's game from a seat in the press box while serving a suspension. The Redbirds led, 6–4, going into the ninth inning at Sportsman's Park. Jim Gilliam came up to bat with two out and Roy Campanella on second base. Reese stood in the on-deck circle. "Get this guy [Gilliam] out!" Stanky yelled. "I don't want 'Happy Birthday' to get up there."[51] And Happy Birthday did not bat. Gilliam popped out to end the game. Brooklyn dropped to six games out of first place. The following day, the Dodgers won, 7–6. Reese, though, went hitless in four at-bats, and his batting average slipped to .299.

Reese climbed above the .300 mark for good after he managed three singles in the series finale. The Dodgers won, 2–1, and improved to 20 games above .500. They still trailed the first-place Giants by four games but led the third-place Braves by 7½ games. Over the month, Reese batted .383 with a .468 on-base percentage and enjoyed 13 multi-hit contests.

During the baseball season, Pee Wee and Dottie Reese rented a house in Bay Ridge, Brooklyn, a quiet, mostly residential area in the borough's southwest corner. The Narrows, a tidal strait that separates Brooklyn from Staten Island, lies to the west. The Fort Hamilton Army base, in use since 1825, stands just to the south. According to a contemporary description, "Bay Ridge is scattered with great history and old landmarks" and "situated in a quiet and peaceful area of New York City, especially when compared to Manhattan."[52] Mostly rural throughout the 1800s, Bay Ridge, along with much of south Brooklyn, grew in the early years of the 20th century as builders looked for open land in the nation's biggest city.

"The sea view from many elevations" in that section of the borough was "superb,"[53] the *Brooklyn Daily Eagle* reported in 1906. "It is the puzzle of many people, visiting this section from Manhattan, why so delightful a territory within a few miles of the heart of New York should not have been fully occupied by residents long ago."[54] Over the next few decades, handsome row houses began to dominate this tidy neighborhood, located about eight miles from Ebbets Field.

Carl and Betty Erskine, Duke and Beverly Snider, and Rube and Mildred Walker also rented homes in Bay Ridge. Snider wrote about this tight-knit group in *The Duke of Flatbush*. The couples went to see movies like *From Here to Eternity*, *Three Coins in the Fountain*, and even a few sci-fi thrillers produced in 3-D, "where we sat wearing cardboard glasses and watched a bunch of actors throw things at each other—only we were the ones doing the ducking."[55] The couples often rode the subway into Manhattan for dinner on Saturday night or to take in a Broadway show.

Another form of entertainment put viewers firmly on the living room couch. In 1939, during the New York City World's Fair, visitors could walk into the RCA exhibit building and buy a "cathode ray tube device" (a.k.a. a television). Eleven years later, only four million U.S. residents owned TVs. By 1954, that number had increased to 26 million. RCA offered four models, ranging from a 17-inch black-and-white model for $189 to a 15-inch color console for $1,000.[56] Popular programs included *The Colgate Comedy Hour*, *Dragnet*, and *I Love Lucy*. "We were watching more TV," Snider wrote, "because there was more TV to watch. We enjoyed all of these things together." He continued, "That's what made us unique, and there's no question in my mind it's also what made us such dominating winners. We were not just good—we were also united like a family and nothing could separate us."[57]

Some friction, of course, is inevitable as a season wears on. Carl Erskine said Reese knew how to calm disgruntled ballplayers.

> See, Pee Wee was a little older than most of us. He'd been around a little longer, and he knew exactly what to say and do. Pee Wee didn't yell, he didn't storm around, and he didn't do a lot of cussing. He was a straight shooter, though. He could find just the right words to use. He could also look at you in a way that would singe your shorts.[58]...We had a team where several players could have been team captain. You also had Gil and Jackie and Campy. But I like to say that Pee Wee was the captain of the captains.[59]

Early in the season, at a forum of the Philadelphia Sports Writers Association, Reese said, "I'm closer to the players than the manager could be, but I'm no stool pigeon. If something's wrong, a player will come and tell me—and I'll talk to the manager about it."[60] He also empathized with Walter Alston, who may have been counting on a few more winning streaks and tough-fought victories from his team. Brooklyn had fallen to 6½ games out of first place in mid–July. After one game, Reese said, "The fellow I feel sorry for, is that guy over there[Alston]. He can't believe it. We're supposed to be a super club. That's what he reads in the paper and then this happens. It's not his fault." Reese pointed out, "He's not swinging a bat. We're out there losing the game. It's us, not him."[61]

The Cubs edged the Dodgers, 6–5, on July 29 at Ebbets Field. Alston sent five pinch-hitters to the plate that day. No one hit the ball out of the infield. Walt Moryn struck out, Jim Gilliam popped out, Billy Cox grounded out, Don Zimmer fanned, and George Shuba grounded out. *The Sporting News* called it "a new high in futility."[62] The team appeared listless at times. One St. Louis player already had said—anonymously—that the Dodgers looked ready to give up on the pennant race and start the off-season. "What's wrong with these guys?" he asked. Reese, though, shook off any idea that he or any of his teammates wanted to go home and play golf. "What team looks good when it gets its brains knocked out?" he asked, not an unreasonable question. "Talk of giving up is ridiculous. This is a veteran club with a number of guys who've been around. They know the race is far from over."⁶³ Walter O'Malley told the press, "No one in his right mind would want to make changes with this club. I wouldn't trade a single man, because I think, man for man, we still have the best team in baseball."⁶⁴

Reese reminded reporters that the Dodgers nearly made up a 9½-game deficit against the Phillies in 1950 and lost a 13½-game lead to the Giants the next year. "However, we're not kidding ourselves," he continued. "We've got to play better ball if we are going to win. We've been good on certain days, but we haven't been good consistently. ... This pennant means more to me than any of the five others I've been in. I've never been on a World Series winner. I may never get another chance to be on one after this one."⁶⁵

The Dodgers did perk up a bit. They traveled to Milwaukee on August 29 and swept a doubleheader, 12–4 and 11–4. The first game was a most unusual blowout victory. The clubs were tied, 4–4, after 10 innings. Brooklyn scored eight runs in the 11th. Gilliam, Snider, and Cox led the way with two-run singles. In the nightcap, Reese rapped out three hits and scored twice. At the end of the day, Alston's Bums trailed the first-place Giants by 1½ games with just more than one month to play. A third straight pennant was within reach. Reese urged caution, though. "We've looked good before, and we've stubbed our toes, too," he said. True to those words, the Dodgers lost the last two games in the four-game series, 7–5 and 2–0.

Unfortunately, problems between Robinson and Alston continued. The fiery infielder disliked Alston's quiet demeanor. He called him passive and unemotional. Once, Robinson ran from the dugout to protest a call made by umpire Bill Stewart. Alston just watched. "If that guy hadn't stood out there at third base like a wooden Indian," Robinson said, "this club might go somewhere."⁶⁶ The manager, though, in *A Year at a Time*, played down any talk that the two ever engaged in a nasty feud. "If ever a man came to play the game of baseball, Jackie Robinson did," Alston wrote. "He was an inspiring player, a born leader who could literally lift a team."⁶⁷

Carl Erskine believed that some of Alston's tactics harkened back to his days as a schoolteacher. The skipper liked to ask players how they might handle a certain situation during a ballgame. "A lot of guys looked at that as a sign of weakness, that he didn't know what to do," Erskine said. "But I think they were wrong. That was his way of testing them, to see whether they had their head in the game."⁶⁸ Alston, in fact, once explained, "Teaching students is very much like managing baseball players. You've got to encourage some. You've got to drive others if you're going to get the best out of every individual."⁶⁹

Alston made it clear that he hoped to return for his sophomore campaign. "I'd be a damned fool not to want to come back," the beleaguered skipper said following a tough, 6–5 loss against the Cardinals on September 8. "It means more to me than it does to anybody else, let me tell you. But I'm not going to worry about it."⁷⁰ Walter O'Malley told reporters that he still had faith in his recent hire. "We felt an organization man was best fitted to handle the rebuilding job that was coming up in a year or two or three."⁷¹ Even so, the Brooklyn executive refused to make any official statement on rehiring Alston for the 1955 campaign. "I don't think that's necessary," he said. "If I were Alston, I would say to himself: 'I've been in the organization for 10 years, working on a one-year contract all the time, and never had to worry, so why should I have to worry about it now?' I believe he feels that way."[72]

The Dodgers had fielded calls from several opposing teams that made "good offers" for many of Brooklyn's veterans. The caveat: All the prospective transactions were cash only. Had the Brooks made any of those deals and still not won the pennant, O'Malley said, "we would have been accused of breaking up a winning team for money. I'm no carpet-bag owner, who wants to bleed a franchise for cash." Then, he added, "I intend to remain in Brooklyn a long time. I want to operate this club right—and to win with it."[73]

Shirley Povich, the esteemed *Washington Post* columnist, wrote a piece on Alston and the Dodgers in the closing weeks of the season. According to Povich, a photographer had recently walked into the Brooklyn dugout and asked, "Which one is Alston?" Players on the bench "snickered." Oh, the photographer said to the man he had just queried, "You're Alston." Povich wrote about the incident not to call out the ignorance of one press photographer, but to call out a manager for being "Mr. Anonymity." Alston, Povich complained, "is bad copy." He did not fill reporters' notebooks with blustery quotes like Charlie Dressen did.

Back in spring, according to Povich, Reese—"a wonderful chap"—figured that it might take a while before the press corps warmed up to Alston. Reese took a few writers aside and pleaded with them, "Don't be hard on Smokey. This fellow is a real nice guy, and you'll end up liking him." Even so, over the ensuing months, reporters did not always go to the skipper for quotes. They went to the captain. "They acknowledge Reese as the take-charge guy, although Pee Wee doesn't want the job," Povich wrote. "It's just that Reese can be talked to and says things that can be written."[74] Carl Erskine agreed that reporters often gathered around Reese for post-game comments before going to other players or even the manager. "Pee Wee was whom the writers would go to first," Erskine said. "And he was deserving of that. He was a little older than the rest of us, he'd been there longer, and he handled himself extremely well with the press. He was an extension of the manager."[75]

During a Dodgers-Giants tussle on September 3 at the Polo Grounds, the score was knotted, 4–4, after six innings. The Giants put two runners on base with two outs in the seventh against Jim Hughes. Hoyt Wilhelm stepped into the batter's box. Would the talented young relief pitcher—and woeful hitter—lay down a bunt? Might the Giants attempt a double steal? From his spot at shortstop, Reese called time-out and motioned for Alston to make a mound visit. According to Povich, Reese was saying, "Get out here and get in the game, and talk to Hughes." It was, Povich wrote, "as close as Reese ever came to getting mad at Alston." Reese "had to remind him that the manager should come off the bench, sometimes, especially, when you're trying to win a pennant."[76] In this case, Wilhelm recorded his only hit of the season and lone RBI. He also pitched three scoreless innings and helped New York to a 7–4 win.

In *Bums*, Carl Furillo unleashed a few unkind words about Alston and more than hinted that Reese had lost all patience with the rookie skipper. "The boys were really down on him, and Pee Wee made a remark, 'If he keeps fooling around like this, I'll take his damn job.' I wish Pee Wee would have. 'Cause Alston was not a manager. I got along good with him—don't get me wrong—but he was no manager."[77]

Later, Buzzie Bavasi assessed Alston this way: "When he had the players, he won. When he didn't have them, he lost."[78]

A young southpaw pitcher provided the brightest highlight for Brooklyn in that final month. The Dodgers called up Karl Spooner, from Oriskany Falls, near Utica, New York. The 23-year-old boasted a crackerjack fastball and earned the promotion. He put together a stellar campaign for the Fort Worth Cats. Despite missing six starts, he won 21 games and struck out 262 batters in 238 innings. The knock on Spooner was his control, or lack of it. Yes, he allowed just 176 hits. He also issued a whopping 162 walks.

Spooner walked to the mound for the first time as a Brooklyn Dodger on September 22 against the Giants and looked like a future ace of the staff. He tossed a three-hit shutout at Ebbets Field and struck out 15, the most punchouts ever for a pitcher making his debut.[79] He only walked three. Brooklyn cruised to a 3–0 victory in front of a paltry crowd of 3,256. The following day, newspapers applauded the borough's latest star. The *Eagle* headline proclaimed: "We Needed Spooner Sooner." Not so fast, Buzzie Bavasi said. "In mid-season, we felt he wasn't ready. He had as many walks as strikeouts. He just wasn't the pitcher he is now."[80] Reese, talking to Spooner, joked, "Is it true that you've asked for my locker already?"[81]

Four days later, Spooner took another turn on the mound. And, as an encore, he pitched another shutout. Why not? This time, at home against the Pirates, he struck out 12, walked three, and gave up four hits. The Dodgers beat the Bucs, 1–0, on a Hodges home run in the seventh inning. Spooner set a National League record with 27 punchouts in two consecutive games, breaking the old mark of 25, set by Brooklyn ace Dazzy Vance. Spooner also equaled the major league record by throwing shutouts in his first two starts.[82] "Karl Spooner—man or mirage?" Tommy Holmes asked.[83]

Brooklyn played just 13–11 baseball in September and slipped into third place for a few days before climbing back into the runner-up spot. Reese hit .352 over the month and put together a 17-for-40 stretch (.425). His average reached .312 on September 15 after he had a single and a double in a 10–4 win against the Reds. "Don't look now," the *Eagle* informed readers, "but Pee Wee Reese isn't only hitting .312, he's in the league's top 10."[84]

The Dodgers won their final four games and ended up 92–62. It wasn't a shabby record, even if it was well off the franchise-best mark from 1953. Walter Alston wrote that his rookie campaign was "a wonderful year in all ways but one. We didn't win."[85] The rival Giants, behind MVP Award-winner Willie Mays (41 home runs, 110 RBI, a league-leading .345 batting average and .667 slugging percentage), swept the Indians in the World Series.

Just as Pee Wee Reese predicted during spring training, the Brooklyn offense took a downturn. The Dodgers scored 778 runs, nearly 200 runs less than in 1953 but still second in the National League. Gil Hodges ripped 42 home runs. Duke Snider smacked 40 and batted .341. Both sluggers drove in 130 runs. Roy Campanella, mostly due to that hand injury, hit just .207 with 19 homers in 111 games. Carl Erskine anchored the pitching staff. He won 18 games and struck out 166 batters. Jim Hughes, in his third season, topped the circuit with 60 appearances and, using today's criteria, would have recorded 17 saves. Joe Black pitched in just five games and gave up nine earned runs over seven innings before the Dodgers demoted him to Montreal on May 30. A doctor there found that he had torn muscles in his right shoulder.

Reese batted .309, 23 points better than his previous high, .286 in 1951, and the ninth-best figure in the league. He also walked 90 times, giving him a .404 on-base percentage. He slugged 10 homers, collected 69 RBI, and scored 98 runs, the seventh straight year in which he crossed home plate at least 94 times. His 171 hits included a career-high 35 doubles and eight triples. Frank Eck called the shortstop's first .300 season "one of the big surprises in National League hitting."[86] Even so, the team-minded shortstop said, "I'd give it back and take a .260 if it would mean we'd have won the pennant."[87]

16

"I said to myself, 'This can't be true'"

Spring training in Vero Beach began on a clunky note. During his first press conference, before most players could unpack their golf bags or even look out at the sparkling ocean water, Walter Alston declared, "Pee Wee is the shortstop." He added, "Unless someone beats him out of it."[1] Well, then.

Dick Young already suspected that Reese's days as a starter might be numbered. He asked, "When did a guy of 36 last put in a full year at shortstop, particularly on a pennant contender?"[2] Don Zimmer stood by as the heir apparent at that position. Zimmer grew up in Cincinnati and starred at Western Hills High School. Scouts from the Dodgers and hometown Reds liked his line-drive swing and hoped to sign him. Brooklyn offered $2,500, or $500 more than Cincinnati, and Zimmer decided to be a Dodger. He feasted on minor league pitching and belted 23 home runs in 81 games for the St. Paul Saints in 1953. He also nearly died. Zimmer suffered a skull fracture after a fastball crashed into his head on July 7. Doctors drilled four holes into his skull "to act like bottle corks"[3] and prevent blood clots.

Recovered, Zimmer hit nine homers in 73 games for St. Paul in 1954 and played 24 games with Brooklyn. He batted a meager .182 in 33 at-bats for the big club. Even so, he told writers in that fresh spring of 1955, "I have a feeling I'm not going to sit on the bench anymore."[4] The brass also liked a young infielder named Humberto "Chico" Fernandez. The Cuban native signed as an amateur free agent in 1951. He spent the 1954 season in Montreal, where he batted .282 and smacked 44 doubles.

Maybe Pee Wee Reese could play second base, at least to spell Gilliam. News about the possible position switch didn't faze the veteran, who seemed his usual accommodating self. He had spent some time at second base as a minor leaguer in 1938 but had never played there in the majors. "I don't care where I play," he said, "but I would like to know a little ahead of time so that I can work out at the position."[5] Walter Alston, though, said Reese might not see any action on the right side of the diamond once the regular season began. "I know what he can do," the skipper said. "I want to see the kids [Zimmer and Fernandez], and I just want Reese to play to get in shape."[6]

Another issue lingered in the salty air. At least one reporter asked Jackie Robinson whether he wanted to take over at third base. "You bet I do," he said. "And I'm taking dead aim at the job."[7] That opportunity opened up after the Dodgers sold Billy

Cox, along with Preacher Roe (who subsequently retired), to the Baltimore Orioles[8] on December 13 for a reported $60,000 in cash.[9] (Robinson played 50 games at third base in 1954. He also got into 62 games in left field, two at second base and one in right field.) Alston said only, "I'll play Jackie where I think it'll do the most good."[10]

The skipper thought about moving Gil Hodges to the outfield or even behind the plate, his original spot on the diamond, "since injuries were wearing down Campanella." Campy, though, predicted a personal comeback and a big season for the Dodgers. "We're gonna run away with this thing," he predicted. "I'm OK, and I don't see how we can fail to run away with it."[11] As for the pitching staff, well, Billy Loes liked it. "We have the best pitching staff in the league, for depth," he boasted. "It can win a pennant easy. It all depends on how it's used."[12] Walter Alston probably chewed over the last sentence in that comment for a minute or two. Or he considered the source and just ignored it.

Alston kept tinkering with the lineup throughout spring training. On March 27, against the Chicago White Sox, he put Hodges in left field, Zimmer at second base, and Fernandez at shortstop. He also penciled in Frank Kellert (acquired March 19 from the Orioles for Erv Palica) at first base. Jackie Robinson, playing the hot corner, made four hits and stole home but still hadn't won the job. "If he's not going to play me," Robinson said, "let him get rid of me."[13] The comment, perhaps understandably, infuriated Alston. "If Robinson had a complaint, why didn't he make it me and not to a writer?" the manager asked. Robinson simply said, "I told him I can't talk to him. I don't know why. I just can't."[14]

Pee Wee Reese answered more questions about his interest in managing a ballclub. Yes, he'd like to take on that job. Someday. Then he asked a question of his own. "Who can tell if you're going to be a good manager? Nobody knows. I think I can manage, but then you don't know until you're in it." He mentioned former teammate Billy Herman, a heads-up ballplayer who struggled in his first season as a skipper. The All-Star infielder led Pittsburgh to a 61–92 mark in 1947 and resigned with one game left in a long campaign. (The Bucs won that finale, 7–0, against the Cubs with Bill Burwell at the helm.) Once again, Reese said he did not want to both play and manage at the same time. If he did that and the club struggled, "Then I'd be out both as a player and a manager. So, I'm going to play out the string at shortstop and then try managing after that."[15]

Young outfielder Sandy Amoros reported late for spring training. The 25-year-old left his home in Havana, Cuba, by boat and planned to drive the 140 miles from Miami to Vero Beach, a nearly straight shot up the coast. The trip should have taken two hours. Instead, it took two days. A peeved Buzzie Bavasi threatened to banish Amoros from camp. "If he turned right, he winds up in the ocean," Bavasi said. "If he turned left, he'd go into the Everglades. How could he get lost?"[16] Bavasi fined Amoros $100. "I didn't fine him for being late but for the story he told,"[17] Bavasi said. Of note, Alston doubted that Amoros could hold down a starting job in the outfield. "He doesn't charge ground balls," the manager said. On the plus side, "he doesn't hurt us with his arm. And he can go get fly balls with the best of them."[18]

Before the season began, Walter O'Malley told Bavasi to negotiate a new lease with Miami Stadium. The Dodgers had been playing a handful of exhibition games in south Florida since 1950 and attracting good crowds. Rumor had it that a jai alai arena might replace the ballpark. "If we can't get Miami Stadium for our exhibitions next spring," O'Malley said, "we will pursue our plans to make a flying trip to California." That contingency, according to *The Sporting News*, "was one of the things leading to the report that Brooklyn's franchise might be transferred to the West Coast."[19]

The Dodgers struggled to go 10-14-1 against spring competition. If that wasn't disappointing enough, Charlie Dressen offered his two cents. Now managing the Washington Senators, Brooklyn's former skipper said in so many words that Walter Alston blew the pennant in 1954. "Even with the injuries, they had enough stuff on the bench to win," he said. "I know those fellows better ... could have gotten more out of them."[20]

Brooklyn opened the season against Pittsburgh on April 13 at Ebbets Field. Alston decided to keep Hodges and Campanella in their usual spots, probably wisely. He penciled in Jim Gilliam at second, Reese at short, and Robinson at third. Amoros, despite Alston's early doubts, won a starting job in left field, with Duke Snider in center and Carl Furillo in right. Behind a complete-game effort from Carl Erskine, plus three RBI from Furillo, the Dodgers won, 6–1. Reese, batting second, doubled and scored a run. Fewer than 7,000 fans attended the game on a rainy, miserable afternoon. "The Dodgers warmed a shivering opening-day crowd,"[21] said the AP.

The Dodgers reeled off 10 straight wins before finally losing, 5–4, to the Giants on April 22. They set the post–1900 record for most consecutive victories to start a season. The 1918 Giants, 1940 Dodgers, and 1944 Browns all won nine straight. A chalkboard inside the Dodgers' locker room read: "The Bums Dood It: 10 Straight." The team gave away a souvenir ashtray to celebrate the achievement.

As to why the Dodgers got off to such a hot start, "You can't put a finger on any one thing," Reese said. "I'd say it is a combination of things. First of all, the attitude is a lot different. For instance, did you ever see a more determined Billy Loes? You know Billy. Last year, it seemed he just didn't give a damn. This year, he's all business. Robinson is in better shape than he's been in a long time, and the way Campanella is playing, you'd never think he had a care in the world."[22]

Furillo smacked five home runs in the first eight games. Snider hit three. Reese began the season in a slump. He hit just .170 in April and finally raised his batting average above .200 by going 3-for-5 in a 12–4 win against the Cardinals on May 4.

So where did all the fans go? The Dodgers drew fewer than 10,000 for an April 20 home game against the Phillies and not even 4,000 the following day. All those empty seats, crummy weather or not, irritated some players. "What happened to the crowds?" Reese asked, "You'd think 10 in a row would get them out. I can remember when we'd come back north and play in snow, and there'd be 20 or 25 thousand people to see us."[23]

A different sort of problem cropped up on May 5 in St. Louis. Don Newcombe refused Alston's order to pitch batting practice that day. "I want to pitch in games, not practice," Big Newk said to coach Joe Becker. "Tell [Alston] I have a sore arm."[24] The skipper, upon hearing that news, told Newcombe to take off his uniform and go home. The Dodgers suspended him indefinitely. At the time, the pitcher was 2–0 but with an ERA north of 5.00. He would be losing $104.79 in salary every day he sat on his couch, and in his own words, "I'm no millionaire."[25] He quickly rejoined the team.

On May 22, the Dodgers knocked off the Cubs, 3–0, behind a one-hitter by Newcombe, and improved to 22–2. Just 24 games into the season, and Brooklyn already led the National League pennant chase by 9½ games. Memorial Day was still a week away. Branch Rickey, who built this juggernaut and now led the Pittsburgh Pirates' front office, feared an apparent runaway to the pennant. Fans, he said, might stop going to games as their favorite team dropped deeper and deeper in the standings. If by July, Rickey said, "Brooklyn has been permitted to widen that lead, it could be a catastrophe. Competitively and economically."[26]

Nothing, though, could stop the Dodgers. Few pitchers could stop Duke Snider, who slammed three home runs in an 11–8 win against the Braves on June 1. He had 15 homers and 48 RBI in 44 games. One of the most dangerous hitters in baseball could still be temperamental, moody, and the occasional object of locker room scorn. Reese, as much as anyone, liked to give him the needle. "Pee Wee would get on him all the time," Clem Labine remembered. "'Who stole his lollipop? Somebody stole Duke's candy. Who was it?'"[27]

Carl Erskine tried to figure out his teammate and Bay Ridge neighbor. He finally came up with this: Snider was an only child growing up and a bit of a "mama's boy." Also, so much was expected of him on the athletic field, and he never took well to criticism. "The other thing was that Duke had a fear he was going to die young," Erskine said. "His dad died of a heart attack at a fairly young age, and his mother had health problems, and it was almost a Mantle story in lesser degree. Mantle had this tremendous fear of dying young."[28]

Reese, Snider, and Erskine often carpooled to Ebbets Field. One afternoon, a police officer pulled over Reese for speeding. The shortstop—and apparent lead foot—apologized for his indiscretion. The officer let him off with a warning. "Geez, take it easy on the pedal, will ya, Pee Wee? Take it easy, fella." The following day, Snider took his turn driving. A different police officer pulled him over for speeding. "I'm Duke Snider of the Dodgers," the star center fielder announced. The officer gave a quick response. "I hate baseball,"[29] he said. Snider paid the fine.

The same day that Snider hit three homers, Pee Wee Reese hit one. He drove in two runs and scored three times. The next day, he rapped two more hits, scored three runs again, and recorded one RBI in a 13–2 shellacking of the Braves. The veteran shortstop batted .321 in June, with four home runs and 21 RBI. He scored 28 runs in 29 games.

On June 24, a young left-hander and graduate of Brooklyn's Lafayette High School made his debut. Alston summoned Sandy Koufax out of the bullpen to start the fifth inning at County Stadium in Milwaukee. The Dodgers already trailed, 7–1. Koufax had signed with his hometown team in December 1954, following a short tryout at Ebbets Field. He agreed to a $6,000 salary and $14,000 bonus. Koufax amazed scouts with his blazing heater. Team executive Al Campanis once famously said, "There are two times in my life the hair on my arms has stood up. The first time I saw the ceiling on the Sistine Chapel and the first time I saw Sandy Koufax throw a fastball."[30] The 19-year-old battled control problems and spent much of his rookie campaign on the bench. He threw two innings against Milwaukee and allowed one hit, walked a batter, and struck out two. "To them [the opposing players], it was just another guy named Koufax," Dick Young wrote in the *Daily News*. "To the Brook brass, however, it marked the start of what they expect to be a fine career."[31]

Brooklyn's delegation to the NL All-Star team, played July 12 in Milwaukee, included Newcombe, Campanella, Hodges, and Snider. Reese, for the first time since 1941 (excluding those three seasons lost due to his service in World War II), sat out the game. The snub didn't bother him, he insisted. The Cubs' Ernie Banks and Braves' Johnny Logan went in his place. Robinson said, "I'll take Pee Wee over the two shortstops named."[32] The senior circuit overcame an early 5–0 deficit and won, 6–5, in 12 innings, thanks to a Stan Musial homer hit off 6-foot-6-inch right-hander Frank Sullivan of the Red Sox.

Reese celebrated his 36th birthday—one day early—on July 22 at Ebbets Field. It was quite a party, and more than 33,000 paid to attend. Vice president and baseball fan Richard Nixon sent congratulations. The Veep wrote, "Anyone who can be a Dodger, in the first place, is quite a man. Anyone who can be a Dodger for 15 years, and rise to be captain of the team, deserves to be a sports immortal." Businesses from throughout the borough donated presents. Gifts included a TV console, movie camera, and sound projector, a still camera, two sets of golf clubs, two deep freezers, 200 pounds of shrimp and meat, two sets of tubeless tires, 100 pounds of coffee, and much more. Dodgers public relations director Irving Rudd, "a Runyonesque character,"[33] put together the entire affair.

"We hustled merchants, not fans, for gifts," Rudd said. "In the past, fans would send in money, and sometimes you'd get situations like the night they threw for Dixie Walker in 1947. They ended up with just enough money to buy him a fishing rod." Pee Wee Reese Night drew about 35,000 fans. "We closed the subways," Rudd said. "You couldn't walk down the streets if you didn't have a ticket in your hand. One of the great, glorious nights in Dodger history."[34] Eleven-year-old Barbara Reese selected a new family car from a set that included a Chevrolet, Buick, DeSoto, Chrysler, Pontiac, Ford, and Plymouth. She reached into a fishbowl filled with ignition keys and picked the Chevrolet. Four trucks carted off the goodies and drove everything to Pee Wee's house in Louisville.

When the fifth inning ended, stadium employees wheeled out two giant birthday cakes and turned off the stadium lights. Fans lit matches or held up cigarette lighters and sang "Happy Birthday" to their favorite shortstop. Reese stepped to a microphone stand behind home plate and addressed the crowd. "Since 1940, you fans have been wonderful to me. When I first came up here, I was a scared kid to tell you the truth. I'm twice as scared now. I've been lucky—one of the luckiest guys in baseball. I just hope these old bones hold up for about two years so I can be with you a little longer."[35]

Fans cheered, and then clapped some more, when Reese smacked two doubles, scored a run, and picked up an RBI. Brooklyn beat Milwaukee, 8–4, and improved to 65–29. Dodgers vice president Fresco Thompson said, "He [Reese] may be a touch slower than in 1940, but he still goes behind second and takes bread and butter away from a batter. And, remember, I said he 'might' be a touch slower. I'm not even sure of that."[36]

What makes Pee Wee Reese tick, a writer asked Walt Alston. The skipper repeated the question. "What makes Pee Wee Reese tick? Character, natural ability, versatility, intelligence and a habit of placing his team ahead of Harold Reese all the time."[37] Roy Campanella answered a similar question in much the same way. "All 'round the league, everybody knows he's never been bad. That's a lot to say about a man." Campanella recalled how Reese supported Jackie Robinson and, later, other African American players. "When we first came up here, he was the guy who went out of the way for us. That doesn't have to be publicized or known in the street, but I know it down deep."[38]

Unfortunately, as part of the celebration on Pee Wee's night at Ebbets Field, some stadium workers displayed a large Confederate flag in full view of fans and players. The gesture enraged Robinson. "Branca, Labine, and I had to cool down Jackie," Carl Erskine recalled. "The stadium workers thought it was a nice gesture, but Jackie was livid. We had to tell Jackie that this was Pee Wee's night, and we didn't want to spoil it."[39]

The Dodgers ended July with an 11–2 win in St. Louis against the struggling Cardinals, who dropped to 46–54. Reese collected two hits and scored two runs. The following day, in a 4–3 win against Milwaukee, he contributed another two hits and drove in the game-tying run in the seventh inning on a bases-loaded walk. Brooklyn improved to 72–32 and led the National League by 14½ games. Reese went 6-for-17 over the next four games and lifted his batting average to .296 and on-base percentage to .374.

Only in August did the Dodgers play losing baseball, going 13–14. Even so, they never enjoyed less than a 10-game lead. Still, some fans grew restless. On August 25, the Dodgers dropped a doubleheader to the Reds, 8–5 and 6–5. Duke Snider went hitless in nine at-bats, and the boo birds sang an ill-tempered tune. Of course, Snider heard every one of them. Afterward, Snider, who once told Kahn that he only played baseball for the money and that he'd like to own an avocado farm back home in California, let loose: "You want a story?" he asked. He didn't hold back: "I'll give you one. These are the lousiest fans in baseball." Oh, boy. Reese tried to give Snider a way out of this mess. "Wait, guys," Reese said to the writers. "Duke doesn't really mean that. Do you, Duke?" Snider refused to backtrack. He just made things worse. "The hell I don't," he said. "I mean every word of it."[40]

On the drive home, Reese looked over at Snider, offered a few soothing words, and told him not to expect a warm greeting the next day at the ballpark. "Well, Duke you really did it this time," Reese said. "You wouldn't listen to me in there, and now you've really put yourself in the soup."[41]

It may seem silly, but Reese decided to sort of babysit his teammate the next day. Wherever Snider went, he followed. Neither player took batting practice. They stayed in the clubhouse rather than give angry fans any chance to cackle. Reese also could intercept reporters looking for more juicy quotes.

Nearly 13,000 fans showed up "ready to let me have it," in Snider's words. Worse, Cincinnati had a left-hander, Don Gross, scheduled to start. "Pee Wee said he didn't like my chances," Snider recalled. "Neither did I." Boos rained down in Snider's first at-bat. He struck out. A few cheers mixed with boos in his second trip to the plate.

He singled. On his third trip, it was half boos, half cheers. Snider singled again. In his fourth at-bat, he lined his third single. "When I reached first base, I got a standing ovation," Snider wrote. "The fans. God bless 'em."[42] The Reds still won, 4–2, and Brooklyn led the pennant chase by 10 games.

Fans, players, and writers noticed a different Walter Alston from 1954. The subject of so much criticism in his rookie campaign—"The Dodgers don't need a manager and that is why they got Alston,"[43] according to one piece—Alston in 1955 demonstrated "a newfound aggressiveness. … He was managing much more aggressively—pinch-hitting, yanking pitchers without so much as a second thought. This was a different man. … As spring turned to summer, Alston kept pushing the Dodgers."[44] Late in the season, Dick Young wrote, "The players feel differently now. They are not ready to concede that Alston is deserving of a reserved room at Cooperstown, but they grant that he is better—quite a bit better."[45]

The Sporting News ran an article on August 31 that focused on the different managers Reese had played for through the years. How would he compare them? The shortstop, "with a twinkle in his eye," said "Now, that's a loaded question." He did not prefer one over the other, he insisted. "You know I don't knock anybody," Reese said. But, publisher J. G. Taylor Spink continued, didn't Pee Wee proclaim himself a "Durocher" man after he got fired. "But I also said that Burt Shotton was all right with me," Reese answered. "Leo helped me so much. He had been a great shortstop, and he showed me a lot about playing the position." Reese acknowledged that "Leo ate me out a few times. I remember once when I was supposed to be in position for a cut-off play and I wasn't there. We lost the game, and he really told me off, but I guess I never made the same mistake again."[46]

Spink egged on Reese and asked if the shortstop could think of anything critical to say about Alston. Reese held up his hands in "mock horror" and asked, "Did you ever notice the size of that man? He might be the strongest man on the club, not excepting Gil Hodges. Who'd be crazy enough to challenge Walt?" The article included a quote from Don Zimmer, who was getting playing time as a part-time second baseman. "I hope Pee Wee never leaves the club," Zimmer said. "He has never done anything but help me. If I'm playing well now, it's because he's playing beside me."[47]

On September 8, "Brooklyn's frolicking Dodgers bombarded their way past Milwaukee's Braves,"[48] and won, 10–2, to clinch the pennant, five days earlier than the 1953 squad. Both Robinson and Hodges drove in three runs. Reese added an RBI single, while Karl Spooner picked up the win in relief of starter Roger Craig. "This, Brooklyn's eighth modern pennant victory," Dick Young began his story, "is not ALMOST the greatest runaway in NL history—it is THE greatest." The Dodgers led the pennant race the entire season. "Nobody chased the Brooks this year,"[49] Young wrote.

The Dodgers won just six of their final 15 games. They still finished 98–55, 13½ games ahead of second-place Milwaukee. Reese, "who refused to get old,"[50] put together another solid season. He hit .282 and smacked 10 home runs, reaching double figures in that category for the seventh and final time. He also drove in 61 runs and crossed home plate 99 times, giving him eight straight seasons with at least 90 runs scored.

Duke Snider, despite traffic tickets and controversy, enjoyed a huge season. He slammed 42 homers, drove in 136 runs, and batted .309. Roy Campanella hit .318, slugged 32 home runs and collected 107 RBI. Don Newcombe overcame his minor act of insubordination and finished 20-5 with a 3.20 ERA and 17 complete games. He even batted .359 and hit seven balls into the seats. Clem Labine won 13 games and saved 10. The Dodgers drew 1,033,589 fans, second-most in the National League. Roger Kahn called the figure "a disappointing total."[51] The Braves drew nearly one million more fans.

On the day Brooklyn clinched, Cleveland led New York by half a game. Joe DiMaggio, retired and on vacation in Italy, was, like many, sure that the Yankees would ultimately prevail and go on to win yet another World Series. It was destiny, as simple as that. DiMaggio couldn't resist a jab at the team his old club had conquered so many times. "[The Dodgers] can't beat the Yankees," a sun-tanned "Yankee Clipper" declared. "I guess the only thing that can cure them is a brain-washing. It has gotten so bad in Brooklyn that they can't ever say the word 'Yankees.'" Billy Cox, playing in his final season, also liked New York to win it all. Again. About his old club, he showed no mercy. "They always fold in the Series," he said. "Maybe it will be different if some other team than the Yankees takes it in the AL, but if it's the Yankees—well; they're the Dodger jinx."[52]

Many fans and maybe a few players—sick and tired of the Yankees achieving October glory at the Dodgers' expense—probably rooted for the Indians to take the pennant. Not Reese, who turned spiritual. "I prayed that some year I'd hit over .300 and last year I did," he wrote. "I also prayed that we would get another crack at the Yankees before I hung up my spikes."[53] His prayers were answered. The Yanks devoured their competition in August and September, going 34–17, and ended up 96–58, three games better than the Indians. Mickey Mantle blasted 37 home runs and batted .306, although he entered the Series with a noticeable limp. He pulled his right hamstring while trying to beat out a bunt on September 16. He made just two more appearances the rest of the season, each time as a pinch-hitter. Yogi Berra hit 27 homers with 108 RBI. Whitey Ford won 18 games and complemented that with a 2.63 ERA.

Reese offered his analysis of the upcoming match-up. "If our pitching comes through, we'll win, no matter who we play,"[54] Yes, he was one of the only players in the game's history to endure five World Series losses without winning one. "How long can it last?"[55] he asked, hopefully. He also knew that time was running out on his dream. Decades later, he admitted what he was thinking in those hours leading up to the first pitch. "I'm 36 years old," he said, "If I don't win this Series, I'll probably never be on a world championship team."[56]

Don Newcombe faced off against Whitey Ford in Game One at Ebbets Field. The Dodgers took a 2-0 lead in the second inning on a Furillo home run and RBI single by Zimmer. That advantage lasted for a few minutes, or until Elston Howard ripped a two-run homer in the bottom half of the frame. New York pulled ahead and won, 6–5. Reese singled in his first at-bat.

In his column, Reese told fans to look out for Brooklyn's big boppers, especially Furillo, who managed three hits in the opener despite battling a cold. "When a guy hits three for four—one of them as long as his second-inning home run—it makes you think a little sinus may be good for hitters."[57] Yankees starter Tommy Byrne, though, gave up just five hits in Game Two and none to Furillo. In fact, the quartet of Snider, Campanella, Furillo, and Hodges—the Dodgers' 3-6 hitters—combined for only one hit in 13 at-bats. New York came out on top, 4-2, in front of 64,707 fans at Yankee Stadium. Reese hit a double and a single. He also scored a run. Charles J. Doyle of the *Pittsburgh Sun-Telegraph* wrote about "the disappointment shown by Capt. Pee Wee Reese, Duke Snider and Gil Hodges as they remain silent following their first two setbacks."[58] Reese, though, did his best to stay upbeat as the Series shifted to Brooklyn. "Okay, so now we're two games down," he said. "That'll make the victory taste even better."[59]

Brooklyn posted four two-run innings in Game Three and won easily, 8-3, behind Johnny Podres. Campanella drove home three runs. Reese drew a bases-loaded walk in the second inning and lined an RBI single in the seventh. "Those Dodgers are a good ballclub," Casey Stengel said. "They're real tough in their own park. They won a lot of games in the National League, and I respect them."[60] Reese told reporters, "We showed we can beat them. And there's no reason why we can't beat them in Yankee Stadium, too."[61] Mickey Mantle, after missing the first two games, homered in this one. He batted 10 times in the Series and had one other hit.

Stengel sent a young fireballer out for Game Four, Don Larsen. The Dodgers called on Carl Erskine. Both pitchers struggled. Larsen gave up five runs in four innings. Erskine allowed three runs before getting pulled with no one out in the fourth. Brooklyn led, 7-3, after five innings and won, 8-5. That quartet of Snider, Campanella, Furillo, and Hodges teamed for nine hits and seven RBI. "Now, we feel better," wrote Reese, who added two base hits and a run scored. "We've squared the Series and we've got the pitching, the hitting, and the spirit to go from here." Reese told fans to "look out."[62]

In fact, Brooklyn won the next day, 5-3. Snider hit two homers; Sandy Amoros added another. Reese walked in his first at-bat and went hitless in his next three. Roger Craig gave up two runs over six innings. Clem Labine allowed one run in three innings of relief. The Dodgers needed one win to claim a championship. "Maybe you think you have seen enthusiasm," Reese wrote, "but you should have been in the clubhouse after the game. Everybody congratulating everyone else and looking forward to tomorrow."[63]

Back at Yankee Stadium, though, Brooklyn struggled to mount any kind of threat with Whitey Ford on the mound. The blond-haired hurler allowed just one run and four hits. He struck out eight as the Yankees won, 5-1. The Dodgers put across their solo run in the fourth inning. Reese led off with a single, advanced to second on a one-out walk to Campanella, and raced home on Furillo's base hit to left field. The Yankees scored all five of their runs in the first inning against Karl Spooner, who failed to retire a single batter. To make things worse, Duke Snider stepped into a small hole in the Yankee Stadium outfield and left the game in the third inning. "Something popped in my left knee," he said. "I better get out."[64] In his column, Reese conceded "that first inning was tough" and "we're all hoping Duke Snider's knee is all right" for Game Seven. He added, "There'll be a last half of the ninth today, and we're looking forward to being there. Don't bet against us."[65]

16. "I said to myself, 'This can't be true'"

On the morning of Game Seven, as the Dodgers rode the team bus from Ebbets Field to Yankee Stadium, Johnny Podres stood up in front of his teammates. The starting pitcher for the finale made both a plea and a promise. "Just give me one run today," he said. "That's all I'll need. Just one."[66] The *Daily News*, in large, bold print on Page One, informed its readers, "ALL EVEN; ONE GAME DOES IT." Casey Stengel said, "We're home and we're confident."[67] Joe Trimble rightly declared, "For the Dodgers, today must be it. …or again the 'Wait 'til Next Year' requiem will be tolled in Brooklyn."[68] *Daily News* weatherman J. Henry Weber predicted "perfect baseball conditions," with fair skies and temperatures in the low 70s.[69]

Duke Snider decided that his knee felt okay enough to play. Jackie Robinson, battling a sore Achilles tendon, sat on the bench. Don Hoak started at third base. Jim Gilliam began the game in left field, and Don Zimmer ran out to second base. Dodgers fan Mike Sharff sat in the bleachers at Yankee Stadium, one of 62,465 fans on hand. "I would guess that the bleachers, unlike the rest of the stadium, were probably evenly divided. There were fanatics on both sides."[70] Before the game, Pee Wee Reese offered some advice to Podres. "Pitch the way Campy calls 'em, Johnny, and we'll make it," he said. "Remember, you don't have to strike 'em all out."[71]

Tommy Byrne started for New York. Over the first three innings, he allowed walks to Gil Hodges and Jim Gilliam. In the fourth, Roy Campanella doubled with one out and rumbled to second on Carl Furillo's groundout. Hodges followed with a run-scoring single. Brooklyn took a 1–0 lead. Would that really be enough for Podres? The young pitcher had squelched a rally in the previous inning. New York put two runners on base with two outs. Gil McDougald, up next, worked the count to three balls, one strike. The Yanks could load the bases with more bad pitch. Reese called time out and walked to the mound. "Got your control, Johnny?" he asked. Podres said he felt okay. "Just keep the pitch down, Johnny," Reese said. "And take your time."[72] Podres paused, stepped off the mound, squeezed the rosin bag, and stepped back onto the mound. He threw a pitch that McDougald hit down the third-base line. It looked like "a tough play"[73] for Don Hoak. The ball, though, smacked into Phil Rizzuto as he slid into the bag. Rizzuto was out, and Podres was out of the inning. Reese met Podres in the dugout. "This looks like your day, Johnny. Just play it cool."[74]

Reese led off the sixth inning with a single to center field. Snider, the next batter, put down a surprise sacrifice bunt. Byrne fielded the ball and threw to Moose Skowron near first base. Skowron dropped the underhand toss for an error. Campanella followed by dropping another sacrifice and advancing the runners to second and third. Casey Stengel ordered Byrne to walk Furillo and load the bases. Stengel also summoned relief pitcher Bob Grim into the game. Gil Hodges lifted a fly ball into left field, deep enough for Reese to tag up and score. Now, Podres had an insurance run.

Walter Alston made an important defensive switch in the bottom half of the inning. He moved the weak-armed Gilliam from left field to second base and brought in Sandy Amoros to play left. (Alston had lifted Don Zimmer for a pinch-hitter in the top of the sixth.) Once again, the Yankees mounted a threat. Billy Martin began the frame by walking on four straight pitches. McDougald followed with a bunt single to bring up Yogi Berra. Alston walked to the mound. "You all right, Johnny?" he asked.

Podres said he felt fine. Pee Wee Reese looked at the manager. "He got out of it with two on before. He can do it again."[75]

Berra launched a high fly ball deep into the left field corner. Amoros, shading toward center field, ran more than 100 feet in pursuit. "The ball stayed up a long time."[76] At last, the outfielder reached out, "gloving it with his right mitt in fair territory."[77] Neither runner thought Amoros could make the grab. Both took off as soon as the drive left Berra's bat. Amoros "gracefully whirled and fired to Reese" in short left field. He made a "perfect throw to Hodges, just getting McDougald as he slid back." Billy Martin already had hustled back to second base. Hank Bauer grounded out to end the inning. As for that catch, Amoros said later, "I ran like a hawk. I ran to the wall, and figured, 'I can get it.'"[78] Podres applauded Reese's throw to Hodges. "[Pee Wee] just spun and knew what he was going to do with the baseball exactly. That made the play."[79]

Reese displayed more sterling defense in the seventh. He handled all three chances. Skowron led off by hitting a grounder to the left side. Reese "charged Skowron's grounder like a ferret, pounced on it" and threw on time to first base. Bob Cerv followed by knocking a ground ball that Reese "almost frantic with need, charged and handled." After Elston Howard singled, Mickey Mantle came to bat as a pinch-hitter for Grim. He popped up near third base. Reese "rushed under it, bounced with eagerness" and "waited as the ball fell into his glove." As Robert Creamer put it, "The seventh inning belonged to Pee Wee Reese."[80]

The Yanks threatened once again in the eighth inning. Rizzuto began with a base hit to left field and advanced to third on McDougald's one-out single that bounced off Don Hoak's arm. Rizzuto raced to third base. Podres next faced the red-hot Berra, who batted .417 in the Series (10-for-24). He got under a slow curveball and lofted it into right field. Carl Furillo made the catch and held Rizzuto at third. Hank Bauer struck out to end the inning.

Skowron led off the bottom half of the ninth and "cracked a sizzler back to Podres."[81] The pitcher, unable to get the ball out of his glove, began running toward first. Finally, he grabbed the ball and tossed it softly to Hodges, in time. Bob Cerv lifted a lazy fly ball to Amoros for the second out. Elston Howard stepped to the plate. Podres ran the count to two balls and two strikes. Howard hit the next pitch straight to Reese, who threw to Hodges—maybe a bit low—for the final out. Podres said, "When Pee Wee saw the ball coming at him, a big grim broke out on his face. I guess he couldn't help it. He made a low throw to first, but Hodges picked it up without any trouble."[82] Snider wrote in *The Duke of Flatbush*, "Hitting it to Pee Wee was perfect."[83]

With the final out recorded at 3:43 p.m. on October 4, 1955, in the Bronx, Johnny Podres leaped high into the air. Roy Campanella ran out to greet him. Ecstatic teammates converged on the field. They congratulated and hugged one another. Fans joined the celebration. Reporters and photographers grabbed quotes and snapped pictures. Brooklyn's popular captain couldn't believe it. Finally. 1941. 1947. 1949. 1952. 1953. Now, 1955. Champions at last. "While I was standing out there in the ninth inning," Reese said, "I said to myself 'this can't be true. Something's got to happen to make us lose.' But it didn't, and when it was over, I had all I could do to keep from crying."[84]

Roger Craig wanted to open a bottle of champagne and get the party started. He looked around the locker room and saw several subdued teammates. The reality of what the Dodgers just did had begun to sink in, especially with the veterans. "I'm looking at Gil Hodges and Jackie Robinson and Pee Wee Reese and Carl Erskine, and they're sitting back in their lockers with tears in their eyes," Craig remembered. "They were crying. They were just so overcome with emotion from getting to the World Series so many times and finally winning it."[85]

Carl Erskine thought about gathering the entire team for a prayer of thanksgiving. This championship, after all those tough October endings of years past, meant so much, and, just maybe, divine intervention played a hand. "I didn't do it," Erskine admitted. "But that was my feeling having won against the Yankees in the stadium after all those many, many, many, many years. It had so much significance. Everybody said, 'The ring.' Yeah, we got a ring, but it wasn't the ring. It was bigger than the ring."[86]

Soon, the smiles brightened again, and the sound of popped champagne corks echoed in the locker room. The players doused one another and guzzled bottles of bubbly. Carl Furillo bellowed out for everyone to hear, "To hell with Billy Cox!" … "And DiMaggio! And Dressen!" He gave the reporters some instructions to pass on to their editors: "Print it in big letters. Tell Billy Cox we didn't choke up! Tell him we won it—without him!"[87]

Reporters fired questions at Johnny Podres, who fired back answers. "My fastball really had it. Mantle? I wasn't worried about him. I keep my fastball up against him, and he can't hit it. … I was never worried about anybody. … I can beat those guys seven days a week." The hero of the day paused. He asked reporters not to print all that braggadocio. Of course, they did. Finally, Podres spotted Reese, the champion at last. "Hey, captain!" Podres yelled. "What did I tell you. Go ahead, tell them what I told you yesterday." So the captain told the story. "That's right, John. You told me not to worry. You said you were going to shut them out."[88]

The veteran Reese issued nothing but praise for the self-confident youngster. "It was one of the finest pitching performances I've ever seen anywhere," he said. "Speed alone won't beat the Yankees. You have to give them that soft stuff and mix it up, and Podres sure mixed 'em up. Had 'em off stride all the time."[89] Decades later, Yogi Berra said, "Johnny was a pretty darn good pitcher. He's the reason the Dodgers finally beat us." The catcher said Podres' change-up and curveball did in the Yanks. "He's a good man, all the Dodgers were good guys and we respected them. I went into their clubhouse after they beat us. I congratulated Pee Wee and Jackie and they were almost in tears. I think they always felt that year was their last chance to beat us. They were aging a bit."[90]

Sandy Amoros stood by his locker. He puffed on a lengthy Cuban cigar and drank from a can of beer. He told all the reporters about his epic catch, one of the greatest in Series history. He kept both eyes on the ball, he explained. Then he recreated the play for reporters. "I never hit the fence," Amoros said. "But I was only this far from it."[91] How far? He spread out his hands. Twenty inches, the length between his one hand, holding the beer, and his other hand, holding the cigar.

Emma Reese's prayers for her son were answered with that final out. "He has waited so long," she told a reporter. "So now, I'm happy. He finally did it and it doesn't matter much what happens now. Of course, I only hope that he keeps on playing, and I'm sure he will. But this was the big thing—being on a winning World Series team just once."[92]

Factory whistles blew throughout Brooklyn, loud and clear. Fans young and old danced and hugged in apartments and in houses and bars and restaurants and on sidewalks. Strangers turned into friends. Fans clanged pots and pans. New signs went up. "We Dood It." Yes, they did. "This Is Next Year." Yes, it was. The Flock faithful had taken so much grief through the years. Yankees supporters said the Dodgers choked every year. Giants fans said the same thing. Finally, an entire borough, filled with nearly three million people, plus all the other Dodgers faithful in Queens, on Long Island and elsewhere, could celebrate an October championship. And celebrate they did. Middle-aged men climbed light poles in triumph. Block parties broke out. Revelers brought out growlers of beer and cooked hamburgers in the street on portable stoves. Drivers honked their horns and steered willy-nilly, zigzagging along avenues and boulevards. Police kept their ticket books hidden. One officer planned to do nothing to stop the mess. Anyway, he said, "I'm a Dodger fan myself."[93]

Fans called other fans, who called more fans. *Can you believe it? ... Neither can I. ... Finally!* "From precisely 3:44 p.m., a minute after the final out, to 4:01 p.m., it was practically impossible to get a dial tone on phones along the east side of Manhattan," Stewart Wolpin wrote in a book about the long-awaited championship season. "According to the phone company, it handled the largest volume of calls since VJ Day 10 years before."[94] The unruly toppled garbage cans. Some plotted even more dramatic, large-scale escapades. "We had the idea of marching up to Yankee Stadium and setting it on fire," Bill Reddy said. "Luckily, someone talked us out of it."[95] The Dodgers didn't just win a World Series. They won a World Series AND they beat the Yankees. Honig said, "If we had beaten Cleveland or the Red Sox, it wouldn't have meant nearly as much."[96]

Carl Furillo said, "Everybody, no matter where in hell you went, everybody couldn't do enough for you. I never in my life saw a town go so wild. We accomplished something. We did something for the people. You did it for yourself, too, but you did it for the people."[97] David Karp handed out free cigars at his Brooklyn food and candy shop. "It's like having a baby,"[98] he cried. An elderly man with a long white beard leaned on a cane and said, "I never thought I'd live so long."[99] Borough resident Jack White declared, "I've gone back to Ireland, and I've seen the Dodgers win. Now, I'm ready to die. May the Lord have mercy on me."[100]

Vin Scully recalled, "When the Yankees won a World Series, the Bronx didn't go bananas, and when the Giants won in their great heyday, I don't think Manhattan danced in the streets. But when Brooklyn won the World Series, the borough went wild. It was like us against the world."[101] Larry King looked for a buddy of his named Herbie, "who was a Yankee fan, just to taunt him, and taunt him. He felt terrible and said Mantle had been hurt; he always had an excuse. I was just jumping up and down."[102]

Later, many of the Dodgers, along with 2,000 of their closest friends, gathered for a post–Series party at the Hotel Bossert in Brooklyn. Over at the *Daily News*, a team of writers, editors, and one talented cartoonist wrapped up a memorable edition. Leo O'Mealia sketched an image of the beloved Brooklyn bum, his eyes and mouth wide open, hair disheveled, beard in need of a shave, and with a lone tooth sticking out of his bottom jaw. The newspaper's assistant managing editor, Gene McHugh, took one look at the artwork and wanted it for Page One. He needed a caption. Copy editor Peter Coutros suggested, "WHO'S A BUM!" McHugh broke out in a smile. "Run it," he ordered.

Pee Wee Reese and Roger Kahn met in the early-morning hours outside of Whyte's, a Brooklyn bar. The two now tipsy gentlemen talked about what happened—finally—just hours earlier. Kahn asked a question. Two outs, bottom of the ninth, Howard up to bat, the Dodgers ahead, a championship—at last—so close at hand. What was going through Reese's mind? The veteran shortstop refused to lie. "I'm thinking," he said, "I hope he [Howard] doesn't hit the ball to me."[103]

17

"You're getting good in your old age"

In *Bums*, Peter Golenbock described Ebbets Field as "personal and familiar. … It was a suitable place for falling in love with the game."[1] Bobby McCarthy recalled how the "homey" park "was small, and everything was close."[2] Ebbets Field never seated more than 35,000 fans. Yankee Stadium, meanwhile, held more than 70,000 in some seasons and 82,000 in 1927. The Polo Grounds had a capacity of 55,000.

The Dodgers' home field, located on the western edge of Crown Heights and next to Flatbush, took on an almost magical glow for many of the faithful. Bill Reddy liked to gaze at the infield diamond. He swore that "it glistened."[3] Bob McGee called his book about Ebbets Field *The Greatest Ballpark Ever*, "where anything can happen and often did."[4] McGee wrote, "Ebbets Field alive teemed with people, the colors of an artist's palette arrayed around its outfield walls, a busting Brooklyn neighborhood right over the top of its right-field fence on Bedford Avenue."[5] Chapter One of *The Greatest Ballpark Ever* is titled "Hallowed Ground." Roger Kahn attended many games at Ebbets Field, both as a boyhood fan and later as a sportswriter. In those years, even when the Dodgers were still daffy, Kahn said, "you didn't worry about midterm exams at the ballpark or how you like to shape your life. The world was a diamond, green and brown and white, and your entire future was the next inning. No one aged at Ebbets Field; nobody died."[6]

The ballpark itself did age, of course. Robert Creamer described the Brooklyn fixture in its later stages and left out the flattery. He scoffed at any romantic reminiscing. "Ebbets Field was not an attractive place," Creamer insisted. "The grandstands were dirty and smelled of stale beer. The clubhouse was so small and cluttered, even the Dodger clubhouse, it was like somebody's attic." As for the visiting clubhouse, well, that was even worse. "It was like the Black Hole of Calcutta," Creamer said. "This was a decrepit, antiquated old ballpark that could just not continue. That's all there was to it. They had to have a change."[7] He added, "So, the glorious Brooklyn Dodgers and the glorious Ebbets Field is a myth. It's a nice myth, but's a myth."[8]

Buzzie Bavasi said the team "always turned a profit," but added, "Ebbets Field was so rundown, the place was on the verge of being condemned several times. Walter had no choice. He had to move the club somewhere."[9] Home attendance had slipped. The team that drew nearly 1.8 million fans in 1946 and just more than that in 1947 was now barely topping the one-million mark. "To be sure, attendance was falling across baseball"[10] in the 1950s, Andy McCue wrote in *Mover and Shaker*. Indeed, major league attendance dropped 22 percent from 1947 to 1956. Dodgers home attendance, though, declined by 33 percent in that same span.[11]

Walter O'Malley worried that the neighborhood was growing poorer and more crime-ridden. Some fans feared going to Ebbets Field at night.[12] "Others noted tensions between Black (fans) and white fans in the stands, mirroring what was happening in Brooklyn neighborhoods,"[13] said McCue. Borough residents struggled as factories closed or were downsized. More and more workers at the Brooklyn Navy Yard were taking home pink slips. "Manufacturing was fleeing,"[14] McCue wrote. Three large department stores had gone out of business. The *Brooklyn Eagle* stopped the presses in early 1955. Unemployment was surging.

Bavasi relayed a story about the day in 1956 when O'Malley asked him to look out the office window and onto the street. "What do you see?" Nearby was the local welfare office. Bavasi gave a blunt, but apparently honest and accurate, answer. "I see a long line of poor Puerto Rican people getting their welfare checks." Bavasi said the "Puerto Rican" part did not bother his boss. It was the "poor" part that did. "He could see the future," Bavasi said. "And the future he saw involved too many people without enough money to adequately support the Dodgers."[15] Roger Kahn, filled with contempt, later wrote, "O'Malley claimed warm memories of Ebbets Field." However, "He was no more sentimental than a hippopotamus, which his enemies claim he resembled. He saw Ebbets Field not as a shrine but as a relic, with rotten parking and smelling urinals, both of which kept the customers away."[16]

In February, the Louisville Bull Pen Club honored World Series champion Reese as its Man of the Year. Warren Giles, seated at the head table, said, "No one in our league has contributed more to the welfare and good of baseball. That is the greatest contribution he has made—even greater than his playing record. I mean, his disposition, his character, his kindness, and his other attributes."[17] The club created a trophy in Reese's name to honor the top amateur baseball player from Louisville each year. Reese told the gathering of approximately 500, "I hope some major league player's name is inscribed on this trophy."[18]

On March 29, Reese and the Dodgers stepped off an airplane at Tampa International Airport and boarded a Greyhound bus. A seven-year-old boy stood in awe. Steven Patrick Garvey, the future Dodgers first baseman (1969–1982), could not believe his good fortune. His dad, Joe Garvey, a transplanted Floridian from Long Island, worked charter routes for Greyhound, often ferrying groups to sporting events or teams to training camps. The previous evening, Joe asked his son, "Do you have any tests tomorrow, and if you don't, do you want to skip school?"[19] Steven's face lit up with a wide smile. For the big day, he put on his royal blue—"almost like Dodger blue"[20]—Ban-Lon shirt and left with his dad at six a.m. The Dodgers were scheduled to play an exhibition game that afternoon against the Yankees at Al Lang Field in St. Petersburg.

Young Steve watched the Dodgers practice and noticed how "Everybody called Reese 'Cap,'"[21] Garvey wrote in *My Bat Boys Days: Lessons I Learned from the Boys of Summer*. "Cap was a leader even to a boy like me. He told me the key to baseball, whether you're batting or fielding, is to never, ever take your eye off the ball from the moment it leaves a pitcher's mitt. Sounds simple, but it's sage advice for a kid learning the game."[22]

Earlier that month, Reese had told Ben Olan of the Associated Press that "I'm more confident than I was last spring," when his legs felt heavy, and "I told my wife that it looked like the beginning of the end." Over the winter, he skipped his running routine and did a bit of bicycling. Reese said he felt "like a kid" as he prepared for the season. "Maybe an injury will stop me," he acknowledged. "But a 21-year-old can get hurt, too. And barring something of that nature, there isn't the slightest doubt in my mind about my ability to have another good year."[23] The next day, Dick Young reported that Reese's back "gave out" and the shortstop "hobbled to the rubdown table," where he spent the next hour. Trainer Harold Wendler admitted, "It could be serious, very serious, at his age."[24] Young speculated that March 1 was "black Friday" and that Dodgers fans might look back on the day as "the beginning of the end for Pee Wee Reese, the greatest guy ever to pull on a Dodger suit."[25]

Reese spent a few nights sleeping on the floor of his bungalow in Vero Beach. Wendler said the veteran suffered some ligament damage but apparently did not injure a disc. Walter Alston said, "I'm more concerned about it than anyone else, naturally. You can never tell about a back injury."[26] The *Brooklyn Daily* reported on March 6 that Reese was "coming along nicely."[27] He expected to work out with the team in about a week.[28]

The Dodgers opened the season April 17, on a chilly but festive day in Brooklyn. A celebration, one befitting world champions, preceded the opening pitch. The *Brooklyn Daily* encouraged fans to attend "the biggest, bestest and finest parade ever," which began at Church and Flatbush Avenues and ended, naturally, at Ebbets Field. Floats representing businesses big and small, plus some from civic groups and local sandlot leagues, took part. In a preview of the festivities, the *Daily* wrote, "They'll parade to the ballpark to watch as manager Walter Alston and captain Pee Wee Reese raise the coveted championship banner."[29]

Pee Wee Reese jogged to his spot at shortstop that afternoon. The Dodgers took their lumps and lost, 8–6. Don Newcombe gave up five runs over 2⅓ innings. Reese doubled, singled twice, and walked. The game drew 24,236 fans. Before the opening pitch, Commissioner Ford Frick (promoted from NL president in September 1951) presented each Brooklyn player with a championship ring for winning the 1955 World Series. Reese stood alone on the first-base line when his name was finally called. "This one, I particularly enjoy presenting,"[30] the commissioner announced. Reese walked over to Frick "amid a thunderous ovation."[31]

Reese admitted to getting emotional during the ceremony. "I just choked up when [Frick] handed me the ring," he told reporters. "I'm a funny guy, I get kind of choked up sometimes just by listening to 'The Star-Spangled Banner' before a World Series game. A lotta things were running through my mind. … You bet I was nervous. After we beat the Yankees last fall, the Commissioner was kidding me about being entitled to a bigger diamond in the ring because I had waited so long."[32]

On April 19, the Dodgers played their first game at Roosevelt Stadium in Jersey City, New Jersey, about six miles from Brooklyn. Walter O'Malley had announced in August, during the heat of the pennant race, that the Dodgers would play seven games at Roosevelt in 1956. According to the *Daily News*, O'Malley called the move to Jersey City "strictly temporary" and "stressed that, while the Dodgers must have a new stadium soon, it should be located in Brooklyn" or within a 30-minute drive or subway trip from the borough.[33] O'Malley told the *Daily News*, "We will consider other locations only if we are finally unsuccessful in our ambition to build in Brooklyn."[34]

Roosevelt Stadium, built on the site of the old Jersey City Airport, served as the home of the New Jersey Giants, the International League affiliate of the New York club, from its opening in 1937 through 1950, and had hosted many top boxing matches, including a heavyweight bout in 1940 that pitted former champion Max Baer against "Two-Ton" Tony Galento. (Baer won by technical knockout in the eighth round and improved his career record to 67–12. Jack Mahon of the *Daily News* reported in graphic detail that "A finish—scrawled in his own blood—was written to the fantastic pugilistic career of Two-Ton Tony Galento as the Battle of the Bums became a part of the madness that is the fight game at Roosevelt Stadium, Jersey City, last night! Smeared with gore, his left hand shattered, his lips shredded, carmine slit in his battered, gargoylish face, Galento fell before the vengeful fists of mad Max Baer...."[35]) Sugar Ray Robinson defended his welterweight title at Roosevelt in 1950.

The Dodgers, according to an AP report, "hauled their floating franchise across the Hudson River" to play "the first major league game on New Jersey soil in the modern era."[36] The contest provided plenty of thrills, and lots of boo-boos, for the 12,214 fans. Brooklyn jumped ahead, 3–0, in the first inning on a bases-clearing double by Hodges and won, 5–4. The Dodgers made five errors, while the Phillies committed three. The scorekeeper marked down Reese for two miscues, both in the ninth inning. First, he bobbled a ball hit by Jim Greengrass and then "heaved wild past first."[37] Neither error hurt the ballclub. Philadelphia left Glen Gorbous, pinch-running for Greengrass, stranded at second.

Reese said the infield at Roosevelt felt a bit hard around shortstop and soft near second and third, but overall, he called the diamond "pretty good." He kind of liked the park, especially the wide-open outfield. "That's for me," he said. "If I try to hit a home run, I'm cooked." He also acknowledged, "Our guys are not too enthused about playing here. The park is strange. The wind is always blowing in toward home plate, I understand, and the background is not good."[38] Other than that.... Duke Snider said the outfield wall looked "a pretty fur piece" away from home plate. Only a mighty swing and a favorable wind could propel a baseball out of Roosevelt Field. Gil Hodges admitted, "Boy, how I wish I was back at dear old Ebbets Field."[39]

Brooklyn pitching took some lickings in the early going. The Bums began the year 8–8 and gave up at least 10 runs four times in one six-game stretch. Billy Loes' oft-injured time with the Dodgers ended in mid–May. The quotable hurler had only pitched one game all year and looked horrendous. Against the Pirates on April 29, he lasted 1⅓ innings and allowed six earned runs. The Orioles purchased Loes' contract for $20,000. Good riddance, Loes said to his hometown team. "I was always under a strain in Brooklyn," he said to reporters on May 15. "I've been asking for two years to be traded and it's finally happened."[40]

Buzzie Bavasi found a way to improve the Brooklyn pitching staff at a bargain price. He acquired old foe Sal Maglie from the Indians for $100. The Giants had traded "Sal the Barber" to Cleveland the previous July. Maglie went 9–7 with a 3.77 ERA in 1955. Dick Young speculated as to how Brooklyn fans might react to the newest Bum, who hurled so many fastballs at Dodgers' noggins through the years. "They will accept him," Young wrote, "just as the Dodger players have accepted him, as one of them. ... Sal never stopped trying. He knew only one way as a Giant, and that's how he can be expected to pitch for Brooklyn—to pitch his aging arm off and win as best as he knows how."[41] Maglie arrived in Brooklyn for a press conference on May 18, the same day his dad died in Niagara Falls, New York. A reporter asked him whether he truly hated the Dodgers, as so many claimed. "Brooklyn was the best, so I hated them," the pitcher said. "I always hated anybody that was the best in any league."[42]

Reese sounded more than willing to let bygones be bygones if Maglie could still throw his wicked curveball. "Based on what he showed us in Cleveland a couple of weeks ago, he's got to help us." Reese decided.[43] During an exhibition game on April 30, Maglie tossed four shutout innings against Brooklyn and allowed just one hit.

One of the all-time great Dodgers pitchers split his time between starting and relieving in 1956. Donald Scott Drysdale, from Van Nuys, in the San Fernando Valley section of Los Angeles, signed a deal with Brooklyn as a 17-year-old. The nearly 6-foot-6-inch right-hander threw an intimidating fastball that kept ambitious batters wary. Brooklyn promoted him to the big club after arm problems sidelined Loes and Karl Spooner, and the Navy took Johnny Podres. "Stuck for pitchers, the club took me, in desperation,"[44] Drysdale conceded. The rookie made his debut on April 17 and threw a scoreless inning against the Phillies at Ebbets Field. Six days later, he made his first start, versus Philadelphia on the road. He tossed a complete game and struck out nine in a 6–1 Brooklyn win. Reese contributed a two-run single in the fifth inning. Dick Young described the 19-year-old rookie as a "red-blooded American (Southern California variety)" and said that by late in the game, he "actually had the normally antagonistic Philly fans cheering him."[45]

Drysdale and Reese were born on the same date—July 23—though 17 years apart and had lockers near one another at Ebbets Field. Pee Wee Reese made a strong impression on the young pitcher. "There's no question, despite the Dodgers' array of strong individuals and different personalities, that Pee Wee Reese was our leader," Drysdale wrote in *Once a Bum, Always a Dodger*. "He had a dry sense of humor, and he could agitate with the best of them." Reese dished it out, and he could take it. Some players had noticed a few wrinkles on his face and dubbed him "Prune." Drysdale said the Dodgers respected one another "regardless of a guy's age or salary status." For that, he credited Reese. "Pee Wee believed that everybody was equal," Drysdale said. "If you wore a Dodger uniform, if you were one of the twenty-five players on the roster, there was always the chance you would make somebody else in that same uniform some money."[46]

During one game, Drysdale got into a jam and Reese walked to the mound. He handed Drysdale a loaded-up baseball. A spitball ready to go. "Just hold the ball in your glove like this," Reese instructed. "Don't move it around. It's ready for you if you want it." Drysdale thanked the veteran, reached for a little resin, and delivered a wet pitch. (Drysdale, in his memoir, recalled the opposing team as the Cardinals.

He wasn't sure about the exact batter. "I want to say Bill Virdon," a talented outfielder with a sweet left-handed swing. Virdon, though, never faced Drysdale during his short stint with St. Louis in 1956. Later in the season, on September 3 at Ebbets Field, after getting traded to Pittsburgh, Virdon collected four hits of his five hits that day against Drysdale.)

The ball never broke. It ran toward home plate with a "hit me" sign on it. The batter lashed a rope off the scoreboard. Drysdale had just thrown one of the straightest, crummiest spitballs of all time. The pitcher took a quick look at his shortstop, who wasn't pleased. "There was nothing worse than screwing up on the field and then looking over at Pee Wee," Drysdale recalled. In this case, Reese stood at his infield spot, glared at the young pitcher, and kicked some dirt. "Pee Wee made you feel like you were about four inches tall." Even so, Drysdale understood the shortstop's motives. "He wanted us to think more, execute better, and win."[47]

Reese took a "finicky" approach to batting practice, as Drysdale remembered. "It was as though he wanted every pitch on a tee," he wrote. Reese didn't like to hit balls off his fists or, at the other extreme, off the end of the bat. One day, Drysdale plunked him in the ribs. "You did that on purpose, you big donkey," Reese yelled, trying to agitate a young teammate. Drysdale shouted back, "We're on the same team, remember. Why would I do that on purpose?" Reese knew the reason. "I was taking too many pitches, that's why. That's why you got mad."[48]

On May 18, in a 7–6 loss to the Reds in Brooklyn, Reese, the Dodgers' "big gunner"[49] in that game, notched four hits and scored three runs. He went 5-for-10 over the next three contests, with four runs scored and three RBI, and raised his average to .319 before going into a slump. By the end of the month, his average had dropped to .281, and it kept falling in June, when he hit just .239.

The Dodgers dropped a doubleheader July 13 against Milwaukee, 8–6 and 6–5, and slipped to 42–35. Braves first baseman Joe Adcock hit a two-run homer in the first game and added another home run, along with five RBI, in the second. "You think you have problems?" asked Ed Wilks of the Associated Press. "Man, take a look at Brooklyn's world champions trying to figure out what not to throw Joe Adcock. He not only hits Dodger pitchers like he owns them, he looks like he has 'em on strings."[50]

Between games of that double-dip, Walter Alston "bawled out" the club. Don Newcombe had given up six runs in just one inning of work, and the team committed three errors, two by reliever Clem Labine and one by Roy Campanella. "We'd blown the game," said Reese, who singled and scored in five at-bats. "There's no denying that. My chin was down in my lap and I sat in front of my locker. Alston stood in front of us and read the riot act." Alston, according to some reports, called the team "gutless." Reese didn't recall that word being used and added, "He was yelling for effect—I know that. He was trying to steam us up, snap us out of it." Similar to what he said when the team struggled in 1954, Reese told reporters, "Alston isn't to blame for anything that has hurt us this season."[51] Carl Erskine echoed that sentiment: "Alston certainly is not responsible because my record is six and six right now."[52]

Alston denied using the word "gutless." But "if I did, I shouldn't have," he said. He hoped to move on from the incident. "I don't think I ever saw anything so exaggerated," he told one writer. "Those things happen all the time. A manager has things to say when his team is not doing well, and perhaps he says things he shouldn't. But this was supposed to be between the players and me. I have never criticized any player and I never will."[53] Walter O'Malley sent telegrams to Reese and Erskine, commending both for supporting their boss. To Reese, O'Malley wrote, "Captain, I had an idea that you would be present when the roll was called to defend the manager and recent anonymous quotes. I predict we will play great ball from here on in."[54]

On July 20, the Dodgers arrived in St. Louis for a two-game series. Reese smacked three singles and a solo home run in the opener. Brooklyn beat the Redbirds, 4–1, behind Newcombe, who improved to 13–5. After his final hit—a single in the ninth—Reese stood beside Stan Musial, who was playing first base. "What's the matter with you tonight?" Musial asked. "You're getting good in your old age." Reese mentioned that he needed just one more hit to reach 2,000. "Is that right?" asked Stan. "Yeah," Reese said. "And my 2,000 came a hell of a lot harder than your 2,700."[55] After the game, Musial commented to Bob Broeg about how much Reese had improved through the years and "developed into a tough little hitter. If he had been able to hit those first couple of years and hadn't missed three years of service, he'd have a lot more base hits."[56]

The following night, Reese hit a line drive that fell to the ground just a few feet from Whitey Lockman in left field. Home plate umpire Stan Landes asked for the ball and lobbed it to Reese, who tossed it into the dugout for safekeeping. He became just the second Dodger to record 2,000 hits. Zack Wheat, a Hall of Famer who retired with 2,884 knocks (2,804 for Brooklyn and 80 for the Athletics in the final year of his illustrious career, 1927), did it first. Reese also stood second in franchise history in games played, at-bats, runs, singles, and doubles.[57]

Finally, the Dodgers perked up. Counting those two wins in the series against St. Louis, the club won eight straight and nine out of 11. On July 29, Newcombe and the Cubs' Jim Davis hooked up in a pitchers' duel in the first game of a doubleheader at Ebbets Field. With one out in the eighth inning, Reese drove a 2–1 pitch "10 rows back into the left field seats"[58] for the only run of the game. Newcombe scattered five hits in his third shutout of the season.

On August 9, Reese scored three times in a 7–3 Brooklyn win against Pittsburgh. The final tally gave him 1,257 runs scored in his career, vaulting him past Wheat and into first place on the franchise's all-time list. It was news to Reese. "I don't remember my first hit, my first homer, anything," he insisted in the August 22 issue of *The Sporting News*. Then, he thought about it for a second. "But I tell you one thing I remember—that home run I hit off Jim Davis,"[59] As for scoring all those runs, Reese gave credit to "those batters who follow me in the batting order."[60]

The Dodgers stayed close most of the way but spent little time in first place. They finally reached a tie with Milwaukee after beating them, 4–2, on September 11 each team sporting an 83–55 mark. The following day, Milwaukee edged Brooklyn, 8–7, to regain first place. Reese had four hits and scored twice. The two teams jockeyed for first place the rest of the way.

On September 25, Sal Maglie, "the amazing 39-year-old reject of the Giants and Indians,"[61] threw the best game of his career, a no-hitter in front of 15,204 fans at Ebbets Field. He struck out three and gave up two walks in a 5–0 win against the

Phillies. Roy Campanella hit a two-run homer in the second inning. Walter O'Malley said Maglie could expect a $500 bonus in his next paycheck.[62] According to the Associated Press, "only once did the Phillies come close to connecting safely."[63] In the second inning, Willie Jones lined a ground ball up the middle. Reese, "playing in his 2,000 [sic] major league game, darted to his left for a fine stop and throw to retire the batter."[64]

A few days later, the Dodgers waited for the rain to stop at Ebbets Field and the game against Pittsburgh to start. Reese spoke in the locker room to columnist Jimmy Cannon about the trials and tribulations of one Walter "Smokey" Alston. The manager can't catch a break, Reese said. "He wins the pennant, he's supposed to. This is supposed to be a great ballclub. If he loses, he's no good, no matter what happens. The way people figure, he can't get any credit. No one wants to give him credit." Alston's record as a player—short as it was—probably did not help matters. "Holding this type of ball club together is no cinch," Reese said. "because this is a fellow who didn't play in the major leagues except for one time at-bat with the Cards."[65]

The rain kept falling, turning the field into a muddy mess. The teams played a doubleheader the next day. Maglie, in his first game following the no-hitter, gave up a two-run homer to Frank Thomas in the opening frame. He settled down after that and held Pittsburgh scoreless over his final eight innings of work. Brooklyn scored three times in the bottom of the first and won, 6–2.

Clem Labine, making just his third start of the campaign, gave Brooklyn another strong effort in the nightcap. He struck out 10 and walked five in a 3–1 victory. The Dodgers led the Braves by one game. They had clinched at least a share of the NL pennant. A confident Jackie Robinson hollered to Buzzie Bavasi: "Were you worried, veep? No need to. We'll wrap it up for you tomorrow."[66] Red Smith wrote, "It was altogether ridiculous, of course. Three days before, the Dodgers were dead, and in no fine state of preservation, either, if one might judge by the twitching noses of those who saw them flounder to wretched defeat by the Phillies. ... Yet, now they were alive again, up and swinging against the bodacious Pirates."[67] In St. Louis, meanwhile, the Cards beat the Braves, 2–1, on Rip Repulski's 12th-inning RBI double.

Don Newcombe opposed Vern Law in the last game of the season. Both pitchers looked tired. Law gave up three runs and retired just two batters. The Dodgers led, 7–2, before Newcombe ran out of gas and allowed three runs in the seventh inning and another in the eighth. Alston asked Don Bessent to provide some relief. The second-year pitcher retired two batters to close out the eighth and pitched a scoreless ninth. Brooklyn held on to win, 8–6. Sandy Amoros and Duke Snider both hit two home runs; Jackie Robinson added another. Reese went two-for-three, drove in one run, and scored once. The Dodgers finished 93–61, one game in front of the Braves. Reese said this was the toughest pennant race of his career. "Maybe it's because I'm older and can't take it like I once could," he told the *Daily News*. "I thought early in the game that we had clinched and then the score was suddenly 7–6 and I began thinking for sure we're going to have to play off against Milwaukee."[68]

Reese hit a modest .257 for the season and scored 86 runs. He also stole 13 bases and finished fifth among NL shortstops with 367 assists. Snider ripped a league-leading 43 home runs, his fourth straight year with at least 40 homers. Gil

Hodges hit 32 round-trippers, and Carl Furillo added 21. Don Newcombe topped the team in most pitching categories. He won 27 games, lost seven, and posted a 3.06 ERA. He also completed 18 games, threw five shutouts, and pitched 268 innings en route to the first-ever Cy Young Award. Sal Maglie went 13–5 with a 2.87 ERA. The Dodgers attracted 1,213,562 fans, the second-highest figure in the league, and the team's best figure since 1951.

New York won the AL pennant with a 97–57 mark. Mickey Mantle put together a huge season and won the Triple Crown with 52 home runs, 130 RBI, and a .353 batting average. He also topped the league in slugging percentage (.705) and runs scored (132). "That season," Mantle wrote in *The Mick*, "I started to do the things they thought I would do," referring to both fans and critics.[69]

The World Series began October 3 at Ebbets Field.[70] President Dwight D. Eisenhower threw out the first pitch. The president also signed a glove for Pee Wee Reese, who told teammates that he asked Ike for a little favor. Could the president—please—"spring" Johnny Podres from his two-year Navy commitment and allow him to pitch against the Yankees. Afterward, one of the reporters asked, "Did you really say that?" Reese just laughed. "Of course not! You think I'm nuts?"[71]

New York took an early lead on Mantle's two-run homer in the first inning off Maglie, who settled down and allowed just one more run over nine innings. Brooklyn came back to win, 6–3. Gil Hodges struck the big blow, a three-run homer in the third. Reese racked up two singles and scored a run. "We won the first one and that's a big help," Walter Alston said afterward to reporters as he grabbed a pack of cigarettes. Even so, he added, "I can't say things are easier now. After all, [the Yankees] won the first two games last time,"[72] just one year ago.

Both Don Newcombe and Don Larsen struggled in Game Two. The Yankees scored six runs in the second inning. Brooklyn matched that total in the bottom half of the frame. Roy Campanella lifted a run-scoring fly ball, Reese added a two-run single, and Duke Snider ripped a three-run homer. Brooklyn outscored New York, 7–2, the rest of the way and won, 13–8. Snider now had 10 career World Series home runs, tying him with former Yankees great Lou Gehrig for second on the all-time list, five behind Babe Ruth. "Duke has a knack for coming through at the right moment," Alston said. "He is a terrific money player."[73] Casey Stengel complained that his staff was throwing too many "fat"[74] pitches. Brooklyn had notched 21 hits and 19 runs through the first two games. Reese said, "If we keep hitting like this, we could beat those guys in a ploughed field."[75]

In Game Three, Enos Slaughter (traded by the Cardinals to the Yankees before the 1954 season, sent to the Kansas City Athletics the following campaign, and reacquired by the Yankees on waivers in August of 1956) belted a three-run homer and led New York to a 5–3 victory. Whitey Ford threw a complete game and struck out seven. Reese singled in the third inning with two out but was left stranded at first base. Three innings later, he tripled into right-center field and scored on Snider's sacrifice fly. New York won the next day, 6–2, and evened the Series. Tom Sturdivant, a 26-year-old right-hander, scattered six hits in his complete game. Reese singled in the sixth inning but struck out twice. Afterward, Sturdivant said, "Yogi called 'em and I threw 'em."[76]

Stengel sent out Don Larsen for Game Five, hoping to get better results this time from his pitcher. No one expected him to throw the greatest game in World Series history. Larsen struck out Jim Gilliam and Reese in the first inning. He fanned Hodges in the second inning and Campanella in the third. After he struck out Snider to end the fourth, Larsen walked back to the dugout and was still perfect. He hadn't allowed a baserunner.

Some players called Larsen "Goony Bird," maybe for his long arms, big ears, and pear-shaped body. Or maybe it was for his care-free, hard-partying habits. Larsen, born in Michigan City, Indiana, later moved with his family to California. He broke in with the St. Louis Browns in 1953 and finished 7–12. The following season, he lost 21 games and won just three for the Orioles. New York picked up Larsen, and the pitcher posted a 9–2 record in 1955. Over the regular season in 1956, he won 11 games and posted a 3.26 ERA.

The Goony Bird kept going and going. Brooklyn only threatened a few times to put a runner on base. In the fifth inning, Gil Hodges ripped a pitch into deep center field that Mickey Mantle ran down, making "a sensational backhanded catch."[77] Sandy Amoros, the next batter, banged a slider that sailed down the right-field line before hooking foul. Larsen barely threatened even to walk a batter. He went to three balls on just one hitter, Reese in the first inning. Larsen retired all 27 Dodgers and jumped into the air following the final out of his perfect game, the only one in Series history. "I'm plumb in another world, and it feels so gosh darn good," Larsen wrote in a column for the next day's newspapers. "I don't think I'm ever coming back. … My legs are still rubbery all over, and I'm so nervous and excited. I don't even know what day it is."[78]

Sal Maglie, Larsen's opponent that day, pitched a strong game himself. He gave up a solo homer to Mantle in the fourth and an RBI single to Hank Bauer in the sixth. He allowed five hits, struck out five, and walked two over eight innings. It was only good enough to be a footnote. October 8, 1956, belonged to Larsen. "His sliders were good, so were his curves, but his fastballs were faster than I've ever seen," Yogi Berra wrote in *Ten Rings*, about all his championship seasons with the Yankees. "Ninety-seven pitches and he was behind on only one hitter,"[79] Reese in that opening frame. (Reese grounded out in the fourth inning and flied out in the seventh in his other at-bats.)

The Brooklyn shortstop also made a play that, according to Larsen, "electrified the crowd."[80] With one out in the fifth inning, Billy Martin stood at first base, safe on a fielder's choice. McDougald ripped a liner that appeared headed to left field. Larson said Reese "leaped into the air, got a glove on the ball, deflected it, and then caught it with his glove." Vin Scully told fans listening on the radio, "It was like Pee Wee Reese was playing catch with himself."[81]

The superb pitching continued in Game Six. Clem Labine and Bob Turley put up a long series of goose eggs. Neither pitcher allowed a run through nine innings. In the 10th, with Turley still on the mound, Jim Gilliam walked with one out and advanced to second on Reese's sacrifice bunt. Turley gave Duke Snider a free pass to bring up Jackie Robinson, who singled to left field as Gilliam sprinted home with the game's only run. Just two Yankees reached second base after the third inning. (This was the 15th one-run game in the 44 World Series contests between the Yankees and the Brooklyn Dodgers. The Yankees won eight and the Dodgers won seven.)

New York easily won Game Seven, 9–0. Yogi Berra hit two home runs, one in the first inning and another in the third. About that first round-tripper, Reese had told Don Newcombe to keep the change-up off the plate. "Instead, he throws a fastball, high and inside," the captain said, "and Yogi parks it."[82] Berra and Moose Skowron drove in four runs apiece for New York. Berra set a record with 10 RBI in one World Series. "I had no idea," the St. Louis native said. "In fact, I'm surprised to hear it."[83] Brooklyn managed just three hits—two by Snider, one by Furillo—against 24-year-old Johnny Kucks.[84]

Lose the deciding World Series game to Kucks, a tall, slender (6-foot-3, 170 pounds) right-hander from Hoboken, New Jersey, albeit an 18-game winner and an All-Star? Jackie Robinson couldn't believe it. "We shouldn't lose to a pitcher like that," said Robinson, who went hitless in that final game and batted .250 (6-for-24) for the entire Series. "Sure, he's got a good sinker," Robinson added, but not much else. "He's not fast, and he has a nickel curve."[85] Newcombe gave up five runs in three innings of work. Roger Craig allowed four runs. Reese, in his final World Series game, went 0-for-2 with two walks. He batted .222 (6-for-27) over the fall classic. "All I know is that he [Kucks] beat us," Reese said, "and beat us good."[86]

The players dressed in a quiet locker room. Someone walked up to Pee Wee Reese and said, "We'll get 'em next year." Reese, tired and yet not in the mood to think about 1957, just said, "Next year is a long way away for me." Don Newcombe didn't say a whole lot after the game, either. Maybe he said nothing. He showered, put on his street clothes, and dashed out of the visiting clubhouse, much to the disappointment of Jackie Robinson. "I think a pitcher should stick around," Robinson said. "You just don't do that kind of thing. He might have gotten permission, though."[87]

It wasn't the best way to begin a goodwill tour halfway around the world. Walter O'Malley had agreed in April to send a mix of players and team employees to Japan following the season. Several teams already had toured the country, including an All-Star contingent in 1934 that included, among others, Babe Ruth, Lou Gehrig, Jimmie Foxx, and Lefty Grove. The Giants visited in 1953 and the Yankees in 1955. Some of the prominent Dodgers who left on this excursion included Reese, Hodges, Campanella, Newcombe, Robinson, Gilliam, Alston, and Drysdale. Vin Scully also traveled with the team. He, along with several others, wondered what to expect, just 11 years removed from the end of World War II. "We went in there with the typical American misconceptions," Scully remembered. "We expected the local teams to be stocked with little yellow, buck-toothed men wearing thick eyeglasses."[88]

Fred Kipp, a young pitcher, wrote about the trip in *The Last Yankee Dodger*. Kipp, a 6-foot-4-inch left-hander from little Piqua, Kansas, 110 miles southwest of Kansas City, won 20 games for the Montreal Royals in 1956 and asked to join the tour. The party took off on the morning after the World Series in a piston-driven DC-7. The engines "revved up, and the whole plane shook," Kipp recalled, on the first leg of a long journey, from New York's Idlewild Airport to Los Angeles.

Cruising at 30,000 feet for several hours leaves the flier with little to do. Some players brought along a bottle of whiskey or two to pass the time and, not surprisingly, the party grew loud. Walter Alston apologized to his wife and daughter for all the commotion and told some players to pipe down. At one point, a drunken Don Newcombe stumbled down the aisle on his way to the restroom, bumping against a few seats. Alston demanded, "Go back and sit down, I've heard enough of you for the day."[89] Newcombe, though, threatened to relieve himself on the manager. Alston, wisely, stepped aside. "You go to the head," the skipper ordered, "and then you get back to your seat and shut up."[90]

The layover in southern California lasted one day, and, Kipp wrote, "none of the players knew that Walter O'Malley was talking with city council members about moving to L.A."[91] From California, the group left for Hawaii. In Honolulu, "thousands of people came out to see us."[92] The Dodgers played three exhibition games in the Aloha State. They knocked off the Honolulu All-Stars, 19–0, and beat the Oahu Red Sox, 7–3. They also defeated a team based in Maui. Following a few relaxing days on Waikiki Beach, the party headed to Wake Island. There, Kipp wrote, the airplane needed repairs, so "we had some time to kill."[93] Reese hit the beach and took a swim. Some guy started screaming "Shark! Shark!" He yelled for everyone to get out of the water. Reese, relaxing in the surf, made a beeline for the shore. Drysdale said he never saw the Brooklyn captain "move any faster than he did that afternoon."[94]

About 100,000 Japanese baseball fans greeted the Dodgers in Tokyo. The team rode in Cadillacs for a parade that began at the airport and ended at the Imperial Hotel. "The Japanese showered us with more flowers than I'd ever seen," said Kipp. The Dodgers lost two of their first three games in Japan, a fact that steamed Walter O'Malley. The owner ordered Alston to read his team the riot act. The skipper obliged. "I'm just repeating what Mr. O'Malley said," Alston told his gathered troops. "Don't think that you'll be getting a raise just for winning the pennant a few weeks earlier. Mr. O'Malley said, 'No way.' Some of you guys might wind up taking cuts if you don't do something more than you've done so far."[95] O'Malley told his team to act as goodwill ambassadors, but to, in his words, "Remember Pearl Harbor."[96]

Those two victories meant everything to Japanese manager Kazuto Yamamoto. "The Dodgers are not as strong as expected," Yamamoto said. "If we had been more careful in sending out our relief pitchers, we might have won." The next day, Brooklyn slammed eight homers and won, 14–0.[97]

Several Dodgers executives and players, including Reese, took part in a ceremony on November 1 to dedicate a plaque placed at the entrance to Hiroshima Stadium. On August 6, 1945, the U.S. B-29 bomber *Enola Gay* dropped an atomic bomb on the city, killing approximately 80,000 people,[98] Three days later, U.S. forces dropped an A-bomb on the Japanese city of Nagasaki. More than 60,000 died in the blast. Japan's Emperor Hirohito announced the unconditional surrender of Japan on August 15, bringing the fighting in World War II to an end. The plaque read, "We dedicate this visit in memory of those baseball fans and others who died by atomic action on Aug. 6, 1945. May their souls rest in peace and with God's help and man's resolution peace will prevail forever, amen."[99]

The tour ended on November 13 at Heiwadai Stadium in Fukuota. The Dodgers beat All-Japan, 3–1, and upped their overall mark to 14-4-1. They played in front of 150,000 total fans, an average of nearly 24,000 per game.[100] The Brooklyn club completed a season in which they played 218 games—35 in spring training, 154 in the regular season, seven in the World Series, three in Hawaii, and 19 in Japan.[101]

Some critics complained that the Dodgers played less than inspired baseball against their Japanese opponents. Reese, though, told writers in Honolulu on November 16 that Japan "should be given credit for playing a good brand of baseball instead of belittling the Dodgers for not putting out. Sure, we could have played better, but we are a tired bunch of fellows. We did our best at all times."[102]

Following the World Series, Buzzie Bavasi had said—maybe in the heat of the moment—"you can bet some changes will be made," with the club. His subsequent remarks sounded a bit cooler. "But we're not going to become panicky. We've got a whole winter to think things out."[103] The Dodgers boasted a strong farm system and a veteran roster. Might some player—or players—be on the move?

Just a few months later, the Dodgers made one of the biggest trades in team history. On December 13, they dealt 37-year-old Jackie Robinson to the Giants—the Giants?!—for pitcher Dick Littlefield and $30,000. Littlefield sported a 31–50 career won-loss record. The 30-year-old left-hander from Detroit played for three teams in 1956—the Pirates, Cardinals, and Giants—and compiled a 4–6 mark with a 4.37 ERA. Jackie Robinson to the hated Giants for journeyman Littlefield and a wad of cash? Egad. "I was surprised and stunned," Robinson wrote in *I Never Had It Made*.[104]

Dick Young ticked off several reasons for the deal, explaining why the Giants gave up so little for "the most dynamic of all Dodgers, maker of social history, screaming headlines, and proud pennants." He mentioned Robinson's age and how Brooklyn wanted to promote some of its minor league talent. "This is the first step in that declared declaration," according to Young. Plus, the market "was limited." Robinson "might have quit rather than go on playing outside New York. At least, he had threatened to do so."[105] Robinson, for his part, said he had no plans to hang up his uniform and glove. "I'm going to do all I can for the Giants,"[106] he declared.

Of course, Robinson never suited up for Brooklyn's great rival. Less than one month after the two teams cut this most surprising of deals, Robinson retired from baseball and took a job as vice-president of Chock Full O'Nuts, based in New York City. Some writers, including Ward, complained that Robinson had "acted and talked as though he would be in a Giant uniform come spring training."[107] Robinson, however, had signed an exclusive agreement with popular *Look* magazine to announce his retirement. "I had to hold out," he said, and allow "*Look* to be the one to break the story."[108]

The *Pittsburgh Press* speculated in early September that Pee Wee Reese might join his double-play partner in retirement.[109] On November 27, though, the shortstop agreed to keep playing, at $36,500. He was the first Dodger to sign, "as is his usual custom,"[110] Dick Young wrote. Buzzie Bavasi and Reese negotiated the contract by telephone. Other Brooklyn players figured to sign over the coming weeks. "They usually do after Reese shows the way," according to Young. "That has become club custom—to line up the captain first thing, and the others follow suit based on a wage scale to conform to Reese's pay."[111]

Looking back, Pee Wee Reese mustered little excitement at reaching so many milestones over the past season. Besides getting his 2,000th hit and passing Zack Wheat on the franchise's all-time list for runs scored, Reese took over the top spot on the Dodgers' career stolen-base chart. "The only thing these records prove," he said, "is that I'm getting old."[112]

18

"So, Pee Wee did it for Walter"

Pee Wee Reese rounded second base "puffin and puffin."[1] He looked for skipper Walter Alston, coaching at third base, to put up the stop sign, happy to watch a veteran infielder smack a triple during an exhibition game. Alston, though, motioned for Reese to keep going.

So he did. He crossed home plate before the tag, safe with an inside-the-park home run. The ball had zipped past White Sox center fielder Larry Doby (traded from Cleveland following the 1955 season) "and hid on the terrace behind the palm trees, near the 410-foot sign at Holman Stadium" in Vero Beach. Later, Reese added a single. He spoke to reporters afterward despite suffering from a cold "or a virus" and with a temperature of 100 degrees. Reese wiped the sweat from his face. He had missed the Dodgers' first four exhibition games. "I didn't even want to make this trip up here from Miami," he said. "I was feeling terrible this morning. But Buzzie asked me to play if I could." Doctors gave Reese a few pills and a shot of penicillin. Duke Snider had a bum knee, and Carl Furillo was nursing a sore arm. "Well," Pee Wee said, "I just had to play up here."[2]

He still hoped to start at shortstop in his 15th season with the Dodgers. Rumor had it that he might be moving to third base with Jackie Robinson now retired. Reese sounded like he wanted to stay put. "I know I can field as well as some of the shortstops on the contending clubs," he said. "If I thought I was hurting the club, I'd be the first one to ask to be moved."[3]

On March 15, Reese hit another home run, in a 9–4 loss to the Red Sox. This time, his drive cleared the fence, and he could take a leisurely trot around the bases. Dick Young joked, "There's a shortstop down here who has a helluva chance of sticking with the club. He's a bit on the small side, but he packs surprising power. ... The kid's name is Harold Reese. They call him Pee Wee."[4]

Weeks earlier, the Reese family grew by one. Pee Wee and Dottie welcomed Mark Allen Reese, born February 4 at Norton Infirmary in Louisville, the couple's second child. Mom and Dad presented baby Mark with a share of stock in the hometown Colonels, making him, *The Sporting News* noted, "possibly the youngest stockholder in organized baseball."[5]

Back in October, Walter O'Malley had sold Ebbets Field to local real-estate developer Marvin Kratter for an estimated $3 million. Kratter planned—someday—to build housing on the site. The Dodgers could play at the ballpark through the 1961 season, but Kratter expected to raise the rent after 1959. "The Dodgers took a big step toward moving into a new home yesterday,"[6] Jim McCulley wrote in the *Daily News*.

On February 21, O'Malley bought the Los Angeles Angels franchise in the Pacific Coast League, as well as that team's home—Wrigley Field in south L.A.—from Cubs owner Phillip K. Wrigley for approximately $3 million.[7] The Cubs, in turn, bought the Dodgers' Texas League franchise in Fort Worth for "a seven-figure sum."[8] Now, the *Brooklyn Daily* pointed out, the Dodgers owned a ballpark in southern California but not one in the borough.[9] O'Malley expected major league baseball to arrive in L.A. by 1960.[10] "Once O'Malley made that announcement, there came to be an unhappy feeling that ran through the team," Furillo said. "We were getting on in years and didn't play baseball as well we used to, but I wouldn't say that the idea of moving was any help to us."[11]

Efforts continued at keeping the Dodgers in New York, although not necessarily in Brooklyn. Mayor Robert F. Wagner supported the construction of a 50,000-seat baseball stadium in Flushing Meadows, Queens, on the site of the 1939 World's Fair. Supposedly, a ballpark and 12,000 parking spots could fit into the space. O'Malley gave the plan a cool response: "If and when this latest reported possibility ever achieves political maturity, I will be pleased to discuss it in detail."[12] The *Daily Brooklyn* contended, "Walter O'Malley would still prefer having his ball club remain"[13] in the borough.

The Dodgers opened at home on April 16 against the Phillies. Pee Wee Reese watched from the bench. He injured himself in the final exhibition game that spring, against the Yankees. "I felt something snap right here,"[14] he said, pointing to an area near his hip. A photograph in the *Daily News* showed Reese lying on a bed in the Brooklyn training room, hooked up to a neuromuscular stimulator. The Dodgers expected him to miss about a week. Don Zimmer answered the call as his replacement. Brooklyn edged Philly, 7–6, in a 10-inning thriller. Gino Cimoli, a 27-year-old, second-year outfielder, hit a game-winning homer in the 12th inning off Robin Roberts.

Zimmer, thanks mostly to a 5-for-6 game on April 30 against the Cubs, batted .317 in the opening month, and the Dodgers won eight of 11 games. Gil Hodges hit .400 with three homers, while Jim Gilliam boasted a .453 on-base percentage. Reese made his season debut on May 6, at home against the Braves, and at shortstop. He went 0-for-2. Gino Cimoli put on another dramatic show. He hit a home run in the 14th inning to break a 4–4 tie. Reese put himself into the hit column the next day with a two-out single against Cincinnati's Hal Jeffcoat. The Reds scored five times in the ninth inning and clobbered the Dodgers, 9–2.

Diehard fan Bill Borst cringed at every news story that reported his favorite team might be moving. Finally, he sensed the inevitable. Borst attended one game at Ebbets Field in 1957, in the outfield cheap seats, on May 8, along with a dozen friends from his school's patrol boy squad. "The feeling seemed to be waning in me already," he wrote in a memoir. "It was as if a good friend had stuck a knife in my back. My absence was supposed to mitigate the pain in some irrational way."[15] Reese singled in the third inning. Brooklyn beat Cincinnati, 7–6. As if that part mattered. "I often wonder how many others of those 10,000 [actually 10,820] were seeing the Dodgers for the last time," Borst said. "Or have the loss I have felt."[16]

Walter O'Malley visited the L.A. area several times, at least once while wearing a "Keep the Dodgers in Brooklyn" button. He also took a few helicopter tours across the basin. He liked an area known to locals as Chavez Ravine, which he described as "the most desirable piece of property right in the center of what is going to be the biggest city in the world."[17]

The Ravine rests in a shallow canyon surrounded by hills, just north of downtown. UCLA professor Thomas S. Hines, called the area a "pleasant, hidden, semi-rural Mexican American Brigadoon. ... The 'Mexican village' was strongly Catholic, and the church and public school were vital centers of its rich urban fabric. Festivals and holidays were celebrated with esprit. Most observers commented on the lush vegetation and the lively street life." Following World War II and the start of the baby boom, city officials envisioned the Ravine as an ideal spot for high-density housing. The architect Richard Neutra designed a community for more than 3,300 families, which would have tripled the population. Plans called for several residential towers, requiring substantial grading and filling. "This meant," Hines wrote, "that virtually the entire population of the ravine had to be temporarily relocated, and most of their village demolished."[18]

City officials removed residents through the use of eminent domain, although not without a fight. Many argued that they were not offered a fair price for their property. Other groups, including the Chamber of Commerce and the *L.A. Times*, called the city's plan for Chavez Ravine an act of "creeping socialism." In 1953, Norris Paulson won the Los Angeles mayoral seat on an anti-housing platform. He cut the housing program in half and nixed the proposal for Chavez Ravine, which, Hines wrote, "lay idle until later in the decade."[19]

Dick Young offered this little note to readers in the May 12 edition of the *Daily News*: "The name 'Dodgers,'" he wrote, "has been registered legally by the Brooklyn ball club in the State of California." Young decided, "Los Angles is still in the lead" to get the Dodgers. But, he added, "O'Malley has not yet made up his mind. He is still listening."[20] Kenneth Hahn, "a young, vigorous career politician," and L.A. native, had "taken leadership in the effort to gain big league baseball for Los Angeles." A member of the county's board of supervisors, Hahn already had failed to bring either the Senators or Athletics to southern California. "I have been burned twice," Hahn admitted, "but I've promised big league ball to the people for five years and I'm not going to give up on it."[21]

On May 21, Pee Wee Reese hit his only home run of the season. He did it in the fifth inning against the Reds at Crosley Field, off Hal Jeffcoat. Ahead in the count, 3–1, he "banged"[22] a ball over the left-field fence with Jim Gilliam on base. The Dodgers won, 6–1. Johnny Podres scattered nine hits over nine innings. Brooklyn improved to 18–10. One week later, National League owners unanimously gave O'Malley and Horace Stoneham of the Giants permission to leave New York for California and a deadline of October 1 to announce their intentions. In other words, Stoneham said, "We have all summer to think about it." A reporter asked O'Malley whether it was too late for Brooklyn to save its baseball team. "It's never too late,"[23] he responded.

Maybe so. Newspapers across southern California celebrated, nonetheless. Under a headline in the *L.A. Times* of "BUMS COMING! ONLY QUESTION IS

WHEN?" Hahn said, "I am extremely pleased. It certainly is good news for all those who love baseball." Norris Poulsen said, "I don't want to say the wrong thing, so I'd better not say anything beyond the fact that the news is good."[24] The *Long Beach Independent-Press Telegram* declared, "Effective in '58 (if requested) OK DODGER TRANSFER TO LA." The *Oxnard Press-Courier* told readers, "Dodger Shift to LA Gets NL Approval." The accompanying wire service article included this quote from Walter O'Malley: "Whether we exercise the permission we've been granted remains to be seen. I am aware that the people of Los Angeles and the government officials there are very anxious to have major league baseball. I think Brooklyn fans have been 100 percent all right, but we want a new ballpark. We need a park where we can park cars and please fans. Right now, we can park only 700 cars."[25]

Cincinnati led the pennant chase for much of the early going. The Dodgers stayed close, always just a few games from the top spot. On June 8, they knocked off the Reds, 9–2, and jumped into first place by half a game. Jim Gilliam and Rube Walker both drove in three runs. Johnny Podres dropped his ERA to 2.03 and improved his record to 6–2. Brooklyn fell back into second place the next day after Cincinnati swept a doubleheader from them.

Pee Wee Reese's career as a starting shortstop essentially ended on June 12. That's when Walter Alston moved him to third base and installed hard-hitting infield prospect Charlie Neal at short. Don Zimmer, whose batting average had plummeted to .217, headed to the bench, relegated to a part-time role at least for the time being. Reese's average, meanwhile, was a paltry .210. In his first game as a starting third baseman, he hit a double and two singles in an 11–9 win against Milwaukee. He played shortstop in just three more games the rest of the year, one in July and two in August.

As late as July 25, Brooklyn trailed the lead spot by just one game. By August 15, that deficit had grown to 8½ games. Lou Smith wrote that the "saddest member of the Dodgers these days is old pro Pee Wee Reese, who sees his team's pennant winning chances slipping away and can't seem to do a thing about it."[26] Smith added, "There is a growing suspicion, even among some of the more cynical New York sportswriters that owner Walter O'Malley is going to keep his Dodgers in whacky old Flatbush at least for a few more years." O'Malley, according to Smith, was still open to some of the New York City stadium proposals. Plus, "he also is reportedly impressed with the potentialities of Long Island."[27]

Horace Stoneham announced the Giants' move to San Francisco on August 19. The team's board of directors voted 8–1 to leave New York, "It's over fellows," Stoneham said to a group of reporters and photographers.[28] He felt bad for the team's young fans, he said. "I've seen lots of them at the Polo Grounds. But I haven't seen many of their fathers lately."[29] Senators owner Calvin Griffith applauded the franchise shift. "It will be great for major league baseball because at last it has a true national scope, from coast to coast."[30] Kenneth Hahn said he expected to hear "good news for Los Angeles within 30 to 60 days."[31]

Reese played his last game at the Polo Grounds on September 8. It was the finale of a three-game set. Johnny Podres threw a 3–0 shutout in the opener. Reese singled in the third inning. The Dodgers also won the second game, 5–4. Reese singled and scored in the sixth inning and lined an RBI base hit in the seventh. He collected two more singles the next day. This time, New York won, 3–2. He handled all 13 chances at third base over the series, including six in the final game. Roscoe McGowen reported, "The Little Colonel made every type of play a third baseman is called up to make during those three games."[32] Russ Hodges also counted himself among the impressed. "Watch that Reese go to his right!" Hodges yelled at one point before Reese had even completed the play.

Hodges told listeners that seven-month-old Mark Reese was teething "and cried most all of last night," making Pee Wee a bit bleary-eyed at game time. Reese swore that he kept this bit of family news a secret. "I didn't tell[(Hodges]. I didn't get much sleep, that's a fact. But I did get a little." Afterward, the Dodgers left for Chicago to play the Cubs. Dottie and Mark were also going on the trip and waiting at LaGuardia Airport. McGowan reported that Mark was "quite calm, contented and non-tearful. He gave pop only a stony stare."[33]

Players suited up for their last game in Brooklyn on September 24, 1957. Only 6,702 fans attended the wake. Ed Corrigan of the Associated Press called Ebbets Field "a ghost ballpark."[34] Duke Snider remembered, "It didn't seem the lights were taking hold. There were a lot more shadows out there. It was an eerie feeling. ... There weren't all that many people, and they weren't very happy."[35] The Dodgers, behind 24-year-old rookie left-hander Danny McDevitt, shut out the Pirates, 2–0. Reese entered the game in the fifth inning as a third baseman and, in the home team's half of the sixth, grounded out to shortstop Dick Groat in his final at-bat as a Brooklyn Dodger.

Following the game, announcer Tex Rickards told fans, as he always did, "Please do not go on the playing field at the end of the game. Use any exit that leads to the street." The souvenir-hunting faithful ignored him. They jumped onto the field and collected dirt and grass. Organist Gladys Gooding played "May the Good Lord Bless You and Keep You." Minutes later, she switched to "Auld Lang Syne," a traditional farewell lament.

Dave Anderson, now with the *New York Journal-American*, grew up in Brooklyn during what he termed "the Pee Wee Reese era."[36] He and Bill Roeder of the *New York World-Telegram* left the Ebbets Field press room two hours after the final out. Anderson let Roeder get a step ahead and then followed him out the ballpark's famous rotunda and onto the street. Anderson planned it that way. He wanted to be the last writer to leave the last Dodgers game played at Ebbets Field. "Put that on my tombstone,"[37] he later said. Reese, according to an AP article, "shook his head" at the thought of never playing another game at the venerable ballpark. He recalled all the good times and said, "I don't think any ballplayer anywhere ever had better treatment that I have had in Brooklyn. It's tough."[38]

After that tearful goodbye, the Dodgers traveled to Philadelphia for one final three-game series as a Brooklyn-based ballclub. The Phillies won two out of three, including the opener, 3–2. Reese got into the middle game as a late-inning defensive replacement at third base. The Dodgers won, 8–4, and then lost the finale, 2–1. They finished 84–70, in third place, 11 games out of first, and fifth in the NL in attendance, drawing 1,028,258 fans. Jim McCulley wrote, "The Dodgers disbanded not knowing whether they had played their last game in Brooklyn or not. ...or whether they would ever see Ebbets Field again. Most of them didn't seem to care; they were tired from a strenuous, unsuccessful campaign."[39] Pee Wee Reese played 103 games over the season and batted .224 with a .306 on-base percentage. He stole five bases in seven attempts and did not record an extra-base hit after June 20.

Walter O'Malley waited until October 7—one week past the deadline—to break Brooklyn's heart. One day earlier, the Los Angeles City Council awarded him the 300-acre Chavez Ravine site "for a ballpark in exchange for Brooklyn-owned Wrigley Field."[40] The team issued a press release that read: "In view of the action of the Los Angeles City Council yesterday and in accordance with the resolution of the National League made October first, the stockholders and directors of the Brooklyn Baseball Club have today met and unanimously agreed that the necessary steps be taken to draft the Los Angeles territory."[41] Norris Poulsen remarked that the Giants and Dodgers should offer "a tremendous boost to California's economy.... The Dodgers have played their last game in Brooklyn. We have taken out of the biggest city in the nation two of its most coveted institutions."[42]

Dick Young wrote his famous "Obit on the Dodgers" in the October 9 edition of the *Daily News*. An obit, he began, "tells of a person who has died, how he lived, and of those who live after him. This is the obit on the Brooklyn Dodgers." The columnist offered no mercy for Walter O'Malley. Young called the Dodgers a profitable franchise and one with a passionate fan base. He skewered O'Malley for lobbying his long-time political allies in New York and for visiting city officials in Los Angeles. While L.A.'s ruling class worked hard to convince the Dodgers executive that sunshine trumped tradition, "New York's officials quibbled, mouthed sweet nothings, and tried to place the blame elsewhere." Young wrote that O'Malley departed from Brooklyn "a rich man and a despised man."[43]

Several days after the season ended, Pee Wee Reese spoke to a reporter about the team's impending move. "I never thought we would go," he said. While he disliked the idea of saying goodbye to old friends in Brooklyn, he was "anxious to make new friends there [in Los Angeles]. I hope I can be with the team out there for a long time." As for all that impending travel to big league cities a few thousand miles from L.A., he said only, "I hope they get us a four-engine plane."[44]

Mark Reese, in a 2001 interview, said his dad had planned to retire as a Brooklyn Dodger. "Then, Walter O'Malley said, 'I need you to come. I need you and Gil Hodges and the old-timers. I want to bring the legacy to L.A., and then gently make the transformation.' So, Pee Wee did it for Walter. But he was past his prime, and so were most of the other Brooklyn stars."[45]

In late October, Reese toured the southland and spoke with *L.A. Times* sportswriter Jeane Hoffman. The veteran player was, Hoffman wrote, "attired like a Brooks Brothers ad, in blue tie, button-down collar, gray pants, and gray hat in hand."[46] Over a cup of coffee, Reese talked about what would be the team's temporary home stadium, the Los Angeles Memorial Coliseum. Opened in 1923 and located three miles south of downtown, the Coliseum had hosted football games, boxing matches, track events, rodeos, the 1932 summer Olympics, and other big events through the years, even a ski-jumping competition. It promised to be an odd venue for America's National Pastime.

Already, there was talk that a tall screen might be built atop the left field fence (just 251 feet from home plate) to prevent lazy fly balls from turning into cheap home runs. Reese looked forward to swatting pitches over a shy barrier. "If they don't put up too high a screen, I'll have a fighting chance," he said. "I'll settle for a few timely singles. At my age, you can't be choosy."[47]

He had not visited Wrigley Field, also rumored as a future Dodgers home stadium, at least for a few games. Instead, he played golf at swanky Hillcrest Country Club and toured Hollywood and Beverly Hills with Duke Snider. "To get back to my encroaching senility, I'm determined to have a good year to make up for last season," he said. He did not expect to move full-time to California. "I never moved to Brooklyn," he said. "I doubt if we'd move here, although I'm tempted when I hear about your golf activity. I play four times a week."[48]

The Coliseum figured to serve as a home run haven for the aging Roy Campanella. His story, though, one so often filled with big home runs and hearty laughter, turned tragic on January 28, 1958. Snow fell a few days earlier, and ice coated some of the roads. Campanella left the liquor store he owned in Harlem at about 1:30 a.m. and stepped into his rented car. "How does a man know when he is taking the last steps of his life," Campanella wrote later. "I haven't taken one since."[49] Just a few miles from his home in the well-to-do Glen Cove area of Long Island, Campanella lost control of the car while steering through a curvy patch of road and crashed into a telephone pole. The violent impact knocked him forward and onto the passenger side floor, trapping him underneath the dash. Officer Frank Poepplein of the Glen Cove Police Department spotted the accident while on patrol and recognized the Brooklyn baseball star.

Campanella, fearing the car might catch fire, asked Poepplein to turn off the engine. Rescuers needed 20 minutes to get Campanella out of the car and then raced him by ambulance to a hospital. The catcher suffered a broken neck and a severed spinal cord. Later, he developed pneumonia and "could barely breathe."[50] A doctor, "with tears in his eyes," said, "I have to operate on you, give you a tracheotomy [cutting open the windpipe]. If I don't, you're not going to live. But I can't give you an anesthetic."[51] Campy said, "If you have to do it, you have to do it,"[52] and he began to recite the 23rd Psalm. "The Lord is my shepherd; I shall not want …."

Southern California's new sports franchise struggled through spring training. Local writers, trying to put a positive spin on all things Dodgers baseball, told fans not to worry. "The spring training campaign never quite demonstrates the potential of a team in the stretch drive of a pennant," *L.A. Times* sports editor and columnist Paul Zimmerman wrote. "In the case of the Dodgers, this is fortunate because they haven't startled anyone."[53]

Reese, now 38 years old, expected to make a few changes and cheat time, if only for a final season. His reflexes had slowed, at least a little bit. "Almost subconsciously, you find yourself revising your pattern of play, trying little schemes, making step-saving experiments, all with a view to compensating what you've lost to the calendar," he said. "You do more thinking about the hitter. You rely more on your sense of anticipation. You try to be where the ball is hit. In short, you let your head help your feet."[54]

Surrounded by the bright lights of Hollywood, Reese made his dramatic television debut on CBS's *General Electric Theater*. He played his mild-mannered self in an episode titled "A Question of Romance." The story centered around a young couple that is preparing for marriage but nearly call off their nuptials due to the future bride's great love for baseball. The boyfriend gets so upset that he takes a punch at Reese, who is walking down the street and minding his own business. Reese explains all this to a judge in court.

Not surprisingly, players razzed the shortstop for taking a Hollywood turn. "They called me Gregory Peck, Tyrone Power and even Frankenstein," Reese said. "They had big plans to throw a TV party so they could sit around and criticize my acting. I was glad that the show, filmed during our last road trip, was scheduled for TV after the season."[55]

L.A.'s version of the Dodgers began play on Tuesday, April 15, at Seals Stadium in San Francisco. The Giants served as rude hosts in front of 23,448 fans tucked into a long-time minor league park. Ruben Gomez scattered six hits and won, 8–0. Don Drysdale lasted just 3⅔ innings and got pounded for six earned runs. Reese, batting second in the order, went hitless in three at-bats and walked twice. A jubilant Phil Norman wrote in the *San Francisco Examiner* about the Giants' victory over "Smogville," He described the first match-up of two teams in California as "the greatest moment in the history of western sports."[56]

After losing two out of three games in San Francisco, the Dodgers flew south to L.A. for the home opener on Friday, April 18, against the Giants. The day began with a parade. Reese sat atop one of the many convertibles that maneuvered down Broadway near downtown. "Enthusiastic thousands" greeted the Dodgers players. Art Ryon wrote about fans who "crowded" the streets and yelled "Hi, Duke!" ... "Next time, Newk!" ... "Coupla home runs today, eh, Gil?" The parade ended at the City Hall steps on Spring Street. Ryon applauded the entire, jubilant affair. "Los Angeles did it yesterday," he wrote. "It gave its Dodgers the goldarnest, warming, howling, confetti-filled, big league welcome it has ever accorded anyone. ... This is supposed to be the city that won't turn out for a parade. Ha!"[57]

The game began in the afternoon. Hundreds of fans waited in line that morning for general admission seats to go on sale at 9:30. Gates opened at 11. Comedian and baseball fan Joe E. Brown served as master of ceremonies for a pre-game program. Some of the Hollywood stars on hand included former cowboy movie star and future California Angels owner Gene Autry, directors John Ford and Alfred Hitchcock, comedian Groucho Marx, actors Jack Lemmon and Burt Lancaster, singer Nat King Cole, and television star Danny Thomas. Edward G. Robinson, famous for his gangster movie roles, brought along "his cigar and wife (not necessarily in that order)." The actor Jimmy Stewart rushed out "to buy a Japanese straw hat to shield wife Gloria from the sun."[58]

Nearly 79,000 fans—78,672 to be exact—piled into the Coliseum to watch the start of a three-game set. Carl Erskine opposed Al Worthington. The Dodgers jumped ahead, 5–2, after five innings and won, 6–5. Reese singled in the fourth inning and walked in the sixth. Giants left fielder Hank Sauer smacked two home runs. The *Times* reported that "the vast Coliseum lay bathed in a warm sun, while fitful breezes stirred the flags, pennants and bunting which decorated the scene. Few coats were visible as the record crowd basked in perfect baseball weather, tailor-made for the occasion."[59]

The Dodgers set an all-time, single-game attendance mark in the National League and accounted for nearly one/third of the 258,566 fans who turned out for the seven home openers held on Friday. Just 23,463 showed up at Yankee Stadium to watch the defending World Series champions beat the Baltimore Orioles, 3–1. The Coliseum crowd fell short of the all-time single-game attendance mark of 86,288, set in Game Five of the 1948 World Series at Municipal Stadium in Cleveland.[60]

Fans settled in for a long season of mediocre baseball. The Dodgers won just three of their first nine games. The Cubs beat them, 15–2, on April 24. Lee Walls, a graduate of nearby Pasadena High School, slammed three home runs and accumulated eight RBI. Reese cautioned that it was early. "I don't know why you guys are burying us because he lost some games," Reese told the press corps. "Man, let's not hang the crepe. Stick with us a little while, and we'll win some ball games for you."[61]

John Roseboro took over the catching duties in place of Roy Campanella, who lay strapped to a bed at the Rusk rehabilitation hospital in New York City. (Dr. Donald Cavalt from Rusk said on May 5, "Campanella remains a quadriplegic case. He can move his shoulders very well, but he has only weak movement in his wrists and there is no muscle function below his arms. It is not a good sign."[62]) An Ashland, Ohio, product, Roseboro batted just .145 over his 69 at-bats in 1958. He got off to a solid start in L.A., posting a .294 mark in April and .299 in May. Like many Black players, he knew how much Reese helped Jackie Robinson in 1947 and subsequent years. "I can believe it, because there was something special about Pee Wee, and it didn't take long to see it," Roseboro wrote. "Reese did everything right, and he was so nice that everyone liked him. I never felt like I was black, and he was white. I felt like he was my captain."[63]

The Dodgers fell to last place on May 12 after getting pummeled by the Giants at home, 12–3. Mays slammed two homers and had five RBIs. L.A. fielders made four errors that led to seven unearned runs in this mess of a game. "The Dodgers struck rock bottom last night," *Times* beat writer Frank Finch informed his readers, for the first time since July 2, 1948. "They spent only one day in the dungeon on that doleful date," Finch wrote. "But the way the bedraggled Dodgers are playing now, it may be that they will never see daylight again."[64]

A few weeks later, on June 7, L.A. met Milwaukee at the Coliseum. Nearly 60,000 fans watched the action. Pee Wee Reese, after grounding out in his first at-bat, led off the third inning by smacking a home run into the left-center field seats off the talented control artist, Lew Burdette. He lined out in the fourth inning and flied out in the sixth. With two out in the eighth, and the Dodgers ahead, 4–2, Reese deposited a Humberto Robinson pitch into the stands. Those were Reese's final two home runs in the majors. He last hit two homers in a game on August 28, 1953. Maybe he was just being modest, but the *Times* quoted him as saying "Zatso? Gee, I don't remember ever doing it before."[65]

By the end of July, the Dodgers had fallen 11 games out of first place and never got closer the rest of the season. They lost to the Giants, 14–2, on August 31, in a "demolition job,"[66] and dropped 15½ games behind the front-running Braves. Sandy Koufax allowed five runs in just two/thirds of an inning. Lately, Finch wrote, "the Dodgers have looked pathetic."[67]

Don Drysdale said the traveling that first year was "terrible. I remember one road trip we were gone three weeks. … When you travel that much, you're worn out. You're constantly flying across time zones, moving in out of ballparks and hotels. It's tough."[68] Just navigating the L.A. freeway system posed a huge challenge for some players. "I'd always leave my house an hour ahead of time because I'd always get lost driving on those freeways," Charlie Neal said. "I'd never take the right exit and go through half of California just to make a U turn. They should have given us highway maps as well as lockers."[69]

Some writers—especially those in New York—liked to poke fun of southern California's laid-back baseball fans, who didn't yell and scream quite as much as their Brooklyn counterparts. They wore sunglasses, cooked hot dogs in the Coliseum parking lot, and listened to Vin Scully on a myriad of transistor radios that echoed throughout the makeshift ballpark. *The Daily News* insisted that the Coliseum made "a mockery of big-league baseball,"[70] the *New York Post* charged that it "turns big baseball into handball,"[71] and the *New York Herald Tribune* called it "an excellent park—for football."[72] Dick Young piled on the most scorn. Young "quoted players complaining about the smog, repeated jokes about the freeways, and noted the crackpot orators in Pershing Square across from the hotel used by most opposing teams. He pointed out items as petty as reversed captions in the Dodger yearbook. He criticized the lights and public address system and the winds."[73]

Fans in L.A. didn't suffer through all those World Series losses or celebrate in the streets after finally winning it all in 1955. Unlike their Brooklyn counterparts, they didn't pray for Gil Hodges after the big first baseman fell into a terrible World Series slump. They didn't cheer for Jackie Robinson on April 15, 1947, or put up with Duke Snider's mood swings in between his big home runs. And they didn't hold dear all those memories of a gentlemanly shortstop from Louisville. Still, comparing the two fan bases hardly made for a fair game, Don Drysdale said. "Because back in the fifties," he insisted, "no other team had fans like the people in Brooklyn. You'll just never have that closeness between team and fans again in America."[74]

Pee Wee Reese saw sporadic action as an L.A. Dodger. He played 11 games in April but just nine in both May and June. His batting average tumbled. A .278 hitter on April 26, he claimed just a .213 mark going into June. Walter Alston penciled him into 17 games in July, but the shortstop hit only .233 with four RBI. On July 29, he enjoyed the final multi-RBI game of his career, against the Braves at County Stadium. In the sixth inning, with one out and two runners on base, the "old pro"[75] lined a double off Joey Jay to put the Dodgers ahead, 2–0, en route to a 4–2 victory. Reese played in 12 games during the August heat and summertime haze. He went 3-for-26, a .115 average. The end seemed near.

He sat down with Harry Grayson following a game at the Coliseum, "the monstrosity," Grayson wrote, "that passes for a baseball park." Reese's back hurt. He was feeling all the aches and pains of a long career and unsure what he wanted to do in 1959. Managing, at least for now, was out. "I don't have the temperament," he said.

Maybe he could get a job in sportscasting, he offered. He sounded "lost," Grayson wrote. Reese said, "This is a cold business. But whatever happens, you won't hear a word of complaint from me. It's been fine up till now."[76]

Reese spent almost all of September on the bench. Finally, on the next-to-last day of a disappointing season, in a meaningless game against the Cubs at the Coliseum, and in the second game of a doubleheader (the Dodgers won the opener, 6–3, behind Drysdale), Reese started at third base and batted second in the order. He hadn't played since August 30. John Buzhardt, a rookie right-hander from South Carolina, stood on the mound for Chicago. Reese walked in his first at-bat and grounded out in the third inning. He led off the sixth by lining a single to center field, his final hit in the major leagues. In the eighth, still against Buzhardt, Pee Wee Reese popped out to second baseman Tony Tyler in his last plate appearance. Sandy Koufax pitched a complete game and struck out nine but walked seven in a 2–1 loss. "He's just too darned liberal with the passes,"[77] Frank Finch wrote in his wrap-up.

The Dodgers finished second in the league in attendance, drawing 1,845,56 fans, while playing in a cavernous, quirky ballpark. Disappointed fans, and at least some writers, expected this team to contend for a pennant. Or at least play .500 baseball. After the team's final game, a 7–4 loss at home to the Cubs on September 27, Finch wrote, "The story of yesterday's Dodger defeat was the story of the Dodgers' life in Los Angeles … a story of ineptitude and frustration … a story of a team that couldn't win the big one."[78] Fewer than 13,000 fans showed up for the contest, about 80,000 short of a sellout.

Reese ended the year with a .224 batting average in 147 at-bats. Buzzie Bavasi announced in December that Reese planned to retire as a player but remain with the team as a coach.

> We are proud of the wonderful record of Pee Wee Reese. He could have remained on the active roster of another major league club. But the Dodgers, in rebuilding their team, must make room for another youngster. That's baseball. We are happy, indeed, that Reese has decided that rather than change uniforms, he would continue his long affiliation with the Dodgers as one of manager Walt Alston's assistants.[79]

Over 16 seasons, Reese played in 2,166 games and collected 2,170 hits. He batted .269 with a .366 on-base percentage and .377 slugging percentage. He hit 126 home runs, 63 at home and 63 on the road. Reese averaged .290 against the Reds, his highest mark against any opponent, and .250 against the Cubs, his lowest. The 10-time All-Star smacked 330 doubles and 80 triples, scored 1,338 runs, and stole 232 bases. He played in every inning of every World Series game played between the Brooklyn Dodgers and the Yankees, the only player to do so.[80] In 44 October match-ups, Reese batted .272 with two home runs and 16 RBI. He scored 20 runs in those seven World Series and stole five bases. He posted a .346 on-base percentage. He certainly put up strong numbers for a shortstop of that era. MVP voters placed him in the top 10 in eight seasons. The statistics, though, tell only a small part of what Reese meant to the Dodgers. Dick Young called him "perhaps the most beloved Dodger in the history of the club."[81]

Reese spoke about the end of his career during an interview at his Louisville home. "When you've played so long, you hate the thought of not being in the thick of things anymore," he said. "But maybe it's for the best. I've had a bad back for a couple of years. ... Maybe it was time to quit"[82] His only regret as a player? He only hit .300 one time. "I could never figure out why I didn't hit more,"[83] he said. About his new position on Walter Alston's staff, Reese said, "I'll try coaching for a year. Maybe I'll like it."[84]

19

"Let's see, folks. Where were we?"

Coach Pee Wee Reese reported to Vero Beach in February 1959. He joined a staff that also included Joe Becker and Greg Mulleavy, in addition to Chuck Dressen[1] and skipper Walter Alston. Back in December, Reese said, "I don't know just what they'll want me to do, whether I'll be on the baseline, working with the youngsters, or what, but I'll be happy to do whatever helps the club most."[2]

He spoke to players in a calm, easy-going manner. Ron Fairly listened closely. A Georgia native, Fairly grew up in Long Beach and played college baseball at the University of Southern California. He signed with the Dodgers in 1958 for $75,000 and posted solid numbers in just 69 minor league games. The outfielder earned a late-season promotion to the big club and hit .283 in 53 at-bats.

One morning, Reese invited Fairly, along with Duke Snider and Gil Hodges, for a round of golf at the Vero Beach Country Club. Afterward, the four stopped at the preverbal 19th hole. Reese quizzed Fairly about going to bat with runners in scoring position. How did he like to handle that situation? The 20-year-old, trying to muster a quick and satisfactory answer, said he just wanted to hit the ball hard. "Well," Reese said, "we'll get a chance to see what you can do."[3]

A few days later, Fairly walked to the plate during an exhibition game against the Tigers with two outs and the tying run on second base. Reese yelled out, "Hey, remember what we talked about the other day. Show me." Fairly worked the count to two balls, one strike and hammered a fastball that the Detroit center fielder grabbed for an out. Reese complimented him on a "very good at-bat," which "really lifted my spirits," Fairly wrote, "because if Pee Wee said I had a good at-bat, then I had a good at-bat."[4]

Reese expected young players to be enthusiastic. "Fellas," he'd say, "you've got to show me you want to play. If you don't, take your uniform off and give it to someone who does."[5] His comment about power-hitting prospect Frank Howard was telling. "If every player worked as hard as Howard," he said, "maybe I wouldn't mind being a manager."[6] Big Frank stood 6-foot-7-inches tall and packed plenty of muscle onto his frame. The Columbus, Ohio, product began working a jackhammer for the local street department at the age of 14 and played both baseball and basketball at Ohio State University. The Dodgers scouted ("Good arm. Fielding below average. Hitting below average, 'good potential.' Running speed slightly below average. Major league power. Definite follow."⁷) and then signed him following his senior year on the Buckeyes basketball team. Howard played in 1958 for the Green Bay Bluejays of the Class B Three-I League and made things look easy. He hit .333 and led the circuit with 37 home runs and 116 RBI.

Howard, always polite, said "Yes, sir" and "No, sir" to every player, coach, and, probably, clubhouse attendant. Reese and Hodges kidded him about those impeccable manners. One day, Hodges called over to Howard. Tell Coach Pee Wee to knock it off, Hodges said to the gentle giant of a rookie. Howard, eager to please, obliged. He stalked over and pulled up Reese by the uniform collar. In mock anger, he growled, "Pee Wee, you quit riding me or I'll punch you right in the nose!" Shortly afterward, Reese walked over to Hodges and said, "The boy seems to be getting more confidence."[8]

The Dodgers entered the season with something to prove. Just one day after that dud of a 1958 campaign ended, Paul Zimmerman wrote, "It is not too much to expect of Walter O'Malley and his staff that they start regrouping their faltering forces immediately."[9] Come spring, though, experts expected more of the same rather than a return to past glory. UPI conducted a preseason poll of 50 baseball people. The L.A. club failed to get a single first-place vote. At least one oddsmaker made the Dodgers a 25–1 long shot to win a pennant.[10]

Wisely, Buzzie Bavasi refused to trade Jim Gilliam to Milwaukee. The Braves were looking for a new second baseman after doctors diagnosed Red Schoendienst with tuberculosis in November. The veteran player felt weak for most of the 1958 campaign and missed nearly 50 games due to colds and respiratory infections.[11] He underwent off-season surgery to remove part of his lung and figured to miss a bulk of the action in 1959.[12] Braves General Manager John McHale talked to Bavasi about Gilliam but was turned away. "So, why should we help them by dealing Gilliam?" Bavasi asked. "Junior is three men-in-one. He hits both ways, he can play infield or outfield, and he's probably the best lead-off hitter in baseball."[13]

In early December, the Dodgers acquired Wally Moon from the Cardinals. Moon, the 1954 NL Rookie of the Year, hit 24 home runs and batted .295 in 1957 but slumped to .238 with just seven homers the following season. "I just couldn't believe he was through," Bavasi said. "Besides, he used to murder our pitchers."[14] The Dodgers sent Gino Cimoli and pitcher Phil Paine to St. Louis. Cimoli, after hitting .293 in 1957, dropped to .246 in 1958. He told Alston at one point, "Play me or trade me."[15] About Moon, Alston said he "isn't a great defensive outfielder, but I know he can play left field at the Coliseum. He's aggressive, he can run, and what I like most about him is his power."[16]

Finally, much to Duke Snider's joy, the team made a few changes to the Coliseum. Now, he and other hitters could take aim at a fence in dead center field that stood 410 feet from home plate rather than 425 feet and a right-center field fence just 385 feet away rather than a ridiculous 440. (After taking a look at the faraway fence during that opening road trip to L.A. in 1958, Willie Mays said to Snider, "Duke, they killed you."[17]) In 1958, the Dodgers hit 92 homers, while opponents hit 101. Only eight of those 193 round-trippers traveled to right field. Snider did not hit any home runs to right.[18] Now, Bavasi said, "Except for left field, which we can't do anything about, the new measurements are an approximate average of the other seven parks in the league."[19]

Despite all that, Walter Alston sounded cautious when he met the press on February 18 in Vero Beach. He never even mentioned the word "pennant," Frank Finch noted. "I'm not going to say anything specific about where I expect the club to finish," Alston said. "I've got to think we're better than a seventh-place club." He remained undecided on whether to name a successor to Reese as team captain. "Nobody is smarter baseball-wise than Hodges, but he's not the fiery type," Alston said. "However, it might restore his confidence if he was given the responsibility of leadership."[20]

The skipper wanted his team to focus more on baseball and less on "horsing around." Alston fined several players in 1958, including two "for playboy antics." Apparently, Don Newcombe and Johnny Podres were "blinded temporarily, by the bright lights of Chicago" on at least one road trip, although Alston refused to divulge any tawdry details. According to Finch, Alston "sounded fair warning that any social lions on his club can expect him to crack the whip like a veritable Clyde Beatty,"[21] the circus king.

Roy Campanella flew out to California on April 11. Paul "Tank" Younger, the retired All-Pro fullback and linebacker for the Los Angeles Rams and Pittsburgh Steelers, carried him off the airplane and to his wheelchair. Three days later, Campanella threw out the first pitch for the Dodgers' home opener against the Cardinals. Pee Wee had wheeled Campy down a specially built runway to a spot behind home plate on the Coliseum floor. Several events preceded the former catcher's dramatic moment. A helicopter flew around the stadium and flashed a sign that read "Welcome Home Dodgers," and a Marine Corps rifle squad "fired its muskets into the Coliseum dew." Actor Howard Keel, the star of *Show Boat* and *Kiss Me Kate*, sang the National Anthem.[22]

The home plate umpire handed a baseball to Reese, who looked a bit nervous. He asked, "Campy, you sure you can throw it?" The catcher grinned. "Just give me the ball, old buddy, and I'll show you." Some doubted the paralyzed former athlete could toss a baseball even a few feet. "But I had a surprise in store for them," Campanella revealed. "What nobody knew was that I had been practicing flipping the ball underhand in the back yard of my home in Glen Cove. I played catch with Roy Jr., and I got so I could even catch the ball when Roy tossed it to me."[23]

Reese gave the ball to Campanella, who flipped it back "sort of like a quarterback making a shovel pass to one of his backs."[24] The two practiced several times while photographers snapped pictures. Campanella offered a short message to the 61,552 on hand. "It is wonderful to be back in baseball," he said, "especially right here in the catcher's box. And from here that left field fence looks great." The Cardinals beat the Dodgers, 6–2. Wally Moon smacked three hits in his southern California debut. Still, Hank Hollingsworth wrote, "Roy Campanella stole the show."[25]

On May 7, the Dodgers once again honored Campanella. An "overflow crowd of 93,103, largest ever to witness a baseball game," attended an exhibition held between the Dodgers and Yankees. "At least 15,000 potential patrons were turned away," and "Police were hard pressed to prevent a riot."[26] About 20,000 people "milled outside after failing to purchase any of the final block of 10,000 general admission tickets that went on sale yesterday."[27] Again, Pee Wee wheeled Campy onto the field, this time to a spot between the pitcher's mound and second base. The program began about an hour before the first pitch, on a "beautiful night," according to Campy. "I have never seen so many people in one place," he said. He spoke to the crowd in a slow, raspy voice. "I thank God I'm living to be here. I want to thank each and every one of you from the bottom of my heart. This is something I shall never forget as long as I live. It's a wonderful tribute. I thank God I'm alive to see it. Thanks a million."[28]

Between the fifth and sixth innings, Pee Wee pushed Campy onto the field one more time. The stadium was darkened, and the PA announcer asked every fan to light a match or cigarette lighter "as if lighting a candle on a cake for Campy," the *Daily News* reported. "As the lights dimmed, the flares made a fine glow, row on row upwards through the 78 rows to the top of the huge horseshoe."[29] Pee Wee, Campy wrote, "stood at my side throughout the entire ceremony,"[30] and at one point took off his L.A. cap and placed it on Campanella's head. "I cried without shame as this tremendous throng—all 93,103 of them—stood up in tribute," Campy wrote, "and shouted a welcome that sounded like a roll of thunder."[31] The Yankees won the game, 6–2. More importantly, the Dodgers' share of the gate was $87,500. Of that, $50,000 was donated to Campy to defray his considerable medical expenses.[32]

The Dodgers got off to a fast start, going 11–6 in April. Wally Moon batted .352 and boasted a .470 on-base percentage. In May, the team hit a slump and stumbled to 25–23 by month's end, five games out of first place. Don Zimmer, a .283 batter in April, tailed off to just .143 in May. Buzzie Bavasi, "in an effort to boast their sagging infield,"[33] promoted Maury Wills, a 26-year-old speedster, to the big club and demoted back-up infielder Bob Lillis to the Spokane Indians of the Pacific Coast League. Wills, from Washington, D.C., had toiled in the minor leagues since 1951. Thus far in 1959, he was batting .313 with 25 stolen bases for the Indians. The *Spokane Chronicle* did not expect this move to make front-page news in Los Angeles. "The swap ... may not be greeted with huzzahs from the man on the street. Still, it isn't the worst exchange in the world. Maury gets to play major league ball and for that all of us are, or should be, happy."[34]

In mid–June, Carl Erskine announced his retirement. Just 28 days short of qualifying for the baseball pension program, the 32-year-old said his oft-sore right arm had thrown more than enough pitches. "I don't mind the pain," he said. "A lot of pitchers work with arms that hurt. But I just don't have a thing on the ball and that's what worries me." He ended his career with a 122–78 record and a 4.00 ERA. Steve Snider of the United Press wrote, "Those who knew him personally will tell you there was no finer gentleman in baseball."[35]

Some of Reese's initial uncertainty about coaching vanished as the season wore on. Mostly, he helped with base running and infield defensive work. "I found that I did like it and also that there was a lot more to coaching that I had realized as a player," he said. "In my playing days, like the other players, I was concerned chiefly with my own problems."[36] Reese usually stayed in the dugout during games, dispensing advice to players and to Alston. He took a turn as the team's third-base coach for a few weeks after Charlie Dressen fell ill.

The most important duty of a third base coach, of course, is to choose between holding a runner or sending him home. "I was lucky in some cases," Reese said. "A couple of times, I waved men home when a good throw might have caught them. But the throw was just a little off and the men scored." Alston, though, said Reese "performed perfectly" in that new, temporary role. "He has to make plenty of snap decisions and from the dugout I couldn't find fault with them."[37]

One night, a group of players stayed out late and then ducked into Reese's hotel room. Someone knocked on the door. It was Alston doing a bed check. Or was it? Many players did Alston impressions. Maybe it was just some joker pulling a prank. Someone in the room, probably inebriated, shouted out, "Hey, Walter, kiss my ass. If it's really Walter Alston, prove it!" So Alston, noted for his strength, did just that. He kicked down the door. Yes, it really was the skipper, who stared down the party. "Is that proof enough?"[38]

The Dodgers spent much of the summer in second place, occasionally in third, and, for a few games, in first. They won seven of their final nine games and finished 86–68, in a tie with Milwaukee for the top spot, setting up a best two-of-three playoff series. Milwaukee hosted the first game. L.A. posted solo runs in the first, third, and sixth innings and won, 3–2.

The following day, the Dodgers earned a 6–5 victory at the Coliseum and clinched a World Series berth. The Braves led, 5–2, going into the bottom of the ninth. The Dodgers, who "appeared hopelessly beaten," led off that frame with three straight singles to load the bases. Norm Larker made it four straight and drove home two runs. Carl Furillo tied the score with his sacrifice fly. In the bottom of the 12th, Furillo, "a money player if there ever was one,"[39] came through once again. He bounced a ball that Felix Mantilla fielded at shortstop but threw in the dirt to Frank Torre at first, allowing Hodges to score the winning run. The *L.A. Times* headline proclaimed: "DODGERS THE CHAMPS! OFF TO SERIES."[40]

Wally Moon, famous for his distinctive unibrow, hit 19 home runs over the season, batted .302, and led the league with 11 triples. He finished fourth in the NL MVP voting. "Moon was fantastic," Buzzie Bavasi exclaimed. The lefty figured out a way to hit balls over the Coliseum screen in left field, using "a calculated slice," he said. "It's simply a matter of bringing your hands closer to your body and slightly delaying your swing," Moon said. "You keep the ball cocked for a split second after the hands have begun to move, and at the last possible moment you flip the barrel of the bat at the ball."[41]

Duke Snider added 23 homers, 88 RBI, and a .308 batting average. Gil Hodges led the team with 25 home runs. Maury Wills played 83 games in his debut campaign at shortstop and hit .260 with seven stolen bases. Don Drysdale won 17 games and threw 15 complete games. Los Angeles native and Fairfax High School graduate Larry Sherry won seven games, lost two, and posted a 2.19 ERA. The Dodgers drew 2,071,045 fans, more than any team in the National League.

For the first time since 1920, the Dodgers got ready to play a team other than the Yankees in the World Series. The Chicago White Sox earned the AL pennant, taking over first place for good on July 28 and finishing with a 94–60 record, five games ahead of the second-place Indians. Chicago's South Side squad hadn't won a flag since the infamous Black Sox team brought one home in 1919. Dubbed the "Go-Go Sox" as a compliment to the team's great speed, the 1959 White Sox stole 113 bases, or 45 more than the Red Sox, the league's next-swiftest team.

The White Sox hosted the first two games at Comiskey Park. Pee Wee Reese wrote a syndicated column that offered his analysis of the Series. The Dodgers boasted strong pitching and a handful of tough hitters, he wrote. He added another reason for the team's success. "The word is 'spirit' and if that sounds corny, I'm sorry," he wrote. Reese looked back on his old Brooklyn teams and decided, "This group [the 1959 squad] beats them all for the will to win. This Dodger team is a team of destiny. They will win the World Series because they honestly think they can, and that's good enough for me."[42]

Most likely, the White Sox players never read Reese's column. Chicago easily won the Series opener, 11–0. Roger Craig gave up five runs in 2⅓ innings; Chuck Churn allowed six. "It was just one of those games where you get the hell knocked out of you,"[43] Walter Alston told reporters. Gil Hodges cautioned that the Series had just begun. "You hate to take a beating like that, but the guys aren't down," he said. "We still have confidence."[44] In his column, Reese wrote, "I guess we forgot to duck." He promised, "It won't happen again."[45] After the first inning of Game Two, he may have been second-guessing himself. The White Sox took a quick 2–0 lead. Charlie Neal, who slammed 19 home runs in the regular season, blasted a solo long ball in the fourth inning to cut the advantage in half. Neal hit another home run as part of a three-run seventh, and L.A. held on to win, 4–3. Don Zimmer, sitting in the team bus after the game, yelled, "Go Go Sox, my ass!"[46]

The World Series shifted to Los Angeles. Huge crowds packed the Dodgers' home park. "The Coliseum was 92,000 for three days in a row," Larry Sherry said. "And it was deafening. You couldn't hear a thing, and this was for baseball games."[47] Reese wrote in his column that the White Sox players might be thinking a little too much about that short fence in the Coliseum. "If they are, it's the worst thing they can do," he wrote. "I've seen pitchers fold because they got licked mentally by the shadow of the fence. I've seen good hitters look like something out of the Cape Cod League because they figured all they needed to hike their batting average was lob a fly ball over, or off, the friendly dimensions of baseball's tallest booby trap."[48]

Chicago managed 12 hits in Game Three but failed to homer. Behind Don Drysdale, with help in the eighth and ninth from Sherry, the Dodgers won, 3–1. Carl Furillo hit a two-run single "before 92,294 fans, the largest crowd ever to witness a series contest."[49] L.A. won again the next day, 5–4. Both teams took turns posting four-run innings. Gil Hodges led off the eighth with a solo home run to put his team ahead. "The Dodgers act like a team dealing off the top of the deck," Reese wrote. "In this series, especially the last two days in the Coliseum, we've won because we've been the better team."[50]

During the Series, Hank Hollingworth spoke with Reese, "a spirited Kentuckian," and asked whether the Dodgers were "one of the luckiest teams in baseball history." Reese shook his head. "Lucky?" he asked. "Good Lord man, no. But I'll sure as the devil say it's the fightingest." He heard "everywhere" that "this Dodger club gets all the breaks." He pointed out that mere lucky teams do not go up three games to one in the World Series. Sure, not every hit that the Dodgers had collected was a ringing line drive. "But we got them when they counted," he insisted. "I'd say it's fighting down to the last out, rather than luck, that's pulling us through."[51]

After 26-year-old right-hander Bob Shaw and two relievers blanked L.A., 1–0, in Game Five, the Series shifted back to Chicago. The Dodgers posted six runs in the fourth inning en route to a 9–3 victory and a championship. Charlie Neal, Wally Moon, and Duke Snider all drove in two runs, while Larry Sherry provided 5⅔ innings of scoreless relief. Hours later, about 5,000 fans greeted their baseball heroes at the airport. Television star Desi Arnaz of *I Love Lucy* fame hosted a short program, and Mayor Paulson gave skipper Walter Alston a scroll that certified October 9, 1959, as "Baseball Champions of the World Day."

Reese wrote, "I think those snide comments remarks about the freaky dimensions of the Coliseum in Los Angeles helped us. Deep down, our ballclub wanted to prove to everybody that they could win the whole thing away from home. ... When the Series started, I made a lot of the fact that this was the most spirited Dodger team I had ever been associated with. I still say that. The 1959 Dodgers had a great talent for keeping their chins up."[52] Years later, Alston called the squad his all-time favorite. "They may not have had as much talent as others, but they had tremendous desire," he wrote in *A Year at a Time*. "They played like a championship team all the way. They were a manager's dream."[53]

Just a few days after the World Series ended, another rumor cropped up that Reese might take a managerial job. This time, the Braves supposedly wanted to hire him. Fred Haney resigned after compiling an admirable 341–231 overall mark, including two pennants and a championship in 1957, during his four years at the helm. His team finished in second place with an 86–70 record in 1959. "[Braves owner Lou] Perini is sold on a name manager,"[54] Bill Lee wrote in the *Hartford Courant*. Til Ferdenzi, a columnist with the *New York Journal-American*, offered an enthusiastic endorsement of Reese. "This man is just great," Ferdenzi said. "He has all sorts of angles—good baseball angles. There aren't many ball players as intelligent as Reese."[55] The Associated Press went so far as to report, "Reese's hiring will be announced in a short time" and that "Reese has been in conference with Milwaukee officials several times."[56]

Ultimately, Reese decided, as he had in the past, that "I'm not ready to manage now."[57] He told Jimmy Brown of the *Louisville Courier-Journal* that, contrary to some reports, he never spoke to anyone from Milwaukee. "I would be flattered if they did consider me," Reese confessed. "It would be an honor. But I wouldn't take it. ... My baseball future is with the Dodger organization. After 20 years with them, and the wonderful treatment I've received, I don't believe I could ever feel otherwise."[58]

Reese, though, left the coaching world after just one season. Ron Fairly counted himself among the disappointed. "I wish Pee Wee hadn't left us after the 1959 season," he said decades later. "It was a big loss for baseball, And certainly a big loss for us."[59]

Reese accepted an offer to join Dizzy Dean as an analyst for CBS's nationally televised "Game of the Week," replacing Buddy Blattner, a former infielder with the Cardinals, Giants, and Phillies. He signed a two-year deal with an option for two more, at $32,000 a year, a nice raise over his $18,000 coach's paycheck. Reese said he wanted to spend more time with his family as well as his storm window and insurance businesses.[60]

The team of Pee Wee Reese and Dizzy Dean met in early 1941 at the New York baseball writers' dinner. Dean showed up in Gotham looking like John Wayne or Tom Mix. He wore cowboy clothes, a 10-gallon hat, and some fancy boots more suitable for Texas than the Big Apple. He couldn't wait for the season to start. "It's going to be a pleasure working with a big leaguer like Reese," Dean proclaimed. "I understand he's a 10-handicap in golf. I'm an eight-handicap. We ought to make a lot of money this summer."[61]

Reese needed some practice before going on air. He devoted much of spring training to making tapes of exhibition games. "Dizzy Dean was playing a lot of golf and advising me, 'Oh, Pee Wee, don't worry. You can do it.'"[62] Reese refused to count the number of errors he made during those never-to-be-heard-from-again broadcasts. "You think I made mistakes in 1940 when I first came up with the Dodgers, you should have heard me when I was practicing play-by-play announcing of spring training games this year."[63]

One duty of a TV broadcaster is to fill out a scoresheet. Reese didn't know how to do that. Seriously. Fortunately, Dottie Reese did. "No kiddin'," Reese admitted. "I never knew anything about scoring a ball game until this spring." Dottie Reese didn't go to many games through the years. When she did, she kept score. Now, Pee Wee said, "it made her feel really good when she was finally able to help me in my work."[64] Other details about broadcasting still eluded him. "They're paying me to talk into a microphone, and I still pronounce the damn word 'th'owed.'"[65]

Working with Ol' Diz could be, uh, different. Dean gave free plugs to products he liked—American Airlines, Lucky Strike cigarettes, the Cadillac division of General Motors, etc., whether that company co-sponsored the telecasts or not. He also gave shout-outs to his favorite restaurants. He liked Antoine's in New Orleans, the Pink Pony in Phoenix, and Bailey's in Mobile, among others. He also endorsed Jack McHenry's Anchor in Wiggins, Mississippi, which served a Dizzy Dean Special—navy beans with cornbread and red onions.

Dean disliked extra-inning games. He hated the scorching heat and the freezing cold. Sometimes he got hungry. One Saturday in Chicago, Dean went out for a burger. Did Reese want one, too? Sure. "Pickles, mustard, or lettuce?" Dean asked. Just onions. "Can you eat two?" Nah, one was fine. So, Dizzy Dean left the booth to go on a burger run. Reese turned his attention back to the game. "Let's see, folks," he said. "Where were we?"[66]

Dean, reminiscing with a reporter in 1973, recalled one broadcast when a pitchers' duel developed. Both hurlers were mowing down opposing batter after batter. Reese suggested that Dean tell the fans what each pitcher was throwing that day. Sure, Dean said. "And I says, 'Yep, Pee Wee, I've been watching them very closely and I believe that's a baseball they're throwin.' And I thought Pee Wee would go crazy."[67] Another time, Dean walked into the booth with a few of his many closest friends. "Let me show you how to do this," he said, and then began singing a favorite song, "The Wabash Cannonball," made famous by Roy Acuff. After a few verses, Dean handed the mic back to Reese and declared, "OK, Podnuh, that's how you do it."[68]

Early on, Reese handled a few broadcasts solo when Dean had something else to do. Was he nervous? No, Reese said, as he ate breakfast at the hotel, hours before game time. He felt fine. "Then, why," a friend asked, "are you pouring coffee on your French toast?"[69]

Reese faced his first health scare in late 1962. He underwent surgery in January for removal of scar tissue from one of his lungs. Afterward, Dr. J. Ray Bryant, a surgeon at Methodist Hospital in Louisville, said Reese was "doing fine" and that the "lesion" was "neither a cancer nor a tumor" but, rather, the result of an arrested case of tuberculosis or other infection. Bryant said Reese would remain in the hospital for about 10 days.[70]

By March, Reese was off to Florida, along with Dottie and six-year-old Mark. (Barbara, now 19, was away at college in Washington, D.C., studying commercial art.) The trio stopped off one day in Dothan, Alabama, and Reese spoke to reporter Terry Everett of the *Dothan Eagle*. At one point, the conversation turned to University of Alabama football coach Paul "Bear" Bryant. "He's a real gentleman," Reese said. Bryant sometimes visited Crosley Field to take in a ballgame "and we'd talk. Last summer, he sent Diz and me a batch of quail. They sure were good." If young Mark ever wanted to play football for Bryant and the Crimson Tide, Pee Wee said, "I'd be flattered." Everett wrote that the dark-haired Mark "looks a lot like his dad." Pee Wee remarked that his son was "a pretty good size for six years." Pee Wee also said he would be "very happy" if Mark opted to play baseball. "The game has been very good to me,"[71] Reese said in typical understated fashion.

A few months into the 1963 season, Reese spoke to Bob Broeg about the current state of baseball, which, he said, "has improved since I broke in." He mentioned the great number of hard-throwing pitchers and the development of the slider. "Guys older than I am like to call it a nickel curve, but they didn't face the kind of slider I've seen Billy O'Dell throw for the Giants this season—a fast pitch with a quick, hard break." Also, more teams were employing bullpen specialists to relieve tired starters and give batters a different look. "It was a novelty to have a good bullpen when we had Hugh Casey at Brooklyn in 1941," Reese told Broeg. "Now, if a club doesn't have one or two good relief pitchers, it can forget about the pennant race." He said the ball seemed a bit livelier in recent years. Players needed the larger gloves to reach balls that rushed toward awaiting outfielders, he said. "The ball really travels through the infield now."[72]

Reese called Willie Mays and Joe DiMaggio "the two best all-round players I ever saw" and Stan Musial "the most amazing player…. At bat, he used to play handball with our walls at Ebbets Field." "Stan the Man" was in the final season of a glorious career and would retire with 475 home runs, a .331 average, and 3,630 hits. In 163 games at Ebbets Field, Musial hit .359 with 37 home runs and 126 RBI. Reese joked that the Redbird "was more popular with the Brooklyn fans than any of us who played with the Dodgers."[73]

Musial returned the compliment later that year. In December, Reese was inducted into the Kentucky Athletic Hall of Fame, along with Happy Chandler and former New York Yankees great Earle Combs. Musial served as one of the speakers for the event. He called Reese "the greatest shortstop I ever saw—without question the best to hit the major leagues over a 15-year period."[74]

In 1966, Reese moved over to NBC and teamed with veteran broadcaster Curt Gowdy on Saturday telecasts. Sandy Koufax joined them the following season after announcing his retirement as a player. The lefty won three Cy Young Awards and hurled four no-hitters over a dynamic, albeit brief, career. In August, Stan Maays wrote a piece that began "Is Pee Wee Reese jealous of Sandy Koufax?" Supposedly, Reese cut off Koufax several times during the recent All-Star telecast. Reese, though, brushed aside any talk of keeping Koufax quiet. "Sandy and I are the best of friends," he said. If the former pitcher did get cut off, Reese said, "it certainly wasn't done deliberately." Maays promised his readers that "it isn't in his [Reese's] make-up to be a jealous or designing person." Reese called himself "basically a shy guy."[75]

NBC fired Reese in early March of 1969. Carl Lindemann, vice-president of the network's sports division, gave him the bad news. "No one could really tell him what he did wrong," Milt Gross wrote for UPI. Reese asked, "Did I talk too much? ... Didn't I talk enough?" Lindemann only said that three broadcasters in one booth was "cumbersome, too many." The network's public relations coordinator, Eddie Wiseman, apologized about the firing. Maybe, Wiseman suggested, NBC could send out a press release stating that the former shortstop quit in order to spend more time with his outside business interests. Reese encouraged NBC to tell the truth. "So, if you're asked, just say my contract wasn't picked up," he said. "If I made up some story and told anything else but the truth, I wouldn't be able to look myself in the mirror."[76]

A few weeks later, the Reds hired Reese to take over for Frank McCormick, the team's former All-Star first baseman, as broadcast analyst and join play-by-plan man Ed Kennedy. Reese had turned down a chance to broadcast Cardinals games in place of the fired Harry Caray. "That meant I would have had to do a lot of traveling," Reese said. "And I don't want to."[77]

In July 1971, Reese began working for local bat maker Hillerich & Bradsby as director of the professional and college baseball advisory staff. J. F. Hillerich's old furniture-making company was now turning out millions of bats every year.[78] "I am extremely happy to stay in baseball,"[79] he said, talking to reporters while playing golf at the Audubon Country Club in Louisville. The following year, Reese gave his last word on managing. He wasn't interested. Mostly, he blamed the ulcers. Maybe he looked cool on the field. Truth be told, Pee Wee Reese was a worrywart. "I guess I fooled a lot of people," he said. He admitted, "There were times I when I dreaded going to bat." He fretted over making an error or going 0-for-5, he said. "I'm not about to start worrying over nine guys doing that," Reese explained. "Mr. O'Malley always used to say I'd be a manager someday, but I said, 'No way.'"[80]

Roger Kahn's book *The Boys of Summer* hit stores and best-seller lists in 1972. The first half is about the writer's Brooklyn boyhood, his love for the Dodgers, and his two years covering that team. The second half offers a portrait of several Dodgers, now retired from playing, now middle-aged, living in New York or California, and points in between, some happier than others. Reese is featured in a chapter called "A Shortstop from Kentucky." The nearly 20 pages offer a brief recap of Reese's life and his time with the Dodgers. He said Roy Campanella was "the best I ever saw at keeping the ball in front of him" and that Billy Cox boasted a better arm than the Baltimore Orioles' Brooks Robinson "and more speed." He spoke of Jackie Robinson, of course, and all the abuse heaped upon him, especially in those early years. "I don't know how he took it, to be frank," Reese said. Reese hated to get booed. He didn't mind so much if fans on the road let him have it, but "being booed in Brooklyn used to kill me." If he made an error, he'd tell his wife to stay home the next day. "I have to do this," he'd say, "but I don't want you there if I'm getting booed."[81]

Kahn asked about an incident at a local bowling alley that Reese owned. A few years earlier, a Black team was told it could not bowl that night. "The paper said your bowling alley was lily white," Kahn said. Reese shook his head. He said the Black team wanted to use the alley on a night when a league already had taken all the lanes. "Now, maybe that *league* was all-white," Reese conceded. "I don't check on all the customers." He added, "I wouldn't run a segregated *anything*."[82]

Los Angeles Times book critic David L. Ulin called *The Boys of Summer* "perhaps the most celebrated baseball book of the last 50 years," one that "brought me to tears more than once ... and to laughter and to that quiet confrontation with enemy Time."[83] George Frazier of the *Boston Globe* wrote, "I cannot conceive that his year, nor next year, nor the year after that, will produce a more important book—a better written one, a more consistently engrossing one than his portrait of the Dodgers in the 1950s, as they were in the sinew and swiftness of their youth as they are now."[84] In 2002, *Sports Illustrated* ranked *The Boys of Summer* as Number 2 of its list of best sports books ever. *SI* called it "a novelistic tale of conflict and change, a tribute, a civic history, a piece of nostalgia, and, finally, a tragedy."[85] *The Sweet Science*, A. J. Liebling's boxing classic, published in 1956, took the top spot.

Two of the "Boys" died in 1972. Gil Hodges, managing the New York Mets, attended church on Easter Sunday, April 2, and then met with some of his coaches to play golf at Palm Beach Country Club. A heavy smoker, Hodges suffered a heart attack and collapsed in the parking lot. Mets bullpen coach Joe Pignatano ran to his side, "I knew he was dead," Pignatano said. "[Mets pitching coach] Rube [Walker] did, too. He said, 'Joe, he's turned blue.' He died in my arms,"[86] just two days short of turning 48 years old. Reese, along with many of the other former Dodgers greats, went to Hodges' funeral mass.

Jackie Robinson, stricken with diabetes and nearly blind, died months later, on October 24, at the age of 53. Reporters reached out to Reese for a comment. He last saw Robinson a few weeks earlier at the World Series in Cincinnati. The two former infielders took part in a pre-game ceremony at Riverfront Stadium. Robinson, overly modest in this case, called himself "just a spoke in the wheel" of the great Brooklyn teams from the 1950s. He described Reese as "a great leader" who "really set the pace."[87] On the day that Robinson passed away, Reese said, "Jackie was quite a person. I grew to know him and admire him a great deal, off the field as well as on. We used to play golf and tennis together, and he was a great competitor in everything he did. ... He was a controversial guy and some of the things he said made some of the players on the old Dodgers teams pretty mad. But for all that, he was a great person and I had to admire him for having the guts to say what was on his mind."[88]

At the time of his death, Robinson was one of only two Brooklyn stars from the 1940s and 1950s to have a plaque at the Baseball Hall of Fame. Writers enshrined him in 1962, his first year of eligibility. Roy Campanella, who won three MVP awards after putting together several stellar campaigns in the Negro Leagues, earned his Cooperstown plaque in 1969. Many writers and fans hoped for more Brooklyn Dodgers to join Robinson and Campy. Some argued for Gil Hodges, who hit 370 career home runs and topped the 100-RBI mark in seven straight seasons (1949–55). Some touted Duke Snider, who slugged 409 career homers and batted .295 lifetime. Still others made a case for the Brooklyn captain. (Writers elected Sandy Koufax to the Hall of Fame in 1972. The lefty with a power fastball and incredible curveball played three seasons in Brooklyn but enjoyed his glory years as an L.A. Dodger.)

Pee Wee Reese gained just 36.3 percent of the vote in 1964, his first year of eligibility, far short of the 75 percent needed for induction. Over the next several ballots, his vote total hovered around 30 percent, not nearly high enough to gain Cooperstown immortality, not nearly low enough to drop off the ballot (less than five percent). Dick Young, in a 1973 column, argued the case for Reese, along with Phil Rizzuto and Marty Marion. "They were great shortstops, great leaders, on winning teams. Shortstops don't build mountains with their bats. They must be seen, game after game, year after year, to be appreciated."[89] Jim Murray lobbied for Reese in his own unique style. "Pee Wee is so cheerful you could spread him on bread," Murray wrote. "He'd have to get grouchier to be merely considered happy-go-lucky." Jackie Robinson, Murray claimed, "would have kicked down the door if they didn't let him in. Pee Wee won't even knock."[90]

Reese topped out on the Hall of Fame ballot at 47.9 percent in 1976, still nearly 30 percentage points shy of induction. Two years later, when he appeared on the regular ballot for the last time, he earned 44.6 percent. Now he would need help from the Veterans Committee. Established in 1939, the Committee, composed of former players, managers, and executives, can elect candidates not voted into the Hall of Fame by the Baseball Writers' Association of America.[91]

One of the greatest shortstops in baseball history didn't lobby for a Hall of Fame plaque. He insisted, "I'm neither bitter or disappointed." He looked back at a long and satisfying career with the Dodgers. "For a kid who graduated high school weighing 110 pounds and who looked like he was going to work for the telephone company his whole life, I consider myself a most fortunate person."[92]

Pee Wee Reese liked to watch his son play baseball. *Courier-Journal* columnist Mike Sullivan wrote about Mark Reese's athletic career in the summer of 1976. Mark batted .450 in his junior year at Atherton High School and .390 in his senior season. The White Sox drafted him in the 30th round of the MLB draft, but Mark opted to play ball at Manatee Junior College in Bradenton, Florida. A former outfielder, Mark Reese switched to first base at Manatee. He also played for a local team in the Metropolitan Amateur Baseball Association, the Combsmen. The team's manager, Brown Lee Combs, swore he did not know—at least right away—that Mark was the son of a former big leaguer. "That wasn't until I saw Pee Wee over in the stands," Combs said. "Then one night, Pee Wee was nice enough to spent 20 or 30 minutes instructing our kids after the game." In the world of sports, Mark said his dad "never pushed me at all. On the other hand, there was never a time when I wanted to work out that he wasn't there. He'll do that until he dies, I think. He still loves the game so much."[93]

20

"He was the heart and soul of the boys of summer"

In early March of 1984, under the still-soft Florida sun, before the start of yet another hot and sticky summer, Pee Wee Reese waited for a telephone call. He happened to be in Winter Haven, site of the Red Sox spring training camp. He flew down to the Sunshine State every year as part of his duties for Hillerich & Bradsby. "I make all the camps I can," he said. He listened to comments and complaints from journeymen and superstars. "If a player picks up an S2 [bat] and maybe likes the feel, he'll tell me, and he'll order some. The Dodgers, they seem to order the most. Some of them order 48 bats at a time."[1]

It was late morning. Reese would know at about noon whether he was a Hall of Famer. "No, I'm not nervous about it," he said. Friends had been wishing him good luck the past few days. "If I make it, fine," he said. "If I don't, I have no hard feelings toward anyone." Funny that he waited out the telephone call while at the Red Sox camp. Boston, after all, bought an entire minor league team just to acquire him. And then sold him to the Dodgers because Joe Cronin thought he was too small to play in the major leagues. "I expected to go with the Red Sox, and that's where I wanted to go," he said. Even so, he regretted that he got upset about being sold to Brooklyn. "I shouldn't have done that, talked like I did,"[2] he told reporters in Florida. The clock ticked closer to noon.

Reese made small talk with Boston manager Ralph Houk. The telephone at the Red Sox publicity office rang at about 12 o'clock, as scheduled. Associated Press writer David O'Hara gave out the news. "He's in," O'Hara said. "Pee Wee is in."[3] Now, someone needed to tell the latest inductee.

His first words were "Really? Really? Really?" Later, he admitted, "You know, I can be an emotional man. I may shed a tear tonight."[4] Newspapers, radio stations, and other media asked for interviews. Reese waited for several hours to call his wife. "I was able to accept it kind of nonchalantly until then," he said. "Then I got a little teary-eyed. When it comes time for the induction ceremony, I just don't know how I'll feel then."[5] Reese spoke about some of his Dodgers teammates who had died in recent years. "I'm sure ol' Jackie, Jim [Gilliam], Gil [Hodges], Billy Cox, Bruce Edwards, all those guys who have passed on, would be very happy for me," he said. "I'm sure they would."[6]

He made several appearances over the next several weeks, in Grand Junction,

Colorado, in Omaha, and, of course, in Louisville. "It still seems strange to be introduced as a Hall of Famer,"[7] he said. "It's a great thrill to me," he said. "I had never given it a lot of thought, to tell you the truth. My feeling was that it was OK if it happened and OK if it didn't."[8] It had been a long wait. "My son Mark once told me if they put me in the Hall of Fame after I was dead and buried, he wouldn't accept it,"[9] Pee Wee said.

Don Drysdale wrote in his memoir, "Why it took Pee Wee so long to get into the Hall of Fame, I don't know." He added, "For my own selfish reasons, it was good that Pee Wee did have to wait as long as he did because we got into Cooperstown together. That was nice, real nice."[10]

"Big D," as some people called Drysdale, retired early in the 1969 campaign due to shoulder problems. He compiled a 209–166 won-loss mark through parts of 13 seasons. The 1962 Cy Young Award winner combined with Sandy Koufax to give the Dodgers a lethal 1–2 starting pitching combination throughout much of the 1960s, one that helped the franchise to three pennants and two championships that decade. Drysdale struck out 2,486 batters and led the National League in that category three times (1959, 1960 and 1962). Maybe most famously, he hit 154 batters, including 20 in 1961. Orlando Cepeda, a hard-hitting first baseman and outfielder for the Giants, Cardinals, and other teams, liked to say, "The trick against Drysdale is to hit him before he hits you."[11] The Dodgers planned to retire Drysdale's uniform Number 53, along with Reese's Number 1, at a ceremony July 1 at Dodger Stadium.

Slugger Harmon Killebrew made it into Cooperstown that year on his fourth try. A native of little Payette, Idaho, near the Oregon state line, the good-natured Killer (as some called him in jest) mashed 573 home runs during a 22-year career, mostly spent with the Washington Senators and Minnesota Twins. He topped the AL in homers six times and earned the MVP Award in 1969. Paul Richards, former manager of the Orioles and White Sox, once said, "The homers he has hit against us would be homers in any park, including Yellowstone."[12]

Baseball writers also voted in Luis Aparicio, the first Venezuelan-born Hall of Famer. "Little Louie" played 18 seasons with the White Sox, Orioles, and Red Sox. A .261 lifetime batter, he—like Reese—reached the .300 mark just one time but won nine Gold Glove Awards. Aparicio made seven All-Star teams and topped the AL in stolen bases every season from 1956–1964.

In addition to Reese, the Veterans Committee elected Rick Ferrell, a former catcher with the Browns and Red Sox. Noted for his defensive talent and adept skill at catching knuckleball pitchers, Ferrell batted .300 in four seasons and hit .281 lifetime.

One day before his induction, Reese enjoyed a round of golf on the Cooperstown course. Fans waited for him near the 12th green and asked for autographs. Reese signed his name on baseballs and postcards and posed for pictures with admirers. He told reporters, "I don't like a lot of fanfare. I guess what is really worrying me is the speech tomorrow.... It could get a little emotional." Kenny Smith, the former Hall of Fame director, spotted Reese on the fairway. Smith told the shortstop, retired now for more than a quarter century, that he looked fresh enough to "play a double-header this afternoon." Reese shook his head and rubbed his knees. No, he could not play two. "Bad wheels, Kenny."[13]

The Hall of Fame program began about 3 o'clock, following a brief rain shower. Killebrew "stole the show" when he spoke about his boyhood and how he grew up with four siblings, including two brothers. Harmon, Sr., encouraged his sons to play rough and compete in sports, no matter what that might do to the Killebrew yard. "We're not raising grass here. We're raising boys," Killebrew recalled his dad saying. With that, "Reese wiped his eyes, and blinked repeatedly."[14]

Reese spoke for about nine minutes. He told the audience that he was "very proud to be inducted into the Hall of Fame today." He introduced his wife, his two children, son-in-law Thomas Dudgeon, and two grandchildren. "Not a bad-looking family," he said. Pee Wee thanked his many fans both in Louisville and Brooklyn. He called Jackie Robinson "a fierce competitor who came to play and to win." He also mentioned Leo Durocher. "He was my biggest booster. He gave a scared kid from Louisville a chance to play."[15] He ended by saying, "I've been married for 42 years to the same woman. If there was a Hall of Fame for baseball wives, she would make it. I wore Number 1 on my back for all the years that I played, but she was Number 1 in my heart."[16]

Legendary broadcaster Vin Scully called Reese "the heart and soul of the Boys of Summer." The Veterans Committee voted Reese into the Hall of Fame in 1984 (National Baseball Hall of Fame Library, Cooperstown, New York).

Groups from Louisville traveled to Cooperstown for the induction. Many of the still-loyal Brooklyn fans also made the trip. Dotty Huelster of Mount Laurel, New Jersey, watched her favorite team play at Ebbets Field many times and on road trips to other ballparks. "We got to know all the Dodgers," she said. "But Pee Wee was always our boy."[17] During Reese's speech, a voice from the crowd shouted out, "Brooklyn still loves you, Pee Wee. You were the original No. 1."[18]

Reese's Cooperstown plaque reads:

Harold Henry "Pee Wee" Reese
Brooklyn N.L. 1940–57
Los Angeles N.L. 1958

Shortstop and captain of great Dodger teams of 1940s and 50s. Intangible qualities of subtle leadership on and off field. Competitive fire and professional pride complemented dependable glove, reliable base-running and clutch-hitting as significant factors in 7 Dodger pennants. Instrumental in easing acceptance of Jackie Robinson as baseball's first black performer.

Going into the Hall of Fame by way of the Veterans Committee suited Reese just fine. "They say I went in through the back door," he told some writers. Then he revealed how much the honor meant to him. "My goodness," he said. "I would've crawled in through the window if that's what I needed to do."[19]

Reese retired from Hillerich & Bradsby in 1985. After traveling for nearly 50 years, he wanted to slow down. "I've been doing it since I was 18 years old," he said. "It will be nice being able to live at home and know I'll not have to go somewhere every two weeks." Reese said he would miss his visits to big league clubhouses, especially the Dodgers.' "I've got a lot of favorites among the players of today," he said, "but some of them are tough to talk to. Some of them have never heard of Pee Wee Reese, you know."[20]

He hoped to see some of his contemporaries gain admission to Cooperstown. "If I made it," he said, "the Phil Rizzutos, the Marty Marions and the Alvin Darks should get in, too."[21] A melancholy Rizzuto vented over not getting a plaque. "I swear, nobody believes in me, but it really doesn't bother me, because I said many times, they never should have lowered the standards for the Hall of Fame. The only time I got upset is that they had promised when Pee Wee went in, he and I would go in together. I'm waiting by the phone, and they put in Rick Ferrell. Holy Cow!"[22] (The Veterans Committee finally voted Rizzuto into the Hall of Fame in 1994, 10 years after it elected Reese. As of 2020, Marion and Dark have not been enshrined.)

In the early 1990s, Pee Wee Reese made his first trip to Brooklyn in more than 30 years. He went there to star in a movie, or more specifically, a documentary about his life in baseball. Mark Reese wrote, produced, and directed the film, titled *Baseball's Quiet Ambassador*, narrated by Roger Kahn. Mark produced other films about Brooklyn Dodgers stars and told Stephen McFarland of the *New York Daily News*, "I've been wanting to do this for a long time."[23]

Pee Wee confessed. "I didn't want to go back. I didn't know what I was going to find. I wanted to remember Ebbets Field the way it was. I wanted to remember the hot dog stands and the people on Bedford Avenue."[24] Wrecking balls knocked down Ebbets Field in 1960. Someone painted at least one of the large spheres to resemble an oversized baseball. About 200 fans watched with sorrow on that first day of destruction as pieces of iron smashed into the fabled yard. "They had a funeral, with all the trimmings, in Brooklyn yesterday,"[25] Dana Mozley wrote. The 69th Regiment Band played "Auld Lang Syne," surely not loud enough to drown out the sounds of demolition. About 1,200 miles to the south, in Vero Beach, Carl Erskine shook his head at the ballpark's demise. "It must be a blow to all the folks in Brooklyn," he said. "I hate to see it come down."[26] Pete Reiser cracked a joke. "I'm sure they won't have any trouble knocking down that center field wall," he said, recalling his many collisions. "I softened it up for them."[27]

The high-rise Ebbets Field Apartments opened at 55 Sullivan Place in 1962. Ten years later, the complex was renamed the Jackie Robinson Apartments. Early in *Baseball's Quiet Ambassador*, Reese stands near the old ballpark site. He is wearing a pair of grey slacks, an argyle sweater, and a cap to protect himself from the sun. He musters some enthusiasm with the camera rolling. "I guess it looks beautiful," he says. "But it doesn't look as good as when Ebbets Field was there."[28]

Roger Kahn, in a column a few years later for the *Los Angeles Times*, wrote about one scene that was left on the cutting-room floor. Pee Wee, along with Mark Reese, Kahn, and Bobby Thomson, were assembled on Bedford Avenue. Residents walked by, and cars rushed past. Mark asked Kahn to talk about the death of his son, Roger Laurence Kahn, and Pee Wee's subsequent telephone call, filled with sorrow.

Roger Laurence Kahn died in the summer of 1987 following a battle with heroin addiction. He was handsome, popular, an athlete, and just 22 years old. After getting news of the tragedy, Pee Wee Reese called his friend, who was sitting alone at home and in a dark state. "What's the use of me going on?" Kahn thought to himself. The telephone rang. It was Pee Wee. "I want to tell you from all the fellas that we are very, very sorry." Kahn relayed this message to a newspaper columnist and said, "What a thing. Do you know how hard it is to call a parent who's just lost a boy?"[29]

The famous writer at first refused to retell the story on the busy avenue, in front of friends. It would be too emotional, he said. "I don't want to get misty in front of your camera." Finally agreeing, thanks to some encouragement from Mark, Kahn made it through fine. Then he looked over at a misty-eyed Pee Wee. The tears, Kahn decided, "were for my son, Roger Laurence Kahn, and they were for my grief, but they were for more than that. They were for all the bereaved, the stricken, the bereft, all mankind."[30]

Baseball's Quiet Ambassador combines interviews, newsreel footage, home movies, and more to tell the story of Brooklyn's favorite shortstop. About Jackie Robinson, Pee Wee said, "I'm just tickled to death that I'm remembered as someone who did help him. [But] when you look at it, I think he ended up helping me more than I helped him. He taught me about life."[31] The first public screening of *Quiet Ambassador* was held Sunday, June 13, 1993, at the central branch of the Brooklyn Public Library. Pee Wee admitted that when Mark first approached him about doing a film, "I didn't know what to think. I had a lot of mixed emotions." After watching the finished product, he admitted, "I had a few tears in my eyes."[32]

Rick Bozich from the *Louisville Courier-Journal* called *Baseball's Quiet Ambassador* a "nostalgic" documentary "without being melodramatic, sentimental without being manipulative, informative without being predictable." Mark Reese spoke of the special bond that existed between the Brooklyn Dodgers and their many fans. "All I can say is that even today my father and I still receive birthday cards from Dodger fans," he said, "and I never played a game for them."[33]

Indeed, Pee Wee Reese still opened 10 to 20 letters every day from fans who wanted autographs. Some sent baseballs for him to sign. He was happy and content in retirement. One way to stir him up was to ask whether the Dodgers of the 1940s and 1950s could compete with the big-league clubs of the 1990s, "I think we could compete with anyone, any year," he said. "Why? Because we had such great ballplayers. They say the guys today are so much bigger and stronger." He rattled off some of the familiar names. Hodges, Robinson, Snider, and Furillo all weighed about 200 pounds. Reese weighed 180. "And we had speed. We didn't run as much, but we had speed. I have no doubt Jackie could have stolen 100 bases. I believe I could have stolen at least 50."[34]

Doctors removed a malignant tumor from one of Reese's lungs in March 1997 and recommended that he undergo 25 radiation treatments—five days a week for five weeks—at a hospital in Venice, Florida, where the former ballplayer and Dottie spent much of their time during the colder months of the year, relaxing and playing golf. "He looks fine, but he's not doing really well," Buzzie Bavasi said following a visit. "The radiation is taking a lot out of him, but he seems in good spirits."[35]

Don Zimmer, hobbled by a bad knee, spent some time with his long-time—now weakened—friend. The two men struggled to keep up with their wives when the four went out for dinner one evening at a popular restaurant. Zim and Pee Wee, who also had recently broken a hip, held on to each other as they took their last steps to the table. Several patrons stopped eating and began to watch. Reese, mustering some additional energy, yelled to his wife, "Hey, Dottie? You ever see two old broken-down shortstops like this?"[36] Everyone in the restaurant "burst out laughing," Zimmer wrote. "I knew how bad a shape Pee Wee was in, but I didn't want to believe he was never going to get well again."[37]

About a week before his dad's passing, Mark Reese wrote a letter to Roger Kahn. He began, "The prognosis is not good." Cancer had spread to several parts of Pee Wee's body, including the brain. He appeared delusional at times. Once, he looked at Mark and said, "All my life I've pondered sleep." One evening, Pee Wee sat down in his wheelchair for dinner. He looked closely at his son. He seemed to be saying, Mark wrote, "Who is this stranger invading my home?" Overwhelmed, Mark got up for a few minutes and composed himself in a different room.[38] He looked at the many pictures on the wall. He noticed something about his dad. "It was his smile. It then dawned on me that my father had a key, a key to the secret of life. He knew how to enjoy life, and never to question a single second of it."[39] Mark returned to the dinner table. He and his dad smiled at one another.

Reese died in the afternoon on August 14, 1999, at his Louisville home. "He was cognizant up until the last couple of hours," Mark said. "Then, he kind of slipped away." The Reverend Bob Russell, pastor at Southeast Christian Church in Louisville, said that shortly before dying, Pee Wee squeezed his wife's hand three times, "a signal they had to indicate 'I love you' when he was unable to talk."[40]

Besides a wife and two children, Pee Wee Reese left behind three grandchildren and two great-grandchildren. The headline on Page One of the *Louisville Courier-Journal* read: "Humanitarian Hall of Famer Dies." Two photographs accompanied the article. One showed Reese celebrating with Jackie Robinson and Preacher Roe after the Dodgers beat the Yankees in Game Three of the 1952 World Series. The other one showed Pee Wee sliding safely into home at Ebbets Field in 1942. Bozich wrote, "On the field, Reese did the little things. But off the field, he did the truly big things, like looking out for others and throwing bigotry out of the ballpark." Reese, Bozich wrote, "treated Robinson the same way he treated everybody—like a friend."[41]

Reporters reached out to many of Reese's old teammates and to the team's long-time broadcaster. Don Newcombe, now employed in the Dodgers' front office, told the *Los Angeles Times*, "It's a sad day. The way he held the club together, Pee Wee was always a calming force. I know he helped me immensely to become the winner I was."[42] Carl Erskine said, "He could look at a guy with a half snarl and burn his shorts off. He never shouted, and he played every day. He didn't have to say anything.

He just showed everyone."[43] Many articles recounted the story of Reese's embrace of Jackie Robinson. Most reported the year it happened as 1947 and the location as Crosley Field. Vin Scully said, "That was a message sent to one and all that a boy from the South put his arms around a black man and said, 'Hey, we're equal, we're teammates, and we're in this together. And that was typical of Pee Wee."[44]

Nearly 2,500 family members, friends, and former teammates attended a service for the Dodgers captain on Wednesday, August 18, at Southeast Christian. Afterward, Vin Scully called Pee Wee Reese "the heart and soul of the Boys of Summer." Duke Snider said, "If you asked anyone on the ballclub how Pee Wee Reese helped him, they would say not only in baseball but in their lives. Without his help, I never would have been a Hall of Fame player. He is the finest person I think I've ever met."[45] Joe Black spoke about how Reese reached out to Robinson and what that meant to other Black players. "When I finally got to Brooklyn, I went up to Pee Wee and said, 'Black people love you. When you touched Jackie, you touched all of us.' With Pee Wee, it was number one on his uniform and number one in our hearts."[46] Don Zimmer, in his autobiography, wrote, "[Pee Wee] treated me like a son when I first came up to the Dodgers, but the truth was, we were like brothers. It was a devastating loss."[47]

Sandy Koufax told reporters, "He was a teammate for four years, a friend for 40."[48] Dodgers president Peter O'Malley said, "Pee Wee had something. Today you'd call it people skills. He knew how to communicate. I think he would have been an extraordinary manager."[49] Rachel Robinson flew in from Los Angeles, where she was attending a golf tournament in support of the Jackie Robinson Foundation. "Pee Wee Reese was more than a friend," she said. "Pee Wee was a good man."[50]

In his August 29 column for the *New York Post*, Jack Newfield suggested that the city build a statue in honor of Reese and Robinson. He even suggested a pose, the Embrace. Newfield wrote, "This instinctive gesture of humanity, between the two Hall of Fame ballplayers representing Brooklyn, should be remembered forever." Newfield spoke to then-New York Mayor Rudy Giuliani, a well-known Yankees fan, about a Reese and Robinson statue. "I love this idea," Giuliani said, and he promised to set up a commission to design the work, raise the money, and select a location.[51] Later, Newfield, a liberal, joked about his conversation with the more conservative Giuliani. "The mayor said he never paid any attention to my political columns, but he liked this one about Pee Wee Reese."[52]

Planners selected a site in the Coney Island neighborhood, the once-bustling Brooklyn getaway, next to the Atlantic Ocean surf. The statue was unveiled November 1, 2005, with Rachel Robinson and Dottie Reese among those in attendance. Dottie called the Embrace "a gesture of friendship." Rachel said the statue, sculpted by William Behrends, offers an important message for everyone. "No one who dares to stand up and challenge the status quo stands alone,"[53] she said. Michael Bloomberg, who took over for Giuliani as New York City mayor in November 2001, spoke at the dedication, as did Mark Reese. Bloomberg called Robinson "a champion of civil rights."[54] Mark Reese said that his dad did some "soul searching" in 1947 as Robinson put on a Dodgers uniform and made major league baseball a game for everyone. "And he knew that some fans, some teammates, and, yes, some family members didn't want him to play with a black man. But my father listened to his heart."[55]

20. "He was the heart and soul of the boys of summer" 253

A baseball rests on Reese's headstone at Resthaven Memorial Cemetery in Louisville. Following his death, Duke Snider said, "He's the finest person I think I've ever met" (photograph courtesy Pam Sparks).

A statue in Louisville also honors the memory of Reese. Just weeks after Reese died, *Courier-Journal* columnist Sheldon S. Shafer wrote, "Pee Wee Reese will live on at the new Louisville Slugger Field," to be built in downtown Louisville. Jim Morrissey, a local businessman and friend of Reese's, said, "My concern for a long time has been a proper monument for Pee Wee. We want to honor a great Louisvillian."[56]

Local artist Raymond Graf created the piece, which was unveiled on June 29, 2000, a few years before the Coney Island sculpture, and shows Pee Wee making an acrobatic throw to first base. Dottie Reese told the assembled crowd of about 200, "[Pee Wee's] received many honors, but this is by far the very best. I hope you love it like I do."[57] Joe Black said, "I want to thank the city of Louisville for honoring a guy not because he was a great baseball player but because he was a great human being."[58] Clem Labine relayed a story about Reese. The shortstop "always knew when to step in when times were bad," Labine said. Sometimes, Pee Wee calmed the young pitcher's unsettled nerves, often during a wild streak, in typical laconic style. "If I was walking somebody, he'd come up to me and say, 'What are you trying to do, throw the game.'"[59]

In 2004, the play "Most Valuable Player: The Jackie Robinson Story," opened at the Kentucky Center's Bomhard Theater. Barbara and Thomas Dudgeon were among those in the audience. One scene involves a threat to Robinson if the ballplayer dared to step onto the field in the third inning. As Jackie does just that, he inches closer to Pee Wee Reese. "I don't think either of them [Reese or Robinson] understood the impact they were making," Thomas Dudgeon said. "They were breaking through color barriers, and it was done through baseball—the national pastime." Pee Wee Reese never made a big deal out of his support for Robinson, Dudgeon said. Reese told him "it was the right thing to do. He didn't think about it." Dudgeon recalled how Reese could be so unflappable. Tom and Barbara had been married since January 1966. The couple had two children. Tom met his future wife on a blind date. He drove to the Reese house and was thinking, "My golly—I'm going to pick up Pee Wee Reese's daughter to go on a date." Pee Wee answered the door, as pleasant as he could be. "He was so real," Tom said. "As famous as he was, he was a humble person."[60]

Major League Baseball retired Jackie Robinson's uniform number 42 in 1997. The former Dodger remains the only player to be honored in such a way. Hollywood released a big-budget Jackie Robinson biopic, titled *42*, in 2013. The movie cost $40 million to make. Brian Helgeland, acclaimed for writing the screenplay to the 1997 noirish hit *L.A. Confidential*, wrote and directed *42*. Chadwick Boseman starred as Robinson, with Harrison Ford as Branch Rickey and Nicole Beharie as Rachel Robinson. Alabama native Lucas Black suited up as Pee Wee Reese. Black, who played a high school quarterback in the movie version of *Friday Night Lights*, said he did some research into Reese's life to prepare for the role. "Pee Wee Reese had such a significant part in helping change baseball by accepting Jackie as a ballplayer and as a friend and making a public gesture toward Jackie," said Black, a four-sport athlete at Speake High School in northern Alabama. "So, I felt there was a little responsibility there to put that on film, and to show that side of my character and how he felt toward racism."[61]

The movie grossed $90 million and earned mostly positive reviews. Lisa Kennedy of the *Denver Post* wrote that "the story inspires and entertains with a vital chapter in this nation's history."[62] Rachel Robinson worked as a consultant on the movie. She gave *42* a solid thumbs-up. "It was important to me because I wanted it to be an authentic piece," she said. "I wanted to get it right. I didn't want them to make him an angry black man or some stereotype, so it was important for me to be in there. … I love the movie. I'm pleased with it. It's authentic, and it's also very powerful."[63]

20. "He was the heart and soul of the boys of summer"

A statue of Reese in action stands outside Louisville Slugger Field in the shortstop's hometown. Dotty Reese said, "Pee Wee would have liked the statue. He would have protested and said he didn't deserve this. But he would have been very pleased" (photograph courtesy Pam Sparks).

Dottie Reese never got to see *42*. She died March 7, 2012, in Louisville. She was 89 years old. A death notice in the *Courier-Journal* listed her as the daughter of Arch C. and Laura Walton and said that she was a member of the local Audubon Country Club, Crescent Hill Presbyterian Church and Southeast Christian Church, as well as Capri Isle Golf Club in Venice, Florida. The notice called Pee Wee and Dottie "a devoted couple who adored their family."[64]

The same year that *42* premiered, vandals defaced the Robinson and Reese statue at Coney Island. Among the epithets: "Hile [sic] Hitler," "Die N-----" and "F--k Jackie Robinson and all N-----s." The *Daily News* offered $10,000 for information leading to the arrest and conviction of the vandals. An 87-year-old Ralph Branca told the *Daily News*, "I have no idea why anyone would do that. The statue signified a great moment in American history." Pee Wee's daughter, Barbara Dudgeon, said, "It's just sad that somebody feels it's necessary to do something like that."[65] In a newspaper column, Mark Reese asked, "Who would do such a thing?" Pee Wee, Mark wrote, would feel "a great sadness" over the crime. "There was nothing my dad hated more than prejudice—of any kind. He believed all, regardless of race, creed, color or sexual orientation, should be judged by their deeds as a member of the human race. Period."[66]

Roger Kahn once wrote, "For all the torment that besets America, there is something profoundly right with a country that can produce a Pee Wee Reese." The Hall of Fame shortstop stood up to bigotry and provided an example for others to follow. He did that before the U.S. Supreme Court decided in *Brown vs. Board of Education* that segregation in public schools is unconstitutional, before Rosa Parks refused to give up her seat to a white man on a Montgomery, Alabama, bus, and before President Eisenhower sent federal troops to Little Rock, Arkansas, and ordered them to escort nine Black students into the halls of Central High School.

Pee Wee Reese, the former ace marble shooter from Louisville, made his mark both as a person and as a player. He led the Dodgers both on the field and off it. One story goes that a young fan saw him in a hotel lobby and asked another player, "What does he do?" The player said, "Anything you want him to."[67] Roy Campanella agreed. "He could do everything to beat you: running, fielding, throwing, stealing, and hitting." Furthermore, Campanella added, "Reese was the captain of our team for ten years. He had real class."[68]

Chapter Notes

Preface

1. Roscoe McGowen, "PEE WEE … Pride of Flatbush," *The Sporting News*, December 26, 1956.
2. Jay Jaffe, *The Cooperstown Casebook: Who's in the Baseball Hall of Fame, Who Should Be In, and Who Should Pack Their Plaques* (New York: Thomas Dunne, 2017), 203.
3. WAR is not a standardized rating system. This book uses the WAR statistics compiled by Baseball-Reference.com. FanGraphs and Baseball Prospectus employ slightly different formulas to calculate WAR.
4. Jaffe, *Cooperstown Casebook*, 203.
5. Bill Borst, *A Fan's Memoir 1953–57* (St. Louis: Krank Books, 1982) 15.
6. William F. McNeil, *The Dodgers Encyclopedia*. (New York: Sports Publishing), 97.
7. Peter Golenbock, *Bums: An Oral History of the Brooklyn Dodgers* (New York: G. P. Putnam's Sons, 1984), 148.
8. McNeil, 97.
9. Steve Bailey, "Reese Remembered as Great, Humble Man," *Indianapolis Star*, August 16, 1999.
10. Hank Kurz, Jr., "Baseball Still Recognizable to Pee Wee," *Indiana Gazette* (PA), August 25, 1997
11. Ibid.

Chapter 1

1. Peter Golenbock, *Bums: An Oral History of the Brooklyn Dodgers* (New York: G. P. Putnam's Sons, 1984), 62.
2. http://visitmeadecounty.org/history/.
3. Ibid.
4. Bob Janiskee, "The New River Raisin National Battlefield Park Highlights One of the Bloodiest Conflicts of a Seldom Mentioned War," December 11, 2009. https://www.nationalparkstraveler.org/.
5. https://www.history.ky.gov/pdf/Community Services/LM42MeadeCounty.pdf.
6. U.S. Census Bureau, "State and County Quick Facts."
7. Visit.meadecounty.org, http://visitmeadecounty.org/frontier-meade-county/.
8. Ibid.
9. A few sources spell the first name of Pee Wee Reese's grandfather as "Blant" rather than "Blent." The headstone at the Ekron Baptist Church Cemetery in Meade County, Kentucky, reads "Marion Reese, 1854–1923."
10. 1900 United States Federal Census—Ancestry.com. Some sources indicate Carl Reese's dad spelled his first name "Blent," while others indicate the spelling as "Blant."
11. Ibid.
12. Gene Shoor, *The Pee Wee Reese Story* (New York: Julian Messner, 1956), 15.
13. Ibid., 17.
14. Kentucky, U.S., Birth Index, 1911–1999—Ancestry.com.
15. 1930 United States Federal Census—Ancestry.com.
16. Pee Wee Reese with Tim Cohane, "Pee Wee Reese's Own Story: 14 Years a Bum!" *Baseball Digest*, May 1954 (condensed from *Look*).
17. Golenbock, *Bums*, 62.
18. Ibid. Six of the Reese children reached adulthood. According to records on ancestry.com and findagrave.com, Emma Reese gave birth to two other children. Emma Reese was born on August 24, 1922, and died the following day. Lucile Reese was born January 7, 1929, and died that same day. The Reeses' oldest child, Pauline Black, died at age 25 on March 1, 1934, while in childbirth, https://www.ancestry.com/discoveryui-content/view/86081314:60525.
19. Isabel McLennan McMeekin, *Louisville: The Gateway City* (New York: Julian Messner, 1946), 70.
20. Ibid.
21. A House Divided: Civil War Kentucky | American Battlefield Trust (battlefields.org), https://www.battlefields.org/learn/articles/house-divided-civil-war-kentucky.
22. Ibid.
23. Ibid.
24. Bob Hill, *Crack of the Bat: The Louisville Slugger Story* (Champaign, IL: Sports Publishing, 2000), 33.
25. https://www.biggestuscities.com/1920.
26. Golenbock, *Bums*, 62.
27. Roger Kahn, *Into My Own: The Remarkable People and Events That Shaped a Life* (New York: Thomas Dunne, 2006), 93.
28. Schoor, *The Pee Wee Reese Story*, 17.

29. Pee Wee Reese with Tim Cohane, "Reese's Own Story: 14 Years a Bum," *Baseball Digest*, May 1954 (condensed from *Look*).
30. Kentucky Historical Society, Kentucky's Civil War: Lexington's Frances Peter, https://history.ky.gov/pdf/Library/LEGM014-Baseball%20in%20Kentucky.pdf.
31. Hill, *Crack of the Bat*, 32.
32. Ibid.
33. Louisville Colonels Attendance, Stadiums, and Park Factors | Baseball-Reference.com (baseball-reference.com), https://www.baseball-reference.com/teams/LOU/attend.shtml.
34. David Magee, *Sweet Spot: 125 Years of Baseball and the Louisville Slugger* (Chicago: Triumph, 2009), 4.
35. Ibid., 11.
36. Hill, *Crack of the Bat*, 34.
37. Magee, *Sweet Spot*, 11.
38. Hill, *Crack of the Bat*, 34.
39. Ibid., 35.
40. Magee, *Sweet Spot*, 14.
41. Hill, *Crack of the Bat*, 36.
42. Magee, *Sweet Spot*, 15.
43. Ibid.
44. Schoor, *The Pee Wee Reese Story*, 19.
45. Milton Richman, "Pee Wee Reese Is Very Content," *Petoskey News-Review* (MI), July 17, 1981.
46. Golenbock, *Bums*, 62.
47. Rick Bozich, "Legend on Diamond, Gem in Life," *Louisville Courier-Journal*, August 15, 1999.
48. Kahn, *Into My Own*, 93.
49. Schoor, *The Pee Wee Reese Story*, 20.
50. "Ballplayer Pee Wee Reese Has Job of Church Deacon—Is 'Just a Rookie,'" *Hartford Currant*, July 28, 1956.
51. Ibid.
52. Marbles.com, https://imarbles/com/historyofmarbles.php.
53. "Game of Marbles Builder of Boys Educator Claims," *Elmira Star Gazette* (NY), April 13, 1932.
54. dupontmanual.com/history.html.
55. The author is no relation to the former church league coach.
56. Rob Edelman, Pee Wee Reese SABR bio, https://sabr.org/bioproj/person/pee-wee-reese/.
57. Schoor, *The Pee Wee Reese Story*, 29.
58. Ibid.
59. Ibid., 30.
60. Kahn, *Into My Own*, 94.
61. Roger Kahn. *The Era: 1947–1957, When the Yankees, the Giants, and the Dodgers Ruled the World*. (New York: Ticknor & Fields, 1993), 94.
62. Roger Kahn, "A Tribute to ... Captain Courageous," *Los Angeles Times*, August 19, 1999.
63. Kahn, *Into My Own*, 94.
64. Golenbock, *Bums*, 62.
65. Schoor, *The Pee Wee Reese Story*, 35.
66. Ibid., 36.
67. Bruce Dudley, "Louisville Hails Bush-Red Sox Purchase; Price Under $200,000," *The Sporting News*, September 15, 1938.
68. Schoor, *The Pee Wee Reese Story*, 38.
69. Kentucky, U.S. Death Records, 1852–1965.

70. David Halberstam, *Summer of '49* (New York: William Morrow, 1989), 133.
71. Ibid.
72. Rob Edelman, Pee Wee Reese SABR bio, https://sabr.org/bioproj/person/pee-wee-reese/.
73. Tommy Fitzgerald, "Brooklyn in $75,000 Deal for Reese, Who 'Didn't Want to be a Dodger,'" *The Sporting News*, July 27, 1939. Most newspaper accounts report that four players, in addition to the $35,000, were sent from Brooklyn to Boston. According to a database on baseball-reference.com, three players were sent from the Dodgers to the Red Sox, although the site only lists pitcher Red Evans and outfielder Art Parks. Neither player ever played a game for the Red Sox. Evans had a lifetime record of 1–11 with a 6.21 ERA. Parks batted .275 lifetime over 255 at-bats.
74. Ibid.
75. Ibid.
76. Ibid.
77. Ibid.
78. Ibid.
79. Schoor, *The Pee Wee Reese Story*, 46.

Chapter 2

1. *Lincoln Star*, February 20, 1932.
2. *Marshall News Messenger* (TX), July 13, 1936.
3. *Muncie Star Press* (IN), September 4, 1937.
4. Sid Keener, "Sid Keener's Columns," *St. Louis Star and Times*, May 21, 1937.
5. Bruce Spinks, "Babe Herman's Son in Tune," *Honolulu Advertiser*, March 7, 1971.
6. "Baseball's Best Put-Downs, Put-Ons," *Los Angeles Times*, February 14, 1986.
7. Tommy Holmes, "Bill Brandt Recalls Babe Herman's Dash," *Brooklyn Eagle*, June 11, 1947.
8. Ibid.
9. Bruce Spinks, "Babe Herman's Son in Tune," *Honolulu Advertiser*, March 7, 1971.
10. Frank Graham, *The Brooklyn Dodgers: An Informal History* (Carbondale: Southern Illinois University Press, 2002) 111.
11. Peter Golenbock, *Bums: An Oral History of the Brooklyn Dodgers* (New York: G. P. Putnam's Sons, 1984), 23.
12. James L. Terry, *Long Before the Dodgers: Baseball in Brooklyn, 1855–1884* (Jefferson, NC: McFarland, 2002), 9.
13. Bruce Chadwick and David M. Spindel, *The Dodgers: Memories and Memorabilia from Brooklyn to L.A.* (New York: Abbeville Press, 1993), 16.
14. Terry, *Long Before the Dodgers*, 18.
15. Ibid., 94.
16. Glenn Stout, *The Dodgers: 120 Years of Dodgers Baseball* (Boston: Houghton Mifflin, 2004), 29.
17. William F. McNeil, *The Dodgers Encyclopedia* (New York: Sports Publishing, 2012), 5.
18. Graham, *The Brooklyn Dodgers*, 23.
19. John Saccoman, Charles Ebbets SABR bio https://sabr.org/bioproj/person/12f35f52
20. William F. McNeil, *The Dodgers Encyclopedia* (New York: Sports Publishing, 2012), 452.

21. *Ibid.*
22. Grantland Rice, "Superbas Open Season with a 1–0 Shutout Defeat," *Brooklyn Daily Eagle*, April 10, 1913.
23. Alex Semchuck, Wilbert Robinson SABR bio https://sabr.org/bioproj/person/5536caf5
24. *Ibid.*
25. Harry Jones, "Uncle Wilbert Robinson Couldn't Stay Serious as Manager of Daffy Dodgers," *Baltimore Evening Sun*, February 11, 1957.
26. *Ibid.*; Harold Rosenthal, "Old Legend Out with Dodgers—Casey Didn't Drop Grapefruit," *The Sporting News*, December 4, 1957.
27. John C. Skipper, *Dazzy Vance: A Biography of the Brooklyn Dodgers Hall of Famer* (Jefferson, NC: McFarland, 2007), 70.
28. "Baseball World Mourns Ebbets; Funeral Tuesday," *Brooklyn Daily Eagle*, April 19, 1925.
29. Golenbock, *Bums*, 20.
30. "When Robbie Learned Bad News," *Brooklyn Daily Eagle*, October 25, 1931.
31. Tommy Holmes, "Max Carey Promises to Be a '12-Month' Manager for Brooklyn," *Brooklyn Daily Eagle*, October 24, 1937.
32. Alex Semchuck, Wilbert Robinson SABR bio https://sabr.org/bioproj/person/5536caf5.
33. Robert Creamer, *Stengel: His Life and Times* (New York: Dell, 1985), 185.
34. Graham, *The Brooklyn Dodgers*, 141.
35. Prescott Sullivan, "The Lowdown," *San Francisco Examiner*, August 24, 1943.
36. Warren Corbett, Red Barber SABR bio, https://sabr.org/bioproj/person/red-barber.
37. John E. Wray, "First Night Baseball game in Majors Real Success; 20,000 Attend," *St. Louis Post-Dispatch*, May 5, 1935.
38. G. Richard McKelvey, *The MacPhails: Baseball's First Family of the Front Office* (Jefferson, NC: McFarland, 2000), 19.
39. "Schott and Holly Are to Face Tigers Today; Dodgers Look Like Dangerous Ballclub," *Cincinnati Enquirer*, March 26, 1938.
40. *Ibid.*
41. McKelvey, *The MacPhails*, 21.
42. Creamer, *Stengel*, 413.
43. Jeffrey Marlett, Leo Durocher SABR bio, https://sabr.org/bioproj/person/leo-durocher/.
44. Leo Durocher with Ed Linn, *Nice Guys Finish Last* (New York: Simon and Schuster, 1975), 70.
45. Hy Turkin, "Durocher to Pilot Dodgers for Year," *New York Daily News*, October 13, 1938.
46. Tommy Holmes, "Durocher Picked as Morale Builder, MacPhail Explains," *Brooklyn Eagle*, October 13, 1938.
47. Maury Allen with Susan Walker, *Dixie Walker of the Dodgers* (Tuscaloosa: University of Alabama Press, 2010), 105.
48. Bill Ritt, "Durocher Does Fine Job as Pilot of Brooklyn Dodgers," *Massillon Evening Independent* (OH), October 5, 1939.
49. Gene Schoor, *The Pee Wee Reese Story* (New York: Julian Messner, 1956), 44.
50. *Ibid.*, 45.
51. *Ibid.*, 46.
52. Lee Scott, "Call Harold Reese, New Dodger Rookie, Fastest Base Runner Since Ty Cobb," *Brooklyn Citizen*, July 22, 1939.
53. Jack Mahon, "Dodgers Reese Tagged as Real Boy Wonder," *New York Daily News*, August 13, 1939.
54. Gerry Moore, "Red Sox Rookie Hurlers Give Cronin Some Tips," *Boston Globe*, August 22, 1939.
55. Rob Edelman, Pee Wee Reese SABR Bio, https://sabr.org/bioproj/person/68671329.
56. Harry Grayson, "The Payoff," *Franklin News-Herald* (PA), September 2, 1939.
57. Tommy Fitzgerald, "Brooklyn in $75,000 Deal for Reese, Who 'Didn't Want to Be a Dodger,'" *The Sporting News*, July 27, 1939.
58. "Reese Glad He's Sold to Brooklyn Club Now," *Hartford Courant* (CT), July 20, 1939.

Chapter 3

1. Dean Eagle, "Ruby's Report," *Louisville Courier-Journal*, May 22, 1949.
2. Roscoe McGowen, "PEE WEE … Pride of Flatbush," *The Sporting News*, December 19, 1956.
3. *Ibid.*
4. Gene Schoor, *The Pee Wee Reese Story* (New York: Julian Messner, 1956), 48.
5. Peter Golenbock, *Bums: An Oral History of the Brooklyn Dodgers* (New York: Putnam, 1984), 63.
6. "Dodgers Boosting Pee Wee Reese as Candidate for 'Rookie-of-the-Year,'" *Marion Star* (OH), March 20, 1940.
7. *Ibid.*
8. Schoor, *The Pee Wee Reese Story*, 50.
9. "Dodgers Boosting Pee Wee Reese."
10. Schoor, *The Pee Wee Reese Story*, 51.
11. Harry Ferguson, "'Pee Wee' Reese Rookie to Watch This Season," *Middleboro Daily News* (KY), March 13, 1940.
12. Golenbock, *Bums*, 63.
13. Charles Dexter, "Reese—Dean of the Dodgers," *Baseball Digest*, June 1952.
14. Tommy Fitzgerald, "Durocher Thinks Peewee Is Great," *Louisville Courier-Journal*, March 9, 1940.
15. *Ibid.*
16. Whitley Martin, "Dodgers Have Good Supply of Fine Shortstops," *Owensboro Messenger* (KY), March 8, 1940.
17. Tommy Holmes, "Reese, Vosmik, Cullenbine among Ten in Joint Debut," *Brooklyn Eagle*, April 12, 1940.
18. *The Sporting News*, March 21, 1940.
19. George Kirksey, "Cincinnati, with Solid Pitching, Is Picked to Win," *Pittston Gazette* (PA), April 5, 1940.
20. "Dodgers Boosting Pee Wee Reese."
21. Leo Durocher, *The Dodgers and Me: The Inside Story* (Chicago: Ziff-Davis, 1948), 50.
22. *Ibid.*, 52.
23. Judson Bailey (Associated Press), "Rival

Bosses Claim All Clubs Stronger as First Day Nears," *Moline Dispatch* (IL), April 15, 1940.
 24. Edward R. Murrow, "The Voice from London," *Reader's Digest Illustrated Story of World War II* (Pleasantville, NY: Reader's Digest, 1969), 131.
 25. https://www.thebalance.com/unemployment-rate-by-year-3305506.
 26. Tommy Holmes, "There's Power Plus in Those New Dodgers," *Brooklyn Eagle*, April 24, 1940.
 27. Tommy Holmes, "Carleton's No-Hitter Replete with Drama, *Brooklyn Eagle*, May 1, 1940.
 28. *Ibid.*
 29. Schoor, *The Pee Wee Reese Story*, 53.
 30. Eddie Brietz, "MacPhail Says He Can Get Medwick for Pee Wee Reese," *Appleton Post-Crescent* (WI), April 16, 1940.
 31. Golenbock, *Bums*, 65.
 32. E. C. "Doc" Osborn, "Dug Outta the Sports Bag," *Harlington Valley Morning Star* (TX), August 16, 1940.
 33. *Ibid.*
 34. *Ibid.*
 35. Tommy Holmes, "Dodgers Aim to Make Hay While Phils Pine," *Brooklyn Eagle*, May 27, 1940.
 36. Lee Scott, "Pee Wee Reese's First Major League Home Run Keeps Dodgers in Lead," *Brooklyn Citizen*, May 27, 1940.
 37. Schoor, *The Pee Wee Reese Story*, 10.
 38. Golenbock, *Bums*, 63.
 39. Schoor, *The Pee Wee Reese Story*, 10.
 40. *Ibid.*, 12.
 41. *Ibid.*
 42. Associated Press, "Pee Wee Reese Resting Easily," *Palm Beach Post* (FL), June 3, 1940.
 43. Harold Parrott, "Hang Up the Pennant! We've Got Medwick," *Brooklyn Eagle*, June 13, 1940.
 44. Ed Hughes, "Ed Hughes' Column," *Brooklyn Eagle*, June 13, 1940.
 45. Derrick Goold, *100 Things Cardinals Fans Should Know and Do Before They Die.* (Chicago: Triumph, 2010), 107.
 46. *Ibid.*
 47. *Ibid.*, 56.
 48. George Kirksey, "Joe Medwick Is Struck by Pitched Ball," *Cushing Daily Citizen* (OK), June 19, 1940.
 49. "O'Dwyer, Frick Probe 'Beaning' of Joe Medwick," *Brooklyn Eagle*, June 19, 1940.
 50. *Ibid.*
 51. W. Vernon Tietjen, "Bob Bowman, Home with Inquiry, Tells of Medwick 'Beaning' and MacPhail's Defiance," *St. Louis Star and Times*, June 25, 1940.
 52. *Ibid.*
 53. Durocher, *The Dodgers and Me*, 57.
 54. *Ibid.*
 55. Harry Forbes, "Dodgers Slug Bucs, 10–8, Fitz Captures Sixth," *New York Daily News*, June 22, 1940.
 56. Golenbock, *Bums*, 65.
 57. *Ibid.*
 58. AP, "Reese Stars as Brooklyn Scores, 7–3," *Richmond Times Dispatch*, July 4, 1940.
 59. McGowen, "PEE WEE … Pride of Flatbush."
 60. Hy Turkin, "Reese's 4-Run Homer Blasts Giants, 7–3," *New York Daily News*, July 4, 1940.
 61. Schoor, *The Pee Wee Reese Story*, 57.
 62. "Cincy's Juggernaut Rolls Over Contenders, Jolts Injury Jinx," *The Sporting News*, August 4, 1940.
 63. *Ibid.*
 64. Donald Honig, *Baseball When the Grass Was Real: Baseball from the Twenties to the Forties, Told by the Men Who Played It* (Lincoln: University of Nebraska, 1975), 285.
 65. Leo Durocher, *Nice Guys Finish Last*, 108.
 66. Hy Turkin, "Cubs Top Dodgers, 2–1; Reese Belts Homer," *New York Daily News*, August 4, 1940.
 67. Harry Forbes, "Dodgers Nip Cubs, 7–6, After Losing, 11–3," *New York Daily News*, August 5, 1940.
 68. *Ibid.*
 69. "Dressen Tells Us Why His Team Will Beat the Reds," *Cincinnati Enquirer*, August 9, 1940.
 70. Harry Forbes, "Reese Lost for Season as Dodgers Bow, 4–2," *New York Daily News*, August 16, 1940.
 71. "Claude Passeau Pitches Cubs to 1–0 Win Over Cincinnati Reds," *Racine Journal Times* (WI), August 16, 1940.
 72. Charles Dexter, "Reese—Dean of the Dodgers," *Baseball Digest*, June 1952.
 73. H. L. Nations, "Peewee Returns—Because He Has To," *Louisville Courier-Journal*, August 21, 1940.
 74. AP, "Durocher Is Bad with the Office," *Palm Beach Post* (FL), September 12, 1940.
 75. AP, "Veteran Brooklyn Pitcher Honored," *Muncie Evening Press* (IN), September 17, 1940.
 76. *Dodgers: From Coast to Coast.* (San Diego: Skybox Press/Abrams, 2012), 47.
 77. *Ibid.*

Chapter 4

 1. Hy Turkin, "Reese's Heel OK, Doctors Find," *New York Daily News*, December 17, 1940.
 2. "Shortstop Situation Improves in New York," *New York Daily News*, January 5, 1941.
 3. Photo caption, *New York Daily News*, January 28, 1941.
 4. J. Roy Stockton, "Born for the Gashouse," *Saturday Evening Post*, May 22, 1937.
 5. *Ibid.*
 6. *Ibid.*
 7. John Lardner, "3,000 Hits Is Goal of Paul Waner When He Joins Brooklyn," *Miami News*, February 7, 1941.
 8. G. Richard McKelvey, *The MacPhails: Baseball's First Family of the Front Office* (Jefferson, NC: McFarland, 2000), 45.
 9. *Ibid.*, 47.
 10. Don Warfield, *The Roaring Redhead* (South Bend, IN: Diamond Communications, 1987), 99.
 11. Hy Turkin, "Dodgers, Farm Clubs to Wear Helmets," *New York Daily News*, March 9, 1941.

12. George Scherck, "Down the Stretch," *Oakland*, March 12, 1941.

13. Victor O. Jones, "Recent Beanings Emphasize Need of Strong Helmets," *Boston Globe*, August 15, 1941.

14. Turkin, "Dodgers, Farm Clubs to Wear Helmets."

15. Frank Graham, *The Brooklyn Dodgers: An Informal History* (Carbondale: Southern Illinois University Press, 2002), 194.

16. Leo Durocher with Ed Linn, *Nice Guys Finish Last* (New York: Simon and Schuster, 1975), 59.

17. Ibid., 60.

18. Ibid., 195.

19. Ibid.

20. Gayle Talbot (Associated Press), "Dodgers Find Cuban Sun Is Fast Worker," *Appleton Post-Crescent* (WI), February 19, 1941.

21. Ibid.

22. United Press, "11 Giants Still Unsigned; Reese Skittish in Practice," *Akron Beacon Journal*, Feb. 17, 1941.

23. Gayle Talbot, "McGrew Praises Ability of Pee Wee Reese," *Tampa Times*, February 13, 1941.

24. Ibid.

25. Ibid.

26. Ibid.

27. Tommy Holmes, "Rizzuto Wins First Round from Reese," *Brooklyn Eagle*, March 18, 1941.

28. Whitley Martin, "Gabby Guy Is Needed on Infield," *Cincinnati Enquirer*, March 15, 1941.

29. Ibid.

30. Tom Meany, "Loyal Watchers Daffy About Dodger Flag Changes; Scribes Already Arguing About World Series Plans, *The Sporting News*, March 20, 1941.

31. "Great American Stories: Winston Churchill's Quote," Realclearpolitics.com, October 23, 2020, https://www.realclearpublicaffairs.com/articles/2020/10/23/great_american_stories_winston_churchills_quote_581769.html.

32. https://detroithistorical.org/learn/encyclopedia-of-detroit/arsenal-democracy.

33. https://www.nps.gov/valr/learn/historyculture/pearl-harbor.htm.

34. Graham, *The Brooklyn Dodgers*, 195.

35. Maury Allen and Susan Walker, *Dixie Walker of the Dodgers: The People's Choice* (Tuscaloosa: University of Alabama Press, 2010), 117

36. Hy Turkin, "Dodgers Rip B's, 8–0, for Hamlin, 8–0, for Wyatt," *New York Daily News*, April 20, 1941.

37. Durocher, *The Dodgers and Me*, 85.

38. Harry Grayson, "Reiser Said He Could Hit any Pitcher ... Dodgers Now Know He Was Right," *Owensboro Messenger* (KY), June 7, 1941.

39. Sidney Jacobson, *Pete Reiser: The Rough-and-Tumble Career of the Perfect Ballplayer* (Jefferson, NC: McFarland, 2004), 99.

40. J. G. T. Spink, "Looping the Loops," *The Sporting News*, September 11, 1941.

41. Dave Anderson. *Pennant Races: Baseball at Its Best*. (New York: Doubleday, 1994), 133.

42. Ibid., 83.

43. Leo Durocher with Ed Linn, *Nice Guys Finish Last*, 120.

44. Ibid.

45. Ibid.

46. Tommy Holmes, "Herman's Brilliant Debut Sparks Flock," *Brooklyn Eagle*, May 7, 1941.

47. Durocher with Linn, *Nice Guys Finish Last*, 120.

48. Gene Schoor, *The Pee Wee Reese Story* (New York: Julian Messner, 1956), 61.

49. Ibid., 63.

50. "Lippy Benches Weak-Hitting Reese and Will Guide Team from Short in Hopes of Putting an End to Slump," *Brooklyn Citizen*, May 21, 1941.

51. Hy Turkin, "Reese Benched, Durocher Returns to Shortstop," *New York Daily News*, May 21, 1941.

52. Hy Turkin, "Cards Lead Dodgers; Reese Back at SS," *New York Daily News*, May 23, 1941.

53. Lou Smith, "Brooks Blow Up in Eighth and Redlegs Score Six Runs," *Cincinnati Enquirer*, June 8, 1941.

54. Tommy Holmes, "Reds Get 6 in 8th, Beat Dodgers, 8–3," *Brooklyn Eagle*, June 8, 1941.

55. Hy Turkin, "Reds Drop Dodgers to 2D as Walters Wins, 8–3," *New York Daily News*, June 8, 1941.

56. Michael Shapiro, The *Last Good Season* (New York: Random House, 2003), 60.

57. Ibid.

58. Jack Smith, "Flock, Cards Divide Before 39,107," *New York Daily News*, August 27, 1941.

59. Lee Scott, "Battle to Finish Looms Between Pace-Setting Dodgers and the Cardinals," *Brooklyn Citizen*, August 27, 1941.

60. Jack Smith, "Flock, Cards Divide Before 39, 107."

61. Dick McCann, "Reese Bemoans Errors Which Cost 2nd Game," *New York Daily News*, August 27, 1941.

62. Leo Durocher, *The Dodgers and Me: The Inside Story* (Chicago: Ziff-Davis, 1948), 82.

63. Ibid.

64. J. Roy Stockton, "Wyatt Beats Copper; 3 Hits for Each Team," *St. Louis Post-Dispatch*, September 14, 1941.

65. "Reese Puts on a Great Show for Home Folk," *Brooklyn Eagle*, September 15, 1941.

66. Ibid.

67. Ibid.

68. Tommy Holmes, "Cards Refuse to Be Brushed Off by Dodgers," *Brooklyn Eagle*, September 15, 1941.

69. Jacobson, *Pete Reiser*, 88.

70. Durocher, *The Dodgers and Me*, 104.

71. Pee Wee Reese, "Pee Wee Reese's Own Story: 14 Years a Bum," *Baseball Digest*, May 1954.

72. "Political Foes Bury the Hatchet to Go to Bat for the Dodgers," *Brooklyn Eagle*, September 30, 1941.

73. Donald Honig, *Baseball When the Grass Was Real: Baseball from the Twenties to the Forties Told by the Men Who Played It* (Lincoln: University of Nebraska Press, 1975), 299.

74. Durocher, *The Dodgers and Me*, 105.
75. *Ibid.*, 106.
76. Judson Bailey (AP), "Curt Davis May Be Dodgers No. 1 Boy and Face Ruffing Today," *Helena Independent* (MT), October 1, 1941.
77. Harry Grayson, NEA, "Brooklyn Dodgers Lauded as National's Best Series Entry Since Cards in '34," *Marshfield News-Herald* (WI), September 30, 1941.
78. Billy Goodrich, "Good Citizens of Brooklyn Rally Behind Dodgers," *Brooklyn Eagle*, September 30, 1941.
79. *New York Herald Tribune*, September 30, 1941.
80. Bob Hill, "Pee Wee Reese Also Knew How to Play the Game of Life," *Louisville Courier-Journal*, August 17, 1999.
81. Jack Smith, "Yanks Nip Flock, 3–2, In Opener as Gordon Smashes Home Run," *New York Daily News*, October 2, 1941.
82. Dick McCann, "Wasdell Muffed Sign, Reese Ran on Own," *New York Daily News*, October 2, 1953.
83. Al Del Greco, "At Random in Sportsdom," *Hackensack Record* (NJ), October 2, 1941.
84. *Ibid.*
85. Tommy Holmes, "Flock Sees Series Victory; Other Guys Really Worried," *Brooklyn Eagle*, October 3, 1941.
86. Game 3 of the 1941 World Series was scheduled for October 3. Heavy rain forced a postponement, and the teams played the following day.
87. Grantland Rice, "Yankee Club Is Heading for Noisiest Ball Park," *Hartford Courant*, October 3, 1941.
88. Graham, *The Brooklyn Dodgers: An Informal History*, 210.
89. Judson Bailey, Associated Press, "Yankees Gain Lead Over Bums in World Series with 2–1 Victory," *Kingsport Times* (TN), October 5, 1941.
90. Durocher and Linn, *Nice Guys Finish Last*, 139.
91. *Ibid.*
92. Judson Bailey, "Yankees Rally to Beat Dodgers, 7–4," *Harrisburg Telegraph*, October 6, 1941.
93. Associated Press, "Owen Is World Series Goat as Yankees Beat Dodgers by 7 to 4," *Billings Gazette* (MT), October 6, 1941.
94. Judson Bailey, "Yankees Rally to Beat Dodgers, 7–4."
95. Tommy Holmes, "MacPhail Confirms the Lip's '42 Post," *Brooklyn Eagle*, October 6, 1942.
96. James L. Kilgallen, "Mickey Owen Takes Full Blame for Pitch That Cost Ball Game," *Wilmington News Journal* (DE), October 6, 1941.
97. Charles Dunkley, Associated Press, "Series Dressing Room," *Muncie Star Press* (IN), October 6, 1941.
98. Associated Press, "Owen Puts All Blame on Himself," *Asbury Park Press* (NJ), October 6, 1941.
99. Peter Golenbock, *Bums: An Oral History of the Brooklyn Dodgers* (New York: G. P. Putnam's Sons, 1984), 74.
100. Lyle Spatz, *Hugh Casey: The Triumphs and Tragedies of a Brooklyn Dodger* (Lanham, MD: Rowman & Littlefield, 2017), 98.
101. Tommy Holmes, "MacPhail Confirms the Lip's '42 Post," *Brooklyn Eagle*, October 6, 1942.
102. Spatz, *Hugh Casey*, 98.
103. Durocher with Linn, *Nice Guys Finish Last*, 139.
104. Warren Corbett, Tiny Bonham SABR biography, https://sabr.org/bioproj/person/d7503bf4.
105. Schoor, *The Pee Wee Reese Story*, 70.
106. *Ibid.*

Chapter 5

1. https://pearlharbor.org/faqs/how-many-people-died-at-pearl-harbor-during-the-attack/.
2. "American People Are United by the Treachery of Japan," *Brooklyn Eagle*, December 8, 1941.
3. "Recruits Rush to Army, Navy Stations Here," *Brooklyn Eagle*, December 8, 1941.
4. United Press, "U.S. Declares War on Axis," *Brooklyn Eagle*, December 11, 1941.
5. http://www.baseball-almanac.com/prz_lfr.shtml.
6. J. G. Taylor Spink, "Player of the Year," *The Sporting News*, January 22, 1942.
7. John Klima, *The Game Must Go On: Hank Greenberg, Pete Gray, and the Great Days of Baseball on the Home Front in WW II* (New York: Thomas Dunne, 2015), 63.
8. International News Service (INS), "War Aid Plan Mapped by Brooklyn Dodgers," *Arizona Republic* (Phoenix), February 18, 1942.
9. "Reese Signs for $9,000; Injured Knee Okay," *New York Daily News*, February 13, 1942.
10. Lee Scott, "Leo Durocher May Decide to Sign Player-Manager's Contract for 1942," *Brooklyn Citizen*, January 15, 1942.
11. *Ibid.*
12. Guy Butler, "Leo Durocher, Here, Says Baseball Men Ready to Render U.S. Every Aid," *Miami News*, February 11, 1942.
13. Dan Daniel, "A Three-Way Problem in National League," *The Sporting News*, April 16, 1942.
14. Guy Butler, "Leo Durocher, Here."
15. Gene Shoor, *The Pee Wee Reese Story* (New York: Julian Messner, 1956), 41.
16. Roscoe McGowen, "PEE WEE … Pride of Flatbush," *The Sporting News*, December 19, 1956.
17. Lyle Spatz, *Dixie Walker: A Life in Baseball* (Jefferson, NC: McFarland, 2011), 103.
18. "Pee Wee Reese and Bride," *Indianapolis News*, April 4, 1942.
19. G. Richard McKelvey, *The MacPhails: Baseball's First Family of the Front-Office* (Jefferson, NC: McFarland, 2000), 56.
20. *Ibid.*
21. Sidney Jacobson, *Pete Reiser: The Rough-and-Tumble Career of the Perfect Ballplayer* (Jefferson, NC: McFarland, 2004), 107.
22. Whitney Martin, "Durocher Insists Pee Wee Reese Is Really Great Player," *Allentown Morning Call*, January 20, 1942.

23. *Ibid.*
24. Schoor, *The Pee Wee Reese Story*, 76.
25. J. G. Taylor Spink, "Looping the Loops," *The Sporting News*, April 9, 1942.
26. *Ibid.*
27. Tommy Holmes, "Reese, Allen Get Dodgers Off Fast," *Brooklyn Eagle*, April 15, 1942.
28. *Ibid.*
29. Hy Turkin, "Dodgers Win in 12th, 4–0, on Reese's Hit," *New York Daily News*, April 23, 1942.
30. *Ibid.*
31. Donna Ford, "Other Women's Lives," *Shreveport Times*, July 12, 1942.
32. Hy Turkin, "Flock Clips Reds, 5–4, in 10th; Ducky Hitless," *New York Daily News*, June 27, 1942.
33. Lee Scott, "Rampaging Dodgers Now Cooling of Cincinnati Reds' Pennant Fever,"+ *Brooklyn Citizen*, June 26, 1942.
34. UP, "Home Runs by Boudreau, York Give A.L. All-Stars 3–1 Win Over Nationals," *Monongahela Daily Republican* (PA), July 7, 1942.
35. Dick McCann, "Flock Tops Reds, 5–0, 3–2; 2d Game Goes 15 Innings," *New York Daily News*, July 12, 1942.
36. "Pee Wee Reese Going Good," *Paterson Morning Call* (NJ), July 28, 1942.
37. Hy Turkin, "Can't Erase Reese," *New York Daily News*, July 24, 1942.
38. *Ibid.*
39. Lee Scott, "Death-Knell of Twilight Sounded as Result of Last Night's Fiasco," *Brooklyn Citizen*, August 5, 1942.
40. Dick McCann, "Giants, Dodgers Tie, 1–1, as Dimout Voids Reese's 4-Run Homer," *New York Daily News*, August 5, 1942.
41. Lee Scott, "Death-Knell of Twilight Sounded as Result of Last Night's Fiasco," *Brooklyn Citizen*, August 5, 1942.
42. *Ibid.*
43. Gene Schoor, *Pee Wee Reese Story* (New York: Julian Messner, 1956), 78.
44. Jack Smith, "Hits Make Heroes," *New York Daily News*, September 12, 1942.
45. Sid Keener, "Sid Keener's Column," *St. Louis Star and Times*, September 12, 1942.
46. Peter Golenbock, *The Spirit of St. Louis: A History of the St. Louis Cardinals and Browns* (New York: William Morrow, 2000), 242.
47. AP, "Circuit Clout by Rook Sinks Dodgers, 2–1," *Arizona Republic*, September 13, 1942.
48. *Ibid.*
49. Judson Bailey, "Cards Edge Dodgers, 2–1, Tie for Lead," *Rochester Democrat and Chronicle*, September 13, 1942.
50. AP, "Circuit Clout by Rook Sinks Dodgers, 2–1," *Arizona Republic*, September 13, 1942.
51. UP, "Cardinals Nip Dodgers, 2 to 1, Tie for First," *Rochester Democrat and Chronicle*, September 13, 1942.
52. Tommy Holmes, "Switch in Starting Hurlers Proves Costly to Dodgers," *Brooklyn Eagle*, September 18, 1942.
53. Don Warfield, *The Roaring Redhead: Larry MacPhail—Baseball's Great Innovator* (South Bend, IN: Diamond Communications, 1987), 144.
54. Hilda Chester http://www.baseballreliquary.org/awards/hilda-award-recipients/hilda-chester/.
55. Sam Davis (NEA), "And When You Hear the Gong, It's Hilda Chester Time at Ebbets Field," *Chillicothe Gazette* (OH), September 9, 1943.
56. *The Brooklyn Dodgers: The Original America's Team*, Virgil Films, 2003.
57. Donald Honig, *Baseball When the Grass Was Real: Baseball from Twenties to the Forties Told by the Men Who Played It* (Lincoln: University of Nebraska Press, 1993), 305.
58. John Keegan, *The Second World War* (New York: Penguin, 2005), 275.
59. McKelvey, *The MacPhails*, 59.
60. "Well, This Is Queer," *Washington Post*, June 29, 1907.
61. Andy McCue, Branch Rickey, SABR bio https://sabr.org/bioproj/person/branch-rickey/.
62. *Ibid.*
63. Murray Polner, *Branch Rickey: A Biography* (Jefferson, NC: McFarland, 207), 69.
64. *Ibid.*, 79.
65. "Fans in 9-Hour Rampage Give Vent to Noisy Joy Over Cardinals' Victory," *St. Louis Post-Dispatch*, October 11, 1926.
66. *Ibid.*
67. "Rickey Is Honored for Assistance in Building Up Cards," *St. Louis Star and Times*, October 19, 1926.
68. Polner, *Branch Rickey*, 96.
69. *Ibid.*, 81.
70. *Ibid.*, 108.
71. Harold Parrott, "Meet Mr. Rickey," *Brooklyn Eagle*, October 30, 1942.
72. Golenbock, *The Spirit of St. Louis*, 248–249.
73. Polner, *Branch Rickey*, 109.
74. Andy McCue, Branch Rickey SABR bio, sabr.org/bioproj/person/branch-rickey/.
75. Polner, *Branch Rickey*, 114.
76. Paul Dickson, *Leo Durocher: Baseball's Prodigal Son* (New York: Bloomsbury, 2017), 111.
77. *Ibid.*
78. *Ibid.*
79. Leo Durocher with Ed Linn, *Nice Guys Finish Last* (New York: Pocket Books, 1976), 207.
80. *Ibid.*
81. Dickson, *Leo Durocher*, 112.
82. *Ibid.*, 113.
83. *Ibid.*, 112.
84. Hy Turkin, "Reese Called by Draft; Braves Get Gomez," *New York Daily News*, January 27, 1943.
85. Lee Scott, "Shortstop Hints He May Join Marines Shortly; Vaughan May Take Over," *Brooklyn Citizen*, January 27, 1943.
86. Dick McCann, "Reese Enlists in Navy; To Seek CPO Rank," *New York Daily News*, January 31, 1943.
87. AP, "Pee Wee Reese Joins Navy; in Tunny Program," *Waterloo Courier* (IA), January 31, 1943.
88. Dick McCann, "Reese Enlists in Navy; To Seek CPO Rank," *New York Daily News*, January 31, 1943.

89. Harold C. Burr, "Leo's 'Best Contract' Demands Club Get First Consideration," *Brooklyn Eagle*, October 26, 1943.
90. Maury Allen with Susan Walker, *Dixie Walker of the Dodgers* (Tuscaloosa: University of Alabama Press, 2010), 129.
91. Ralph Moses, Arky Vaughan SABR bio, https://sabr.org/bioproj/person/arky-vaughan/.
92. Hiram "Hi" Bithorn was the first native of Puerto Rico to play in the major leagues. The right-handed pitcher made his debut on April 15, 1942, for the Chicago Cubs. Bithorn played four seasons and compiled a 34–31 record with a 3.16 ERA for the Cubs (1942–1943, 1946) and crosstown White Sox (1947).
93. Steve Rudman, Dave Eskenazi, and Mark Armour, Eddie Basinksi SABR bio https://sabr.org/bioproj/person/cc60b79b.
94. *Ibid.*
95. "Another Double Is on Today; Watch Us in '46, Says the Lip," *Louisville Courier-Journal*, September 10, 1945.
96. Michael Shapiro, *The Last Good Season: Brooklyn, the Dodgers, and Their Final Pennant Race Together* (New York: Random House, 2003), 60.
97. "Reese Drives in Winning Run," *The Sporting News*, July 1, 1943.
98. "In the Service," *The Sporting News*, June 17, 1943.
99. Schoor, *The Pee Wee Reese Story*, 82.
100. "Big Leaguers Show Talent in Hawaii," *The Sporting News*, May 18, 1944.
101. "Reese Chosen Top Athlete of the Week," *Honolulu Advertiser*, August 6, 1944.
102. https://www.baseballinwartime.com/baseball_in_wwii/baseball_in_wwii.htm.
103. Bob Drury and Tom Calvin, *Halsey's Typhoon: The True Story of a Fighting Admiral, an Epic Storm, and an Untold Rescue* (New York: Atlantic Monthly Press, 2007), 272.
104. Bob Feller with Bill Gilbert, *Now Pitching, Bob Feller: A Baseball Memoir* (New York: Sports Publishing, 2014), 119.
105. Jack Doherty, "Victory But Half Won: Truman," *New York Daily News*, May 9, 1945.
106. National World War II Museum web site. https://www.nationalww2museum.org/students-teachers/student-resources/research-starters/research-starters-worldwide-deaths-world-war.
107. Schoor, *The Pee Wee Reese Story*, 83.

Chapter 6

1. Michael O'Keefe, "Reese: The Man of Summer," *New York Daily News*, August 15, 1999.
2. "Pee Wee Reese Plans to Join Dodgers Soon," *Spokane Spokesman-Review*, February 19, 1946.
3. Gene Schoor, *The Pee Wee Reese Story* (New York: Julian Messner, 1956), 93.
4. *Ibid.*
5. *Ibid.*
6. *Ibid.*
7. *Ibid.*
8. *Ibid.*
9. *Ibid.*
10. Jack Smith, "Dodgers Meet Yanks in 23 of 44 Tune-ups," *New York Daily News*, January 17, 1946.
11. Ralph Berger, Dolph Camilli SABR Bio, https://sabr.org/bioproj/person/dolph-camilli/.
12. Bill Littlefield, "South of the Color Barrier," wbur.org, https://www.wbur.org/onlyagame/2008/03/13/south-of-the-border-2.
13. Lawton Carver (INS), "Durocher Discusses Leading Shortstops," *Troy Times Record* (NY), March 28, 1946.
14. Warren Corbett, Marty Marion SABR bio, https://sabr.org/bioproj/person/marty-marion/.
15. Lawton Carver (INS), "Durocher Discusses Leading Shortstops," *Troy Times Record* (NY), March 28, 1946.
16. Harold C. Burr, "Brooklyn Dodgers," *The Sporting News*, April 18, 1946.
17. Carl T. Rowan with Jackie Robinson, *Wait Till Next Year* (New York: Random House, 1960), 21.
18. *Ibid.*, 20.
19. Jackie Robinson, *I Never Had It Made* (New York: HarperCollins, 1995), 9.
20. *Ibid.*
21. Rob Ray, "The Sports X-Ray," *Los Angeles Times*, February 9, 1940.
22. Arnold Rampersad, *Jackie Robinson* (New York: Arnold A. Knopf, 1997), 74.
23. Jackie Robinson, *My Own Story* (Brattleboro, VT: Echo Point Books & Media, 2019), 9.
24. Robinson, *I Never Had It Made*, 10.
25. Rampersad, *Jackie Robinson*, 95.
26. Robinson, *I Never Had It Made*, 19.
27. Jackie Robinson, *I Never Had It Made*, 24.
28. *Ibid.*, 11.
29. *Ibid.*
30. *Ibid.*
31. Arnold Rampersad, *Jackie Robinson* (New York: Arnold A. Knopf, 1997), 116.
32. *Ibid.*, 25
33. *Ibid.*, 24.
34. Rampersad, *Jackie Robinson*, 116.
35. *Ibid.*, 117.
36. Robinson, *I Never Had It Made*, 25.
37. Major League Baseball elevated the Negro Leagues of 1920–1948 to major league status. These included the Negro National League (I) (1920–1931); the Eastern Colored League (1923–1928); the American Negro League (1929); the East-West League (1932); the Negro Southern League (1932); the Negro National League (II) (1933–1948), and the Negro American League (1937–1948).
38. Andy McCue, Branch Rickey SABR bio, https://sabr.org/bioproj/person/branch-rickey/.
39. Polner, *Branch Rickey*, 133.
40. *Ibid.*
41. *Ibid.*, 134.
42. *Ibid.*, 30.
43. *Ibid.*
44. *Ibid.*, 31.
45. Harold Kaese, "Johnny Sain Does Artistic

Job, Beating Dodgers, 5–3," *Boston Globe*, April 17, 1946.
 46. *Ibid.*
 47. *Ibid.*
 48. Dick Young, "Braves Trip Flock, 5–3," *New York Daily News*, April 17, 1946.
 49. AP, "Pee Wee Reese Leads National League Batters," *Paterson Morning Call*, May 14, 1946.
 50. Lee Scott, "Dodgers Hope to Resume Winning Ways at Home," *Brooklyn Citizen*, May 10, 1946.
 51. Gayle Talbot (AP), "Durocher Turns to Veterans," *Orlando Evening Star*, May 14, 1946.
 52. Tommy Holmes, "Higbe Finds Winning Formula in Walker," *Brooklyn Eagle*, May 23, 1946.
 53. *Ibid.*
 54. Dick Young, "Dodgers Nips Cubs in 13th, 2–1, as Dixie Doubles; 2 Banned," *New York Daily News*, May 23, 1946.
 55. Hy Turkin, "Dixie, Merullo Fined $150 and Suspended for Brawl," *New York Daily News*, May 24, 1946.
 56. Harold C. Burr, "Cubs Again Shut Out Dodgers by 2 to 0," *Brooklyn Eagle*, June 9, 1946.
 57. Lee Scott, "Brilliant Relief Pitching Major Factor in Keeping Dodgers in First Place," *Brooklyn Citizen*, July 3, 1946.
 58. *Ibid.*
 59. *The Sporting News*, November 1, 1945.
 60. *Ibid.*
 61. Polner, *Branch Rickey*, 151.
 62. *Ibid.*, 153.
 63. *Ibid.*, 167.
 64. Rampersad, *Jackie Robinson*, 142.
 65. Peter Golenbock, *Bums: An Oral History of the Brooklyn Dodgers* (New York: G. P. Putnam's Sons, 1984), 139.
 66. *Ibid.*, 141.
 67. Robinson, *I Never Had It Made*, 43.
 68. *Ibid.*, 47.
 69. Wendell Smith, "Jackie Robinson Sensational in Opening Game," *Pittsburgh Courier*, April 27, 1946.
 70. Swaine, Jackie Robinson SABR bio, sabr.org/bioproj/person/jackie-robinson/.
 71. Wendell Smith, "The Sports Beat," *Pittsburgh Courier*, August 31, 1946.
 72. Gollenbock, *Bums*, 144.
 73. Carl Lundquist, "Dodgers Just Can't Beat First Division Clubs," *Brooklyn Citizen*, July 18, 1946.
 74. Harold C. Burr, "Pressure Off Flock as Cards Take Lead," *Brooklyn Eagle*, July 19, 1946.
 75. Terry Flynn, "Losing Streak Doesn't Worry Dem Bums," *Montgomery Advertiser*, July 20, 1946.
 76. Dick Young, "Reese's Triple Stops Dodgers' Slide, 8–4," *New York Daily News*, July 20, 1946.
 77. *Ibid.*
 78. Dick Young, "Flock Tops Reds, 5–4, on Squeeze in 14th," *New York Daily News*, August 5, 1946.
 79. Dick Young, "Dodgers, Reds in 19 Scoreless Heats; Cards Lead Cut to 1½," *New York Daily News*, September 12, 1946.
 80. *Ibid.*

 81. The Dodgers and Reds made up the game on September 20. Dixie Walker drove home three runs and Brooklyn won, 5–3.
 82. Lou Smith, "Deacon May Go East, Word from That Sector," *Cincinnati Enquirer*, September 15, 1946.
 83. Gerald Eskenazi, *The Lip: A Biography of Leo Durocher* (New York: William Morrow, 1993), 196.
 84. Jimmy Cannon, "Jimmy Cannon Says…," *St. Louis Star-Times*, October 2, 1946.
 85. Sid C. Keener, "It's Dickson or Brecheen for Cards in Flatbush Tomorrow," *St. Louis Star-Times*, October 2, 1946.
 86. Joe Trimble, "Cardinals Rap Dodgers, 4–2, in First Playoff," *New York Daily News*, October 2, 1946.
 87. *Wilmington Morning News* (DE), October 4, 1946.
 88. Tommy Holmes, "Cardinals Proved Better Ballclub," *Brooklyn Eagle*, October 4, 1946.
 89. Donald Honig, *Baseball When the Grass Was Real: Baseball from the Twenties to the Forties Told by the Men Who Played It* (Lincoln: University of Nebraska Press, 1975), 283.
 90. Schoor, *The Pee Wee Reese Story*, 90.

Chapter 7

 1. Peter Golenbock (*Bums: An Oral History of the Brooklyn Dodgers* (New York: G. P. Putnam's Sons, 1984), 148.
 2. Arnold Rampersad, *Jackie Robinson* (New York: Arnold Knopf, 1997) 160.
 3. Ted Reed, *Carl Furillo: Brooklyn Dodgers All-Star* (Jefferson, NC: McFarland, 2010), 29.
 4. Golenbock, *Bums,* 148.
 5. Roger Kahn, *Rickey and Robinson: The True, Untold Story of the Integration of Baseball* (New York: Rodale, 2014), 117.
 6. Donald Honig, *Baseball When the Grass Was Real: Baseball from the Twenties to the Forties Told by the Men Who Played It* (Lincoln: University of Nebraska, 1995), 312.
 7. Maury Allen and Susan Walker, *Dixie Walker of the Dodgers: The People's Choice* (Tuscaloosa: University of Alabama Press, 2010), 157.
 8. Golenbock, *Bums*, 150.
 9. Lyle Spatz, *Dixie Walker: A Life in Baseball* (Jefferson, NC: McFarland, 2011), 167.
 10. Allen with Walker, *Dixie Walker of the Dodgers*, 3.
 11. *Ibid.*, 153.
 12. *Ibid.*
 13. *Ibid.*, 152.
 14. Jules Tygiel, *Baseball's Great Experiment: Jackie Robinson and His Legacy* (New York: Oxford University Press, 2008), 170.
 15. *Ibid.*
 16. *Ibid.*, 35.
 17. *Ibid.*
 18. *Ibid.*
 19. Roger Kahn, *The Era: 1947–57 When the*

Yankees, Giants, and Dodgers Ruled the World (New York: Ticknor & Fields, 1993), 35.
  20. Eskenazi, *The Lip: A Biography of Leo Durocher* (New York: William Morrow, 1993), 210.
  21. *Ibid.*
  22. *Ibid.*, 179.
  23. Paul Dickson, *Leo Durocher: Baseball's Prodigal Son* (New York: Bloomsbury, 2017), 150.
  24. *Ibid.*
  25. Eskenazi, *The Lip*, 204.
  26. Kahn, Roger, *The Era*, 30.
  27. Gerald Eskenazi, *The Lip*, 208.
  28. *Ibid.*, 209.
  29. *Ibid.*, 210.
  30. Leo Durocher, *The Dodgers and Me* (Chicago: Ziff-Davis, 1948), 271.
  31. Carl T. Rowan with Jackie Robinson, *Wait Till Next Year* (New York: Random House, 1960), 177.
  32. Jonathan Eig, *Opening Day: The Story of Jackie Robinson's First Season* (New York: Simon & Schuster, 2007), 48.
  33. *Ibid.*, 49.
  34. Bob McGee, *The Greatest Ballpark Ever: Ebbets Field and the Story of the Brooklyn Dodgers* (New Brunswick, NJ: Rivergate Books, 2006) 196.
  35. Hal Bock (AP), "Jackie Robinson: The Man Who Changed Baseball and America," *Staunton News-Leader* (VA), March 23, 1997.
  36. Hy Turkin, "Robinson Bought by Dodgers; Hitless as Royals Win, 4–3," *New York Daily News*, April 11, 1947.
  37. Dave Anderson, "Clyde Sukeworth Is Dead; Steered Robinson to Majors," *New York Times*, September 6, 2000.
  38. Jack McCulley, "Larry Hints Backing If Dressen Appeals Ban," *New York Daily News*, April 11, 1947.
  39. Jonathan Eig, *Opening Day: The Story of Jackie Robinson's First Season* (New York: Simon & Schuster, 2007), 55.
  40. Dick Young, "Robinson Hunts Home, Looks Like He'll Stick," *New York Daily News*, April 17, 1947.
  41. Harold C. Burr, "'Old Reiser,' 'New Hermanski' Stars of Dodgers' Day Triumph," *Brooklyn Eagle*, April 16, 1947.
  42. *Ibid.*
  43. Eig, *Opening Day*, 52.
  44. *Ibid.*
  45. *Ibid.*
  46. Golenbock, *Bums*, 157.
  47. *Ibid.*
  48. https://www.fangraphs.com/tht/the-story-of-kindly-old-burt-shotton/.
  49. Rob Edelman, Burt Shotton SABR bio, https://sabr.org/bioproj/person/97735d30.
  50. *Ibid.*
  51. Stanley Woodward, "Views of Sport," *The Sporting News*, May 21, 1947.
  52. *Ibid.*
  53. Peter Golenbock, *The Spirit of St. Louis: A History of the St. Louis Cardinals and Browns* (New York: William Morrow, 2000), 381.
  54. *Ibid.*, 383.
  55. *Ibid.*, 384.
  56. *Ibid.*
  57. McGee, *The Greatest Ballpark Ever: Ebbets Field and the Story of the Brooklyn Dodgers* New (Brunswick, NJ: Rutgers University Press, 2005), 197.
  58. Dick Young, "Flock Nips Cards, 7–6, On Reese HR in 7th," *New York Daily News*, May 7, 1947.
  59. *Ibid.*
  60. Dick Young, "Reiser Hurt Crashing Wall; Flock Wins, 9–4," *New York Daily News*, June 5, 1947.
  61. Dick Young, "Dodgers Collar Cubs Again, 5–1," *New York Daily News*, June 20, 1947.
  62. *Ibid.*
  63. *Ibid.*
  64. Dick Young, "Dodgers Rowe, Rowe, Rowe Over Phils, 7–4," *New York Daily News*, July 1, 1947.
  65. Schoor, *The Pee Wee Reese Story*, 102.
  66. John McMurray, Larry Doby SABR Bio, https://sabr.org/bioproj/person/4e985e86.
  67. *Ibid.*
  68. "Reese Appointed to NL All-Stars," *New York Daily News*, July 6, 1947.
  69. Honig, *Baseball When the Grass Was Real*, 313.
  70. Golenbock, *Bums*, 246.
  71. W. C. Heinz, *What a Time It Was: The Best of W.C. Heinz on Sports* (Cambridge, MA: Da Capo Press, 2001), 30.
  72. Reed, *Carl Furillo*, 10.
  73. *Ibid.*, 11.
  74. *Ibid.*, 40.
  75. *Ibid.*, 39.
  76. Harold C. Burr, "Bums Look Around, Ask 'Who's Better Than Us,'" *The Sporting News*, July 9, 1947.
  77. "Pee Wee Qualifies for Dodger 'Cub,'" *New York Daily News*, July 13, 1947.
  78. *Ibid.*
  79. Bob Broeg, "Redbirds Make Up 10-Run Deficit but Lose Wild Night Game in 10th," *St. Louis Post-Dispatch*, July 31, 1947.
  80. *Ibid.*
  81. Joe Reichler, AP, "Blackwell's Streak Ends; Dodgers Capture Thriller," *Ithaca Journal* (NY), July 31, 1947.
  82. Cornelius Ryan, UP, "Reese Beats Cards Again," *Binghamton Press and Sun-Bulletin* (NY), August 1, 1947.
  83. AP, "Pee Wee Reese's Hit Again Nips Cards," *Palm Beach Post*, August 1, 1947.
  84. Schoor, *The Pee Wee Reese Story*, 95.
  85. Hal Bock, "Pee Wee Was a Giant Friend to Robinson," *Hazelton Standard-Speaker* (PA), March 23, 1997.
  86. Jules Tygiel, *Baseball's Great Experiment*, 194.
  87. Eig, *Opening Day*, 128.
  88. Tygiel, *Baseball's Great Experiment*, 169.
  89. Robinson, *I Never Had it Made*, 63.
  90. Pee Wee Reese, "Jackie Robinson … Reese Remembers Him as 'Great Influence on Our Lives,'" *Louisville Courier-Journal*, July 17, 1977.

91. Schoor, *The Pee Wee Reese Story*, 96.
92. Kahn, *Rickey and Robinson*, 117.
93. Enos Slaughter and Kevin Reid, *Country Hardball: The Autobiography of Enos "Country" Slaughter* (Greensboro, NC: Tudor Publishers, 1991) 111.
94. AP, "'We'll Win It,' Exuberates Dyer; Rhubard Over Robinson Spiking," *St. Louis Post-Dispatch*, August 21, 1947.
95. Golenbock, *The Spirit of St. Louis*, 385.
96. Enos Slaughter and Kevin Reid, *Country Hardball*, 111.
97. Stan Baumgartner, "Galen Hurls 'Cry-Baby' Taunt at Dodgers After Roughing-Up by Reds," *The Sporting News*, September 3, 1947.
98. Dick Young, "Reese, Stanky Spiked in Red-Flock Feud," *New York Daily News*, August 24, 1947.
99. Stan Baumgartner, "Galen Hurls 'Cry-Baby' Taunt at Dodgers After Roughing-Up by Reds."
100. *Ibid.*
101. Harold C. Burr, "Dodgers Don't Know Own Strength Until They Call to Bench," *The Sporting News*, September 3, 1947.
102. Lou Smith, "Bums Beat Reds Twice, Lead by Seven Contests," *Cincinnati Inquirer*, September 15, 1947.
103. John Ebinger, "Conquering Bums Return as Faithful Go Nertz," *New York Daily News*, September 20, 1947.
104. AP, "Bums Get Rush in Tumultuous Welcome by Dodger Fans," *Rochester Democrat and Chronicle*, September 20, 1947.
105. Ebinger, "Conquering Bums Return as Faithful Go Nertz."
106. Oscar Fraley, "Opener to Lure 73,000 Fans," *Rochester Chronicle and Democrat*, September 30, 1947.
107. John Ebinger, "Scribes Pick Yanks to Win Series, 3–1." *New York Daily News*, September 30, 1947.
108. Jim McCulley, "Dodgers Unawed by Yankee 'Might'; Winners More Interested in Gate," *New York Daily News*, October 1, 1947.
109. AP, "Staggering Dodgers Series Hosts to Yanks Today," *Montana Standard* (Butte), October 2, 1947.
110. AP, "Yanks and Dodgers Tie Two Marks, One by Belting, One by Watching," *Hartford Courant*, October 2, 1947.
111. Schoor, *Pee Wee Reese Story*, 107.
112. Kahn, *The Era*, 121.
113. Hy Turkin, "Lavagetto Mussed Up by Dodgers; Yanks Funereal, Bev Near Tears," *New York Daily News*, October 4, 1947.
114. Dick Young, "Cookie Hit with 2 Out in 9th Spoils Bevins' No-Hitter, Nips Yanks, 3–2," *New York Daily News*, October 4, 1947.
115. "All-Night Line at Bleachers Noisy, Happy," *Brooklyn Eagle*, October 4, 1947.
116. Harold C. Burr, "No Dodger Pitcher Has Gone Route," *Brooklyn Eagle*, October 6, 1947.
117. Joe Trimble, "Yanks Champs! Trim Flock, 5–2; M'Phail Retires from Baseball," *New York News*, October 7, 1947.
118. Tommy Holmes, "As Dodgers Reached End of the Line," *Brooklyn Eagle*, October 7, 1947.
119. Arky Vaughan returned to the Dodgers in 1947 and hit .325 in 126 at-bats. Vaughan played one more season, batted .244 and joined the San Francisco Seals of the Pacific Coast League. He hit .288 and retired as a player. Vaughan died in a boating accident in 1952 at the age of 40. The Veterans Committee voted him into the Hall of Fame in 1985.
120. Schoor, *The Pee Wee Reese Story*, 97.
121. "Brooks Still in the Making," *Brooklyn Eagle*, October 7, 1947.
122. *Ibid.*

Chapter 8

1. Gerald Eskenazi, *The Lip: A Biography of Leo Durocher* (New York: William Morrow, 1993), 219.
2. Lou Niss, "Dodgers Sign Leo at '47 Figure—Shotton Is Shifted," *Brooklyn Eagle*, December 7, 1947.
3. Tommy Holmes, "Scatter Shot at the Sports Scene," *Brooklyn Eagle*, December 8, 1947.
4. Dick Young, "Leo Flock '48 Manager; Shotton Farm Overseer," *New York Daily News*, December 1947.
5. AP, "Dixie Walker Praises Brooklyn Baseball Fans," *Wilmington Morning News* (DE) December 9, 1947.
6. John Vorperian, Gene Mauch SABR bio, https://sabr.org/bioproj/person/36a8c32a.
7. "Walker, Gregg, Lom Traded to Pirates," *Brooklyn Eagle*, December 8, 1947.
8. Hy Turkin, "Rickey in Double Play; Nabs Stanky and Reese," *New York Daily News*, March 2, 1948.
9. Dick Young, "Stanky Well Paid; Reese Worth More, Says Leo," *New York Daily News*, February 28, 1948.
10. *Ibid.*
11. Hy Turkin, "Rickey in Double Play; Nabs Stanky and Reese," *New York Daily News*, March 2, 1948.
12. Joe King, "Diamond Dossier … Pee Wee Reese," *The Sporting News*, October 15, 1952.
13. Paul Dickson, *Leo Durocher: Baseball's Prodigal Son* (New York: Bloomsbury USA, 2017), 183.
14. Leo Durocher and Ed Linn, *Nice Guys Finish Last* (New York: Simon and Schuster, 1975), 244.
15. Jimmy Powers, "The Powerhouse," *New York Daily News*, March 9, 1948.
16. *Ibid.*
17. J. G. Taylor Spink, "Looping the Loop," *The Sporting News*, March 31, 1948.
18. Murray Polner, *Branch Rickey: A Biography* (Jefferson, NC: McFarland, 2007), 124.
19. Eskenazi, *The Lip*, 149.
20. *Ibid.*, 150.
21. Roy Campanella, *It's Good to Be Alive* (Boston: Little, Brown, 1959), 137.
22. Dick Young, *Roy Campanella* (New York: Grosset & Dunlap, 1952), 14.
23. Roy Campanella, *It's Good to Be Alive*, 114.

24. *Ibid.*, 118.
25. *Ibid.*, 134.
26. Mark Langill, *Dodgertown* (Charleston, SC: Arcadia, 2005), 11.
27. Rody Johnson, *The Rise and Fall of Dodgertown* (Gainesville: University Press of Florida, 2008), 9.
28. http://historicdodgertown.com/history/historic-timeline/years-1940s.
29. Lingill, *Dodgertown*, 9.
30. *Ibid.*, 15.
31. Zeke Handler, "Touch of Brooklyn in Texas—Reese, Rookie in Rhubarb," *The Sporting News*, April 14, 1948.
32. *Ibid.*
33. "CBS to Air Life of Pee Wee Reese," *The Sporting News*, April 7, 1948.
34. *Ibid.*
35. *Ibid.*
36. Gene Schoor, *The Pee Wee Reese Story* (New York: J. Messner, 1956), 123.
37. Rex Barney with Norman L. Macht, *Rex Barney's Thank Youuuu for 50 Years in Baseball from Brooklyn to Baltimore* (Centreville, MD: Tidewater, 1993), 123.
38. *Ibid.*
39. *Ibid.*, 119.
40. Arnold Rampersad, *Jackie Robinson* (New York: Alfred A Knopf, 1997), 200.
41. Harold C. Burr, "Dodgers Deep at All Positions, Especially Second, Lippy Proves," *Brooklyn Eagle*, April 22, 1948.
42. *Ibid.*
43. "Leo Didn't Forget Shuffle—66 Players in Four Tilts," *The Sporting News*, May 5, 1948.
44. Dick Young, "Lip's Luck: Reese Reaps Rain's Reward—Rest!," *New York Daily News*, May 6, 1948.
45. Dick Young, "Flock 14, Bucs 2, in 1st; Reese Grand Slams," *New York Daily News*, May 10, 1948.
46. Dick Young, "Flock Hits 9th on 8th Loss by .008; Reds Win, 6–5, on Hatton Homer," *New York Daily News*, May 24, 1948.
47. AP, "Dodgers Defeat Chicubs, 4 to 2," *Wilmington Morning News* (DE), May 28, 1948.
48. "One Game Dodger Winning Streak in Acid Test Under Boston Moon," *Brooklyn Eagle*, May 28, 1948.
49. "Parrott Credited as Author. Proofs Went to Chandler," *The Sporting News*, May 26, 1948.
50. *Ibid.*
51. *Ibid.*
52. Red Smith, "Views of Sport," *The Sporting News*, May 26, 1948.
53. Bill Roeder, "Lip's Book Startles Brass Hats," *The Sporting News*, May 26, 1948.
54. Arch Murray, "Durocher Defends Book as 'Accurate,'" *The Sporting News*, May 26, 1948.
55. Campanella, *It's Good to Be Alive*, 138.
56. Dick Young, "Cubs Sweep Flock, 6–3, As Lip Scouts Talent," *New York Daily News*, June 21, 1948.
57. "Umpire Stewart Has Fan Given the Heave-Ho," *Brooklyn Eagle*, June 21, 1948.
58. Lee Lowenfish, *Branch Rickey: Baseball's Ferocious Gentleman* (Lincoln, NE: Bison Books, 2009), 458.
59. Dick Young, "Dodgers Edge Giants, 13–12, With 4 in 9th," *New York Daily News*, July 5, 1948.
60. *Ibid.*
61. *Ibid.*
62. Durocher and Linn, *Nice Guys Finish Last*, 246.
63. AP, "Mel Ott Quits Giants; Durocher Named to Post," *Salt Lake City Deseret News*, July 16, 1948.
64. *Ibid.*
65. Paul Dickson, *Leo Durocher*, 189.
66. *Ibid.*, 189.
67. Harold C. Burr, "Dodgers Welcome Shotton Back with Hair-Raising Win Over Reds," *Brooklyn Eagle*, July 17, 1948.
68. "Dodgers Sorry for Lippy," *Brooklyn Eagle*, April 17, 1948.
69. *Ibid.*
70. Schoor, *The Pee Wee Reese Story*, 125.
71. Carl Erskine, *Tales from the Dodger Dugout: A Collection of the Greatest Dodgers Stories Ever Told* (New York: Sports Publishing, 2017), 6.
72. Lou Smith, "Bums Trip Reds, Gain on Boston; Homer by Reese Is Bat Highlight," *Cincinnati Enquirer*, August 27, 1948.
73. Dick Young, "Dodgers Pummel Cards, 12–7; Robby Hits for Cycle," *New York Daily News*, August 30, 1948.
74. UP, "Pinch-Hitters Click in Rout of Cardinals," *Elmira Star-Gazette* (New York), August 31, 1948.
75. AP, "Brooklyn Dodgers Climb into National Loop Lead," *Calgary Herald* (Alberta, Canada), August 30, 1948.
76. Harold C. Burr, "Dodgers Carry Title Look," *Brooklyn Eagle*, August 30, 1948.
77. Jim McCulley, "Are the Dodgers Dead? Lip Hedges the Question," *New York Daily News*, September 13, 1948.
78. Barney with Macht, *Rex Barney's Thank Youuuu*, 115.
79. *Ibid.*, 123.
80. Jim McCulley, "'Just Knew I Was Due,' Flock's Barney Beams," *New York Daily News*, September 10, 1948.
81. Barney with Macht, *Rex Barney's Thank Youuuu*, 6.
82. Andrew Paul Mele, *Tearin' Up the Pea Patch* (Jefferson, NC: McFarland, 2015), 101.
83. Jon Thurber, "Preacher Roe Dies at 92; Pitcher for the Brooklyn Dodgers," *Los Angeles Times*, November 11, 2008.
84. *Ibid.*
85. *The Sporting News*, August 30, 1950.
86. "Reiser Says He Won't Play Any More for Brooklyn," *The Sporting News*, October 13, 1948.
87. Oscar Fraley (UPI), "Is Pete Reiser Finished? Dodger Star Ailing," *Monongahela Daily Republican* (PA), August 4, 1948.
88. *Ibid.*
89. Schoor, *The Pee Wee Reese Story*, 121.
90. Harold C. Burr, "Shotton Back for New

Term—Dodger Overhaul in Sight," *The Sporting News*, October 20, 1948.

91. Harold C. Burr, "Dodgers Nine Outfielders Put B.R. Behind Eight-Ball," *The Sporting News*, November 17, 1948.

92. "Reese's Blood Saves Boy," *The Sporting News*, November 24, 1948.

Chapter 9

1. Bob Herbert, "Louisville's Pee Wee Reese and 'Baseball's Finest Moment,'" *Louisville Courier-Journal*, March 15, 1997.
2. Joe Posnanski, "The Embrace," https.sportsworld.nbcsports.com/the-embrace/.
3. Ira Berkow, "New Brooklyn Statue Honors Pee Wee's Simple Gesture," *Louisville Courier-Journal*, November 2, 2005.
4. Ken Burns on Famous Jackie Robinson/Pee Wee Reese Embrace—Bing video
5. *Jackie Robinson*, Directed by Ken Burns, Sarah Burns, and David McMahon, 2016.
6. Ken Burns on Famous Jackie Robinson/Pee Wee Reese Embrace—Bing video
7. Arnold Rampersad, *Jackie Robinson: A Biography* (New York: Ballantine, 1998), 182.
8. Ibid., 183.
9. Ibid.
10. http://baseballdeworld.com/2012/08/19/jackie-robinson-pee-wee-reese-statue-brooklyn/.
11. Lou Smith, "Bums Humble Braves to Take Second Spot," *Cincinnati Enquirer*, May 13, 1947.
12. Peter Golenbock, *Bums: An Oral History of the Brooklyn Dodgers* (New York: G. P. Putnam's Sons, 1984) 161.
13. Ibid.
14. Jonathan Eig, *Opening Day: The Story of Jackie Robinson's First Season* (New York: Simon and Schuster, 2007), 128
15. Ibid., 127.
16. Ibid.
17. Ibid., 124.
18. Ibid.
19. "Blackwell to Face Hatten Today; Tatum Goes Well in Debut Here," *Cincinnati Enquirer*, May 14, 1947.
20. Harold C. Burr, "Epidemic of Walks Sickens Flock," *Brooklyn Eagle*, May 14, 1947.
21. Dick Young, "Redlegs Leading Dodgers Under Arcs in Cincy," *New York Daily News*, May 14, 1947.
22. Lou Smith, "Blackwell Trims Brooklyn by 2–0 Margin," *Cincinnati Enquirer*, May 15, 1947.
23. "Dodgers Take Over Second Place; Shotton Lifts Ban on Card Playing," *Cincinnati Enquirer*, June 22, 1947.
24. Dick Young, "Dodgers Lead Redlegs; Taylor Opposes Vandy," *New York Daily News*, June 22, 1947.
25. AP, "Chapman Praises Jackie Robinson," *New York Daily News*, June 22, 1947.
26. Christian Red, "Did Jackie Robinson-Pee Wee Reese Embrace Happen? Ken Burns Doc Explores Dodger's Life," *New York Daily News*, April 9, 2016.
27. Eig, *Opening Day*, 128.
28. Brad Snyder, "Jackie Robinson Myth-Busting Gone Wrong," Slate, April 15, 2016, https://slate.com/culture/2016/04/where-ken-burns-jackie-robinson-documentary-goes-awry.html.
29. Joe Posnanski, "The Embrace," NBC Sports, https://sportsworld.nbcsports.com/the-embrace/.
30. Dick Young, "Dodgers Nip Braves, 5–3, on Reiser's One-Man Show," *New York Daily News*, April 16, 1947.
31. Mike Klingaman, "Robinson Was Covered in Mainstream Press Mostly by Ink: AN AMERICAN HERO," *Baltimore Sun*, April 15, 1997.
32. Brad Snyder, "Jackie Robinson Myth-Busting Gone Wrong."
33. Ibid.
34. Jackie Robinson and Ed Reid, "Jackie Robinson Tells His Story," *Brooklyn Eagle*, August 24, 1949.
35. Ibid.
36. Ibid.
37. Brad Snyder, "Jackie Robinson Myth-Busting Gone Wrong."
38. Jackie Robinson with KMOX's Jack Buck on 'race relations' (audacy.com), https://www.audacy.com/kmox/articles/news/jackie-robinson-with-kmoxs-jack-buck-on-race-relations.
39. Carl Thomas Rowan with Jackie Robinson, *Wait Till Next Year: The Life Story of Jackie Robinson* (New York: Random House, 1960), 228.
40. Ibid.
41. Jackie Robinson, *I Never Had It Made: An Autobiography* (New York: G. P. Putnam's Sons, 1972), 64.
42. Eig, *Opening Day*, 129.
43. Ibid., 172.
44. Bill Roeder, *Jackie Robinson*.
45. Schoor, *The Pee Wee Reese Story*, 97.
46. Rampersad, *Jackie Robinson*, 182.
47. Jules Tygiel, *Baseball's Great Experiment: Jackie Robinson and His Legacy* (New York: Oxford University Press, 1983), 195.
48. Dave Kindred, "Better than Fiction."
49. Ibid.
50. Bruce Cronin, "Did Reese Really Embrace Robinson in '47," espn.com, April 13, 2013, https://www.espn.com/blog/playbook/fandom/post/_/id/20917/did-reese-really-embrace-robinson-in-1947.

Chapter 10

1. Duke Snider with Bill Gilbert, *The Duke of Flatbush* (New York: Zebra Books, 1989), 63.
2. Ibid.
3. Ibid., 64.
4. Ibid., 63.
5. Gene Schoor, *The Pee Wee Reese Story* (New York: Julian Messner, 1956), 127.
6. Ibid.
7. Roscoe McGowen, "PEE WEE ... Pride of Flatbush," *The Sporting News*, December 26, 1956.

8. Schoor, *The Pee Wee Reese Story*, 127.
9. *Ibid.*, 128.
10. *Ibid.*
11. *Ibid.*, 129.
12. *Ibid.*
13. Harold C. Burr, "Branca Gives Dodgers Head Start on Casualties," *The Sporting News*, March 9, 1949.
14. Joe Reichler, Associated Press, "Brooklyn Dodgers Picked to Win Flag," *Tallahassee Democrat*, March 31, 1949.
15. *Ibid.*
16. Neil Lanctot, *Campy: The Two Lives of Roy Campanella* (New York: Simon & Schuster Paperbacks, 2011), 179.
17. *Ibid.*
18. Snider with Gilbert, *The Duke of Flatbush*, 38.
19. *Ibid.*, 55.
20. *Ibid.*
21. Dick Young, "Speedy Robby Just Learning How to Slide," *New York Daily News*, March 5, 1949.
22. Red Smith, "Men vs. Machines at Vero Beach; The Mahatma Has Assembly Line," *The Sporting News*, March 16, 1949.
23. *Ibid.*
24. *Ibid.*
25. *Ibid.*
26. Dick Young, "Reese Stays in Game Despite Muscle Injury," *New York Daily News*, April 1, 1949.
27. Dick Young, "Flock to Test Reese in Nat Tilt Tonight," *New York Daily News*, April 14, 1949.
28. Dick Young, "Flock Hurlers Fail, Phils Win, 12–4; Reese Hits 2," *New York Daily News*, May 1, 1949.
29. Dick Young, "Robby Drives in 6 Runs as Dodgers Romp, 15–6," *New York Daily News*, May 22, 1949.
30. Dean Eagle, "David Among Goliaths—That's Our Pee Wee Reese Who Plays in Cincy Today," *Louisville Courier-Journal*, May 22, 1949.
31. Jules Tygiel, *Baseball's Great Experiment: Jackie Robinson and His Legacy* (New York: Oxford University Press, 2008), 68.
32. Dick Young, "Cards Drub Dodgers, 6–2, Blast Newcombe's Debut," *New York Daily News*, May 21, 1949.
33. Harold C. Burr, "Newcombe Stiffens Flock Mound Corps," *Brooklyn Eagle*, May 23, 1949.
34. Dick Young, "Tip on All-Star Poll; NL Goes for Reese," *New York Daily News*, June 21, 1949.
35. Harry Grayson, "Pee Wee Reese Steps In as Dodgers' 'Take-Charge Guy,'" *Warren Times Mirror* (PA), June 7, 1949.
36. Carl Lundquist (UPI), "Bums Bombard All Opposition for Imposing Record," *Murfreesboro Daily News-Journal* (TN), June 27, 1949.
37. Dick Young, "Tip on NL All-Star Poll; NL Goes for Reese," *New York Daily News*, June 21, 1949.
38. Ira Berkow, "At Robinson's Side, Reese Helped Change Baseball," *St. Louis Post-Dispatch*, April 20, 1997.
39. *Ibid.*
40. Bob Herbert, "Louisville's Pee Wee Reese and 'Baseball's Finest Moment,'" *Louisville Courier-Journal*, March 15, 1997.
41. Roger Kahn, *Into My Own: The Remarkable People and Events That Shaped a Life* (New York: Thomas Dunne, 2006), 107.
42. Harold C. Burr, "Flatbush Says It's Over—Except for the All-Star Picks," *The Sporting News*, June 22, 1949.
43. Harold C. Burr, "National Loop Seeks Win Formula in Vain," *Brooklyn Eagle*, July 13, 1949.
44. *Ibid.*
45. Harold C. Burr, "Missouri Murder Inc.; Pushes Cardinals into First," *Brooklyn Eagle*, July 25, 1949.
46. *Ibid.*
47. Pee Wee Reese and Tim Cohane, "Reese's Own Story: 14 Years a Bum," *Baseball Digest*, May 1954.
48. https://www.history.com/news/polio-fear-post-wwii-era.
49. https://www.gosanangelo.com/story/news/2019/06/12/san-angelo-center-polio-epidemic-summer-1949/1421514001/.
50. *Ibid.*
51. https://www.history.com/news/polio-fear-post-wwii-era.
52. *Ibid.*
53. *Ibid.*
54. Jeffrey A. Tucker, "No Lockdowns: The Terrifying Polio Pandemic of 1949–52," *American Institute for Economic Research*, May 10, 2020.
55. *Ibid.*
56. Mary Bellis, "History of the Iron Lung-Respirator," ThoughtCo, January 8, 2018.
57. Reese and Cohane, "Reese's Own Story: 14 Years a Bum," *Baseball Digest*, May 1954.
58. Dick Young, *Roy Campanella* (New York: Grosset & Dunlap, 1952), 119–120.
59. Harold C. Burr, "Calling Dr. Kildare—Report to St. Louis, Patient Flattened by Hit-and-Run Dodgers," *Brooklyn Eagle*, September 23, 1949.
60. Joe Reichler (AP), "Nearly Everybody Thinks St. Louis Cardinals 'In,'" *Monroe Star-News* (LA), September 26, 1949.
61. Harold C. Burr, "'Twas a Great Fight and a Great Victory," *Brooklyn Eagle*, October 3, 1949.
62. John Ebinger, "Banta's Hurt Finger Didn't Curb Speed," *New York Daily News*, October 3, 1949.
63. Roger Kahn, *The Boys of Summer* (New York: Harper & Row, 2006), 313.
64. Roger Kahn, *The Era: 1947–1957, When the Yankees, the Giants, and the Dodgers Ruled the Word* (New York: Ticknor & Fields, 1993), 166.
65. Violet Brown, "10,000 Wait Hours in Rain for Bleachers," *Brooklyn Eagle*, October 5, 1949.
66. *Ibid.*
67. Tommy Holmes, "Even Casey Stengel Mourns Newcombe Loss," *Brooklyn Eagle*, October 6, 1949.
68. Oscar Fraley (U.P.), "Sports Parade," *Latrobe Bulletin* (PA), October 7, '1949.
69. Schoor, *The Pee Wee Reese Story*, 137.
70. Oscar Fraley, "Sports Parade."

71. Harold C. Burr, "Yankee Magic Casts Spell Over Flock as Four Singles Overpower 3 Homers," *Brooklyn Eagle*, October 8, 1949.
72. Dana Mozley, "Mize Belted Tiny Darry, "Sports Patter," *Lebanon Daily News* (PA), October 8, 1949; "One He Wasn't Supposed to Hit: Branch," *New York Daily News*, October 8, 1949.
73. Pee Wee Reese, "Reese: Branca Hurls His Best Game of Season," *Lebanon Daily News* (PA), October 8, 1949.
74. "Lopat to Hurl 4th Game; Don Looms Dodger Choice," *New York Daily News*, October 8, 1949.
75. Pee Wee Reese, "Pee Wee Insists the Bad Pitch Was One Brown Hit for a Single," *Hackensack Record* (NJ), October 8, 1949.
76. Steve Snider, "Dodgers Give No Alibis for Their Defeat," *Rochester Democrat and Chronicle*, October 9, 1949.
77. Roger Kahn, *The Era* (New York: Ticknor & Fields, 1993), 239.
78. Dick Young, "Yanks Win '49 Championship," *New York Daily News*, October 10, 1949.
79. Clarence Greenbaum, "Dodger Fans Stunned by Blow; Some Blame Shotton for Loss," *Brooklyn Eagle*, October 10, 1949.
80. Dana Mozley, "Defeat a Bitter Pill—But Dodgers Take It Sweetly," *New York Daily News*, October 10, 1949.
81. Gayle Talbot, "Yanks Wrap Up 12th World Series Title in Five Games," *Ottawa Journal* (Canada), October 10, 1949.
82. Mozley, "Defeat a Bitter Pill—But Dodgers Take It Sweetly."
83. Tommy Holmes, *Dodger Daze and Knights: Enough of a Ball Club's History to Explain Its Reputation* (Philadelphia: David McKay, 1953), 248.
84. Roger Kahn, *The Era*, 239.
85. "Proclamation: It's Pee Wee Reese Week," *Louisville Courier-Journal*, October 23, 1949.
86. Tommy Fitzgerald, "For Once Pee Wee Reese Is a Little Plate Shy," *Louisville Courier-Journal*, October 27, 1949.
87. Tommy Fitzgerald, "Reese Tabbed as Managerial Material by Rickey at Testimonial in Louisville," *The Sporting News*, November 9, 1949.
88. *Ibid.*
89. *Ibid.*
90. "Jackie Robinson Most Valuable; May Retire at the End of Next Year," *Pittsburgh Post-Gazette*, November 19, 1949.
91. Schoor, *The Pee Wee Reese Story*, 134.
92. McGowen, "PEE WEE … Pride of Flatbush," *The Sporting News*, December 26, 1956.

Chapter 11

1. Dick Young, "Operation on Pee Wee Is 'Highly Successful,'" *New York Daily News*, January 4, 1950.
2. *Ibid.*
3. John M. Hightower (AP), "State Dept. Said to Weigh Another Bid to Russia for Atomic Controls," *St. Louis Post-Dispatch*, February 1, 1950.
4. UP, "Atom Experts Predict U.S. Will Test First H-Bomb Within Year," *St. Louis Post-Dispatch*, February 1, 1950.
5. Gayle Talbot, "Branch Rickey Is Reported Thinking of Selling Robinson," *Owensboro Messenger-Inquirer* (KY), January 10, 1950.
6. Joe Reichler, "Jackie Robinson's $35,000 Tops All Dodgers," *Windsor Star* (Canada), January 25, 1950.
7. AP, "$30,000 Contract Inked by Pee Wee," *Middletown Journal* (OH), February 4, 1950.
8. Harold C. Burr, "Rickey Ready with Cigars to Traders with Pitchers," *The Sporting News*, February 15, 1950.
9. *Ibid.*
10. Dick Young, "After Shotton? Reese Best Guess," *New York Daily News*, March 23, 1950.
11. *Ibid.*
12. Stan Opotowsky, "Brooklyn Dodgers Will Win—Rickey," *Mansfield News-Journal* (OH), January 27, 1950.
13. *Ibid.*
14. Robin Roberts and C. Paul Rogers III. *The Whiz Kids and the 1950 Pennant*. (Philadelphia: Temple University Press, 1996), 193.
15. *Ibid.*, 215.
16. *Ibid.*, 216.
17. *Ibid.*, 16.
18. "Phillies Startle the Baseball World by Selling Alexander and Killefer to the Chicago Cubs," *Philadelphia Inquirer*, December 12, 1917.
19. *Ibid.*
20. Todd Zolecki, *The Good, the Bad, & the Ugly: Philadelphia Phillies: Heart-Pounding, Jaw-Dropping, and Gut-Wrenching Moments form Philadelphia Phillies History* (Chicago: Triumph, 2010), 164.
21. Roberts and Rogers, *The Whiz Kids and the 1950 Pennant*, 32.
22. Red Barber and Robert Creamer, *Rhubarb in the Catbird Seat*. (New York: Doubleday, 1968), 261.
23. Rob Edelman, "The Many Faces of Happy Felton," https://sabr.org/research/many-faces-happy-felton.
24. https://www.youtube.com/watch?v=KsQuqhWhm8o.
25. Author interview with Carl Erskine, December 4, 2020.
26. Dick Young, "Reese Heaved, Flock Wins, 10–2," *New York Daily News*, May 5, 1950.
27. *Ibid.*
28. *Ibid.*
29. AP, "Pee Wee Reese Gets 1,000th Hit," *York Daily Record*, May 10, 1950.
30. Harold C. Burr, "Podbielan's Arm Hurt, Reese's Ankle Sprained," *Brooklyn Eagle*, May 21, 1950.
31. Joe King, "Pee Wee's Value to Brooks Shown During Absence," *The Sporting News*, June 14, 1950.
32. AP, "U.S. Fighters KO 4 Red Planes, M'Arthur Says," *Brooklyn Eagle*, June 27, 1950.
33. https://www.marfork.marines.mil/About/History

34. http://ushistoryscene www.marfork.marines.mil/About/History; http://ushistoryscene.com/article/levittown/.
35. *Time 1950: The Year in Review*, 1950 and 1999, 40.
36. http://ushistoryscene.com/article/levittown/.
37. Ben Gould, "Mahatma Publicly Lashes Dodgers for Complacency," *The Sporting News*, August 16, 1950.
38. *Ibid*.
39. Jim McCulley, "Dodgers Sweep Giants, 8–6, 5–1, in Twin Bill," *New York Daily News*, August 18, 1950.
40. Harold C. Burr, "Gil Only Living Player to Hit 4 Homers in Game," *Brooklyn Eagle*, September 1, 1950.
41. *Ibid*.
42. *Ibid*.
43. *Ibid*.
44. *Ibid*.
45. C. Paul Rogers III, Robin Roberts SABR bio https://sabr.org/bioproj/person/robin-roberts/.
46. Stan Baumgartner, "Brooks Route Phils, 11–0, on 2–Hitter; Lead Now 5," *Philadelphia Inquirer*, September 25, 1950.
47. Jimmy Kennan, Bob Miller SABR bio, https://sabr.org/bioproj/person/bob-miller-4/.
48. George Vescey. *Baseball's Most Valuable Players*. (New York: Random House, 1966), 93.
49. Roberts and Rogers, *The Whiz Kids and the 1950 Pennant*, 311.
50. Harold C. Burr, "Dodgerdom Awaits Today's Game with Bated Breath," *Brooklyn Eagle*, October 1, 1950.
51. Stan Baumgartner, "Dodgers Beat Phils, 7–3, Move One Game from Tie," *Philadelphia Inquirer*, October 1, 1950.
52. *Ibid*.
53. Sid Frigaud, "Boro Fans See Visions Very Bright and Gay," *Brooklyn Eagle*, October 1, 1950.
54. *Ibid*.
55. Roger Kahn, *The Era: 1947–1957 When the Yankees, the Giants, and the Dodgers Ruled the World* (New York: Ticknor & Fields, 1993), 253.
56. Stan Baumgartner, "Whiz Kids Win on Sisler Homer; Roberts Gets 20th," *Philadelphia Inquirer*, October 2, 1950.
57. Kahn, *The Era*, 253.
58. Roberts and Rogers, *The Whiz Kids and the 1950 Pennant*, 314.
59. Carl Lundquist (UP), "Phils 2–1 Underdogs Against Yanks," *Lincoln Journal Star*, October 2, 1950.
60. Harold C. Burr, "Fighting Dodgers Rated Team of Year," *Brooklyn Eagle*, October 2, 1950.
61. Milt Stock, SABR bio, https://sabr.org/bioproj/person/e410fef6.
62. Roberts and Rogers, *The Whiz Kids and the 1950 Pennant*, 319.
63. Bob McGee, *The Greatest Ballpark Ever: Ebbets Field and the Story of the Brooklyn Dodgers* (New Brunswick, NJ: Riverdale Press, 2006), 219.
64. Fred Down (UP), "Ashburn's Throw Stuns Dodgers," *Philadelphia Inquirer*, October 2, 1950.
65. *Ibid*.
66. Joe King, "Flatbush Shivers at Threat of Being Passed by Giants," *The Sporting News*, September 20, 1950.
67. Murray Polner, *Branch Rickey: A Biography* (Jefferson, NC: McFarland, 2007), 201.
68. *Ibid*.
69. *Ibid*.
70. *Ibid*., 193.
71. *Ibid*., 194.
72. Andy McCue, *Mover & Shaker: Walter O'Malley, the Dodgers, & Baseball's Westward Expansion* (Lincoln: University of Nebraska, 2014), 69.
73. Harold C. Burr, "Rickey Still Unaware of His Fate as Dodger Conferences Continue," *Brooklyn Eagle*, October 24, 1950.
74. Michael Shapiro, *The Last Good Season: Brooklyn, the Dodgers and Their Final Pennant Race Together* (New York: Doubleday, 2003), 20.
75. *Ibid*.
76. *Ibid*., 21.
77. *Ibid*.
78. Dick Young, "Rickey Resigns, Owners Pick O'Malley President," *New York Daily News*, October 27, 1950.
79. Jimmy Powers, "The Powerhouse," *New York Daily News*, May 10, 1950.
80. Fred Hayden (AP), "2 V.P.'s Replace 1 G.M. at Brooklyn; Reese 'In,'" *Dayton Daily News*, November 3, 1950.
81. AP, "Reese Leader? He Plays Coy," *New York Daily News*, October 26, 1950.
82. "Flatbush Futurity Field," *New York Daily News*, November 4, 1950.
83. *Ibid*.

Chapter 12

1. Tommy Holmes. "Newk Totes the Mail," *Brooklyn Eagle*, October 3, 1951.
2. Many sources report that the Dodgers held a 13½ game lead. Technically, that is true. Roger Kahn explained in *The Era* that the Dodgers never led the Giants by 13½ games "at sundown" in 1951. The Dodgers won the first game of a doubleheader against the Braves on August 11 and did pull ahead by 13½ games for a short time. The Dodgers lost the second game, though, and led the Giants by an even 13 games at the end of the day.
3. Duke Snider with Bill Gilbert, *The Duke of Flatbush* (New York: Zebra, 189), 127.
4. Ray Robinson, *The Shot Heard 'Round the World: The Dramatic Story of the 1951 Giants-Dodgers Pennant Race* (Mineola, NY: Dover Publications, 1991), 64.
5. Rob Edelman, Burt Shotton SABR bio, https://sabr.org/bioproj/person/burt-shotton/.
6. *Ibid*.
7. Joe Reichler (AP), "Charlie Dressen Named Brooklyn Manager, O'Malley Hints Shotton Going with Bucs," *Elmira Advertiser* (NY), November 29, 1950.
8. Dave Anderson, *Pennant Races: Baseball at Its Best* (New York: Doubleday, 1994), 216.

9. Hal Wood (UP), "Dressen Says Dodgers to Be Pennant Race," *Wilmington Press Journal* (CA), February 2, 1951.

10. AP, "Pee-Wee Reese in Fold for $30,000," *Hazelton Standard-Speaker* (PA), January 4, 1951.

11. Joe King (NEA), "Dodgers Need Good Relief Hurler, Slugger, Reese Says," *Shamokin News-Dispatch* (PA), March 5, 1951.

12. Dick Young, "Flock Nips Braves in 11, 4–3; Pee Wee Solid Guy," *New York Daily News*, April 2, 1951.

13. Tommy Holmes, "Clinical Openings on Opening Day," *Brooklyn Eagle*, April 18, 1951.

14. *Ibid.*

15. Anderson, *Pennant Races*, 216.

16. AP, "Durocher Retains Faith in His New York Giants Despite Losses," *Hazelton Plain Speaker* (PA), April 25, 1951.

17. Dick Young, "Robby's Boot, 6 in 8th Clip Flock for Cards, 11–7," *New York Daily News*, May 7, 1951.

18. AP, "Robinson's Life Threatened, Police Scan Crowd Closely," *Cincinnati Enquirer*, May 21, 1951.

19. Arnold Rampersad, *Jackie Robinson* (New York: Alfred A. Knopf, 1997), 237.

20. Roger Kahn, *The Era: 1947–1957 When the Yankees, the Giants, and the Dodgers Ruled the World* (New York: Ticknor & Fields, 1993), 269.

21. Dick Young, "Flock Gets Pafko in 8-Man Deal," *New York Daily News*, June 16, 1951.

22. Bobby Thomson with Lee Heiman and Bill Gutman, *"The Giants Win the Pennant! The Giants Win the Pennant!"* (New York: Citadel, 2001), 130.

23. AP, "Brooklyn Manager Hails Dodgers as Greatest in City's History," July 14, 1951, *Spokane Spokesman-Review*, July 14, 1951.

24. Joe King, "$3,000,000—Player Value of Dodgers," *The Sporting News*, August 8, 1951.

25. Anderson, *Pennant Races*, 214.

26. Clay Felker, "Dodger Taunts Fired Giants to Fury," *The Sporting News*, October 10, 1951.

27. William F. McNeil, *The Dodgers Encyclopedia* (New York: Sports Publishing, 2012), 277.

28. Anderson, *Pennant Races*, 214.

29. Ted Reed, *Carl Furillo: Brooklyn Dodgers All-Star* (Jefferson, NC: McFarland, 2010), 82.

30. Golenbock, *Bums*, 274.

31. Lee Allen, *Giants and the Dodgers* (New York: G. P Putman's Sons, 1964), 11.

32. *Ibid.*, 12.

33. *Ibid.*

34. *Ibid.*

35. *Ibid.*, 13.

36. *Ibid.*, 14.

37. Robinson, *The Shot Heard 'Round the World*, 169.

38. Anderson, *Pennant Races*, 223.

39. Gene Ward, "Clutch Baseball," *New York Daily News*, September 2, 1951.

40. *Ibid.*

41. "Mueller's 3 Homers Sparks Giants, 8–1," *Brooklyn Eagle*, September 3, 1951.

42. Jim McCulley, "Giants Sweep Dodgers, 11–2; Mueller Belts 2," *New York Daily News*, September 3, 1951.

43. Snider with Gilbert, *Duke of Flatbush*, 127.

44. AP, "Dodger Team is Downcast, Not Through," *Richmond Times-Dispatch* (VA), September 26, 1951.

45. Harold C. Burr, "Final Hope Rests on Newcombe, Roe," *Brooklyn Eagle*, September 29, 1951.

46. Will Grimsley, "Brooklyn Still Hopes for Title Despite Defeat," *Glens Falls Post-Star* (NY), October 2, 1951.

47. Jeff Findley, Bobby Thomson SABR bio, https://sabr.org/bioproj/person/bobby-thomson/.

48. Anderson, *Pennant Races*, 213.

49. Harold C, Burr, "Branca's 2 Mistakes—BOOM! BOOM!" *Brooklyn Eagle*, October 2, 1951.

50. Anderson, *Pennant Races*, 241.

51. Tommy Holmes, "Zero Hour at Hand in N.L. Flag Chase," *Brooklyn Eagle*, October 3, 1951.

52. Joseph F. Wilkinson, "Fans Say It's in the Bag," *Brooklyn Eagle*, October 3, 1951.

53. *Ibid.*

54. "THIS IS IT! MAGLIE AGAINST NEWCOMBE!" *New York Daily News*, October 3, 1951.

55. Kahn, *The Era*, 273.

56. Robinson, *The Shot Heard 'Round the World*, 218.

57. *Ibid.*

58. Anderson, *Pennant Races*, 244.

59. *Ibid.*

60. Robinson, *The Shot Heard 'Round the World*, 217.

61. Anderson, *Pennant Races*, 246.

62. *Ibid.*, 247.

63. Author interview with Carl Erskine, December 4, 2020.

64. Leo Durocher with Ed Linn, *Nice Guys Finish Last* (New York: Pocket Books, 1976), 267.

65. Anderson, *Pennant Races*, 248.

66. *Ibid.*

67. Robinson, *The Shot Heard 'Round the World*, 225.

68. Anderson, *Pennant Races*, 248.

69. Thomson with Heiman and Gutman, *The Giants Win the Pennant! The Giants Win the Pennant!*, 235.

70. *Ibid.*, 238.

71. *Ibid.*, 239.

72. *Ibid.*, 250.

73. *Ibid.*, 226.

74. Anderson, *Pennant Races*, 249.

75. Robinson, *The Shot Heard 'Round the World*, 226.

76. Kahn, *The Era*, 277.

77. Thomson with Heiman and Gutman, *The Giants Win the Pennant! The Giants Win the Pennant!*, 252.

78. Snider with Gilbert, *The Duke of Flatbush*, 131.

79. *Cincinnati Enquirer*, October 4, 1951.

80. Durocher and Linn, *Nice Guys Finish Last*, 267.

81. AP, "Branca Glum after Defeat; Bums Silent," *Cincinnati Enquirer*, October 4, 1951.
82. Anderson, *Pennant Races*, 250.
83. Bobby Thomson (As told to the United Press), "Thomson Rode Around the Bases on a P.G. Cloud," *Brooklyn Eagle*, October 4, 1951.
84. Gayle Talbot AP, "Bobby Thomson Blasts 3-Run Homer in Great Come-from-Behind Drive," *Bristol Herald Courier* (TN), October 4, 1951.
85. Thomson with Heiman and Gutman, *The Giants Win the Pennant! The Giants Win the Pennant!*, 256.
86. Snider with Gilbert, *The Duke of Flatbush*, 132.
87. "Brooks Take Disaster Like Champs," *Brooklyn Eagle*, October 4, 1951.
88. Author interview with Carl Erskine, November 4, 2020.
89. Richard Goldstein, "Bobby Thomson Dies at 86; Hit Epic Home Run," *New York Times*, August 17, 2010.
90. Joe King, "Giants' Playoff Win Sets New High in Drama," *The Sporting News*, October 10, 1951.
91. Joe Trimble, "Thomson Hero, Branca Goat in the Big Payoff," *New York Daily News*, October 4, 1951.
92. Ibid.
93. Harold C. Burr, "Victory Just Wasn't in Books for Us," *Brooklyn Eagle*, October 4, 1951.
94. Ibid.
95. Durocher with Linn, *Nice Guys Finish Last*, 267.
96. Ibid., 268.
97. Ibid.
98. AP, "Branca Glum After Defeat; Bums Silent," *Cincinnati Enquirer*, October 4, 1951.
99. Joshua Prager, *The Echoing Green: The Untold Story of Bobby Thomson, Ralph Branca and the Shot Round the World* (New York: Pantheon, 2006), 31.
100. Ibid.
101. Ibid.
102. Ibid.
103. Ibid., 46.
104. Richard Goldstein, "Sal Yvars Dies at 84; Revealed Baseball Scheme," *New York Times*, December 11, 2008.
105. James Elfers, "Focus on the Giants' Cheating Scandal in 1951," https://sabr.org/journal/article/focus-on-the-giants-cheating-scandal-of-1951/.
106. James Elfers, Sal Yvars SABR bio, https://sabr.org/bioproj/person/sal-yvars/.
107. Goldstein, "Sal Yvars Dies at 84; Revealed Baseball Scheme."
108. Joshua Prager, "Was the '51 Giants Comeback a Miracle, or Did They Simply Steal the Pennant," *Wall Street Journal*, January 31, 2001.
109. Bill Shaiken, "Bobby Thomson, Who Hit Dramatic 1951 Home Run, Dies," *Los Angeles Times*, August 17, 2010.
110. William F. McNeil, *The Dodgers Encyclopedia* (New York: Sports Publishing, 2012), 279.
111. Schoor, *The Pee Wee Reese Story*, 143.
112. Thomson with Heiman and Gutman, *The Giants Win the Pennant! The Giants Win the Pennant!*, 261.
113. Ibid., 256.
114. *Brooklyn Dodgers—The Original America's Team*, Virgil Films, 2005.

Chapter 13

1. Gayle Talbot, "Yankees Again ('49), Again ('50) and Again ('51)," *Elmira Advertiser* (NY), October 11, 1951.
2. AP, "Brooklyn Dodgers Eager to Get Even with Giants," *Pensacola News Journal*, March 31, 1951.
3. Roscoe McGowen, "Brooks 'To Put Out a Little More This Year,' Says Jackie," *The Sporting News*, February 20, 1952.
4. Ibid.
5. Jim McCulley, "The Flock's in the Fold! Reese, Ralph, King Sign," *New York Daily News*, February 14, 1952.
6. Dick Young, "18 Wins Roe '52 Goal; Need Luck to Get 22," *New York Daily News*, February 27, 1952.
7. Gregory H. Wolf, Billy Loes SABR bio. https://sabr.org/bioproj/person/b5095a12.
8. Peter Dreier, Joe Black SABR bio https://sabr.org/bioproj/person/b5095a12.
9. "Dodgers Rated 'Most Solid' N.L. Team in Poll of Rivals," *The Sporting News*, April 2, 1952.
10. Roger Kahn, *Into My Own: The Remarkable People and Events That Shaped My Life* (New York: Thomas Dunne, 2006), 103.
11. Ibid., 104.
12. Ibid., 105.
13. Oscar Ruhl, "An Innovation of '52—Frustrated '51 Idea," *The Sporting News*, April 30, 1952.
14. Paul Lukas, Uni Watch, "Revealed: The Story Behind the Dodgers' Red Numbers." https://uni-watch.com/2013/10/16/revealed-the-story-behind-the-dodgers-red-numbers/.
15. Dick Young, "Dodgers Nip Braves, 2–1, in First Game," *New York Daily News*, April 23, 1952.
16. AP, "Fans Taunt Dressen for Lifting Reese," *Austin American-Statesman*, April 23, 1952.
17. Schoor, *The Pee Wee Reese Story*, 148.
18. Stan Baumgartner, "Missed Pop Foul Helps Nats Trip A's, 5–2, in 11; Dodgers Tops Phils, 4–3, on Unearned Run in 10th," *Philadelphia Inquirer*, May 12, 1952.
19. "Doesn't Agree 'Best Years' Behind Jackie and Pee Wee," *The Sporting News*, May 7, 1952.
20. Lou Smith, "Tree Grows in Brooklyn, Falls on Reds," *Cincinnati Enquirer*, May 22, 1952.
21. Harold C. Burr, "It Wasn't Thunder—It Was the Dodgers!" *Brooklyn Eagle*, May 22, 1952.
22. Ibid.
23. Sid Frigand, "Labine Picked to Bury Reds Dazed by 15-Run Record," *Brooklyn Eagle*, May 22, 1952.
24. Ibid.
25. Black's scoreless streak lasted another two

appearances and 1⅓ innings, https://www.baseball-reference.com/players/gl.fcg?id=blackjo02&t=p&year=1952.

26. Dick Young, "Flock's Black Stops Cubs, 3–2; Take 1st," *New York Daily News*, June 2, 1952.

27. Martha Jo Black and Chuck Schoffner, *Joe Black: More Than a Dodger* (Chicago: Academy Chicago 2015), 3.

28. "Dean Predicts Dodger Hurler Will Reach Top," *Brooklyn Eagle*, May 2, 1952.

29. Associated Press, "Carl Erskine Hurls No-Hit, No-Run Game," *Anderson Herald* (IN), June 20, 1952.

30. United Press, "Fear of Rain Spoiled Carl's Perfect Game," *Indianapolis News*, June 20, 1952.

31. "Braw Laddie on the Way," *New York Daily News*, June 29, 1952.

32. United Press, "Now, Gals, No Swoonin,'" *Cincinnati Enquirer*, June 29, 1952.

33. Robert M. Grannis, "Butch Did Not Come Here for a Loan, Folks," *Brooklyn Eagle*, July 2, 1952.

34. AP, Reds Lose 6–4 to Brooklyn," *Louisville Courier-Journal*, June 7, 1952.

35. Lou Smith, "Reds' Rally Falls Short, Brooks Win," *Cincinnati Enquirer*, June 7, 1952.

36. UP, "Dodgers Tune Up for Cardinals with 22-Hit Blast in Chicago," *St. Louis Post-Dispatch*, July 13, 1952.

37. Roger Kahn, "A Tribute to ... Captain Courageous," *Los Angeles Times*, August 19, 1999.

38. Ibid.

39. Lyn Connelly, "A Peek at the Stars," *Opp News* (AL), July 10, 1952.

40. Carl Erskine, *Tales from the Dodgers Dugout: A Collection of the Greatest Dodger Stories Ever Told* (New York: Sports Publishing, 2012) 157.

41. Tommy Fitzgerald, "Reese Still Fast Despite 33 Years," *Louisville Courier-Journal*, August 20, 1952.

42. Tommy Fitzgerald, "Even Umpires Like Reese, Who'll Be Honored Tonight," *Louisville Courier-Journal*, August 19, 1952.

43. Dick Young, "Dodgers Clinch! Split with Phils," *New York Daily News*, September 24, 1952.

44. Ibid.

45. Stan Baumgartner, "'Reese a Pickpocket on Base! He Catches Foes Asleep'—B.R.," *The Sporting News*, April 26, 1950.

46. "Dodgers Undefeated in 4 Parks in Loop in First Half," *The Sporting News*, July 16, 1952.

47. "55 Grand-Slam Homers in '52, Eight for Dodgers and Red Sox," *The Sporting News*, December 31, 1952.

48. Roger Kahn, *The Era: 1947–1957 When the Yankees, the Giants, and the Dodgers Ruled the World* (New York: Ticknor & Fields, 1993), 244.

49. George Vescey, *Baseball's Most Valuable Players* (New York: Random House, 1966), 128.

50. Jane Leavy, *The Last Boy: Mickey Mantle and the End of America's Childhood* (New York: HarperCollins, 2010), 13.

51. Dick Young, "Yanks 6–5 Over Dodgers in Series Opener Today, *New York Daily News*, October 1, 1952.

52. "Warm Series," *New York Daily News*, October 1, 1952.

53. Joe Trimble, "Rhubarbs Won't Grow in Brooklyn, Rules Frick," *New York Daily News*, October 2, 1952.

54. Ibid.

55. Roscoe McGowen, "Reese Still a Dazzler After Dozen Years with Dodgers," *The Sporting News*, October 8, 1952.

56. Dorothy O'Keefe, J. F. Wilkinson, and Al Salerno, "Faithful Jam Ebbets Field," *Brooklyn Eagle*, October 1, 1952.

57. Walter F. O'Malley, "O'Malley Stresses Need for Arena," *Brooklyn Eagle*, October 1, 1952.

58. Hy Turkin, "There Is No Fan Like Dodger Fan!" *New York Daily News*, October 2, 1952.

59. AP, "From Rags to Riches in Less Than Year Is Joe Black Saga," *Hazelton Standard-Sentinel* (PA), October 2, 1952.

60. Ibid.

61. Ibid.

62. Kahn, *The Era*, 244.

63. Jim McCulley, "Reese Hurt," *New York Daily News*, October 2, 1952.

64. "Dodger Tickets for Sale," *Brooklyn Eagle*, October 3, 1952.

65. Jim McCulley, "'It Was My Fault,' Berra Says; Legwork Won: Chuck," *New York Daily News*, October 4, 1952.

66. Tommy Holmes, "That Yankee Genie Goes Out to Lunch," *Brooklyn Eagle*, October 4, 1952.

67. Dave Anderson, "Flock 'Runs' Away on Yanks, *Brooklyn Eagle*, October 4, 1952.

68. Jim McCulley and Dick Young, "Aging Mize Not So Sure He'll Quit Net Season," *New York Daily News*, October 5, 1952.

69. Martha Jo Black and Chuck Schoffner, *Joe Black: More Than a Dodger* (Chicago: Academy Chicago, 2015), 234.

70. Roger Kahn, *The Era: When the Yankees, the Giants, and the Dodgers Ruled the World* (New York: Ticknor & Fields, 1993), 306.

71. Ibid., 307.

72. Dick Young, "It's Great to Be a Dodger! Yanks Beef Over Umpiring," *New York Daily News*, October 6, 1952.

73. Dana Mozley, "Snider HRs Tie Ruth, Gehrig; Casey's Ouija Says 'Gorman,'" *New York Daily News*, October 7, 1952.

74. Clarence Greenbaum, "Stunned, Bewildered Fans Take It on Chin for 6th Time," *Brooklyn Eagle*, October 8, 1952.

75. Leo H. Peterson (UP), "Yankees Are Still Champions; Brooklyn Dodgers Are Still 'Bums,'" *Coos Bay Times* OR), October 8, 1952.

76. Will Grimsley, "'They Didn't Miss Joe DiMaggio—Mantle Killed Us,' Says Robby," *Elmira Advertiser* (NY), October 8, 1952.

77. Joe Reichler, "Mixed Emotion Fill Brooklyn's Dressing Room; Reese Dejected," *Elmira Star-Gazette* (NY), October 8, 1952.

78. Ibid.

79. *Ibid.*

80. Joe Reichler, "Mixed Emotion Fill Brooklyn's Dressing Room; Reese Dejected."

81. Will Grimsley, "'They Didn't Miss Joe DiMaggio—Mantle Killed Us,' Says Robby."

82. Kahn, *The Era*, 310.

Chapter 14

1. Andrew Paul Mele, *Tearin' Up the Pea Patch* (Jefferson, NC: McFarland, 2015), 1.

2. William F. McNeil, *The Dodgers Encyclopedia* (New York: Sports Publishing, 2012), 193.

3. Besides leading the NL in runs scored for the fifth straight year, the Dodgers also topped the league in home runs, slugging percentage, and runs batted in (887) for the fifth straight campaign. *Ibid.*

4. *Ibid.*

5. Dana Mozley, "Reese, Campy, Robby Hit Flock for 98G, Giants Give Sal 35," *New York Daily News*, January 13, 1953.

6. Roger Kahn, *Into My Own: The Remarkable People and Events That Shaped a Life* (New York: Thomas Dunne, 2006), 108.

7. Earl Ruby, "Ruby's Report," *Louisville Courier-Journal*, February 3, 1953.

8. Hy Hurwitz, "Tribe Gives Hartsfield, Cash for Veteran Dodger Slugger," *Boston Globe*, January 18, 1953.

9. AP, "Pafko Is Disappointed on Moving to Braves," *Cincinnati Enquirer*, January 19, 1953.

10. Saul Wisnia, Lou Perini SABR bio, https://sabr.org/bioproj/person/lou-perini/.

11. Mele, *Tearin' Up the Pea Patch*, 43.

12. *Ibid.*

13. Roger Kahn, *The Boys of Summer* (New York: Harper, 2006), 175.

14. Mele, *Tearin' Up the Pea Patch*, 45.

15. Kahn, *The Boys of Summer*, 177.

16. Schoor, *The Pee Wee Reese Story*, 155–56.

17. AP, "Hall of Fame Shortstop Reese Dies at Age 81," *Arlington Heights Daily Herald* (IL), August 15, 1999.

18. Dick Young, "Eyes Shipshape Again, Furillo Future Bright," *New York Daily News*, February 26, 1953.

19. Lester J. Biederman, "Phils Ogle Buc Pitchers for Swap," *Pittsburgh Press*, April 16, 1953.

20. Harold G. Burr, "Gilliam a Natural in Leadoff Role," *Brooklyn Eagle*, April 20, 1953.

21. Tom Meany, *The Artful Dodgers* (New York: Grosset & Dunlap, 1958), 118.

22. AP, "Dodgers Gain Loop Lead on Reese Homer in 8th; ChiSox Beat Yankees," *Rochester Democrat and Chronicle*, May 2, 1953.

23. Roscoe McGowen, "18,178 Cheer Slump-Ridden Hodges for First '53 Homer," *The Sporting News*, May 13, 1953.

24. *Ibid.*

25. Harold C. Burr, "Gilliam a Natural in Lead-off Role."

26. Jim Angus, Jim "Junior" Gilliam SABR bio. https://sabr.org/bioproj/person/3c15c318.

27. Milton Richman, "Pee Wee Reese Places Approval on Junior Gilliam," *Alexandria Times-Tribune* (IN), April 29, 1953.

28. Harold C. Burr, "Erskine Just What Doctor Ordered," *Brooklyn Eagle*, May 18, 1953.

29. "'Good Bunt,' Says Erskine, After Bell Spoils No-Hitter," *The Sporting News*, May 27, 1953.

30. Dick Young, "Dozen Dodgers Score in 8th for Record; Phils Bow, 16–2," *New York Daily News*, May 25, 1953.

31. UP, "NL Shortstops Name Pee Wee Reese Tops," *Palm Beach Post*, June 23, 1953.

32. Roger Kahn, *Into My Own: The Remarkable People and Events That Shaped a Life* (New York: Thomas Dunne, 2006), 107.

33. *Ibid.*, 106.

34. AP, "Dodgers Regain League Top Spot with 11–1 Triumph over Braves," *Elmira Advertiser* (NY), June 29, 1953.

35. Joe Reichler (AP), "Dressen Still Mad at Maglie," *Terre Haute Tribune*, July 6, 1953.

36. Dick Young, "Flock Ties for 1st, 4–3, on Reese HR in 10th," *New York Daily News*, June 28, 1953.

37. Dave Anderson, "Home Run Bug Finally Bites Roe as Dodger Sluggers Set NL Mark," *Brooklyn Eagle*, July 8, 1953.

38. AP, "Pee Wee Reese Happiest Guy on NL Team," *Altoona Tribune*, July 15, 1953.

39. Earnest Hoberecht, "Fighting Ends," *Brooklyn Eagle*, July 27, 1953.

40. Bill Roeder, "Bustin' Bums Challenge Slugging Marks," *The Sporting News*, August 26, 1953.

41. *Ibid.*

42. Dave Anderson, "Reese Muscles into Homer Act as Dodgers Aim for Two Goals," *Brooklyn Eagle*, August 29, 1953.

43. "Brooklyn Ties Home Run Mark," *Janesville Daily Gazette* (WI), August 29, 1953.

44. Dave Anderson, "Reese Muscles into Homer Act as Dodgers Aim for Two Goals," *Brooklyn Eagle*, August 29, 1953.

45. AP, "Dodgers Score 12 Runs in 7th to Crush Cards, 20–4, Tie Record; Campy Had 122 RBIs," *Oneonta Star* (NY), August 31, 1953.

46. *Ibid.*

47. Bob Broeg, "Something Snaps as Cards Lose, 20–4; It Wasn't Rabbit Ball," *St. Louis Post-Dispatch*, August 31, 1953.

48. Dave Anderson, "Pennant Clinched on Earliest Date in N.L. History," *Brooklyn Eagle*, September 13, 1953.

49. Tommy Holmes, "Flock Almost Blasé About Flag Triumph," *Brooklyn Eagle*, September 13, 1953.

50. Joe King, "'53 Dodgers Best of Five Winners, Says Reese," *The Sporting News*, September 30, 1953.

51. *Ibid.*

52. *Brooklyn Eagle*, September 30, 1953.

53. Al Salerno, "Freed of Jury Duty to See Dodgers Win," *Brooklyn Eagle*, September 28, 1953.

54. "The Dope, Straight from Dodgers' Mouths," *Brooklyn Eagle*, September 30, 1953.

55. Oscar Fraley, "Dodgers' Hopes Ride on Ol' Preach Today," *Cincinnati Enquirer*, October 1, 1953.

56. AP, "'Mickey Parked Low Screwball,' Says Roe," *Los Angeles Times*, October 2, 1953.
57. Mele, *Tearin' Up the Pea Patch*, 157.
58. Jack Hand (AP), "Erskine Sets Whiff Mark, Beats Yanks 3–2," *Jacksonville Daily Journal* (IL), October 3, 1953.
59. Joe Lee, "Yanks Sing Praises of Erskine's 'Stuff,'" *Brooklyn Eagle*, October 3, 1953.
60. Jack Hand (AP), "Erskine Sets Whiff Mark, Beats Yanks 3–2," *Jacksonville Daily Journal* (IL), October 3, 1953.
61. Mele, *Tearin' Up the Pea Patch*, 159.
62. Oscar Fraley (UP), "'Team Job' Wins for Brooklyn," *Mansfield News-Journal* (OH), October 4, 1953.
63. Ibid.
64. Tommy Holmes, "Yanks on Their Game— Our Guys Weren't," *Brooklyn Eagle*, October 6, 1953.
65. AP, "Yankees and Dodgers Acclaim Billy Martin as the Series Hero," *Kingston Daily Freeman* (NY), October 6, 1953.
66. Ibid.
67. Hugh Fullerton Jr. (AP), "Winning Ball Game, Not Record, Important Thing to Billy Martin," *Newport News Daily Press* (VA), October 6, 1953.
68. Tommy Holmes, "Yanks on Their Game— Our Guys Weren't," *Brooklyn Eagle*, October 6, 1953.
69. UP, "Futility Strikes Brooks," *Binghamton Press and Sun-Bulletin* (NY), October 6, 1953.
70. Ibid.
71. AP, "Manager Charlie Dressen Quits Dodgers in Contract Tiff," *Great Falls Tribune*, October 15, 1953.
72. Joe Reichler, "Pee Wee Reese Seen Likely Dressen Successor; Latter May 'Change Mind,'" *Newport Daily News* (RI), October 15, 1953.
73. Joe Reichler (AP), "Peppery Pilot Who Won Pennant for Bums Says He Is 'Very Happy,'" *Billings Gazette*, October 17, 1953.
74. Ibid.
75. Joe Reichler, "Dressen Calls Pee Wee Logical Choice for New Dodgers' Manager," *Newport Daily News* (RI), October 17, 1953.
76. Buzzie Bavasi with John Strege, *Off the Record* (Chicago: Contemporary Books, 1987), 53.
77. Frank Eck (AP), "Reese is Seen as Dodger Playing Manager," *Bryan Eagle* (TX), November 10, 1953.
78. Ibid.
79. Ibid.
80. Ibid.
81. AP, "Pee Wee Reese Decides Not to Manage Dodgers," *Hanover Evening Sun* (PA), November 6, 1953.

Chapter 15

1. United Press (UP), "Alston, of Montreal, Dodger '54 Manager," *Boston Globe*, November 24, 1953.
2. Joe Trimble, "Montreal's Alston to Pilot Dodgers," *New York Daily News*, November 25, 1953.
3. Milton Richman, "O'Malley Hints That Walt Alston Had Better Beat the Yanks Next Season," *Berkshire Eagle* (Pittsfield, MA) November 25, 1953.
4. Joe Trimble, "Montreal's Alston to Pilot Dodgers." *New York Daily News*, November 25, 1953.
5. Buzzie Bavasi with John Strege, *Off the Record* (Chicago: Contemporary Books, 1987), 54.
6. Tommy Holmes, "Dodgers Introduce Their '54 Skipper," *Brooklyn Eagle*, November 25, 1953.
7. Bill Johnson, Walter Alston SABR bio, https://sabr.org/bioproj/person/walter-alston/.
8. Walter Alston with Jack Tobin, *A Year at a Time* (Waco, TX: Word Books, 1976), 51.
9. Harold Tuthill, "Warneke Victor Over Dizzy Dean in Finale," *St. Louis Post-Dispatch*, September 28, 1936.
10. Bavasi with Strege, *Off the Record*, 54.
11. Ibid.
12. Harold C. Burr, "Alston Story a Page Out of Horatio Alger," *Brooklyn Eagle*, November 25, 1953.
13. AP, "Reese SS?," *New York Daily News*, November 25, 1953.
14. Ibid.
15. Dick Young, "Reese Okays Flock Terms, *New York Daily News*, January 14, 1954.
16. Ibid.
17. Dave Anderson, Reese Sees New Shuffle for Cards," *Brooklyn Eagle*, March 2, 1954.
18. Steve Snider, "Weight Loss May Spark Dodger Catcher Again," *Billings Gazette*, March 12, 1954.
19. UP, "Bums Laugh Off Complacency Rumor," *Long Beach Independent Press-Telegram*, March 14, 1954.
20. Roscoe McGowen, "Brooks Regulars Again Bar Way to Blue-Ribbon Subs," *The Sporting News*, March 10, 1954.
21. Dick Young, "Jackie Avoids Weigh-In, Hopes to Hit 140 Games," *New York Daily News*, March 1, 1954.
22. Ibid.
23. Peter Golenbock, *Bums: An Oral History of the Brooklyn Dodgers* (New York: G. P. Putnam's Sons, 1984), 372.
24. Roscoe McGowen, "Dodgers Find Alston Knows the Score," *The Sporting News*, March 17, 1954.
25. C. C. Johnson Spink, "The Low-Down on Majors' Big Shots," *The Sporting News*, January 6, 1954.
26. Roscoe McGowen, "Dodgers Find Alston Knows the Score," *The Sporting News*, March 17, 1954.
27. Pee Wee Reese and Tim Cohane, "Reese's Own Story: 14 Years a Bum," *Baseball Digest*, May 1954.
28. Roscoe McGowen, "Dodgers Find Alston Knows the Score."
29. Bill Lee, "With Malice Toward None," *Hartford Courant*, March 6, 1954.
30. Alston with Tobin, *A Year at a Time*, 104.
31. Ibid., 106.
32. UP, "Jackie Robinson to Quit Baseball After '54," *Pittsburgh Press*, March 3, 1954.

33. Roy Campanella, *It's Good to Be Alive* (New York: Little, Brown, 1959), 185.
34. Dave Anderson, "Maglie Draws Praise from Dodgers," *Brooklyn Eagle*, April 14, 1954.
35. Dave Anderson, "Durocher Up to Old Beanball Tricks," *Brooklyn Eagle*, April 15, 1954.
36. *Ibid.*
37. *Ibid.*
38. *Ibid.*
39. *Ibid.*
40. *Ibid.*
41. Roy Campanella, *It's Good to Be Alive*, 186.
42. Stan Baumgartner, "2-Run Blast Off Dickson in 5th Wins; Rain Halts Game After 6," *Philadelphia Inquirer*, May 9, 1954.
43. "Pee Wee Reese Pulls Off 200th Theft as a Dodger," *The Sporting News*, June 9, 1954.
44. Jim McCulley, "Reese's Homer, Erskine's Hurling Beats Giants, 4–2," *New York Daily News*, May 30, 1954.
45. Roscoe McGowen, "Pee Wee Hits 100th Homer as Dodgers—Aims at Another Hundred in 10 Years," *The Sporting News*. June 30, 1954.
46. Dana Mozley, "Snider and Reese Hurt, Lost to Flock for Series," *New York Daily News*, June 30, 1954.
47. Dana Mozley, "Reese Injury Serious; Zimmer May Return," *New York Daily News*, July 1, 1954.
48. Les Biederman, "The Scoreboard," *Pittsburgh Press*, "July 13, 1954.
49. "Mays Pushes Duke Around," *Brooklyn Eagle*, July 14, 1954.
50. Roscoe McGowen, "Does Smokey Lack Fire as Pilot? Opinions of Older Dodgers Differ," *The Sporting News*, July 28, 1954.
51. Schoor, *The Pee Wee Reese Story*, 165.
52. http://www.travelthruhistory.tv/bay-ridge/.
53. "Future of South Brooklyn and Its Suburbs," *Brooklyn Daily Eagle*, March 18, 1906.
54. *Ibid.*
55. Duke Snider with Bill Gilbert, *The Duke of Flatbush* (New York: Zebra Books, 1988), 172.
56. Reference.com. https://www.reference.com/technology/much-did-television-cost-1950s-9dcede5123bfef9.
57. Snider with Gilbert, *The Duke of Flatbush*, 173.
58. Author interview with Carl Erskine, December 4, 2020.
59. *Ibid.*
60. "'Keeping Players Satisfied Captain's Chief Job'—Reese," *The Sporting News*, May 5, 1954.
61. AP, "Pee Wee Reese Says Alston Not to Blame for Brooklyn Slump," *Fort Myers News-Press*, July 18, 1954.
62. "5 Brook Pinch-Hitters Fail to Hit Ball Beyond Infield," *The Sporting News*, August 11, 1954.
63. Joe Reichler, "Pee Wee Reese Denies Cardinal Player's Charge of Listless Play by Dodgers," *Alabama Journal* (Montgomery), August 6, 1954.
64. "O'Malley Has Faith, Thinks Bums Will Overtake Giants," *The Sporting News*, July 28, 1954.
65. *Ibid.*
66. Jackie Robinson, *I Never Had It Made* (New York: Putnam, 1972), 118.
67. Alston and Tobin, *A Year at a Time*, 105.
68. Bill Madden, *1954: The Year Willie Mays and the First Generation of Black Superstars Changed Major League Baseball Forever* (Boston: Da Capo, 2014), 64.
69. *Ibid.*
70. Dave Anderson, "O'Malley Calls Walt Best Man to Rebuild Club," *Brooklyn Eagle*, September 9, 1954.
71. Dick Young, "Alston Is Set as Manager for '55, O'Malley Hints," *New York Daily News*, September 9, 1954.
72. *Ibid.*
73. *Ibid.*
74. Shirley Povich, "Mr. Anonymity of the Dodgers—That's Alston," *The Sporting News*, September 15, 1954.
75. Tom Clavin and Danny Peary, *Gil Hodges: The Brooklyn Bums, the Miracle Mets, and the Extraordinary Life of a Baseball Legend* (New York: Berkley, 2012), 98.
76. *Ibid.*
77. Golenbock, *Bums*, 173.
78. Bavasi with Strege, *Off the Record*, 55.
79. UP, "More History in Spooner's 2nd Shutout," *Binghamton Press and Sun-Bulletin*, September 27, 1954.
80. Dave Anderson, "We Needed Spooner Sooner," *Brooklyn Eagle*, September 23, 1953.
81. "Reese Sure to Bat .300 for First Time," *Brooklyn Eagle*, September 23, 1954.
82. UP, "More History in Spooner's 2nd Shutout."
83. Tommy Holmes, "Spooner's Second Masterpiece Almost Duplicate of First Start," *Brooklyn Eagle*, September 27, 1954.
84. "Robinson Made Right Play," *Brooklyn Eagle*, September 16, 1954.
85. Walter Alston, *A Year at a Time*, 107.
86. Frank Eck, "Second-Half Feast Lifted Mays, Kuenn High on Swat Table," *The Sporting News*, December 22, 1954.
87. Schoor, *The Pee Wee Reese Story*, 166.

Chapter 16

1. Dick Young, "Flock's 1st Flash: Reese Is SS," *New York Daily News*, March 1, 1955.
2. Stewart Wolpin, *Bums No More! The Championship Season of 1955* (New York: St. Martin's, 1995), 31.
3. Bill Hurte, Don Zimmer SABR bio, https://sabr.org/bioproj/person/don-zimmer/.
4. *Ibid.*
5. United Press, "Pee Wee Due to Shift Over, Play Keystone," *Cincinnati Enquirer*, March 24, 1955.
6. Roscoe McGowen, "'Who's on Third?' Routine No Joke to Dodger Rivals," *The Sporting News*, March 16, 1955.
7. *Ibid.*
8. Claire Hall, Billy Cox SABR bio, https://sabr.org/bioproj/person/billy-cox/.

9. *Ibid.*
10. *Who's a Bum! The 1955 Brooklyn Dodgers* (New York: *New York Daily News* Publications, 1995), 22.
11. *Ibid.*
12. *Ibid.*
13. Wolpin, *Bums No More!*, 32.
14. *Ibid.*
15. "Quote 'Em Poll," *Des Moines Register*, February 14, 1955.
16. *Who's a Bum!*, 130.
17. Roscoe McGowen, "Tardy Amoros Fined $100, Not for Lateness, But for Story," *The Sporting News*, March 16, 1955.
18. Wolpin, *Bums No More!* 32.
19. Jimmy Burns, "O'Malley Seeks New Lease on Miami Stadium," *The Sporting News,* March 2, 1955.
20. *Who's a Bum!* 24.
21. AP, "Snider Sparks Dodger Assault," *Elmira Advertiser.* April 14, 1955.
22. AP, "7 Dodgers Give 7 Reasons for Winning Streak," *LaCrosse Tribune* (WI), April 22, 1955.
23. Wolpin, *Bums No More!* 36.
24. *Who's a Bum!*, 32.
25. *Ibid.*, 38.
26. Bob Broeg, "Catastrophe for N.L. Unless Dodgers Are Halted," *The Sporting News*, May 25, 1955.
27. Peter Golenbock, *Bums: An Oral History of the Brooklyn Dodgers* (New York: G. P. Putnam's Sons, 1984), 350.
28. *Ibid.*, 351.
29. *Ibid.*, 350.
30. Carl M. Cannon, "When Koufax Made a Pitch for Jews Everywhere," Realclearpolitics.com, November 18, 2019, https://www.realpolitics.com/articles/2019/11/18/when_koufax_made_a_pitch_for_jews_everywhere_141759.html.
31. Dick Young, "Braves Win 7th in Row, Diverting Brooks, 8-2," *New York Daily News*, June 25, 1955.
32. Gene Schoor, *The Pee Wee Reese Story* (New York: Julian Messner, 1956), 168.
33. Richard Sandomir, "Irving Rudd, Press Agent in Baseball, Racing, Boxing," *New York Times*, June 4, 2000.
34. Golenbock, *Bums*, 392.
35. "Clambake 'Scares' Reese," *Louisville Courier-Journal*, July 23, 1955.
36. Jimmy Breslin, "Dressen Last to Express Concern for Pee Wee Reese," *Council Bluffs Nonpareil* (IA), July 24, 1955.
37. Schoor, *The Pee Wee Reese Story,* 167.
38. *Ibid.*, 167.
39. Author interview with Carl Erskine, December 4, 2020.
40. Duke Snider with Bill Gilbert, *The Duke of Flatbush* (New York: Zebra, 1989), 183.
41. *Ibid.*
42. *Ibid.*, 184.
43. *Who's a Bum!*, 62.
44. *Ibid.*, 63.
45. *Ibid.*, 64.
46. J. G. Taylor Spink, "Looping the Loop," *The Sporting News*, August 31, 1955.
47. *Ibid.*
48. AP, "Flock Flies Flag After Crushing Braves," *Glens Falls Post-Star* (NY), September 9, 1955.
49. Dick Young, "Brook Victory 'the Greatest,'" *New York Daily News*, September 9, 1955.
50. *Ibid.*
51. Roger Kahn, *The Era: When the Yankees, the Dodgers, and the Giants Ruled the World* (New York: Ticknor & Fields, 1993), 318.
52. *Who's a Bum!*, 65.
53. Pee Wee Reese, "Pee Wee Reese Picks Dodgers to Beat Yankees In Six," *Edmonton Journal* (Canada), September 26, 1955.
54. *Ibid.*
55. Schoor, *The Pee Wee Reese Story*, 168.
56. *The Brooklyn Dodgers: The Original America's Team*, Virgil Films, 2005.
57. Pee Wee Reese, "Pee Wee Says: The Difference was Collins," *Pittsburgh Sun-Telegraph*, September 29, 1955.
58. Charles J. Doyle, "It Looks Bad for Our Team' *Pittsburgh Sun-Telegraph*, September 30, 1955.
59. Schoor, *The Pee Wee Reese Story*, 170.
60. AP, "Spooner May Go Sunday," *Elmira Star-Gazette*, October 1, 1955.
61. AP, "Win Inspires Dodgers; Team Sure of Series Title," *Spokane Chronicle*, October 1, 1955.
62. Pee Wee Reese, "Pee Wee Sees His Brooks Going on to Series Title." *Syracuse Post-Standard*, October 2, 1955.
63. Pee Wee Reese, "Pee Wee Reese Says: 'It Was the Toughest Yet,'" *Pittsburgh Sun-Telegraph*, October 3, 1955.
64. *Who's a Bum!*, 110.
65. Pee Wee Reese, "Dodgers Confident There'll Be Last Half of Ninth Today," *Lincoln Star*, October 4, 1955.
66. *Who's a Bum!*, 13.
67. AP, "Casey Stengel Is Confident in Home Park," *Edmonton Journal* (Canada), October 4, 1955.
68. Joe Trimble, "Yanks Square Series, Win 6th, 5-1," *New York Daily News*, October 4, 1955.
69. "Skies Clear," *New York Daily News*, October 4, 1955.
70. Wolpin, *Bums No More!*, 95.
71. Schoor, *The Pee Wee Reese Story*, 172.
72. *Ibid.*, 173.
73. *Ibid.*
74. *Ibid.*
75. *Ibid.*, 174.
76. *Who's a Bum!*, 126.
77. *Ibid.*
78. *Ibid.*, 131.
79. *The Brooklyn Dodgers: The Original America's Team*, Virgil Films, 2005.
80. Robert Creamer, "When Brooklyn Won," *Sports Illustrated*, October 17, 1955.
81. *Who's a Bum!*, 127.
82. Bob Bennett, John Bennett, and Robert S. Bennett, *Johnny Podres: Brooklyn's Only Yankee Killer* (Bloomington, IN: AuthorHouse, 2005), 45.
83. *Duke of Flatbush*, 192.

84. Ted Smits, "Dodgers Cut Loose with Celebration after Capturing First World Series," *Troy Times Record*, October 5, 1955.
85. Bob McGee, *The Greatest Ballpark Ever: Ebbets Field and the Story of the Brooklyn Dodgers* (New Brunswick, NJ: Rutgers University Press, 2005), 249.
86. Golenbock, *Bums*, 405.
87. Wolpin, *Bums No More*, 116.
88. Dick Young, "Dodgers Delirious—Yanks Take It in Stride," *New York Daily News*, October 5, 1955.
89. Bennett, Bennett, and Bennett, *Johnny Podres*, 43.
90. *Ibid.*, 53.
91. Wolpin, *Bums No More*, 116.
92. Roscoe McGowen, "Mom's Prayers Answered, Reese Finally on a Winner," *The Sporting News*, October 12, 1955.
93. Wolpin, *Bums No More!*, 107.
94. *Ibid.*, 105.
95. Golenbock, *Bums*, 407.
96. *Ibid.*
97. *Ibid.*, 405.
98. Wolpin, *Bums No More!*, 109.
99. *Ibid.*
100. *Ibid.*
101. *Ibid.*, 119.
102. *Ibid.*, 109.
103. Kahn, *Into My Own*, 110.

Chapter 17

1. Peter Golenbock, *Bums: An Oral History of the Brooklyn Dodgers* (New York: G. P. Putnam's Sons, 1984), 26.
2. *Ibid.*, 25.
3. Golenbock, *Bums*, 26.
4. Bob McGee, *The Greatest Ballpark Ever: Ebbets Field and the Story of the Brooklyn Dodgers* (New Brunswick, NJ: Rivergate Press, 2006), 5.
5. *Ibid.*, 4.
6. Roger Kahn, *The Era: 1947–1957 When the Yankees, the Giants, and the Dodgers Ruled the World* (New York: Ticknor & Fields, 1993), 159.
7. Steve Delsohn, *True Blue: True History of the Los Angeles Dodgers, Told by the Men Who Lived It* (New York: William Morrow, 2001), 12.
8. *Ibid.*
9. Buzzie Bavasi with John Strege, *Off the Record* (Chicago: Contemporary Books, 1987), 78.
10. Andy McCue, *Mover & Shaker: Walter O'Malley, the Dodgers, & Baseball's Westward Expansion* (Lincoln: University of Nebraska, 2014), 120.
11. *Ibid.*
12. *Ibid.*, 122.
13. *Ibid.*
14. *Ibid.*
15. Bavasi with Strege, *Off the Record*, 77.
16. Kahn, *The Era*, 299.
17. Tom Fitzgerald, "Pee Wee Hailed as Louisville's Man of Year," *The Sporting News*, February 8, 1956.
18. *Ibid.*
19. Steve Garvey, *My Bat Boy Days: Lessons I Learned from the Boys of Summer* (New York: Scribner, 2008), 6
20. *Ibid.*, 7.
21. *Ibid.*, 21.
22. *Ibid.*, 22.
23. Ben Olan (AP), "Veteran Reese Confident of Another Good Season," *Gastonia Gazette* (NC), March 2, 1956.
24. Dick Young, "Reese Out; Back Injured," *New York Daily News*, March 3, 1956.
25. *Ibid.*
26. UP, "Pee Wee Reese Ordered to Take Complete Rest," *Hartford Courant*, March 4, 1956.
27. Steve Wyman, "Fernandez in Shape if Pee Wee Isn't," *Brooklyn Daily*, March 6, 1956.
28. "Podres Called for Army Duty," *Louisville Courier-Journal*, March 6, 1956.
29. "Everyone in Step," *Brooklyn Daily*, April 17, 1956.
30. United Press (UP), "Pee Wee Reese 'Choked Up' When Presented with Ring," *Ottawa Journal* (Canada) April 18, 1956.
31. *Ibid.*
32. *Ibid.*
33. Dana Mozley, "Dodgers to Play 7 in JC Park in '56," *New York Daily News*, August 7, 1955.
34. *Ibid.*
35. Jack Mahon, "Baer Stops Galento in 8th," *New York Daily News*, July 3, 1940.
36. AP, "Dodgers Open Jersey Season," *Ithaca Journal*, April 19, 1956.
37. Dick Young, "Diamond Dust—Campy Gets 1,000 Hit," *New York Daily News*, April 20, 1956.
38. AP, Joe Reichler, "Big Park, Soft Turf, Strong Wind, Poor Crowd, Irks Bums," *Hackensack Record* (NJ), April 20, 1956.
39. *Ibid.*
40. AP, "Billy Loes Glad to be Departing from Brooklyn," *Troy Times Record* (NY), May 16, 1956.
41. Dick Young, "The Sports of Kings and Queens," *New York Daily News*, May 20, 1956.
42. Jack Hand, "Sal Maglie Joins Bums, Tells Tales," *Montpelier Evening Argus*, May 19, 1956.
43. AP, "Bums Had 'Names' for Maglie But Now He's 'Our Pal Sal.'" *Binghamton Press and SunBulletin*, May 16, 1956.
44. Joseph Wancho, Don Drysdale SABR bio, https://sabr.org/bioproj/person/don-drysdale/.
45. Dick Young, "Drysdale Whiffs 9, Baffles Phils, 6–1," *New York Daily News*, April 24, 1956.
46. Don Drysdale with Bob Verdi, *Once a Bum, Always a Dodger* (New York: St. Martin's, 1990), 97
47. *Ibid.*, 99.
48. *Ibid.*
49. Lou Smith, "Jablonski's Homer Gives Reds 7–6 Win," *Cincinnati Enquirer*, May 19, 1956.
50. Ed Wilks (AP), "Joe Adcock Drives in 7 Runs in Braves Sweep into Lead," *Ithaca Journal* July 14, 1956.
51. Tommy Holmes, "Alston Okay, Says Pee Wee," *Miami News*, July 21, 1956.
52. Roscoe McGowen, "Dodgers Big Happy

Family After Blistering by Alston," *The Sporting News*, July 25, 1956.
53. *Ibid.*
54. Roscoe McGowen, "O'Malley Commends Reese, Erskine for Backing Alston," *The Sporting News*, July 25, 1956.
55. "Hats Off," *The Sporting News*, August 1, 1956.
56. Bob Broeg, "Reese Just One Hit Away from 2,000 After Belting 4 Against Cards," *St. Louis Post-Dispatch*, July 21, 1956.
57. *Lancaster Intelligencer Journal*, July 21, 1956.
58. Dana Mozley, "Brooks win, 1–0, Bow, 4–2; Newk, Rush Cop 100th Tilts," *New York Daily News*, July 30, 1956.
59. Roscoe McGowen, "Schedule Gives Brooks a Hand, but Their Hands Are Crossed," *The Sporting News*, August 22, 1956.
60. "Pee Wee Reese Sets New Dodger Scoring Record," *Alabama Journal* (Montgomery), August 10, 1956.
61. Dick Young, "Dodgers Beat Phils on Sal's No-Hitter," *New York Daily News*, September 26, 1956.
62. This was the second Dodger no-hitter of the 1956 season. Carl Erskine threw the first one—and the second of his career—on May 12 against the Giants at Ebbets Field. He needed 102 pitches and allowed only two runners to reach first base. Oisk walked two batters on 3-and-2 counts. "I was faster than I had been in any game this season, I think," Oisk said. "But my curveball was my best pitch today. It was fooling them pretty good." Source: Dick Young, "Exercise with Steel Balls Relaxed Carl's Muscles," *New York Daily News*, May 13, 1956.
63. AP, "Maglie New Idol of Ebbets Field," *Kingston Daily Freeman* (NY), September 26, 1956.
64. *Ibid.*
65. Shapiro, *The Last Good Season*, 277.
66. AP, "Excited Dodgers Predict League Pennant Wrap-up Today," *Rochester Democrat and Chronicle*, September 30, 1956
67. Red Smith, "Dodgers Live Once More," *Rochester Democrat and Chronicle*, September 30, 1956.
68. Jim McCulley, "Champagne Flows Amid Bedlam in Clubhouse," *New York Daily News*, October 1, 1956.
69. Mickey Mantle with Herb Glock, *The Mick* (New York: Jove, 1986), 135.
70. This was the tenth straight year that the World Series included at least one team from New York City. The streak began in 1947 and would continue through 1958, when the Yankees beat the Braves. In seven of those seasons, the Series was an all-New York event. That streak ended in 1959 when the Los Angeles Dodgers beat the Chicago White Sox. It was not until 1967, when the St. Louis Cardinals beat the Boston Red Sox, that the World Series did not include a team that once called New York its home state.
71. AP, "Campanella Calls Pitch for Sal, and Ike Too," *Elmira Star-Gazette*, October 4, 1956.
72. Ed Wilks, "Alston Ready to Pull Sal if Berra Walked," *Elmira Star-Gazette*, October 4, 1956.
73. AP, "Duke at Best When Chips Are Down, Ties Gehrig with 10 Series Homers," *Binghamton Press and Sun-Bulletin*, October 6, 1956.
74. AP, "Managers Doubt Stadium Switch Will Help Yanks," *Binghamton Press and Sun-Bulletin* , October 6, 1956.
75. *Ibid.*
76. AP, "Sturdivant Credits Berra, Stengel for Victory in 6–2 Series Win," *Troy Record* (NY), October 8, 1966.
77. Jack Hand, "Don Larsen's Perfect Game Gives Yankees 3-2 Edge in World Series," *Troy Times Record* (NY), October 9, 1956.
78. Don Larsen, "Dodger Batters in Ninth Looked Like Williams," *Lebanon Daily News* (PA) October 9, 1956.
79. Yogi Berra with Dave Kaplan, *10 Rings: My Championship Seasons* (New York: William Morrow, 2003), 151.
80. Larsen, Don with Mark Shaw, *The Perfect Yankee: The Incredible Story of the Greatest Miracle in Baseball History* (Champaign, IL, Sagamore, 1996), 114.
81. *Ibid.*
82. Dana Mozley, "Don Didn't Choke; Young Hurlers," *New York Daily News*, October 11, 1956.
83. *Ibid.*
84. The Brooklyn Dodgers and New York Yankees met in the World Series seven times. The Yankees won six of them and 27 of the 44 games.
85. Mozley, "Don Didn't Choke; Young Hurlers."
86. *Ibid.*
87. *Ibid.*
88. Neil Lanctot, *Campy: The Two Lives of Roy Campanella* (New York: Chelsea House, 1996), 354.
89. *Ibid.*, 123.
90. *Ibid.*
91. Kipp, *The Last Yankee Dodger*, 124
92. *Ibid.*, 124
93. *Ibid.*, 126.
94. Drysdale with Verdi, *Once a Bum, Always a Dodger*, 49.
95. *Ibid.*, 51.
96. Fred Kipp and Scott Kipp, *The Last Yankee Dodger: Fred Kipp, from Brooklyn to LA and the Bronx*, Kindle Direct Publishing, 2018, 130.
97. AP, "8 Homers Give Dodgers Victory," *Abilene Reporter-News* (TX), November 2, 1956.
98. https://www.history.com/topics/world-war-ii/bombing-of-hiroshima-and-nagasaki#.
99. Walteromalley.com, https://www.walteromalley.com/en/dodger-history/international-relations/1956-Japan-Tour_Page-1.
100. *Ibid.*
101. https://www.walteromalley.com/en/dodger-history/international-relations/1956-Summary_Postscript.
102. *Ibid.*
103. AP, "No Pain for Dodgers at 'End,'" *Binghamton Press and Sun-Bulletin*, October 11, 1956.
104. Jackie Robinson, *I Never Had It Made* (New York: HarperCollins, 1995), 123.

105. Dick Young, "Robby Sold to Giants for Littlefield + 30G," *New York Daily News*, December 14, 1956.
106. Ibid.
107. Gene Ward, "Inside Sports," *New York Daily News*, January 8, 1957.
108. Robinson, *I Never Had It Made*, 123.
109. Lew Biederman. "Lew Biederman's Scoreboard," *Pittsburgh Press*, September 1, 1956.
110. Dick Young, "Reese Okays 36½ Gs; Operation for Campy," *New York Daily News*, November 28, 1956.
111. Ibid.
112. Ibid.

Chapter 18

1. AP, "A Shot Got Reese in Time for Pierce," *Binghamton Press and Sun-Bulletin*), March 14, 1957.
2. Ibid.
3. UP, "Pee Wee Reese Still Thinks He Can Stay as Dodgers Regular Shortstop," *Hartford Courant*, March 19, 1957.
4. Dick Young, "Reese HRs, But Sox Win, 9–4," *New York Daily News*, March 17, 1957.
5. "'Little Colonel for Pee Wee Gets His Start as Stockholder," *The Sporting News*, February 13, 1957.
6. Jim McCulley, "Ebbets Field Sold, but Dodgers Stay," *New York Daily News*, October 31, 1956.
7. Frank Finch, "Brooklyn Dodgers Buy L.A. Angels," *Los Angeles Times*, February 22, 1957.
8. Ibid.
9. "O'Malley 'Cool' to Stark Plan; Eyes L.A. in '60," *Brooklyn Daily*, March 27, 1957.
10. Finch, "Brooklyn Dodgers Buy L.A. Angels."
11. Ted Reed, *Carl Furillo, Brooklyn Dodgers All-Star* (Jefferson, NC: McFarland, 2010), 120.
12. AP, "O'Malley Cool to NY Proposal for Queens Stadium Location," *Elmira Advertiser*, April 20, 1957.
13. "O'Malley 'Cool' to Stark Plan; Eyes L.A. in '60."
14. Dick Young, "Reese Strains Back, Misses Flock Opener," *New York Daily News*, April 16, 1957.
15. Bill Borst, *Brooklyn Dodgers: Fan's Memoir 1953–57* (St. Louis: Krank Press, 1982), 63.
16. Ibid.
17. Dick Young, "What's It Going to Be with Dodgers," *New York Daily News*, May 12, 1957.
18. Thomas S. Hines, "The Battle of Chavez Ravine," *Los Angeles Times*, April 20, 1997.
19. Ibid.
20. Dick Young, "What's It Going to Be with Dodgers."
21. Ibid.
22. "Podres Just Too Tough," *Cincinnati Enquirer*, May 22, 1957.
23. AP, "Can Bums Still Stay? 'It's Never Too Late,'" *Binghamton Press and Sun-Bulletin*, May 29, 1957.
24. Paul Zimmerman, "Bums Coming! Only Question is When," *Los Angeles Times*, May 29, 1957.
25. AP, "Dodger Shift to LA Gets NL Approval," *Oxnard Press-Courier*, May 29, 1957.
26. Lou Smith, "Paul May Seek Bums' Big Newk," *Cincinnati Enquirer*, August 21, 1957.
27. Ibid.
28. AP, "Giants Will Move to San Francisco Next Year," *Greenville News* (SC), August 20, 1957.
29. Bill Reddy, "Keeping Posted," *Syracuse Post-Standard*, August 24, 1957.
30. AP. "Giants' Move Hailed as 'Good for Baseball,'" *Rochester Democrat and Chronicle*, August 20, 1957.
31. AP, "Good News Promised for West Coast Fans on Dodgers' Transfer," *Rochester Democrat and Chronicle* August 20, 1957.
32. Roscoe McGowen, "Dodgers Find News Third Base Star—It's Old Pro Reese," *The Sporting News*, September 18, 1957.
33. Roscoe McGowen, "Sleepless Night with Baby Fails to Slow Reese in Field," *The Sporting News*, September 18, 1957.
34. Ed Corrigan, "Ebbets Now Ghost Park to Dodgers," *Elmira Star-Gazette*, September 25, 1957.
35. Bob McGee, *The Greatest Ballpark Ever: Ebbets Field and the Story of the Brooklyn Dodgers* (New Brunswick, NJ: Rivergate Press, 2006), 8.
36. Glenn Stout, *The Dodgers: 120 Years of Dodgers Baseball* (Boston: Houghton Mifflin, 2004), 212.
37. Ibid., 214.
38. AP, "Ebbets Field Looks Same as Usual," *Johnson City Press* (TN), September 25, 1957.
39. Jim McCulley, "Phils Put Flock to Sleep 2–1, on Rookie's Four-Hitter," *New York Daily News*, September 30, 1957.
40. "Welcome L.A. Dodgers," *Long Beach Independent-Press Telegram*, October 9, 1957.
41. Reed, *Carl Furillo: Brooklyn Dodgers All-Star*, 121.
42. "Welcome L.A. Dodgers," *Long Beach Independent-Press Telegram*, October 9, 1957.
43. Dick Young, "Lust for More $s Kills Brooks," *New York Daily News*, October 9, 1957.
44. UP, "Move Surprises Pee Wee Reese, *Indianapolis Star*, October 9, 1957.
45. Steve Delsohn, *True Blue: The Dramatic History of the Los Angeles Dodgers, Told by the Men Who Lived It* (New York: William Morrow, 2001), 23.
46. Jeane Hoffman, "Reese Hopes for Homers," *Los Angeles Times*, October 31, 1957.
47. Ibid.
48. Ibid.
49. Norman L. Macht, *Roy Campanella: Baseball Star* (New York: Chelsea House, 1996), 19.
50. Ibid.
51. Ibid.
52. Ibid.
53. Paul Zimmerman, "Sportscripts," *Los Angeles Times*, April 14, 1958.
54. Joe Williams, "How Much Longer Can Pee Wee Go," *The Sporting News*, April 4, 1958.
55. AP, "Pee Wee Reese Makes TV Dramatic Debut Tonight," *Long Beach Independent Press-Telegram*, November 9, 1958.

56. Phil Norman, "Fans Have a Ball, Take Giants to Heart," *San Francisco Examiner*, April 16, 1958.

57. Art Ryon, "Enthusiastic Crowds Jam Broadway to Cheer for Players," *Los Angeles Times*, April 19, 1958.

58. Jeane Hoffman, "Star-Studded Crowd Sees Opener," *Los Angeles Times*, April 19, 1958.

59. "Ceremonies at Coliseum Thrill Throng," *Los Angeles Times*, April 19, 1958.

60. UP, "Dodgers' Crowd One-Third Major League Attendance, *Valley Times* (North Hollywood, CA), April 19, 1958.

61. Paul Zimmerman, "Sportscripts," *Los Angeles Times*, April 24, 1958.

62. Roy Campanella, *It's Good to Be Alive* (Boston: Little, Brown), 214.

63. John Roseboro with Bill Libby, *Glory Days with the Dodgers and Other Days with Others* (New York: Atheneum, 1978), 107.

64. Frank Finch, "29,770 See Giants Tumble Dodgers into Cellar, 12–3," *Los Angeles Times*, May 13, 1958.

65. "Pee Wee Either Very Modest, or Has Bad Memory," *Los Angeles Times*, June 8, 1958.

66. Walter Judge, "Giants Win 14–2, Tie for 2nd," *San Francisco Examiner*, September 1, 1958.

67. Frank Finch, "Giants Trample Dodgers, 14 to 2," *Los Angeles Times*, September 1, 1958.

68. Bruce Chadwick and David M. Spindel, *The Dodgers: Memories and Memorabilia from Brooklyn to L.A.* (New York: Abbeville Press, 1993), 96.

69. *Ibid.*, 95.

70. Andy McCue, *Mover and Shaker: Walter O'Malley, the Dodgers, & Baseball's Westward Expansion* (Lincoln: University of Nebraska Press, 2014), 221.

71. *Ibid.*

72. *Ibid.*

73. *Ibid.*, 223.

74. *Ibid.*, 91.

75. Frank Finch, "Drysdale, Dodgers Whip Braves, 4–2," *Los Angeles Times*, July 30, 1958.

76. Harry Grayson, NEA, "Pee Wee Reese 'Has a Good Thing in Louisville,'" *Chillicothe Constitution-Tribune* (MO), September 3, 1958.

77. Frank Finch, "Dodgers Win, Then Lose to Cubs, 2–1," *Los Angeles Times*, September 27, 1958.

78. Frank Finch, "Dodgers Close Year with 7–4 Loss, Finish Seventh," *Los Angeles Times*, September 28, 1958.

79. AP, "Reese Accepts Job as Dodgers Coach," *San Francisco Examiner*, December 19, 1958.

80. Roger Kahn, *The Era: When the Yankees, the Giants, and the Dodgers Ruled the World* (New York: Ticknor & Fields, 1993), 226.

81. Dick Young, "Reese Becomes LA Coach," *New York Daily News*, November 15, 1958.

82. UPI, "Pee Wee Reese Hangs Up," *Windsor Star* (Canada), December 19, 1958.

83. *Ibid.*

84. *Ibid.*

Chapter 19

1. Dressen rejoined the team in 1958 following two full seasons and a small part of one more campaign as manager of the Senators. He compiled a woeful 116–212 mark with Washington.

2. UPI, "Maybe for Best," *San Francisco Examiner*, December 19, 1958.

3. Ron Fairly and Steve Springer, *My Turn at Bat* (San Dimas, CA: Back Story Publishing, 2018). 52.

4. *Ibid.*, 53.

5. *Ibid.*, 64.

6. Frank Finch, "Frank's Size Earns Respect," *Los Angeles Times*, February 24, 1959.

7. Mark Armour, Frank Howard SABR bio https://sabr.org/bioproj/person/frank-howard/.

8. Bob White, "Klippstein 'Scores' at Baseball Night," *Green Bay Press-Gazette*, January 22, 1960.

9. Paul Zimmerman, "L.A. Fans Entitled to Stronger Team," *Los Angeles Times*, September 29, 1958.

10. Brian M. Endsley, *Bums No More* (Jefferson, NC: McFarland, 2009), 104.

11. Schoendienst played just five games in 1959 due to the effects of tuberculosis and went hitless in three at-bats. He played 68 games in 1960.

12. Schoendienst made his 1959 debut on September 2 and played five games that season.

13. Endsley, *Bums No More*, 99.

14. *Ibid.*

15. *Ibid.*, 100.

16. *Ibid.*

17. *Ibid.*, 59.

18. *Ibid.*, 102.

19. *Ibid.*

20. Frank Finch, "Alston Declines Flag Prediction," *Los Angeles Times*, February 19, 1959.

21. Frank Finch, "'Too Much Horsing Around Last Year,' Alston Warns Dodgers," *Los Angeles Times*, February 19, 1959.

22. Hank Hollingworth, "Campy Returns to Catcher's Box," *Long Beach Independent*, April 15, 1959.

23. Campanella, *It's Good to be Alive*, 292.

24. *Ibid.*, 293.

25. Hank Hollingsworth, "Campy Returns to Catcher's Box."

26. Frank Finch, "93,103 Watch Yanks Defeat Dodgers, 6–2," *Los Angeles Times*, May 8, 1959.

27. Al Wolf, "Greatest Baseball Crowd Cheers Campanella," *Los Angeles Times*, May 8, 1959.

28. Norman L. Macht, *Roy Campanella* (New York: Chelsea House, 1996), 95.

29. Joe Trimble, "Record 93,103 in Tribute to Campy; Yanks Win, 6–2," *New York Daily News*, May 8, 1959.

30. Campanella, *It's Good to be Alive*, 297.

31. *Ibid.*, 298.

32. Buzzie Bavasi with John Strege, *Off the Record* (Chicago: Contemporary Books, 1987), 86.

33. "Dodgers Trade Lillis for Spokane Shortstop Wills," *Los Angeles Times*, June 2, 1959.

34. Bob Johnson, "My Nickel's Worth," *Spokane Chronicle*, June 2, 1959.

35. Steve Snider, "Retiring Carl Erskine Regarded as One of Finest Men in Baseball," *Billings Gazette*, June 24, 1959.
36. UPI, "Pee Wee Reese Likes Job as Dodger Coach," *Pomona Progress-Bulletin* (CA), July 2, 1959.
37. Ibid.
38. Steve Delsohn, *True Blue: The Dramatic Story of Los Angeles Dodgers, Told by the Men Who Lived It* (New York: William Morrow, 2001), 31.
39. Frank Finch, "Dodgers Champs! Ready for Series," *Los Angeles Times*, September 30, 1959.
40. "DODGERS THE CHAMPS! OFF TO SERIES," *Los Angeles Times*, September 30, 1959.
41. Endsley, *Bums No More*, 100
42. "'We Will Win This Series on Spirit'—Pee Wee Reese," *Pittsburgh Sun-Telegraph*, October 1, 1959.
43. Al Wolf, "Players Unshaken by Loss," *Los Angeles Times*, October 2, 1959.
44. Ibid.
45. Pee Wee Reese, "Won't Happen Again: Reese," *San Francisco Examiner*, October 2, 1959.
46. Don Zimmer with Bill Madden, *Zim: A Baseball Life* (Kingston, NY: Sports Illustrated Books, 2001), 43.
47. Delsohn, *True Blue*, 33.
48. Pee Wee Reese, "Screen May Win," *San Francisco Examiner*, October 4, 1959.
49. Braven Dyer, "Furillo's Clutch Hit Beats Chisox," *Los Angeles Times*, October 5, 1959.
50. Pee Wee Reese, "'LA Faster Than Sox,'" *San Francisco Examiner*, October 6, 1959.
51. Hank Hollingworth, "Sports Merry-Go-Round," *Long Beach Independent*, October 7, 1959.
52. Pee Wee Reese, "Duke's HR 'key blow' to Reese," *San Francisco Examiner*, October 9, 1959.
53. Bob Bennett, John Bennett, and Robert S. Bennett, *Johnny Podres: Brooklyn's Only Yankee Killer* (Bloomington, IN: AuthorHouse, 2005), 80.
54. Bill Lee, "With Malice Toward None," *Hartford Courant*, October 12, 1959.
55. Ibid.
56. AP, "Rumor Pee Wee Reese Next Milwaukee Braves Manager," *Lancaster Intelligencer Journal* (PA), October 10, 1959.
57. AP, "Pee Wee Reese 'Not Interested' in Braves' Job," *Winona Daily News* (MN), October 10, 1959.
58. Jimmy Brown, "Pee Wee 'Not Interested' in Managing Milwaukee," *Louisville Courier-Journal*, October 10, 1959.
59. Fairly and Springer, *My Turn at Bat*, 66.
60. "Reese Signed to Air Games," *Louisville Courier-Journal*, November 4, 1959.
61. *Fort Myers News-Press*, Jan 31, 1960
62. Jim Morrissey, "The Old Ball Game," *Louisville Courier-Journal*, June 16, 1968.
63. AP, *Binghamton Press and Sun-Bulletin*, September 25, 1960.
64. Ibid.
65. Roger Kahn, *The Boys of Summer* (New York: Harper & Row, 2006), 313.
66. Robert Gregory, *Diz: The Story of Dizzy Dean and Baseball during the Great Depression* (New York: Viking, 1992) 389.
67. AP, "'Ol Diz to Take Shot at Covering Monday Baseball," *Bismarck Tribune*, May 15, 1973.
68. Jim Morrissey, "The Old Ball Game," *Louisville Courier-Journal*, June 16, 1968.
69. Ibid.
70. "Pee Wee Reese 'Doing Fine,'" *Louisville Courier-Journal*, January 5, 1963.
71. Terry Everett, "Pee Wee Visits—Likes Bear, Yanks," *Dothan Eagle* (AL), March 10, 1963.
72. Bob Broeg, "Good Old Days? Baseball Better Now, Says Reese," *St. Louis Post-Dispatch*, June 3, 1963.
73. Ibid.
74. "Pee Wee Reese in Hall of Fame," *Owensboro Messenger-Inquirer* (KY), Dec 18, 1963.
75. Stan Maays, "Pee Wee Jealous of Sandy Koufax? Not on Your Life," *Jackson Sun* (TN), August 10, 1967.
76. Milton Richman, "Pee Wee Reese No Longer a Television Commentator," *Sheboygan Press* (WI), March 9, 1969.
77. Don Boykin, "Pee Wee Supports Bristol," *Palm Beach Post*, December 27, 1969.
78. Bob Hill, *Crack of the Bat: The Louisville Slugger Story* (Champaign, IL: SportsMasters, 2000), 76.
79. "Pee Wee Reese Accepts Job with Bat-Making Firm," *Louisville Courier-Journal*, July 2, 1971.
80. NEA, "Managing? Not for Pee Wee Reese," *Poughkeepsie Journal* (NY), May 6, 1972.
81. Kahn, *The Boys of Summer*, 319.
82. Ibid., 315.
83. David L. Ulin, "The Reading Life: The Nine Best Baseball Books," *Los Angeles Times*, March 31, 2011.
84. George Frazier, "Living: The Boys of Summer," *Boston Globe*, March 1, 1972.
85. "The Top 100 Sports Books of All Time," *Sports Illustrated*, December 16, 2002.
86. Tom Calvin and Danny Peary, *Gil Hodges: The Brooklyn Bums, the Miracle Mets, and the Extraordinary Life of a Baseball Legend* (New York: New American Library, 2012), 360.
87. *The Brooklyn Dodgers—The Original America's Team*, Virgil Films, 2005.
88. Joe Carnicelli, "Reese Admired Robinson for Speaking His Mind," *Raleigh Register* (Beckley, WV), October 25, 1972.
89. Dick Young, "Spahn, Roberts, Ford, Top Hall of Fame List," *Orlando Sentinel*, January 21, 1973.
90. Jim Murray, "Pee Wee Reese Still Number 1," *Lebanon Daily News* (PA), June 15, 1977.
91. https://www.baseball-reference.com/bullpen/Committee_on_Baseball_Veterans.
92. Larry Schwartz, "Why Not Reese, Duke, Rizzuto," *Hackensack Record* (NJ), January 23, 1976.
93. Mike Sullivan, "Pee Wee's Son Not 'Pushed,' but Dad Always There When Needed," *Louisville Courier-Journal*, August 2, 1976.

Chapter 20

1. Michael Madden, "Perfect Ending to a Perfect Day for Reese," *Boston Globe*, March 5, 1984.

2. *Ibid.*
3. *Ibid.*
4. *Ibid.*
5. Billy Reed, "Pee Wee Reese Elected to Baseball's Hall of Fame," *Louisville Courier-Journal*, March 5, 1984.
6. Gordon Edes, "Pee Wee Is Finally Elected to Hall of Fame," *Los Angeles Times*, March 5, 1984.
7. Jerry Zgoda, "Reese: It Was a Long Time Coming," *Asbury Park Press* (NJ), August 12, 1984.
8. Billy Reed, "Pee Wee Reese Elected to Baseball's Hall of Fame."
9. Dave Anderson, "The Captain Finally Arrives," *Miami News*, March 5, 1984.
10. Don Drysdale with Bob Verdi, *Once a Bum, Always a Dodger: My Life in Baseball from Brooklyn to Los Angeles* (New York: St. Martin's, 1990) 100.
11. Don Drysdale Baseball Hall of Fame bio, https://baseballhall.org/hall-of-famers/drysdale-don.
12. AP, "Five Enter Hall of Fame Class Today," *Asbury Park Press* (NJ), August 12, 1984.
13. Jim Adams, "Hall of Fame Gains a Modest Fellow Today: Pee Wee Reese," *Louisville Courier-Journal*, August 12, 1984.
14. Jim Adams, "Reese Praises Wife in His Hall of Fame Speech."
15. Los Angeles Dodgers Highlights—Pee Wee Reese's Hall of Fame Speech—Bing video, https://www.bing.com/videos/search?q=pee+wee+HOF+speech&docid=608014008808653021&mid=EDC8DDEA9A0877642DEAEDC8DDEA9A0877642DEA&view=detail&FORM=VIRE.
16. Adams, "Reese Praises Wife in His Hall of Fame Speech."
17. *Ibid.*
18. *Ibid.*
19. Mike Lupica, "Good Player—But 'a Better Guy," *New York Daily News*, August 15, 1999.
20. "Pee Wee Reese Retires," *Mattoon Journal Gazette* (IL), February 20, 1985.
21. Stephen McFarland, "Reese Is in the Lineup for the 'Return-to' Fete," *New York Daily News*, June 10, 1993.
22. "Scooter Enters Hall ... in Jersey," *New York Daily News*, May 21, 1993.
23. Stephen McFarland, "Reese Is in the Lineup for the 'Return-to' Fete," *New York Daily News*, June 10, 1993.
24. Manuel Perez-Rivas, "Pee Wee Returns," *New York Newsday*, June 3, 1993.
25. Dana Mozley, "Wreck-Ball Caps Ebbets Rites," *New York Daily News*, February 24, 1960.
26. Dick Young, "Dodgers Recall Flatbush Era," *New York Daily News*, February 24, 1960.
27. *Ibid.*
28. *Brooklyn Dodgers—Original America's Team*, Virgil Films, 2005.
29. Ray Weiss, "The Man Behind 'Boys of Summer,'" *White Plains Journal News* (NY), September 30, 1997.
30. Roger Kahn, "A Tribute to ... Captain Courageous," *Los Angeles Times*, August 19, 1999.
31. *Brooklyn Dodgers—Original America's Team*, Virgil Films, 2005.
32. Rick Bozich, "'Quiet Ambassador' a Son's Labor of Love for Bums of Summer," *Louisville Courier-Journal*, June 13, 1993.
33. *Ibid.*
34. Rick Bozich, "It Was Oct. 3, 1951, and Pee Wee Reese Will Never Forget It," *Louisville Courier-Journal*, September 17, 1991.
35. "Hall of Famer Reese Has Ling Cancer, Starts Radiation Treatments," *Baltimore Sun*, March 9, 1997.
36. Don Zimmer with Bill Madden, *Zim: A Baseball Life* (New York: Total Sports, 2001), 260.
37. *Ibid.*
38. Mark Reese, "He Knew the Secret of Life," *Los Angeles Times*, August 19, 1999.
39. *Ibid.*
40. Rick Bozich, "Reese Taught Us Courage and Class," *Louisville Courier-Journal*, August 19, 1999.
41. *Ibid.*
42. John Thurber and Jason Reid, "This Pee Wee Was a Giant," *Los Angeles Times*, August 15, 1999.
43. *Ibid.*
44. Michael O'Keefe, "Reese: The Man of Summer," *New York Daily News*, August 15, 1999.
45. Steve Bailey, "Reese Remembered as Great, Humble Man," *Indianapolis Star*, August 16, 1999.
46. Baseball-almanac.com Pee Wee Reese Baseball Stats by Baseball Almanac, https://www.baseball-almanac.com/players/player.php?p=reesepe01.
47. Zimmer with Madden, *Zim*, 260.
48. AP, "Reese Is Remembered as a Man Among 'Boys,'" *Los Angeles Times*, August 19, 1999.
49. *Ibid.*
50. Rick Bozich, "Reese Taught Us Courage and Class."
51. Jack Newfield, "Brothers Arm-in-Arm: Monument Due for Pee Wee and Jackie," *New York Post*, August 29, 1999.
52. Dave Kindred, "An Eternal Gesture Will Get an Enduring Honor," *Austin American-Statesman*, April 9, 2002.
53. Rivka Burkowsky, "Hug Felt 'Round Word," *New York Daily News*, November 2, 2005.
54. *Ibid.*
55. Ira Berkow, "New Brooklyn Statue Honors Pee Wee's Simple Gesture," *Louisville Courier-Journal*, November 2, 2005.
56. Sheldon S. Shafer, "Tribute to Pee Wee Reese," *Louisville Courier-Journal*, August 28, 1999.
57. Shannon Tangonan, "Statue Honoring Reese Is Unveiled at Ballpark," *Louisville Courier-Journal*, June 30, 2000.
58. Brian Bennett, "Pee Wee's Stature Put Up Statue," *Louisville Courier-Journal*, June 30, 2000.
59. *Ibid.*
60. Christa Ritchie, "Stage One Tells of Jackie Robinson, Pee Wee Reese," *Louisville Courier-Journal*, February 1, 2004.
61. www.Al.com, Alabama's Lucas Black gets back in uniform to play Pee Wee Reese in the Jackie Robinson movie '42,' https://www.al.com/entertainment/2013/04/post_148.html.
62. Lisa Kennedy, "'42 Gives Baseball Great Jackie

Robinson, But also Heroism, Its Due," denverpost.com, April 11, 2013.

63. "Rachel Robinson Reflects on Role in Making *42*." Foxsports.com, April 15, 2013. https://www.foxsports.com/west/story/rachel-robinson-reflects-on-role-in-making-42-041513.

64. "Reese, Dorothy Walton," *Louisville Courier-Journal*, March 9, 2012.

65. Richard Botte, Roger Rubin, Nicholas Wells, and Richard Schapiro, "Find the Scum," *New York Daily News*, August 9, 2013.

66. *Ibid.*

67. Zgoda, "Reese: It Was a Long Time Coming."

68. McNeil, *Dodgers Encyclopedia*, 98.

Bibliography

Books

Allen, Lee. *Giants and the Dodgers*. New York: G. P Putnam's Sons, 1964.

Allen, Maury, with Susan Walker, *Dixie Walker of the Dodgers*. Tuscaloosa: University of Alabama Press, 2010.

Alston, Walter, with Jack Tobin. *A Year at a Time*. Waco, TX: Word Books, 1976.

Anderson, Dave. *Pennant Races: Baseball at Its Best*. New York: Doubleday, 1994.

Barney, Rex, with Norman L. Macht. *Rex Barney's Thank Youuuu for 50 Years in Baseball from Brooklyn to Baltimore*. Centreville, MD: Tidewater Publishers, 1993.

Bavasi, Buzzie, with John Strege. *Off the Record*. Chicago: Contemporary Books, 1987.

Bennett, Bob, John Bennett, and Robert S. Bennett, *Johnny Podres: Brooklyn's Only Yankee Killer*. Bloomington, IN: AuthorHouse, 2005.

Black, Martha Jo, and Chuck Schoffner. *Joe Black: More Than a Dodger*. Chicago: Academy Chicago, 2015.

Borst, Bill. *Brooklyn Dodgers: Fan's Memoir 1953–57*. St. Louis: Krank Press, 1982.

Broeg, Bob. *Bob Broeg: Memories of a Hall of Fame Sportswriter*. Champaign, IL: Sagamore Publishing, 1995.

Campanella, Roy. *It's Good to Be Alive*. Boston: Little, Brown, 1959.

Chadwick, Bruce, and David M. Spindel, *The Dodgers: Memories and Memorabilia from Brooklyn to L.A.* New York: Abbeville Press, 1993.

Clavin, Tom, and Danny Peary. *Gil Hodges: The Brooklyn Bums, the Miracle Mets, and the Extraordinary Life of a Baseball Legend*. New York: Berkley, 2012.

Creamer, Robert. *Stengel: His Life and Times*. New York: Dell, 1985.

Delsohn, Steve. *True Blue: True History of the Los Angeles Dodgers, Told by the Men Who Lived It*. New York: William Morrow, 2001.

Dickson, Paul. *Leo Durocher: Baseball's Prodigal Son*. New York: Bloomsbury, 2017.

Dodgers: From Coast to Coast. San Diego: Skybox Press/Abrams, 2012.

Drury, Bob, and Tom Calvin. *Halsey's Typhoon: The True Story of a Fighting Admiral, an Epic Storm, and an Untold Rescue*. New York: Atlantic Monthly Press, 2007.

Durocher, Leo. *The Dodgers and Me: The Inside Story*. Chicago: Ziff-Davis, 1948.

Durocher, Leo, with Ed Linn. *Nice Guys Finish Last*. New York: Simon and Schuster, 1975.

Eig, Jonathan. *Opening Day: The Story of Jackie Robinson's First Season*. New York: Simon & Schuster, 2007.

Endsley, Brian M. *Bums No More: The 1959 Los Angeles Dodgers, World Champions of Baseball*. Jefferson, NC: McFarland, 2009.

Erskine, Carl. *Tales from the Dodger Dugout: A Collection of the Greatest Dodgers Stories Ever Told*. New York: Sports Publishing, 2017.

Eskenazi, Gerald. *The Lip: A Biography of Leo Durocher*. New York: William Morrow, 1993.

Fairly, Ron, and Steve Springer, *My Turn at Bat: My 50 Years in Baseball, from the Batter's Box to the Broadcast Booth*. San Dimas, CA: Back Story Publishing, 2018.

Feller, Bob, with Bill Gilbert. *Now Pitching, Bob Feller: A Baseball Memoir*. New York: Sports Publishing, 2014.

Garvey, Steve. *My Bat Boy Days: Lessons I Learned from the Boys of Summer*. New York: Scribner's, 2008.

Golenbock, Peter. *Bums: An Oral History of the Brooklyn Dodgers*. New York: G. P. Putnam's Sons, 1984.

_____. *The Spirit of St. Louis: A History of the St. Louis Cardinals and Browns*. New York: William Morrow, 2000.

Gould, Derek. *100 Things Cardinals Fans Should Know and Do Before They Die*. Chicago: Triumph, 2010.

Graham, Frank. *The Brooklyn Dodgers: An Informal History*. Carbondale: Southern Illinois University Press, 2002.

Halberstam, David. *Summer of '49*. New York: William Morrow, 1989.

Heinz, W. C. *What a Time It Was: The Best of W. C. Heinz on Sports*. Cambridge, MA: DeCapo, 2001.

Hill, Bob. *Crack of the Bat: The Louisville Slugger Story*. Champaign, IL: Sports Publishing, 2000.

Holmes, Tommy. *Dodger Daze and Knights: Enough of a Ball Club's History to Explain Its Reputation*. Philadelphia: David McKay, 1953.

Honig, Donald. *Baseball When the Grass Was Real: Baseball from the Twenties to the Forties, Told by the Men Who Played It.* Lincoln: University of Nebraska, 1975.

Jacobson, Sidney. *Pete Reiser: The Rough-and-Tumble Career of the Perfect Ballplayer.* Jefferson, NC: McFarland, 2004.

Jaffe, Jay. *The Cooperstown Casebook: Who's in the Hall of Fame, Who Should Be in, and Who Should Pack Their Plaques.* New York: Thomas Dunne, 2017.

Johnson, Rody. *The Rise and Fall of Dodgertown.* Gainesville: University Press of Florida, 2008.

Kahn, Roger. *The Boys of Summer.* New York: Harper Perennial Modern Classics, 2006.

_____. *The Era: 1947–1957 When the Yankees, the Giants, and the Dodgers Ruled the World.* New York: Ticknor & Fields, 1993.

_____. *Into My Own: The Remarkable People and Events That Shaped a Life* New York: Thomas Dunne, 2006.

_____. *Rickey and Robinson: The True, Untold Story of the Integration of Baseball.* New York: Rodale, 2014.

Kipp, Fred, and Scott Kipp. *The Last Yankee Dodger: Fred Kipp from Brooklyn to LA and the Bronx.* Kindle Direct Publishing, 2018.

Klima. John. *The Game Must Go On: Hank Greenberg, Pete Gray, and the Great Days of Baseball on the Home Front in WW II.* New York: Thomas Dunne, 2015.

Lanctot, Neil. *Campy: The Two Lives of Roy Campanella.* New York: Simon & Schuster Paperbacks, 2011.

Langill, Mark. *Dodgertown.* Charleston, SC: Arcadia, 2005.

Larsen, Don, with Mark Shaw. *The Perfect Yankee: The Incredible Story of the Greatest Miracle in Baseball History.* Champaign, IL: Sagamore, 1996.

Leavy, Jane. *The Last Boy: Mickey Mantle and the End of America's Childhood.* New York: HarperCollins, 2010.

Lowenfish, Lee. *Branch Rickey: Baseball's Ferocious Gentleman.* Lincoln, NE: Bison Books, 2009.

Macht, Norman L. *Roy Campanella: Baseball Star.* New York: Chelsea House, 1996.

Madden, Bill. *1954: The Year Willie Mays and the First Generation of Black Superstars Changed Major League Baseball Forever.* Boston: Da Capo Press, 2014.

Magee, David. *Sweet Spot: 125 Years of Baseball and the Louisville Slugger.* Chicago: Triumph, 2009.

McCue, Andy. *Mover & Shaker: Walter O'Malley, the Dodgers, & Baseball's Westward Expansion.* Lincoln: University of Nebraska Press, 2014.

McGee, Bob. *The Greatest Ballpark Ever: Ebbets Field and the Story of the Brooklyn Dodgers.* New Brunswick, NJ: Rutgers University Press, 2005.

McKelvey, G. Richard. *The MacPhails: Baseball's First Family of the Front Office.* Jefferson, NC: McFarland, 2000.

McMeekin, Isabel McLennan. *Louisville: The Gateway City.* New York: Julian Messner, 1946.

McNeil, William F. *The Dodgers Encyclopedia.* New York: Sports Publishing, 2012.

Mele, Andrew Paul. *"Tearin' Up the Pea Patch": The Brooklyn Dodgers, 1953.* Jefferson, NC: McFarland, 2015.

Polner, Murray. *Branch Rickey: A Biography.* Jefferson, NC: McFarland, 2007.

Prager, Joshua. *The Echoing Green: The Untold Story of Bobby Thomson, Ralph Branca and the Shot Heard Round the World.* New York: Pantheon, 2006.

Rampersad, Arnold. *Jackie Robinson.* New York: Arnold A. Knopf, 1997.

Reed, Ted. *Carl Furillo: Brooklyn Dodgers All-Star.* Jefferson, NC: McFarland, 2010.

Roberts, Robin, and C. Paul Rogers III. *The Whiz Kids and the 1950 Pennant.* Philadelphia: Temple University Press, 1996.

Robinson, Jackie. *I Never Had It Made.* New York: HarperCollins, 1995.

_____. *My Own Story.* Brattleboro, VT: Echo Point Books & Media, 2019.

Robinson, Ray. *The Shot Heard 'Round the World: The Dramatic Story of the 1951 Giants-Dodgers Pennant Race.* Mineola, NY: Dover Publications, 1991.

Roeder, Bill. *Jackie Robinson.* New York: A. S. Barnes, 1950.

Rowan, Carl T., with Jackie Robinson, *Wait Till Next Year: The Life Story of Jackie Robinson.* New York: Random House, 1960.

Schoor, Gene. *The Pee Wee Reese Story.* New York: Julian Messner, 1956.

Shapiro, Michael. *The Last Good Season: Brooklyn, the Dodgers and Their Final Pennant Race Together.* New York: Doubleday, 2003.

Skipper, John C. *Dazzy Vance: A Biography of the Brooklyn Dodgers Hall of Famer.* Jefferson, NC: McFarland, 2007.

Slaughter, Enos, and Kevin Reid, *Country Hardball: The Autobiography of Enos "Country" Slaughter.* Greensboro, NC: Tudor Publishers, 1991.

Snider, Duke, with Bill Gilbert, *The Duke of Flatbush.* New York: Zebra Books, 1989.

Spatz, Lyle. *Hugh Casey: The Triumphs and Tragedies of a Brooklyn Dodger.* Lanham, MD: Rowman & Littlefield, 2017.

Stout, Glenn. *The Dodgers: 120 Years of Dodgers Baseball.* Boston: Houghton Mifflin, 2004.

Terry, James L. *Long Before the Dodgers: Baseball in Brooklyn, 1855–1884.* Jefferson, NC: McFarland, 2002.

Thomson, Bobby, with Lee Heiman and Bill Gutman, *The Giants Win the Pennant! The Giants Win the Pennant!* New York: Citadel, 2001.

Tygiel, Jules. *Baseball's Great Experiment: Jackie Robinson and His Legacy.* New York: Oxford University Press, 2008.

Vescey, George. *Baseball's Most Valuable Players.* New York: Random House, 1966.

Warfield, Don. *The Roaring Redhead.* South Bend, IN: Diamond Communications, 1987.

Who's a Bum! The 1955 Brooklyn Dodgers. New York: New York Daily News Publications, 1995.

Wolpin, Stewart. *Bums No More! The Championship Season of 1955.* New York: St. Martin's, 1995.

Zimmer, Don, with Bill Madden. *Zim: A Baseball Life.* Kingston, NY: Sports Illustrated Books, 2001.

Zolecki, Todd. *The Good, the Bad, & the Ugly: Philadelphia Phillies: Heart-Pounding, Jaw-Dropping, and Gut-Wrenching Moments form Philadelphia Phillies History.* Chicago, IL: Triumph, 2010.

Magazines

Baseball Digest
Saturday Evening Post
Sports Illustrated
Time

Websites

aier.com
al.com
ancestry.com
baseball-almanec.com
baseball-reference.com
baseballreliquary.org
baseballrenationalww2museum.org
battlefields.org
biggestuscities.com/1920
detroithistorical.org/learn/encyclopedia-of-detroit/arsenal-democracy
dupontmanual.com
facebook.com
gosangelo.com
historicdodgertown.com
history.ky.gov
marbles.com
marfork.marines.mil
nationalparktraveler.org/
nbcsports.com
nps.gov
pearlharbor.org
realclearpolitics.com
sabr.org
slate.com
thebalance.com
thoughtco.com
travelthruhistory.tv/bay-ridge
ushistoryscene.com
visitmeadecounty.org/history/reference.com
youtube.com
walteromalley.com
wbur.org

Newspapers

Abilene News-Record (Texas)
Akron Beacon Journal (Ohio)
Alabama Journal (Montgomery)
Alexandria Times-Tribune (Indiana)
Allentown Morning Call (Pennsylvania)
Altoona Tribune (Pennsylvania)
Anderson Herald (Indiana)
Appleton News-Crescent (Wisconsin)
Arizona Republic (Phoenix)
Arlington Heights Daily Herald (Illinois)
Ashbury Park Press (New Jersey)
Austin American-Statesman (Texas)
Baltimore Evening Sun
Baltimore Sun
Billings Gazette (Montana)
Binghamton Press and Sun-Bulletin (New York)
Boston Globe
Brooklyn Citizen
Brooklyn Daily
Brooklyn Eagle
Bryan Eagle (Texas)
Calgary Herald (Alberta, Canada)
Chillicothe Constitution-Tribune (Missouri)
Chillicothe Gazette (Ohio)
Cincinnati Enquirer
Coos Bay Times (Oregon)
Council Bluffs Nonpareil (Iowa)
Cushing Daily Citizen (Oklahoma)
Dayton Daily News (Ohio)
Des Moines Register (Iowa)
Edmonton Journal (Alberta, Canada)
Elmira Advertiser (New York)
Elmira Star-Gazette (New York)
Fort Myers News-Press (Florida)
Franklin News-Herald (Pennsylvania)
Glen Falls Post-Star (New York)
Great Falls Tribune (Montana)
Green Bay Press-Gazette (Wisconsin)
Greenville News (South Carolina)
Hackensack Record (New Jersey)
Hanover Evening Sun (Pennsylvania)
Harrisburg Telegraph (Pennsylvania)
Hartford Courant (Connecticut)
Hazelton Standard-Sentinel (Pennsylvania)
Helena Independent (Montana)
Honolulu Advertiser (Hawaii)
Honolulu Star-Bulletin (Hawaii)
Indiana Gazette (Pennsylvania)
Indianapolis News (Indiana)
Indianapolis Star (Indiana)
Ithaca Journal (New York)
Jacksonville Daily Journal (Illinois)
Janesville Daily Gazette (Wisconsin)
Kingsport Times (Tennessee)
Kingston Daily Freeman (New York)
La Crosse Tribune (Wisconsin)
Latrobe Bulletin (Pennsylvania)
Lebanon Daily News (Pennsylvania)
Lincoln Journal-Star (Nebraska)
Lincoln Star (Nebraska)
Long Beach Independent (California)
Long Beach Independent-Press Telegram (California)
Los Angeles Times
Louisville Courier-Journal
Mansfield News-Journal (Ohio)
Marion Star (Ohio)
Marshall News Messenger (Texas)
Marshfield News-Herald (Wisconsin)
Massillon Evening Independent (Ohio)
Mattoon Journal Gazette (Illinois)
Miami News (Florida)
Middleboro Daily News (Kentucky)

Middleton Journal (Ohio)
Minneapolis Star
Monongahela Daily Republican (Pennsylvania)
Monroe Star-News (Louisiana)
Montgomery Advertiser (Alabama)
Montpellier Evening Argus (Vermont)
Mount Carmel Item (Pennsylvania)
Muncie Evening Press (Indiana)
Muncie Star Press (Indiana)
Murfreesboro Daily News-Journal (Tennessee)
New York Daily News
New York Newsday
New York Post
New York Times
Newport Daily News (Rhode Island)
Newport News Daily Press (Virginia)
Oakland Tribune (California)
Opp News (Alabama)
Orangeburg Times and Democrat (South Carolina)
Orlando Evening Star (Florida)
Ottawa Journal (Ontario, Canada)
Owensboro Messenger (Kentucky)
Oxnard Press-Courier (California)
Palm Beach Post (West Palm Beach, Florida)
Pensacola News Journal (Florida)
Petoskey News-Review (Michigan)
Philadelphia Inquirer
Pittsburgh Courier
Pittsburgh Post-Gazette
Pittsburgh Press
Pittsburgh Sun-Telegraph
Pittston Gazette (Pennsylvania)
Racine Journal Times (Wisconsin)
Pottsville Republican and Herald (Pennsylvania)
Richmond Times-Dispatch (Virginia)
Rochester Democrat and Chronicle (New York)
Salt Lake City Deseret News (Utah)
San Francisco Examiner
Shamokin News-Dispatch (Pennsylvania)
Shreveport Times (Louisiana)
Spokane Chronicle (Washington)
Spokane Spokesman-Review (Washington)
St Louis Post-Dispatch
St Louis Star and Times
Staunton News-Leader (Virginia)
Syracuse (NY) *Post-Standard* (New York)
Tallahassee Democrat (Florida)
Tampa Times (Florida)
Terre Haute Tribune (Indiana)
The Sporting News (St. Louis)
Troy Record (New York)
Troy Times Record (New York)
Valley Morning Star (Texas)
Valley Times (North Hollywood, California)
Warren Times Mirror (Pennsylvania)
White Plains Journal News (New York)
Wilmington Morning News (Delaware)
Wilmington News Journal (Delaware)
Wilmington Press Journal (California)
Windsor Star (Ontario, Canada)
York Daily Record (Pennsylvania)

Index

Abell, Ferdinand 16
Abrams, Cal 119, 135–137, 147
Acuff, Roy 241
Adcock, Joe 213
Aiea Barracks Receiving Team 64
Al Lang Field 209
U.S.S. *Alabama* 65
Alameda Naval Air Station 54
Alexander, Grover Cleveland "Pete" 130–131
All-Japan 219
All-Star Game 103, 121–122
Allen, Gus 6
Allen, Jack 165
Allen, Lee 146
Allen, Maury 96
Aloha Stadium 64
Alston, Walter 130, 140, 182–186, 189–192, 194–196, 200, 203, 210, 212, 215–216, 218–219, 225, 231, 233–240
American Airlines 241
American Association 8, 13, 16, 19, 75
American Locomotive 42
Amoros, Sandy 195–196, 203–205, 215–216
Amsterdam News 75
Anderson, Carl 68
Anderson, Dave 148, 150–151, 176, 183, 185, 226
Aparicio, Luis 1, 247
U.S.S. *Arizona* 52
Arnaz, Desi 240
Ashburn, Richie 131, 137
Associated Press 28, 41, 45, 48, 50, 140, 213
Astoria, Queens 157
Atherton High School 245
Atomic Energy Commission 129
Atwater, Caleb 6
Audubon, James 6
Audubon Country Club 243
Autry, Gene 229

Baer, Max 211
Bagby, Elmer 18

Bailey, Judson 48, 50, 58
Baker, William H. 130–131
Baltimore Elite Giants 172
Baltimore Orioles 230, 247
Baltimore Orioles (later the Yankees) 163
Bancroft, Dave 1, 25, 92
Banks, Ernie 198
Barber, Walter "Red" 21, 63, 84, 108, 131
Barney, Rex 83, 87, 100, 105, 110, 112, 115, 126
Barr, George 36
Baseball Digest 27, 123, 184
Baseball When the Grass Was Real 47
Baseball Writers Association of America (BBWAA) 128
Baseball's Great Experiment 81, 115
Baseball's Quiet Ambassador 249–250
Basinski, Eddie "The Fiddler" 63
Battle of Guadalcanal 65
Battle of Iwo Jima 65
Battle of Midway 59
Battle of Okinawa 65, 134
Battle of Raisin River 5
Battle of Saipan 65
Battle of the Bulge 65, 174
Bauer, Hank 65, 125, 179, 204, 216
Baumgartner, Stan 137
Bavasi, Buzzie (earlier) 140, 180–181, 183–184, 186, 191, 195, 208, 211, 215, 220, 231, 235, 238, 251
Bay Ridge, Brooklyn 188–189
Beatty, Clyde 236
Beaumont High School 35
Beazley, Johnny 58
Becker, Joe 196, 234
Beggs, Joe 76
Beharie, Nicole 254
Behrman, Hank 93
Bel Geddes, Norman 165
Bell, Gus 173
Bell, Les 60

Belmont Park 51
Bennett, George 40
Berra, Yogi 92, 163, 166, 178–179, 201, 204–205, 216=218
Bessent, Don 215
Bettie, Bettie 6
Betts, Mookie 2
Bevens, Bill 92–93
Biederman, Lester J. 171
Birmingham Black Barons 144
Black, Joe 160, 252, 254
Black, Lucas 254
Blackwell, Ewell 90, 111, 159, 159, 167
Blattner, Buddy 240
Bloomberg, Michael 252
Blumberg, Max 48
Bolero 82
Bomhard Theater 254
Bonds, Barry 1
Bonham, Ernest "Tiny" 51
Boone, Daniel 5
Boone, Squire 5
Borowy, Hank 120
Borst, Bill 2, 223
Bostic, Joe 75
Boston Braves 14, 29, 43, 65, 114, 125, 163, 170
Boston Globe 244
Boston Red Sox 11–13, 48, 89, 163, 176, 222, 239, 246–247
Boston University 131
Bottomley, Jim 60
Boudreau, Lou 57, 87
Bowman, Bob 32–34
Bowman Field 37
Boyer, Cloyd 143
Boys High School 153
The Boys of Summer 243–244
Bozich, Rick 250–251
Bragan, Bobby 63, 80–81, 140
Branca, Ralph 78, 82, 87, 92, 103, 121, 126, 141, 147–154, 199, 256
Braves Field 29, 113–114
Breadon, Sam 61, 85
Brecheen, Harry 75, 123
Bresnahan, Roger 40
Bridge at Remagen 65

291

Index

Bridges, Everett "Rocky" 143
Brietz, Eddie 30
Broeg, Bob 85–86, 90, 176, 214, 242
Bronx Bombers 48, 177
Brooklyn, New York 15, 17
Brooklyn Athletics 16
Brooklyn Atlantics 16
Brooklyn Brown Dodgers 71, 98
Brooklyn Charter Oaks 16
Brooklyn Chronicle 59
Brooklyn Citizen 36, 44, 46
Brooklyn Daily 210
Brooklyn Eagle 15–16, 19, 31, 41, 46, 48, 125–126
Brooklyn Greys 16
Brooklyn Navy Yard 209
Brooklyn Public Library 250
Brooklyn Putnams 16
Brooklyn Times 17
Brooklyn Trust Company 21, 60, 107
Brown, Bobby 126
Brown, Jimmy 45, 240
Brown, Joe E. 229
Brown, Tommy 63, 137
Brown, Violet 125
Brown Hotel 127
Brown vs. Board of Education 256
Browning, Pete 8
Bryant, Dr. J. Ray 242
Bryant, Paul "Bear" 242
Buck, Jack 114
Bums 26, 191, 208
Bunderick, Tom "Duke" 84
Bunn, Jack 107
Burdette, Lew 230
Burge, Lee 99
Burick, Si 186
Burns, Ken 108, 112–113
Burr, Harold C. 68, 75, 93, 100, 111, 120, 122, 124, 133, 136
Burwell, Bill 195
Bush, Donie 12
Buzhardt, Don 231
Byrne, Charles 146
Byrne, Tommy 126, 202–203

Cadillac 241
California Angels 229
Camilli, Dolph 21–22, 27, 28, 29, 37, 43, 46–47, 67, 172, 177
Camp Lee, Virginia 81
Campanella, Ida 98
Campanella, John 98
Campanella, Roy 1, 97–98, 100, 102, 105–106, 118–119, 121, 123, 125, 133, 135–136, 141, 143, 145, 148, 150, 153–154, 158–159, 162–163, 166, 168–169, 171, 175–176, 178–180, 183–185, 187, 191, 195–196, 198–199, 201–204, 215–216, 228–229, 237, 243, 245
Campanis, Al 197
Cannon, Jimmy 78, 215
Cape Cod League 239
Capri Isle Golf Club 255
Caray, Harry 243
Carey, Max 19
Carleton, James "Tex" 30
Carpenter, Bob 157
Carpenter, Robert Ruliph Morgan "Ruly" 131
Casey, Hugh 6, 29–30, 49–50, 64, 67, 80, 93, 100, 177, 242
Catholic Youth Organization (CYO) 83
Cavalt, Dr. Donald 230
Cavarretta, Phil 73
CBS Game of the Week 240
CBS Radio 29
Central High School 256
Cepeda, Orlando 247
Cerv, Bob 204
Chadwick, Abraham 153–54
Chamber, Cliff 133
Chandler, Happy 82–83, 95, 164, 242
Chandler, Spurgeon Ferdinand "Spud" 49, 92
Chapman, Ben 85, 112
Chapman, Ray 34, 40
Charter Oaks 16
Chavez Ravine 224, 227
Chester, Hilda 59
Chicago Black Sox 238
Chicago Cubs 24, 31, 35, 44, 72–73, 88, 120, 153, 161, 168–170, 172, 175–176, 186, 189
Chicago White Sox 13, 195, 222, 238–240, 247
China-India-Burma Theatre 65
Chipman, Bob 73
Chock Full O'Nuts 220
Church, Bubba 135
Churchill, Winston 42
Churn, Chuck 239
Cimoli, Geno 223, 235
Cincinnati Enquirer 21, 91, 110, 111, 112, 159
Cincinnati Reds 13, 21–22, 30–32, 37, 39, 42, 45–47, 75–77, 90, 109–110, 120, 142, 160, 163, 172, 176, 186, 194, 199–200, 213, 223, 231
City of Churches 160
Clarke, Fred 19
Clay, Dain 76
Clearwater, Florida 26
Clearwater Athletic Field 26
Cleveland Indians 18, 34, 177, 192, 201, 212, 214, 238
Cleveland Municipal Stadium 187
Clifty, Arkansas 53

Cobb, Ty 24, 41–42, 60
Cold War 129
Cole, Nat King 229
Coleman, Jerry 126
The Colgate Comedy Hour 189
Collins, Jack 136
Columbia University 9
Columbus (Ohio) Red Birds 20
Combs, Brown Lee 245
Combs, Earle 242
Comiskey Park 70, 239
Compton High School 118
Coney Island 16, 108, 254
Connie Mack Stadium 177
Coombs, "Colby Jack" 18
Cooper, Mort 34
Cooper, Walker 58, 176
The Cooperstown Casebook 1
Coos Bay Times (Oregon) 168
Cornell University 131
Corrigan, Ed 226
Corum, Bill 19, 122
Coscarat, Pete 30, 44
The Cotton Club 62
County Stadium 197
Coutros, Peter 207
Cox, Billy 96, 100, 105, 117, 119, 124, 133, 135, 141, 145, 149, 151, 159, 167, 171, 174–175, 189–190, 194–195, 201, 205, 243, 246
Craig, Roger 200, 203, 205, 218, 239
Craver, Bill 7
Creamer, Robert 204, 208
Crescent Hill Presbyterian Church 255
Crespi, Creepy 46
Crone, Ray 187
Cronin, Joe 12–13, 25
Crosley, Powell, Jr. 21
Crosley Field 21, 30, 46, 91, 108, 110–111, 115, 120, 224
Crusade in Europe 97
Cuddy, Jack 97
Cuidad Trujillo 97
Cullenbine, Roy 28, 30
Culver Academy 139
Cumberland Gap 6
Curtis High School 148
Curtiss-Wright 42
Cuyler, Kikki 186

Dahlgren, Babe 57
Daily Brooklyn 223
Daily Racing Forum 63
Daily Worker 110
Daley, Arthur 112, 170
Dandy, Walter 40
Dark, Alvin 143, 147, 149–150, 173, 187, 249
Dascoli, Frank 137
Davis, Curt 32, 49, 56
Davis, George 2
Davis, Jim 214

Davis, Dr. John F. 31–32
Day, John 146
Day, Laraine 82–83, 86
Dayton Daily News 186
Daytona Beach, Florida 54
Dean, Dizzy 3, 32, 61, 160, 240–242
DeBerry, Hank 15
Del Greco, Al 49
Denver Post 254
Derringer, Paul 28
Desmond, Connie 131, 177
Detroit Tigers 13, 24, 27, 32, 37
Devlin, Jim 7
Dexter, Charles 27
Dickey, Bill 50, 66
Dickson, Murry 186
Dickson, Paul 62
Diering, Chuck 120
Dillhoeffer, William "Pickles" 130–131
DiMaggio, Joe 3, 48, 50, 125, 163, 175, 201, 205, 242
Doby, Larry 87, 121, 222
Dockweiler, George A. 82
Dr. Kildaire Goes Home 82
Dodger Stadium 247
The Dodgers and Me 101
The Dodgers Encyclopedia 154
Dodgertown 99, 118
Doerr, Bobby 96
Dominican Republic 97
Donald, Atley 50
Doolittle, Gen. James "Jimmy" 60
Dothan Eagle 242
Downs, Rev. Karl 68
Doyle, Carl 32
Doyle, Charles 16
Doyle, Charles J. 202
Dragnet 189
Dressen, Charles "Chuck" 28, 36, 49, 78, 142–143, 145, 149–150, 152, 156, 158–160, 163, 165, 167, 171, 174, 176–180, 184, 188, 196, 205
Dressen, Ruth 180
Drysdale, Don 212–213, 217, 219, 229, 231–232, 234, 237–239, 247
Dudgeon, Thomas 248, 254
Duke of Flatbush 116, 141, 189, 204
Dunbar, Bob 62
duPont Manual High School 9–10
Durocher, Leo 1, 22, 25–28, 30–32, 34–35, 37, 40–46, 48–49, 62–63, 68, 76, 78, 81–84, 86, 95, 97, 100–102, 104, 143–146, 149–150, 152–54, 180, 184–185, 188, 200, 234, 248
Dyer, Eddie 78

Eagle, Dean 120
East Dixie League 182
East Orange High School 150
Eastern Shore League 88
Eau Claire Commissioners 20
Ebbets, Charles 16–17, 19, 85
Ebbets, Genevieve 17
Ebbets Field 2, 14, 17, 21, 24, 29, 36–37, 43, 72, 78, 84–85, 87, 90, 92, 101–102, 104, 121, 126, 130, 135–137, 143, 145, 159–160, 162, 164–165, 168, 170, 176–178, 189, 196–198, 203, 208–210, 212–216, 222, 226=227, 242, 249, 251
Ebbets Field Apartments 249
The Echoing Green 153
Eck, Frank 193
Eckfords 16
Edelman, Rob 142
Edwards, Bruce "Bull" 84, 87, 92–93, 101, 118, 144, 246
Eig, Jonathan 84, 110, 115
Eilperin, George 178
Eisenhower, Dwight D. 97, 216, 256
Ekron, Kentucky 6
Elfers, James 154
Eliot, T.S. 147
Engleberg, Memphis 62, 82
Ennis, Del 131
Enola Gay 219
The Era 137
Erasmus Hall High School 52, 70, 157
Erautt, Ernie 110
Erickson, Paul 47
Errickson, Dick 30
Erskine, Betty 188
Erskine, Carl 1, 3, 104, 116, 132, 143, 148, 150, 152, 160–161, 166–167, 171, 173, 176–179, 184–192, 196–197, 205, 212, 214, 229, 249, 251
Erskine, Matt 104
Eskanazi, Gerald 82
European Radio Network 160
Evans, Billy 11–12
Everett, Terry 242
Excelsiors 16

Fairfax High School 238
Fairly, Ron 234, 240
Feller, Bob 65
Felton, "Happy" Francis 132, 177
Fenway Park 73, 131
Ferdenzi, Til 240
Ferguson, Harry 27
Fernandez, Humberto "Chico" 194–195
Ferraris, Ronald 132
Ferrell, Rick 247, 249
Fette, Lou 35
Fewster, Chick 15

Finch, Frank 230, 232, 236
Fitzgerald, Tommy 13, 31, 67, 127, 166
Fitzsimmons, Freddie 37, 46, 49, 67
Flushing Meadows, Queens 223
Focus 113
Fondy, Dee 99, 160
Forbes, Alistair "Butch" 160–161
Forbes, Harry 34, 36
Forbes Field 121, 133, 161, 171
Ford, Harrison 254
Ford, John 229
Ford, Whitey 178–179, 201–202, 216
Ford Motor Company 7, 42
Fordham University 50, 131, 139
Foreign Correspondent 82
Fort Hood (Texas) 70
Ft. Worth Cats 99, 118, 192
42 (movie) 111, 254, 256
Fox, Howie 159
Foxx, Jimmie 218
Fraley, Oscar 106, 179
Frankenstein 229
Franks, Herman 29, 154
Frazier, George 244
Frey, Lonnie 45
Frick Ford 34, 73, 85, 164, 210
Friday Night Lights 254
Frigland, Sid 160
From Here to Eternity 189
Frost, Robert 158
Fullerton Union High School 53
Furillo, Carl 1, 72, 76–77, 80, 85–86, 88, 92, 101, 118, 123–124, 128, 133, 137, 143–144, 146–147, 161, 163, 167–168, 171, 174–179, 191, 196, 201–202, 204–206, 216, 228, 238–239, 250
Furillo, Filomena 88
Furillo, Michael 88

Gabionwitz, Joe 125
Gable, Clark 91
Galan, Augie 57, 90–91
Galento, Tony "Two-Ton" 211
Gallagher's 155
Galyean, Crystal 133
Gandhi, Mahatma 61
Ganzel, Babe 13
Garagiola, Joe 78, 123
Garcia, Mike 175
Garvey, Joe 209
Garvey, Steve 209
Gas House Gang 22
Gedeon, Lt. Elmer 65
Gehrig, Lou 10, 167, 175, 216, 218
Gelbert, Charles 22
Gene Tunney School 62
General Electric Theater 229
General Motors 241

George Washington Elementary School 118
Gettel, Al 154
Giants and the Dodgers 146
Gifford, Dick 178
Gilbert, Charlie 30, 35, 44
Giles, Warren 120–21, 162
Gilliam, Jim 171–172, 174–177, 186–190, 194, 196, 217–218, 222--225, 235, 246
Gionfriddo, Al 93
Giuliani, Rudy 252, 254
Glen Cove Police Department 228
Glenn, Dr. Frank 39
Goetz, Larry 50
Goldstein, Martin "Bugsy" 34
Golenbock, Peter 208
Gomez, Ruben 229
Gooding, Gladys 162, 226
Goodman, Ival 30
Goold, Derrick 32
Gorbous, Glen 211
Gordon, Joe (sportswriter) 15, 48
Gorman, Tom 166
Gowdy, Curt 243
Graf, Raymond 254
Graham, Frank 17, 24, 45, 50
Grand Central Station 48
Grannis, Robert M. 161
Grayson, Harry 48, 121, 130, 231
The Greatest Ballpark Ever 208
Green Bay Bluejays 235
Greenbaum, Clarence 167
Greenberg, Hank 65, 85
Greengrass, Jim 211
Greenwood Chiefs 182
Gregg, Hal 76, 87, 92–93, 96
Griffith, Calvin 225
Grim, Bob 203
Grimes, Burleigh 20–23, 180
Grimm, Charlie 72
Grissom, Marv 187
Groat, Dick 226
Grodzicki, Johnny 86
Gross, Don 196, 199
Gross, Milt 79, 171, 243
Grove, Lefty 218
Gumbert, Harry 76
Gurino, Vito "Socko" 34

Haas, Bert 32, 90
Hackensack Record 49
Hahn, Kenneth 224–225
Hall, Bob 174
Hall, George 7
Hall of Fame 87, 244–245, 247–249
Halsey, Adm. William "Bull" 65
Halsey's Typhoon 65
Hamner, Granville 'Granny" 131
Haney, Fred 240
Hanlon, Luke 24, 31, 45

U.S.S. *Hannan* 60
Happy Felton's Knothole Gang 132
Harlem River 141
Harris, Bucky 92
Harrocks, John 52
Hart, Bill 63
Hartford Courant 240
Hartnett, Gabby 35, 44, 176
Hartsfield, Roy 170
Hartung, Clint 85, 141
Harwell, Ernie 131
Hatten, Joe 72, 78–79, 92, 104, 119, 126, 144
Hatton, Grady 76
Hayden, Frank 140
Haynes, Sammy 70
Head, Ed 80
Heiwadai Stadium 219
Hemus, Solly 173
Hendricks, Ray 82
Henrich, Tommy 48, 93, 125
Herman, Billy 44, 46, 62, 72, 177, 195
Herman, Bob 15
Herman, Floyd Caves "Babe" 14–15, 141
Herman, John 15
Hermanski, Gene 71, 81, 84, 88, 105, 118–119, 125, 144
Herring, Art 73
Heusser, Ed 32
Heydler, John A. 19
Higbe, Kirby 31, 37, 39, 44–45, 47, 50, 79, 81
Hillcrest Country Club 228
Hillerich J.F. 7, 243
Hillerich, John A. "Bud" 8
Hillerich & Bradsby 3, 243, 246, 249
Hilltop Park 163
Hines, Thomas S. 224
Hirohito, Emperor 219
Hiroshima Stadium 219
Hiss, Alger 129
Hitchcock, Alfred 82, 229
Hitler, Adolf 65
Hoak, Don 203
Hodges, Charles 134
Hodges, Gil 1, 98, 102, 117, 119, 121, 123, 125, 133–137, 145, 147–148, 150, 153–154, 162–163, 167, 169, 172, 174–176, 179, 194–185, 187–188, 192, 195–196, 198, 200, 202–204, 211, 215–218, 223, 226, 231, 234–236, 238–239, 244–246, 250
Hodges, Irene 134
Hodges, Joan (Lombardi) 134–135
Hodges, Russ 152, 226
Hoffman, Jeane 227
Hogan, Frank S. 82
Hollingworth, Hank 239

Holman, Bud 98–99
Holman, Bump 98
Holman Stadium 222
Holmes, Tommy (manager) 157
Holmes, Tommy (sportswriter) 19, 22, 30, 42, 45, 47, 50, 59, 78, 95–6, 106, 139, 141, 143, 149, 157, 177, 180, 182
Holy Ghost Elementary School 35
The Home Run Heard 'Round the World 141
Honig, Donald 35, 87, 206
Honolulu 52
Honolulu Advertiser 64
Honolulu All-Stars 219
Honolulu Bears
Honolulu Stadium 64
Hood, Gen. John Bell 70
Hopper, Clay 74, 84, 130, 140
Horbrect, Ernest 175
Hotel Bossert 139, 206
Hotel Nacional 81
Hotel New Yorker 32
Hotel St. George 134
Houk, Ralph 246
Houston, Texas 55
Howard, Elston 201, 204, 207
Howard, Frank 234–235
Howerton, Bill 123
Hubbell, Carl 56, 103
Hudson, Johnny 37, 44
Huelster, Dottie 247
Hughes, Ed 32
Hughes, Jim 184, 191–192
Hurst, Patricia 54

I Love Lucy 189, 240
I Never Had It Made 89, 114, 220
Idlewild Airport 218
Immerman, Connie 62, 82
Imperial Hotel 219
Indianapolis Indians 13
International League 74, 172
Inter-State Association of Professional Baseball Clubs 16
Interstate League 183, 211
Into My Own 10, 173
Irvin, Monte 149–150, 153–154
Ivars, Sal 154

Jack McHenry's Anchor 241
Jackie Robinson Foundation 252
Jackie Robinson: My Own Story 114
Jackson, Travis 1
Jacobson, Sidney 54
Jaffe, Jay 1–2
James Madison High School 119
Jansen, Larry 102, 122, 148, 157
Jay, Joey 231
Jeffcoat, Hal 223–224

Index

Jennings, Hughie 1
Jersey City Airport 211
John Muir Technical High School 69
Johnny Angel 82
Johns Hopkins Hospital 40, 87
Johnson, Ban 163
Johnson, Don 72
Johnson, Walter 2, 53
Jones, Sheldon 102
Jones, Victor O. 40
Jones, Willie 128, 136, 215
Jorda, Lou 76
Jorgensen, John "Spider" 84, 92–93, 101

Kahn, Joan 173
Kahn, Roger 9–10, 82, 90, 137, 157–158, 167–169, 171, 173, 199, 207–209, 243–244, 249–251, 256
Kahn, Roger Laurence 250
Kaiser Shipyards 42
Kansas City Blues 13
Kansas City Monarchs 70
Karp, David 206
Keel, Howard 236
Keener, Sid 14, 58, 78
Kegan, John 60
Keller, Charlie 48, 50
Kellert, Frank 195
Kennedy, Ed 243
Kennedy, Lisa 254
Kentucky Athletic Hall of Fame 242
Kerr, Buddy 106
Kieran, John 19
Killebrew, Harmon 247–48
Killebrew, Harmon, Sr. 247
Killefer, Bill 130–131
Kimball, Newt 35
Kimmel, Ralph 10, 99
Kindred, Dave 115
Kiner, Ralph 100, 135, 170
King, Clyde 176
King, Joe 133, 138, 152
King, Larry 206
Kipp, Fred 218–19
Kirksey, George 28
Knothole Club 83
Konstanty, Jim 135–36
Korean War 133
Koschnick, Carrie 165
Koufax, Sandy 197–98, 231, 242–243, 247, 252
Koy, Ernie 31–32, 45
Kratter, Marvin 222
Kurowski, Whitey 58, 78
Kuzava, Bob 167

L.A. Confidential 254
Labine, Clem 135, 148, 150, 177, 179, 184, 197, 204, 213, 215, 217, 254

Lafayette High School (Brooklyn) 197
Lamanno, Ray 57
Lancaster, Burt 229
Landes, Stan 214
Landis, Kenesaw Mountain 32
Lanier, Max 58, 123
Largione, Richard 166
Larker, Norm 238
Larsen, Don 217
Lary, Lyn 13
The Last Yankee Dodger 218
Latham, Arlie 8
Lavagetto, Harry "Cookie" 24, 27, 29, 33, 49, 54, 93, 145, 177
Law, Ruth 18
Law, Vern 215
Lazzeri, Tony 10–11
Lea, Col. Luke 20
Leachman, Dr. George 129
Lee, Bill 240
LeFebvre, Wilfred 25
Lend-Lease Act 42
Leonard, Emil "Dutch" 172
Lepke, Louis, 34
Levitt, William J. 133–34
Levitt & Sons 133
Levittown, 133
Lewis and Clark, 41
Lexington Hotel 169
Lieberman, Hank 137
Liebling, A.J. 244
Lillis, Bob 237
Lincoln, Abraham 6
Lincoln, Tom 6
Lindell, Johnny 71, 92
Lindemann, Carl 243
Little World Series 75
Littlefield, Dick 220
Livingston, Mickey 39
Lockman, Whitey 141, 143, 151, 214
Loes, Billy 157, 160, 163, 166, 174, 184, 195–196, 211–212
Logan, Johnny 173, 198
Lohrman, Bill 36
Lombardi, Ernie 28
Lombardi, Joan 134–35
Lombardi, Vic 79, 91, 93, 96
Look 113, 123, 220
Lopat, Eddie 126, 161, 163, 173
Lopata, Stan 137
Los Angeles, CA 53
Los Angeles Angels 223
Los Angeles City Council 227
Los Angeles Dodgers 229–232, 235–240, 245, 247
Los Angeles Memorial Coliseum 227–232, 235–40
Los Angeles Rams 236
Los Angeles Times 224, 227–228, 230, 238, 244, 250–251
Louis, Joe 78
Louisville & Nashville Railroad 7

Louisville Colonels 9–13, 25, 28, 222
Louisville Courier-Journal 9, 13, 27, 120, 162, 240, 245, 250–251, 253
Louisville Eclipse 7
Louisville Greys 7
Louisville Slugger Field 253, 255
Lowery, Harry "Peanuts" 73
Lucadello, Johnny 64
Lucky Strike 241
Luken, Eddie 77
Lundquist, Carl 121, 131
Lynch, Tom 146

Maays, Stan 243
MacArthur, Gen. Douglas 133
Mack, Connie 18, 85
Macon, Max 58
Macon, Georgia 89
MacPhail, Larry 20–25, 30, 33–34, 37–41, 43, 48, 96, 101
MacPhail, Lee 21
Maddux, Greg 3
Maglie, Sal "The Barber" 143, 147–149, 174, 185–186, 212, 214–217
Magoffin, Beriah 6–7
Mahon, Jack 25
Malton, Sam 75
Manatee Junior College 245
Mancuso, Gus 40
Mantilla, Felix 238
Mantle, Elvin "Mutt" 163
Mantle, Mickey 163, 166–168, 178–179, 197, 201–202, 204, 216–217
Mapes, Cliff 126
Marion, Marty 46, 58, 67–68, 77–78, 86, 245, 249
Marshall Islands 65
Martin, Billy 166–167, 178–179, 203, 217
Martin, Pepper 61
Martin, Whitney 27–28, 42
Marx, Groucho 229
Masi, Phil 71
Massachusetts Institute of Technology 131
Mathewson, Christy 60
Mauch, Gene 96, 100
Mays, Carl 18, 34
Mays, Willie 2, 144, 149–151, 185–186, 192, 230, 235, 242
McAlpin Hotel 83, 183
McCann, Dick 46
McCarthy, Bobby 208
McCarthy, Joe 28
McCormick, Frank 28, 45, 243
McCormick, Mike 106
McCue, Andy 209
McCulley, Jim 147, 186, 223, 226
McCullough, Clyde 88
McDeviit, Danny 226

Index

McDougald, Gil 167, 203–204, 217
McFarland, Stephen 249
McGee, Bill 58
McGee, Bob 208
McGowen, Roscoe 115, 161, 170, 184, 226
McGraw, John 18, 103
McGrew, Harry "Ted" 24–26, 41
McGriff, Burton 68
McHugh, Gene 207
McKee Jungle Gardens 99
McKelvey, G. Richard 21
McKinney, Frank E. 12
McLaughlin, George V. 71
McNeil, William F. 154, 169
McQuinn, George 92
Meade, Gen. George 5
Meade County, Kentucky 5–6
Meany, Tom 42
Medwick, Joe "Ducky" 28, 30, 32–34, 37, 39, 42–43, 61, 67
Mele, Andrew Paul 170
Mendocino County 53
Merullo, Lennie 72
Methodist Hospital (Louisville) 242
Mexican League 98
Meyer, Russ "The Mad Monk" 101, 170-1
Miami Stadium (Florida) 195–96
Miami University 182
The Mick 216
Miksis, Eddie 93, 124, 133, 144
Miley, Jack 40–41
Miller, Bob 135, 186
Miller, Clyde R. 9
Miller, Eddie 37, 87
Miller, Stuart 107
Milliken, Bill 177, 184
Milwaukee Braves 174, 176, 197–198, 201, 213, 215, 222, 231, 238, 240
Milwaukee County Stadium 170, 174, 231
Minneapolis Millers 144
Minner, Paul 151
Minnesota Twins 247
Minnesota-Wisconsin League 20
U.S.S. *Missouri* 65
Mix, Tom 241
Mize, Johnny "Big Cat" 28, 45, 56, 64, 125–126, 166, 168
Monterrey Sultans 98
Montreal Royals 73, 160, 182, 218
Moon, Wally 235–236, 238, 240
Moore, Terry 58
Mooty, Jake 31
Morgan, Bobby 159, 176
Morrison, Jane 48
Morrissey, Jim 253

Moryn, Walt 187, 189
Most Valuable Player: The Jackie Robinson Story 254
Mover and Shaker 209
Mozley, Dana 169
Mueller, Don 141, 147
Mulleavy, Greg 234
Muncie Star Press 14
Municipal Stadium 48, 187, 230
Murder, Inc. 34
Murphy, Eddie 19
Murphy, Johnny 50
Murray, Arch 106
Murray, Jim 245
Murrow, Edward R. 29
Musial, Stan 56, 76, 86, 105, 121–122, 144, 157, 163, 169, 198, 214, 242
My Bat Boy Days 209–210

Naham, Sam 32
Nashua Dodgers 98, 183
Nashville Cumberlands 7
Nashville Vols 142
National League 7, 14, 16, 19, 21, 34, 37, 87
Nations, H.L. 37
Navin Field 32
NBC 243
NCAA 69
Neal, Cap 10–12
Neal, Charlie 225, 231, 239–240
Negro Leagues 70–71, 74, 98, 120, 160, 172, 174
Neutra, Richard 224
New Covenant Presbyterian Church 9
New England League 98
New Guinea 65
New Jersey Giants 211
New Orleans Zulu Social Aid and Pleasure Club 74
New York American 15
New York City World's Fair 189
New York Daily News 22, 25, 34, 45–46, 118, 120, 129, 149, 163, 198, 203, 206–207, 211, 215, 223, 227, 237, 249, 256
New York Evening World 17
New York Giants (MLB) 18, 29, 34–35, 37, 40, 42–43, 45, 91, 95, 100, 102–103, 105, 134–135, 141–155, 173–175, 177, 185–187, 190–192, 196, 214, 218, 220, 224–225, 227, 229–230, 240, 247
New York Giants (NFL) 131
New York Herald Tribune 47, 85, 152, 231
New York Journal-American 226
New York Knicks 131
New York Mets 244
New York Mirror 73
New York Post 79, 171, 231, 252
New York Sun 19

New York Times 153, 161, 170
New York World-Telegram 226
New York Yankees 17, 22, 28, 48–51, 60, 92–94, 125–127, 139, 142, 156, 163–168, 251, 177–180, 201–207, 209, 216–218, 223, 236–238
New Yorker Hotel 48
Newark Eagles 74, 87, 120, 154
Newcombe, Don 120–126, 128, 131, 135, 136–137, 147, 149, 155–156, 171, 183–184, 186, 196, 198, 201, 210, 213–216, 218–219, 236–251
Newcombe, Roland 120
Newfield, Jack 252
Newport News Dodgers 118
Newsom, Bobo 63, 92, 101
Newspaper Enterprise Association 121, 130
Nice Guys Finish Last 22, 150, 152–153
Nichols, Al 7
Nixon, Richard 198
Norfolk Naval Training Station 64
Norman, Phil 229
Northey, Ron 123
Now Pitching, Bob Feller 65
Nugent, Gerry 39–40

Oahu Red Sox 219
Oakland Oaks 67, 125, 142, 180
O'Dell, Billy 242
O'Dwyer, William 34, 48
Off the Record 180, 183
O'Hara, David 246
Ohio River 5–6
Ohio State University 234
Ohio Wesleyan University 61
Olan, Ben 210
Old Louisville neighborhood 7
Oldfield, Barney 85
Olmo, Luis 63, 123–24
Olsen, Vern 64
Olson, Ivy 18
O'Malley, Alma 139
O'Malley, Edwin 139
O'Malley, Kay 139
O'Malley, Peter 139, 252
O'Malley, Terry 139
O'Malley, Walter 132, 139–140, 142, 158–160, 165, 169, 173, 179–180, 182–183, 190, 196, 209–211, 214–215, 218–219, 222–225, 227, 235, 243
O'Mealia, Leo 207
Once a Bum, Always a Dodger 212
O'Neil, Mickey 15
O'Neill, Harry 65
Opening Day 110
Oppenheimer, Joel 51
Osborn, E.C. "Doc" 31

Index

Oshinsky, David M. 23
Ott, Mel 10, 77, 102–103
Owen, Marv 32
Owen, Mickey 37, 39, 42, 56
Oxford Press-Courier 225

Pacific Coast Conference 69
Pacific Coast League 67, 237
Pafko, Andy 144–145, 147–149, 151, 166–168, 170
Paige, Satchel 70
Paine, Phil 235
Palica, Erv 135, 195
Palm Beach Country Club 244
Paris Peace Conference 20
Parker, Dan 73
Parks, Rosa 256
Parrott, Harold 61, 81, 101, 103, 115
Pasadena High School 230
Pasadena Junior College 69
Pasquel, Jorge 67
Passeau, Claude 36
Paul, Gabe 127
Paulson, Norris 224–225, 227, 240
Pearl Harbor 42, 52
Pearson, Ike 47
Peck, Gregory 229
Pecko, Joe 172
The Pee Wee Reese Show 161
The Pee Wee Reese Story 116
Pennant Races 148, 150
Pepper Street Gang 68
Perini, Lou 170, 240
Petersburg High School 134
Peterson, Kent 173
Phelps, Ernest "Babe" 41
Philadelphia Athletics 18, 85, 92, 175
Philadelphia Inquirer 130, 159, 186
Philadelphia Phillies 21, 31, 36, 47, 85–86, 120–121, 130, 134–136, 142–143, 159, 162, 170, 173–174, 177, 186, 190, 196, 211, 215, 223, 226, 240
Philadelphia Sportswriters Association 189
Piatkowski, Harry 186
Piccadilly Circus 65
Picone, Mario 185
Piedmont League 118
Pignatano, Joe 244
Pigtown 17
Pikard, Cully 87
Pinelli, Babe 132–133
Pinter, John 40
Pitler, Jake 177
Pittsburgh Courier 75
Pittsburgh Pirates 13, 15, 34, 40, 86, 96, 106, 121, 133, 161, 163, 170, 186, 192, 197, 211, 215, 220, 226

Pittsburgh Press 171, 220
Pittsburgh Steelers 236
Pittsburgh Sun-Telegraph 202
Pittsburgh Symphony Orchestra 132
Play Ball 99
Pocomoke City Chicks 88
Podres, Johnny 179, 184, 186, 202–205, 212, 216, 224–225, 236
Poepplein, Frank 228
Pofahl, Jimmy 25
Polio: An American Story 123
Pollet, Howie 78
Polner, Murray 62
Polo Grounds 34–35, 45, 91, 100, 106, 119, 134, 141, 146, 148, 151, 153, 155, 185, 187, 191, 208, 225
Posnanski, Joe 112
Postove, Harry 172
Poulsen, Norris 215, 227
Povich, Shirley 191
Powell, the Rev. Vincent A. 83
Power, Tyrone 56, 229
Powers, Jimmy 97, 139–140
Prager, Joshua 153
Prendergast, Mike 130
Presko, Joe 172
Priddy, Jerry 25
Pride and Judea Home and Jewish Sanitarium for Chronic Diseases 48
Prospect Park 16
Pueblo Dodgers 183
Purple Heart 65

Queen, Mel 100
Quickstop Club 16
Quinn, Bob 29

Racine, Hector 130
Radcliffe, Ted "Double Duty" 70
Raffensberger, Ken 36
Raft, George 82
Rampersad, Arnold 108–109
Raschi, Vic 125, 163, 166–167
Reading Times 88
Reardon, John "Beans" 15
Reddy, Bill 31, 206, 208
Reese, Barbara (Dudgeon) 64, 123, 198, 231, 248, 254, 256
Reese, Blent Marion 5–6
Reese, Carl 5–9, 12
Reese, Carl, Jr. 9, 37
Reese, Dorothy "Dottie" 58, 64, 91, 129, 155, 188, 222, 226, 231, 242, 248, 251–252, 255
Reese, Elizabeth 7
Reese, Elizabeth "Lizzie" 6
Reese, Emma 6, 99, 127, 155, 205–6
Reese, Mark 222, 226–227, 231, 242, 245, 247, 252, 254, 256

Reese, Mary 7
Reese, Pauline 7
Reese, Willie 7
Reichler, Joe 89, 124
Reiser, Pete 35–37, 42, 47, 78, 80–81, 87, 93, 101, 103, 106, 145, 249
Reiser, Sally 81
Repulski, Rip 215
Resthaven Memorial Cemetery 6, 253
Reynolds, Allie 125, 163, 165, 167, 175, 178–179
Rhodes, Dusty 187
Rhubarb in the Catbird Seat 131
Rice, Grantland 49
Richards, Paul 247
Richmond Hill High School 49, 164
Rickards, Tex 226
Rickey, Branch 22, 39–40, 60–63, 71, 73, 81, 93–97, 102–103, 106, 116–119, 126–127, 129–130, 134–134, 138–39, 141, 159, 162, 170, 197, 254
Rickey and Robinson 90
Rikard, Cully 87
Ripken, Cal 2
Ripple, Jimmy 45
Ritt, Bill 24
Riverfront Stadium 244
Rizzo, Johnny 55
Rizzuto, Phil 23, 126, 132, 164–65, 204, 245, 249
Robb, Scotty 102
Roberge, Skippy 71
Roberts, Robin 130–131, 135, 137, 143, 148, 223
Robinson, Brooks 243
Robinson, Edward G. 229
Robinson, Humberto 230
Robinson, Jackie 1–2, 65–66, 68–70, 73, 80, 81, 83–87, 89–90, 93–94, 97, 100–101, 103–104, 108–117, 119, 121–22, 125, 128–129, 131, 133, 137, 141, 145, 148–149, 152, 154, 156, 159, 162, 165–166, 168–172, 174–175, 178, 181, 184–185, 187–188, 190, 195–195, 199, 203, 205, 211, 215, 218, 220, 231, 243–244, 246, 248, 250–252, 254, 256
Robinson, Jerry 68
Robinson, Mallie 68
Robinson, Rachel 69, 75, 108, 252, 254
Robinson, Ray 141, 149
Robinson, "Sugar" Ray 211
Robinson, Wilbert "Uncle Robbie" 15, 18–19, 101
Rodney, Lester 110
Rodriguez, Alex 2
Roe, Preacher 96, 105–6, 121, 123, 125–126, 135, 138, 145, 154,

156–158, 162, 166, 174–175, 178, 195, 251
Roeder, Bill 101, 175, 226
Rojek, Stan 106
Rolfe, Red 50
Roosevelt, Franklin D. 21, 42, 52–53, 65
Roosevelt, Theodore 68
Roosevelt Stadium 210–11
Roseboro, John 230
Rosen, Al 177–178, 187
Rowan, Carl T. 114
Rowell, Carvell "Bama" 97
Rozelle, Pete 118
Rudd, Irving 198
Ruffing Red 49
Rusk rehabilitation hospital 230
Russell, the Rev. Bob 251
Russell, Jack 34
Russo, Marius 49
Ruth, Babe 2, 18, 22, 41, 52, 91, 167, 176, 216, 218
Rutherford, Johnny 162, 166
Ryan, Connie 71, 85
Ryan, Cornelius 89
Ryon, Art 229

SABR (Society for American Baseball Research) 142
Sain, Johnny 84, 163, 167
St. Joseph's College (Indiana) 134
St. Louis Browns 60, 217, 247
St. Louis Cardinals 20, 28, 32–35, 39–40, 42–43, 46–47, 75, 78, 85–86, 90, 120, 122–123, 143–144, 169, 173, 176–177, 182, 188, 190, 199, 212, 214–215, 220, 235–236, 240, 247
St. Louis Post-Dispatch 46, 60, 85, 182
St. Louis Star and Times 58
St. Paul (Minnesota) Saints 13, 102, 118, 160, 183, 194
Salk, Dr. Jonas 123
San Francisco Examiner 229
San Francisco Giants 229–230, 242
Sanders, Ray 97
Santa Monica Municipal Airport 82
Sauer, Hank 170, 229
Sawyer, Eddie 130–131, 135–136
Scales, George "Tubby" 172
Scarborough, Ray 165
Scarface (1932) 82
Schenz, Harry 153
Schmitz, Johnny 72, 86, 144
Schoendienst, Red 135, 235
Schoor, Gene 44, 51, 99, 171
Schultz, Howie 76
Schumacher, Hal 72
Schwebel, Jack 54
Scott, Lee 31, 53–54

Scully, Vin 131, 147, 206, 217–218, 231, 248, 252
Seals Stadium 229
Seaton, Tom 17
Sewell, Joe 1
Sewell, Rip 73
Shafer, Sheldon S. 253
Shapiro, Michael 139
Sharff, Mike 203
Shaw, Bob 240
Shea, Merv 22
Shea, Spec 92–93
Sherry, Larry 238–40
Shibe Park 31, 47, 73, 121
Shotton, Barney "Burt" 85–86, 93, 95–96, 103–4, 106, 117–119, 126–127, 137, 139–140, 142, 184, 200
Shoun, Clyde 56, 76
Shuba, George "Shotgun" 104, 158, 175, 189
Sid Mercer Memorial Award 169
Siegel, Bugsy 82
Simmons, Curt 131
Singleton, Elmer 86
Sisler, Dick 86, 136–137
Sisler, George 86
Sistine Chapel 197
Skowron, Moose 203
Slaughter, Enos "Country" 28, 58, 78, 90, 123, 175, 216
Smith, Elmer 18
Smith, Hilton 70
Smith, Jack 46, 49, 66
Smith, Kenny 247
Smith, Lou 45, 77, 110, 159, 225
Smith, Red (coach) 73
Smith, Red (sportswriter) 101, 118–119, 132, 215
Smith, Wendell 75, 111, 119
Smith, William E. 12
Snider, Beverly 188
Snider, Duke 1–2, 116, 118–119, 124, 133, 136–138, 143, 145, 147, 149, 151, 160, 162, 165, 167–169, 171, 176–179, 184–190, 192, 196–199, 201–204, 211, 215–217, 226, 228, 234–235, 238, 240, 245, 252–254
Snider, Florence 118
Snider, Steve 237
Snider, Ward 118
Snyder, Brad 113
Southeast Christian Church 251–2, 255
Southern Bell Telephone Company 10
Southworth, Billy 34
Spahn, Warren 65, 134, 158, 174
Sparks, Keith 9–11, 99
Speake High School 254
Spence, Stan 87
Spencer, Don 110

Spink, J.G. Taylor 43, 56, 200
Spokane Chronicle 237
Spokane Indians 237
Spooner, Karl 192, 202, 212
The Sporting News 9, 12, 28, 35, 37, 42–43, 64, 68, 107, 125, 129, 130, 145, 152, 158, 163, 175, 184, 189, 196, 200, 214
Sports Illustrated 244
Sportsman's Park 46, 104, 120
spring training 18, 25–28, 35, 40–43, 54–55, 97–99, 117–119, 171, 183–185, 193–196, 194, 209–210, 222, 234, 236
Stanky, Eddie 63, 72, 76, 80, 84–85, 87–88, 96–97, 100, 113, 116–117, 143, 145, 147, 149, 172, 188
Staten Island 148
Staten Island Ferry 148
Statue of Liberty 148
Steiner, Dr. Morris 123
Stengel, Casey 17–20, 125–127, 156, 163–166, 180, 202–203, 216–217
Stevens, Ed 79
Stewart, Bill 102
Stewart, Gloria 229
Stewart, Jimmy 229
Stock, Milt 137
Stockton, J. Roy 46
Stoneham Horace 103, 224–225
Strincevich, Nick 29
Stringer, Lou 44
Sturdivant, Tom 216
Sturm, Johnny 25, 50
Sukeworth, Clyde 71, 83, 133, 140, 150
Sullivan, Mike 245
Summer Olympics (1932) 227
Susan Miller Dorsey High School 69
The Sweet Science 244
Syracuse Chiefs 75

Talbot, Gayle 41–42, 129, 152
Tamuis, Vito 28
Tatum, Tommy 90
Taylor, Eddie 15
Taylor, Harry 87, 92, 110
Tearin' Up the Pea Patch 170
Ten Rings 217
Terry, Bill 35, 103
Terwilliger, Wayne 144
Texas League 118
Thomas, Danny 229
Thompson, Don 143
Thompson, Fresco 14, 198
Thompson, Hank 174
Thomson, Bobby 141, 143, 149–156, 158, 250
Thomson, James Ray 148
Thorn, John 112
Three Coins in a Fountain 189

Three-I League 235
Titusville, Florida 54
Tobin, Jim 56
Todd, Al 31
Tokyo, Japan 65, 219
Toledo Mud Hens 19
Torre, Frank 238
Trenton Packers 183
Trickle, Ken 100
Trimble, Joe 164
Trujillo, Gen. Rafael 97
Truman, Harry S 129, 133
Turkin, Hy 22, 72–73, 166
Turkus, Barton 3, 4
Turley, Bob 217
Turner, Jim 37
Tygiel, Jules 81, 89, 115
Tyler, Tony 232

U.S. Supreme Court 256
UCLA 69, 114, 224
Ulin, David L. 244
United Press 52, 77, 121, 235, 237, 243
U.S. Civil War 6, 16, 80
U.S. Congress 42
U.S. Marine Corps 65, 133–134, 236
U.S. Naval Station Vero Beach 98
U.S. Pacific Fleet 42
University of Alabama 242
University of Buffalo 63
University of Florida 21
University of Georgia 49
University of Maryland 131
University of Michigan 65
University of Missouri 69
University of Notre Dame 35
University of Pennsylvania 139
University of Southern California 69, 234
U.S. Steel 156
USA Today 154

Vance, Dazzy 19, 141, 192
Van Cuyk, Chris 159
Vandenberg, Hy 34–5
Vanderbilt, Alfred, Jr. 51
Vander Meer, Johnny 76, 110
Van Robays, Maurice 57
Vaughan, Arky 2, 53, 62- 64, 101–102
Veeck, Bill 87
Veracruz Blues 67
Vernon, Mickey 178
Vero Beach Airport 98
Vero Beach Cadillac Company 98
Vero Beach Country Club 234
Veterans Committee 2, 249
Victoria Club 173
Virdon, Bill 213

Voiselle, Bill 113
Vosmik, Joe 28, 32–33, 36

The Wabash Cannonball 241
Wade, Ben 177, 184
Wagner, Charley 25
Wagner, Honus 25, 99
Wagner, Robert F. 223
Wai Mami 42
Waikiki Beach 219
Waikus, Eddie 88, 137
Wait Till Next Year 114
Waldorf Astoria Hotel 19, 169
Walker, Dixie 24, 30–31, 33, 36–37, 42–43, 49–50, 54, 63, 72, 76–77, 80–81, 84–85, 87–88, 92, 96, 97, 100-1-1, 140, 177
Walker, Estelle 54
Walker, Mildred 188
Walker, Rube 141, 144, 148–151, 159, 172, 175, 225, 244
The Wall Street Journal 153
Wallis, Lee 230
Walters, Bucky 28, 45–46
Walton, Arch C. 255
Walton, Laura 255
Wambsganss, Bill 18
Waner, Lloyd "Little Poison" 40
Waner, Paul "Big Poison" 40–42
WAR (Wins Above Replacement) 1–2
War of 1812 5
Ward, Gene 147
Warren, Tommy 63
Wasdell, Jimmy 45, 49
Washington, Kenny 69
Washington D.C. Elite Giants 98
Washington Park (Brooklyn) 16
Washington Post 60, 191
Washington Senators 13, 119, 178, 224–225, 247
The Wasteland 147
Wayne, John 241
Weber, J. Henry 163, 203
Weintrub, Phil 63
Weiss, George 142
Wendler, Harold 210
Werber, Bill 46
West, Dick 39
West, Max 77
Western Hills High School 194
Western Union 43
Wheat, Zack 18, 214, 221
White, Jack 206
Whitman, Walt 15–16
Wilhelm, Hoyt 191
Wilhelm II, Kaiser 20
Wilkinson, Joseph 149
Wilks, Ed 213
William Cullen Bryant High School 157
Williams, Dick 186

Williams, Ted 48, 73
Williams Equipment Company Award 64
Wills, Maury 237–238
Wilson, Jim 174
Wiseman, Eddie 243
WMGM Radio 131
Wolpin, Stewart 206
Wolter, Harry 17
Woodling, Gene 167, 179
Woodward, Stanley 85, 171
Wooster, Leo 17
WOR TV 131–32
World Series: (1915) 92; (1916) 18; (1920) 18; (1929) 92; (1934) 32; (1941) 48–51; (1947) 91–94; (1948) 230; (1949) 125–127; (1950) 139; (1951) 156; (1952) 163–168, 251; (1953) 177–180; (1955) 201–207; (1956) 216–218; (1959) 238–240; (1972) 244
World War I 20, 52
World War II 2, 52–53, 59–60, 65, 87, 134, 164, 170, 175, 218
Worthington, Al 174, 229
Wright, Johnny 74–75
Wrigley, Phillip K. 223
Wrigley Field (Chicago) 31, 35, 44, 120, 132, 153
Wrigley Field (Los Angeles) 223, 228
Wyatt, Whitlow 21, 29, 37, 43, 46–47, 49, 67, 177
Wyte's 207

Yamamoto, Kazuto 219
Yankee Stadium 10–11, 49, 91, 93, 125, 166, 178, 202–203, 208, 230
Yawkey, Tom 12–13
A Year at a Time 190, 240
Yochim, Ray 120
York, Rudy 57
U.S.S. *Yorktown* 60
You Can't Hit with the Bat on Your Shoulder 83
Young, Cy 2
Young, Dick 72, 76, 100–101, 104, 111–112, 119–120, 130, 132, 144, 158, 161, 173–174, 176, 194, 198, 200, 210, 212, 220, 222, 227, 231–232, 245
Younger, Paul "Tank" 236
Yvars, Sal 154

Ziff-Davis 101
Zimmer, Don 189, 194, 200–201, 203, 223, 225, 237, 239, 251–252
Zimmerman, Paul 228

www.ingramcontent.com/pod-product-compliance
Lightning Source LLC
Chambersburg PA
CBHW060336010526
44117CB00017B/2849